Social Structure and
Forms of Consciousness

VOLUME 2

THE DIALECTIC
OF STRUCTURE AND HISTORY

WORKS BY THE SAME AUTHOR

Satire and Reality, 1955

La rivolta degli intellettuali in Ungheria, 1958

Attila József e l'arte moderna, 1964

Marx's Theory of Alienation, 1970

The Necessity of Social Control, 1971

Aspects of History and Class Consciousness, ed., 1971

Lukács's Concept of Dialectic, 1972

Neocolonial Identity and Counter-Consciousness, ed., 1978

The Work of Sartre: Search for Freedom, 1979

Philosophy, Ideology and Social Science, 1986

The Power of Ideology, 1989

Beyond Capital, 1995

L'Alternativa alla Società del Capitale, 2000

Socialism or Barbarism, 2001

A educação para além do capital, 2005

O desafio e o fardo do tempo histórico, 2007

The Challenge and Burden of Historical Time, 2008

The Structural Crisis of Capital, 2010

Social Structure and Forms of Consciousness, Volume I, 2010

Social Structure and Forms of Consciousness

VOLUME 2

THE DIALECTIC OF STRUCTURE AND HISTORY

by ISTVÁN MÉSZÁROS

MONTHLY REVIEW PRESS
New York

Library of Congress Cataloging-in-Publication Data

Mészáros, István, 1930–

  Social structure and forms of consciousness, volume 2 / by István Mészáros.

    p. cm.

  Includes index.

  ISBN 978-1-58367-236-5 — ISBN 978-1-58367-235-8 (pbk.)

  1. Social structure. 2. Consciousness. 3. Marxian school of sociology.

I. Title.

  HM706.M47 201

  301–dc22

                          2010002973

Monthly Review Press

146 West 29th Street, Suite 6W

New York, NY 10001

www.monthlyreview.org

5 4 3 2 1

Contents

For Donatella

INTRODUCTION

The investigation of the dialectical relationship between *structure and history* is essential for a proper understanding of the nature and the defining characteristics of any social formation in which sustainable solutions are being sought to the encountered problems. This is particularly important in the case of capital's social formation, with its inexorable tendency toward an all-embracing, structurally embedded determination of all aspects of societal reproduction and the—feasible for the first time ever—global domination implicit in that form of development. It is therefore by no means accidental that in the interest of the required *structural change* Marx had to focus critical attention on the concept of *social structure*, in the historical period of crises and revolutionary explosions of the 1840s when he articulated his own—radically new—conception of history.

In his first great synthesizing work, the *Economic and Philosophical Manuscripts of 1844*, Marx put into relief that in the course of modern historical development natural science, through its close integration with the material practices of capitalist industrial production, had become *in an alienated form* the basis of social life; a circumstance considered by Marx "a priori a lie."[1] In his view this had to be rectified by extricating science itself from its alienating integument. At the same time science had to be retained—in a qualitatively modified form, remade as "the science of man"[2] in its inseparability from "the science of history"—the enriching and gratifying basis of actual human life. But to achieve this fundamental transformation, it was absolutely necessary to understand and lay bare the deep-seated *structural determinations* through which the creative potentiality of human labor, including the scientific endeavor of the social individuals, had been subjugated by the alienating imperatives of fetishistic/uncontrollable capital-expansion and accumulation.

For this reason the category of *social structure* had to acquire a seminal importance in the Marxian vision in a completely tangible form. Contrary to the speculative philosophical approaches to these problems dominant at the time, there could be nothing mysterious about the required analysis of the social structure. Nor could political vested interests be allowed to obfuscate the issues at stake in the interest of speculatively transubstantiated state-apologetics.

As far back as 1845 Marx forcefully underscored, in his contribution to the book written with Engels, *The German Ideology,* that in the envisaged theoretical analysis *all* of the relevant factors were amenable to empirical observation and rational assessment. For the overall conceptual framework of explanation had to be made fully intelligible on the basis of the ongoing practices of societal reproduction in which the particular human beings happened to be constantly engaged in their daily life. In this sense Marx insisted that the only valid theoretical investigation was a type capable of bringing to the fore

> without any *mystification and speculation* the connection of the social and political structure with *production.* The *social structure and the state* are constantly evolving out of the *life-process of definite individuals.*[3]

This demystifying theoretical approach, which concerned not only the conditions of Marx's own time but had a general validity as a structurally anchored historical explanation for the past as well as for the future, served a radical emancipatory purpose under the circumstances of the revolutionary explosions of the 1840s. And it continues to have a vital emancipatory mandate ever since that time.

By focusing attention on the actual life-process of the social individuals who were engaged in capitalistically alienating industrial production, it became possible to perceive, in Marx's words, "the *necessity,* and at the same time the *condition,* of a *transformation* both of *industry and the social structure.*"[4] That is to say, it became possible to see both the *necessity* of a profound transformation itself and the objective nature of the *conditions* that had to be changed. And the latter corresponded to the *structurally determined characteristics* of social life, highlighting at the same time the deepening severity of the crisis itself. For it was the innermost structural determination of these objective conditions themselves that called for the tangible and far-reaching *practical leverage* indicated by Marx. Due to the inherent characteristics of the encountered problems, the required leverage for successfully overcoming the historical crisis could not be other than the radical transformation of *industry and the social structure.*

This is why in Marx's view a change in the political circumstances alone could not match the magnitude of the historic task. What was really needed was nothing less than a qualitative *structural change* capable of embracing the fundamental modality of societal reproduction in its entirety. Naturally, that kind of change had to include the political domain, with all of its general legislative as well as more limited local regulatory institutions. But it could not be confined to the political field. For in their traditional way even the greatest political upheavals of the past tended to change only the ruling personnel of society while leaving the *exploitative structural framework* of material and cultural reproduction in its hierarchical *class articulation* standing.

Thus, according to the Marxian conception, the "*social and political structure*" had to be transformed in its integrality, and such transformation had to be accomplished by the social individuals referred to in our last quotation from *The German Ideology*. As Marx also made it very clear in another work written in the same period of revolutionary upheavals, the historic task had to be accomplished by the social individuals by restructuring "from top to bottom the conditions of their industrial and political existence, and consequently *their whole manner of being.*"[5]

The question of *social structure* cannot be put in its correct perspective without a multifaceted *dialectical* assessment of the complex factors and determinations involved. For the plain truth of the matter is that in *any* particular type of humanity's reproductive order the *social structure* is unthinkable without its properly articulated *historical dimension*; and vice versa, there can be no real understanding of the *historical movement* itself without grasping at the same time the corresponding *material structural determinations* in their specificity.

In this sense, history and structure in the human context are always deeply intertwined. In other words, there can be no structure of relevance abstracted from history in its dynamic course of unfolding in any conceivable social formation, nor history as such without the associated structures that bear the essential defining characteristics of the determinate social formation in question.

Ignoring, for whatever reason, the substantive dialectical interrelatedness of structure and history carries with it harmful consequences for theory. For an undialectical approach can only result either in a philosophically irrelevant anecdotal depiction of historical events and personalities, by presenting some chronological sequence of "before and after" as its assumed self-justification for "story-telling," or in a mechanical cult of "structuralism."

The first defect is well illustrated by the fact that already Aristotle ranked historical writing known to him as philosophically inferior to poetry and tragedy, in view of the anecdotal particularism of such story-telling accounts of events and circumstances,[6] in tune with the original Greek term of history—"*istor*"—which means "eye-witness." As to the structuralist violation of the dialectical interconnection between structure and history, and its replacement by a positivistically oriented mechanical reductionism, the once highly influential work of Claude Lévi-Strauss offers us a prominent example, as we shall see in considerable detail in the final chapter of the present study.[7] At this point a single quotation—from one of his most celebrated books—should suffice to make clear the anti-historical as well as anti-dialectical approach adopted to these problems by Claude Lévi-Strauss:

> History is a *discontinuous set* composed of domains of history, each of which is defined by a characteristic frequency and by a differential coding of *before* and *after*. . . . The *discontinuous* and *classificatory* nature of historical knowledge emerges clearly. . . . In a system of this type, *alleged historical continuity* is secured only by dint of *fraudulent outlines*. . . . We need only recognize that history is a *method* with no distinct *object* corre-

sponding to it to reject the equivalence between the notion of history and the notion of *humanity* which some have tried to foist on us with the unavowed aim of making *historicity* the last refuge of a *transcendental humanism:* as if men could regain the *illusion of liberty* on the plane of the *"we"* merely by giving up the "I"'s that are too obviously wanting in consistency. In fact history is tied *neither to man nor to any particular object.* It consists wholly in its *method,* which experience proves to be indispensable for *cataloguing* the elements of *any structure* whatever, human or non-human, in their entirety.[8]

Thus the profound dialectical relationship between *continuity* and *discontinuity* in historical development is tellingly rejected by Lévi-Strauss—a rejection, moreover, even insultingly underlined by accusing those who uphold the dialectical character of this relationship as being guilty of presenting "fraudulent outlines"—in order to enable himself to confine the allegedly "objectless method" of history itself, in a mechanical reductivist fashion, to the subsidiary role of *"cataloguing* the elements of any structure whatever." In this way the literally vital objective determinations of actually existing history are completely obliterated.

However, paradoxically for Claude Lévi-Strauss himself, as a result of his adoption of a mechanical reductivist approach to history, "human or non-human," also his key concept of structure—amounting to no more than an equally mechanical definition of structure as what is supposed to be "catalogued" in the form of its positivistically dissectable and cataloguable elements—is deprived of any real explanatory significance in relation to social development. And all this is done, according to Lévi-Strauss and his followers,[9] at the peak of the structuralist influence in Western Europe and in the United States, in the name of the most fashionable "anti-ideological scientific rigor."

To be sure, the general orientation of the various "post-structuralist" and "postmodernist" approaches by no means could be considered any better. They all share an extremely skeptical attitude to history and a complete disregard for objective dialectical relations and determinations. At times this attitude produces utterly mystifying pronouncements, bordering on vacuous sophistry. Thus the leading theoretician of "postmodernity," Jean-François Lyotard—a repenter who once belonged to a left political group in France assembled around the periodical called *Socialisme ou Barbarie*—offers this kind of programmatic definition: "What, then, is the *postmodern*? It is undoubtedly a part of the *modern*. . . . A work can become *modern only if it is first postmodern*. Postmodernism thus understood is not modernism at its end but in the *nascent* state, and this state is *constant*."[10] In the same sense, Lyotard's anti-dialectical programmatic counter-position of the *parts* (the metaphorically eulogized "little narratives" or *"petits récits"*)[11] to the *whole* (the aprioristically rejected "grand narratives") is no less incoherent and no less capitulatory.

The issue we are concerned with here—that is, the profound dialectical interrelationship between structure and history—is not only theoretical, let alone purely academic. Its great relevance arises from the far-reaching practical implications of this relationship for the much needed *emancipatory intervention* of committed human beings in the unfolding trends of historical development. For without understanding the true character of the hierarchically articulated *structural determinations* of capital's increasingly more destructive societal reproductive order, with its organic system in which the *parts sustain the whole*, and *vice versa*, in their now *paralyzing circular reciprocity*, there can be no significant improvement in the time still available to us.

The Marxian revolutionary science, addressing the difficult problems of how to secure an *all-embracing structural change*—feasible by firmly grasping the strategically vital objective leverages of material and cultural transformation—was formulated precisely for that purpose. Conservative anti-historical and anti-dialectical structuralist discourse, à la Lévi-Strauss, about "cataloguing" the dubiously identified constituents of the existent and its mythologized past, coupled with utterly pessimistic laments about "humanity as its own worst enemy" while exempting from blame the destructive forces and institutions of capitalist social and political development, is diametrically opposed to that. The same goes for the conservative postmodern chatter and prattle about the "little narratives," devised in order to be able to arrogantly dismiss not only by implication but even *explicitly*, in Lyotard's words, "the great narratives of emancipation,"[12] so as to break with all progressive tradition in the historical past.

The deepest meaning of the Marxian conception is the passionate advocacy of a *structural change* to be accomplished in a *global epochal sense* directly affecting the whole of humanity. Without focusing on this dimension of Marx's work neither the central message nor the animating spirit of his approach is comprehensible.

Evidently, the global epochal orientation of the structural change advocated by Marx, with its stress on the great urgency of the tasks to be confronted by the social individuals, due to the danger of humanity's self-destruction, could only arise at a determinate point in historical time. Every social formation known to human beings has its inexorable historic limits, and—despite all idealization of capitalism by the classical political economists of the eighteenth century as "the natural system of perfect liberty and justice," not to mention the theories propounded by the later defenders of even the worst contradictions of this mode of production—the capital system can be no exception to such limitations.

The radical novelty of Marx's conception was made possible at a time when the objective *need for an epochal change* from capital's social order to one *qualitatively* different in all of its fundamental determinations as a mode of humanity's social metabolic control appeared with its peremptory finality on the historical agenda, with the *onset of the capital system's descending phase of development*. This fateful reversal of capital's historically unprecedented and in many ways highly positive advancement in societal reproduction coincided with the period of crises and revolutionary explosions to which Marx himself was a profoundly insightful witness. Due to this radical historic change the capital system became alterable ever since that time only in some partial respects, no matter how extensive in scale, but not in its *overall perspective*, despite the grotesquely self-serving propaganda slogan of "people's capitalism" proclaimed by the beneficiaries of the ruling order.

As we constantly witness, "globalization" is mystifyingly depicted in our time by the vested interests of the entrenched powers as an unproblematical extension of the capital system's viability into the *timeless future*. As if "globalization" was a totally new characteristic of our own days, representing the happily eternalizable climax and the absolute positive fulfillment of capital's societal reproductive destination. However, the inconvenient truth of the matter is that the Marxian critical vision was inherently *global* almost from the beginning, and decidedly so from the years 1843–44 onward, forcefully indicating at the same time the *irreversibility* of capital's *descending phase* of development.

The onset of the descending phase carried with it grave implications pointing in their *overall historic sense* toward humanity's destruction unless a radically new mode of societal reproductive control could be instituted in place of the existing order. This painful truth objectively appeared on the historical horizon as an *epochal irreversibility* around the middle of the nineteenth century, even if in some parts of the planet the *ascendancy* of capital was still far from its conclusion, as explicitly acknowledged later by Marx himself.[13]

The new historic phase conceptualized by Marx represented a fundamental contrast to capital's *ascending systemic phase* of development. For capital's triumphantly advancing phase opened up in the first decades of the sixteenth century resulted—notwithstanding its alienating impact on all aspects of human life—in the greatest productive accomplishment in all history. Disconcertingly, however, in the course of the final decades of the ascending phase of development a capitalistically insuperable problem had arisen that could only worsen as time went by. Namely, the growth of a crisis-producing destructiveness—understood with all of its perilous implications by Marx himself more deeply well before anyone else[14]—foreshadowing the *implosion* of capital's reproductive order. An implosion not through some natural calamity but under the weight of its own insoluble systemic contradictions and explosive antagonisms at the *height* of capital's societal dominance and global encroachment.

This contradictory inner determination carried with it as the ultimate horizon of the descending systemic phase the irreversible maturation of the historic limits of by far the most powerful societal reproductive order known in history. In other words, this grave historical maturation of capital's *absolute structural limits* was foreshadowing not simply yet another periodic crisis and corresponding hardship, as the recurrent normality of capital, but the total destruction of humanity, as farsightedly anticipated by Marx. This is why he wrote in *The German Ideology*, in his own version of the stark alternative of "socialism or barbarism" well over half a century before Rosa Luxemburg's famous warning, that in the development of productive forces there comes a stage when productive forces and means of intercourse are brought into being which, under the existing relations, only cause mischief, and are no longer productive but *destructive forces*.[15] Thus things have now come to such a pass that the individuals must appropriate the existing totality of productive forces, not only to achieve self-activity, but, also, *merely to safeguard their very existence*.[16]

Moreover, parallel to this qualitative change from the ascending to the descending historic phase, also the theoretical evaluation of the problems at stake as formulated from capital's vantage point was fundamentally changing. Thus in contrast to "the anatomy of civil society"[17] depicted in the "scientific bourgeois economy" by the great representatives of classical political economy in the eighteenth and in the first third of the nineteenth century, and generously praised for their "genuine scientific research" by Marx, the uncritical defense of the capital system became the deplorable general rule.

This change in attitude and perspective was fully in tune with the need to ideologically rationalize and attenuate the *systemic contradictions* that erupted and intensified at the onset of capital's descending phase of development. Accordingly, the theoretical transformation for much the worse was characterized by Marx in his "Afterword to the Second German Edition" of *Capital* with these words:

> Political Economy can remain a science only so long as the class struggle is *latent* or manifests itself only in isolated and sporadic phenomena. [However] In France and in England the bourgeoisie had conquered political power. Thenceforth, the class struggle, practically as well as theoretically, took on more and more outspoken and threatening forms. It sounded the knell of *scientific bourgeois economy*. It was thenceforth no longer a question, whether this theorem or that theorem was *true*, but whether it was *useful to capital or harmful*, expedient or inexpedient, politically dangerous or not. In place of disinterested inquirers, there were *hired prize fighters;* in place of genuine scientific research the *bad conscience* and the evil intent of *apologetics*.[18]

It is enough to compare in this sense the writings of F. A. Hayek with the work of Adam Smith to see the devastating intellectual consequences of switching in the descending phase of the capital system's development from the scholarly concern with the requirements of *truth* to the glorification of what is *"useful and expedient to capital."* We find a crass hostility to anything to do even with the mention of a less obscurantist position displayed in a most pronounced way in the Austrian economist's writings. It is particularly clear in Hayek's blindly pursued crusade against the ideas of socialism, denounced by the author of *The Road to Serfdom* and *The Fatal Conceit*—as well as by his equally reactionary Austrian and other stable mates—as politically dangerous to capital.

Characteristically, Hayek's pseudo-scientific and often even *openly irrational* capital-apologetics is most eager to do away with *causal explanations* altogether. He insists that "the creation of wealth . . . cannot be explained by a chain of cause and effect."[19] And in a telling summation of his aggressively capital-apologetic position Hayek pontificates that *"mysterious money* and the financial institutions based on it"[20] must be exempt from all criticism, adding in the spirit of his obsessive condemnation of the spectre of socialism, which he claims to have discovered as far back as the time of ancient Greece, that "the high-minded socialist slogan, 'Production for use, not for profit,' which we find in one form or another from Aristotle to Bertrand Russell, from Albert Einstein to Archbishop Camara of Brazil (and often, since Aristotle, with the addition that these profits are made 'at the expense of others'), betrays ignorance of how productive capacity is multiplied by different individuals."[21]

The severity of these problems is underlined not simply by the apologetic character of the economic theories dominant in capital's descending phase of development but by the *objective reason* why the formulation and the highly promoted practical implementation of such theories has become the deplorable general rule. What has fundamentally changed since Adam Smith is not the orienting standpoint and the class allegiance of the theoreticians in question but the *historical ground* of the standpoint itself from which their conceptions arise, in accordance with the change from the ascending to the descending phase.

Adam Smith, who conceptualized the world from the vantage point of capital, was no less committed to advocating the viability of the capital system than F. A. Hayek. The big difference is that in Adam Smith's age capital's social metabolic order in the ascendant represented the most advanced form of societal reproduction feasible to humankind. Also, the class struggle itself, on the side of, or against, labor's qualitatively different hegemonic alternative order to the capitalist modality of social metabolic control, was in Adam Smith's age still "latent or manifested itself only in isolated and sporadic phenomena."

By contrast, in Hayek's time the growing *destructiveness* of capital's socioeconomic system, due to its irreversible descending phase of development, together with the eruption of its antagonistic inner contradictions in the form of even two devastating global wars in the twentieth century, could be denied—again from capital's vantage point, but this time with a really "Fatal Conceit" capable of dismissing no less a thinker than Aristotle as an "ignorant socialist"—only in the service of the crudest and most belligerent form of capital-apologetics. Given this fundamental change in the objective historical ground of capital's vantage point from the ascending to the descending phase, the need for a *structural change* in a *global epochal sense*—to be accomplished by the social individuals "not only to achieve self-activity, but, also, *merely to safeguard their very existence,*" as spelled out in the dramatic alternative between "socialism or barbarism," could not be removed from the historical agenda.

Perhaps the most effective way of postponing the historical "moment of truth" and thereby prolonging the dominance of capital over human life, despite its growing destructiveness and deepening structural crisis, is the *hybridization* of capitalism. This hybridization in capitalistically advanced countries assumes the form of the massive injection of *public funds* into the revitalization of the pretendedly "free market" capitalist enterprises by the direct involvement of the capitalist state. This trend has been demonstrated already at the time of the—subsequently quite easily reversible—"nationalization" of large-scale capitalist bankruptcy in several vital economic sectors of Great Britain in 1945 by the Attlee government of the "old" Labour Party, and not by "New Labour." A necessary postwar rescue operation of British capitalism was characteristically misrepresented as a genuine socialist achievement.[22]

This kind of operation is carried out in order to defend and secure the continuing *viability* of the established reproductive order, thanks to a great variety of system-apologetic—and in that sense politically moti-vated—direct economic contributions by the state (from the funds of gen-eral taxation, of course), which Adam Smith could not even dream about. They range from the astronomical magnitude of the resources put at the disposal of the *military/industrial complex* on an ongoing basis to the *trillions of dollars of financial rescue funds* given to private capitalist banks and insurance companies not only in 2008 and 2009 but also in 2010, accepting liability to the tune of 90 percent for their future losses.

In historical terms this is a relatively recent phenomenon in the devel-opment of capitalism. Its potential extent and significance were still very far from evident in Marx's lifetime. For "in the nineteenth century the possibilities of adjustment for capital as a *'hybrid' system* of control—which became fully visible only in the twentieth century—were as yet hid-den from theoretical scrutiny."[23]

To be sure, this systemic hybridization is by now overwhelmingly important in prolonging the life-span of the capital system. However, its modality of direct state involvement in "saving the system"[24]—through the transfer of immense public funds and even the full-scale "nationaliza-tion" of ever more serious capitalist bankruptcy—has its own limits and far-reaching implications for future development, and therefore it should not be imagined as a permanent *structural remedy*.

In 1972, as part of my critique of Max Weber's definition of capital-ism, I stressed that

it is quite inaccurate to describe capitalism in general as characterized by the "investment of *private* capital." Such a characterization is valid only of a determinate historical phase of capitalistic development, and by no means as an "ideal type" in its Weberian sense. By stressing the invest-ment of *private* capital Weber uncritically champions the subjective standpoint of the individual capitalist, disregarding at the same time *one of the most important objective trends of development* of the capitalist mode of production, namely, the ever-increasing involvement of *state-capital* in the continued reproduction of the capitalist system. In princi-ple the outer limit of this development is nothing less than the transformation of the prevailing form of capitalism into an all-comprehensive system of *state-capitalism,* which theoretically implies the complete abolition of the specific phase of capitalism idealized by Weber. But precisely because of such implications, this crucial trend of development must be excluded from the ideological framework of Weber's "ideal type."[25]

Naturally, this trend of ever greater direct involvement by the state in the transfer of *public funds* for the purpose of prolonging the reproductive viability of the capital system is totally misrepresented by the "hired prizefighters" and propagandists of the established order.

In some parts of Britain, as in Northern Ireland for instance, the—capitalistically managed and exploited—share of the "public sector" in administrative, health and educational employment and other economic activity by now exceeds 71 percent, and the overall *national average* is approaching 50 percent. Yet the actual state of affairs which prevails in undeniable forms of greatly increasing hybridization is described, with characteristic neoliberal distortion and hypocrisy, as *"rolling back the boundaries of the state,"* as well as with variants of the same misrepresentation, like *"the retreat of the state."*

In this way, just like *The Economist,* another prominently class-conscious press organ of the international bourgeoisie, the London-based *Financial Times,* advocates a new "Beveridge moment," in obvious reference to Lord Beveridge, an influential Liberal politician who toward the end of the Second World War theorized the welfare state in his book programmatically titled *Full Employment in a Free World.* And this is how the editors of the *Financial Times* formulate the problem of the so-called "retreat of the state" in their lead article under the present conditions of an extremely serious global economic crisis, in the midst of the campaign for British parliamentary elections, when it is already anticipated that the "national debt" will exceed well over *£1.5 trillion* (approximately *2.4 trillion dollars* at the current rate of exchange) in four to five years:

> *Public wages, pensions and jobs must be cut. So must services.* The Budget ought to spell out how that pain would be distributed were Labour to be returned to office. . . . The government is right not to cut too much too fast, but that is no excuse not *to plan.* . . . Labour's deliberate vagueness

is forcing what should be a *deep debate about the role of the state*—a *Beveridge moment*—into shallow waters. . . . Whoever wins this election will oversee the *retreat of the state*.[26]

Thus the real meaning of the "retreat of the state"—or, for that matter, of the cynical neoliberal slogan of "rolling back the boundaries of the state" propagandized everywhere for a very long time—is the editorially camouflaged but totally self-serving advocacy of *"planning"* (and in this revealing sense the ideological champions of the "free market" are even in favor of "planning") how to transfer the financial benefits released by drastically cutting *"public wages, pensions and jobs"* as well as social *"services"* into the bottomless pockets of the ever more dangerously bankrupt capitalist enterprise. In other words, the new "Beveridge moment" advocated by the leader writers of the *Financial Times* means in reality the savagely "planned" liquidation of the remnants of the welfare state by the capitalist state itself.[27] This is done, of course, for the "good cause of saving the system" by securing through massive state involvement, to the tune of *literally astronomical* sums, the slipping viability of capital's reproductive order in the descending historic phase of its systemic development indelibly marked by the deepening structural crisis.

However, the kind of class-conscious editorializing we can read in *The Economist* and in the *Financial Times* is only a mixture of quixotism and hypocrisy. The combination of these two ingredients is well illustrated by the fact that on the *same page* of the *Financial Times,* dated March 23, 2010, printed in the immediately adjoining column of the paper to the quoted editorial, an article criticizes the Labour government's "Strategic Investment Fund" which has been recently announced as the by no means negligible sum of *£950 million,* listing from it several items amounting to nearly *half a billion.*

The criticism expressed in this article is not directed at all against the yet again increasing *state handouts* to private capitalist enterprise—and in that sense there can be no question of "the retreat of the state." On the contrary, the state is always most welcome to continue with its generous handouts. The "criticism" is directed only against the *name* of the announced fund, which in the journalist's view should be called "Strategic Reelection Fund."[28] Thus the author of this article did not want to question the essentials without which the system fully supported by him could not survive at all; he simply wanted to make what he thought to be a witty electioneering point.

The simultaneously hypocritical and quixotic character of arguing in the editorial article in favor of "the retreat of the state" is revealed by the fact that at the present historic phase of capitalist development it is really *unthinkable* to cut out the great variety of the *public sector economy* and corresponding employment expenditure that the editors of the *Financial Times* would like to see in the interest of strengthening the shaky private capitalist productive and financial system. For the *systemic hybridization* in the last hundred years had assumed such proportions—now amounting to nearly 50 percent of the total in the capitalistically advanced countries, as mentioned before, despite all protests by various conservative political forces (including "New Labour") against it—that the now "planned" savage intervention in favor of abolishing this trend is bound to fail again. These self-righteous "sound capitalist bookkeeping" protests are monotonously combined with repeated failed promises to "redress the balance in favor of the private sector." All they are likely to achieve is the imposition of increasing hardship on the masses of the people but not the abolition of the contradictory trend of systemic hybridization itself.

In truth, the issue

> concerns the structure of present-day capitalist production as a whole, and not simply one of its branches. Nor could one reasonably expect the state to solve the problem, no matter how much public money is poured down the drain in the course of its revealing rescue operations. . . . The power of state intervention in the economy—not so long ago still widely believed to be the wonder drug of all conceivable ills and troubles of 'modern industrial society'—is strictly confined to accelerating the maturation of these contradictions. The larger the dose administered to the convalescing patient, the greater is its dependency on the wonder drug.[29]

In this sense, we are confronted here by a fundamental contradiction of the capital system in general. Whichever side of the contradictory determinations is pushed forward by its advocates, it is bound to be countered and nullified by its opposite. Thus in the long run, on the one side, the *astro-*

nomical sums required for resourcing the hybridization of the productively most problematical, and financially adventurist and even fraudulent, capital system through the extension of the capitalistically managed "public sector"—now manipulated even in the form of the cynically private-capital-favoring "PPPs," i.e., "Private-Public Partnerships"[30]—are bound to be exhausted, and thereby the viability of ever-expanding state handouts are seriously undermined.

At the same time, on the other side of this equation imposed on capital by historical development, the virtuously self-congratulatory advocacy of "living within the available means and resources"—that is, a necessarily diminishing economic activity in tune with the proposed drastic cuts of *"public wages, pensions and jobs"* as well as social *"services"* in the interest of reducing the already multi-trillion and all the time still inexorably growing "national debt"—in a societal reproductive system that functions on the basis of its *self-mythology of growth:* an ultimately self-destructive "growth" that means nothing more than the alienating but absolute necessity of *capital expansion and accumulation irrespective of the consequences*—a reproductive system of this kind, operating on the basis of such contradictory principles, can only *implode.*

This is why only a *structural change* in a *global epochal sense* can offer any hope of overcoming capital's *systemic contradictions* in the historic phase of its *structural crisis.* An epochally sustainable structural change whose fundamental orienting principle is the creation of a radically different societal reproductive order.

The systemic hybridization we see extended in our time, despite various consensual political attempts aimed at containing it, in tune with the mythology of the superior "private enterprise system" and its "sovereign individual consumers," is part of a more general and a significantly worsening problem that continued to gather strength in the course of the last hundred years. The underlying causal determination of this problem could be described as the *historically narrowing margin* of capital's objectively feasible *alternatives* for displacing and managing its *antagonistic contradictions.*

The now painfully obvious *three-pronged destructiveness* of the capital system—(1) in the military field, with capital's interminable wars since the onset of monopolistic imperialism in the final decades of the nineteenth century, and its ever more devastating weapons of mass destruction in the last sixty years, (2) through the intensification of capital's obvious destructive impact on ecology directly affecting and endangering by now the elementary natural foundation of human existence itself, and (3) in the domain of material production and ever-increasing waste, due to the advancement of *"destructive production"* in place of the once eulogized "creative" or *"productive destruction"*—is the necessary consequence of this narrowing margin.

Disconcertingly for capital, however, neither the perilously growing destructiveness nor the consensus-generating hybridization of the established antagonistic system—a hybridization that has been used for a long time for the purpose of displacing capital's antagonisms in the capitalistically most powerful countries, and it will be used in that way for as long as its economic and political viability is not undermined by the intensifying structural crisis—cannot offer any long-term solution to the objectively narrowing margin.

It is part of the essential defining characteristics of any *antagonistic* system that it is *structurally incapable of resolving* its inner contradictions. That is precisely what objectively defines it as an antagonistic system. Accordingly, such a system must institute other ways of dealing with or managing—for as long as it can—its *systemic contradictions* in the absence of the possibility or viability of *solving* or *resolving* them. For a historically viable and sustainable solution would turn the capital system itself into a *non-antagonistic* way of *"doing away with"* its de facto *structurally entrenched* and *hierarchically exploitative* determinations that, contrary to the wishful projection of "people's capitalism," in reality define it as an insuperably antagonistic societal reproductive order. Unsurprisingly, therefore, by far the most favored and ubiquitously promoted ideology of capital-apologetics is precisely the elaborate or blatant denial of even the remote possibility of historically created (and historically supersedable) *systemic antagonism,* tellingly misrepresented as *individual conflict,* which is supposed to be determined forever by "human nature itself."

Nevertheless, such denial of systemic antagonism by the ruling ideology, irrespective of how elaborately camouflaged or cynically blatant it might be, cannot spirit away the underlying problem itself. Indeed, this problem can only grow in severity in the time ahead of us, as it has already done under the historical circumstances of the last few decades, marked by capital's worsening structural crisis. For there are only two ways in which an antagonistic societal reproductive order can deal with its fundamental systemic contradictions: (1) by temporarily *displacing* or *exporting* them, or indeed (2) by *imposing* them with all means at its disposal on its adversary, including the most violent and destructive ones. In this twofold sense:

1. *displacing the antagonisms,* in whichever way is practicable under the prevailing conditions—as, for instance, in all varieties of *exporting* the internal contradictions in the form of the well-known British Empire "gunboat diplomacy" of socially mystifying, and chauvinistic consensus-generating *imperialist* domination, transubstantiated and propagandized as "the white man's burden"; or by engaging in the practices of the militarily less obvious but economically/politically most effective post–Second World War "modernizing" *global encroachment* by "advanced capital" over the less developed areas of the planet[31] in agreement with the pretendedly "post-imperialist" ideology—for as long as this displacing/exporting modality of the management of capital's *systemic antagonisms* by the internationally for the time being dominant powers (and, of course, only by *some* of them, at the expense of *others)* remains feasible;

2. by ruthlessly *imposing* on the *class adversary* the violently repressive imperatives of capital's intensified class rule in situations of worsening crisis and sharpening class conflict, casting aside—in the name of socially required and "justified" states of emergency—even the pretenses of "democracy and the rule of law"; or, in the case of *inter-imperialist* systemic confrontations, by imposing on the weaker rivals and state antagonists the "non-negotiable" demands and interests of the most dominant military power or powers—on the widest scale, with all possible means, including the weapons of a *total war*—as demonstrated by two world wars in the twentieth century.

The trouble for the ruling order is that neither the *exporting displacement* of the capital system's antagonistic contradictions through capital's global encroachment, together with its devastating impact by now even on nature, which could be sustained with relative ease for a very long time in the past, nor the *violent imposition* of the systemic antagonisms on the adversary to be subdued by the ultimate force of a *total war* is readily feasible in our time. Today there remain no significant areas of the planet to be encroached upon by the dominant capitalist powers. Neither by direct military imperialist invasion nor by newly instituted "modernizing" economic domination. For the *global ascendancy of capital* described by Marx in his earlier mentioned letter to Engels[32] has been historically accomplished. In other words, capital's global encroachment is now complete, even if not in the idyllic form of "globalization"[33] glorified by its professional ideologues and "hired prizefighters." Capital now dominates and exploits our entire planet in every way it can, in the increasingly unstable form of its three-pronged destructiveness; but it can neither resolve nor suitably displace its structural antagonisms and explosive contradictions in the interest of untroubled capital-expansion and accumulation.

Moreover, capital's traditional "ultimate solution" of the aggravating problems, through *unlimited war* waged in the past against the potential or real enemy, has become impracticable, as a result of the invention of the now fully operational weapons of mass destruction that would totally destroy humanity in the event of yet another global war. The continuing *partial wars*—even when using the callously idealized military strategy of "overwhelming force," with immense and even more callously named "collateral damage" inflicted upon the people, as in Vietnam and elsewhere—can only deepen the capital system's structural crisis, instead of offering a way out of it in the traditional mold of the imperialist victor and the defeated.

In this way, the narrowing margin of capital's alternatives for managing its internal antagonisms—which is inseparable from capital's descending phase of development—carries serious implications for the future. For the sobering truth is—and always remains—that *structural problems* require *structural solutions*. And that calls, as we shall see below, for epochally sustainable structural remedies in a genuine socialist spirit, feasible only through the *reconstitution of the historical dialectic* which has been radically *subverted* by capital's antagonisms in the course of the descending phase of its systemic development. That is how capital's social metabolic order that once achieved by far the greatest productive advancement in history has been turned into its opposite, articulated as by far the most destructive system of structural determinations directly endangering humanity's survival in our planetary household.

However, notwithstanding all vested interests to the contrary, the irrepressible historical dimension of the established order should not be ignored, and the actual character of the determinations at its roots should not be misconceived. For social structures—even the most powerfully entrenched ones, like capital's societal reproductive order—cannot prevail as the "law of gravity" asserting itself in the world of natural necessity. Nor should one imagine *historical necessity* on the model of the natural law, as capital-apologists like to misrepresent the claimed eternal validity of their own system while falsely accusing Marx of viewing the world as an "economic determinist." In Marx's dialectical conception the unfolding phases of historical necessity are envisioned as in due course necessarily "vanishing necessity," and the social structures—described by him as "constantly evolving out of the life-process of definite individuals"—are subject to the deepest historical qualifications. This is what the dialectic of structure and history amounts to. For history and structure in the human context are always profoundly intertwined and history itself is necessarily *open-ended*. The complexities and contradictions of globalization unavoidable in our time cannot alter that. They can only underline the heightened responsibility for confronting the challenges involved, as it is made clear in the present study. Truly, "the stakes are not a row of beans" ("nem babra megy a játék"), as a Hungarian adage appropriately puts it.

NOTES

1. Marx, *Economic and Philosophical Manuscripts of 1844,* Lawrence and Wishart, London, 1959, 110.
2. Ibid., 111.
3. Karl Marx and Frederick Engels, *Collected Works,* Lawrence and Wishart, London, 1975, 5:35 (henceforth MECW).
4. Ibid., 41.
5. Marx, *The Poverty of Philosophy,* Lawrence and Wishart, London, 1936, 123. Written in the winter of 1846–47, this book was first published in French in 1847.

6. See Aristotle, *Poetics*, chapters 8 and 9.

7. See Section 6.4.

8. Claude Lévi-Strauss, *The Savage Mind*, George Weidenfeld and Nicolson Ltd., London, 1966, 261–62. The French original, *La pensée sauvage*, was published by Plon, in Paris, in 1962. Lévi-Strauss's tirades against "transcendental humanism" were later echoed by Louis Althusser and his circle as a key defining characteristic of their "structuralist Marxism," with its curious "theoretical anti-humanism."

9. See the first three pages of Section 6.4.

10. Jean-François Lyotard, *The Postmodern Condition: A Report on Knowledge*, Manchester University Press, 1979, 79.

11. Ibid., 60.

12. Lyotard, "Universal History and Cultural Differences," *The Lyotard Reader*, Basil Blackwell, Oxford, 1989, 318.

13. See in this respect Marx's seminally important letter to Engels, 8 October 1858.

14. As his great companion in arms, Engels recognized and highlighted it: "Marx stood higher, saw further, and took a wider and quicker view than all the rest of us." Engels, "Ludwig Feuerbach and the End of Classical German Philosophy," in *Karl Marx and Frederick Engels: Selected Works*, vol. 2, Foreign Languages Publishing House, Moscow, 1951, 349.

15. MECW, 5:52.

16. Ibid., 5:87.

17. Marx's expression used in his "Contribution to the Critique of Political Economy" about the major theoretical achievements conceived in the spirit of capital's standpoint by the outstanding intellectual figures of the bourgeoisie in the ascendant.

18. Marx, *Capital*, 1:14.

19. F. A. Hayek, *The Fatal Conceit: The Errors of Socialism*, Routledge, London 1988, 99.

20. Ibid., 101. This blatant apologetics of what is "useful and expedient to capital" must be music to the ears of those who could see no reason why we should even try to control the catastrophically dangerous global financial system that now engulfs irresponsibly misappropriated and wasted *trillions* of dollars in the field of production. Many years ago I quoted from a London *Sunday Times* article that "to cover some cash shortages General Motors has dipped into its $15 billion pension fund, as it can under American law. But now $8.9 billion of money set aside for pensioners is unfunded." And I commented in my book *Beyond Capital* that in this sense *"fraudulence* is not marginal or exceptional but belongs to the *normality of the capital system."* Recently the industrial giant General Motors, once boasting about its own might by saying that its budget exceeded that of the state of Belgium, had to be rescued from its bankruptcy by the state, despite

its revealing treatment of its workers' pension funds "under American law."

21. Hayek, *The Fatal Conceit,* 104.

22. This kind of misrepresentation goes back a very long time in history. Engels criticized it in a note attached in 1892 to the English edition of his *Socialism: Utopian and Scientific* by pointing out, "Of late, since Bismarck went in for State-ownership of industrial establishments, a kind of spurious Socialism has arisen, degenerating, now and again, into something of flunkeyism, that without more ado declares *all* State-ownership, even of the Bismarckian sort, to be socialistic." Quoted from *Marx & Engels, Selected Works,* Moscow, 1951, 2:135.

23. István Mészáros, *Beyond Capital,* Merlin Press, London, 1995, xxi.

24. See the open admission by one of the most obviously class-conscious weekly publications of the international bourgeoisie, *The Economist,* that the fundamental merit of the trillions of dollars "invested" in the good cause of capitalist bankruptcy during the recent crisis is *"saving the system,"* as explicitly highlighted with oversized characters on the *front cover* of its issue dated October 11, 2008.

25. István Mészáros, "Ideology and Social Science," paper presented to an Interdisciplinary Seminar of the Division of Social Science at York University, Toronto, January 1972. First published in *The Socialist Register,* in 1972. *Ideology and Social Science* republished it in India as a separate volume (Critical Quest, New Delhi, 2010). The quotation is taken from page 10 of this easily accessible recent volume.

26. "Darling [the name of the British Labour Chancellor of the Exchequer] must give a reality Budget: The UK state will be cut back; Labour must tell us how." Editorial, *Financial Times,* March 23, 2010.

27. This means, of course, the ever more active *direct* involvement of the state in economic matters, rather than its *"retreat."*

28. See Brian Groom, "Call It the Strategic Re-election Fund," *Financial Times,* March 23, 2010.

29. From *The Necessity of Social Control,* my Isaac Deutscher Memorial lecture delivered at the London School of Economics on January 26, 1971, quoted from page 82 of my book *The Structural Crisis of Capital,* Monthly Review Press, New York, 2010.

30. It transpires even through *The Economist* how absurdly wasteful and mismanaged such "Partnerships" are for generously compensating the shareholders of bankrupt capitalist enterprises, heavily promoted by the "New Labour" government. Thus we read in *The Economist* on May 15, 2010, under the title "The Tube upgrade deals. Finis: The end of the line for Britain's biggest private finance initiative," that "In theory the PPP was meant to harness the efficiency of the private sector and, in return for healthy profits, transfer risks to the firms doing the work. In fact neither Tube Lines nor Metronet could make the deals work. Metronet was badly

managed, and risk transfer proved to be a mirage: the firm went bankrupt in 2007 and the government bailed out its creditors to the tune of about £2 billion" (40; the following quotes are ibid.). This kind of arrangement means that in the "Private-Public Partnership" the word "Private" equals *"healthy profits,"* and the word "Public" the huge *losses* (in this particular case nearly *3 billion dollars)* transferred to the shoulders of the working classes at the mercy of capitalist bankruptcy eagerly bailed out by the state. Nor is it possible to exempt from responsibility the "impartial consultancy firms" which help to "expertly" justify and impose on society such fictitiously beneficial ventures. Thus "as the partnership was being put together, PricewaterhouseCoopers, a [prominent] consultancy, predicted that the private sector could extract savings of up to 30%, a figure that informed the entire project. But the consultancy 'published no adequate evidential basis for that figure,' says Stephen Glaister, an academic who has followed the saga." And that is by no means the end of the story regarding this *system of institutionalized irresponsibility.* For "On May 11 Chris Bolt, the PPP's referee, published a review of Metronet's old contracts, now also run in-house by TFL [Transport for London]. It was 'disappointing,' he said, to note that TFL had changed the way it did the accounts making comparison with Tube Lines and pre-takeover Metronet *impossible.*" Accordingly, in full conformity to the usual legally complicitous system of institutionalized irresponsibility, no one can be taken to task for the colossal waste. But who can seriously believe that this system of state-sponsored and catastrophically wasteful irresponsibility in the service of capitalist bankruptcy can be sustained forever?

31.   Also in this respect the *historical dimension* of the structurally prevailing displacement is obvious. The pretended justification of "modernizing" strategies is provided by the historically acquired (but unmentioned) *exploitative privileges* of the handful of capitalist countries involved, falsely promising the *universal diffusion* of the projected "development" in the total absence of any real ground in its support, as for instance in Walt Rostow's grotesque theory of "takeoff and drive to maturity." (See his book *The Stages of Economic Growth: A Non-Communist Manifesto,* Cambridge University Press, 1960.) Also in the direction of the future, such "developmental theories" become totally vacuous as soon as the privileged "model countries" have to confront their own serious problems in the midst of capital's structural crisis, *despite* their accumulated privileges, as they are forced to do in our time.

32.   See n. 13 above.

33.   See Martin Wolf, *Why Globalization Works: The Case for Global Market Economy*, Yale University Press, New Haven, 2004.

CHAPTER ONE

The Nature of Historical Determination

1.1 Material Imperatives and the "Active Side"

At Marx's graveside, his lifelong friend Engels assessed in the following terms one of the greatest achievements of the founder of historical materialism:

> Just as Darwin discovered the law of development of organic nature, so Marx discovered the law of development of human history: the simple fact, hitherto concealed by an overgrowth of ideology, that mankind must first of all eat, drink, have shelter and clothing, before it can pursue politics, science, art, religion, etc.; that therefore the production of the immediate material means of subsistence and consequently the degree of economic development attained by a given people or during a given epoch form the foundation upon which the state institutions, the legal conceptions, the ideas on art, and even on religion, of the people concerned have been evolved, and in the light of which they must, therefore, be explained, instead of vice versa, as had hitherto been the case.[1]

And yet, notwithstanding the plain transparency of what Engels called a "simple fact," the true character and significance of Marx's discovery remains in the present a highly contested issue: no less concealed today "by an overgrowth of ideology" than ever before.

Nor is the systematic misreading and distortion of Marx's views on historical development confined to his adversaries who, for understandable reasons, a priori reject anything they consider threatening to their established positions—even if it has the character of an obvious "simple fact"—with unconcealed hostility. More puzzling is the "agreement" we find in "vulgar-Marxist" interpretations that tend to reduce Marx's complex dialectical explanations to some simplistic caricature, postulating a crude, immediate correspondence between determinate changes in the material base and the mechanical emergence or modification of even the most abstract ideas.

To be sure, the ideological motivation of Marx's adversaries needs no further explanation beyond the self-evident hostility of its negative posture: The position of "vulgar-Marxism," however, is much more complicated than that. For the views of its representatives range from the fatalistic determinism of the Second International to the subjective voluntarism of Stalin and his followers, and well beyond; all the way down to the paradoxical voluntarism of "structuralist Marxism," which manages to combine a mechanical conception of determination and "homology" with a complete depreciation of the subject of socio-historical action.

Thus historically different situations of relative social immobility—with regard to the basic confrontation between capital and labor—produce characteristically static ideological conceptualizations of the social process itself. Such vulgar-Marxist reflections of the temporarily prevailing social immobility separate theory and practice from, and oppose them to, one another in a fatalistic/voluntaristic vision of historical determination as such, substituting a fetish-like view of "science" (some main figures of the Second International), or an arbitrary/subjective conception of the "class struggle" (Stalin and his followers), or a combination of the two ("structuralist Marxism") for the Marxian dialectic of base and superstructure and the irrepressible social dynamism implicit in it.

Marx is often accused of "historical determinism," "economic determinism," or quite summarily of "determinism" in general. However, if we bear in mind that even an idealist like Hegel defines freedom as "recognized *necessity*," it is very difficult to imagine what meaning, if any, could be given to a historical conception that tries to do away with the need for rigorous determinations in tracing historical events and developments, explaining them, instead, with the help of some "principle of *indeterminacy.*" For all historical theories properly so called, whether materialist or idealist, must operate within the framework of some coherent set of determinations through which they can locate and identify the relative weight and significance of particular events, linking them to one another, and pinpointing through their determinate linkages some historically specific, and more or less far-reaching or comprehensive, tendencies of development. Thus the real question is not "determinations or indeterminacy," but what *kind* of historical explanation one adopts: a mechanical-determinist or a *dialectical* overall framework.

Marx's conception of historical materialism from the very outset rejected all mechanical explanations, stressing that "the chief defect of all previous materialism (that of Feuerbach included) is that things [*Gegenstand*], reality, sensuousness are conceived only in the form of the object, or of contemplation, but not as *sensuous human activity, practice,* not subjectively. Hence, in contradistinction to materialism, the *active* side was set forth abstractly by idealism—which, of course, does not know real, sensuous activity as such."[2]

When it comes to genuine historical explanations, their plausibility hinges on whether or not they can account for the "active side" through which history is constantly being *made,* and not merely *given* as a brute conglomeration and fatalistic conjuncture of self-propelling material forces.

Admittedly, such forces are everywhere in evidence in history known to us: the history of class society, or "pre-history" as Marx called it, in contrast to the coming "real history" when the human agency is envisaged to be fully in control of its own destiny. But even when the strictly material forces are still preponderant, in the darker phases of that "pre-history," there is nevertheless an increasing tendency toward their being mastered, thanks to the controlling potential of the "active side." And how much more favorable could be this correlation between the material forces and the human agency in our own time, if the productive powers of society potentially available for the satisfaction of genuine human needs were not gravely distorted and crippled by their necessary subordination to the alienating imperative of capital's expanded self-reproduction? At a historical stage, that is, when the removal of the constraints of natural scarcity would be no longer beyond human reach, if it were not for the self-paralyzing—but in principle transcendable—impact of antagonistic *social* contradictions? For it is the latter that create the false appearance of a humanly uncontrollable *material* force being responsible for the crises of *plenty* (overproduction), imposing themselves in the form of a brutal paradox as chronic *"scarcity,"* thanks to the "own goals" of the selfsame active side.

1.2 Philosophical Foundations of Historical Materialism

In his attempt to spell out the real historical potentialities of the "active side" of human involvement in the complex network of social determinations—in its active character defined as an objective movement from "prehistory" to the "realm of the new historic form"—Marx had to set out from a position diametrically opposed to that of Hegel on every key issue. Hence he put into relief *labor* in the form in which it actually constituted the foundation of both historical determinacy and emancipation: as "sensuous productive activity," and thereby also as the ground of even the most complex and mediated *intellectual production*. Similarly, he rejected all forms of *theological* teleology, focusing attention at the same time on the dynamic material/intellectual *telos of labor:* both as human *self-production* and as the production of the conditions of emancipatory social transformation in the direction of that "realm of freedom."

In the same spirit, he conceived the nature of historical determination and the unfolding of historical necessity—in contrast to the self-anticipating circularity of such concepts within the confines of Hegel's truncated dialectic—as the necessarily *"disappearing* necessity"[3] of actual historical transformations which, through the growing mastery of material life's objective constraints, also create the growing margin of freedom. Accordingly, there could be no such thing as "the end of history." For history had to remain *radically open* to qualify as history in order to make any sense at all of "self-activity" and "freedom" in terms of the objective potentialities of human self-realization.

Furthermore, if history as such had to remain radically open, how could one possibly assume an uncritical attitude toward the state as the permanent framework of all future historical development? This contradiction in terms could only be propounded by those who arbitrarily identified the modern state with the elementary conditions of *social life* in general, as indeed happened in much of liberal political theory.

Hegel adopted a more ingenuous scheme than his predecessors: by opposing an inward-oriented "ideal realm" to the world of practical interest, insisting that "mind receives in its *inner life* its truth and concrete essence, while in *objectivity* it is at home and *reconciled* with itself."4 Thus he interweaved the themes of a "reconciliation with the actual" and of "enjoying the present" with his discourse on the end of history and on the ultimate consummation—in "objectivity" and "actuality"—of such end, under the supremacy of Europe, through the absolute permanence of the idealized state. In this way he created the *semblance* of a genuine history by allowing the emergence of objective forces in the form of their *genesis* and expelling them through the back door: by envisaging the necessary culmination of all such historical movement in the apriori anticipated "return of the Spirit into itself." Thus, however ingenious the Hegelian scheme in its details, the "end of history" and the permanence of the state were ideologically wedded together in its overall construct.

Understandably, Marx's rejection of the idea of the "end of history" necessarily implied a radically critical attitude toward the state as a historical product as well as toward all theories—whether the original liberal conceptions or the Hegelian variant—which failed to treat the state in a consistently historical manner. All social institutions, no matter how elementary or all-embracing, had to be accounted for in strictly historical terms, rather than being merely assumed "ready made," like Pallas Athene emerging fully armed from Zeus's head. And they had to be accounted for with regard to both their origin and historical dissolution, in the generally ignored Marxian sense of historical necessity, defined as necessarily "disappearing, vanishing necessity."

In this respect, the methodologically vital critique of theories that ahistorically "assume what needs to be proved" is a guiding thread of Marx's approach not only to Hegel (particularly to his theory of the state) but equally to Hobbes and Locke as well as to the classics of political economy in general. For all these theories tend to equate the modern state and the capitalist market-relations with the elementary conditions of social life, thereby a priori excluding the possibility of situating the dominant social institutions within the dynamic horizon of their ultimately necessary supersession.

In Marx's conception of objective and open-ended historical determinations both philosophy and its categories had to be assigned a role qualitatively different from that of his predecessors. For even within the Hegelian scheme of things (which stressed the importance of the "active side") philosophy, as the "owl of Minerva," was presented as the consolation prize for an unavoidable *resignation* to the false positivity of the established world. Defined as "the rose in the cross of the present," philosophy was destined to provide the necessary "reconciliation to the actual" and to authenticate—with the help of its "eternal" categories—the apologetic circularity of beginning and end in the "essentially present" ahistorical "actuality." Thus philosophy, as the "owl of Minerva," had to culminate in the atemporal categories of the Hegelian logico/dialectical circle in order to fulfill its function of reconciliatory resignation; and vice versa: the conception of the categories fit to produce the formal/sequential deduction of "actuality"—as corresponding to the a priori anticipated "return of the Spirit into itself"—could only result in an essentially pessimistic worldview of unavoidable reconciliation and inward-oriented resignation.

In Marx's view, by contrast, philosophy was itself inherently historical and, as such, subject to materially identifiable objective determinations. At the same time, as an *active* constituent of the complex dialectic of the social base and its superstructure, it was also a necessary instrument of the struggle for self-emancipation from the real "cross of the present": that unholy rule of dehumanization in the exploitative "actuality" of the established world. To be sure, it was the prevailing state of affairs that made it *necessary* to orient philosophy toward "changing the world," in polemics with its contemplative/interpretative role in the past. However, only a dialectical conception of the social base and its superstructure— which acknowledged philosophy's materially articulated active potential and thereby emancipatory intervention in the complicated network of historical determinations—made it realistically *possible* to do so.

As to the categories themselves, their historical character had to be stressed with equal radicalism. Accordingly, Marx insisted that they are produced by objective historical development as "forms of being" [*Dase-insformen*], becoming manifest in the practical interrelations of the social world before they can be conceptualized by philosophers and "political economists" in a general form. Thus the general category of "labor," for instance, appears in theory only after the displacement or marginalization of its particular forms—e.g., agricultural labor as the key concept in the physiocratic system—in reality itself. For

> as a rule, the most general abstractions arise only in the midst of the richest possible concrete development, where one thing appears as common to many, to all. Then it ceases to be thinkable in a *particular* form alone. On the other side, this abstraction of labour as such is not merely the mental product of a concrete totality of labour. Indifference toward specific labours *corresponds* to a form of society in which individuals can with ease transfer from one labour to another, and where the *specific* kind is a matter of *chance* for them, hence of indifference. Not only the *category* of labour, but labour *in reality* has here become the means of creating wealth in general, and has ceased to be organically linked with particular individuals in any specific form. Such a state of affairs is at its most developed in the most modern form of existence of bourgeois society—in the United States. Here, then, for the first time, the point of departure of modern economics, namely the abstraction of the category, "labour," "labour as such," labour pure and simple, becomes *true in practice.* . . .[5] In the succession of the economic categories, as in any other historical, social science, it must not be forgotten that their subject—here, modern bourgeois society—is always what is given, in the *head* as well as in *reality,* and that these categories therefore express the *forms of being,* the characteristics of existence, and often only individual sides of *this specific society, this subject,* and that therefore this society by no means begins only at the point where one can speak of it *as such.*[6]

Thus the categories of philosophy could not be produced by the "self-activity of the Idea" but as "forms of being" had to reflect in an adequate form some essential relationship. Nor could they be exempted from historical determinations but, on the contrary, as forms of an irrepressibly changing social being, they qualified as true conceptualizations of that being only by putting into relief the inherent historical dynamic of the whole process in question. Hence philosophy could only come into its own by "letting reality speak" its own truth, instead of compressing the latter into the Procrustean bed of preconceived categories, in the name of some abstract "eternal truth."

As already mentioned, philosophy, according to Marx, had to play a vital role in the process of self-emancipation. However, in order to be able to do so, first it had to emancipate itself from the tyranny of its own mystifications and preconceptions, grounding itself at every level—from the most immediate and particular propositions to the most abstract categories and generalizations—in the real historical dynamics of social being. The materialist conception of history was meant to provide precisely such grounding.

Thus far from being an "economic determinist," Marx was in fact deeply concerned with the freedom of human self-emancipation arising from the real possibilities of the "active side" to transcend the antagonisms of "prehistory" and to move toward the "realm of the new historic form." However, both the tangible liberating potentials and the objective constraints of this emancipatory movement had to be defined with precision, in contrast to the vacuity of "freedom" conceived as the philosophical contemplation of the Idea's self-realization in the enslaving actuality and "eternal present" of the capitalist state.

The objective constraints of social development that frustrated the aim of going beyond "prehistory" had to be fully acknowledged and put in perspective in order to make feasible a meaningful intervention in the *real* world. In this sense, the materialist conception of history, with its view on the relationship between *"base and superstructure,"* provided the necessary corrective to all previous accounts of the "active side": by situating the potential impact of ideas within a coherent framework of determinations, instead of either ignoring them or idealistically ascribing to them mythical powers in an unreal world.

At the same time, the determinations of base and superstructure had to be conceived as dynamic *interdeterminations*—thus decidedly not a mechanical one-way traffic, as the Marxian view is often misrepresented—

if the claimed and advocated intervention of the "active side" was to achieve any significance at all. Accordingly, the materialist conception of history had to be articulated from the very outset as the objective *dialectic* of base and superstructure, with all of its complex reciprocities and autonomy-producing interdeterminations.

This is how Marx in *The German Ideology* spelled out—in opposition to idealist conceptions—his view of history and the dialectic of "reciprocal action" among the various factors and forces that constitute the overall social complex of base and superstructure:

> This conception of history relies on expounding the real process of production—starting from the material production of life itself—and comprehending the form of intercourse connected with and created by this mode of production, i.e., civil society in its various stages, as the basis of all history; describing it in its action as the state, and also explaining how all the different theoretical products and forms of consciousness, religion, philosophy, morality, etc., etc., arise from it, and tracing the process of their *formation* from that basis; thus the whole thing can, of course, be depicted in its totality (and therefore, too, the *reciprocal action* of these various sides on one another). It has not, like the idealist view of history, to look for a *category* in every period, but remains constantly on the real ground of history; it does not explain practice from the idea but explains the *formation* of ideas from material practice, and accordingly it comes to the conclusion that all forms and products of consciousness cannot be dissolved by *mental criticism,* by resolution into "self-consciousness" or transformation into "apparitions," "spectres," "whimsies," etc., but only by the *practical overthrow* of the actual social relations which gave rise to this idealistic humbug; that not criticism but revolution is the driving force of history, *also of religion, of philosophy and all other kinds of theory.* It shows that history does not end by being resolved into "self-consciousness" as "spirit of the spirit," but that each stage contains a material result, a sum of productive forces, a *historically created* relation to nature and of individuals to one another, which is handed down to each generation from its predecessor; a mass of productive forces, capital funds and circumstances, which on the one hand is indeed *modified* by the new generation, but on the other also *prescribes* for it its conditions of life and

gives it a definite development, a special character. It shows that *circum-stances make men* just as much as *men make circumstances*.[7]

As we can see, even though in this work Marx's immediate target was idealism, determining the need to put sharply into relief—some might say overemphasize—the material dimension of the necessary corrective standpoint, he did not leave out of sight the complex dialectical interconnections. This is clearly in evidence through the following qualifications in terms of which the fundamental relationship between the "mode of production"—the material "basis" of society—and social consciousness is assessed:

1. A distinction is made between the different "theoretical products" and the "forms of consciousness" (religion, philosophy, morality, etc.) *within* which those theoretical products themselves arise. Thus attention is drawn to the *specificity* and relative *autonomy* of the various forms of social consciousness as the necessary—and to a significant extent *transhistorical*—intermediary or *mediation* between the given material base and the particular ideas as they are being produced at any particular time.

2. In conjunction with the previous point, the accent is on *the formation* of ideas (from the "basis," "real ground" and "material practice" of social life), which is primarily concerned with the *original constitution* of the "*forms* and *products* of consciousness." For once the various forms and modalities of consciousness already exist in their relative autonomy and transhistoricity, the reproduction and transformation of ideas—just as much as the production of even the most "radically new" ideas—is, of course, deeply affected by the specific forms within which all ideas must be produced.

3. Characteristically, Marx insists on the importance of the concept of *totality* in terms of which "the whole thing" can and must be depicted and without which the intricate nature of social interaction is thoroughly unintelligible. For only if we treat the various sides and aspects of the relationship between "material practices" and the production of

ideas as *inextricable constituents* of a coherently structured overall complex,[8] only then can we avoid the danger of mechanical reductionism.

4. It must be also noted that Marx is talking about the *"reciprocal* action of the *various sides* on one another," and not about a one-to-one connection between a given social base and the corresponding ideas—let alone about some form of mechanical determination of the ideas in general by the material base as such. In a coherently structured totality—the way in which Marx depicts the social complex, with all its intricate constituents and multiple dimensions—this could not be otherwise. For every single constituent has a variety of significantly different aspects through which a virtually inexhaustible range of combinations becomes possible:

    a) *within* each level (i.e., between ideas and ideas, or between different material factors, for instance), at a determinate time in history;

    b) *between* one level and another (e.g., between a material factor and a superstructural complex), again considered simply at a given point in time;

    c) through the *interplay* of a multiplicity of very different factors, thanks to the appropriate linkages and *mediations* that enable even the more or less temporary reversal of fundamental structural hierarchies at specific times in history, in contradistinction to the model of a straightforward determination directly asserting the power of the material base (e.g., the structurally dominant role of politics in Antiquity or of Christianity in the Middle Ages);

    d) through the dialectic of *structural and historical* determinations the insertion and more or less prolonged retention of different layers of temporality (i.e., of social complexes corresponding to qualitatively different historical determinations in their original constitution) into the overall structure of the social totality, and the all-round determination of the functioning of the social complex as a whole through *continuity in discontinuity* (and vice versa) with regard to its temporal dimensions no less than with respect to its manifold material and superstructural articulations or structures. (As an example, we can go back to an earlier point. We have seen that in the "*formation* of ideas" one must distinguish between the *original* constitution or production of ideas and forms of consciousness on the one hand, and the *ongoing* formation, reproduction and transformation of ideas on the other. Through the dialectic of structure and history—and its discontinuity in continuity as much as the other way round—the reality of this "formation of ideas" asserts itself simultaneously both as the production of more or less new ideas within an inherited framework or "form of consciousness," in a direct or mediated response to some more or less clearly conceptualized requirement of the social base, and as a more or less weighty pressure for the modification of both the conceptual framework within which the idea is produced and of the social complex, or part of it, to which the newly produced idea actively responds.)

Thus the "reciprocal action of the various sides on one another" and the creative potentialities resulting from the newly discovered and socially reinforced combinations open up growing areas of social practice for conscious intervention, constantly pushing back at the same time the boundaries of the original material structures and determinations. If nothing else, such a view of "reciprocal action" should make any mechanical/reductionist reading of Marx impossible.

5. In contrast to idealist "mental criticism," Marx indicates *revolution* as "the driving force of history, also of religion, of philosophy and all other kinds of theory." Thus again we are not offered some simple material mechanism for explaining historical and ideal/theoretical changes but an immensely complicated, dynamic *social complex* which itself is simultaneously as much the crystallization and summation of a great variety of pressures, determinations, and forces—including, of course, a multiplicity of ideal factors—leading to it, as indeed the new point of departure for all further development. This becomes all the more obvious if we remember that, just a few lines

before the passage we are concerned with, Marx insists on the necessity of producing "on a mass scale" what he calls "communist consciousness," linking it to revolution as the condition of its production,[9] and that the next paragraph reiterates the great importance of this "revolutionary mass," with its revolutionary consciousness, in contrast to the—no matter how advanced—"idea"[10] that remains separated from the objective dynamic of mass movements. To see *revolution*, therefore, merely as a material mechanism would be a gross oversimplification.

6. The last point that needs stressing is related to a widely diffused misreading of Marx. The misreading referred to here interprets Marx's conception of history as if he were only concerned with stating that "circumstances make men," completely ignoring his dialectical qualifications with regard to the active/creative impact of men themselves on their circumstances. This is particularly strange in view of the fact that one of Marx's most forceful *Theses on Feuerbach*—written at the same time as *The German Ideology*—explicitly rejects[11] precisely the same mechanical/materialistic one-sidedness that nevertheless continues to be attributed to him. Also, in the passage quoted from *The German Ideology* the necessary critique of idealism in no way diverts Marx from his dialectical assessment of the issues involved. For the dialectical character of the "reciprocal action" we are concerned with could hardly be put more clearly than by saying that "men make circumstances *as much as* they are made by them."

As we can see, this first systematic presentation of historical materialism in *The German Ideology* contains all of its principal defining characteristics as they later appear in Marx's famous "Preface" to his *Contribution to the Critique of Political Economy*. The passage we have looked at constitutes the obvious direct inspiration of the 1859 "Preface."

The only term missing from the earlier work is "superstructure." However, even though that term is absent from *The German Ideology*, the concept is decidedly not. It is there by way of describing how ideas "arise" out of real social practice, and also in the unavoidable implication of concepts like "foundation," "real ground," "basis," etc. (in German:

Grundlage, Geschichtsboden, realer Grund, and *Basis*) with which the formation and production of ideas and forms of consciousness is contrasted.[12] And what is more important, *The German Ideology* contains not only the main defining characteristics of historical materialism but simultaneously also the necessary dialectical qualifications that clearly set it apart from all previous conceptions of materialism. Thus the Marxian view of history is articulated from the outset not merely as historical *materialism*—in contrast to idealism—but simultaneously and inseparably also as *dialectical* materialism: in conscious opposition to all varieties of "*naturalistic* materialism."[13]

1.3 The Poverty of "Anti-Historicism"

The most famous passage in which Marx sums up his position on the dialectical relationship between base and superstructure reads like this:

> My inquiry led me to the conclusion that neither legal relations nor political forms could be comprehended whether by themselves or on the basis of a so-called general development of the human mind, but that on the contrary they originate in the material conditions of life, the totality of which Hegel, following the example of English and French thinkers of the eighteenth century, embraces within the term "civil society"; that the anatomy of this civil society, however, has to be sought in political economy. . . .
>
> In the social production of their existence, men inevitably enter into definite relations, which are independent of their will, namely relations of production appropriate to a given stage in the development of their material forces of production. The totality of these relations of production constitutes the economic structure of society, the real foundation on which arises a legal and political superstructure and to which correspond definite forms of social consciousness. The changes in the economic foundation lead sooner or later to the transformation of the whole immense superstructure. In studying such transformations it is always necessary to distinguish between the material transformation of the economic conditions of production, which can be determined with the pre-

cision of natural science, and the legal, political, religious, artistic or philosophic—in short, ideological forms in which men become conscious of this conflict and fight it out.

Just as one does not judge an individual by what he thinks about himself, so one cannot judge a period of transformation by its self-consciousness, but, on the contrary, this consciousness must be explained from the contradictions of material life, from the conflict existing between the social forces of production and the relations of production. No social order is ever destroyed before all the productive forces for which it is sufficient have been developed, and new superior relations of production never replace older ones before the material conditions for their existence have matured within the framework of the old society. Mankind thus inevitably sets itself only such tasks as it is able to solve, since closer examination will always show that the problem itself arises only when the material conditions for its solution are already present.[14]

In the first place, one must underline here the importance of Marx's remark that "it is always necessary to distinguish" between the material transformations and the ideological forms. For, astonishingly, interpretations often not only completely miss the point but manage to turn his views into their *exact opposite*. Yet an attentive reading makes it amply clear that Marx's aim is

1. to focus on the distinction itself, emphasizing the vital importance of keeping constantly in mind the qualitative differences implicit in it;

2. to insist that the superstructure cannot be determined with the same precision as the strictly "material transformation of the economic conditions of production";

3. to indicate that since there is a dialectical interaction between the superstructure and the material base—and thus both profoundly affect one another, thereby together constituting an organic whole— by implication: the overall development of the whole complex cannot be "determined with the precision of natural science."

Strangely, however, the passage is often interpreted as if Marx had said: "One should *never distinguish* between the material transformations and the ideological forms." Once such vital qualifications are disregarded, the road is wide open for constructing a totally unrecognizable edifice of Marxism, in accordance with a fetish-like view of science. The necessary result of this kind of misreading is a reductionist distortion, irrespective of the subjective intent behind it: be it the aim of producing some structuralist/Marxist "revival," or, on the contrary, that of supplying the grateful audience of bourgeois cultural/political expectations with yet another "final refutation" of Marxism and its alleged "historicism."

We can see the consequences of identifying the Marxian conception with a model of natural science in Popper's celebrated attack on Marxism. In *The Poverty of Historicism*[15]—a title, according to the author, "intended as an allusion to the title of Marx's book *The Poverty of Philosophy*"[16]—he proudly announces that "I have succeeded in giving a refutation of historicism."[17] And this is how the line of reasoning of this much acclaimed "refutation" runs:

1. The course of human history is strongly influenced by the growth of human knowledge. (The truth of this premise must be admitted even by those who see in our ideas, including our scientific ideas, *merely the by-products* of material developments of some kind or other.)

2. We cannot predict, by rational or scientific methods, the future growth of our scientific knowledge.

3. We cannot, therefore, predict the future course of human history.

4. This means that we must reject the possibility of a theoretical history; that is to say, of a historical social science that would correspond to *theoretical physics.* [Popper's emphasis.] There can be no scientific theory of historical development serving as a basis for historical prediction.

5   The fundamental aim of historicist methods is therefore misconceived; and historicism collapses.[18]

As we can see, the whole "refutation" sets out from the invention of a straw-man that later can be knocked down or made to "collapse" with the greatest ease. This obliging strawman is produced by substituting for the complex dialectical model of base and superstructure an absurdly reductionist caricature according to which ideas are "merely the by-product of material developments." This is, of course, a rather crude way of begging the question, since the author prefabricates for his own use a convenient target that is "made to measure" for the circularly anticipated refutation.

And this is only the outer perimeter of the web of tautologies from which the Popperian "refutation" is constructed. The next circle is spun by definitionally—and, of course, arbitrarily—*separating* the production of knowledge from the social and historical conditions of its production, so as to be able to *oppose* this artificially disembodied knowledge to social/historical developments and determinations.

To be sure, this kind of disembodied knowledge is immune to social influences and to the possibility of prediction. However, by circularly defining knowledge in a way that fits in with the requirements of the self-anticipating "refutation," the reality of knowledge—together with the actual conditions of its production—must disappear without trace. For in the real world the development of knowledge is dialectically intertwined with social processes, and it is a matter of *degree* how much they (a) *influence* and (b) are *predictable* with regard to their reciprocal impact on one another.

Thus, though it is indeed impossible to predict the appearance of this or that particular *item* of knowledge at a determinate time in history—just as it is impossible to predict the particular events through which a social/historical trend asserts itself—it is by no means impossible to grasp the connection between the emergence and further development of a certain *type* of knowledge and the broad social/historical determinations on the basis of which *both* the scientific knowledge of an age and the institutional/instrumental framework of the corresponding social formation articulate themselves in their manifold details.

Significantly, from Popper's deductions both qualifiers are omitted. The *degree* to which the development of knowledge can or cannot be predicted becomes a *categorical denial* of the possibility of its prediction. At the same time, no attempt is made at specifying the *degree* to which the "non-predictable" development of knowledge—which is itself subject to the necessary dialectical qualifications—vitiates social/historical prediction in general. (In other words, what is crudely distorted here is that, since the development of knowledge is in fact predictable *up to a certain degree* in the sense indicated a moment ago, and since the advancement of knowledge is itself only *one* of the factors involved in social development, historical prediction is indeed possible to a quite *significant degree*.) It sounds much better—and supports the claim "I have succeeded in giving a refutation of historicism" more convincingly—if one can *categorically* state that, since the growth of knowledge is unpredictable as a matter of logical impossibility therefore historical prediction is a priori impossible on other than the most myopic scale. The trouble is, though, that the all too eager omission of the necessary qualifications makes the Popperian deduction/"refutation" fallacious even in its own terms of reference.

But perhaps the most revealing part of the Popperian web of tautologies is its inner circle and "ultimate proof" as enunciated in point 4. According to this "there can be no scientific theory of historical development" because no historical conception can aspire at being like *"theoretical physics."* Here again an arbitrary measure is definitionally assumed as the self-evident orienting principle of all rational discourse on science and history, and thus the "refutation" is accomplished by circularly concluding that "historicism" does not match up to the arbitrarily assumed measure.

In truth the supposedly self-evident measure is only a sieve, made of enormous holes—the latter so big, in fact, that even a great deal of *natural science* would fall through them, not to mention the totality of *social science*—held together by nothing more sound and solid than crusading ideological hostility toward Marxism.

The title of another crusading book by Popper—*The Open Society and Its Enemies*—speaks for itself in this respect. Anything that cannot fit into the pattern of apologetically patching up and papering over the cracks of the established order—especially the idea of the self-management of a socialist society by the associated producers, in accordance with an overall plan they set for themselves—is categorically rejected by appending the labels of "holism" and "pre-scientific perfectionism." We can see the ideological interest beneath the surface of such exorcism-by-labeling in the following lines: "An additional reason for considering the holistic approach to social science as pre-scientific is that it contains an element of perfectionism. Once we realize, however, that we cannot make heaven on earth but can only improve matters a *little,* we also realize that we can only improve them *little by little.*"19

The logic of this "scientific" procedure is really telling. First the idea of improving the conditions of life through major changes in society is turned into "an element of perfectionism" (and ipso facto consigned to the devil as "pre-scientific"). Next, the alleged *element* of perfectionism is rhetorically equated with wanting to have wholesale *"heaven on earth"* (and dismissed as self-evident absurdity by the force of the image itself). Having thus cleared the ground—not by proof or reasoning but through rhetoric and labeling—the author can now introduce the totally unsupported assertion (the underlying aim of the whole exercise) according to which "we can only improve matters a *little.*" Finally, the arbitrarily assumed "little" stipulates the one and only conceivable "scientific method" appropriate to its object: the *"little by little"* of apologetic "social engineering" confined to technological manipulation.

Naturally, sympathy for this crusading posture dulls the philosophical sensitivity of those who should know better—at least at the level of formal logic. Instead, the true character of Popperian "refutation"— that its inner core is a self-referential tautology (the mythical model of "theoretical physics") wrapped up in a double circularity, as we have seen already— remains hidden and the enterprise is hailed as ultimate wisdom. Thus, thanks to a large extent to the fetish of "science" it uses in its circular "refutations," blatant ideological hostility—wedded to logical fallaciousness— can successfully misrepresent itself as "the logic of scientific discovery."

Characteristically, even the most far-fetched speculation is seriously entertained in this "scientific discourse" so long as it promises to yield some useful ammunition against the ideological adversary. We read in *The Poverty of Historicism:*

> There is, for example, a trend toward an 'accumulation of means of production' (as Marx puts it). But we should hardly expect it to persist in a population which is rapidly decreasing; and such a decrease may in turn depend on extra-economic conditions, for example, on chance inventions, or conceivably on the direct physiological (perhaps biochemical) impact of

an industrial environment. There are, indeed, countless possible conditions; and in order to be able to examine these possibilities in our search for the true conditions of a trend, we have all the time to try to imagine conditions under which the trend in question would disappear. But this is just what the historicist cannot do. He firmly believes in his favorite trend, and conditions under which it would disappear are to him unthinkable. The poverty of historicism, we might say, is a poverty of imagination.[20]

Here we are again presented with a caricature of Marx as a mechanical materialist and crude determinist. For Marx does not speak generically about an "accumulation of means of production" but defines with great precision the objective conditions of the historically identified trend in terms of the "organic composition of capital," the "declining rate of profit," the "centralization and concentration of capital," etc. What he "fails" to do, of course, is to supply capital's apologists with a list of grotesquely fanciful "conditions" (self-congratulatorily praised by Popper as "imagination") which would *a priori invalidate* his concern with the inner contradictions of capital foreshadowing the system's breakdown.

Surely, Popper must know that if science wasted its time on speculating about possible "chance inventions" and about all "conceivable possibilities" as well as counter-possibilities, one would never get as far as lifting one little finger for the realization of any task whatsoever, thinking that "possibly" they are all doomed to failure as a result of some "conceivable" intervening counter-condition. For just as practical activity of real life in general—subject to a multiplicity of objective constraints—so science, too, is not concerned with the "bad infinity" of fancifully abstract "conceivable possibilities" but with *concrete possibilities and probabilities*, which are defined in more or less direct terms with *some relevance* to the problems at stake.

Thus to dismiss Marx in an age of dramatically rising population as a "hopelessly unimaginative historicist" for his alleged failure to talk a century earlier about a "rapidly decreasing population" as the sound counter-condition to his own theory is rather astonishing. For even if we disregard how wide Popper's own counterexamples miss their mark, the fact remains that the only way to satisfy the conditions laid down by the author—namely to water down the validity of the identified social/economic trends by conjuring up possible "chance inventions" and "countless possible extra-economic conditions" as well as other "imagined" and "conceivable" counter-conditions—is not to have any critical theory at all about actual social/economic trends. But, of course, that is precisely the purpose of the much celebrated Popperian undertaking.

1.4 Concepts and Metaphors: A Problem of Method

In contrast to all fetishistic views of science and their crude models of causation—which equate social determination with the necessity of a mechanical natural science (hence their notion of "historical inevitability") and lead to reductionism even when not motivated by ideological hostility—it is important to grasp *social causation* by preserving the great complexity of determinations involved in its manifold interacting dimensions. The Marxian theory of base and superstructure is meant to put into relief such qualitatively different dimensions and their complicated interrelations, instead of providing a magic formula for bringing everything under the lowest common denominator, as some interpretations do while attempting to find inadmissible shortcuts.[21]

Admittedly, it is much easier to operate with neat reductions and schematic models than to take hold of the elusive social process in a way that adequately reproduces, within the categorial framework employed, the objective dynamic of the dialectical movement. Furthermore, in the "shorthand" notation of our own thinking we all tend to sum up—often by images and similes—whole networks of complicated categorial interconnections, with reference to shifting, and through their reciprocity meaningful, sets of relations. Such shorthand is a necessary part of the economy of thought, although by no means devoid of its own complications and drawbacks. For though on the one hand it enables us to bring simultaneously into focus a multiplicity of interconnections, together with their complex ramifications (which simply could not be recalled in any other way with such simultaneity), on the other hand, all this is accomplished only in the form of more or less obvious *implications* and allusions. The latter, in turn, are open to further expansion or completion and are subject to a number of possible interpretations in the light of which particular members of the interconnected sets are pushed into the foreground. Indeed, the shorthand or graphic image itself may even be an obstacle to a proper understanding of the complex relations at issue if it is not coupled with an adequate conceptual articulation of the relevant constituents involved.

In this sense, "base and superstructure," "reflection," and even "reciprocal action," represent insurmountable difficulties if taken *literally,* as, unfortunately, all too often happens to be the case. For in their immediacy they are only *similes* (in everyday language also described as "metaphors")[22] whose straightforward conceptual translation is—of necessity—one-sided, if not altogether mechanical.

The most problematical of these images, surrounded by interminable controversy, is the "reflection" theory of art and knowledge. At the roots of it stands the proposition according to which the various forms of social consciousness *originate* on the material ground of social being, as spelled out in *The German Ideology* and in the 1859 "Preface" quoted above: a proposition very difficult to object to on other than purely speculative, idealist grounds. However, the simile of "reflection," especially as linked to the image of the mirror, cannot help slanting the issue in the direction of a mechanical account. Taken in its literal/immediate sense, this graphic image cannot reproduce the dialectical complexity of the manifold interactive processes referred to but tends to compress them into a simple one-to-one relationship of which—to make things worse still—the "reflected" part is merely a *passive* constituent.

Nor would the difficulties ipso facto disappear by pointing to a "reciprocal action" between the two sides. For the primary problem lies in the *mechanical literal meaning* of this provisional simile itself, which can only serve as a point of departure to the required flexible and dynamic explanation. It is of little consequence to suggest that the object is not only reflected in the mirror but also "reacts back" on the mirror itself, since it is very difficult to imagine what meaning, if any, one could ascribe to such "reaction" within the literal sense of the simile.

In any case, the idea of a "reciprocal action" by no means constitutes on its own a self-evident dialectical qualifier, since prima facie it recalls the third law of motion of Newtonian *mechanics* in the framework of which it originally acquired its meaning. The problem is not only that the real situation reveals a *multiplicity* of reciprocally interpenetrating and structurally modifying/modified elements in the dialectic of base and superstructure, but that the various constituents involved are not *homogeneous* entities or forces. Thus an additional complication has to be faced, in the sense that the "homogenization" of the material and the ideal factors—or something equivalent to such homogenization—must be first established before one could take for granted the possibility of a "reciprocal action" between base and superstructure.

Similarly, the notion of "base and superstructure" presents us with a whole range of difficult problems. As a spatial simile, it lends itself with particular ease to mechanical distortions, suggesting an ossified, uni-directional determination which in no way can be redressed by some vague and rather incoherent talk about "overdetermination." For once the shorthand summing up of "base and superstructure"—which stands for a great multitude of dialectical determinations and interconnections—is reduced to the one-sided simplicity of its *literal* meaning, no amount of patching up will turn the static architectural skeleton into a living organism so as to match the inherently dynamic character of the social metabolism, with all its arterial as well as capillary processes.

Methodologically, the distortions in all these cases do not arise simply from the restrictive imagery itself but from the use to which the particular images are put. Similes and analogies cannot help being what they are, and even the best of them are bound to break down sooner or later. Nor is it conceivable to do without them. For it is an inherent characteristic of the thought process that it proceeds by stages, requiring a number of provisional summations before the envisaged end can be reached. These summations in turn represent progressively higher plateaus or "base camps" from which the final assault on the chosen summit may be eventually attempted. As such the provisional summations do not carry the meaning of the enterprise itself, only that of its necessary instrumentality.

Of course, by no means are all "base camps" made of similes, analogies, etc., even if many of them are. What matters here is that *all* such provisional summations—be they graphic or not in character—must be further articulated in the course of the discursive analysis, in accordance with the particular requirements of the shifting contexts to which they are related. If, therefore, the imagery is confined to the immediacy of its literal meaning, no further articulation and enrichment of its original connotations is possible. Consequently, the "base camp" becomes an end in itself, and all newly arising data as well as their correlations are manipulated so as to compress everything into its restrictive confines, rationalizing at the same time this "Procrustean" practice of manipulation as if it were the fulfillment of the given task in its integrality. This is why it is essential to recognize the strictly summary and provisional character of all similes and comparisons, treating them with great caution within the limits of their usefulness and discarding them the very moment they tend to constrain the necessary conceptual articulation and elucidation toward which even the best of them can only supply a stepping-stone.

1.5 Technological Determinism and Dialectics

In Marx's conception of social processes and transformations every single element is considered in its dialectical linkages with all the others. The overall complex can be visualized as dialectical only because its "moments" themselves are dynamically interconnected constituents of a structured whole. In other words, there is a fundamental coherence between the global structure and its "microstructures" without which one could only speak of some chaotic aggregate of disparate elements, and not of a developing social totality, with identifiable tendencies of its own.

In this sense, the relationship between base and superstructure can be dialectical because *both* complexes are constituted in an irreducibly dialectical way. Forgetting this elementary truth leads to mechanical distortions of the Marxian conception, like the "technological determinism" of Kautsky and Bukharin as well as of many less well-known figures. In one of his early essays Lukács rightly emphasizes that

> Bukharin attributes to technology a far too determinant position, which completely misses the spirit of dialectical materialism. . . Bukharin remarks: "Every given system of social technique determines human work relations as well." He attributes the predominance of a natural economy in classical times to the low level of *technical* development. He insists: "If technique changes, the division of labour in society also

changes." He asserts that "in the last analysis" society is dependent on the development of *technique,* which is seen as the *"basic determinacy"* of the "productive forces of society," etc. It is obvious that this final identification of technique with the forces of production is neither valid nor Marxist. Technique is a *part,* a moment, naturally of great importance, of the social productive forces, but it is neither simply identical with them, nor (as some of Bukharin's earlier points would seem to imply) the final or absolute moment of the changes in these forces.[23]

In such approaches, the oversimplifying interpretation of the base/superstructure model as a rigid one-to-one correspondence between its two key terms of reference—stipulating a unilateral determination of the world of ideas by the material world—is founded on the mechanical reduction of the base itself to *one* of its manifold constituents, carrying with it the disappearance of all the relevant dialectical linkages and the replacement of the concept of *social structure* (or socioeconomic structure) by that of the "base" narrowly identified with the fetishistic objectivity of *technology.*

Thus the unwarranted literal interpretation of the base/superstructure model reveals a conceptual rigidity at the core of all such mechanical/reductionist theories. It is not the Marxian graphic simile that pushes this kind of approach toward the mechanical one-sidedness of its technological determinism. On the contrary, it is the fetishistic view of necessity, science, objectivity, and technology of its propounders that reaches out for a crude literal interpretation of base and superstructure as the authoritative legitimation and grounding of extremely dubious positions.

In complete contrast, Marx defines the socioeconomic structure in the passage quoted earlier from the 1859 "Preface" as "the totality of the relations of production," which is an inherently dialectical concept. Furthermore, the latter constitutes the necessary framework into which all material and work processes are inserted and embedded, including, of course, every conceivable form of technology. Thus there is an inescapable dialectical relationship between the forces and the relations of production on the foundation of which it is possible to think of the social whole as a dialectically structured complex: one made up of dynamically interacting parts that reciprocally determine one another in all directions through their "embedding embeddedness."

The dialectic is either everywhere or nowhere. If we exclude it from the social determination of the productive forces and technology, we turn dialectic into a pseudo-historical conceptual device incapable of explaining social transformations, depriving thereby the base/superstructure model of its explanatory value as well.

The dialectical intent implicit everywhere in the Marxian conception is forcefully put into relief when Marx insists on the "dialectic of the concepts productive force (means of production) and relation of production, a dialectic whose *boundaries* are to be determined, and which does not suspend the *real difference.*"[24] It is this dialectic that makes the graphic imagery acceptable and illuminating. For if at the core of a theory we find instead a rigid, mechanically linked set of relations, no amount of pictorial flourish is going to turn such a view of reality into a flexible dialectical conception. And by the same token, if a "mechanical Marxist" thinker wants to fit things into his own conceptual scheme, he must radically change the original base/superstructure model, too, with all of its corollaries, so as to make them compatible—by means of a one-sided, "literal" interpretation and reduction—with the reductionist meaning of technological determinism as such.

The dialectical approach is concerned with bringing to the fore the objective internal connections of a complex while drawing the necessary lines of demarcation—defining the *boundaries,* as Marx puts it—between the multiplicity of constitutive "moments" that make up the overall structure.

Both steps are vitally important. Concentrating on the great variety of objective interconnections enables one to grasp the constantly unfolding process in its inner dynamism. At the same time, "defining the boundaries" makes it possible to preserve the *"real differences"* in their tangible specificity without which the first step could not produce a dialectical approximation of its object but only a *chaotic flux* of shapes and hues merging into one another.

A "dialectic" devoid of firm lines of demarcation and "overriding [*über-greifenden*] moments" could amount to no more than tautology, or to the unenlightening truism according to which "everything is connected with everything else." For it is the *determinate* character of what is connected as well as the *specific mode* of the prevailing connections that matters, not the mere fact of connectedness. Accordingly, the object of a dialectical inquiry must be grasped as a totality whose parts are not merely interconnected, nor equally important, but constitute a *structured* whole, with its appropriate internal *order* and determinate *hierarchies*, even if the latter must be understood as dynamically shifting and changing, in accordance with the inherent nature of a *dialectical* complex.

The validity of Marx's model of base and superstructure arises precisely from its ability to set boundaries on a firm foundation, by focusing on the relevant historical specificities in the structural framework of dialectical interconnections: a procedure that simultaneously unfolds and puts into perspective the real differences. Since structural and historical determinations constitute an inseparable unity in this conception, there can be no room for absolutes, for any "eternalization of the relations of production," nor indeed for their opposite: a totally disorienting "historical relativism."

Historical materialism, as its name implies, explains the various social processes and intellectual developments in their coherently ordered complexity in relation to their material ground without reducing them to some abstract material entity. For, on the one hand, being dialectically *related* to a material structure is very far from being *identical* to it; and on the other, the material foundation referred to is itself inherently *historical* in character.

To appreciate the anti-relativist stance and at the same time the complete flexibility of Marx's approach, it is necessary to present here the broad outlines of his conception of dialectical interdeterminations.

The social metabolism is the ultimate framework of reference of this conception, since it comprehends the totality of determinations, from the direct material processes to the most mediated intellectual practices. The structural foundation of all social processes is the *transhistorical* objectivity *of social ontological determinations* in virtue of the inescapable fact that the social metabolism is rooted—and remains so even at the highest conceivable level of social and technological development—in the *metabolism between humankind and nature.*

However, two qualifications are necessary in order to avoid misunderstanding. *First,* and this cannot be repeated often enough, "transhistorical" means precisely what it says: namely, *trans*-historical and not *supra*-historical. The concept of "transhistorical" expresses the continued reproduction—even though with changing weight and relative significance in relation to the given social totality—of determinate conditions or processes *across* historical boundaries, whereas the idea of anything "*supra*-historical" is no more than a metaphysical mystification.

The *second* point to stress is that although the fundamental material determinations of social life persist throughout history, they do not by any means occupy the same position at all times in the overall hierarchy of interacting forces that regulate the historically always specific social metabolism. Obviously, even at the highest conceivable level of development they remain *latent* and therefore may surface with brutal suddenness under the circumstances of an all-embracing structural crisis. Since, however—thanks to the achievements of progressive socioeconomic transformations—the most elemental material determinations become latent only, far more mediated superstructural factors may assume a key position in the historically prevailing order of structural hierarchies.

The social totality at any particular time in history is constituted from a multiplicity of interdeterminations, with a—changing—relative weight of each (hence the concept of "*übergreifendes* [overriding] Moment") in the overall complex. The relative weight of the various factors and determinations depends on the functions they are called upon to fulfill in the social metabolism, which in turn depends both on the attained degree of historical/economic development of the society in question and on the successful functioning of the given set of determinations in the prevailing order of hierarchies for reproducing the conditions of existence of that society. As long as the function of reproduction is successfully carried out, the "brute" material determinations need not be *directly* operative but may be displaced by superstructural mechanisms and determinations, as mentioned above. However, they are *reactivated* again at times when we experience a serious disruption in the social metabolism, thus calling for a major restructuring of the existing structural hierarchies.

1.6 The Dialectic of Structure and History

To sum up, the following points must be emphasized:

1. The social complex is defined as a rigorously structured whole (in contrast to all "historical relativism"), with its—dynamically changing

and shifting—internal hierarchies and more or less dominant "*über-greifenden*" moments.

2. The Marxian simile of "reflection" must be understood—in conjunction with the base/superstructure model and the manifold "reciprocities" implicit in it—in the context of this historically articulated and flexible conception of structural hierarchies, and not as a *static* determination, established once and for all in a *mechanical* order of things.

3. The superstructural complexes—from law and politics to art and morality—only *originate* (as *The German Ideology* and the 1859 "Preface" make amply clear) in the basic material determinations of social life, but do not always remain *directly* dependent on them. Hence the possibility of their relative *autonomy* and to a significant extent independent development with regard to the original material determinations. To attempt to make sense of every particular superstructural nuance or permutation in terms of the given material determinations is, therefore, rather nonsensical.

4. The relative autonomy of superstructural complexes establishes the *possibility* of breaking the stranglehold of direct material/economic determinations under favorable circumstances. Without the relative autonomy that arises out of the interplay of superstructural mediations upon which the possibility of a break is founded, the Marxian discourse on socialism—which stipulates the necessity of such a break—would be totally incoherent.

5. The original material determinations are progressively *displaced* in the course of historical development, and their severity greatly diminishes parallel to the multiplication of the productive forces. At the same time, they are never completely superseded but remain *latent* under the surface of the displacing mechanisms and consumptive modalities of social reproduction; indeed, they violently reassert themselves at the time of a major breakdown in the social metabolism with greater intensity the more *generalizable* the conditions causing

the breakdown are in an increasingly integrated global framework of social reproduction.

6. The *superstructural mediations* are not suspended in thin air and follow a course entirely of their own but, notwithstanding their *relative* autonomy, are sociohistorically specific carriers of determinate material functions with which they are *reciprocally embedded* through appropriate forms and modes of mediation. Such embeddedness is particularly pronounced at earlier stages of social development.

7. A more advanced stage of social development is by no means synonymous with a smaller degree of economic determination, as capitalism testifies. Nevertheless, such "advanced" forms of the domination of society by the material/economic processes can only operate through highly sophisticated and complex institutional mediations, encompassing not only the material base but the superstructure in its entirety. Accordingly, the crisis of such forms of socioeconomic metabolism of necessity embraces all dimensions of social life, underlining the need for a radical overhaul of society as a whole, with all its vital reproductive practices. (Evidently, the move from limited consumption to socially being able to sustain "luxury" requires not only the provision of the strictly material conditions of such a process but also the simultaneous mobilization of a great variety of superstructural mechanisms and mediations, from fashion and market research to the manipulation of taste and the creation and consolidation of "consumer-oriented" systems of value. Less obviously, perhaps, capitalistic market transactions imply a highly articulated system of state and inter-state relations, notwithstanding the mythology of "private" enterprise and "individual" incentive. The transition from handling metalmoney to electronically transmitting capital sums and profit figures of transnational companies from one computer terminal to another in different parts of the globe is hardly conceivable without a massive co-involvement of the capitalist state—as the ultimate guarantor for the viability of all such operations—either directly or from behind the stage.)

8. The relative autonomy of superstructural mediations mentioned in points (3) and (4) emphasized the possibility of a socialist break with capital's material determinations. It is, however, necessary to add to that some considerations concerning the ambivalent political character of this break, on account of the following circumstances: since the transition from the rule of capital to the "realm of the new historic form" involves the radical restructuring of the existing internal hierarchies dominated by the economy, the necessary *break* with the dominant practices in the first place must take a directly political form; but whereas capital's material/economic domination is being exercised on a *global* scale, the political break—in view of the structural articulation of the political as subsumed under particular states—cannot be other than *limited* in scope and extent in its initial stages, instead of being global, in accordance with the inherent requirements of the task to be accomplished.

These points put together throw into sharp relief the fundamental inseparability of the structural and the historical. For the *structural* is, so to speak, soaked in history and the *historical* is always articulated as a specific set of *structural determinations.*

NOTES

1. Frederick Engels, "Speech at the Graveside of Karl Marx" (March 17, 1883), in Karl Marx and Frederick Engels, *Selected Works,* Foreign Languages Publishing House, Moscow, 1951, 2:153.
2. Karl Marx, "Theses on Feuerbach," in Karl Marx and Frederick Engels, *Collected Works,* Lawrence and Wishart, London, 1975, 5:3 (henceforth MECW).
3. See the treatment of this issue particularly in Marx's *Grundrisse.*
4. Hegel, *Philosophy of Right,* Clarendon Press, Oxford, 1942, 220.
5. Karl Marx, *Grundrisse,* Penguin Books, Harmondsworth, 1973, 104–5.
6. Ibid., 106.
7. MECW, 53–54.
8. In his *Ontology of Social Being* (Merlin Press, London, 1978), Lukács makes the important point that even the smallest constituents of the social complex are themselves complexes. Thus, in describing the social totality,

we have to talk about a "complex of complexes," and not of the mere combination of more or less easily isolable, atomistic constituents.

9.   "Both for the production on a mass scale of this communist consciousness, and for the success of the cause itself, the alteration of men on a mass scale is necessary, an alteration which can only take place in a practical movement, a revolution; the revolution is necessary, therefore, not only because the ruling class cannot be overthrown in any other way, but also because the class overthrowing it can only in a revolution succeed in ridding itself of all the muck of ages and become fitted to found society anew." MECW, 5:52–53.

As we can see, the accent is on the revolution being practical, rather than simplistically material, since its primary concern is the production and ongoing development of the necessary revolutionary consciousness on a mass scale. Furthermore, it is equally stressed that this revolution is constantly self-renewing: a restless "permanent revolution" through which the revolutionary masses "become fitted to found society anew." Thus, also under this aspect, to think of the constantly self-renewing revolution—concerned with the production of a revolutionary consciousness—as a simple material mechanism would be a contradiction in terms.

10.   "If these material elements of a complete revolution are not present—namely, on the one hand the existing productive forces, on the other the formation [*Bildung*] of a revolutionary mass, which revolts not only against particular [*einzelne*] conditions of the existing society, but against the existing 'production of life' itself, the 'total activity' on which it was based—then it is absolutely immaterial for practical development whether the idea of this revolution has been expressed a hundred times already, as the history of communism proves." Ibid., 54.

Thus, the point is not to oppose the practical reality of the revolutionary masses to the idea but to emphasize their necessary unification. For the revolutionary masses quite simply do not exist without the consciousness of both having to, and being fitted to, radically transform the "total activity" of society; which is truly a matter of Bildung, dialectically meaning "objective constitution" as well as education.

11.   "The materialist doctrine concerning the changing of circumstances and upbringing forgets that circumstances are changed by men and that the educator must himself be educated. This doctrine must, therefore, divide society into two parts, one of which is superior to society. The coincidence of the changing of circumstances and of human activity or self-change can be conceived and rationally understood only as revolutionary practice." MECW, 5:4.

12.   The real novelty of the 1859 "Preface" in this respect consists in stressing the key mediating role of the legal and political superstructure.

13. A great deal of nonsense is written about the alleged opposition between Marx and Engels, on the flimsy ground that the terms "historical and dialectical materialism" are not used by Marx. This kind of "discovery" amounts to no more than making a fetish out of some half-understood words. For Marx in fact speaks of the "materialist conception of history," stressing its inherently dialectical character and the vital importance of reciprocal determinations and interactions. He opposes this dynamic, historical/dialectical conception of materialism to "naturalistic materialism," defending himself against "Accusations about the materialism of this conception. Relation to naturalistic materialism." And this is how the lines just quoted continue: "Dialectic of the concepts productive force (means of production) and relation of production, a dialectic whose boundaries are to be determined, and which does not suspend [*aufhebt*] the real difference." (*Grundrisse*, 109.) Thus the meaningful line of demarcation is not between Marx and Engels but between dialectical/historical and naturalistic materialism.

14. Karl Marx, *A Contribution to the Critique of Political Economy*, Lawrence & Wishart, London, 1971, 20–21.

15. Karl Popper, *The Poverty of Historicism*, Routledge & Kegan Paul, London, 1957.

16. Ibid., xi.

17. Ibid., ix.

18. Ibid., ix–x.

19. Ibid., 75, Popper's emphases.

20. Ibid., 129–30.

21. For instance, by suggesting that everything can be handled "with the precision of natural science."

22. See in this respect my essay, "Metaphor and Simile," in *Philosophy, Ideology and Social Science*, Harvester Press, 1986. See also chapter 3 in this volume, "Key Concepts in the Dialectic of Base and Superstructure."

23. Georg Lukács, *Political Writings, 1919–1929*, N.L.B., London, 1972, 136.

24. Marx, *Grundrisse*, 109.

CHAPTER TWO

Dialectical Transformations: Teleology, History, and Social Consciousness

2.1 Social Interaction and Uneven Development

According to Marx, the potential impact of the interaction between the material base and the superstructure can be both positive and negative, from early stages of historical development right up to that point in history when human beings consciously take control over the conflicting social forces of their situation. Hence ideology, too, appears in his conception with diametrically opposed connotations. On the one hand, it is presented in its negativity as a mystifying and counterproductive force which greatly hinders development. Yet on the other hand, it is also seen as a vital positive factor—bent on overcoming determinate social constraints and resistances—without whose active contribution the forward driving potentialities of the given historical situation quite simply could not unfold.

Some critics see an "ambiguity" in this view and try to remove it by giving ideology a one-sidedly negative connotation. The trouble with such interpretations is that they end up with a circular definition of both science and ideology as self-referential opposites to one another. To quote one example:

The comprehensive view [of the Marxian conception of ideology] holds that *all* philosophical, political, legal, etc., forms are ideological, though this is not said in so many words. The restrictive interpretation holds that only those philosophical, political, legal, etc., forms *which are ideological* can be opposed to science, without implying that they are always necessarily so. I think this interpretation is more consistent with Marx's other tenets, but one has to accept that an ambiguity exists in Marx's text.[1]

Unfortunately, the evidence put forward by the people who argue on these lines in support of their curious approach is rather flimsy. Thus we read in the same book: "In the 1859 Preface Marx referred to the 'forms of social consciousness' which correspond to the economic structures, *but he does not equate them with ideology, nor does he use the term superstructure to refer to them.*"[2]

This sounds very firm and conclusive indeed, establishing in the author's view the negative conception of ideology on Marx's authority. For if this is how Marx sees things, then it would appear to follow, as Larrain in fact later asserts, that "the superstructure of ideas refers to a global societal level of consciousness, whereas ideology is only a restricted part of the superstructure which includes specific forms of *distorted consciousness*."[3]

Surprisingly, however, our quote from page 171 continues like this: "*None the less, in a subsequent passage* Marx affirmed that"—and there follows a quotation (from the 1859 Preface) in which Marx clearly states the very *opposite* of what he was supposed to have said earlier in the same passage, namely he refers in general terms to "the legal, political, religious, aesthetic or philosophic—in short, *ideological forms* in which men become conscious of this conflict and fight it out."

Hence one cannot quite understand the meaning of "none the less," nor the vagueness of "in a subsequent passage" that implies some ambiguous second thought on Marx's part. For the fact is that the so-called subsequent passage is part of the *same paragraph*, just a few lines from Marx's reference to the correspondence between the material/economic base and "definite forms of social consciousness," written in the same breath and representing the logical continuation, not the ambiguous opposite of that thought.

Thus the claimed ambiguity is not a feature of the Marxian conception. Rather it is a requirement of the construct that wants to establish the one-sidedly negative characterization of ideology on Marx's authority, at the cost of oversimplifying his views by removing the alleged "ambiguity" (in truth the dialectical complexity) from the Marxian approach. For the real dynamics and vitality of multidimensional dialectical determinations disappear without trace if one opts for the tempting simplicity of an "unambiguously" negative conception of ideology.

In truth, there can be no a prioristic predetermination as to how the historical dialectic will unfold on the basis of the original correlates of the social metabolism. Nor can one a priori prejudge the way in which new material and intellectual factors—emerging at subsequent stages of historical development—will affect the overall complex in its temporary synthesis of the interacting forces at a progressively higher plateau from which later advances may be attempted.

To say that the plateau is progressively higher—thanks to the cumulative and at times dramatic advancement of the social productive forces—does not mean that there is something even vaguely resembling a *linear* progression. It simply means that *if and when* (or inasmuch as) the conflicting "moments" of the dynamic social interaction *resolve* their tensions—through devastations and revivals, relapses and qualitative improvements, the destruction of some forces and communities and the injection of new blood into others; in short, through the complicated trajectory of "uneven development"—then humanity finds itself at a higher level of actual productive accomplishment, with new forces and potentialities of further advance at its disposal. However, there can be no guarantee of a positive resolution of the social antagonisms involved, as the suggestions that the struggle may end "in the common ruin of the contending classes"[4] and that the historical alternative is "socialism *or* barbarism"[5] clearly acknowledge.

2.2 Problematical Character of Labor's Spontaneous Teleology

Looking back from a certain distance at actual historical development—a distance from which the *already consolidated* plateaus stand out as "necessary stages" of the whole itinerary, while the manifold specific struggles and contradictions leading to them (which contain numerous pointers toward possible alternative configurations) fade into the background—one may have the illusion of a "logically necessary" progression, corresponding to some hidden design. Viewed from such a perspective, everything firmly established acquires its *positive* sense, and the consolidated stages by definition must appear to be positive/rational—in virtue of their actual consolidation.

The historical images conceived in this way represent a rather problematical achievement, as manifest in the idealist conceptions of history. Understandably, there is a tendency to treat teleology in general as a form of theology. This is due to a large extent to the long prevailing conjunction of the two in an important current of the European philosophical tradition that formulated its explanations in terms of "final causes" and identified the latter with the manifestation of the divine purpose in the order of nature. However, the summary equation of teleology and theology is quite unjustifiable since the objective teleology of labor is an essential part of any coherent materialistic historical explanation of social development. Such an explanation, dealing with actually unfolding causal factors and not with a priori preconceived schemes, has nothing whatsoever to do with *theological* assumptions, even though determinate *teleological* propositions are inseparable from it.

Indeed, human history is not intelligible without some kind of teleology. But the only teleology consistent with the materialist conception of history is the objective and open-ended teleology of labor itself. At the fundamental ontological level such teleology is concerned with the way in which the human being—this unique "self-mediating being of nature"—creates and develops itself through its purposeful productive activity.

In this process, labor fulfills the function of active mediation in the progressively changing metabolism between humankind and nature. All potentialities of the socialized human being as well as all characteristics of the social intercourse and social metabolism emerge from the objective teleology of this mediation. And since the labor involved in these processes and transformations is men's own labor, the active mediation between humans and nature, too, cannot be considered other than *self-mediation*, which, as a framework of explanation, is radically opposed to any theological conception of teleology.

In this sense, history must be conceived as necessarily open-ended in virtue of the qualitative change that takes place in the natural order of determinations: the establishment of a unique framework of ontological necessity of which *self-mediating human teleology* itself is an integral part.

The *historically created* radical openness of history—human history— is therefore inescapable in the sense that there can be no way of theoretically or practically *predetermining* the forms and modalities of human *self*-mediation. For the complex teleological conditions of this self-mediation through productive activity can only be satisfied—since they are constantly being created and recreated—in the course of this self-mediation itself. This is why all attempts at producing neatly self-contained and closed systems of historical explanation result either in some arbitrary reduction of the complexity of human actions to the crude simplicity of mechanical determinations or in the idealistic superimposition of one kind or another of *a priori transcendentalism* on the *immanence* of human development.

However, the radical openness of the historical process—which is responsible for the simultaneously "positive negativity" and "negative positivity" of its results—is by no means fully characterized by emphasizing the *immanent* and *self-mediatory* nature of the teleology of labor. There are three further major considerations that must be mentioned in this context:

1. In accord with the inherent characteristics of the labor process, the *purpose* envisaged in its immediacy can only be a *partial* one, directly related to the task at hand, even if the cumulative partial solutions are always inserted into an increasingly broader context. Hence the "*positivity*" of a successful solution is necessarily defective inasmuch as it cannot possibly control the *global* consequences and implications of its own success, which may in fact turn out to be utterly disastrous despite the positivity originally posited and implemented in the specific teleological activity in question.

   As the multiplicity of limited teleological designs is realized in the course of practical productive activity, interlinking and integrating the specific results in a more or less coherent overall complex, a "totalization" of some kind takes place. However, it is a "totalization without a totalizer"[6] and therefore the conscious partial projects must suffer the (negative, unintended) consequences of being inserted into a "blind" overall framework that seems to defy any attempt at being controlled. As a result, not only is the originally posited meaning of the partial projects deflected and distorted, but at the same time the unconscious totalization of the partial results—later rationalized as the benevolent "hidden hand" of market society—becomes the necessary foundation and structurally vitiated (i.e., from the very beginning distorting and alienating) presupposition and guiding principle of the partial teleological activities themselves.

Undoubtedly, historical development—through the growing division of labor, coupled with the unfolding interconnectedness, indeed integration of the social organization of production—makes the particular purposes envisaged by the labor process increasingly more global even in their limited specificity. Thus at a highly advanced (e.g., capitalist) stage of the social division of labor, not only the *solution* of partial tasks cannot be envisaged without bringing into play a whole network of scientific, technological and social processes but the *tasks themselves* cannot be conceptualized without keeping in mind an equally complex network of linkages, both to the immediacy of the given labor process from which the specific tasks arise and to the broader context of their *destination* as products and *commodities*.

Nevertheless, this circumstance per se, notwithstanding its potentially far-reaching positive implications, does not carry with it a greater effective control over the social metabolism as a whole, nor even over a more positive orientation of the partial positing activities that remain in fact more strictly than ever subordinated to the irrationality of the prevailing global determinations.

The positive meaning of this objective tendency toward a global integration of the labor process is that it opens up the possibility of a conscious control over the social metabolism as a whole. For the latter is either controlled *in its integrality* or, due to the contradictions between its constituent parts on a global scale, it continues to elude human control, no matter how devastating the consequences. At a primitive stage of social development—when the teleology of labor is hopelessly constrained by the crude immediacy of its positing activity as sternly confronted, and to a large extent directly dominated, by nature—the question of a conscious control over the social metabolism cannot conceivably arise. The removal of such constraints through the full development of the forces of production creates the potentiality of making the partial tasks and processes homogeneous with the overall structures, thereby producing the possibility of conscious action both at the level of the immediate/limited tasks and at that of an overall social plan and coordination. But of course the historical unfolding of labor's objective teleology creates only the *potentiality* of a successful control of the conditions of human self-mediation and self-realization. This potentiality can only be translated into *actuality* through a radical *break* with the prevailing system of determinations as a result of a *conscious human enterprise* that envisages itself as its own end, in contrast to the present modality of labor's teleology in which the positing activity is dominated by alien ends, from the fetishism of commodity to antagonistic contradictions between states.

2. Another inescapable condition that reinforces the radical openness of the historical process, with all its positive/negative as well as negative/positive implications, concerns the *permanent structural presence of basic material determinations* in the changing social metabolism. For no matter what degree the direct material determinations are displaced in the course of historical development, they remain always *latent* under the surface of the displacing mechanisms and may massively reemerge on the horizon of even the most advanced society, including a genuinely socialist one. The jungle may be cleared with great effectiveness, nevertheless it is bound to reassert with even greater effectiveness its original claim if the necessary conditions for its successful banishment are not constantly renewed.

    Nor could one consider the expansion of historically created needs an a priori guarantee in this respect. Quite the opposite. Although the development of complex needs—the "luxury" of erstwhile political economy—may indeed displace the realm of bare necessity, it can do so only at the cost of activating a new, and far more extensive, order of necessity whose mastery becomes increasingly more difficult within the framework of capital's perverse logic. As a result, we have to reckon not only with the permanent *latency* of the basic material determinations but also with the increasing *fragility* (or vulnerability) of the globally more and more intertwined social metabolism. This is why, at the present juncture of history, the "positive negativity" and "negative positivity" of open-ended social development can only be pictured in the image of Janus, with one of his two faces pointing in the direction of humanity's triumph, the other confronting in anguish the hell of self-destruction.

But even if we envisage the successful mastery of capital's perverse logic, the latency of basic material determinations remains the implicit premise of all future social interaction, notwithstanding its qualitatively changed meaning. For "real history" is not the *end* of history but, on the contrary, a full *awareness* of its radical openness. Such awareness, however, by its very nature cannot wish out of existence the paradoxical ambivalence of objective determinations, including the permanent structural vulnerability of a globally intertwined and managed—or, for that matter, mismanaged—social metabolism. In view of the necessary reproduction of this latency as the natural foundation of human existence even at the highest conceivable level of social development, the path between success and failure is bound to remain extremely narrow, even if not threatened at every turn by capital's inherent irrationality. One may envisage successfully threading such a narrow path only *on condition* that the required full awareness of the positive/negative meaning of history's radical openness asserts itself as the permanent orienting force of all social enterprise.

3. The third major point to stress is closely connected with the previous two. It concerns a characteristic that happens to be totally ignored by all kinds of utopianism—irrespective of their political/ideological orientation—including the capitalistically inspired technological idealizations of the "third industrial revolution." The point is that any increase in the powers of *production* is simultaneously also an increase in the powers of *destruction*. Indeed, a careful examination of the balance sheet of history in this respect reveals the sobering fact that the underlying trend is the worst kind of *"uneven development."* For

though it is not only unrealistic but totally inconceivable to envisage a technology that solves all of humanity's problems with one clean swoop and on a permanent basis, notwithstanding the wishful postulates of "post-industrial" ideology, we have *already* reached the stage where the existing destructive devices of technology—fully deployed in fact to spring into action at the push of a button—could right here and now put an end to human life on this planet.

Thus technology, as constituted throughout history—far from being "neutral"—is inherently *problematical* in itself. Nor is its connection with natural science (in the name of which the ideologies of technological manipulation legitimate themselves) such a blessing as many people try to make us believe. Natural science, as we know it, has a gravely problematical side that is ignored by all those who counterpose their positivistically idealized "science" to "ideology" *tout court.*

What needs to be stressed in the present context is that the inescapable material reality of the powers of destruction *necessarily* arises from all advances in productivity known to us. Evidently the metabolism between human beings and nature has to subdue nature with nature's own might. Hence, the more extensive and multiform society's needs vis-à-vis nature (necessarily implying an equivalent and ever-growing resistance on nature's side, too), the greater—and also potentially more destructive—the forces that must be constantly activated to secure their satisfaction. The irony inherent in this relationship is that it is a matter of total indifference to nature whether its explosive forces move mountains and dig navigable canals in the service of humanity, or irreversibly destroy the elementary conditions of human existence itself.

However, the problems are further aggravated by the way in which the fundamental metabolic relationship between socially produced needs and nature is articulated and reproduced in the course of historical development, with regard to the instruments and productive forces as well as the social organization of production. The teleology of both technology and natural science is rooted in the primitive technology of labor, and the original limitations of the latter—the constraining results of the necessary *partiality* of its positing activity earlier referred to—are reproduced even at the most advanced phase of capitalistic developments. This partiality, which tends to render technology totally blind to the destructive implications of its own mode of operation, is greatly aggravated by three additional conditions:

a) Technological teleology is necessarily linked to determinate instruments and material structures, with a limited life span and a corresponding "economic imperative" (cycle of amortization, etc.) of their own; such limited material objectivations inevitably impose their logic—the problematical logic of their material and economic dictates—on the labor process as a whole, tending to intensify the original partiality and fragmentariness of labor's teleological positing, instead of pushing it in the opposite direction.

b) Technology fights the *latency* of basic material determinations in accordance with its own material *inertia* by pursuing "the line of least resistance" that best suits its direct material/economic dictates, even if it means producing "artificial appetites," nay a tendency toward the destruction of non-renewable resources, etc., rather than real solutions.

c) The inherently limiting and problematical characteristics of technology per se are devastatingly enhanced and multiplied by its *embeddedness in class society*, articulated in the service of the rulers so as to secure the permanent subjugation of the dominated. The development of technology in the course of history is inseparable[7] from this structure of domination and subordination: the *technological* division of labor is a subordinate moment of the *social* division of labor, rather than the other way around, as it is misrepresented in the camera obscura that produces the upside-down images of ruling–class–inspired mystification.[8] The destructive sides and implications of technological developments, which otherwise would be easily visible on strictly technical and scientific ground, are systematically repressed and rationalized as a result of this lopsided social embeddedness of technology in the ruling order.

Naturally, technological utopianism—which refuses to see the negative side of technological/scientific developments—has nothing whatever to do with the Marxian approach, even if it has penetrated the working-class movement quite a long time ago. As Walter Benjamin rightly observed:

> The conformism which has been part and parcel of Social Democracy from the beginning attaches not only to its political tactics but to its economic views as well. It is one reason for its later breakdown. Nothing has corrupted the German working class so much as the notion that it was moving with the current. It regarded technological development as the fall of the stream with which it thought it was moving. From there it was but a step to the illusion that the factory work which was supposed to tend toward technological progress constituted a political achievement. . . . Josef Dietzgen proclaimed: "The saviour of modern times is called work. The . . . improvement . . . of labor constitutes the wealth which is now able to accomplish what no redeemer has ever been able to do." This vulgar-Marxist conception of the nature of labor bypasses the question of how its products might benefit the workers while still not being at their disposal. It recognizes only the progress in the mastery of nature, not the retrogression of society.[9]

Under the disorienting impact of capital's postwar success, and influenced by the technologically oriented idealizations of this success by "scientific" neopositivism, structuralist vulgar Marxism pursued the direction first embarked upon by early Social Democracy, even if the crudeness of its message—linked for a while to a pseudo-radical political rhetoric—was carefully wrapped in several layers of hermetic jargon. The "self-critical" conversions and intellectual collapses that later followed merely brought the verbal radicalism of the original political posturing in line with the right from the beginning thoroughly conformist theoretical substance.

Nor should it be surprising to witness the ideological manifestations of capital's technological rationalization under so many different—and apparently even contradictory—forms. For the practical field in which such ideologies are formulated is dominated by capital's mighty material structures, many of which are explicitly or implicitly taken for granted, as unquestionable premises, by these rationalizing conceptualizations of the "scientifically" sound and feasible mode of action. And they are taken for granted whether they positively identify themselves with capital's practical domain, or try to devise within its framework strategies of limited opposition that remain structurally constrained and effectively contained by the criticized material structures. It is by no means accidental that by far the most durable form of ideology in the age of globally articulated and technologically legitimized capital is *positivism*, from its early nineteenth-century manifestations (Comte, Taine, neo-Kantianism, etc.) to "sociologism," "pragmatism," "relativistic positivism," "instrumentalism," "juridical positivism," "logical positivism," "linguistic analysis," "structural functionalism," "relationalism," "structuralism," etc., and to many fashionable neopositivistic "philosophies of science."

2.3 Interdependence and Global Control

All this takes us back to the problem raised at the beginning of this chapter, concerning the ambivalent position of social consciousness in the dialectical interrelationship between base and superstructure. For though all three fundamental structural constraints discussed above— namely the *partial* character of labor's original teleology, the *permanent latency* of basic material determinations in the ontology of social being, and the inseparable *destructive* dimension of all productive advance—are only amenable to a *conscious* solution, there seems to be no way out of the dilemma this solution presents us with, since social consciousness itself, as manifest in all history known to us, is severely affected and vitiated by the overbearing determinations of its own ground: the material base of society.

It is not difficult to see that the partial character of labor's teleological positing is constitutional to the labor process itself, inasmuch as the latter cannot help being directed at specific tasks. Hence the comprehensive dimension can only be a later addition, coupled with conscious coordination at the highest level, provided that the material prerequisites of structural coordination are successfully produced and reproduced—with a high degree of homogeneity and on a global scale—by an advanced stage of social/economic development. Furthermore, the material conditions themselves, no matter how advanced, cannot amount to more than *mere prerequisites* to a conscious control of the social metabolism in all its dimensions, and never to some a priori guarantee of its continued success. The conditions of a successful global control of the social interchange by consciousness must be constantly reproduced, just as much as those directly required for the trouble-free functioning of the material infrastructure, and *none* of the constituents involved in this complex dialectical relationship can be taken for granted. This is the real magnitude of the task facing consciousness with regard to labor's spontaneous teleology and its necessary—indeed qualitatively different and higher— completion by social consciousness itself.

In regard to the permanent latency of basic material determinations in the social ontology of the natural/human being, the role of consciousness in preventing its reemergence with a vengeance is, obviously, of paramount importance. For natural necessity can never be *abolished*, only *displaced* by socially mediated material determinations of increasingly higher complexity. The dialectical tension between socially created needs and the conditions of their gratification means—since the production process, through the challenge of meeting the demand inherent in a given set of needs, must raise itself above its immediate object in order to succeed, and thus it must itself generate new needs while satisfying old ones—that the mode of reproduction of human needs cannot help being a constantly *enlarged* one. This implies not only the growing mobilization of the available material resources but simultaneously an ever-increasing sophistication in "working them up," both as directly consumable goods and as instruments/skills/technology and the institutional/organizational framework required by the appropriate processes of production and distribution. To expect a *material mechanism* to deal with the growing complexities of this situation would be, of course, an absurd suggestion. As to whether consciousness itself will be able to do so remains at this stage a completely open question. What is clear, nevertheless, is that *if* consciousness is to cope with the situation it is called upon to confront, it must be an adequately "totalizing" social consciousness: namely, one free from the structurally vitiating dimensions of antagonistic material determinations.

Equally, since the destructive side of productive advance is not simply attached to isolated objects and processes but to the social complex as a whole, in which the negative partial features become cumulative and reciprocally intensify one another, an adequate control over the growing threat is conceivable only as the work of globally coordinated social consciousness. Thus, in view of the measure and severity of the issues at stake, advocating their solution by "piecemeal social engineering" is as rational as expecting to defeat Hitler's armies by firing shots in the dark with blank cartridges.

2.4 The Structural Constraints of Social Consciousness

The problems surveyed so far lead to the uncomfortable conclusion that the necessary precondition for finding a real solution to them—in place of rationalizations and manipulative diversions—is the ability (if it is feasible to have one) to successfully challenge the existing mode of interaction between the base and superstructure, with the aim of minimizing the structurally vitiating determinations that emanate from the material base of social life. The practical relevance of understanding the dialectic of base and superstructure consists in its help to identify the mechanisms and distorting constituents of this relationship, without which the question of their corrigibility (or otherwise) cannot be seriously raised.

Are the distortions of social consciousness we can pinpoint throughout history corrigible or not? Are the objective structural constraints that result in ruses of rationalization and "false consciousness" contingent to antagonistic forms of social interaction, hence in principle removable or, on the contrary, are they inherent "in the structure of consciousness itself" and in the necessary failure of consciousness in its attempt to reach any object not immanent to its individualistic self-constitution? For if the latter is the case, as many philosophers argue,[10] then the fundamental problems and challenges we encounter cannot be really tackled, except in the form of struggling against *symptoms* but not *causes*, producing thereby necessarily inconclusive results in accordance with the very nature of such a priori derailed confrontations.

As we have seen, the problems discussed earlier (which seem to escape human control) all involve the necessity of "totalization." For the fundamental contradictions inherent in the growing structural dysfunctions of the social metabolism are amenable to a solution only in the event of a conscious control of the *totality* of the relevant processes, and not merely the more or less successful temporary management of *partial complexes*. However, though teleological positing in relation to specific, limited objects can point to *individual* consciousness as its carrier, the controller of a *totality* of social processes is an intensely problematical concept.

Thus we find ourselves in a truly paradoxical situation. On the one hand, the limited teleology of individual consciousness is constitutionally incapable of dealing with the global challenges that must be faced. At the same time, on the other hand, the seat of "true collective consciousness"—as contrasted with socially determined collective conceptualizations that manifest more or less pronounced characteristics of "false consciousness"—cannot be readily identified. Furthermore, while the dominant individualistic ideologies have their institutional counterpart—including the practical teleology of the market and the "hidden hand" of its "parallelogrammatic"[11] interactional instrumentality—which effectively operate in accordance with the prevailing structures of material inertia, the successful functioning of a collective "true consciousness," engaged in a lasting global control of its tasks, requires a *non-inertial* institutional framework nowhere in sight, even in an embryonic form, today.

This raises a number of important questions that help to define the scope of ideology and draw the necessary line of demarcation between modalities of true and false consciousness:

1. In view of the growing failure of "unconscious social interaction," described as a "totalization without a totalizer," is it possible to constitute a "collective totalizer" in a sense that is completely free from the idealistic connotations of theological teleology; or, to put it more precisely, how is it possible to envisage the conditions of a *conscious collective totalization* and the material articulation of its necessary *non-inertial instrumentality*?

2. How is the interaction between the material base and the superstructure possible through which social consciousness can actively and positively intervene in the operation and transformation of the fundamental social metabolism?

3. What are the salient characteristics of ideology, in its positive and negative senses, and how is it possible to differentiate between various forms of true and false consciousness?

4. How does it come about that consciousness becomes structurally vitiated by its own material ground; or, to put it in a different way, what are the contradictory social determinations through which social consciousness acquires an independent existence and, through its alienation, becomes a predominantly negative instrument of domination, instead of emancipation?

5. How is it possible to minimize the negative dimension of social consciousness on the ground of a radically open history? That is to say, how is it possible to envisage extricating social consciousness from its structural vitiation by its material ground without being trapped by the contradictions of postulating, however unwittingly, a "closure" of and an end to history?

These and related questions are also discussed in my books *The Power of Ideology* (1989) and *Beyond Capital* (1995). The aim in this chapter has been to situate our problems within the overall social framework in which they inescapably arise, and to underline their importance for understanding the dialectical nature of historical transformations.

NOTES

1.   Jorge Larrain, *Marxism and Ideology,* Macmillan, London, 1983, 172. Larrain's emphases.

2.   Ibid., 171.

3.   Ibid., 173.

4.   Karl Marx and Frederick Engels, *Manifesto of the Communist Party,* in

Marx and Engels, *Collected Works,* Lawrence and Wishart, London, 1975, 6:484.

5. Rosa Luxemburg's expression. Marx asserts much the same in *The German Ideology.*

6. See Jean-Paul Sartre's *Critique of Dialectical Reason* (N.L.B., London, 1978), a much neglected work. For even if Sartre's solutions are rather problematical, the questions he raises in the *Critique* are of the greatest importance.

7. See in this respect Stephen Marglin's excellent study, "What Do Bosses Do?: The Origins and Functions of Hierarchy in Capitalist Production," *Review of Radical Political Economics* 6 (1974): 60–112. See also a well-documented book by Stewart Clegg and David Dunkerley, *Organization, Class and Control*, Routledge & Kegan Paul, London, 1980.

8. One must resist the temptation of *"personifying"* technology as an autonomous evil; a temptation to which even some major figures of twentieth century "critical theory" succumbed. Underrating the social embeddedness of technology inevitably carries with it a shift of perspective in that direction.

9. "Theses on the Philosophy of History," in Walter Benjamin, *Illuminations,* ed. and with an introduction by Hannah Arendt, Jonathan Cape, London, 1970, 260–61.

10. Sartre, for instance. Indeed he does so not only in *Being and Nothingness,* where he stipulates the "ontological solitude of consciousness," but even in his "marxisant" (Sartre's expression) *Critique of Dialectical Reason*. It must be emphasized, however, that this is by no means some special characteristic of an existentialist approach. On the contrary, it seems to be the rule rather than the exception in the last few centuries of philosophical development dominated by atomistic conceptions of the relationship between individual and society.

11. A term used by Engels, although in a broader sense, intended by him to identify the "unwanted outcome" of individual interactions in general.

CHAPTER THREE

Key Concepts in the Dialectic of Base and Superstructure

3.1 Hasty Rejection of the Marxian Conceptual Framework

In recent years Marx's theory of base and superstructure has been subjected to a great deal of criticism. Indeed, it has become quite fashionable to engage in a wholesale rejection of the Marxian conceptual framework. Moreover, this rejection is often coupled with attempts to replace the criticized Marxian concepts by some vague neo-Weberian notion of "culture," or by an even vaguer—as well as circularly self-referential—talk about "material and immaterial rights" and similar suggestions.

In place of proofs to support the advocated rejection of the Marxian conceptual framework, we are offered declarations of faith and a "critique" amounting to mere insult. In the first category we find this curious "argument" in favor of the recommended neo-Weberian position: "Many Marxists I know will admit, in private, to being closet Weberians. But never in public."[1]

An argument that may indicate something about the questionable intellectual consistency and public behavior of the author's acquaintances, but absolutely nothing about the respective merits of either the Marxian or the Weberian position.

At the same time, in the second category we are presented with the totally unsustained assertion according to which "The attempt to preserve the model of base and superstructure, and to force it onto all cultures, inevitably involved resorting to Jesuitical casuistries and intellectual and verbal contortions of the kind pioneered by Engels."[2]

In the end, the rejection of Marx's views on these matters tends to be categorical, even when its presentation is more polite. We are invited to subscribe to the astonishing proposition that "the basic theoretical blockage [in Third World studies] is a concept incompatible with a dialectical sociology: the materialist image of base and superstructure," coupled with the "solution" of the diagnosed problem in the following terms:

> It is time, now, to pay tribute, a century after Marx's death, to his own criticality . . . by *consigning that concept* to the same place to which Engels wanted to consign the State: "the *Museum of Antiquities*, alongside the spinning-wheel and the stone axe."[3]

And in the same spirit, though with commendably less sugar-coated consignatory words, another writer declares—on the basis of a far too literal interpretation of the debated concepts—that the Marxian differentiation between base and superstructure is "a dead, static, architectural metaphor, whose potential for illumination was never very great and which has for too long cast nothing but shadows over Marxist theory and Marxist practice," concluding his reflections with the rhetorical question that clearly indicates the desired answer: "Is it not time to *consign it to the scrap-heap*?"[4]

It seems to me rather unfortunate and less than productive that people should try to settle these issues by talking about "Jesuitical casuistries," "intellectual and verbal contortions," "Museums of Antiquity," "scrap-heaps," and similar terms of a prioristic disqualification.[5] Particularly since quite often the rejection is constructed on the ground of nothing but generic references to the "images," "model," "metaphors," etc. of base and superstructure, in place of a concrete examination of the numerous contexts in which Marx addresses himself to the relevant issues.

As a rule, only his brief remarks from the 1859 Preface to *A Contribution to the Critique of Political Economy* are taken into account.

Yet due to the very nature of that particular undertaking—which attempted to compress a monumental new conception of history into a few paragraphs: consciously and explicitly presented by Marx as a popularization of his theory—the treatment of "base and superstructure" could not help being other than summary in the 1859 Preface, even though by no means undialectical, as the critics claim. In his work as a whole, however, we can find a great deal more on the complicated interrelations of base and superstructure from *The German Ideology* to *Capital* and *Theories of Surplus Value*.

Whereas the few lines dedicated to the discussion of base and superstructure in the 1859 Preface are undoubtedly *compatible* with the rest of Marx's writings on this complex subject, they are no more than just that, and therefore should not be used to obliterate the ideas he offers elsewhere as their necessary corollaries. In other words, the "telegraphic" presentation of the dialectical interconnection between base and superstructure in the Preface could in no way be considered an adequate *substitute* for his carefully qualified and "shaded" views as formulated in several books, articles, and letters. Indeed, as we shall see later on, the striking propositions of the 1859 Preface itself only acquire their proper meaning if read in conjunction with his analysis of some other major aspects of the same problematic, whereas without such reading one is tempted to ascribe a mechanical intent to the much quoted passage.

One cannot reach a theoretically viable conclusion about such key categories without taking on board at least the principal arguments in terms of which their author attempts to articulate them. This is why it is necessary to acquaint ourselves with some neglected dimensions of Marx's account of the relationship in question—which are not even hinted at in the Preface—before we can really appreciate or question the explanatory value of "base and superstructure."

Central to these concerns is the need to focus attention on the Marxian distinction between superstructure *as such* and the more limited concept of "*legal and political* superstructure," which refers to qualitatively different sociohistorical conditions and determinations. The two concepts are often hopelessly conflated, carrying with them the failure to make the necessary distinction and a tendency to offer thoroughly implausible mechanical interpretations and explanations. For only with reference to the historically constituted, and at a certain stage of social development antagonistically determined transformation of the super-structure into a separate and ever more alienated sphere of legal and polit-ical domination, can some of Marx's seminal ideas—including his radical critique of politics itself—be made intelligible at all.

However, before we can turn to these matters, it is necessary to address first some directly relevant methodological issues.

1. It is quite wrong to suggest, in neo-Weberian terms, that "Marxist conceptions of the mode of production, of the institutions of civil society, and of the State are, of course, all *ideal types*. Ideal types are all *abstractions*, perfect models which *rarely occur* in reality."[6] Far from being "of course" in relation to the Marxian categories, such interpretation seems to be confused even as regards the meaning of Weber's own concept of "ideal types." For the latter, in the words of their originator, only attempt to locate "the theoretically conceived *pure type* of *subjective meaning* attributed to the *hypothetical actor or actors* in a given type of action."[7]

    Thus the Weberian "ideal type" is not an "*abstraction*," derived by way of sifting through the specific characteristics of *real* situations (be they frequent or rare), but a deliberate "*construction* of a purely rational course of action,"[8] devised for the explicitly stated purpose of enabling the sociologist to "account for the *deviation* from the line of conduct which would be expected on the hypothesis that the action were *purely rational*."[9] Moreover, Weber is anxious to stress in another work that his pure or ideal type "has *nothing* to do with any type of *perfection* other than a *purely logical* one."[10] Hence to talk about "ideal types" as "perfect models that occur in reality" is logi-cally incoherent.

    Such misplaced and confused attempts to turn the Marxian cate-gories into Weberian "ideal types" are purportedly made in the name of a critical appropriation and synthesis of Marx and Weber. In truth, they represent a far less critical understanding of the issues involved than what we are offered even in the partial insights of the conservative Talcott Parsons. For as recognized by the American advocate of "structural functionalism":

> Ideal type theory is perhaps the most difficult level on which to develop a coherent generalized system. Type concepts can readily be formulated ad hoc for innumerable specific purposes and can have a limited usefulness in this way. This does not, however, suffice for a generalized system. For this purpose they must be arranged and classified in a definite order of relationship. Only then will they have highly generalized significance on either a theoretical or an empirical level. Such systematization cannot, however, be developed on an *ad hoc* empirical basis. Logically it involves reference both to considerations of extremely broad empirical scope and to comprehensive theoretical categories.[11]

The fundamental incompatibility of Weberian categorization with Marx's account of the categories becomes clear if we compare their ideas on the nature of collective agency and collective consciousness.

For Weber "there is no such thing as a *collective personality* which 'acts' . . . *only* a certain kind of development of actual or possible actions of individual persons."[12] Given the fact that Weber's concern is "the *subjective understanding* of the action of the component individuals,"[13] within his conceptual framework "*collectivities* must be treated as *solely* the *resultants* and modes of organization of the *particular acts of individual persons*, since these alone can be treated as *agents* in a course of *subjectively* understandable action."[14] He grants to the category of "collective agency" only the status of being the application of "the *juristic concept*."[15] This is because he wants to describe even the modern state "as a complex of social interaction of *individual persons* . . . oriented to the belief that it [the state] exists or *should exist*, thus that its acts and laws are *valid in the legal sense*."[16] Thus the Weberian conception of a merely aggregative "collective" agency corresponds to an equally aggregative "collective" consciousness whose meaning is exhausted by predicating the individual person's recognition (or "should-be" recognition) of how legitimate and valid the state's "acts" and laws are, by definition. Obviously, this conception of the collective agency is so firmly locked into the advocated formal/juristic model that even Sartre—whose thought was formed within the confines of the same individualistic tradition to which Weber belongs—goes well beyond its horizon when he counterposes to strictly aggregative "seriality" the "fused group in action" in his *Critique of Dialectical Reason.*

As to Marx's own views with regard to the constitution of collective groups and the concomitant articulation of collective consciousness, the contrast with Weber could not be more pronounced. For, very far from being satisfied with the notion of the state-oriented "resultant" of individualistic interaction (a socially apologetic stipulative concept) as the explanatory category of collective formations and modes of consciousness, Marx defines the latter—the emergence of the proletariat, for instance, as a "class in-itself," and its transformation into a "class for-itself"—in substantive/material terms, on the ground of actual historical development. Moreover, he clearly states that the categories—again, far from being "ideal types"—"express the *forms of being,* the characteristics of existence"[17] of actually developing society. For instance, "labor" as a category is produced not by idealistically self-referential "brainwork" (or "head-activity," *Kopfarbeit,* as Marx teasingly refers to it in the *Grundrisse*), but by tangible material developments conceptualized by socially conditioned "brainwork." For

> "*labor* is as modern a category as are the relations which create this simple abstraction. The Monetary System, for example, still locates wealth altogether objectively, as an *external thing,* in money. Compared with this standpoint, the commercial, or manufacture, system took a great step forward by locating the source of wealth not in the object but in a subjective activity—in commercial and manufacturing activity—even though it still always conceives this activity within narrow boundaries, as money-making. In contrast to this system, that of the Physiocrats posits a certain kind of labor—agriculture—as the creator of wealth, and the object itself no longer appears in a monetary disguise, but as the product in general, as the

general result of labor. . . . It was an immense step forward for
Adam Smith to throw out every limiting specification of
wealth-creating activity—not only manufacturing, or commercial or agricultural labor, but one as well as the others. With
the abstract universality of wealth-creating activity we now
have the universality of the object defined as wealth, the product as such or again *labor as such.* . . . Indifference towards
specific labors corresponds to a form of society in which individuals can with ease transfer from one labor to another, and
where the specific kind is a matter of chance for them, hence
of indifference. Not only the category, labor, but labor *in reality* has here become the means of creating wealth in general,
and has ceased to be organically linked with particular individuals in any specific form. . . . "Labor as such," labor pure and
simple, becomes *true in practice.*[18]

Thus the general category of "labor" is not a *"mental abstraction"*; nor is it indeed a theoretical "construction" that "serves the
sociologists as a type"[19] in relation to which they can describe what
they consider "deviations" from some stipulated Weberian model.
Rather, it is a highly significant *"practical abstraction,"* brought
within the compass of theoretical consciousness by the objective logic
of the advancing productive developments themselves.

Likewise, the Marxian concept of "class consciousness" is not an
"ideal type"; nor is it the "theoretical discovery of a new continent."
It is the recognition of a determinate modality of conscious collective
action, with hegemonic class interest as its driving force, corresponding to the historical potentialities and attainments of the capitalist
age, but decidedly not to those of earlier periods.[20] Accordingly, when
Marx speaks of the consciously fulfilled "world-historic role" that the
"socialist writers ascribe to the fully formed proletariat,"[21] it is radically different from describing class consciousness in terms of an
alleged "deviation from the line of conduct which would be expected
on the hypothesis that the action were purely rational," as required by
the Weberian categorial framework of "ideal types." For Marx clearly
states that he is concerned with "absolutely imperative *need*—the

practical expression of *necessity*," which is not a matter of ideally hypostatized "subjective meaning," not even

> a question of what this or that proletarian, or even the whole proletariat, at the moment *regards* as its aim. It is a question of *what the proletariat is*, and what, in accordance with this *being*, it will historically be compelled to do.[22]

In other words, in the Marxian conceptual framework the categories are treated as "forms of being" (*Daseinsformen*) that encapsulate the objective "characteristics of existence" in their dynamic historical unfolding, and not as "*regulative concepts*" that the theoreticians can devise more or less at will (or "ad hoc," if one prefers to use Talcott Parsons's fitting expression), with the aim of "purely logical perfection," having in mind as their guiding principle the—by Weber explicitly stated—intellectual "merit of clear understandability and lack of ambiguity,"[23] and nothing more.

2. According to Marx's critics:

> The image of base and superstructure is an image, a metaphor which uses *extra-social analogies* to describe social arrangements. All such images, whatever their value in illuminating the subject, are profoundly distorting as well. *Society* is not a machine; it is not an organism, nor does it follow sequences of gestation and birth (Marx's favourite, obstetric imagery) or of decay and death. . . . The model reposes on the assumption that the economic base is material. It is not. . . . The organization of production involves internalizing or at least complying with norms of behaviour . . . norms of output and working conditions. But the system as a whole reposes upon even more fundamental concepts: of the *right* of some people to own the means of production and to appropriate the product.[24]

What is forgotten or deliberately disregarded in all such reasoning is that *both* the material transformations and the established systems of norms and rights must be dialectically accounted for in terms of their *historical genesis,* instead of being arbitrarily assumed as already given, so as to be able to conclude, with triumphant circularity, that "freeman and slave, patrician and plebeian, lord and serf, are not categories determined by relationship to the means of production at all: they are *extra-economic statuses into which people are born.*"[25] Yet even if one talks about "statuses into which people are born," setting aside the issue for the time being whether or not they could be legitimately considered "extra-economic," the crucial question remains to be answered: how did (and do) such "status groups" come into being?

Replacing the Marxian analysis of *specific* social determinations and relations by vague references to a generic *"society"* can take us absolutely nowhere. For such generic propositions about "society" as such are usually presented in purely negative form, asserting that "society is not this" and "society is not that," without attempting to indicate at the same time in affirmative terms what society actually *is* on the basis of which the negative judgments—by themselves thoroughly unenlightening—are commended.[26]

To be sure, if one's frame of reference is a generic "society," directly equated with the aggregate of separate individuals, in that case there is no room for a historical/genetic enquiry into the "obstetric" origin and life-cycle—including not only the necessary period of "gestation" but also the progressive decay and death—of determinate social complexes and formations, since the ahistorically assumed subject remains, by definition, always the same. "There are characteristics which all stages of production have in common, and which are established as general ones by the mind; but the so-called general preconditions of all production are nothing more than these abstract moments with which no real historical stage of production can be grasped."[27]

This is even more true of "society in general." For existing society is always a historically specific and evolving totality. There is no such thing as society in the abstract, which would, by definition, "comprehend" everything in its a prioristic timelessness, and consequently no conceivable vantage point of critical understanding could be envisioned in relation to it. Real society exists only in its concrete determinateness. As such, it is made of a multiplicity of historically changing complexes and totalities, including, of course, the always given totality of real social individuals. Social individuals, that is, who are inseparable from the historically determinate institutional complexes within which they must function (and which define, of course, their social specificity), as opposed to the fictitious "genus-individuals" depicted by all those who consciously or unconsciously adopt "the standpoint of civil society," from early bourgeois thought all the way down to the abstract "human beings" of recent neo-Weberian conceptions.

Even if some people dislike Marx's "obstetric imagery," the fact remains that the very nature of the constantly shifting particular social complexes is practically defined within the given social totality—corresponding to the manifold dialectical interrelations of the "real historical stage of production"—in the sense that at any particular time in history some of them are in the process of growth and development, while others, on the contrary, are on the way to "withering away," disintegration, and decay. A proposition that, obviously, one could not assert about "society as such" (a most generic "abstraction of the mind") in its vacuous indeterminateness. At the same time, the historical specificity of the social complex as a whole is itself practically defined and constantly redefined by the *changing overall configuration* and interrelationship of the particular complexes and partial totalities among themselves within the objective dynamics of the unfolding transformations. Moreover, even though the scale itself is different, the social complex as a whole is also subject to the determinations that bring about under favorable circumstances a historical phase of "ascent," whereas under conditions when disturbances and antagonisms predominate in the overall configuration, they set in motion the phase of "decline" and ultimate disintegration. This could not be otherwise since the *"macro-structure"* of any particular social formation is itself made of inherently historical *"micro-structures"* that cannot escape the necessary limitations—and corresponding life span—of their social specificity.

Although no one should deny that every analogy has its limits, one can take the implied objection to varieties of comparison rather too far: ultimately to the point of absurdity, denying the legitimacy of using *adjectives* in general, which happen to be "analogies" of sorts. Strangely enough, people who are so dogmatic in their rejection of the allegedly "extra-social" analogy of "base and superstructure" are perfectly happy to commend their own preferred imagery, such as "*developed* consciousness" and "*shared* culture." Yet, not only is there no reason given why social analogies alone should be able to throw light on determinate social connections; equally, the propounders of this a prioristic constraint fail to notice that there is nothing inherently social about the approved terms of comparison, like "developed" or "shared." As a matter of fact, the latter are both applicable to the natural universe in general, and by no means only to the social world. It is enough to think in this respect of "fully developed" plants and animals, or of the "sharing" involved among the members of any class whatsoever that happen to be objectively defined by the same determinations. Unhappily, on closer examination of the recommended alternative imagery we end up with the singularly unilluminating tautology that only *socially developed* development and *socially shared* sharing may be considered inherently social.

It is quite simply not true that all analogies and images are "profoundly distorting." Those that are should not be used in the first place. However, it must be stressed again that the relevant question—as far as the legitimacy of using similes and analogies in theoretical discourse is concerned—is whether or not the adopted forms and varieties of comparison are adequately "translatable" into a significant and *discursively viable* message, irrespective of how many explanatory sentences one needs in order to accomplish the necessary conversion. In other words, their legitimacy hinges on whether or not they have a fully transliterable *conceptual substance*—a real *conceptual equivalent*—that is encapsulated, summarized, or graphically brought into relief by the relevant simile or analogy. What is objectionable, by contrast, is the introduction of mere "literary flourishes," or of the kind of metaphors (appropriately used in poetry) that are (and in poetry are meant to be) untranslatable into literal, strictly discursive, propositions in virtue of the unique structure of predication—namely reciprocal predication—that characterizes the logical syntax of poetic metaphors, in contradistinction to similes and analogies.

Marx's conception of "base and superstructure," just as his references to "*organic* systems" and to their dynamic conditions of development, etc., fully satisfy this requirement of "translatability." Their function is to focus attention on significant social relations and interdeterminations that can be ascertained on the basis of historical and empirical research. At the same time, their validity as "images" and analogies depends on the conceptual viability of both the propositions complementary to them in Marx's own writings and those we can readily derive from the Marxian "models." Furthermore, in their turn all such propositions and "translations" are subject to the selfsame conditions of practical verification that Marx indicated as the necessary criteria of evaluation for all meaningful theoretical discourse.

The justification for using the analogy of "base and superstructure" is that, far from being a rigid and mechanical constraint, it offers a dialectical line of demarcation with reference to which the more comprehensive totality of *superstructure* can adequately mark the historical limits of the *legal and political* superstructure in its socially defined specificity. Similarly, the characterization of the capitalistic formation as an "*organic* system" does not turn this social complex into an atemporal *natural mechanism*, as indeed happens to be the case with the use of the organic analogy in bourgeois thought. On the contrary, it enables Marx to raise the question of *limits* in terms of which the historical formation of capital can be dialectically understood, as well as *delimited* with regard to its social viability in the direction of both the past and the future. To quote Marx:

> It must be kept in mind that the new forces of production and relations of production do not develop out of *nothing*, nor drop from the sky, nor from the womb of self-positing Idea; but from within and in antithesis to the existing development of production and the inherited, traditional relations of property. While in the *completed* bourgeois system every economic relation *presupposes* every other in its bourgeois economic form, and *everything posited is also a presupposition*, this is the case with every *organic system*. This organic system itself, as a *totality*, has its *presuppositions*, and its *development* to its totality consists precisely in

subordinating all elements of society to itself, or in creating out of it the organs which it still lacks. This is *historically* how it *becomes a totality*. The process of becoming this totality forms a moment of its process, of its *development*.[28]

As we can see, far from being a "profoundly distorting imagery," the meaning of "organic" is defined with great conceptual precision as a type of system in which "everything posited is also a presupposition." At the same time it is correctly recognized by Marx that in the *completed* economic system "every economic relation presupposes every other" in a form appropriate to the totalizing requirements of the—historically specific—system, which itself quite simply could not become a completed system without successfully "subordinating all elements of society to itself." The point, however, is to grasp these relations in their historical dynamism in terms of which one can make sense of the undeniable fact that all systems of social reproduction are characterized by a very high degree of "*self-regulation*," "*reciprocity*," and "*feedback*," even if the forms and modalities of self-regulatory feedback significantly differ if compared across the overall trajectory of historical development.

Failure to assess the given social totality in its historical genesis means substituting for the dialectical conceptualization of the prevailing part/whole-relations (in terms of the *Daseinsformen* of developing social being) the "flat tautologies"[29] that one can derive from assuming the *pernicious practical circularity* of capital's self-regulating totality—with all its characteristically modern reifications—as a priori inseparable from the requirements of social reproduction as such. This amounts not only to disregarding how the established socioeconomic totality "*became a totality*" but simultaneously also to obliterating the fact that capital's antagonistic "subordination of all elements of society to itself" necessarily circumscribes the historical boundary of its social viability. Just as the category of "labor" is produced within the objective logic of the unfolding socioeconomic developments themselves, in the same way the theoretical circularity of the political economists criticized by Marx arises from the *practical circularity* of the given organic system, with its *objectively posited presuppositions* which the economists take for granted as the unmentioned premises of their generalizations. At the same time, significantly, the actual part/whole-relations are arbitrarily *reversed* by them in the interest of the "eternalization of the bourgeois relations of production." As Marx points out:

> The aim is to present production—see e.g. Mill—as distinct from distribution, etc., as encased in eternal natural laws independent of history, at which opportunity bourgeois relations are then quietly smuggled in as the inviolable natural laws on which *society in the abstract* is founded. . . . All production is appropriation of nature on the part of an individual within and through a specific form of society. In this sense it is a *tautology* to say that property (appropriation) is a precondition of production. But it is altogether ridiculous to leap from that to a *specific* form of property, e.g. *private property*. (Which further and equally *presupposes an antithetic form, non-property*.) . . . History rather shows *common property* (e.g. in India, among the Slavs, the early Celts, etc.) to be the original form, a form which long continues to play a significant role in the shape of *communal property*.
>
> . . . That there can be no production and hence no society where some form of property does not exist is a *tautology*. An appropriation which does not make something into property is a *contradictio in subjecto*. . . . When these trivialities are reduced to their real content, they tell more than their preachers know. Namely that every form of production creates its own legal relations, form of government, etc. In bringing things which are *organically* related into an *accidental* relation, into a merely reflective connection, they display their crudity and lack of conceptual understanding.[30]

Thus the actual relationships are turned upside down in conceptualizations of this kind. For the truly *organic* and primary modality of social determinations—which is *historical* in the most *comprehensive* sense: i.e. in that it embraces the totality of social formations, the highest possible stage of socialism included—becomes *accidental*, so as to enable the political economists to transform the incomparably more *limited* historical specificity (and in that sense "accidentality") of the bourgeois formation into the unalterable organicity of an alleged *natural order*.

We can see now the relevance of the much criticized Marxian "imagery." For both the "organic system" (or "organic totality") and "base and superstructure" assert a structurally ordered relationship between the social whole and its constituent parts. A relationship is made intelligible by Marx with reference to the objective dialectic of historically articulated *reciprocal determinations*. This is what is really at issue beneath the controversy about the "extra-social metaphor" of base and superstructure. The rejection of "imagery" is not motivated by a quest for greater conceptual precision, but by a desire to abandon the Marxian theoretical framework of *objective determinations*. What critics find unpalatable, in fact, is the Marxian proposition we have just seen—namely that "every form of production creates its own legal relations, form of government, etc."—and not the analogy of "base and superstructure" of which the quoted sentence is a partial and strictly discursive conceptual equivalent.

3. The final point, which can be treated briefly for the purposes of the present context, concerns the primacy of material determinations and its characterization in terms of the *"ultimate* determinant." Expressed in another way, this means that the determinations that emanate from the material basis of society prevail "in the *last analysis*."

    As a matter of historical record, this qualification was made in order to guard against mechanical reductionism and one-sidedness, insisting that the role of material determinations must be assessed dialectically, in conjunction with complex ideal and ideological factors that interact with them and significantly modify their potential impact. Subsequently, however, critics started to query the heuristic value of this methodological proviso, ending up with the skeptical formula according to which the hour of the "last analysis" (or "last instance") *never comes*. This carried rather unfortunate implications for the Marxian theory as a whole. For, in view of the rejection of the advocated dialectical qualifier, it appeared that either we had to give up the primacy of material determinations, in favor of some vague "culturalist" alternative, or we had to opt for impaling ourselves on the stake of precisely the kind of narrow mechanical reductionism— later characterized as "vulgar Marxism"—that was already emphatically condemned by Marx and Engels.

Yet there are perfectly good reasons for maintaining that the primacy of material determinations remains valid. The field of application of this principle is, in fact, twofold.

First, it refers to the original *historical* course of development in the framework of which whatever "culture" had been created by the social interchange of the people involved obviously was done so on tangible natural and material foundations. In this sense, the "last analysis" in question applies to the remote *historical past*, to a period, that is, when the "material basis" simply could not help having a massive direct primacy over the slowly emerging social consciousness.

The second sense, by contrast, embraces all dimensions of temporality, the present not less than the past and the future. It concerns the innermost *structural determinations* of social production and reproduction, including what Marx calls their "natural prerequisites," as we shall see in a moment.

Theoreticians, who have in front of them the characteristics of highly advanced stages of socioeconomic development, tend to forget that cultural production itself must be materially grounded. They tend to forget it because under their own circumstances the necessary material preconditions of cultural activity can be taken for granted with relative justification, at least for the time being. The situation may precipitously change, however, in the event of a profound *structural crisis* that affects the whole of society and in a tangible way the mode of existence of every individual. It is at such times that the "moment of truth" arrives even for the productively most advanced, and with regard to their accumulated wealth the richest societies whose wealth and productive power may collapse almost from one moment to the next, practically refuting thereby the dictum that the hour of the last instance never comes. For the complex multiplicity of social determinations constitutes a *structurally ordered* whole in which the ultimately brute "facticity" of the natural and material prerequisites of the overall reproduction process can *never* be permanently left behind. It can only be more closely integrated with superstructural determinations than what we find under the conditions of early social formations.

In this objective structural sense, the elementary factors of material determination preserve—whatever the given historical circumstances might be—their dialectical primacy "in the last analysis," in that their naked power may be reactivated and superimposed over everything else if securing the necessary natural and material *prerequisites* of social reproduction suffers a structural breakdown. This remains true despite the fact that under the "normal" (i.e. materially well provided) conditions of highly advanced production various configurations of superstructural determination may predominate as a matter of course.

3.2 Reproduction of the Operating Conditions of Production

Let us now consider an important but little known passage from Marx's *Capital*. It deals with the relationship between the objective conditions and necessary requirements of the material production process on the one hand, and the specific forms of the legal and political superstructure on the other, described by Marx in the following terms:

> That the product of the serf must suffice to reproduce his conditions of labor, in addition to his subsistence, is a circumstance which remains the same under *all modes* of production. For it is not the result of their *specific form*, but a *natural requisite* of all continuous and reproductive *labor in general*, of any continuing *production*, which is always simultaneously *reproduction*, i.e., including reproduction of *its own operating conditions*. ... Should the direct producers not be confronted by a private landowner, but rather, as in Asia, under direct subordination to a state which stands over them as their landlord and simultaneously as sovereign, then rent and taxes coincide, or rather, there exists no tax which differs from this form of ground-rent. Under such circumstances, there need exist no stronger political or economic pressure than that common to all subjection to that state. The state is then the supreme lord. Sovereignty here consists in the ownership of land concentrated on a national scale. But, on the other

hand, no private ownership of land exists, although there is both private and common possession and use of land.

The *specific economic form*, in which unpaid surplus-labor is pumped out of direct producers, determines the relationship of rulers and ruled, as it grows directly out of production itself and, in turn, *reacts* upon it as a determining element. Upon this, however, is founded the entire formation of the *economic community* which grows up out of the *production relations* themselves, thereby simultaneously its *specific political form*. It is always the *direct relationship* of the *owners* of the conditions of production to the direct *producers*—a relation always *naturally corresponding* to a definite stage in the development of the methods of labor and thereby its social productivity—which reveals the *innermost secret*, the *hidden basis* of the entire *social structure*, and with it the *political form* of the relation of *sovereignty and dependence*, in short, the corresponding *specific form of the state*. This does not prevent the same economic basis— the same from the standpoint of its main conditions—due to innumerable different empirical circumstances, *natural* environment, *racial* relations, *external historical* influences, etc., from showing *infinite variations and gradations* in appearance, which can be ascertained only by analysis of the empirically given circumstances.[31]

To grasp the meaning of the relationship between the legal and political superstructure and the material base in its dialectical complexity, it is necessary to understand the precise character of the various—qualitatively different—"correspondences" here referred to by Marx in his attempt to elucidate the underlying dynamic interconnections. It is by no means sufficient simply to stipulate a *"reciprocity"* between the superstructure and the material base. By itself that would neither account for the *genesis* of the "political form of the relation of sovereignty and dependence" nor its mode of *present functioning*, not to mention its potential or real *transformations* in the future, including the possibility of its complete "withering away" as a separate "political form" (which happens to constitute the central concern of Marx's political theory). Talking generically about "reciprocity," without focusing attention on the necessary materialist underpinning as well as on the actual historical dynamism of the relations involved, would amount to no more than empty tautology.

All actual sociohistorical complexes characterized by "reciprocity" in their mode of functioning have some *"uebergreifendes Moment"* (a moment or factor of overriding importance) among their interacting sets of relations, both "absolutely"—i.e., with regard to their structural determinations that transcend the given historical form—and relative to the particular historical circumstances of the social formation within which they are situated. It is with reference to the appropriate *uebergreifendes Moment* that the category of reciprocity acquires its dialectical meaning, in contrast to the empty circularity of all talk about "reciprocal determination" that fails to indicate the structurally articulated and historically valid dominant aspects of the interrelationships in question. If, therefore, it is necessary to stress, as Marx does, that under determinate circumstances (in ancient Athens and in Rome) *politics*, while in the Middle Ages *Catholicism* "reigned supreme," it is equally important to situate such historical variations within their proper *materialist ontological perspective*, insisting that

> the Middle Ages could not live on Catholicism, nor the ancient world on politics. On the contrary, it is the mode in which they gained a livelihood that explains why here politics and there Catholicism, played the chief part. For the rest, it requires but a slight acquaintance with the history of the Roman republic, for example, to be aware that its secret history is the history of its landed property. On the other hand, Don Quixote long ago paid the penalty for wrongly imagining that knight errantry was compatible with all economic forms of society.[32]

Thus it is of no use to go on repeating that superstructural dimensions come into prominence, as obviously they do, under certain historical conditions. For the real question is *why?*—unless we are willing to treat "politics" or "Catholicism" as idealistically "self-explanatory" *assumptions*.

What is at issue here is the *specificity* of the various social formations in their overall defining characteristics, which inevitably affect the functioning of the subordinate parts of the *social whole*. In this sense, to concentrate on the economic mechanism *alone*, to the exclusion of all the other aspects of the overall social complex, or to attempt *directly* to derive the various dimensions of the latter from the given economic forces and imperatives, is hopelessly one-sided. But it is just as one-sided to suggest that, since our frame of reference is the *social whole*, we must abandon the idea that the economic foundation of society remains the *ultimately* determining ground of all social formations (in the sense indicated at the end of section 3.1).

To explain why in the Middle Ages Catholicism and in the ancient world politics "played the chief part," we must focus attention on the objective requirements of reproducing the *operating conditions* of production. For it is the latter that combine the material/structural and the superstructural determinations into a coherent and dialectically interdependent whole, objectively defining—through their historically developed modality of *practical mediation*—the *specificity* of the given system of productive reproduction.

As we have seen with reference to the *Grundrisse*, a *particular* social system—*once* it is historically constituted and articulated in its principal dimensions, in terms of which it successfully regulates the manifold partial functions of social interchange—can be validly considered an "*organic whole*." This means two things. First, that the "organicity" of a given social totality must be historically qualified in that any particular social system both *becomes* and, beyond a certain point, *ceases to be* the viable overall regulator of the social metabolism under all its aspects. *("Viable overall regulator"* represents the literal meaning of social organicity.) And second, that within the framework of the established social formation the different levels of material/structural and superstructural determinations, notwithstanding their tensions and even contradictions, *coalesce* and *reinforce* one another: so long as the *ultimate limits* of the material production system itself are not reached.

Accordingly, the reason why Catholicism or politics can "reign supreme" under determinate historical circumstances is not some mysterious cultural force, for a while strangely illuminating the individual members of the concerned societies only to desert them with equal strangeness at some later date. Rather, what we encounter in these cases are specific forms of regulating the production process itself in such a way that the *continuity of production*, simultaneously with the reproduction of the *necessary operating conditions* of social reproduction, is secured. And the implicit orienting principle of all such forms of metabolic regulation, whatever their differences among themselves, is to achieve as high a degree of *economy* and *stability* as feasible in terms of the socially available forces, instruments and institutions. (The "economy" and "stability" here referred to must be understood in their primary sense of which the capitalist variants—oriented toward safeguarding the continued extraction of surplus-value and the expansion of exchange-value under the conditions of generalized commodity production—are only particular, and historically very limited, instances.)

So long as the *dominant* structural and superstructural determinations coalesce (or act relatively undisturbed in the same direction) in the ongoing process of societal reproduction, it is difficult to draw a sharp line of demarcation between the "operating conditions of production" and the various superstructural factors. While the "ascending phase" of socioeconomic development lasts, the impression of "organic finality" tends to prevail in the various conceptualizations that accept as unalterably self-sustaining the practical premises of the given order. And even the phase of gradual decline—marked by the increasing prominence of so-called dysfunctions—defines the superstructural dimension of the operating conditions strictly in terms of the required "correctives" so that the superstructure as such appears to constitute a *vicious circle* of interlocking determinations with the material imperatives of the established productive system, and therefore cannot be recognized as a meaningfully autonomous factor. This is particularly pronounced at times when the material dictates of an internationally articulated and antagonistic reproductive system reduce the margin of "active superstructural intervention" to that of an uncritically *supportive* role, as clearly identifiable from the onset of the monopoly phase of capitalist development. At such times not only the representatives of the ruling ideology rationalize the existent by proclaiming that "there is no alternative" to the measures prescribed by the established system of production. Equally, oppositional forces that articulate their strategies from the false premise of capital's unchallengeable vitality end up in supportive and "corrective" blind alleys, from Bernstein's "evolutionary socialism" to recent varieties of "Euro-communist" inspired social democracy (or the other way around).

Paradoxically, to talk of "*reciprocal* determination" between base and superstructure under the circumstances of the "ascending phase" of socioeconomic development appears to be somewhat redundant, since the reproduction of the given system—together with its required operating conditions—is considered "organically" unproblematical in the light of its daily demonstrated success. Likewise, during the phase of gradual decline that may embrace many decades, the *dominant* superstructural forces can successfully exercise their regulatory/reproductive functions in view of the "*practical circularity*" that tends to prevail between the material imperatives and the superstructural dimensions of a fully articulated—and in that sense organic—system. Nevertheless, it would be quite wrong to identify the superstructure in general with its constituent parts that happen to be *dominant* under the prevailing historical circumstances, however long. For just as the productive system is torn by antagonisms, the superstructure itself is very far from being a homogeneous entity. After all, one should not forget that broadly the same period that was responsible for the emergence and consolidation of revisionist social democracy also produced the revolutionary conceptions and political movements of Lenin and Rosa Luxemburg.

It is in periods of transition from one social formation to another that the true relationship between the material base and its superstructure transpires with great clarity. For under such conditions both the productive foundation and the superstructure of the established order must be radically restructured—a task whose realization is inconceivable without the most active intervention of superstructural factors in resolving the crisis of social reproduction through the establishment of a new set of viable operating conditions and practicable rules of "reciprocity." This must be done so that, again, all levels of social practice, including the most mediated "cultural" ones, can be brought into play and coalesce in an economy- and stability-enhancing new "organic" framework. In this sense, it is by no means accidental

1. that the first coherent theories of ideology appeared in the aftermath of the French Revolution, with the crowning act of the bourgeoisie that consciously tried to distance itself from the feudal order, irrespective of how "unconscious" and uncritical it remained with regard to the inherent contradictions of its own—capitalist—social formation;

2. that some of the most original contributions to the development of Marxism in the twentieth century, involving a major reexamination of the problems of ideology and "false consciousness," emerged after the Russian Revolution, which put on the historical agenda not only the practical problems of transition to a socialist society but also the unavoidable challenge to assume a critical posture vis-à-vis the available social agencies and the advocated strategies of radical transformation.

To turn now to a particularly important question, the reciprocities between the given political form and the social structure to which that political form corresponds cannot be explained by the mere fact of their "correspondence." They must be accounted for through a deeper level of dialectical determinations—namely the social ontology of a self-reproducing natural being—which fully integrates the unavoidable requirements of the *natural* factors with the specific conditions of the objectively changing *social* relations. It is possible to talk about the (historically specific) correspondence between a given social structure and its political form only because they are both grounded in the "*natural* correspondence" between the attained degree of "social productivity" and the established relations of production—i.e., the existing structure of domination—summed up under their common denominator as the prevailing structural-hierarchical (and not simply functional) social division of labor.

There are indeed such things as the "*natural requisites*" of all continuous and reproductive "labor in general" that remain in force "under all modes of production": namely the absolute conditions of the *social metabolism as such* that correspond to the needs and self-reproductive determinations of a historically unique natural being. And since these conditions do exist, the ongoing metabolism between human beings and nature necessarily implies not only successful material production and reproduction as such but also the effective reproduction of the socially vital "*operating conditions*" of continued production without which sustainable production, quite simply, could not take place.

In other words, the imperatives of the social metabolism, as grounded on the historically "humanized" (in the straightforward sense of being affected by human beings) and constantly modified foundations of nature, imply not only an adequate level of material productivity but also the reproduction (or maintenance) of the existing *power relations* that regulate the given mode of production as its inherent "operating conditions." The *"natural requisites"* of continued production and reproduction (their nature-determined unavoidability) explain the need for such regulatory "operating conditions" in an absolute sense. At the same time, the given degree of development of the productive forces determines the relative, historically specific modality of regulatory constraints as more or less directly wedded to determinate *social hierarchies* for the whole of what Marx calls "humanity's pre-history," with the exception of its most primitive stages.

Admittedly, to envisage the replacement of such structural social hierarchies by the self-determining and conscious control of their interchanges by the "associated producers" (who are expected to institute a qualitatively different system of "operating conditions") presupposes a sufficiently favorable change in the objective constraints and necessities of material production itself. It must be emphasized that the presentation of this problem as a *temporal sequence* in which the required productive advancement *precedes*—on the ground of its own scientific/technological and "purely economic" determinations—the possibility of radically altering the motive forces and operating conditions of social reproduction is a crude and mechanical conception that befits only the ideologists of the ruling order. For, in the spirit of their "uncritical positivism," they eternalize the *present*—from the standpoint of which they can arbitrarily rewrite also the *past* [33]—and locate the feasibility of any socially meaningful transformation in a *future* that lies well beyond the life span of the individuals to whom such discourse is addressed. [34]

The illusory character of such (explicit or implicit) idealizations of technology arises from the failure to recognize a *structural necessity* inherent in all social forms of productive reproduction. In other words, the false diagnosis and concomitant prognosis of being able to find an adequate solution to deep-seated social problems by means of technological achievements are not due to the absence of ample evidence to the contrary. They are due to a defective theoretical matrix that obliterates the "obverse side"—the iniquitous social costs—of the advances made in limited areas at the expense of the overwhelming majority. This is how the thinkers concerned end up projecting the viability of *technological* solutions per se whose general implementation is in fact radically incompatible with the *social premises* of the established productive order. In this sense, well beyond questioning the merits of the particular propositions and wishful anticipations of various economists and social theorists, what we are concerned with here is a general theoretical issue of quite fundamental importance.

The point is that the *operating conditions* of production cannot be simply identified with, or submerged into, production as such. The two constitute a dialectical complex whose elements—even under the best possible circumstances—cannot amount to a relationship of *identity*, but only to that of an interactive, and in class societies of necessity contradictory, *unity*.

Depending on the precise configuration of the constituents of such interaction, this unity may be more or less stable and enduring. Equally, depending on how distant a given system of social reproduction happens to be at a particular point in time from its ultimate limits of productive advancement, the regulatory framework of material production may appear to be purely "organic" and unproblematical—as indeed the idealized "hidden hand" seemed to be in the age of "laissez-faire"—or display signs of "dysfunctionality" and "maladjustment" even in the view of its passionate defenders.

But even so, the operating conditions of productive reproduction can *never* be reduced to production itself, since they are not merely *technological* but simultaneously also *social*. They possess a relatively *autonomous* dimension that, far from being just "dysfunctional," can be extremely disruptive with regard to the objective requirements of the whole productive system under determinate historical circumstances.

The necessity for the establishment of a relatively autonomous framework of operating conditions arises in the case of social production for two—historically untranscendable—reasons. First, because every constituent part of the ongoing production process requires a set of manmade rules, however primitive (e.g. simple repetition), once labor intervenes in the metabolic process between the "tool-making animal" and nature, thereby embarking on the first emancipatory steps in the direction of overcoming the direct domination of nature's being by nature itself.

And second, the multiplicity of productive units must be somehow coordinated and protected—through modes of cooperation and reciprocity, however rudimentary—to secure their chances of survival and advancement in the face of the forces they have to confront, be such forces groups of hostile men or the power of nature. The "society of bees" needs neither of the two, since direct natural determinations regulate its "productive" activity both internally (through instinctual mechanisms) and in relation to the totality of nature.

Thus the structural foundation of the superstructure is not *materiality* in its *immediacy*, but the underlying necessity to establish properly regulated operating conditions even in the case of the most primitive forms of social production. Operating conditions, that is, which cannot help being *relatively autonomous* in their assumed regulatory functions from the very moment of their inception.

This is a matter of great theoretical importance. For these relatively autonomous operating conditions of production constitute the material ground on which the superstructure can historically arise. Naturally, superstructure cannot be simply identified with the regulating conditions themselves, just as the latter could not be simply submerged into production as such. The relatively autonomous operating conditions of production constitute the objective *mediating ground* between the strictly material and the specifically superstructural determinations of social intercourse. Consequently, the relative autonomy of the superstructure is not a subjective afterthought, devised by Engels with "Jesuitic casuistry"[35] so as to extricate the materialist conception of history from the self-imposed dilemmas of its alleged "mechanical reductionism." On the contrary, it is a *dialectical category of social being* that makes its first appearance in the operating conditions of productive reproduction already at a very early stage of historical development.

The advancement of social production and the multiplication of historically created human needs greatly enhance this relative autonomy, especially when the internal divisions of early reproductive practices become consolidated with the active help of the regulatory framework itself. Thus, once the internal divisions are structurally articulated and safeguarded, the question of control objectively defines itself under three principal aspects:

1. how to control the production process itself with the help of the available set of rules and regulatory devices;

2. how to secure the strategic positions of control in the established system of productive reproduction for one particular social class or group rather than for another; and

3. how to assume real control over the operating conditions themselves, which seem to have a life of their own and resist even the "corrective strategies" of the socially dominant forces.

Parallel to the general diffusion of the social division of labor as inextricably tied to the structurally enforced conditions of class domination, the superstructure—more and more formally articulated as a legal and political superstructure—assumes an increasingly greater role in the overall regulatory framework of productive reproduction. Accordingly, it not only *arises* and *rests* on the material basis of the given socioeconomic formation, but simultaneously also *superimposes* itself on that basis, graphically demonstrating also in this respect its relative autonomy.

To be sure, its power of superimposition can prevail—on the strength of the necessary regulatory functions effectively fulfilled by the superstructure in the system of social reproduction—only so long as the interests of the fundamental social metabolism are not endangered. Nevertheless, short of an elemental structural crisis the power of the superstructure—for better or worse—is truly immense. For in virtue of its vital regulatory functions it constitutes a closely *interlocking complex*—a real vicious circle in capitalist society—with its material basis of productive reproduction. This is why the much heralded triumph of "science and compound interest" (Keynes)[36] over scarcity within the structural parameters of capitalist society is, at best, only a pipedream. For the elementary condition of taking even the first steps in the direction of that triumph is to break the vicious circle between capitalist material production and its necessary operating conditions. To achieve such an aim is conceivable only as a dialectical process of reciprocity through which both dimensions of the interlocking complex are radically—and simultaneously—restructured, in contrast to the fantasy of establishing a temporal sequence between them, irrespective of which of the two we might place first in the chronological order.

In accordance with this line of reasoning, the historically changing superstructural forms can "correspond," in the Marxian sense, to the specificities of the given social structure precisely because they constitute the *necessary regulatory framework* of continued reproduction, dialectically interacting with the latter and *co-determining* its transformations, on the basis of the "natural correspondence" between the given forces and relations of productive reproduction.

By the same token, the reciprocities of interaction may also manifest, and indeed explode, in the form of *acute contradictions*, in case the regulatory interventions themselves seriously contribute to the emergence and aggravation of *structural blockages* in the system of continued reproduction instead of helping to increase the given society's productivity. This happens when the existing framework of regulatory interventions is no longer sufficient to displace the various manifestations of the system's contradictions, in contrast to earlier phases of their unfolding, when they can still be treated as mere "dysfunctions," corrigible with relative ease within the objective structural parameters of the established order. Under such circumstances the normally stabilizing superstructural forms themselves paradoxically disrupt the dynamics of "correspondence-by-reciprocal-adjustments" and, as a result, ultimately endanger even the most elementary requirements of the basic social metabolism.

We must distinguish between very different levels of "correspondence" that constitute an integrated system of determinations, structured in an ascending order of *"uebergreifenden"* moments. At the same time, it must be emphasized that even the most mediated levels actively "react back" on the more fundamental ones, dialectically contributing to the historical transformation of the social complex as a whole.

The principal aspects of this system of reciprocal interactions and correspondences may be described, in ascending order, as follows:

1. the *natural requisites* of *all* modes of production and of all continuous and reproductive labor in general;

2. the *natural correspondence* between the *given* forces and relations of

production, in accordance with the historically attained level of social productivity;

3. the correspondence between the historically specific *social structure* and its *superstructure,* which assumes the form of *legal and political* superstructure under a variety of social formations;

4. the correspondence between determinate *ideas* and *forms of social consciousness* and the *material base* of the society in question as *mediated* by, and articulated through, the inextricably material as well as ideological instruments and institutions of this society in the overall framework of its superstructure.

Without grasping the problematic of dialectical "reciprocity" and "correspondence" in the above sense—i.e., as an integrated complex of material and ideal determinations, with the *ultimate* priority vested in the former—we would end up with some tautological structural-functionalist conception that stipulates an unfailingly successful system of "reciprocal adjustments," with the necessary elimination of "social dysfunctions," in the interest of social apologetics.

In this sense, a dialectical conception of the complex interactions and reciprocal determinations between base and superstructure means, first of all, to grasp the various factors involved as an *objectively structured and ordered* set of relations, with a precisely definable relative weight attached to each element at any given time, as well as transhistorically. (The latter in accordance with the priorities pertaining to the different structural constituents in virtue of their more or less strategic location with regard to one another in the general framework of the basic social metabolism. In other words, what we perceive as *transhistorical* trends of development— e.g., the stubborn persistence of class formations, notwithstanding their manifold contradictions, over a very long historical period—correspond in reality to some *structurally primary* interests and determinations of social interchange. Their nature and function within the established structural parameters of society is such that for the time being, however long, they must be reproduced in the historical dialectic between continuity and discontinuity predominantly under the sign of *continuity*, given the objective constitution of the established metabolic system and of the inherent operating conditions of its deeply entrenched modality of productive reproduction.)

Such a dialectical approach to the interconnections between base and superstructure requires, of course, the most careful assessment of the various levels and principal structural relations themselves, with particular attention to the necessary historical qualifications that concern the specific social formation in its entirety. As we have seen earlier, Marx's remark on the politics of Athens and Rome and on the Catholicism of the Middle Ages forcefully underlines the importance of identifying the historical specificities of determinate social formations at the level of their superstructural/ideological mechanisms and modes of interaction with the material base, without weakening in the least the materialist underpinning of his explanatory framework as a whole.

These considerations, concerned with some central characteristics of different social formations, acquire their full significance only in relation to the "innumerable different empirical circumstances"—such as the characteristics of the "natural environment, racial relations, external historical influences, etc."—which are responsible for creating those "infinite variations and gradations" that constitute the tangible reality of any historical situation in the overall framework of the given social formation. However—and this must be strongly emphasized, since it is often disregarded—the concrete assessment of the "innumerable different empirical circumstances" becomes meaningful (and possible at all) only within this firmly ordered general framework of the structural relations of the social formation as such, and not the other way around. That is to say, no matter how hard we might try, we shall never be able to squeeze out of the survey of the numerous empirical circumstances, however "complete," a coherent theoretical framework capable of illuminating the various social formations both by themselves and in relation to one another.

The two together: i.e., the full inventory of the relevant empirical data on the one hand and the conceptual framework of "base and superstructure" on the other as the condition of situating and evaluating the former, provide the necessary constituents of an adequate theoretical explanation of these complex dialectical relations. In this way it becomes possible to give due weight both to the strictly material and to the not directly material factors, from the natural productivity of the land to compulsion and tradition, and from the genesis of "explicit law" as a principal regulatory force of the social metabolism under several different socioeconomic formations to the subtle functioning of even the most mediated forms of social consciousness.

3.3 Customs, Tradition and Explicit Law: Historical Boundaries of the Legal and Political Superstructure

Talking about the emergence of rent, for instance, Marx stresses the vital importance of:

1. a sufficiently large surplus of labor-power, and

2. the natural productivity of the land, as the necessary conditions for introducing rent.

At the same time he adds: "It is not this possibility which creates the rent, but rather *compulsion* which turns this possibility into reality. But the possibility itself is conditioned by subjective and objective natural circumstances."[37]

From such considerations he moves on to assess the role of *tradition* and the emergence of *law* in terms of the requirements of the fundamental social metabolism by saying:

> It is evident that *tradition* must play a dominant role in the primitive and undeveloped circumstances on which these social production relations and the corresponding mode of production are based. It is furthermore clear that here as always it is in the interest of the *ruling* section of society to *sanction the existing order as law* and to legally establish its limits given through *usage and tradition.* Apart from all else, this, by the way, comes about of itself as soon as the *constant reproduction* of the basis of the existing order and its fundamental relations assumes a *regulated and orderly form* in the course of time. And such *regulation and order* are themselves indispensable elements of *any* mode of production, if it is to

assume *social stability* and independence from mere chance and arbitrariness. These are precisely the form of its social stability and therefore its relative freedom from mere arbitrariness and mere chance. Under backward conditions of the production process as well as the corresponding social relations, it achieves this form by mere *repetition* of their very reproduction. If this has continued on for some time, it *entrenches* itself as *custom and tradition* and is finally *sanctioned* as an *explicit law*.[38]

As we can see, though the truly extra-economic category of *naked compulsion* needs no historical explanation (the spontaneous exercise of brute force on the basis of differential natural strength is sufficient to set it into motion), the appearance of *legalized* compulsion (i.e., legally sanctioned and institutionally enforced compulsion) is an entirely different matter.

To explain the genesis of law, it is necessary to bring into play a number of very different factors, from the elementary requirements of the social metabolism as such to much more mediated superstructural mechanisms. "Continued reproduction," "regulation and order," "social stability," and "independence from mere chance and arbitrariness" are all vital requirements of any mode of production, irrespective of its relative degree of historical development. Thus "regulation" and "orderly reproduction" arise as the elemental material imperatives of social stability as such, prior to any conceivable legal regulation. Law itself must be first established on the same material basis before it can determine the specific form in which subsequent social interaction may legitimately take place. As the point of departure for a theoretically viable account, it is not possible to assume more than the mere fact of *"repetition"* as the necessary condition of any successful societal reproduction. (This much, of course, one may rightfully assume, since it is simply inconceivable to envisage any mode of socioeconomic reproduction, no matter how "innovative," in which "repetition"—or "continuity"—does not play a significant part.)

The social practice (and the corresponding category) of "repetition" represents the necessary point of departure toward the establishment of law, through the mediation of *"usages," "customs," and "tradition."* Once reproduction is reinforced and stabilized through continued repetition of its fundamental processes to the point of becoming well-established "usages and customs" of the given society—thereby securing and safeguarding the "regulated and orderly form" of reproduction in the interest of social stability—the transition from *direct material determinations* (subject to the rule of "mere chance and arbitrariness") to the active intervention of *superstructural* constituents is in fact successfully accomplished. For inasmuch as usages and customs "*entrench themselves*" and acquire the power of *tradition*, the door to formally codifying the more or less generally accepted (and at any rate effectively working) normativity of tradition by explicit law is wide open, together with the possibility of manipulating the beliefs associated with all forms of customs and tradition. By the same token, those who happen to be in some key position with respect to the implementation of customs and tradition (as guardians of the associated ritual practices, for instance) ipso facto not merely have a vested *interest* in reinforcing their own relatively privileged position but also the *ability* to do so.

Another point of great importance is that the existence of a regulatory system of customs and traditions makes it not only possible (and relatively easy) to establish "explicit law" as the watchdog of the ruling order, but also facilitates the task of the latter by exercizing many of its controlling functions, thereby reducing to a minimum the need for a direct repressive (legal) intervention in areas over which customs and traditions can maintain effective control. Hence there is always a dialectical relationship between tradition and law in that

1. no society can regulate itself on an enduring basis by the power of "explicit law" alone;

2. there is a "two-way traffic" between law and tradition inasmuch as one can reinforce the other; or take over some functions of the other when the latter fails in effectively exercising them; or initiate some new functions and later assign them to the other, etc.;

3. the more customs and traditions successfully embrace, the less explicit or codified law needs regulating;

4. the broad framework of the law itself is powerfully conditioned by the existing system of customs and traditions (i.e., no legal system can

diametrically oppose the established system of customs and traditions without losing its own credibility and efficacy);

5. major socioeconomic changes initiate corresponding transformations in tradition and law alike, but the effective unfolding and implementation of such changes may be retarded for a considerable time by the power of inertia of the latter;

6. by definition, law can respond more quickly than tradition to basic socioeconomic determinations (and in general to the need for significant social change); however, due to the interdeterminations referred to in point (4), the pace at which law can effectively respond to the requirements of major social change cannot ignore the limitations (and potentialities) of tradition itself as an integral part of the overall transformation;

7. *in the last analysis*, in the dialectical relationship between *law* and *tradition* the latter is structurally more important, even though, as a matter of brute fact, law assumed the dominant position in the course of history. What this vital consideration with regard to the alienating historical reversal of the objective structural primacy of tradition over the legal and political superstructure amounts to is that the progressive transcendence of explicit law—envisaged by Marx in order to do away with its negative, repressive dimension: inseparable from independently articulated law and *"Staatswesen"*[39] as such—is conceivable only if society can transfer all the regulative functions of explicit law to the "self-activity" (i.e., the conscious or spontaneous "customs and tradition") of the social body itself.

It is also clear from the Marxian account that the superstructure must be constituted and articulated within the framework of customs and traditions *well before* it can assume the form of "legal and political superstructure." The prominence of legal and political determinations in exercising the essential functions of the social metabolism is characteristic of *class societies*, including the long historical period of transition from the capitalist social formation to the "higher phase of socialism" (or communism). According to Marx, only the latter can bring a radical change in this respect, when—beyond the earlier regulatory constraints—the self-determined interaction of the social individuals is governed by the principle "to everyone according to their need," rather than by the institutionalized rule of a separate legal system and its corresponding "state form," be that of the most enlightened kind.

Once the superstructure takes on the characteristic form of "legal and political superstructure" in the course of historical development—a form appropriate to various modes of "orderly" reproduction within the confines of the hierarchical-structural division of labor—the whole of the superstructure, even its most mediated dimensions (religious beliefs, artistic practices, philosophical conceptions, etc.), must be brought under its determinations, though, of course, in the earlier seen dialectical sense of the term. For the legal and political superstructure is by its very nature a "totalizing," all-comprehensive structure. It reaches down to the most fundamental levels of social interchange, regulating the social metabolism itself by imposing and safeguarding the property relations of the given mode of production.

We must recall in this context Marx's characterization of the completed capitalist order as a historically constituted totality and, as such, an "organic system."[40] Within the framework of this "organic system," everything must be in tune with the necessary *practical presuppositions* of the dominant mode of production, based on a perverted form of "*universality.*" This is in reality a pseudo-universality in that it is determined negatively, by way of *exclusion*, so that citizenship, for instance, is circumscribed with reference to barriers and various disqualification clauses; and, likewise, the pseudo-positive concept of "conformity to the law" is defined in terms of the conditions of its violation, together with a set of more or less arbitrarily stipulated sanctions. All this is, of course, in perfect agreement with the dictates of *exclusivistic* (rather than just private) *property relations* which assign control over the vital reproductive functions of society to a small minority, in sharp contrast to genuinely all-inclusive *communal* property relations that embrace all members of society.

Since the development of such social formations takes place on the material foundations (and regulatory premises) of structurally divided class society, those parts of the "organic system" in question possess the greatest strategic relevance—and a corresponding ability to extend their power over every sphere—which are the most directly involved in reproducing the iniquitous *structural parameters* and operating conditions of the overall social complex. This is the principal reason why the *legal and political* superstructure acquires its paramount importance in the course of historical development.

Parallel to the consolidation of exclusivistic property ownership and the emergence of the ruling order's need for a radical redefinition of universality in the sense mentioned above, the legal and political superstructure becomes the *"uebergreifendes Moment"* (and in the end a one-sidedly dominant constituent) of the superstructure as a whole. For no other part of the superstructure can satisfy this need—from the point of view of the ruling order absolutely vital—with a comparable practical effectiveness.

Religion and art, for instance, must maintain their claims to potentially all-inclusive and communally shared universality (from which in principle not even the members of the most hostile foreign state can be excluded), however illusory and "other-worldly" their terms of reference might be, if they are not to contradict their self-definition and thereby lose their authenticity and credibility. Accordingly, the practical role they are allowed to play must be on the whole a subsidiary one with regard to the structural parameters and operating conditions of established society. The more so, in fact, the greater the complexity of the reproductive interconnections within an increasingly more integrated, and in the end globally intertwined, socioeconomic framework.

In this sense one can truly say that several dimensions of the superstructure become "marginalized" and condemned to an essentially supportive role in the course of historical development, in direct proportion to the rise of the legal and political superstructure. At the same time, "practical reason" under all its aspects must remain subjected to the materially determined normative requirements directly manifest in the coordinating and "totalizing" function of the legal and political *uebergreifendes Moment*. It is by no means accidental in this respect that precisely those dimensions of the non-legal/political superstructure that happen to be the most sensitive from the point of view of the societal reproduction process are brought under the direct control of the ever-more-powerful legal and political superstructure (in contrast to the pre-capitalist past when they were much more directly influential), as evidenced not only in the relationship between the modern state and the churches (notwithstanding all talk about their separation) but also in the way in which the artistic and educational institutions of society are being controlled.

As we have seen, the normative dominance of law and politics becomes possible only at a relatively recent stage of historical development. The original constitution and long drawn-out transformation of the regulatory principles necessary to sustained social reproduction can be identified in the following terms:

1. the exposure of primitive communities to the rule of chance and arbitrariness; *naked compulsion* as the only feasible regulatory force, with all its *wastefulness* and *instability*; total absence of normativity;

2. the emergence of stabilizing factors through *repetition*, on the basis of "trial and error," representing the first—*spontaneous*—steps in the direction of emancipation from chance and arbitrariness;

3. the consolidation of the positive achievements of repetition in the form of—instrumentally oriented—*specific usages*;

4. the coordination of a multiplicity of recurrent usages into a fairly coherent body of *customs*; normativity is still primarily concerned with the objective requirements of production and reproduction, i.e., with the enforcement of predominantly instrumental necessities; this remains the case for a long time, even though the imperatives associated with the reproduction of the operating conditions of production (articulated as a set of well-marked customs) introduce a strong element of social normativity, preparing the ground for a much more problematical social division of labor;

5. the integration of the most varied and long established customs into the *universally respected tradition* of the given community, representing a mode of regulation that lays great stress on *values* transmitted from generation to generation, coupled with ritual reinforcement that involves the active participation of all; societies regulated by the nor-

mativity of tradition may remain for an indefinite period of time thoroughly egalitarian in character, as historical records show, although the entrenchment of the new regulatory modalities opens the door to the development of separate forms of institutional enforcement and to the structural hierarchies that go with them;

6. the emergence of *explicit law*; tradition *selectively* elevated to the status of law, with its *sanctions* and separate organs of law-enforcement at the service of the *ruling order*; the exploitative minority interests of the established social formation codified as "the law," self-interestedly redrawing the boundaries of legitimate social intercourse and redefining the meaning of "society," "communality" and "universality" in accordance with the a prioristic requirements of *structural domination,* so that the concept of "social organism" acquires a profoundly conservative and apologetic meaning. At the same time, the potentially dissenting social forces are strictly (and punitively) subordinated to the new, rather abstract and instrumentally enforced system of overall coordination and normativity, hence the inescapably *negative* articulation of the legal and political regulatory framework.

Thus, though it is undoubtedly true that the various "moments" referred to here become not only practically but also formally *subsumed* under the fully articulated legal and political superstructure, they nevertheless remain directly or indirectly *operative* within the totalizing framework of the latter, however unpalatable this may sound to those who continue to idealize and "eternalize" the triumph of "Leviathan" as equivalent to civilized human existence, from the earliest theorists of "social contract" to present-day apologists of the capitalist state. For the historically recent legal and political regulatory machinery simply could not fulfill its vital metabolic functions without effectively bringing into play all the other—structurally more fundamental—moments as well, redefined as subordinate parts of its own "orderly" self-constitution. Even *naked compulsion* remains an integral part of the (no matter how "refined") legal and political superstructure, convenient though it might be to ignore this fact as far as the established socioeconomic order is concerned, since it happens to clash with the self-mythology of the dominant interests. As Marx rightly observed:

All the bourgeois economists are aware of is that production can be carried on better under the modern police than e.g. on the principle of might makes right. They forget only that this principle is also a legal relation, and that the right of the stronger prevails in their 'constitutional republics' as well, only in another form.[41]

Indeed, the right of the stronger—i.e., the necessary dominance of those who own and/or control the means of production—must prevail, ultimately at all costs, since the stability of the *relations* of production (the material underpinning of the legal and political superstructure) is crucial to the successful reproduction of the operating conditions of production, as we have seen. Law and the institutions of its enforcement are eminently suitable to such a role under the conditions of social antagonism, that is, when the management of the essential reproductive structures of society remains irreconcilably contested. Consequently, only the radical supersession of social antagonisms could do away with naked compulsion and institutionalized violence, however "civilized" and liberally "sophisticated," which must be at least "implicit"—and at times of major crises openly reactivated—in all forms of "explicit law."[42]

All this does not alter the fact that the historically primary and ontologically fundamental—and in that sense "absolute"—moment is the necessity of *orderly regulation,* in the interest of socioeconomic advancement and the expansion and satisfaction of historically produced needs on the ground of such advancement, and not its *specific form.* All the less since the form in question can only secure the required reproduction at the devastating social cost of reproducing at the same time the structural hierarchies and antagonisms of the established order both on an expanding scale and with a growing intensity, which carry grave implications for the future.

The most problematic aspect of the historically evolved and up until the present time dominant mode of social regulation (from which many others follow) is that *appropriation* falls under the rule of minority-controlled property and alienated legality that sustains such property in the form of separately constituted political power. Indeed, one of the vicious circles we can identify in this sphere is that the separately articulated legal and political superstructure necessarily implies the material dominance of exclusivistic/minority controlled property (and the corresponding modality of iniquitous appropriation at all planes) and vice versa. Thus in class societies the legal and political form is both a regulator of the social intercourse and a usurper in the service of the usurpers of social wealth. And even after the intended post-revolutionary break with the past it represents one of the greatest challenges to extricate the new society of "associated producers" from the clutches of these determinations, which tend to resist or subvert precisely their practical self-definition as associated producers.

It is by no means surprising that so long as the legal form remains dominant, the structural iniquities of discriminatory appropriation are reproduced with it. This is particularly revealing in the light of some major reversals to which modern history bears witness. For in the course of revolutionary upheavals conscious efforts are made, at times, to introduce some truly egalitarian principles for the regulation of production and appropriation—as for instance during the initial phase of the Russian Revolution—which are later reversed, parallel to the reconstitution of the state that emerges more powerful than ever from the crisis. Such reversals, rooted in the vicious circle between separate legality and iniquitous appropriation, underline the hopeless inadequacy of explaining these problems in terms of "postrevolutionary bureaucratization"— and associated categories—which at best only beg the question. One cannot reduce a whole range of objective structural determinations to subjective defects.[43]

Historically the emergence and consolidation of the legal and political superstructure runs parallel to the conversion of communal appropriation into exclusivistic property. The more extensive the practical impact of the latter on the prevailing modality of social reproduction (especially in the form of fragmented private property), the more pronounced and institutionally articulated the totalizing role of the legal and political superstructure must be. It is therefore by no means accidental that the centralizing and bureaucratically all-invading *capitalist* state—and not a state defined by vague geographic terms as "the modern Occidental state"—acquires its preponderance in the course of the development of generalized commodity production and the practical institution of the property relations in tune with it, notwithstanding the "free market" and "laissez-faire" mythology of its beneficiaries. Once this connection is omitted, as indeed for ideological reasons it must be in the case of all those who conceptualize these problems from the standpoint of the ruling order, we end up with a mystery as to why the state assumes the character it happens to have under the conditions of generalized commodity production. A mystery that becomes a complete mystification when Max Weber tries to unravel it by suggesting that "it has been the work of jurists to give birth to the modern Occidental state."[44] Hegel's idealism at least offered us the good services of the "World Spirit" in explanation of such monumental miracles, not the misty "*Kopfarbeit*" of drunken judges.

The more fully articulated the legal and political superstructure is, the more closely it embraces and dominates not only the material practices but simultaneously also the most varied "ideal forms" of social consciousness. As a result, the theoretical, philosophical, artistic, etc., forms of activity cannot directly reflect, or respond to, the needs and demands of the social base. They must do so via the necessarily *biased mediation* of the legal and political superstructure.

Two sets of questions are particularly important in this respect. The first concerns the nature of practical mediations within the capitalistic framework of social reproduction, and the second the perverse overall configuration of this formation as an "organic system."

Since these problems are discussed in considerable detail in *Beyond Capital,* let it suffice to say here briefly, with regard to the first set, that the mediations in question—which negatively affect the production of all forms and modalities of social consciousness—are the structurally vitiated and reified *second-order mediations* of WAGE LABOR, PRIVATE PROPERTY and EXCHANGE, asserting themselves through the controlling power of capital (which arises from its monopoly over the means of production) and the corresponding hierarchical social division of labor. Naturally, given the way in which class society is constituted on the ground of objective contradictions (held together by a multiplicity of interlocking determinations), the legal and political superstructure formally regulates and reinforces this network of alienated second order mediations, enlisting in its task the contribution of all the other parts of the superstructure as well, and thereby it plays a vital role in the successful reproduction of the entire system.

As to the second set of problems, what is directly relevant in the present context is that the practically crucial role of the legal and political superstructure in the overall reproduction process—which turns it into the *uebergreifendes Moment* of the entire superstructure—confers upon the legal and political superstructure a highly privileged status in the "organic system" of the established social order. As a result, the other parts of the superstructure cannot gain access to the necessary means of their own activity without the (explicit or implicit) stamp of approval by the legal and political superstructure. In this sense, the "organic system" of capital articulates itself also at the plane of the superstructure as a complex network of subordinations and superordinations, even if intellectuals tend to forget about the paradoxical relationships of superstructural dependency into which they are, as individuals, inescapably inserted.

On both counts, therefore, the "full emancipation" of art, philosophy, etc., from the rule of capital is inseparable from the "withering away" of the legal and political superstructure as such. Since under the prevailing system, as mentioned already, the non-legal/political parts of the superstructure can only gain access to the conditions of their effective functioning through the necessarily biased mediation of the legal and political superstructure, there is a prima facie tension between the two. Under favorable circumstances this tension can assume the form of critical emancipatory contestation. Indeed, one may rightfully assert that there is a genuine emancipatory interest on the side of art, critical social theory, etc., opposed to the legal and political superstructure for as long as the latter retains its normative preponderance in the overall reproduction process. Such emancipatory interest, though, must be located in an empirically identifiable social agency as its carrier, rather than hypostatized on a fictitiously self-supporting ideal/intellectual terrain, as often happens with the representatives of the Frankfurt School, including Marcuse's desperate yet mysteriously emancipatory "Aesthetic Dimension."[45] Moreover, since by its very nature "explicit law" can never acquire the character of *self-activity*, in that it must set itself up above all members of society in its spurious claims to universal validity, the practical realization of socialist emancipation envisaged by Marx is in principle unthinkable within the structural constraints of the legal and political superstructure as such. In other words, according to the Marxian conception the legal and political superstructure not only in its capitalist form but *in all conceivable forms* must be considered the necessary target of emancipatory social practice.

In relation to these considerations it becomes clear why the historical boundaries of the legal and political superstructure must be drawn with great care, both with regard to the past and in the direction of the future. For, as no one could seriously dispute it, no society can adequately reproduce itself and advance in its capacity to satisfy an expanding range of human needs without creating reliable normative structures and institutions, in accordance with the cumulative regulatory requirements of an increasingly more complex and intertwined social metabolism. In this sense, once the phase regulated by the crudest material determinations is left behind, social intercourse is inconceivable without the growing intervention of superstructural factors, with their corresponding forms of normativity. Nor is it conceivable to do away with normativity as such in a socialist society. If anything, its role, on the contrary, is bound to increase with the mastery of material necessities and the successful removal of external constraints. For the fully acknowledged *reciprocity* of the interacting social individuals as "associated producers" necessarily implies as its precondition the *internal normativity* of a new mode of action, oriented within, and envisaging the reproduction of, a consciously adopted overall societal framework from which the a prioristic (materially prejudged and vitiated) predominance of partial interests has been removed in the course of historical development.

Thus, although the "new historic form"—Marx's code name for a truly socialist society—is totally unthinkable without its properly articulated superstructure, it is quite another matter as far as the legal and political superstructure is concerned. For the normativity of the latter, very far from being *internal* and thus suitable to the exercise of consciously pursued and fully equitable reciprocity, is in fact *external* and alienated normativity par excellence.

With respect to the past, the historical boundary of the legal and political superstructure is marked by the radical displacement and domination (though, for reasons already indicated, by no means the liquidation) of the earlier—in their inception spontaneously all-embracing and participatory—forms of normativity. Furthermore, throughout its long history the

legal and political superstructure is characterized by the practical reproduction of yet another, somewhat paradoxical, vicious circle. Through
this circle it *sustains* the dominance of minority-controlled property, and
at the same time—in regard to its ultimate *sanction* that materially
grounds (in principle at least) its own power of domination over all particular individuals—*it is itself sustained by property*, in the form of its
selectively exercised negation of the right of determinate individuals to
enjoy their property and the freedoms associated with their possessions,
without disrupting thereby in the least its own subservience to the dominant class or classes at the level of collective relations.

As for the future, the historical boundary of the legal and political
superstructure can only be drawn in practical terms by the structural crisis of the mode of social interchange that must rely on minority-controlled
property as the principal motivating force of its system of productive
reproduction. For so long as the operating conditions of social production remain tied to the structural hierarchies of the established social division of labor, the vicious circle just referred to is bound to be reproduced
with them, even if in an altered form.

This means that under such conditions the dominance of the alienating normativity of the law—deeply rooted in the reproductive processes
themselves—cannot be superseded. At the same time it is also clear that
the retention of the alienating normativity of the legal and political superstructure is totally incompatible with the idea of socialist emancipation. It
is not surprising, therefore, that the Marxian project had to be spelled out
from the very beginning as a revolutionary critique of the state. A critique
that envisaged the state's complete transcendence already in Marx's very
early writings (such as the *Critique of the Hegelian Philosophy of Right*,
among others), reiterating the same point with great emphasis in the
assessment of the Paris Commune's historical significance and in some
passages of the *Critique of the Gotha Program* that envisage the necessary
historical supersession of the state form and the radical transcendence of
the law (or "explicit law") as such. Thus there can be no compromise as
far as the "withering away of the state" and the progressive "*Aufhebung*"
of the legal and political superstructure—in favor of a qualitatively redefined and correspondingly restructured superstructure—are concerned.
In terms of the Marxian vision, any accommodation on this point

amounts to abandoning the idea of a socialist transformation of society altogether.

This is why concern with the relationship between the material base and the superstructure of the various socio-historical formations occupies such an important place in the Marxian conception.

As we have seen, according to Marx the "superstructure" in its primary sense is *radically* different from superstructure articulated as "legal and political superstructure." The emergence and consolidation of a separate legal and political framework to which all the other parts of the superstructure must be subjected is due to much more recent socio-historical factors and determinations than the original constitution of the *superstructure as customs and tradition.* Appropriately, therefore, the latter thus assumes a particular significance in the assessment of the issues at stake. For it remains the structurally and ontologically fundamental constituent, notwithstanding the dominant position of law and politics throughout the history of class societies.

Ultimately, it is the Marxian way of drawing the line of demarcation between the ontologically untranscendable *superstructure* and the historically limited *legal and political* superstructure that makes it possible to anticipate the "withering away" of the state and the end of the domination of social life by separate legality and abstract normativity, with all the emancipatory potential inherent in such "withering away" with regard to both the primary material and the corresponding regulatory superstructural practices of the "freely associated producers."

NOTES

1. Peter Worsley, *The Three Worlds: Culture and World Development*, Weidenfeld and Nicolson, London, 1984, 37.
2. Ibid., 32. Sadly, in reality it is Peter Worsley himself who finds it necessary to resort to "verbal contortions" and distortions. He declares in his refutationary zeal—which is perhaps also a form of self-criticism for his own dogmatic Marxist and Maoist past—that "It is simply not true that man must eat before he can *think.* People would not find food at all if they did not *think.*" Ibid., 36.

    In truth, Marx's critique of idealism is not concerned with "thinking" as such, but with denying the primacy and self–referential autonomy of *philos-*

ophizing over the historically unfolding production and reproduction of the material conditions of human existence that itself is—as a matter of truism—totally inconceivable without thinking. And even Engels's deliberately simplified formulations of the materialist conception of history make it quite clear that Worsley's "refutation" is a crude caricature. For the way in which Engels puts it in his "Speech at the Graveside of Marx": "Mankind must first of all eat, drink, have shelter and clothing, before it can pursue *politics, science, art, religion, etc.*" (Marx and Engels, *Selected Works*, Foreign Languages Publishing House, Moscow, 1958,2:153.) Furthermore, it is a cornerstone of precisely the Marxian tradition to insist that *homo faber* (man the worker and tool-bearer) cannot be separated from and opposed to *homo sapiens* (man the thinker).

3.   Ibid., 41.

4.   Steven Lukes, "Can the Base Be Distinguished from the Superstructure?," in *The Nature of Political Theory*, ed. David Miller and Larry Siedentop, Clarendon Press, Oxford, 1983, 119.

5.   For an illuminating counterexample see Raymond Williams, "Base and Superstructure in Marxist Cultural Theory" (1973; repr. in *Problems in Materialism and Culture*, N.L.B., London, 1980, 31–49); and part 2 of his *Marxism and Literature* (Oxford University Press, 1977, 75–141). For though Williams is justifiably critical of mechanical reductionism, he also offers a positive alternative. Particularly valuable is his analysis of "incorporation" which integrates Gramsci's concept of "hegemony" into the Marxian theoretical framework of historical and cultural developments.

6.   Worsley, *The Three Worlds*, 28.

7.   Max Weber, *The Theory of Social and Economic Organization*, ed. with an Introduction by Talcott Parsons, Free Press, New York, 1964, 89. "Pure type" is italicized by Weber.

8.   Ibid., 92.

9.   This is how Weber illustrates his "typological scientific analysis" that has as its frame of reference what he calls "a conceptually pure type of rational action":

> For example a panic on the stock exchange can be most conveniently analysed by attempting to determine first what the course of action *would have been* if it had not been influenced by *irrational effects*; it is then possible to introduce the irrational components as accounting for the observed *deviations from this hypothetical course*.[Ibid., 92]

10.   Weber, "Objectivity" (1904), in *The Methodology of the Social Sciences*, ed. E. A. Shils and H. A. Finch, Free Press, New York, 1949, 99. For a more detailed discussion of these problems, see my essay on "Ideology and Social Science" (*The Socialist Register*, 1972; repr. in I. Mészáros, *Philosophy, Ideology, and Social Science*, Harvester Press, Brighton, 1976), particularly sections 2: "Max Weber and Value-Free Social Science," 3:

"Ideological Character of the Ideal Types," and 4: "Theory and Meta-Theory."

11. Talcott Parsons, introduction to Max Weber, *The Theory of Social and Economic Organization*, Free Press, New York, 1964, 28.

12. Weber, *The Theory of Social and Economic Organization*, 102. "Only" underlined by Weber.

13. Ibid., 103.

14. Ibid., 101. "Solely" italicized by Weber.

15. Ibid., 102.

16. Ibid.

17. Karl Marx, *Grundrisse*, Penguin Books, Harmondsworth, 1973, 106.

18. Ibid., 103–5.

19. Weber, *The Theory of Social and Economic Organization*, 92.

20. In this sense, it is by no means accidental that the category of "class consciousness" is so recent. For just like "labor as such," it is produced by actual historical development, reaching its climax in the capitalist social formation. Thus modern historians and philosophers "discover" its relevance to the analysis of social conflict when the assertion of the motivating force of class consciousness "becomes true in practice." This does not mean, of course, that it is not applicable—*mutatis mutandis*—to earlier conditions. However, again, just like "labor as such" the concept of "class consciousness," too, "achieves *practical truth* . . . only as a category of the *most modern society*." (Marx, *Grundrisse*, 105.) Marx's methodological principle that contrasts "human anatomy" with the "anatomy of the ape" is relevant also in this respect. As he puts it:

    Bourgeois society is the most developed and the most complex historic organization of production. The categories which express its relations, the comprehension of its structure, thereby also allow insights into the structure and the relations of production of all the vanished social formations out of whose ruins and elements it built itself up, whose partly still unconquered remnants are carried along within it, whose mere nuances have developed explicit significance within it, etc. Human anatomy contains a key to the anatomy of the ape. The intimations of higher development among the subordinate animal species, however, can be understood only after the higher development is already known. [Ibid.]

21. Karl Marx and Frederick Engels, *Collected Works*, Lawrence and Wishart, London, 1975, 4:36 (henceforth MECW).

22. Ibid., 37. Marx's italics.

23. Weber, *The Theory of Social and Economic Organization*, 92.

24. Worsley, *The Three Worlds*, 28–29. Worsley's italics.

25. Ibid., 36.

26. It is interesting to note that Peter Worsley, after declaring that society is not

this and not that, immediately changes the subject from "society" to "human beings" when he tries to offer an affirmative statement. As he puts it: "The crucial difference, anthropologists have long insisted, is that human beings possess a developed consciousness and, collectively, a shared, cumulative culture." (Ibid., 28.) However, simply to equate "society" with "human beings" is blatantly fallacious. For such equation wishfully omits the *institutional inertia*—Sartre's "practico-inert"—that confronts and often destructively negates the "developed consciousness" of human beings.

27. Marx, *Grundrisse*, 88.

28. Ibid., 278.

29. Marx often scorns the tautologies with the help of which even the classics of bourgeois political economy "deduce" the existent from their own assumptions. The expression "flat tautologies" is from the *Grundrisse,* 86.

30. Ibid., 87–88.

31. Karl Marx, *Capital*, Foreign Languages Publishing House, Moscow, 1959, 3:771–72.

32. Ibid., 1:82. In view of its importance, it is worth quoting this passage in its entirety:

> I seize this opportunity of shortly answering an objection taken by a German paper in America, to my work, *Zur Kritik der Politischen Oekonomie*, 1859. In the estimation of that paper, my view that each special mode of production and the social relations corresponding to it, in short, that the economic structure of society, is the real basis on which the juridical and political superstructure is raised, and to which definite social forms of thought correspond; that the mode of production determines the character of the social, political, and intellectual life generally, all this is very true for our own times, in which material interests preponderate, but not for the middle ages, in which Catholicism, nor for Athens and Rome, where politics, reigned supreme. In the first place it strikes one as an odd thing for any one to suppose that these wellworn phrases about the middle ages and the ancient world are unknown to anyone else. This much, however, is clear, that the middle ages could not live on Catholicism, nor the ancient world on politics. On the contrary, it is the mode in which they gained a livelihood that explains why here politics and there Catholicism, played the chief part. For the rest, it requires but a slight acquaintance with the history of the Roman republic, for example, to be aware that its secret history is the history of its landed property. On the other hand, Don Quixote long ago paid the penalty for wrongly imagining that knight errantry was compatible with all economic forms of society.

Marx's acknowledgment of the "chief part" played by politics, or by Christianity, under determinate historical conditions, tends to be greatly exaggerated by those who one-sidedly insist on the "autonomy" (by which they mean complete independence) of such superstructural factors. In truth, however, Marx's pejorative references both to the shallowness of the "well-worn phrases" about the middle ages and the ancient world—phrases that want to assign a role to politics and religion idealistically out of proportion to the material dimensions of social life—and to the unreality of "knight-errantry," forcefully reiterate his general position, rather than provide a fundamental corrective to it, as had been claimed.

The fact is that Marx always stressed the inherently active function of ideological forms in producing social change (see his "Introduction" to the *Critique of Hegel's Philosophy of Right* and the *Economic and Philosophical Manuscripts of 1844*, for instance), but within the framework of the overall socioeconomic structure and in terms of the appropriate historical conjuncture. And precisely because one needs the proper historical qualifications to explain the relative prominence of some specific ideological factor at determinate times, the possibility of the relative dominance of ideological components of the social complex put into relief by Marx in the passage quoted above underlines the validity of his general conception, instead of undermining it, as some interpreters suggest or imply.

33.   John Maynard Keynes, for instance, idealizes the capitalist epoch to such an extent that the rest of human history is curtly (and circularly) dismissed by him as the "absence of important technical improvements" and "the failure of capital to accumulate." ("Economic Possibilities for Our Grandchildren" [1930], in *Essays in Persuasion*, W. W. Norton, New York, 1963, 360.) Indeed, he goes so far as to say, "Almost everything which really matters and which the world possessed at the commencement of the modern age was already known to man at the dawn of history." (Ibid.)

34.   Characteristically, the most influential of all those who worked out the strategies for capital's revitalization in the twentieth century, John Maynard Keynes—whose ideological allegiances are unashamedly spelled out when he declares that "the *class war* will find me on the side of the educated *bourgeoisie*"—offers the most rigid and dogmatic separation of material/productive advancement ("the solution of the *economic problem*" in his terminology), and the betterment of the conditions of human existence in all respects, in accordance with the potentialities of consciously adopted objectives. Keynes, "Am I a Liberal?" (1925), in ibid.,324. He describes the process of productive reproduction from the "vulgar materialist" standpoint of what he himself calls "the economic machine" ("The End of Laissez-Faire" [1926], in ibid., 319, arguing that science, technical efficiency and capital accumulation—and the latter thanks to "the principle of compound interest" ("Economic Possibilities for Our Grandchildren", ibid., 371), and not of indigenous and colonial exploitation) are well on their way to solve, "*gradually*" of course, "humanity's economic problem,"

which in his view should be considered "a matter for *specialists*—like dentistry" (ibid., 373). If we are still experiencing troubles, like "the prevailing world depression" and the "anomaly of unemployment in a world full of wants" (ibid., 359), that is only because:

> For the *moment* the very rapidity of these changes [in technical efficiency] is hurting us and bringing difficult problems to solve. Those countries are suffering relatively which are not in the *vanguard of progress*. We are being afflicted with a new disease . . . namely, *technological unemployment. . . .* But this is only a *temporary phase of maladjustment*. All this means in the long run that *mankind is solving its economic problem*. [Ibid., 364.]

As we can see, the tune does not seem to have changed much in all the intervening years. For our own growing unemployment is equally supposed to be no more serious than "a temporary phase of maladjustment," due to the "rapidity of changes in technological efficiency," all in the good cause of remaining in the "vanguard of progress."

The difference is that Keynes can still confidently anticipate—in 1930—that "mankind's economic problem" will be solved within one hundred years in the "progressive countries" (ibid., 364). However, through his qualifications it transpires that for Keynes the concept of "mankind" that is declared to be in the process of solving the economic problem is confined to the "progressive countries" and "vanguards of progress." This, again, underlines the total unreality of his diagnosis.

Moreover, in agreement with the age-old postulate of bourgeois political economy according to which nature itself implanted the "money-motive" into all human individuals, Keynes asserts that: "we have been expressly evolved by nature—with all our impulses and deepest instincts—*for the purpose of solving the economic problem*. If the economic problem is solved, mankind will be deprived of its traditional purpose" (ibid., 366). And yet, this is how he describes the coming positive change with regard to the selfsame individuals who are said to be so deeply determined by nature itself in their innermost "impulses and instincts":

> When the accumulation of wealth is no longer of high social importance, there will be great changes in the code of morals. . . . All kinds of social customs and economic practices, affecting the distribution of wealth and of economic rewards and penalties, which we now maintain at all costs, however distasteful and unjust they may be in themselves, because they are tremendously useful in promoting the accumulation of capital, we shall then be free, at last, to discard. . . . We shall honour those who can teach us how to pluck the hour and the day virtuously and well, the delightful people who are capable of taking direct enjoyment in things, the lilies of the field who toil not, neither do they spin. [Ibid., 369–70.]

The miraculous conversion of nature's instinctual moneymaker, which is here anticipated to occur a century or so after 1930, is, of course, a totally gratuitous suggestion. For without any supporting ground whatsoever, nay against his own arguments enunciated on the authority of "nature" itself just a moment earlier, Keynes counterposes with wishful arbitrariness nothing but the impotent world of "ought" to the given reality of "is," underlying their polarity also by the temporal abyss he puts between them.

In any case, the hypostatized quasi-religious redemption is not the real purpose of the Keynesian discourse. He offers the moralizing/religious carrot of "ultimate reward" to the individuals—for whom the promised land lies in the world of beyond, since in one hundred years they will be all dead—on condition that they trade in their quest for a possible radical change in the not so distant future for its *postponement* well beyond their own life expectancy, accepting thereby with sanctified resignation the established order of things. Accordingly, Keynes, immediately after the lines just quoted, takes us back with a highly developed sense of hypocrisy to his own rather prosaic and utterly mystifying vision of reality. For this is how he continues his "Essay in persuasion" after praising the lilies in the field:

> But beware! The time for all this is not yet. For at least another hundred years we must pretend to ourselves and to every one that fair is foul and foul is fair; for *foul is useful and fair is not*. Avarice and usury and precaution must be our gods for a little longer still. For only they can lead us out of the tunnel of *economic necessity* into daylight. [Ibid., 372.]

Keynes mystifies his audience by deliberately conflating (and confusing) "*useful*" with *profitable* (the real operative term beneath his diversionary phraseology). He is convinced—or rather, he wants to convince *us*—that the problems of "economic necessity" are *technical* problems, to be assigned to our "*specialists*" in usury management and economic tooth extraction. In this spirit, Keynes insists that the "humble but competent" specialists recommended by him are destined to lead us out of "the tunnel of economic necessity" to our own "destination of economic bliss" (ibid., 373), provided that we entrust ourselves to them—just as no toothache sufferer in his or her right mind would query the wisdom of consigning themselves to the pain-relieving competence of dental specialists. Keynes is in fact so convinced of the validity of his dentist/specialist vision of the "economic problem" that he concludes his essay with these words: "If economists could manage to get themselves thought of as humble, competent people, on a level with dentists, that would be splendid" (ibid.).

Unfortunately, however, a mere twenty-one years from reaching our promised destination of economic bliss we are much more distant from the mouth of the tunnel than seventy-nine years ago, *despite* the tremendous advances in productivity accomplished in all these decades. The reason why this is so is that the "economic problem" of which Keynes speaks is in reality not that of "economic necessity"—which in his view is bound to be automatically eliminated in due course by the blissful "accumulation of wealth"—but a profoundly *social* (or *socio*economic) problem. For no amount of accumulated wealth can do as much as even begin to remove the paralyzing constraints of the now prevailing socioeconomic determinations if the growing social wealth is poured down—as happens to be the case today—into the bottomless pit of the military-industrial complex, as well as of other varieties of wasteful wealth absorption, instead of satisfying human needs. Similarly, despite the self-absolving—and in our own time for the same reasons highly popular—Keynesian treatment of the problem, there is no such thing as "*technological unemployment*." For mass unemployment—much greater today than in 1930, when Keynes promised us daylight "before long" at the end of the tunnel—could be eliminated in principle virtually *overnight*. Not by the new job-creating miracles of a "third" and "fourth industrial revolution," but by the consciously adopted social strategy to reduce the amount of labor-time undertaken by the members of society, in accord with the real needs and productive objectives of the available workforce.

The apologetic intent behind the Keynesian rationalization of the relationship between material developments and human emancipation is fairly obvious once we assemble its constituents. The same is true of more recent and much cruder apologists of capital than Keynes, like Daniel Bell and Robert Tucker, for instance. The only difference is that for the latter the future has already become present in our own so-called post-industrial society, which is said to have solved the "economic problem." Thus they declare: "Marx's concept of communism is more nearly applicable to present-day America, for example, than is his concept of capitalism" (Robert Tucker, *Philosophy and Myth in Karl Marx*, Cambridge University Press, Cambridge, 1961, 235), which leaves us merely with the problems of abundance and "leisure" that already worried Keynes in his description of the world of "daylight" beyond the economic tunnel.

However, the mechanistic optimism that took for granted the realization of technologically produced abundance was by no means confined to the faithful defenders of capital's contradictions. It was in fact extremely widespread among intellectuals in general at the height of postwar prosperity and political consensus. What was rather surprising, though, was that the selfsame optimism infected even some leading Western Marxist scholars. They seemed to forget that predicating, as they did, that the triumph of abundance over scarcity was well on its way to solve all our material problems must be applicable to the globally interconnected social world—and in that sense it must be generalizable—instead of being a wishful projection of the conditions that happened to prevail, for the time being, in relatively small areas of even their own privileged, neo-colonially exploitative, countries. To take one example, even the distinguished Canadian Marxist, C. B. Macpherson, argued in "A Political Theory of Property," in *Democratic Theory: Essays in Retrieval* (Clarendon Press, Oxford, 1973, 138–39):

> The *conquest of scarcity* is now not only foreseeable but *actually foreseen*. . . . In the conditions of material scarcity that have always prevailed up to now, property has been a matter of a right to a material revenue. With the *conquest of scarcity* that is now foreseen, property must become rather a right to an *immaterial revenue*, a revenue of enjoyment of the quality of life. Such a revenue cannot be reckoned in material quantities.

We find a similarly disoriented perspective in the writings of the Frankfurt School. The objective significance of the necessary operating conditions of capitalist reproduction is ignored, producing a thoroughly unrealistic assessment of capitalist technology and production. Moreover, since this major dimension of the dialectic of base and superstructure is left out of sight, the ideological critique of "advanced industrial society" articulated by the representatives of this school suffers accordingly, in that it cannot point to any foundation except itself. The moralizing negativity in evidence in so many works of "critical theory" is the necessary consequence of such omission.

Theodor Adorno, for instance, defines the conditions of an emancipated society in terms of its being "so organised as the productive forces would *directly permit it here and now*, and as the conditions of production *on either side* relentlessly prevent it" (*Negative Dialectics*, Seabury Press, New York, 1973, 203).

The weaknesses of this conception are threefold. First, the *global misery* upon which the apparently successful productive forces are built is not seriously taken into account, and therefore the vital question of how generalizable is the dominant productive technology—which in the end decides whether it is viable at all, not to mention its actual suitability to ground the necessary socialist transformation—is not even raised. Second, inasmuch as the available level of productive technology is declared to be adequate even for the purposes of an emancipated society, its deepseated objective contradictions—inherent in the necessary operating conditions of the established mode of productive reproduction, which steer it in a perilous direction and thereby constrain it in all major respects, "here and now," with ultimately explosive implications with regard to its future development—escape all criticism. And third, since in the *capital/labor* relationship the responsibility for "relentlessly preventing" the emergence of the envisaged emancipated society on the already given foundations of productive technology is ascribed as much to one side as to the other, the possibility of finding an agency of emancipation equal to the task disappears completely. Once, however, the situation is diagnosed in such terms, Adorno is forced into the dubious posture of a generic moral denunciation of the existent from his (conceived from the point of view of the elite) "negative dialectic."

Despite some differences in emphasis and terminology, Marcuse's position is not fundamentally different from that of Adorno. For although the author of *One-Dimensional Man* detests the capitalist system and has great sympathy for "the wretched of the earth," his perspective is based on much the same misdiagnosis of capital's inherent potentialities and accomplishments. He too, greatly overrates them, asserting that as a result of "the greater happiness and fun available to the majority of the population" (Marcuse, *An Essay on Liberation*, Allen Lane/ Penguin Press, London, 1969, 13), "the working class . . . has become a conservative, even *counterrevolutionary* force" (ibid., 16).

Paradoxically, Marcuse admits that he is trapped by "the vicious circle: the rupture with the selfpropelling conservative continuum of needs must *precede* the revolution which is to usher in a free society, but such rupture itself can be envisaged only in a revolution" (ibid., 18, Marcuse's italics). Yet he can only offer an abstract moral imperative—the mysterious "emergence of a morality which might precondition man for freedom" (ibid., 10)—as a way out of his self-imposed "vicious circle," advocating the strategy of "passing from Marx to Fourier" (ibid., 22) and even to Kant: "Here too, Kant's aesthetic theory leads to *the most advanced notions*: the beautiful as 'symbol' of the moral" (ibid., 32).

To make things worse for himself, Marcuse not only categorically asserts "the integration of the organized (and not only the organized) laboring class into the system of advanced capitalism" (ibid., 14), but even tries to offer a *biological* underpinning to the alleged fateful integration by predicating that "it is precisely the *excessive adaptability of the human organism* which propels the perpetuation and extension of the *commodity form*" (ibid., 17) in place of the Marxian explanation of the—prevailing—historically and socially qualified—form of "false consciousness" in terms of the "fetishism of commodity." Furthermore, Marcuse also insists that the "utopian possibilities," which he advocates, "are inherent in the *technical and technological forces* of advanced capitalism" on the basis of which one could "terminate poverty and *scarcity* within a very foreseeable future" (ibid., 4). Just as Macpherson hypostatized that the question of "material revenue" is now obsolete and therefore we must concern ourselves, instead, with the difficulties of "immaterial revenue," Marcuse asserts that "the question is no longer: how can the individual satisfy his own needs without hurting others, but rather: how can he satisfy his needs without hurting himself" (ibid.).

Given such assumptions, Marcuse ends up with a picture that closely resembles the technologically premised postulates of John Maynard Keynes noted above. These are Marcuse's words:

Is such a change in the "nature" of man conceivable? I believe so, because *technical progress* has reached a stage in which reality no longer need be defined by the debilitating competition for social survival and advancement. The more these *technical capacities* outgrow the framework of exploitation within which they continue to be confined and abused, the more *they propel* the drives and aspirations of men to a point at which the *necessities of life cease to demand* the aggressive performances of "earning a living," and the "nonnecessary" becomes a vital need. [Ibid., 5]

Thus, similarly to the Keynesian diagnosis, a radical change in "human nature" is postulated. And just like in Keynes, no indication is given how such change might actually come about. Only that "this qualitative change *must* occur in the needs, in the infrastructure of man" (ibid., 4), to the point that the stipulated moral "ought" of "the rebellion would then have taken root in the very nature, the 'biology' of the individual" (ibid., 5), establishing in the "organism" itself "the instinctual basis for freedom" (ibid., 4) and "the biological need for freedom" (ibid., 100).

35. Worsley, *The Three Worlds,* 32.

36. Keynes presents an almost unbelievable rationalization of even British colonial plundering in terms of "compound interest." This is how he argues his case in "Economic Possibilities for Our Grandchildren" (*Essays in Persuasion,* 361–62):

> The value of British foreign investments today is estimated at about £4,000,000,000. This yields us an income at the rate of about 6 and 1/2 per cent. Half of this we bring home and enjoy; the other half, namely 3 and 1/4 per cent, we leave to accumulate abroad at compound interest. Something of this sort has now been going on for about 250 years. For I trace the beginnings of British foreign investment to the treasure which Drake stole from Spain in 1580. [Which is fine, of course, since Spain stole it from *her* colonies.] . . . Queen Elizabeth found herself with about £40,000 in hand. This she invested in the Levant Company—which prospered. Out of the profits of the Levant Company, the East India Company was founded; and the profits of this great enterprise were the foundation of England's subsequent foreign investment. Now it happens that £40,000 accumulating at 3 and 1/4 per cent compound interest approximately corresponds to the actual volume of England's foreign investments at various dates, and would actually amount today to the total of £4,000,000,000 which I have already quoted as being what our foreign investments now are. Thus every £1 which Drake brought home in 1580 has now become £100,000. *Such is the power of compound interest.*

37. Karl Marx, *Capital,* Foreign Languages Publishing House, Moscow, 1959, 3:773.

38. Ibid., 773–74.

39. The term often used by Marx, *Staatswesen*—rather than simply "*Staat,*" or

"state"—approximately translatable as "state–matter," refers to a number of specific functions exercised by the state institutions that articulate the material relations of sovereignty and dependence in a political form. Many of these functions are absolutely vital to the process of social reproduction, but by no means in the form which they assume in class societies. Thus the project of socialist transformation is defined by Marx in this respect as the *restitution* of the vital metabolic functions of separate *Staatswesen* to the social body itself, thereby superseding their alienated character.

40.   See the passage quoted above in Marx's *Grundrisse*, 86–87.

41.   Ibid., 88.

42.   The emergence of Fascism out of the crisis of liberal-democratic capitalism in Italy and Germany speaks for itself in this respect, just as in 1973 the violent destruction of Allende's democratic regime in Chile, or the conspiratorial attempt by none other than the president of the Italian Republic, Pietro Segni—supposedly the custodian of the constitution—to overthrow the "constitutional republic," or indeed a little later yet another attempt, with the same objective in mind, by prime minister Tambroni failed not for want of trying hard enough but thanks to the successful mobilization of the popular forces. Less well known but equally serious in its overall impact was the destruction of militant trade unionism in the United States with the help of armed violence, supported by the state institutions not only in the form of closing both eyes to the lawless acts of private armies but in the direct intervention of law-enforcing agencies themselves in the struggle to suppress all radical opposition to the rule of capital.

Anti–trade union legislation in Britain under Margaret Thatcher only followed well-established tradition for creating an up-to-date framework in which the "full might of the law" can be "legitimately" exercised against labor in the event of crisis and confrontation, as the weapons used against the miners in their one-year-long strike clearly demonstrated. A more recent case, that of press magnate Rupert Murdoch and his self-metamorphosing companies against the printers' unions, highlighted the oppressive character of the law devised to facilitate the performance of the *"vanishing capitalist"* trick for the purpose of emasculating the trade union movement. The point is that, thanks to the law in question, capitalists engaged in a trade union dispute can now "disappear" through the convenient device of a legal fiction, and reappear at once in a suitably transubstantiated form— under a different business name; the *same* capitalists, confronting the *same workers*—whereupon the formerly legitimate trade union dispute of the workers suddenly becomes *unlawful*, so that the full might of the law can be turned against them. Thus, institutionalized and legally enforced violence is only the other side of the coin of "explicit law" as such.

We must also notice here that the *vanishing capitalist* trick, performed with the active complicity of the law, is only the *"legal"* adaptation of the long-established and widespread *material* practice of capitalist fraudulence—the normality of capitalist "civil society"—to the regulatory requirements of changing class relations in the sphere of politics. For there is an obvious *structural homology* between the legal fiction that allows capitalist enterprises to "go out of existence" in order to reappear almost instantly—under a new name, with the same "actors" pulling the strings of continued exploitation, sometimes openly, sometimes only from the background—and then, thanks to their fictitious reconstitution, be conveniently freed in the eyes of the law from their former material liabilities and legal obligations. Thus the primacy of the material base asserts itself also on this terrain, producing legislative devices for political domination on the model of ubiquitous capitalist material structures.

43. Lenin's legendary sense of realism would never allow him to offer explanations on the model of "the revolution betrayed." Yet even he had to face some insurmountable dilemmas with regard to the relationship between post-revolutionary state power and the associated producers in his recommendations concerning what he called "the central distribution of labor-power." For a discussion of these problems see my essay on "Political Power and Dissent in Postrevolutionary Societies," *New Left Review* 108 (March–April 1978): esp. 4–17 (repr. in part 4 of *Beyond Capital*).

44. H. H. Gerth and C. Wright Mills, eds., *From Weber: Essays in Sociology*, Routledge & Kegan Paul, London, 1948, 299. As usual, Weber turns everything upside down. For it would be much more correct to say that the objective needs of the modern capitalist state give birth to its class-conscious army of jurists, rather than the other way around, as Weber claims, with mechanical one-sidedness. Besides, Weber's curious followers—some of them former "vulgar Marxists"—fail to notice that their newfound idol uses the idealist version of the selfsame "obstetric metaphor" for which they castigate Marx.

Of course, in reality we must speak also in this respect of a dialectical reciprocity, and not of a one-sided determination. But we must also recall that it is not possible to make more than tautological sense of such reciprocity unless we recognize—something that Weber cannot do, because of his far from neutral ideological allegiances—that the *"uebergreifendes Moment"* in this relationship between the ever more powerful capitalist state (with all its material needs and determinations) and the "jurists" happens to be the former, notwithstanding the Weberian-type rationalizations that hypostatize the heroic birth pangs and "fiercely independent" deliveries of "legal brains."

45. See Marcuse, *Die Permanenz der Kunst*, Carl Hanser Verlag, Munich, 1977; in English: *The Aesthetic Dimension*, Macmillan, London, 1979.

CHAPTER FOUR

Material Transformations and Ideological Forms

4.1 Historical Conditions and Limits of "Free Spiritual Production"

It might come as a surprise to Marx's detractors that he should entertain the notion of "free spiritual production" even for a moment. Yet he forcefully argues in *Theories of Surplus-Value*:

> The distinction between productive labours and unproductive labours is of decisive importance for what Smith was considering: the production of *material* wealth, and in fact one definite form of that production, the *capitalist* mode of production. In *spiritual* production another kind of labour appears as productive. But Smith does not take it into consideration. Finally, the *interaction and the inner connection* between the two kinds of production also do not fall within the field he is considering; moreover, they can only lead to something more than empty phrases when material production is examined in its own form. Insofar as he speaks of workers who are not directly productive, this is only to the extent that they participate *directly* in the consumption of material wealth but not in its production.

With Storch himself the *theory of civilisation* does not get beyond trivial phrases, although some ingenious observations slip in here and there—for example, that the material division of labour is the pre-condition for the division of intellectual labour. How much it *was inevitable* that Storch could not get beyond trivial phrases, how little he had even *formulated* for himself the task, let alone its solution, is apparent from one single circumstance. In order to examine the connection between spiritual production and material production it is above all necessary to grasp the latter itself not as a general category but in *definite historical* form. Thus, for example, different kinds of spiritual production correspond to the capitalist mode of production and to the mode of production of the Middle Ages. If material production itself is not conceived in its *specific historical* form, it is impossible to understand what is specific in the *spiritual production* corresponding to it and the *reciprocal influence* of one on the other. Otherwise one cannot get beyond inanities. This because of the talk about "civilisation."

Further: from the specific form of material production arises in the first place a specific *structure* of society, in the second place a specific relation of men to *nature*. Their *State* [*Staatswesen*] and their *spiritual outlook* is determined by *both*. Therefore also the kind of their *spiritual production*.

Finally, by spiritual production Storch means also all kinds of *professional activities of the ruling class,* who carry out social functions as a trade. The existence of these strata, like the function they perform, can only be understood from the *specific historical structure* of their production relations.

Because Storch does not conceive material production itself *historically*—because he conceives it as production of material goods in general, not as a definite *historically developed and specific form* of this production—he deprives himself of the basis on which alone can be understood partly the *ideological component parts* of the *ruling class*, partly the *free spiritual production* of this particular *social formation*. He cannot get beyond meaningless general phrases. Consequently, the relation is not so simple as he presupposes. For instance, capitalist production is *hostile* to certain branches of *spiritual production*, for example, *art and poetry*. If this is left out of account, it opens the way to the illusion of the French in the eighteenth century which has been so beautifully satirised by Lessing. Because we are further ahead than the ancients in mechanics, etc., why should not we be able to make an epic too? And the *Henriade* in place of the *Iliad!*[1]

Several important considerations arise in this passage:

I.   The "inner connection" and "interaction" (or "reciprocal influence") of the two basic kinds of production: "material production" and "spiritual production."

II. To grasp the determinate *historical* character (or "specific historical form") of the different *modes of production* (e.g., capitalist in contrast to that of the Middle Ages) is a vital condition for understanding the nature of the different kinds of spiritual production which *correspond* to any given mode of material production. (Such "correspondence" must be understood, of course, in the sense of an active *reciprocity*— as emphasized in point (I.)—whose terms of reference must be further defined, with all the necessary dialectical qualifications.)

III. Any given form of material production articulates itself as:

1) a specific *social structure* (or "structure of society," i.e., a historically specific relationship of *human beings to other human beings*); and

2) a specific relation of *human beings to nature* (corresponding to the various constraints of their productive forces and of their structurally secured relationship among themselves).

These two *together* determine:

a) their *State,* as *Staatswesen* (or the "legal and political superstructure," as the 1859 "Preface" puts it);

b) their "spiritual outlook" (or ideas); and

c) their "spiritual production" (which is the concrete articulation and embodiment of those ideas, the historically specific *"dis-*

courses," from moral and political discourse to art and literature, in accordance with the specific characteristics of the instruments and institutional forms employed in the process of this "spiritual production").

For the sake of greater precision, it is necessary to stress here—before moving on to (IV)—that the 1859 "Preface" speaks of a determinate *"economic structure"* that stands for the "totality of the *relations of production."* The *"economic structure"/*"totality of the *relations of production"* in its turn "corresponds" to the given degree of development of the *material productive forces* upon which the legal and political superstructure is erected, together with "definite forms of social consciousness," again in a relationship of *dialectical* correspondence and reciprocity. Thus the 1859 "Preface" subsumes a set of complex relationships under the term "economic structure," for the sake of brevity and simplicity. This must be constantly borne in mind if we are to do justice to Marx's dialectical conception of the relationship of "material base" and "superstructure," with their manifold aspects and active "reciprocities," together with their highly complex "correspondences" which are often reduced even in sympathetic Marxology, not to mention its broadly promoted hostile varieties, to some mechanical *"one-to-one correspondence"* between the economy and the crudely/mechanically determined ideas.

By contrast, the essential terms of reference in this regard are:

1) the historically specific material productive forces;

2) the equally specific *"structure* of society";

3) the historically prevalent (i.e., determinate, "historically developed and specific") relationship of human beings to nature;

4) the "specific *historical structure* of the production relations";

5) the "economic structure" of society (or "the real foundation"): a term which, in fact, *summarizes the first four complexes;*

6) the legal and political *superstructure* (summarily presented at times as the state, or *Staatswesen*);

7) the historically determinate and changing "spiritual outlook" (*geistige Anschauung*) of human beings, which includes the conceptualization of their relationship to nature;

8) the different kinds and modes of "spiritual production" (*geistige Produktion*);

9) the "definite forms of social consciousness" in their historical specificity as well as in their detailed articulation, under determinate historical conditions, as conflicting forms of ideology.

Again, number (9) may be considered a *summary* of (7) and (8) in that the determinate "forms of social consciousness" incorporate the historically feasible varieties of "spiritual outlook" (or "worldview") in terms of which the opposing classes of people fight out their conflicts, in accordance with, and with the help of, the available instruments and institutions of "spiritual production."

IV. A firm distinction is drawn between the "ideological component parts of the ruling class" and the "free spiritual production of a particular social formation." The latter indicates the relevant limits both in a positive and in a negative sense:

a) *Positively* it marks the objective potentialities of the social formation in question—its genuine achievements in the field of spiritual production toward a greater degree of freedom and corresponding intellectual insight, as compared to that of a previous social formation, on the basis of the advancing attainments of the new formations in the field of material production and the practical understanding of nature—which are available also to the intellectual interpreters of the ruling class, irrespective of the prevailing material interests.

b) *Negatively* it indicates some characteristic limitations of the social formation as a whole, irrespective of the class situation and ideological position of the intellectuals involved. Hence the reference to capitalism as such being "hostile to art and poetry" in general, rather than taking them to a higher degree of development in line with the productive achievements of the material base, frustrating thus the attempts of Voltaire and others to produce great epic poetry on the soil of a social formation that *objectively* opposes such attempts, whoever might be the artist involved.

V. The expression *"ideological component parts of the ruling class"* needs further qualifications. For it cannot be simply assumed that the limits arising from the class determinations themselves remain—for better or worse—the same throughout history. Nor indeed that one should be able to speak of some *unilinear* development with regard to the potentialities and necessary limitations of "ruling class consciousness," mechanically parallel to the fact that the class assumes an increasingly parasitic position in the structure of production.

First of all, therefore, an important distinction must be made between different *phases of development* of the same social formation. Accordingly, a few pages further on in *Theories of Surplus-Value*[2] Marx contrasts the contemporary spokesmen (calling them "mouthpieces") of the ruling class to their "interpreters" at an earlier phase of development. With reference to Nassau Senior and others he writes:

These insipid literary flourishes used by these fellows when they polemise against Adam Smith show only that they are representatives of the "educated capitalist," while Smith was the *interpreter* of the frankly brutal bourgeois upstart. The educated bourgeois and his mouthpiece are both so stupid that they measure the effect of every activity by its effect on the purse. On the other hand, they are so educated that they *grant recognition* even to functions and activities that have nothing to do with the production of wealth; and indeed they grant them recognition because they too "indirectly" increase, etc., their wealth, in a word, fulfil a "useful" function for wealth.[3]

The value of such apologetic and often merely tautological "theories," based on arbitrary assumptions, is no more than the self-serving *rationalization* and the blatant ideological justification of the given state of affairs. The political economists here referred to unquestioningly justify the prevailing mode of socioeconomic and cultural interchange as the only feasible one, together with their own participation in it as the necessary "superstructure of ideological strata, whose activity—*whether good or bad*—is good, because it is necessary."[4]

At the same time, the complexity of these interrelations clearly warns us against any attempted explanation in the form of reductionism. The complexity which must be acknowledged manifests itself also in the sense that at a historically more progressive or less crisis-prone stage of society the level of ruling-class consciousness is by no means ipso facto higher. Indeed, the exact opposite may be the case under determinate historical circumstances. Thus, in the midst of the great turmoil of the French Revolution, for instance, the bourgeoisie has a powerful motivation, and also a relative justification, for presenting its own interests as the "general interest" of society. This kind of misrepresentation of the real state of affairs—paradoxically not only not *despite* but, on the contrary, precisely *thanks to* the obvious "false consciousness" involved in it—is one of the most important factors in the success of the bourgeoisie under the then prevailing historical circumstances.

In a more general sense, a situation of *crisis* does not necessarily carry with it a *decrease* in the level of ruling-class consciousness. For, as regards the bourgeoisie, for instance, under normal circumstances "capital has no awareness whatever of the nature of its process of realization, and has an interest in having an awareness of it *only in times of crisis*."[5] Thus, under the impact of the crisis—but, obviously, depending on the exact nature of the crisis in question (which must be always concretely grasped in its socio-historical specificity)—the ruling class's degree of self-awareness may indeed be *heightened,* rather than diminished, thereby strengthening the efficacy of its rule, instead of immediately undermining it.

By the same token, as regards labor on the other side of the irreconcilable social divide, it would be thoroughly naive, to say the least, to expect a dramatic intensification of combative working-class consciousness under the immediate impact of the crisis itself. For under such circumstances there is a tendency to follow "the line of least resistance," instead of embarking on the perilous journey on the uncharted territory that must be traversed by capital's hegemonic antagonist in the direction of the radical alternative order. Indeed, the institutionally/organizationally conditioned and constraining actual political trends, because of the historically still prevailing relation of forces strongly in capital's favor, may induce the representatives of labor to move in the opposite direction, becoming thereby responsible for a *counterproductive retreat* from the required militant position, as we have seen in the recent past.

The weighty implications of these conditions, especially if taken in conjunction with one another—that is to say, by adding the improved effectiveness of the ruling class's control of society as a result of its increased self-awareness and greater sense of reality to the negative consequences of "following the line of least resistance" by capital's historic adversary, labor, under the pressure of the unfolding crisis—must be obvious for the elaboration of revolutionary strategies.

Naturally, the objective historical conditions of free spiritual production cannot be bypassed or disregarded by any thinker or creative artist. This is so no matter at how advanced a stage of societal development they may appear in the overall course of historical development, and of course also quite irrespective of how progressive a stance they may assume as responsible individuals in relation to the fundamental social antagonisms of the particular social formation of which they are active participants, together with those at the most conservative end of the conflicting value-determinations of the established order in all class societies.

In this sense, being situated at a more advanced historical stage does not give to a thinker or to a creative artist, ipso facto, any a prioristic guarantee of a more viable and lasting intellectual achievement. Even putting aside the negative consideration mentioned by Marx, namely that "capitalist production is *hostile* to certain branches of *spiritual production*, for example, *art and poetry*," the question remains: What can he or she *actively make* of the available conditions of free spiritual production, whatever they might be under the given historical circumstances in their innermost character? Lukács's famous comparison of the "mighty elephant of the plain" (be that a Goethe or a Balzac of the capitalist social formation) with the "rabbit at the high plateau" of a socialist society—a comparison for which he had been sharply taken to task by his Stalinist critics—tried to encapsulate both the general social and the creative personal dimensions of this relationship.

The important correlation in this context is that in the actually existing world no one can really avoid assuming a determinate position with regard to the dominant societal interests—which in all class societies are inevitably value-laden class interests and corresponding conflicts—no matter to what extent they may continue to nourish the well-known illusions of "value-neutrality" about the position they actively make their own. At the same time, though, they cannot claim exemption from the implications their adopted position objectively carries, be they conscious of such implications or not, for the unfolding social and historical development.

Understandably, there is a major difference in this respect between the political economists of the great Scottish Enlightenment tradition (like Adam Smith) and the vulgar economists of the capital system's descending phase of historical development sarcastically criticized by Marx. The latter presume for themselves as thinkers, as well as for the exploitative economic order of their society, which they do not hesitate to idealize for a moment, that the object of their boundless admiration could not be questioned at all, because "*whether it was considered good or bad*," it had to be "*good,* because it was *necessary*." That kind of self-identification of the thinkers concerned with the blindly accepted "necessity" of the established order's structural determinations, as self-evidently *good,* represented the crudest form of social apologetics. In its theoretical formulation it was hopelessly defective not only on account of conferring positive value on the most problematical, even destructive, aspects and antagonistic contradictions of societal reproduction, but also with regard to its shallowest notion of "necessity."

Nevertheless, not only the vulgar economists but even such outstanding intellectual figures of the bourgeoisie who conceptualized the world from capital's vantage point at their system's ascending phase of development, like Kant, Adam Smith, and Hegel, showed their inclination to equate what they considered commendable, despite its problematical and even most iniquitous character, with some kind of necessity. And the necessity stipulated by them ranged from what they called natural necessity to that of the claimed Divine Providence, and even the necessity predicated by the Absolute Reason of the Hegelian World Spirit. In this way Kant could openly justify the most iniquitous social relations on the stipulated ground that human beings were made from "crooked timber," as ordained by Nature's Lawgiver,[6] while Adam Smith could see no difficulty about asserting that the socioeconomic order of capital, as benevolently guided by the "invisible hand" in its mysterious work for the good of every individual in society, constituted nothing less than "the *natural* system of *perfect liberty and justice*."[7]

The same problem appeared in the Hegelian philosophy, even if in a more complicated form, due to the much greater social and political upheavals of the French Revolution and the Napoleonic Wars under the circumstances of which that philosophy was conceived. For Hegel, on the one hand, was perfectly willing to stress that it was "just as absurd to fancy that a philosophy can transcend its contemporary world as it is to fancy that an individual can overleap his own age, jump over Rhodes."[8] On the other hand, however, he could easily reconcile this genuinely historical view with his absolutized reconciliatory philosophical postulate according to which "*what is rational is actual and what is actual is rational*."[9] Thus the interest of reconciliation in the end had to prevail. As a result, in Hegel's speculative philosophical universe the historical dimension of human affairs, including the actual conditions of free spiritual production, had to be obliterated by the self-enclosed determinations of the World Spirit's "eternal present" temporality, as conceived from capital's incurably eternalizing vantage point shared by Hegel with even the greatest figures of classical political economy. In this way the historical process could be proclaimed by Hegel to be "the true Theodicaea, the justification of God in History,"[10] closely linked to the equally absolutized and timeless characterization of the political domain as "the *true reconciliation* which discloses the *State* as the image and actuality of *Reason*."[11]

The fundamental difference between the outstanding intellectual figures of the bourgeoisie and the vulgar political economists of capital's descending phase of development is that the latter must "measure the effect of every activity by its *effect on the purse*."[12] That is what decides in their view everything, in conformity to the self-serving rules of crass social apologetics.

In Hegel's conceptualization of the world the religious imagery, as *Theodicaea*, in its affinity with his monumental vision of the World Spirit and the Absolute Mind, was perfectly genuine. It was an integral part of presenting the dialectical progression from the Oriental world to the projected permanence of the Germanic present (which included in his conception the successfully colonizing English), with its climax in the "Protestant principle" and its "Rational State." But by the time we reached our own historical circumstances, with Hayek—appropriately Margaret Thatcher's guru and "Companion of Honor"—as one of the grotesquely idealized mouthpieces of the established order, even the potentiality of religion had to be measured by its feared "effect on the capitalist purse," though hypocritically wrapped up as a parcel of pretended "concern" for the people that directly contradicted Hayek's principal political economic tenets of callous disregard for their plight. Thus he condemned liberation theology—just as Pope John Paul the Second did, together with his "Defender of the Faith,"[13] Cardinal Ratzinger (who tellingly became his successor as Pope Benedict the Sixteenth)—in this way: "*'liberation theology'* may fuse with nationalism to produce a powerful religion with disastrous consequences for people already in dire economic straits."[14] At the same time, not surprisingly, Hayek kept the secret to himself. How could it be held tenable to glorify the capital system in the way he did—as the best conceivable "extended economic order"—in which in his view the overwhelming majority of the people found themselves "already in dire economic straits." Nor could Hayek restrain himself from yet another boundless glorification of the ruling order by answering his own rhetorical question directed against the working people, who find themselves truly "in dire economic straits" all over the world, in this blatantly capital-apologetic way: "If we ask what men most owe to the moral practices of those who are called *capitalists* the answer is: *their very lives.* . . . Although these folk may *feel*[15] exploited, and politicians may arouse and play on these feelings to gain power, most of the *Western proletariat,* and most of the millions of the *developing world,* owe their existence to the opportunities that advanced countries have created for them."[16] No wonder that his high-ranking politician pupil, British prime minister Margaret Thatcher, responded in Hayek's spirit to a major crisis of the British capital system in this way: "We had to fight the *enemy with-*

out in the Falklands. We always have to be aware of the *enemy within,* which is more dangerous to *liberty*."[17]

To be sure, the crudely apologetic way of bringing up to date in our time the ideological forms in the interest of capital's continued rule over society, in the spirit of aggressively reactionary "neoliberalism," corresponds to the material transformations accomplished in the last few decades, well in tune with the established social metabolic order's deepening structural crisis. But irrespective of that, when we consider the capital system in its entirety we find in this regard a major problem that cannot be satisfactorily resolved even by the greatest bourgeois thinkers of the more distant past. It concerns the way in which *necessity* in general is conceived—and *must be conceived*—from capital's vantage point even at the most progressive phase of the system's development.

The radical novelty and emancipatory character of the Marxian conception is striking in this respect. The contrast of Marx's views on the viability of human intervention in the historic process, as compared with the position assumed by even the outstanding thinkers of the Enlightenment, concerning the crucial issue of how one must visualize *necessity* and its relevance to actual societal development, is absolutely fundamental. This is a seminal issue because so much else depends on it in all theories, whether formulated from the vantage point of capital or from the perspective of its hegemonic alternative. It is all the more important because assuming a reconciliatory position, in the name of some kind of (frequently ambiguous) absolutized conception of necessity—whether it is postulated as "natural necessity" (as for instance in the political economy of Adam Smith) or as a speculative kind (as in Kant and Hegel)—may very well be associated with an explicit claim to the realization of freedom. And that carries with it a tendency to trap in a conceptual maze the unsuspecting reader, who is conditioned by the dominant ideologies to react with automatic consent to the very mention of the words "freedom" and "liberty," no matter how shaky the ground on which they rest. At the same time, the Marxian conception, which evaluates the thorny issue of necessity in a thoroughly emancipatory way, in its practically vital and historically changing context, is dismissed—sometimes as a result of genuine theoretical disorientation and ignorance, but more often than not through hostile ideological misrepresentation—with the labels of "mechanical determinism" and "economic determinism." Yet nothing could be further off the intended target than such dismissal. For no thinker in all history has formulated a more liberating view of the complex issues concerned with the assessment of necessity than Marx. He did that in his profoundly *dialectical* approach to the subject, not only by giving their proper weight to the *objective determinations* manifest in both natural and historical necessity, but also by putting those determinations in *historical perspective* without which they could have only a most distorted sense. That is how Marx could lay the theoretical foundation to what he passionately advocated and called *"the realm of freedom."*

The problematical conceptions of necessity we find in the writings of the major figures of bourgeois political economy and philosophy can be summed up by stressing, on the one hand, that they tend to *conflate* natural and historical necessity, and, on the other, that they extend the validity of these concepts well beyond the limits to which they could be legitimately applied. And they formulate such theories in conjunction with a *purely individualistic* explanation offered to the conflicts perceived in what they call "civil society." Conflicts that are decreed by them to be directly attributable to *"human nature,"* or to some other form of alleged necessity. That is how the conflation of a *historically determined* mode of human behavior (the "egotism" of the individuals in "civil society") with the pretended *"natural necessity"* of arbitrarily and fallaciously stipulated unalterable *"human nature"* is eternalized and fulfills in such conceptions its revealing ideological function.

In this way some of the thinkers here referred to almost completely *block out* from view—while others *obliterate* altogether—the irreconcilable *structural antagonisms* of the social metabolic order they represent from capital's vantage point. Moreover, the tendentious theoretical conflation we find in their theories is by no means confined to natural and historical necessity. It is closely connected with other instances of illegitimately merging into one another some clearly distinguishable concepts of key importance in the functioning of the established mode of societal reproduction.[18] This is done in the service of the same cause of conflict-attenuation and the transfiguration of the capital system's structural antagonisms, which is of course ideologically understandable (even if very far from justifiable) in theories formulated from the standpoint of capital. In this way the strong impression of *stability* is created in all such theories on account of the purely individualistic, and consequently in principle with relative ease reconcilable, conflicts of the individuals in "civil society," as we find them in the conceptions formulated from the standpoint of capital directly linked to, and fully sanctioned by, the envisaged "natural system"—or by "Divine Providence," by "Nature's Lawgiver," by the "World Spirit," and the like, establishing thereby the timeless validity and permanence of capital's social metabolic order of reproduction on a "rationally unquestionable" basis.

Naturally, Marx's approach to the same problems could not have been more different, from the very beginning. As an acute observer and participant in the Europe-wide unfolding social and political conflicts of his time, he was interested in a radical change to the established iniquitous societal order. Thus he subjected to a far-reaching critical scrutiny every constituent of the complex relations involved in maintaining, despite its explosive structural antagonisms, the ruling order in his analyses. He did that so as to be able to identify the leverage that had to be grasped in order to accomplish the required change.

Understandably in this sense, the question of *historical genesis* had to be at the forefront of his attention, in view of its great theoretical *and practical* relevance. For it was totally unthinkable to find a viable solution to the pressing issue of how to intervene in the actual historic process unless one could give proper weight to the material and intellectual forces that confronted one another—including by that time the first articulation of labor as capital's promising structural antagonist—in the political turmoil of the early 1840s, when Marx began to formulate his new conception.

A fixed view of natural necessity and its corresponding "human nature," which constituted the helpful crutch and the self-serving prejudice of some important theories of the past, could have been only a millstone around the neck of a revolutionary thinker who was looking for sustainable answers under those circumstances. Accordingly, the theory advocated by Marx had to be *historical* through and through, with the proposed investigation of the objective and subjective conditions needed for the formation of the transformatory historical agency—the potentially revolutionary social subject of organized labour—at the center of it. All of his early writings—from the *Economic and Philosophic Manuscripts of*

1844 and *The Holy Family* to *The German Ideology* and the *Communist Manifesto*—made that amply clear. This was also the reason why the radical critique of the theories of "civil society," with their unreal theorizations of the purely individual conflicts put into relief both in political economy and in philosophy, had to become an integral part of the Marxian emancipatory enterprise. Thus the many-sided issue of *necessity,* natural as well as historical, had to be put in its proper place in this new perspective, envisaging the institution of labor's radically different mode of controlling societal reproduction as the hegemonic alternative to capital's established social order.

Such reassessment of necessity had to be undertaken in part for gaining an adequate conception of past historical development, intended by Marx as the clear articulation of a deep-rooted dialectical explanation of both natural and historical determinations in their relationship to the active human agency of social development, spelled out by the young German philosopher in sharp contrast to the speculative idealist as well as the mechanical materialist doctrines in vogue at the time. But the radical critique of the dominant theories had to be pursued above all in order to demonstrate in a tangible way the feasibility of a much needed emancipatory strategy for the present and the future, unhindered by the paralyzing false conceptions of self-servingly assumed *natural* or speculative *metaphysical* necessity. The concluding essay of Marx's "Theses on Feuerbach," written in the spring of 1845, summed it all up by insisting, "The philosophers have only *interpreted* the world in various ways; the point is to *change* it."[19]

In Marx's dialectical conception every aspect of social life had to be explained in terms of its historical genesis and transformations. The self-evident point of departure could only be that human beings are an integral part of nature and therefore must continue to reproduce the conditions of their existence through a productively viable metabolic interchange with nature. And the metabolic interchange in question, in order to be feasible at all, had to include a socially sustained, even if for a long historical period antagonistic, relationship of the human individuals, as well as the social groups and classes to which the individuals actually belonged, among themselves.

This vision, concerned not only with the positive prospects but also with the potentially destructive limitations of the unfolding historical developments, could not be derived from a totally unexplainable world of *"natural necessity"* and *"human nature,"* relying on the mysterious "invisible hand" for its viability, as decreed by the political economists, nor could it "drop from the womb of self-positing Idea,"[20] as postulated by speculative philosophy. Moreover, in view of the immense productive and destructive power at the disposal of human beings by the time the Marxian conception was formulated, under the conditions of capital's apparently irresistible expansionary drive toward its global integration— when talking about "world history" had become meaningful in a most tangible sense[21]—it was not only legitimate but also imperative to raise the question: For how much longer was it possible for human beings to carry on reproducing their conditions of existence in a form of social metabolic control characterized by *structural antagonisms* without putting an end to their own history?[22]

The boundless dominance of *natural necessity* was confined in this vision to the *most primitive* phase of human development, when our ancestors, due to their massively uneven confrontation with the forces of nature, had to live literally "from hand to mouth," in accordance with the hard-fought satisfaction of the most elementary needs capable of securing little more than bare survival.

One could talk about the first steps in the historical process only in conjunction with changing needs. The changes involved in that respect amounted to a certain degree of displacement—even if at first only an absolutely minimal displacement—of strictly natural determinations. However, already in relation to that point in time and circumstance, when, looking back on it, is it possible to identify only the satisfaction of the most elementary need of bare survival through the interaction of human beings with nature, it is necessary to bring into the picture a *dialectical* view of the unfolding changes, which *begin* to open up the road toward their genuine historical development. For "the satisfaction of the first need, the *action* of satisfying and the *instrument* of satisfaction which has been acquired, leads to new needs; and *this creation of new needs is the first historical act.*"[23] As to the pertinent question *"Why history?,"* it was answered by saying, "Men have history because they must *produce* their life, and because they must produce it moreover *in a certain way.*"[24]

This is how the creation of new needs in human history starts to push back the boundaries that originally mark the absolute tyranny of *natural necessity*. Such transformation is pursued by progressively displacing natural necessity through a qualitatively different set of determinations. For in the new type of determinations the human agency—this *unique* part of nature whose members are not *"genus-individuals"* directly merging with their species[25]—is *actively* involved as the *subject* of history in the proper sense of the term. In this way the historical subject *begins* to set out on the immensely long and contradictory road toward its *potential self-emancipation,* thanks to the advancement of productive powers and to the "acquisition of instruments" required for the satisfaction of the historically produced new needs.

Thus a new form of *causality,* and a corresponding new kind of necessity—that is, by human beings generating *historical necessity*—enters the order of nature via the societal reproductive domain. It is a qualitatively different type of causality/necessity that points—far ahead in time—to the possibility of full human emancipation. Paradoxically, the same type of necessity is also capable of imposing *its own kind of tyranny* on the social individuals, threatening them even with collective self-annihilation, for as long a historical process as they are unable to bring their contradictory—at first unavoidable, but with the dramatic advancement of humanity's productive powers less and less justifiable—*self-imposed necessity* under their *conscious control.*

The fundamental difference between the original natural necessity and this new type of causality is that the former, at the outset of history, directly dominates the entire human species. But only at first, in contrast to all other natural species of animals which have no way of productively mediating the relationship among their particular members, nor their relationship to nature as a whole, hence they must always remain *genus-individuals*. Accordingly, their character—which in their case is directly conferred upon them by nature—could never be described in the way Marx defined "human nature" relevant to his own time, as *the ensemble of historically changing social relations.* For in the animal world everything must be regulated by continued natural necessity, even the "perfect architecture" of the bees. Not so in the case of the human individuals. For humans are capable of articulating the vitally important and potentially

most emancipatory *self-mediation* of their relationships among themselves and nature at large, as well as among themselves as developing
social groups and social individuals.

At the same time, however, human beings are also responsible for the
hostile discriminatory and structurally/hierarchically imposed—*antagonistic mediation* of their reproductive relations among themselves, in the
form of the *alienating second-order mediations* they institute and perpetuate in all class societies, and by no means only in its capitalist variant.
What distinguishes the capital system from the earlier reproductive formations is that it introduces and brings to a perverse perfection a historically specific form of all-embracing antagonistic second-order mediations
on a fully extendable global scale, with its ultimately unlimited—and
indeed, for as long as this system remains dominant, unlimitable—destructive implications on an equally global scale. Moreover, quite understandably, in the twofold mediatory relationship between nature and
human beings in general, on the one hand, and among the class-ordained
social individuals, on the other, the primacy goes to the latter in a far from
reassuring way under the historically prevailing circumstances. As a
result, the *antagonistic* modality of mediating their reproductive relations
by the individuals and their social groups among themselves under the
rule of capital entirely *subverts* humanity's vital relationship to nature,
threatening it with destruction on a monumental scale that fully matches
the historically acquired devastating powers of human beings, and consequently threatens at the same time humankind as a whole with self-
destruction.

However, precisely because the problematically self-imposed necessity that goes with the capital system's antagonistic second-order mediations is *historical* and not *natural necessity,* there can be no question of
fatalistically unsurpassable determinations, as necessity is often fallaciously conceptualized in philosophy and political theory. The dynamic
nature of historical relations is incompatible with any idea of *fixity,* either
on the model of *natural laws,* like the law of *gravity,* or as projected in the
form of *metaphysical absoluteness,* the way we find it depicted in speculative idealist philosophy.

In the Marxian conception historical necessity is understood in a very
different way, in virtue of being *historical* in its innermost determination.

Conceived in that way means that historical necessity must be envisaged to prevail under the specific conditions that not only *define* its effective *power* but at the same time also *set to it* some historically determinate and clearly identifiable *limits*. Consequently, such necessity must leave the place once held by it in history when the objective conditions themselves—which at some point in time gave rise to it, and which include, of course, the (no matter how problematical and throughout the long history of class societies antagonistic, but nonetheless always active) contribution by the human subject of history—are actually *superseded*. And of course the supersession in question is inconceivable without fully incorporating the active contribution (including not only the material but also the "free spiritual production") of the human historical subject.[26] That is the reason why Marx calls this kind of necessity *"merely* historical necessity," making it also explicit that in due course, in conformity to its changing nature considered inherently *historical,* brought into being by the historical subject under determinate circumstances, it *must* become a *"disappearing necessity"* (that is, *"eine verschwindende Notwendigkeit"*). Defining these important issues in the way in which we have seen them discussed by Marx—by stressing the role of the *dialectic* in their interrelations in contrast to rigid *"naturalistic* determinations"—is an integral part of the Marxian emancipatory conception of human development, as we shall see in greater detail in chapter 5.

If we now look at the conflation of the concepts of *work* in general with capitalist *wage labor,* and of the production of *use-values* necessary in all forms of society with the capitalistically dominant *exchange-values,* as mentioned in note 18, we find that with Adam Smith "labor" is in principle the source of value only insofar as in the division of labor the surplus appears just as much a *gift of nature*—a natural force of society, as the soil is for the Physiocrats. Hence the weight Adam Smith lays on the *division of labor.* Capital, on the other hand, appears to him—because, although he defines labor as productive of value, he conceives it as *use-value,* as productivity for itself, as *human natural force in general* (this distinguishes him from the Physiocrats), but not as *wage labor,* not in its *specific* character as formed, in *antithesis to capital*—not as that which contains wage labor as its *"internal contradiction* from its *origin."*[27] Similarly, Ricardo conceives the relationship of wage labor and capital:

"as a *natural*, not as a *historically specific* social form . . . just as wealth itself, in its *exchange-value* form, appears as a *merely formal mediation* of its *material* composition; thus the specific character of *bourgeois* wealth is not grasped—precisely because it appears there as *the adequate* form of *wealth as such*. . . . Instead, he always speaks about distribution of the general product of labour and of the soil among the three classes, as if the form of wealth based on *exchange-value* were concerned only with *use-value*, and as if exchange-value were merely a *ceremonial* form, which vanishes in Ricardo just as money as medium of circulation vanishes in exchange."[28]

Thus by both of these great representatives of bourgeois political economy the historically specific is turned into the allegedly "natural," and thereby that which is in reality necessarily *transient*, in its Marxian sense of unavoidably "disappearing necessity," thanks to the historically feasible superseding action of human beings who had brought it upon themselves, is given the status of unchallengeable *natural necessity*. Accordingly, in tune with the *eternalization* of capital's mode of social metabolic control which we find even in the classics of political economy who consider their productive order much like the *natural order* in which laws like the law of *gravity* operate and unalterably prevail, in such a view only the gratuitous projection of a—rationally unjustifiable—system of societal reproduction, based on a totally different set of natural laws as its causal foundation, could offer an (obviously inconceivable) alternative.

Once a conception of this kind prevails, reifying the historically produced capitalist system on the model of the natural law of gravity, arbitrariness and irresponsibility in the pursuit of productive targets can easily go with it. Especially when the structural antagonisms of the established order assert themselves with ever greater intensity in the descending phase of capitalist development. When, that is, the originally almost unlimited scope for economic growth and capital-accumulation turns out to be increasingly more problematical and untenable, due to *systemic limitations,* and not to some more or less easily remediable *conjunctural crises.* Not surprisingly, therefore, under such circumstances it becomes impossible to adopt an appropriate *measure*—given capital's profit-oriented self-expansionary drive *at all cost,* irrespective of the consequences—which could judge what might be historically viable and sustainable even in the longest run, rather than wasteful and utterly destructive. As a result, the once idealized *"productive* destruction" of the capital system tends to impose itself on society in the form of a historically unsustainable and ultimately explosive *destructive production.*

Putting into relief this perspective, which is tangibly unfolding before our eyes, is by no means an unjustifiable "leveling down" objection that would tend to hem in the productive potentialities of human beings. Far from it. For productive advancement is considered a positive value in socialist theory, provided that it arises from a humanly meaningful and historically viable ground. Marx made that very clear in his discussion of "luxury" and "naturally necessary." This is how he put it:

> *Luxury* is the opposite of *naturally necessary.* Necessary needs are those of the individual himself *reduced to a natural subject.* The development of industry *suspends this natural necessity* as well as this former luxury— in bourgeois society, it is true, it does so only in *antithetical form.*[29]

Clearly, then, in view of the fact that in the course of socioeconomic development the "luxury" of a more backward stage of production is turned into a normal and even necessary object of "productive consumption," thereby potentially stimulating further development, the real issue is the imperative to overcome the *antithetical form* in which productivity unfolds under the rule of capital, and not the restriction of positive and humanly enriching productive potentialities.

However, if an appropriate measure of evaluation for the viability of productive activity is missing, since it cannot be instituted in the form of consciously planned productive targets based on *genuine human needs,*[30] in that case *wastefulness* is bound to run riot, as we experience it today, *multiplying scarcity* in the most absurd way by means of the *vicious circle* created between *scarcity and waste,* instead of progressively consigning to the past scarcity as such.

Indeed, we should not forget that the imposition of that vicious circle in our existing reproductive order is not confined to what is routinely discarded by the everyday life of the "throw-away society" of every capitalistically advanced country, due to the irrational pursuit of the mindlessly profit-oriented decreasing rate of utilization in production no less than in consumption. It embraces the *directly destructive purposes* to which the natural and social resources are being put, affecting humanity as a whole, on a frightening scale, including the two world wars of the twentieth century and the genocidal wars of our own time, as we know it only too well from actual historical experience.

Naturally, it is not difficult to visualize the negative impact of such destructive practices on intellectual and political developments. Such practices prevail under our particularly grave historical circumstances, when the need for *consciously* facing up to these perilous changes, by mobilizing also the potential emancipatory resources of "free spiritual production" at our disposal, is obviously greater than ever before. However. that kind of conscious intervention in the unfolding historical process would be possible only if the various forces and relations involved in it could be grasped in their proper perspective. And that would require addressing the issues within the framework of their complex dialectical interdeterminations.

Understandably in this sense, the nature of "free spiritual production" can only be made intelligible at all in its close relationship to the actual historical conditions and their underlying material transformations in *any* social formation whatsoever. For the historical conditions in question also set the specific limits within which "free spiritual production" itself becomes feasible and practicable.

Thus, if for some weighty ideological reasons, arising from the now dominant system of social antagonisms, the actual correlations and complex interdeterminations are ignored or tendentiously distorted in the theories conceived from the vantage point of capital, in that case the historically specific is bound to be transformed into a *timeless absolute*. And in that respect it makes no difference at all whether the postulated absolute is justified in the name of a proclaimed *"natural order"* or of a *speculative metaphysical* kind, as we had the opportunity to see above in some of their distinct varieties, and indeed even in the writings of some of the greatest figures of classical political economy and philosophy. What really matters is that the capital-eternalizing transfiguration of the historically specific into a timeless absolute inevitably carries with it far-reaching implications both for theory and for the relevant socioeconomic and political practice.

For that reason it is important to bear in mind Marx's words according to which "if labour as *wage-labour* is taken as the *point of departure*"—as, of course, it *must be* taken from capital's self-serving standpoint—"so that the identity of labour in general with wage-labour appears to be *self-evident,* then capital and monopolized land must also appear as the *natural form* of the conditions of labour in relation to *labour in general.* To be capital, then, appears as the *natural form* of the *means of labour* and thereby as the purely real character arising from their function in the *labour-process in general.*"[31]

Here the issue is not just a distortion of the historically observable actual relationships but their ideologically most revealing *complete reversal.* If, however, this kind of reversal of the actual historical conditions and of the corresponding structural relations between capital and labor, as described by Marx in the last quotation, is not challenged, theoretically as well as practically, in that case all emancipatory ideas and efforts are bound to remain hopelessly trapped in the worst form of vicious circle from which there can be no escape. For the complete reversal, which we encounter in this upside-down relationship between capital and labor, is not simply the mystifying invention of the theories conceived from the vantage point and in the interest of capital. It is abundantly visible in everyday social practice, in the reified appearance of a perverse "natural absoluteness" to which people in all walks of life become "naturally" accustomed.

The ideological/theoretical forms represent the *active embodiment* of the powerful *material and historical transformations* that had *practically produced*—through their *primacy,* which, however, should not be tendentiously confused with some kind of one-sided mechanical *exclusiveness*—the enduring reversal of the original interrelations in question in the course of actual historical development, thereby turning labor itself into *"the property of its own product"* through the structural imposition of such *practical fetishism* on society as a whole.

This is why the meaning of "free spiritual production" cannot be understood in an idealistically absolutized sense, no matter how great the temptation might be to do so. For even in the work of the greatest intellectual figures, be they creative artists or theoreticians, including the classics of bourgeois political economy and philosophy, spiritual production continues to *respond in its own way*—in the form of a *dialectical recipro-*

city—to the actually given conditions by making *its own significant impact* upon the emerging transformations of the existent. This is and remains the undisputable case even if, understandably, spiritual production must make its own contribution within the well-defined framework of the *overall* historical conditions.

Nonetheless, "free spiritual production" is *free* in a genuine sense— and for the same reason also carries a great *responsibility* as an intellectual enterprise—precisely in virtue of its undeniable *active role* in intervening, *for better or worse,* in the unfolding historical process of which it is an *integral part.*

4.2 Key Aspects of Mediation in the Dialectic of Base and Superstructure

Marx's famous 1859 "Preface" to his *Contribution to the Critique of Political Economy* gave a concise assessment of the relationship between the superstructure and the material basis of society with reference to capital's mode of societal reproduction. Naturally, the issue is much broader than that, as we can find it discussed in some of Marx's other works, including the important passages quoted from his *Grundrisse* and from *Capital* in chapter 3.

In regard to the mode of social metabolic reproduction under the rule of capital, the relationship in question is ultimately determined by the absolute imperative of labor's *permanent structural domination* at all cost. Everything must be subordinated to that overarching systemic capital-interest that inevitably vitiates all structural determinations and inter-relations. For capital is *absolutely nothing* in this—*non-symmetrical*—relationship between itself and the class of living labor without the unalterable *structurally secured hierarchical imposition* of the *self-expansionary reproductive imperatives* of its system of social metabolic control on its historical adversary, callously ignoring even the most destructive consequences on society as a whole.

This means that all of the functions of *direction and command*—fully in tune with the vital *practical premises* and objective imperatives of unquestioned and totally unquestionable *capital-expansion* (whose failure would make the system implode)—must be expropriated and exercised by the blindly mandated "personifications of capital" not simply at the expense of the class of labor but in general at the expense of society in its entirety. This must be the case no matter how much more irrational and unstable the *antagonistic structural imposition* of the self-expansionary practical imperatives of capital on society at all cost becomes with the passing of historical time from the ascending to the perilously descending phase of the system's development. The earlier mentioned fetishistic correlation whereby the very possibility of the economically necessary exercise of labor power is at the mercy and under the privileged *"property of its own product"*—on the abusive ground of the structurally imposed expropriation and self-serving allocation of the creations of human productive activity by an alien force originating in, and confronting in a hostile fashion, living labor itself—well encapsulates not only the institutionalized absurdity of this way of regulating expanded societal reproduction but also its total untenability in the longer run.

Naturally, the incurably vitiated articulation and mediation of the relationship between the material basis of society and its superstructure under the rule of capital is an essential constituent of making the fundamental imperatives of this system prevail. The incurably vitiated character of the relationship we are presented with under the established conditions arises from the fact that the interchange between capital and labor is—and must always remain, despite all manipulation and mystification to the contrary, including the constantly propagandized fantasies of "people's capitalism"—an insuperably *antagonistic* one.

To be sure, no societal relationship of continued reproduction is conceivable without its own type of *mediation* of the interchanges between human beings and nature, on the one hand, and among the social individuals themselves as well as among the groups to which they belong, on the other. That also goes, self-evidently, for the capital system. Besides, such circumstance by itself is in no way the necessarily vitiating circumstance in this respect. The insoluble problem arises from the historically specific character of the *type of mediations* that are inseparable from capital's mode of social metabolic reproduction.

The historically specific type of the capital system's necessary mediatory interchanges, which happens to be anti-historically eternalized even

by the greatest intellectual figures who conceptualize the world from capital's vantage point, as we have seen on numerous occasions in the course
of this study, is the modality of—in principle globally extendable—*antagonistic second-order mediations* without which this societal reproductive
order could not function at all. It is precisely the necessity to make prevail
on a permanent basis the antagonistic innermost determinations of the
capital system that incurably vitiates the globally unfolding relationship
between the material basis of society and its superstructure. Every constituent of capital's systemic determinations and interrelations, including
obviously the powerful superstructure, must be dedicated to this literally
vital operational purpose.

Moreover, quite understandably, this relationship between the material basis of society and its superstructure, as closely intertwined with
capital's antagonistic second-order mediations, is by far the most complex in all history. And that is so not least because of the inexorable tendency toward the *global* domination of the capital system as a mode of
societal reproduction, the first time ever in history.

At the same time, however, the intensely contradictory character of
capital's unique—since *structurally necessary*—global expansionary drive
must also be put into relief. For capital's structurally necessary *global
drive* does not at all mean that such drive can also prevail as a *productively
viable and historically sustainable* global domination of societal reproduction on a permanent basis, as the theoretical and ideological eternal-
izers of the system would like us to believe. Far from it, since precisely at
the point where this historically specific system extends to its maximum
power it also greatly overreaches itself.

The overreaching in question asserts itself with far-reaching consequences in the vital domain of the most problematical articulation of the
capital system's antagonistic legal and political superstructure, carrying
with it the activation of massive *structural impediments*—with their
unavoidable implications for nothing less than the destruction of the elementary conditions of human existence itself—to its continued global
domination, as we shall see below.

As mentioned at the beginning of this section, the relationship
between the superstructure and the material basis of society is much
broader than the way we find it articulated under the specific historical

circumstances of capital's mode of societal reproduction. There is also an important transhistorical dimension, on the basis of which it is possible to envisage the supersession of the now predominant contradictions of this relationship.

However, before turning to the discussion of such problems, it is necessary to clarify the principal characteristics of the deeply constraining interchange between the material basis of society and its superstructure under capital's rule. With regard to the *trans*historical dimension of our problem let it now suffice to anticipate that, similar to the question concerning the untranscendable dimension of productive activity itself—that is, "production in general" or "labor as such," without which human life on this planet would be inconceivable—which means that in this respect we must focus attention on the relationship between (always necessary) *purposive productive activity,* together with its *material and means of production,*[32] and not on the historically unique relationship between *wage labor* and *capital.* And this means that in virtue of the here relevant transhistorical dimension the elimination of the structurally evident difference between the material basis as such and its superstructure is inconceivable, even if overcoming the historically generated destructive aspects of their relationship is both necessary and feasible. The transhistorical dimension in this regard remains in force in the sense that the superstructure as such could never be assimilated by, nor indeed could it be reduced to, the material basis of society, except in mechanistic theories that indulge in the gross violation not only of the dialectic but even of elementary logic. And by the same token, only in the most grotesque capital-apologetic fantasies of "post-industrial society" can one project the "fully automated" realization of materially necessary productive activity as the unproblematical ground of "boundless leisure."

The real issue for us is the radical supersession of the dehumanizing *tyranny* of the material basis, as manifest under the rule of capital, and not the fictitious removal of the distinct characteristics and determinations of materiality itself from the life of human beings who are, and must always remain, an integral—even if the uniquely self-mediating and thereby in a genuine sense potentially self-liberating—part of nature. Marx, who is often accused of utopian illusions, always insisted, with the greatest sense of reality, on the need for acknowledging the objective determinations that must be respected in all human affairs, including of course the interchange of human beings with nature. He did that with great clarity even when he was firmly drawing the line of demarcation between humanity being unavoidably subjected to the power of necessity and the prospects of really feasible emancipation, by underlining:

> Just as the savage must wrestle with nature to satisfy his wants, to maintain and reproduce life, so must civilized man, and he must do so in all social formations and under all possible modes of production. With his development the realm of necessity expands as a result of his wants; but, at the same time, the forces of production which satisfy these wants also increase. Freedom in this field can only consist in socialized man, the associated producers, rationally regulating their interchange with nature, bringing it under their common control, instead of being ruled by it as by the blind forces of nature; and achieving this with the least expenditure of energy and under conditions most favourable to, and worthy of, their human nature. But it nonetheless still remains a realm of necessity. Beyond it begins that development of human energy which is an end in itself, the true realm of freedom, which, however, can blossom forth only with this realm of necessity as its basis.[33]

And yet, notwithstanding the clarity with which these matters are spelled out by Marx, his conception of the relationship between the material basis of society and its superstructure is often tendentiously misrepresented in the most absurd fashion, as befits the hostile requirements of capital-apologetic ideology. To take an example, it is asserted in a particularly crude account of "historical explanation" that in Marx's view "people's thoughts and ideas are a kind of *vapour* ... which mysteriously rises from the 'material foundation.'"[34]

But even when the characterization of the Marxian conception is not as primitive and blatantly hostile as this one, the attribution of a mechanical *one-to-one correlation* between the material basis of society and its superstructure frequently tends to prevail in the depiction of the Marxist position. Sometimes we find this kind of approach presented not only without any hostile intent but even with full approval, due simply to the mechanical predilection of the thinkers who put forward such views. In this way the *dialectical mediations,* which form an essential part of this vital explanatory complex of the unfolding developments, completely disappear from view. As a result, the dynamic interrelationship between the material and the superstructural factors and determinations which characterize the historical genesis and the transformations of the capital system cannot be made intelligible at all.

What is particularly important in this respect is the institutionally secured and safeguarded legal and political superstructure in its vital intermediary role between the material foundation of society and "the legal, political, religious, artistic or philosophic—in short, *ideological forms* in which men become conscious of their conflict and fight it out."[35] Accordingly, what we are really concerned with here is not a *mechanically* projected *one-to-one* correspondence between materiality and ideas but a *threefold* interrelationship characteristic of this vital social complex that *dialectically* constitutes the dynamic interchange between the material base and the superstructure of society.

In this sense, first we have the "relations of production" that constitute "the economic structure of society, the real foundation." Second, on that *real foundation* "arises a legal and political superstructure." And the third essential factor is constituted by the manifold variety of "the ideological forms" that enter the picture as "definite forms of social consciousness," and as such "correspond to the legal and political superstructure."[36]

Accordingly, the "correspondence" in question is not that between the material base and the ideas (or ideological forms through which humanity's practical social consciousness is articulated and asserted in the course of history) but that between the *legal and political superstructure,* on the one hand, and the various *ideological forms* themselves, on the other. Ideas as such cannot arise in, let alone can they make their impact on the real world from, a vacuum. Nor could indeed they "drop from the womb of self-positing Idea,"[37] as speculative idealist philosophy circularly postulates their appearance. Especially not under the conditions of the globally unfolding capital system, with its contradictory tendency to utmost centralization of its productive and distributive processes as well as to the all-encroaching material subjugation of even the most sublime ideas by the structurally entrenched vested interests. For ideas appear and assert themselves, if they have the strength to do so, within this threefold framework of dialectical interchanges, as depicted by Marx.

What is also relevant to put into relief is that in the course of historical development the earlier mentioned "ideological forms" have also assumed the form of determinate types of *discourses:* from *political* and *moral* to *religious* and *aesthetic.* Such discourses all have clearly identifiable defining characteristics of their own, in terms of which they respond to, and embody within their own, transhistorically consolidated, specific framework, the real world, deeply affecting the behavior of human beings in their clearly articulated domain.

In this sense the understanding of religion, politics, and morality, or the proper appreciation of the nature and development of art and literature, is impossible without focusing attention on the constitution and structurally relevant characteristics of these specific discourses. Moreover, these discourses, in their objective constitution, should not be confused with the corresponding *theories of discourses*—ranging from theology and political philosophy to ethical and aesthetic theory—which legitimately arise on the practically operative ground of the socially articulated practical discourses themselves.

The function of the particular theories of discourses is to generalize in their own, conceptual terms of reference the operative principles that objectively manifest themselves in the well-circumscribed practical discourses. In that way these theories of discourses transform the respective practical operative principles, in accordance with the relevant historical conditions and requirements that confront the particular thinkers concerned—as for instance we find this in the monumental Hegelian vision of Aesthetics, which happens to be a closely integrated part of his time-bound philosophical system as a whole—into historically determinate conceptions organically linked to the ideological panorama of their own age.

Two important considerations must be added here. The first is that the vital practical discourses without which developed social life is unthinkable are not at all intelligible by themselves. In other words, they are not intelligible without their close links to the given institutional framework of the historically dominant legal and political superstructure. The *"correspondence"* between the various discourses and the legal and political superstructure in question can be rightfully asserted precisely on that ground.

This kind of interconnection is perfectly obvious when we talk about the practical reality of the *political discourse* that happens to be inseparable from the frequently most direct state political practices. As an example, it is enough to think of the promotion and the justification of the parliamentary form of legislation and decision making as such. That form of interrelationship is in clear contrast to the much more indirect mode of articulating the various *theories of political discourse.*

Nevertheless, when the connection is not as obvious as in the case of practical political discourse, with its essential concern with securing the most effective *means/ends* relationship for *overall* societal reproduction, even then similar determinations prevail. For instance, when we think of religious practices, they are also unimaginable as simply the spontaneous adherence of the individuals to determinate rituals and beliefs. For such beliefs and rituals are in fact practically embraced and maintained, as well as significantly modified, within the complex institutional framework of the various *churches* (and their less formally defined organizational equivalents) which in their turn are themselves closely linked to, and in some cases even openly integrated into, the legal and political superstructure and into the modern state.[38] The once radically proclaimed principle of the "separation of the Church and the State" has never been translated into social practice in the originally intended sense. Its reality turned out to be in the final analysis a greater willingness by the diverse religious bodies to accept the *preeminence* of the legal and political superstructure.

Regarding the practice of *moral discourse,* we should not be deceived by the fact that its institutional framework is more diffused than those of political and even religious discourse. For also in that domain the links to the legal and political superstructure are very intense. In this respect it is enough to remind ourselves of the way in which all of the given *educational practices* and bodies of society are regulated by the modern state, from the family to all levels of institutionalized learning, including the kindergartens at one end and the universities at the other. Nor should we forget the way in which also the various religious institutions of society participate—often under direct legislative regulation—in the moral education of individuals. Through their more diffused institutional network they are all involved in transmitting the dominant values of the established social order from the present generation to the future ones. And, of course, in regulating this transmission of the dominant value system of society from the present toward the future the legal and political super-structure plays the preeminent regulatory role.

At the same time, even the highly mediated social practice of *aesthetic discourse* is an integral part of these processes, which cannot be divorced from the legal and political superstructure of the prevailing social order. This is so notwithstanding the well-known illusions characteristic of more recent historical times (since the second half of the nineteenth century), including the artistic creed programmatically spelled out under the slogan of *l'art pour l'art,* for instance. Significantly, Plato had no use whatsoever for such illusions. On the contrary, he made it amply clear that he wanted to integrate the various practices of artistic endeavor into the vital educational framework of his *Republic.*

In any case, the production and consumption of the works of art and literature, as we actually know them today, are also quite unimaginable without the far-reaching regulatory impact of the legal and political super-structure. This goes from the direct and indirect political supervision of theatrical and other literary productions, including magazine and book publishing as well as television programming and the film industry—and all that not just under openly authoritarian modes of control but also under the liberal democratic forms of the state, and, moreover, by no means only as confined to the existing openly censorial regulatory offices of the latter, but even more tellingly under the subtle varieties of promot-ing effective self-censorship—as well as the strict legislative control of the educationally important state museum network. Besides, the dominant legal and political superstructure of society actively participates even in the obviously profit-oriented, and pretendedly most independent, enter-prise of private art galleries that could not sustain themselves for any length of time without receiving the direct and indirect benefits of the state-regulated national and international financial network. Naturally, all this could not be further removed from the ideologically convenient illu-sions of "free art" and its claimed "sovereignty" as divorced from practi-cally relevant social functions, a fictitious view promoted as a rule in the service of the powerful vested interests of the ruling class.

The illusions associated with the denial of the vital interconnection between the legal and political superstructure and the ideological forms of social consciousness tend to be reinforced by the objective difference between the *forms* of discourse—i.e., the *directly practical* operational reality of political, moral, religious, and aesthetic discourse as such—and the corresponding *theories* of discourses within which the respective *ideas* are more or less systematically spelled out. For, in contrast to the specific *practical forms of discourse*—which in addition to the work of outstanding particular representative figures also include folk art and popular culture, as well as spontaneous political and other mass participatory activities and responses to ongoing developments, without any clearly identifiable "individual author" in their forefront—the various *theories of discourses* are elaborated and combined into some kind of a (periodically changing) system by *individual* philosophers, political and moral theorists, and theologians, with a pronounced tendency to put into relief their own "sovereignty" over the subject of their analysis.

This is why Marx had to stress that "philosophers have only interpreted the world, the point is, though, to change it." But even when the thinkers in question declined the idea of *changing* the world, as Hegel explicitly did when he compared the role of philosophy to the "owl of Minerva" spreading its wings only with the "falling of the dusk," he contributed in a most powerful way to the *preservation* of the existing order. Thus, directly or indirectly, the "sovereign" outstanding intellectual figures of the last few centuries who formulated their relevant theories of discourses nonetheless did so by inescapably participating in the same interrelationship between the ideological forms and the legal and political superstructure of their time, even when they had no intention at all of changing the order they viewed and theorized from capital's standpoint. We should not forget that Hegel was responsible not only for the creation of the greatest theory of aesthetic discourse all the way up to his own time but also for the elaboration of the most comprehensive and boundlessly apologetic conception of the modern capitalist state in his *Philosophy of Right,* which retains its representative role and importance even today.

Although the individual authors who conceive their *theories* of discourse directly *reflect on,* and generalize across history, the nature of the various practical discourses in their own intellectual activity, whether we think of their evaluations of practically embedded political activity and its organizational setting, or of the seminal characteristics of artistic creation and consumption—and thus in a sense they are "one step removed" from the direct connection of their subject of inquiry to the institutionalized legal and political superstructure—this fact makes that connection only more complicated and more mediated but cannot fundamentally alter its character.

The undeniable circumstance here referred to only underscores the complex *dialectical mediations* involved in these activities, warning against any attempt at mechanistic reductionism. Also in this way the Marxian depiction of the actually prevailing relationship in these matters clearly puts into relief that, notwithstanding all tendentiously distorting accusations to the contrary, there can be in this regard no suggestion of a direct, one-to-one correlation between *materiality and ideas*. On the contrary, since ideas must have their appropriate vehicles through which they can assert their viability, the two kinds of distinctly different activity *together*—that is, the practically operative discourses of social consciousness on the one hand, from politics and religion to morality and artistic creativity, and the relevant theories of discourses that reflect on and generalize across history the specific defining characteristics of the practical discourses themselves, on the other—are integral parts of the *dialectically mediated ideological forms of social consciousness*. Thus they *conjointly* constitute the dialectical interrelationship, which itself cannot be divorced from the vital explanatory complex of the legal and political superstructure as it fulfills its dynamic role in the course of social change. This is the case irrespective of how problematical might be the role of the legal and political superstructure under determinate socioeconomic circumstances in the overall historical development.

The earlier mentioned second important consideration that needs to be underscored in the present context, before we can turn to the final points of this section, is a corollary to the first. It serves to put the transhistorical dimension of our problem—concerned with the inherent nature of the various practical discourses as such—in its proper perspective. For it should always be remembered that everything in human affairs has, and must have, its *historical genesis* and transformations.

To be sure, the various practical discourses, from religion and politics to art and literature, have their clearly identifiable defining characteristics. These important defining characteristics are by no means confined to a particular historical period. They embrace all of those in which the respective activities that objectively define the discourses in question are carried on in one way or another. This is why we can rightfully refer to the *trans*historical dimension of all of the practical discourses that we are concerned with here.

However, it is also an obvious aspect of their innermost nature that none of them could "drop from the womb of self-positing Idea," as we know. They all had to be *constituted* in the form of their clearly identifiable substantive characteristics in the course of *actual historical development*. In this sense the objective *trans*historical determinations of the practical discourses—which should never be subsumed under some kind of *supra*-historical speculative projection, as alas frequently happens to be the case—are inseparable from the equally objective *historical* characteristics of their *actual constitution*. In fact, there can be nothing mysterious about the transhistorical determinations of their reality. They represent, within the specific framework of any one of them, the persistent *reproduction* and *consolidation* of determinate ways of *practically relating* to the existent, with a view to significantly influencing human behavior in their respective domain.

This is undoubtedly the case whether we think of the practical reality of political discourse or of the less direct practical intervention of art and literature in social life. In this sense, they are all transhistorical *and historical* at the same time. And we find the same determination of simultaneously transhistorical and historical characteristics in the practical reality of religion. This is in obvious contrast to the often tellingly one-sided *theological* conceptions and generalizations we encounter in the multiple *theories* of religious discourse. For no matter how one-sidedly the latter theorize the powerful *practical reality* of religious discourse as such—and irrespective of whether they do that in harmony with the institutional reality of their respective church or in sharp conflict with it, as we find such conflicts spelled out in the programmatic writings of the early representatives of dissenting Protestantism, for instance—no one could seriously suggest to us that the striking move in religious practices from the virtually countless gods of Greek and other mythologies all the way to the now overwhelming prevalence of monotheism, as an example, has nothing to do with actual historical development.

The significant reality of the *trans*historical dimension is always made of *inherently historical constituents*. This circumstance is very important for a proper understanding of the necessary structural determinations of society—their continuity in change and change in continuity—if we want to grasp in a viable perspective their all-embracing dialectical interactions, extending from the material basis of the elementary reproductive structures to the manifold interrelations of the superstructure mediated in the most complex way, as indicated above.

At the same time the same circumstance is equally important for making intelligible the changing historical process as a whole not simply in terms of the unavoidable constraints and limitations at work in it. If we confined our attention only to the inevitable socio-historical constraints that would offer us only one side of the picture. To have a historically accurate conception we must simultaneously also bear in mind the objectively grounded emancipatory potentialities of the developments unfolding across history. For what is most relevant in this regard—and cannot be stressed often enough in view of its customary neglect—is that what is *historically constituted* in the course of the ongoing dynamic transformations of society is in principle also *subject to potential future historical change,* once the appropriate objective and subjective conditions are fulfilled. This is so even if, by no means surprisingly, the genuine historical picture is in sharp contrast to the self-serving *eternalizations* of the established states of affairs as characteristically represented from the standpoint of capital.

Without this important dialectical interrelationship, which objectively defines the connection between the *historical* and the *transhistorical* as being inseparable from one another, we could not have any genuine historical advancement. Nor could we have, of course, on the ground of such advancement, the feasibility of real emancipatory change.

Furthermore, in focusing attention on the inseparability of the historical from the transhistorical, we can also gain insight into the vitally important dialectic of the *historical* and the *structural.* For the structurally significant and renewed *transhistorical consolidation* of some major *historical* determinations and characteristics of the unfolding process of societal development has a direct bearing on the ultimate *social-ontological limits* within which a specific social formation—like, for instance, the capital system as a mode of all-embracing social metabolic control—can maintain its historical viability or flounder under the weight of its irrepressible antagonisms through the eruption of its *structural crisis.*

Naturally, this dialectical interchange between the structural and the historical factors of societal transformation works in both directions. At first, in the ascending phase of a system's development, the transhistorical consolidation of some important historical and structural determinations positively enhances its overall controlling power and the potentialities of its self-assertive productive advancement. This is the case despite the fact that the development in question might well be associated with an understandable (and not simply short-sighted but even destructively blind) tendency to disregard the more distant implications of the *type of productivity* of the given reproductive system, as happens to be under capital's mode of social metabolic control, together with its ultimately unfulfillable demand on material and human resources.

In the descending phase of systemic development, however, inevitably even the longest term implications come to the fore with a vengeance, no matter how elaborate might be the machinery and the corresponding ideology of eternalization. In this way, in the course of the descending phase, the unfolding determinations negatively contribute to deepening the structural crisis itself, paradoxically through the impact of the intended "remedial measures," which *more or less directly contradict* the projected outcome. For such measures cannot work in the final analysis in the descending phase for the simple reason that they cannot fit into the *structural limits* once they are objectively overstepped—and in that way violated—by the system in question, in that it had become *anachronistic* in an epochal historical sense. A strikingly obvious example for the counterproductive character of the "remedial measures" irrationally adopted and ruthlessly enforced today is the way in which the aggressive personifications of capital are attempting to redress in vain the growing *destructiveness* of the capital system in our time through the constant *intensification of destructiveness* not only in the *economic and financial* but also in the *political/military* domain.

With regard to the interrelationsip between the legal and political superstructure and the ideological forms of social consciousness, the most problematical determination is that in the course of actual historical developments in the last four to five centuries the legal and political superstructure itself had acquired a *preponderant role*. Accordingly, in the objective dialectic of the structural and the historical it became responsible for the production of some increasingly negative—and ultimately most destructive—characteristics as time went by, due to the antagonisms asserting themselves in an increasingly more pronounced form in the *descending phase* of the capital system's development, culminating in our time in the all-pervasive structural crisis. As a concomitant of this overall systemic crisis, under the present circumstances the legal and political superstructure is characterized by an ever-extensive *legislative jungle* that dominates all processes of societal reproduction, and—instead of positively enhancing them—casts over the whole of society the dark shadow of uncontrollability.

Naturally, all this is the antagonistic corollary of the capitalist material processes that must prevail in the form of the ever more destructive domination of even the most wasteful forms of *exchange-value* over humanly meaningful *use-value*. In their negativity they assert themselves today not only through the dominance of the directly destructive military-industrial complex but also through the institutionalized adventurism of insanely parasitic speculative finance. And, of course, both the military-industrial complex and the parasitic financial adventurism of our time require the generous facilitating services of the capitalist legal and political superstructure for the purpose of making their operations rationally impenetrable and uncontrollable. Compared to this painful reality, which we can clearly identify and tangibly pinpoint in actually existing capitalist society, the assertions of even some major bourgeois thinkers, like Max Weber— who invites us to accept that the apparently unstoppable legislative jungle, with the growing army of its "virtuoso bureaucrats" (Weber's expression), must be positively hailed in his sense according to which "it has been the work of jurists to give birth to the modern Occidental state,"[39] as mentioned before—are not only grotesquely superficial and idealist in character but also the unashamed apologetic and question-begging theorizations of the modern capitalist state.

It goes without saying that even the normatively regulating superstructure, which we have to confront in our time in its form as the highly developed and perilously preponderant legal and political superstructure, with its drive toward global self-assertion, was very different in its historical origin. In the distant past of its original constitution it had to emerge from the socioeconomically essential *operating conditions* of the material reproduction process with which it formed at first an organic unity, as we have seen in the last chapter.[40] It required the elapse of many centuries before some of the original regulatory determinations of productive development could be separated out from their organic setting and transformed into the now ubiquitous preponderance of the legal and political superstructure, under the requirements of capital's mode of social metabolic reproduction.

At the same time, when we refer to this circumstance, it is also important to put into relief that with regard to the actual constitution of the legal and political superstructure the earlier mentioned vital relationship between the *historical* and the *transhistorical* should not be misconceived in the sense of attributing to the capitalistically dominant form a one-sidedly *supra*historical role, as happens to be the case in its self-serving conceptualizations from capital's vantage point. For by its implications that would amount to the acceptance of the now prevailing determinations of the existent as insuperable.

Naturally, we should not disregard or underrate the relevance and the nature of the *structurally primary* determinations in this respect. In other words, we should not overlook the enduring reality of both the material base and the corresponding superstructure in these equations, attributing an ephemeral role to the latter on the mistaken understanding of its definition as superstructure. For, due to the actuality of their constitution and to their ongoing necessary dialectical interchanges, neither the material base of societal reproduction, nor the superstructure as such, can be conceptualized as historically superseded at some future point of development on a permanent basis.

The insurmountable reality of the *superstructure* itself, in its dialectical correlation to the always necessary foundation of humanity's societal reproduction process on the ground of the appropriate *material basis,* can only fallaciously—and *anti-historically*—be equated with the *specific legal and political superstructure* of capital's social formation. This is so because the actual historical constitution of the highly formalized legal and political superstructure of capital's social formation is simply inconceivable without the corresponding *labor process,* with its inexorable tendency toward the all-embracing dominance of *abstract labor* oriented toward universal *quantification* and toward the corresponding *formal-reductive equations* of generalized commodity production. And, of course, these determinations are organically linked to the ever-expanding complexity of the characteristic *contractual* relations (required by the labor process of capital's mode of social metabolic reproduction) that must emerge from the irrepressible—even if in the last analysis insuperably contradictory—drive of the capital system forward from its *local* units of production toward their attempted *global* integration.[41]

The irrepressibly growing *legislative jungle* of the now obviously preponderant legal and political superstructure—and here it is irrelevant whether that jungle is somewhat circularly condemned on the left as an allegedly self-explanatory "bureaucratization"—or idealized not only by Max Weber but in his own way also by Hegel as the domain of the allegedly most beneficial "universal class" of civil servants wishfully postulated by him—is the necessary embodiment of this process right from the time of its inception. This is the real ground for the constitution and massive expansion of the state of the capital system, and not the fictitiously declared sovereign brainwork of Occidental jurists.

It is the fundamental difference between the *superstructure as such* and the *historically specific* and incorrigibly antagonistic legal and political superstructure of capital's social formation that enables us to envisage extricating societal reproduction from the destructiveness of the overbearing state, together with the all-pervasive second-order mediations of the capital system in general. Without the fundamental difference between the transhistorically reshaped actuality of the superstructure in general and its historically specific and limited variety under the rule of capital, there could be no way of overcoming the "iron cage" of the capital system. Clearly, this is very far from being simply a political matter, despite the reductive and ultimately self-defeating sectarian preconceptions advocated on this score. The exclusivistic stress on politics, at the expense of the much broader strategies of structurally viable and historically in all reproductive domains to be sustained transformation, cannot be a viable approach to these issues, no matter how important a role radical political intervention must play in the overall emancipatory process, especially at the time of breaking the stranglehold of alienated politics over societal change in the first place.

In envisaging a qualitative advancement to the "new historic form" advocated by Marx, we are concerned with the *entire* complexity of societal reproduction, as resting on a secure material foundation that must be capable of maintaining a harmonious relationship to nature. This means, in other words, that without the profound restructuring of the totality of society's reproductive relations—from the elementary material prerequisites of the labor process to the most mediated regulatory interchanges in the domain of social consciousness and the emancipatory production of ideas, including the qualitative switch from the now dominant modality of externally imposed normativity to internally embraced and positively pursued evaluation of the objectives consciously chosen by the individuals[42]—it is impossible to expect, in terms of the required enduring basis, the solution of the problems we have to face.

Since the earlier mentioned dialectical interchange between the structural and the historical factors and determinations asserts itself, of necessity, both in a positive and in a negative way, according to the ascending or the descending phase of a social reproductive system's development—i.e., by enhancing its productive potentialities in the ascending phase (while the problematical impact of the adopted reproductive practices would be visible only from a more distant perspective), or by significantly intensifying its antagonistic contradictions, to the point of causing explosions, when even the most wastefully resourced efforts applied to securing the continued domination of the ruling order in question as an all-embracing system of social metabolic control, beyond the objective structural limits of its productive viability, can only worsen the systemic crisis—the role of the superstructure is very important in contributing to the eventual outcome. It is in this context that the potential transformatory significance of the superstructure as such becomes clearly visible also with regard to the institution of a radically different future.

It goes without saying that the historically specific structural articulation of the established order can successfully work as the vital *structural support* to the societal reproductive strategies pursued under the favorable circumstances of its genuine reproductive viability. Naturally, however, it can also assert its power in the opposite direction, in the form of some major *structural disturbances and impediments*—and, indeed, even as insurmountable *structural blockages* causing havoc in the functioning of the system as a whole—when the "tide is turned," so to speak, and the continued *historical sustainability* of the prevailing societal reproductive practices, in contrast to the strictly *conjunctural success or failure* of their customary mode of operation, is being called into question. The grave *structural crisis* of an all-embracing social metabolic order is defined precisely in terms of its *overall historical sustainability and viability*, measured on the *epochal* scale, and not on the ground of its *periodic*, more or less easily supersedable, *conjunctural* vicissitudes and crises.

This is the point where we can return to the opening considerations of this section. Namely, that the question concerning the structurally and historically vital relationship between the material basis of any particular society and its superstructure is much broader than its brief characterization in Marx's 1859 "Preface" to his *Contribution to the Critique of Political Economy*. That "Preface" was intended only as a concise assessment of the historical specificity of this issue, with reference to capital's unique and necessarily transient mode of societal reproduction.

If we want to envisage an actually feasible solution to the now encountered—and constantly aggravating—problems of capital's antagonistic mode of social metabolic control, with its dangerously worsening, and by now suicidally wasteful, second-order mediations of the required societal reproduction process, we have to reassess the relationship between the inescapable material basis of human life and its potentially positive superstructural determinations from a much longer-term perspective. A perspective capable of subjecting to a *radical critique* the capital system's destructively preponderant legal and political superstructure itself.

This must be done in view of capital's not only destructive but ultimately even *self-destructive* transformation of its once *organic* reproductive order—which used to secure its productive advancement as a matter of course in the *ascending* phase of its systemic development—into the *vicious circle* of its historically no longer sustainable productive practices, in our time attempted to be imposed on a global scale. A vicious circle in which the more fully capital succeeds in achieving its intended self-expansionary targets the worse it is for the prospects of human survival, in view of the prohibitive constraints imposed in every domain by the system's antagonistic contradictions, under the escalating authoritarian supremacy of the state.

Precisely for this reason it is by no means surprising that Marx envisaged—and as a matter of vital theoretical consistency *had to envisage*—the "withering away of the state" as the only feasible solution to the structural antagonisms of our existing social order. Those who are willing to abandon that Marxian idea altogether, as we have seen it done all too readily and frequently in the labor movement ever since his sharp *Critique of the Gotha Program*, should also face up to the necessary implications of doing so for the future. For by turning their backs to the difficult task of making the required contribution to the "withering away of the state," for whatever reason, they abandon—knowingly or not—the Marxian strategic project engaged in the socialist transformation of society. Our historical experience in the twentieth century is a dire warning in that respect.

The positive outcome of a historically sustainable socialist transformation is inconceivable without the most *active* contribution by the superstructure to the realization of the envisaged target. The Marxian conception in this regard is not only different from its tendentious misrepresentations, whenever his critics describe it as a "mechanical reflection" of materiality—not to mention the mindless insult leveled against Marx according to which in his view "people's thoughts and ideas are a kind of *vapour* . . . which mysteriously rises from the 'material foundation'"—but the *diametrical opposite* to the dynamic account of his profoundly dialectical characterization of the complex historical development, giving their full weight in this relationship to the various forms and modalities of social consciousness. Only the crudest kind of reductivism could depict these matters in a different light, in view of the inherently active nature and role of the manifold, dialectically mediated, superstructural factors and determinations that assert themselves in the overall historical process.

However, fully acknowledging the active role of the superstructure, as must be done, does not mean that the superstructure itself can be exempted from quite fundamental changes, as required by the envisaged qualitative transformation of the societal complex in its entirety. For the unavoidable historical challenge of radically restructuring the capital system necessarily involves overcoming the *preponderance* of the legal and political superstructure, with its deep roots not only in the historical past but also in the existing material reproductive constituents of the dominant social metabolic process. The fact that in the course of capital's descending phase of historical development the earlier *organic* unity of the various material and ideal factors—once greatly contributing to the positive productive advancement of the system—had been turned into the *vicious circle* of the cancerously expansionary imposition of its power on society, sinking ever deeper into the morass of the *antagonistic second-order mediations* of capital's socioeconomic order while completely disregarding the consequences, this painful fact cannot be redressed without superseding the dangerous preponderance of the legal and political superstructure, with its constantly growing militaristic accretion ever since the onset of modern imperialism.

The concern about the necessary "withering away of the state" is inseparable from these considerations. The politically difficult and revealing question why the Marxian theorization of the necessary "withering away of the state" had been cast aside ubiquitously[43] in the twentieth century will have to be confronted one day. It will surface again when the need to move toward its realization will become much more pressing than in the past, as it is bound to be in due course.

The great problem for the future of humanity is how to liberate itself from the straitjacket of capital's antagonistic second-order mediations, constantly reinforced by its powerful superstructure. For the once positive potential of capital's *organic system*—characterized in the ascending phase by the *reciprocal support* of its constituent parts among themselves which made it possible to secure in those days the productive advancement of societal reproduction as a whole—had been turned into the *vicious circle* of defending at all cost even of the most wasteful and destructive systemic determinations under the circumstances of sharpening antagonisms and deepening structural crisis. Understandably, the present articulation of capital's legal and political superstructure, thanks to its preponderant power, with the capitalist state at its apex, plays a massive role in the preservation and global dominance of the established social metabolic order. In this respect, too, the most *active role of superstructural reciprocity* is clearly visible, even if it asserts itself not in a positive way, for the better, but for the worse.

However, it is not written in some sacred book that the capital system's antagonistic second-order mediations, with their perverse reciprocity, should always prevail. The *superstructure as such* can be equated only in a fallacious and anti-historical way with its—in our time most retrograde—variant of the legal and political superstructure under the rule of capital. Equally, only from the vantage point of the narrowest vested interests can the transhistorical necessity of social metabolic *mediation as such* be equated with the *antagonistic second-order mediations* of the capital system. For, as discussed already, human beings are also capable of articulating the potentially emancipatory *self-mediation* of their relationship among themselves and nature at large, as well as among themselves as developing social groups and individuals. This is what confers upon them their unique status in the order of nature.[44]

At the peak of its productive development capital's organic system was responsible for unprecedented social transformation and advancement, thanks to the *positive reciprocity* and interdependency of its reproductive processes in which its superstructural dimension—from anti-feudal political commitment to the great emancipatory contribution of art and literature, as well as to the genuine universalist, even if somewhat naïve and in the end disappointed, aspirations of Enlightenment philosophy—played a most significant role. All that had dramatically changed as time went by. But no matter how contrasting and problematical the overall impact of the established mode of social metabolic control happens to be today, the socialist order cannot define itself simply in terms of saying no to capital's systemic control. For the socialist project cannot constitute a viable alternative to the established reproductive order unless it is successfully articulated in a positive way, as a historically sustainable *organic system*, with its own kind of reciprocity based on the *conscious self-mediation* of its social individuals. It is this form of potentially emancipatory self-mediation that is expected in the socialist alternative to take the place of the vicious circle of the capital system's interactive constitutive parts that assign to the legal and political superstructure in our time a totally apologetic role.

As underscored, the greatly constraining and in many ways under our present-day circumstances counterproductive historical necessity that continues to prevail through the antagonistic second-order mediations of the capital system is the assertion of a—changeable—*man-made causality*, imposed by human beings upon themselves in the course of historical development. Paradoxically, this qualitatively different form of causality, in contrast to the strictest determinations of the natural law, was imposed by humans upon themselves as a step forward on the contradictory road toward their *potential self-emancipation*, parallel to the increasingly more complex articulation of the totality of their forms and instruments of reproductive interchanges, including the ever more mediated superstructure of their life activity since that time. Accordingly, this new type of causality—of man-made historical necessity—is not intelligible at all without focusing attention on the most active role of the changing superstructure in its constitution and renewed assertion. The historically feasible solution to this challenge is to bring the self-imposed necessity in question under control by overcoming the capital system's antagonistic second-order mediations through a self-mediated—because consciously self-managed—alternative. Naturally, the potential emancipatory role of the qualitatively reconstituted superstructure could not be greater in this respect.

4.3 Ideology and "False Consciousness"

One of the most frequent misconceptions about ideology is its attempted direct identification with false consciousness. We have seen in chapter 2 that even without any hostile intent Marx's position is at times completely misquoted and distorted to fit it in with that kind of simplistic reduction of ideology to false consciousness.[45]

In truth, ideology appears in the Marxian conception not in a unilateral sense but with diametrically opposed connotations. In one sense it is presented, in its negativity, as a mystifying and counterproductive force that greatly hinders social development. On the other hand, however, it is also seen as a vital positive factor—serving the purpose of overcoming determinate social constraints and resistances—without whose active contribution the productive potentialities of the given historical situation could not unfold and assert themselves.

The misconceived attempts to reduce ideology to false consciousness are often associated with a rigid, fetishistic view of science. The holders of such views tend to disregard or ignore even the most obvious differences between *natural* science and the *social* sciences. However, when we recall Marx's views directly relevant in this respect, he made it absolutely clear that in the analysis of the complex dialectical interchanges of social life not everything can be determined with the precision of natural science. This is how he put it:

> The changes in the economic foundation lead sooner or later to the transformation of the whole *immense superstructure.* In studying such transformations it is *always necessary to distinguish* between the material transformation of the economic conditions of production, which can be *determined with the precision of natural science,* and the legal, political, religious, artistic or philosophic—in short, *ideological forms* in which men become conscious of this conflict and fight it out.[46]

Nothing could be clearer and theoretically more precise than this way of contrasting the "ideological forms"—through which it becomes possible "to fight out the conflict" between the rival hegemonic forces of society: a way of settling many vital socioeconomic and political issues, which happens to be characteristic of development under the conditions of class rule—and the analysis of the economic foundation (the material ground) from which the most varied ideological forms arise in a dialectical sense, as we have already seen it discussed. But, of course, the fetishistic conception of science, and the complete misrepresentation of Marx's own views in that spirit, makes it impossible to understand both the nature of *ideology as such* and the very real problem of *false consciousness* in its own appropriate context. The two of them—i.e., ideology and false consciousness—*may or may not* be inseparably linked together under determinate circumstances. However, it is precisely the social and historical specificity of those circumstances that decides the issue.

Naturally, the right and proper acknowledgement that in the field of social inquiry not everything can be determined with the precision of natural science does not mean that those aspects of one's critical concerns which cannot be ascertained in that way can be consigned to the mercy of arbitrary and gratuitous judgements, as doing so might suit the convenience of some vested interests. But most certainly it means that in relation to the particular field in question, which is being investigated or con-tested, the criteria and method applied to solving the problems that arise must be *appropriate* to the nature of the problems in their *full societal complexity and conflictuality*. And, of course, the *dialectical investigation* of the social structure, together with the forms and modalities of inter-change that must take place within its framework, including the great vari-ety of the ideological forms of social consciousness, requires an appropri-ate way of dealing with the highest level of complexity.

It is highly relevant in this respect that in his Afterword to the second German edition of *Capital* Marx quotes with approval a Russian com-mentator who wrote on the Marxian method that "the old economists misunderstood the nature of economic laws when they likened them to the laws of *physics* and *chemistry*. A more thorough analysis of phenom-ena shows that *social organisms* differ among themselves as fundamen-tally as plants or animals. Nay, one and the same phenomenon falls under quite different laws in consequence of the different structure of those organisms as a whole, of the variations of their individual organs, of the different conditions in which those organs function. . . . [according to Marx] With the varying degree of development of productive power, social conditions and the laws governing them vary too. . . . The scientific value of such an inquiry lies in the disclosing of the *special laws* that reg-ulate the origin, existence, development, death of a given *social organism* and its replacement by another and higher one. And it is this value that, in point of fact, Marx's book has."[47] And Marx adds at that point: "Whilst the writer pictures my method . . . what else is he picturing but *the dialec-tical method*."[48] In other words, since there cannot be in human affairs a higher level of complexity than the overall societal complex, with its inter-acting—and under the conditions of class society *conflictually interacting* social individual and collective subjects—the application of the *dialectical method* concerns the social and historical *specificity* of the relevant inter-changes and their ensuing outcome in the form of their *dynamic unfold-ing*. Thus, any attempt at reducing this vital dialectical approach to a fetishistic view of natural science, so as to be able to simplistically disqual-ify ideology on that ground, makes no sense at all.

With regard to ideology an important aspect of these issues becomes visible when we consider the scientific claims associated with the social sciences. The *pursuit of truth* in scientific inquiry can never be avoided. Thus, the critical examination of the claims regarding their own truth value is no less important in the social sciences than in the natural sciences.

Talking about the nature of an important domain of the social sciences, political economy, Marx firmly puts into relief the way in which *class struggle* has a major impact on the scientific potentialities and limitations of bourgeois political economy. Evidently such direct impact could not be found in *physics* and *chemistry* with which the earlier quoted Russian commentator on *Capital,* with Marx's approval, contrasted his own account of the Marxian dialectical method in 1871. This is how Marx characterizes the vital relationship between the pursuit of truth and the class struggle:

> In so far as Political Economy remains within the [bourgeois] horizon, in so far, i.e., as the capitalist regime is looked upon as the absolute final form of social production, instead of as a passing historical phase of its evolution, Political Economy can remain a *science* only so long as the *class struggle is latent* or manifests itself only in isolated and sporadic phenomena. [However, by 1830] in France and in England the bourgeoisie had conquered political power. Thenceforth, the class struggle, practically as well as theoretically, took on more and more outspoken and threatening forms. It sounded the knell of *scientific bourgeois economy.* It was thenceforth no longer a question, whether this theorem or that theorem was *true,* but whether it was *useful to capital or harmful,* expedient or inexpedient, politically dangerous or not. In place of disinterested inquirers, there were *hired prize fighters;* in place of *genuine scientific research,* the *bad conscience* and the evil intent of *apologetics.* . . . The Continental revolution of 1848–9 also had its reaction in England. Men who still claimed some scientific standing and aspired to be something more than mere sophists and sycophants of the ruling classes, tried to harmonise the Political Economy of capital with the claims, no longer to be ignored, of the proletariat. Hence a shallow syncretism, of which John Stuart Mill is the best representative. It is a declaration of bankruptcy by bourgeois economy, an event on which the great Russian scholar and critic, N. Tschernyschewsky, has thrown the light of a master mind in his "Outlines of Political Economy According to Mill."[49]

In this sense, the pursuit of truth is deeply affected by the class struggle. It can be affected both in a negative and in a positive sense. For the question itself is inseparable from the objective determinations of *class interest* and the theoretically valid—or indeed false—evaluation of their own class position by the thinkers concerned in relation to the *historically sustainable,* or on the contrary *historically retrograde,* role of the social class whose vantage point they adopt under the circumstances of the sharpening class struggle. Accordingly, when in place of pursuing the question of *truth* with scientific integrity—in accordance with the requirements of *genuine scientific research*—they reduce their own theoretical enterprise to "whether it was *useful to capital or harmful,* expedient or inexpedient," under the pressure of the sharpening class antagonism and the corresponding *vested interests* of their class, they turn themselves into *apologists* and *"hired prize fighters,"* abandoning thereby the vocation once clearly visible in, and beneficial to, the field of social science in which they are active. This is how the classical political economy of capital's ascending phase of development is transformed into the *"vulgar economy"* (in Marx's terminology) of the descending phase.

In contrast to the negative impact of these determinations in political economy and in other fields of the social sciences, the unfolding and sharpening of the class struggle can also be positive for theoretical development. For this reason it is impossible to imagine even the bare outlines of the Marxian approach, let alone its coherent synthesizing achievements, without the earlier undreamed-of stage in the historically developing class struggle—characterized at the time by the explosion of the deepening structural antagonisms of the system in the form of Europe-wide revolutions—without the epoch of socioeconomic and political ferment in which radically different theoretical insights had become feasible from a new vantage point. But again this question cannot be divorced from the objective historical viability and sustainability of the underlying social interests. This is why Marx insists in the same analysis of the necessary impact of the class struggle on the feasibility of lasting scientific achievements that the *criticism* of the bourgeois economy, in order to be theoretically viable, must be closely linked to the appropriate (i.e., in an *epochal sense* viable) social interests. As Marx puts it: "So far as such criticism represents a class, it can only represent the class whose vocation in history is the overthrow of the capitalist mode of production and the final abolition of all classes—the proletariat."[50]

Naturally, the question concerning the *pursuit of truth* applies also to the assessment of ideology. It is precisely that question which helps to draws the line of demarcation—in the sharpest possible way, in contrast to the confused obliteration of that important line of demarcation—between *positively sustainable ideology* on the one hand, and *ideology as false consciousness* on the other.

Of course, the pursuit of truth is not the only criterion by which we judge the historical validity of a forward-looking ideology. It is a *necessary* requirement that must be complemented by others, even if ideology as *false consciousness* falls far short of its claimed self-justification already in view of the necessary *absence of truth* from its core.

In this sense, one of the principal defining characteristics of ideology is that it is closely *practice-oriented.* No ideology can escape this kind of determination, arising from the historical conditions under which ideology, as a form of social consciousness, arises and must assert its claims to validity. This is so whether a particular ideology defines itself with regard to its fundamental *value-orientation* in the spirit of a forward-looking progressive vision, or, on the contrary, of a conservative retrograde view of the social order. For it happens to be an inescapable condition of our life that we live in—and have to confront the deep-seated problems and antagonisms of—*class society.*

Marx's way of highlighting the negative impact of the sharpening class struggle for the scientific potentialities of theories conceived from the vantage point of the ruling order—in contrast to less openly conflictual circumstances when "the *class struggle is latent* or manifests itself only in isolated and sporadic phenomena"—acquires its relevance on that inescapable historical ground. That ground is what radically separates *positive emancipatory ideology*—including the Marxian conception itself, passionately committed to the perspective of life made possible in the "new historic form"—from the *false consciousness* of socially apologetic, and in our historical epoch inevitably *capital-apologetic* ideology, wedded to the "hired prize-fighting" defense and *eternalized* maintenance of a historically *anachronistic,* and under the now prevailing determinations also tangibly *destructive,* order of social metabolic reproduction.

Accordingly, ideology is the *inescapable practical consciousness of class societies,* concerned with the articulation and assertion of *rival sets of values and strategies.* Not for the sake of some pseudo-scientific "detached theoretical reflection," and nothing else, self-delusorily fantasized about under the navel-gazing slogan of strictly "theoretical practice," but for the vital purpose of *fighting out the fundamental conflict* in the social arena, since the rival sets of values are inseparable from the objectively identifiable *hegemonic alternatives* of the given historical situation. This is how the *socialist vision*—embodied in a practical way in labor's *historically sustainable hegemonic alternative* to the established order, oriented with great programmatic precision toward the *substantive equality* of all social individuals in their radical confrontation with *capital's hierarchical exploitative domination* of society—firmly defines itself in class-conscious terms, embracing the class-determination of its *mandate* with defiant combativeness. Take away the class struggle from this picture—as all of the absurd projections of the *"third way"* attempted to do for a very long time, from the deceptive catchphrase of "people's capitalism" to its social democratic variants vainly propagandized in the course of the twentieth century—and you are left with nothing.

In truth, the antagonistic class determinations of our existing social order make it impossible to run away from the stark reality of the *structurally* anchored *epochal hegemonic conflict,* no matter how insistently the various *"pacificatory"* ideologies are trying to impose such perspective on the masses of the people. This is why the fundamental issues of our epoch must find their manifestations in the practice-oriented "ideological forms in which men become *conscious* of this conflict and *fight it out.*"[51] And that way of drawing the fundamental line of demarcation must remain the case for as long as humanity continues to live under the structurally determined conflicts and antagonisms of class society.

The role of ideology—as an integral part of the superstructure as such, in contrast to the crippling constraints of the capitalist historical specificity of the superstructure—can only change under radically different historical circumstances, in the sense in which it has been discussed in the last section, in the context of the dialectical relationship between the *historical* and the *transhistorical* aspects of the underlying issues. This is a matter not only of the vital objective structural determinations of the historical process but at the same time of the *conscious involvement* of the social individuals in realizing the positive potentialities of the unfolding historical conditions without which the new structural order could not be envisaged.

Understandably, the fundamental practical challenge for all those who identify themselves with a determinate set of values, whether conservative or progressive—including of course the values associated with an emancipatory vision of the envisaged alternative historical order—is how to fight out to a *successful conclusion* the major conflict in which the rival social forces are involved. Inevitably, the question of the *interest* pursued by the rival forces cannot be excluded from the assessment of the nature of the confrontation in question, with a view to judging the ideology of the contending classes. For the conflicting parties are materially, politically, and ideologically interested in the outcome of their hegemonic confrontation, asserting their position in favor of their own side, with all means at their disposal.

However, this circumstance by itself does not turn their ideology into *false consciousness*. What decides the issue one way or another is the *viability* and *sustainability* (or not) of the *position* that the rival social forces occupy in the *objective historical situation*. And that cannot be a matter of peremptorily proclaimed and imposed self-interest but must have some objective ground. What transforms the ideology of capital's personifications into sharply pronounced *false consciousness* is the *objectively prevailing historical anachronism* of the social order itself whose untenable values they continue to assert at a critical juncture of their system's descending phase of development. At a time, that is, when the once sustainable values of capital's successful productive expansion have been turned by the objectively unfolding historical process itself into the dangerous *counter-values* of an increasingly destructive way of controlling the mode of social metabolic reproduction.

This is why the question of *truth* must be eliminated from the picture by the "hired prizefighters" of capital, replaced by the narrow vested interests of their retrograde ideology articulated as false consciousness in place of the pursuit of genuine scientific research. What the "prizefighters" of capital, like Hayek, proclaim to be eternally valid under such circumstances is a particularly regressive type of false consciousness that—

in Marx's words—can assume even the form of *"bad conscience* and the evil intent of apologetics." This is so not simply as a result of some more or less easily corrigible personal failure but because the *capital system itself* had actually lost its once progressive *historical mandate* in the course of the objectively prevailing sociohistorical development. Thus, because of the transformation of the capital system as such into a *historical anachronism* which by its continued self-assertion, totally disregarding the consequences even in its impact on nature, threatens the very survival of humankind, it is for this reason that the ideology of the personifications of capital, whether they exercise their role as "captains of industry" or as "hired prizefighters" in the field of political economy, cannot be other than *false consciousness.*

The same criterion of *objective historical mandate* applies to the evaluation of the ideology of the rival social class that puts forward its claim and design for the institution of a sustainable alternative to capital's reproductive order. Accordingly, also in the case of those who identify themselves with the emancipatory values leading toward the "new historic form," the validity of the ideology embraced by them for the purpose of fighting out the hegemonic conflict to its successful conclusion will depend on the position they occupy in the objectively unfolding course of development.

Also in this regard the matter is decided on the ground of the objectively arising and challenging *mandate* and historical *vocation* of the social force called upon to institute a qualitatively different reproductive order. This means a historical mandate and vocation whereby the class opposed to capital defines its own ideology and emancipatory role in the sense not simply of overcoming its *class antagonist,* so as to entrench itself as the *new ruling class* in place of the defeated one, but by radically overcoming the historical anachronism of the control of societal reproduction on the structurally entrenched ground of antagonistic and productively wasteful class divisions and confrontations. This is why Marx defines the nature of the only historically viable form of *practical criticism* by insisting that "so far as such criticism represents a class, it can only represent the class whose *vocation in history* is the overthrow of the capitalist mode of production and the *final abolition of all classes*—the proletariat."

No doubt the historical role of a progressive social force cannot be abstracted from the evaluation and appreciation of what is involved in the practical realization of its *self-interest*. Indeed, the ideology of the class of labor fighting for its own emancipation cannot be even imagined without the effective exercise of such vital self-interest. Without it the advocacy of that ideology could amount to nothing more than some abstract speculative rhetorics, convincing nobody and achieving absolutely nothing. However, the fundamental issue in this respect is whether the self-interest in question *excludes* the legitimate interest of others or, on the contrary, is capable of *embracing and enhancing them* in the course of its own combative emancipatory self-assertion, as an integral part of the *overall perspective* guiding its own way of "fighting out the conflict." And that is, again, a matter of what is *objectively realizable* by capital's historical antagonist through the potentialities of the unfolding process. For the viability of the overall perspective adopted by capital's historical antagonist implies carrying alongside itself all those forces with which a common cause can be positively maintained in the course of the envisaged constitution of the "new historic order," in affinity with its own vision of the sustainable hegemonic alternative.

In view of the irreversible historical anachronism of the capital system that instituted the most sophisticated form of *class exploitation* in history, hitting in our time the buffers of its once overwhelmingly successful productive horizon, it is imperative to find a radically different solution to the assertion of the structurally prejudged self-interest of the ruling order, in opposition to the known forms of exploitative *vested interest*. But the only way to bring to a *common denominator* the *genuine self-interest* of the now subjected class of labor and *the general interest of society* as a whole—on the basis of the *objectively unfolding historical development,* beyond the antagonisms of the capital system's destructive second-order mediations—is by instituting the *substantive equality* of all social individuals feasible only in a classless society.

This means instituting substantive equality not as an abstract speculative desideratum but as the historical mandate and vocation emerging with practical force from the *objective trends of development* of the societal reproductive relations. The attained level of development in our time makes the institution of a productive order based on substantive equality *possible*, provided that this qualitatively different productive order is consciously planned and managed by the associated producers. At the same time, the destructive antagonisms and the catastrophic wastefulness of capital's irreversible historical anachronism makes the institution of that kind of social metabolic control also *necessary*. This is why the type of ideology "fighting out the conflict" toward that end, inasmuch as it is conscious of its essential transformatory mandate, cannot be identified with false consciousness. Only the crudest form of mechanical reductionism can equate ideology in general with false consciousness. For it is precisely the objective ground of tangible sociohistorical determination, in its inseparability from the dynamically unfolding trends of development, that forcefully counterposes the *positive* nature of emancipatory ideology to the *necessary false consciousness* of all ideology wedded to the cause of defending at all cost the interests of the established, historically anachronistic, order.

The criteria of viability are thus defined in terms of the objective historical trends of development. The same criteria were used by Marx when he contrasted his understanding of the nature of the communist movement with the idealistic rhetorics of Feuerbach and others. He talked about this problem already in one of his earliest writings in the same spirit as we have seen him discussing it in *Capital*. This is how he put it then: "Communism is for us not a *state of affairs* which is to be established, an *ideal* to which reality [will] have to adjust itself. We call communism the *real* movement which abolishes the present state of things. The conditions of this movement result from the now existing premise."[52]

Admittedly, the difficulties that need to be overcome include the weighty circumstance, put into relief by Marx, that since the ruling class controls the means of material production it can also control the means of intellectual production. Accordingly, "The ideas of the ruling class are in every epoch the ruling ideas."[53] However, the control of intellectual production by the ruling class, no matter how powerful it might be under determinate sociohistorical circumstances in material and political terms, can never be *absolute*. Marx's revolutionary lifework itself is a clear demonstration of this important—and for the ruling order rather uncomfortable—truth.

The domination of the ideas of the ruling class cannot be absolute precisely because the objectively unfolding trends of historical transformation—which greatly enhance the productive potentialities of the capital system in its ascending phase of development—make that impossible when the modality of capital's *"productive destruction"* is objectively turned into *destructive production* at the stage when the same system reaches its irreversible *historical anachronism*. Nevertheless, even under such historical circumstances the required fundamental change cannot be accomplished without bringing into play the *active role of ideology*. To be sure, ideology not as false consciousness, but as the *emancipatory ideology* deeply engaged in the *pursuit of truth*. Indeed, the form of ideology engaged in the pursuit of truth as the necessary condition for "fighting out the conflict to its successful conclusion," in the interest of establishing a historically sustainable social reproductive order.

4.4 Radical Transformation of the Legal and Political Superstructure

Several aspects of the necessary "withering away of the state," as envisaged by Marx, are discussed in the last chapter of this book. In the present context only the most comprehensive dimension of the complex of problems to which the historically specific issues of the capitalist state belong can be focused upon. This is done in direct relationship to the central theme of the present chapter, concerned with the dialectical interchange between the material transformations and the ideological forms. For it is precisely such dialectical interchange that sets the overall historical boundaries within which the unavoidable challenge for the withering away of the state, through the radical transformation of the legal and political superstructure as a whole, must be faced and accomplished in due course.

As we know, the modern state was not formed as a *result* of some direct economic determination, as a mechanical superstructural outcrop, in conformity to a reductivist view of the supposedly *one-sided material domination* of society, as presented in the vulgar Marxist conception of these matters. Rather, it was dialectically constituted through its necessary *reciprocal interaction* with capital's highly complex material ground. In this sense, the state was not only *shaped* by the economic foundations of society, but it was also *most actively shaping* the multifaceted reality of capital's reproductive manifestations throughout their historical transformations, both in the ascending and in the descending phase of development of the capital system.

We have also seen that in this complex dialectical process of reciprocal interchange the historical and the transhistorical determinations have been closely intertwined,[54] even if in the course of the capital system's descending phase of development we had to witness a growing violation of the historical dialectic, especially under the impact of the deepening *structural crisis*. For the defense of the established mode of societal reproduction at all cost, no matter how wasteful and destructive its impact by now even on nature, can only underscore the *historical anachronism* and the corresponding untenability of a once all-powerful mode of productive societal reproduction, which tries to extend its power in a *"globalized form"* at a time when the *absolute systemic limits*[55] of capital are being activated on a global scale.

Moreover, the fact that the historical phase of modern imperialism that used to prevail prior to and during the Second World War—a form of imperialism in which a number of *rival powers* asserted themselves in the world, in contention with one another, as theorized by Lenin during the First World War—is now replaced by the *global hegemonic imperialism* of the United States of America, attempting to impose itself everywhere as *the global state of the capital system in general*, does not solve any of the underlying contradictions at all. On the contrary, it can only highlight the gravity of the dangers inseparable from the structural crisis of capital's mode of controlling societal reproduction. For the imposition of global hegemonic imperialism of our time by the now dominant military power is no less untenable in the longer run than the traditional imperialist state rivalry that produced two devastating world wars in the twentieth century. Far from successfully constituting the state of the capital system in general, as a vain attempt to remedy capital's great historic failure on that score, the global hegemonic imperialism of the United States, with its growing military domination of the planet as an *aggressive nation-state*, the present phase of imperialism is the potentially deadliest one.

As mentioned already, in the course of the capital system's historical unfolding the legal and political superstructure assumed an ever more *preponderant* role. The present phase of global hegemonic imperialism is the most extreme manifestation of that, marking at the same time the end of a, for the time being practicable, but in the longer run absolutely untenable, road, given the still prevailing relation of forces in which some countries with massive population and matching military potential, including China, are marginalized. For nothing could be more preponderant in terms of its domination of all aspects of social life—from the elementary conditions of material reproduction and their grave impact on nature all the way to the most mediated forms of intellectual production—than the operation of a state system that directly and indirectly threatens the whole of humanity with the fate of self-destruction. Even a return to the formerly experienced violent state confrontations is feasible in the not too distant future, which would certainly terminate human life on this planet, if the destructive antagonisms of the capital system are not resolved in a historically sustainable way within the time still at our disposal. Accordingly, only a *qualitative transformation* of the established legal and political superstructure in its entirety, together with the radical restructuring of its no longer viable material ground, can show a way out of this blind alley. This means an *all-embracing transformation* which is conceivable only in the spirit of the envisaged socialist hegemonic alternative to capital's mode of social metabolic control.

The historically specific and necessarily transient, no matter how preponderant, legal and political superstructure of capital emerged in the course of systemic development in conjunction with some vital structural requirements of the unfolding overall societal complex.

In sharp contrast to the feudal type of material productive and political relationship that had to be replaced by the capital system, a *direct political control* of the countless particular productive units—the locally articulated *microcosms* of the newly developing material ground, with its *abstract* and "free" labor force (i.e., abstract also in the sense of being propertyless, because totally deprived of the means of production, and "free" in its concomitant hierarchical structural determination of being forced by *economic compulsion,* and not by *direct political bondage,* to put its labor power at the service of the new productive system)—was neither feasible nor conducive to the irresistible process of capital expansion. It was controlled in a most *contradictory* way by the individual "personifications of capital"[56] as masters of their *particular* enterprises, who, however, could by no means control, as individual capitalists acting in the economic domain, the capital system as a whole.

Thus in the course of historical development we witnessed the emergence of an inherently *centrifugal* material productive system in which the particular microcosms dynamically interacted with one another, and with society as a whole, by following their self-oriented and self-expansionary capital interests. This kind of productive practice was, of course, fictionalized in the form of the claimed "sovereignty" of capital's individual personifications, and even idealized as late as the last third of the eighteenth century by one of the greatest political economists of all time, Adam Smith, with the naïve stipulative suggestion according to which it was necessary to *exclude the politicians* from the reproductive logic of the system, since the system itself was supposed to function insuperably well under the beneficial guidance of the mythical "invisible hand." However, no fictional postulate of "entrepreneurial sovereignty," nor indeed the idealized projection of the mysterious, yet by definition necessarily and forever successful "invisible hand," could in actuality remedy the *structural defect* of the capital system's productive microcosms: their self-oriented and self-asserting *centrifugality,* devoid of a systemically tenable overall/totalizing *cohesion.*

This is where we can clearly see the *necessary reciprocal interrelationship* between the unfolding and *systemically consolidating* material reproductive ground of capital and its historically specific state formation. For it was inconceivable that the new modality of reproduction, with its inherently centrifugal material productive microcosms, should be able to consolidate itself in actuality as a *comprehensive system,* without acquiring an appropriate *cohesive dimension.* At the same time, it was no less inconceivable that the required totalizing/cohesive dimension—the answer to the *objective imperative* to remedy in some way, no matter how problematically, the *structural defect* of potentially most disruptive centrifugality—should be able to emerge from the *direct materiality* of the productive practices pursued by the individual personifications of capital in the particular economic microcosms.

As far as the material productive units of capital were concerned, the size of the enterprises was (and remains) of secondary importance in this respect. As we know only too well, even in our time the giant quasi-monopolistic transnational corporations, characterized by an extremely high degree of the centralization of capital, retain the severe structural defect in question. Thus, given the *insuperably centrifugal* determination of capital's material productive microcosms, only the modern state could assume and fulfill the required vital function of being the *overall command structure* of the capital system. The *cohesive dimension,* without which even the potentially most dynamic type of productive units could not constitute a sustainable reproductive *system,* was therefore acquired by capital's mode of controlling societal reproduction in this historically specific and unique form.

Accordingly, the critically important process of capital expansion—not simply with regard to the increasing size of the particular productive units but, much more importantly, in terms of the ever more intensive penetration of the new reproductive principles, with the unchallengeable domination of *exchange-value over use-value,* together with its fundamental *corollaries*[57]—into every domain, was made possible through this *reciprocal interchange* between the economic microcosms and the legal and political superstructure, producing thereby capital's mode of social metabolic reproduction in its integrality as a *cohesive overall system.* Naturally, the dialectical reciprocity had to prevail in the other direction also, through the dynamic transformation and massive expansion of capital's state formation itself.

Such transformation and expansion of the legal and political superstructure had to take place parallel to the growing centralization and concentration of capital in the economic microcosms. For this kind of—in terms of its self-serving expansionary logic in principle unlimitable—economic expansion could not help putting ever greater requirements on the all-embracing political dimension of this historically unique modality of social metabolic control. In this sense the modern capitalist state was expected to favorably respond, in a most active way, to the apparently unlimitable expansionary demands emanating from the material basis of societal reproduction.

The state was required to fulfill its dynamic—and, despite all neoliberal mythology of "pushing back the boundaries of the state," increasingly more *directly interventionist* role during the descending phase of the capital system's development—in accordance with its own logic. And that logic could only amount to ever greater legal/political, and even military (hence in the case of the most powerful states inevitably imperialist), preponderance. Moreover, this kind of development could be readily imposed on society only for as long as fulfilling the state's all-encroaching role, with its reciprocal interchange with capital's material ground, was practicable under the globally prevailing circumstances. That is what had to be rendered untenable in our time through the direct military danger of humanity's self-destruction, on the one hand, and through the ongoing destruction of nature, on the other.

However, well before the activation of capital's absolute limits, in close conjunction with the—in earlier historical epochs inconceivable—development of the material reproductive units of the system, the modern state had acquired an ever greater importance and dynamism of its own. In this important sense, as a most powerful articulation and assertion of its own logic, the historically unfolding modern capitalist state cannot be abstracted from the reciprocal determinations and the objective dynamism of the developing capital system as a whole. Accordingly, the ever more powerful modern state is intelligible in its historical emergence and transformations only as constituting an *organic unity* with the system as a whole, inseparably from its continuing interrelationship with the constantly expanding material reproductive domain.

This is the tangible reality of capital's advancement, sustainable throughout the ascending phase of its systemic development as a dynamic reproductive order. Indeed, it cannot be stressed strongly enough: the unfolding productive development of the capital system was a historic advancement that would be inconceivable without the massive contribution by the legal and political superstructure to the all-embracing structural determinations of the system as a whole.

However, it must be kept in mind that the earlier mentioned tendency of capital's legal and political superstructure *to acquire an all-pervasive preponderance* was an essential condition of the same advancement right from the beginning. Nor can we ignore the necessary corollary of this type of systemic development. Namely, that the *tendency* to all-pervasive preponderance ultimately had to run *out of control,* carrying with it great problems for the future. For the impact of the tendentially all-encroaching legal and political superstructure on overall societal development was very different in the two contrasting phases of historical transformation.

In the ascending phase of capital's development the remedy offered to the structural defect of centrifugality of the particular material reproductive units—by the state providing the missing *cohesive* dimension in the form of a most dynamic overall political command structure—*objectively enhanced* the positive expansionary potentialities of the system in its entirety. Paradoxically, the state's growing appetite for the appropriation of significant amounts of resources, in the interest of its own enlargement, was for a long historical period an integral part of this reproductive dynamics, in that it was beneficial to the internal material expansion as well as to the global extension of capital's social metabolic order.

By contrast, in the descending phase of the capital system the ultimately incurable *negative* constituents of this kind of *state-imperatival* involvement and the corresponding transformation of societal reproduction have become ever more dominant, and with regard to their growing *wastefulness and destructiveness* totally untenable in the longer run. Imposing such wastefulness and destructiveness on society under the now prevailing circumstances, while brushing aside all concern about the consequences, would be impossible without the most active, and often directly authoritarian, role of the capitalist state. The earlier mentioned direct state interventionism in the economy on a growing scale, and the escalating military adventurism justified under false pretenses, are the necessary manifestations of the underlying contradictions. This is why the radical transformation of the legal and political superstructure is a vital requirement for the constitution of a historically sustainable hegemonic alternative to the capital system.

We have seen earlier how forcefully capital's legal and political superstructure encroached upon, and continues to dominate, every domain of social consciousness.[58] The various practical discourses without which societal reproduction could not function at all are now closely linked to and deeply affected by the overpowering determinations of the legal and political superstructure. In this sense the cause of human emancipation inevitably requires also the liberation of the various practical discourses from the severe limitations imposed upon them, on the basis of capital's vested interests, by the increasingly preponderant legal and political superstructure itself.

That goes not only for the need to emancipate moral, political and aesthetic discourse[59] from their domination by state-imperatival determinations, but also for religious discourse and liberation theology, that is, liberation theology committed to fighting for the emancipation of the countless millions of the exploited and the oppressed. Marx's remark about religion is often deliberately quoted in a truncated form, cynically omitting the continuation of his words on "the opiate of the people," when he strongly underscores that religion is *"the heart of a heartless world."* That role of religion is what makes it possible for socialists to create common ground with liberation theologians who try to live up to the requirement of uniting theory and practice, in the Marxian sense of not only interpreting but also changing the world, by dedicating themselves to the cause of human emancipation in our heartless world.

The increasingly negative role of the legal and political superstructure in the material reproductive processes, prevailing in the course of the capital system's descending phase of development, is not only obvious but also most dangerous. For it affects directly, in the literal sense of the term, the prospects of humanity's survival. The historical unfolding of *monopolistic imperialism* in the descending phase clearly indicates the perilous nature of these developments, including the two world wars of the twentieth century, in addition to countless smaller ones, and the ultimate danger of total human annihilation if the system's antagonistic contradictions are not overcome in the not too distant future.

Moreover, in our time the capitalist state is even the *direct purchaser* of the catastrophically wasteful *destructive production* of the military-industrial complex. In this way the modern state of the capital system not only facilitates (by means of its growing legislative jungle) but also hypocritically legitimates the most fraudulent—and of course immensely profitable—capital expansion of militarist production in the name of the "national interest."

Contrary even to the most elementary *economic rationality*, it does not seem to matter to the personifications of capital today that *global material bankruptcy* looms large at the end of such a road. For, in tune with it, they are already bent on imposing moral and political bankruptcy on society, in the form of the system's *counter-values* even in the form of genocidal wars, for the sake of eternalizing capital's historically no longer tenable domination. Thus, totally false priorities of direct military destruction must prevail, under the false pretenses decreed by the preponderant state, together with the ongoing destruction of nature. Moreover, as a bitter irony, humanity is forced to suffer in our time even the callously imposed *global food crisis,* with the prospect of causing the starvation of countless millions, *at the peak of capital's productive development.* This is the dehumanizing reality of the established order's "all-round beneficial globalization," putting into relief the completion of capital's destructive full circle.

The radical transformation of the legal and political superstructure can only be accomplished in its actually developing historical perspective by countering the destructive antagonisms of the established order as a mode of social metabolic reproduction from the standpoint of its feasible hegemonic alternative.

The accomplishment of this task requires, in due course and on a continuing basis, the *conscious management* of the totality of societal reproductive practices to be able to overcome the boundless irrationality of the now existing order. For the unique way in which the structural defect of centrifugality had been managed in the course of capital's historical development could only mean the *complete alienation* of the powers of *overall decision making* from the social individuals.

There could be no exception to that. The *state-imperatival* overall decision making of the capital system, as a most problematical remedy to centrifugality that in due course had to run out of control, was in no way the realization of the comprehensive vision of a conscious social subject. On the contrary, it was the necessary imposition of an objective, but in the final analysis blind, *structural imperative*—the lopsided reflection and self-serving preservation of the underlying *structural defect*—in antagonistic opposition to the only feasible *real subject* of historically sustainable societal reproduction, labor.[60] Even the particular economic personifications of capital had to be strictly mandated to carry out the *structural imperatives* of their system. For in the event of failing to do so, they would quickly find themselves marginalized in, and—as bankrupt "surplus to requirements"—even completely ejected from, the material reproduction process. Thus, the modern state, in its inseparability from the necessary material ground of the capital system as such, had to be the *paradigm of alienation* regarding the powers of *comprehensive/totalizing decision making.*

Since the combined totality of the material reproductive determinations and the all-embracing political command structure of the modern state *together* constitute the overpowering reality of the capital system, it is necessary to submit to a radical critique the complex *interdeterminations* of the entire system in order to be able to envisage a historically sustainable societal change. This means that the historically specific overall material articulation of the capital system must be *qualitatively* changed, through a laborious process of comprehensive restructuring, no less than its corresponding multifaceted political dimension. Fulfilling the task of a coherent socialist transformation of the direct materiality of the established order is absolutely vital in this respect.

The necessary radical transformation of capital's preponderant legal and political superstructure is not conceivable in any other way. Partial political changes, including even the legislative expropriation of the private capitalist expropriators of the fruits of labor, can constitute only the first step in the envisaged direction. For such measures are more or less easily reversible, in the interest of capitalist restoration, if the *combined totality* of the deep-rooted—direct material as well as the corresponding but highly mediated political—interdeterminations of the system are dealt with in a politically reduced voluntaristic way, even if that kind of approach is pursued under the weight of difficult historical circumstances. Our painful historical experience in the twentieth century provided an unmistakable warning in that regard.

In our own time we see a particularly damaging *symbiosis* between the legal/political framework and the material productive as well as the financial dimension of the established order, managed often with utterly corrupt practices by the privileged personifications of capital. For no matter how transparently corrupt such practices might be, they are fully in tune with the *institutionalized counter-values* of the system, and therefore legally quite permissible, thanks to the facilitating role of the state's *impenetrable legislative jungle* in the financial domain. Fraudulence, in a great variety of its practicable forms, is the normality of capital. Its extremely destructive manifestations are by no means confined to the operation of the military-industrial complex. By now the direct role of the capitalist state in the parasitic world of finance is not only fundamentally important, in view of its forbiddingly all-pervasive magnitude, but also potentially catastrophic.

The gravity of this fact has been recently highlighted by the monumental financial crisis in the United States of America in the banking and mortgage sector (in June–July 2008), including the vainly camouflaged bankruptcy and the de facto default of some giant companies, like Bear Stearns, Indy Mac Bancorp of California, and, above all, Fannie Mae (founded as the rock of the more affordable and safe housing enterprise during Roosevelt's presidency, in 1938) and Freddie Mac. Under the present circumstances of crisis even the customarily most apologetic and hypocritical economic and political weekly magazine of London, *The Economist*, has been forced to concede that "At Fannie and Freddie— and, shockingly at the investment banks—*the profits were privatized, but the risks were socialised.*"[61]

At the same time, this is how *The Economist* tries to justify in a transparently cynical but utterly ridiculous way the massive state intervention that runs counter to all neoliberal self-mythology:

> Capitalism rests on a *clear principle:* those who get the profits should take the pain. For the system to work, bankers sometimes need to lose their jobs and investors their shirts. Yet were a collapsing Bear Sterns or Fannie Mae to sow destruction *for the sake of a principle,* it would impose a terrible price in lost jobs and output on everyone else. The unpalatable truth is that by the time a financial crisis hits, the state often has to *compromise*—to impose as much pain as it can, *of course,* but to shoulder a large part of the losses nonetheless.[62]

The total hypocrisy of talking about "principle" while dangling in front of the reader *The Economist*'s own bleeding heart about "job losses," which are supposed to quickly justify discarding the—utterly fictitious, for never really observed—"clear principle of capitalism"! It shows the unquestioning subservience of the ideological "hired prize fighters of capital" (in Marx's words) to their system. Even the use of the words "compromise" and "of course" is revealing. For the state's so-called "compromise" over dishing out pain "of course," and at the same time shouldering "a large part of the losses"—as if the state had a pocket filled with the fruits of its own productive efforts—"gently" avoids to mention, or rather, characteristically diverts attention from, the question of who suffers the pain, and who really pays for the losses, both for the massive financial losses and for the concomitant even greater job losses in the capitalist economy as a whole. This time really *of course* neither the bankers, nor the giant U.S. mortgage companies, like Fannie Mae and Freddie Mac (which were corruptly supported and generously supplied with profitable guarantees by the American state's *legislative jungle* in the first place, as well as through the personal services of political corruption)[63] and least of all the capitalist state itself. The burden for the growing pain and for the monumental losses must be carried by the great masses of the people.

Under the circumstances of the capital system's deepening *structural crisis*, understandably but in no way justifiably, without the most active facilitating and supporting role of the capitalist state, in its pronounced *symbiotic* relationship with the incorrigible material framework of *destructive production* in every domain, including the parasitic world of financial speculation, the extremely problematical reality of the now ruling social metabolic order could not be maintained in dominance for any length of time. Its explosive contradictions erupt from time to time even in the form of headline catching scandals with global ramifications, like the notorious case of Enron, as well as in major economic crises threatening the "meltdown" of the international financial system. However, we have seen so far only the tip of the colossal iceberg under the water level of capital's poisonous sea. No wonder, therefore, that as a rejoinder to the latest spectacular crisis "traders in the credit-default swaps market have recently made *bets on the unthinkable: that America may default on its debt.*"[64] Such traders react even to events of this nature and gravity the only possible way they can: squeezing profit out of it.

The trouble for the capital system is, though, that the *default of America is not unthinkable at all*. On the contrary, it is—and it has been for a very long time—a coming certainty. This is why I wrote many years ago that

In a world of financial *insecurity* nothing suits better the practice of gambling with astronomical and criminally unsecured sums on the world's stock exchanges—foreshadowing an earthquake of magnitude 9 or 10 on the Financial Richter Scale—than to call the enterprises which engage in such gambling *"Securities* Management"; ... When exactly and in what form—of which there can be several, more or less brutal, varieties—the U.S. will default on its astronomical debt, cannot be seen at this point in time. There can be only two certainties in this regard. The first is that the *inevitability of the American default* will deeply affect everyone on this planet. And the second, that the preponderant hegemonic power position of the U.S. will continue to be asserted in every way, so as to make the rest of the world pay for the American debt for as long as it is capable of doing.[65]

Naturally, the aggravating problem today is that the rest of the world—even with the historically most ironical massive Chinese contribution to the balance sheet of the American Treasury—is less and less capable of filling the "black hole" produced on an ever-growing scale by America's insatiable appetite for debt financing, as demonstrated by the global reverberations of the recent U.S. mortgage and bank crisis. This brings the necessary default of America, in one of its "more or less brutal varieties," that much closer.

The truth of this painful matter is that there can be no way out of these ultimately suicidal contradictions, which are inseparable from the *imperative of endless capital expansion*—arbitrarily and mystifyingly confounded with *growth as such*—without radically changing our mode of social metabolic reproduction by adopting the much needed responsible and rational practices of *the only viable economy*.[66] However, this is where the overwhelming impediment of capital's self-serving interdeterminations must be confronted. For the absolutely necessary adoption and the appropriate future development of the only viable economy is inconceivable without the radical transformation of the legal and political superstructure of our existing social order.

To understand the great difficulties involved in attempting to overcome the *vicious circle* of capital's self-serving interdeterminations, in their inseparability from the preponderant power of the legal and political superstructure, the unique character and bewilderingly complex artic-ulation of this system must be put in its historical perspective.

The formerly unimaginable dynamism of the capital system unfolded on the basis of the radical separation of productive activity from the pri-mary determinations of *use* and the corresponding degree of *self-sufficiency* in the former (feudal and earlier) reproductive units, in the interest of ever enlarged commodity exchange. This meant the total subordination of *use-value* to the unlimitable requirements of *exchange-value* without which *generalized commodity production* would be impossible. For the paradoxi-cal, and indeed in an ultimately untenable way contradictory nature of cap-ital's mode of societal reproduction is that "all commodities are non-use-values for their owners, and use-values for their non-owner. Consequently they *must* all change hands. But this change of hands is what constitutes their exchange, and the latter puts them in relation with each other as val-ues. Hence commodities must be realised as *values* before they can be realised as *use-values*."[67] Inevitably, therefore, generalized commodity pro-duction is dominated by an *abstract formalized value-relation* that must be sustained on an appropriate *economy-wide scale,* as a vital condition of its operational feasibility and continued expansion.

However, the earlier discussed *structural defect* of this societal repro-ductive order—the *insuperable centrifugality* of its economic micro-cosms—*prevents* the realization of the dominant value-relation on the necessary economy-wide scale, contradicting thereby capital's systemic potentiality. For the value-relation must be in principle unlimitable in accordance with the innermost determinations of the unfolding capital system, so as to become a *cohesive system.* Thus, since the cohesion required cannot be achieved on the *substantive* basis of the self-expan-sionary material microcosms themselves, only the *formal universality* of the *state imperatival* determinations can complete capital's mode of social metabolic reproduction as a system, thereby offering a way out from the contradiction of insuperable centrifugality. And even this unique way out is feasible only on a strictly temporary basis. Until, that is, the *overall structural/systemic limits* of this kind of societal reproduction are historically reached, both in terms of the necessary *material* requirements of its unlimitable self-expansionary productive microcosms (deeply affecting in a destructive way nature itself), as well as in relation to the *nationally constrained legal and political superstructure* that brings the productive units together and drives them forward in its own way, as their comprehensive/totalizing power of decision making and condition of systemic advancement.

However, the inexorable self-expansionary drive of the material productive units is not brought to a point of rest by being contained within the national boundaries. The wishful projection of *unproblematical globalization,* most powerfully promoted today by the United States as the dominant *aggressive nation-state,* is the manifestation of this contradiction, in view of capital's historic failure to create the *state of the capital system as such.* But even if the existing nation-states could be somehow put under a common umbrella—by military force or by some kind of formal political agreement—that could only be ephemeral, leaving the underlying contradiction unresolved. For it would still maintain the innermost *structural defect* of the capital system—the *necessary self-expansionary centrifugality* of its material reproductive microcosms—in its place, totally devoid of an effective and cohesive operational rationality. Indeed, it would remove even the limited and fairly *spontaneous negative cohesion* in the face of an identified "common enemy," generated within the particular national boundaries on the basis of some shared interests and/or grievances, as demonstrated under the circumstances of a major emergency, like war.

That kind of relatively spontaneous negative cohesion can be effective not only *across class boundaries,* as experienced in a disheartening way in which the European social democratic parties sided with their class antagonists at the outbreak of the First World War, but also among the otherwise competitively/adversarially related personifications of capital in positions of key economic command in the particular economic enterprises, witnessed during the Second World War.[68] The relatively spontaneous cohesive impact of facing the declared "common enemy" was attempted to be even morally justified, although in a most questionable way, in view of its destructive implications, by Hegel himself. He retorted—in undisguised ironical reference to Kant's postulate of a League of Nations that was expected to guarantee world peace—by saying that "corruption in nations would be the product of prolonged, let alone 'perpetual' peace."[69]

In our time the major military undertaking in the name of the so-called "war on terror," without a commensurate identifiable enemy, as pursued and imposed by the dominant imperialist nation-state of North America on others, lacks the ability to generate even the minimal negative cohesion among the populations of its dubiously "willing" partners; and in virtue of the untenable self-definition and justification of the real purpose behind such operations also among a most significant part of its own population. This is how the promotion of "beneficial globalization" reveals itself as the imperialist adventure of the militarily for the time being most powerful nation-state, in accordance with capital's self-contradictory logic, putting into relief not an isolated and contingent development but a particularly grave manifestation of the deepening structural crisis of the established order of social metabolic reproduction.

In their historical perspective the developments leading to this kind of perilous blind alley are inseparable from the fundamental contradiction manifest in the way in which the *substantive* is reduced to the *formal* in the capital system. To put it more precisely, capital's systemic development necessarily involves the fetishistic reduction of the *substantive determinations* of objects and social relations into *formally generalizable* characteristics, both in the material reproductive domain and at the level of the corresponding legal and political superstructure. For that is the only way in which the self-oriented and self-asserting *partiality* of capital's commodity relations, centrifugally operated in the productive *microcosms*—requiring in and through their interchanges the apparently absurd *equation of incommensurability*[70]—can be transformed into the *pseudo-universality* of the formally homogenized abstract value-relations coalescing into a systemic *macrocosm*.[71] And all within the all-embracing framework of the modern capitalist state's legal and political totalizing practices that rest on *formal* principles of claimed *universal rationality*. That is what Hegel proclaims to amount to *"the rationality of actuality."*

Hegel asserts: "The nation-state is mind in its *substantive rationality* and immediate *actuality* and is therefore the *absolute power* on earth. It follows that every state is *sovereign* and autonomous against its neighbours. It is entitled in the first place and *without qualification* to be sovereign from their point of view, i.e. to be recognized by them as sovereign."[72] However, he must introduce a qualification immediately by adding that "this title is *purely formal* . . . and recognition is *conditional* on the neighbouring state's judgement and will."[73]

This solution of working with "purely formal" principles leaves the door wide open to the most violent effective *denial of other nations' sovereignty* through war, fully approved by Hegel himself, in total agreement with the normal practice of capital's inter-state relations up to the present time. And this is how Hegel rationalizes the most *arbitrary* practice of breaking the "purely formal" treaty obligations by the more powerful states at the expense of those they can subdue:

> A state through its subjects has widespread connexions and many-sided interests, and these may be readily and considerably injured; but it remains *inherently indeterminable* which of these injuries is to be regarded as a specific breach of treaty or as an injury to the honour and autonomy of the state. The reason for this is that a state may regard *its infinity and honour* as a stake in each of its concerns, *however minute,* and it is all the more inclined to susceptibility to injury the more its strong individuality is impelled as a result of *long domestic peace* to seek and create a *sphere of activity abroad.*[74]

Thus even one of the greatest thinkers of all history is pushed to the edge of cynical apologetics when he has to find justification for the crude violation of his own solemn principle: the unqualified sovereignty and unconditional autonomy of the nation-state. For he has to do that fully in tune with the *colonial imperialist* expansionary phase of the capital system's development, decreeing that "Europe is absolutely the end of history" and accepting the imposition of extreme forms of injury—imposed "in rational actuality"—on the weaker states. Characteristically, Hegel must adopt such a position when he formulates his monumental historical conception from the vantage point of capital, with its state theory finding self-justification even for the most brutal deeds of the powerful on the ground of the "*inherently indeterminable* injuries" which can be (and of course are) arbitrarily proclaimed by the "world historical nations."

Naturally, it is utterly incoherent to predicate the all-round beneficial condition of globalization and the permanence of peace required for it in positive international relations while maintaining, as we know from historical experience, the unrestrainable self-expansionary dynamics of the capital system's material reproductive basis. To introduce the required change in the domain of interstate relations, in order to realize the now absolutely imperative condition of safeguarding peace on a global scale, it would be necessary to radically reconstitute the elementary operative principles of the capital system's material practices, from the smallest cells of the productive microcosms to the most comprehensive structures of transnational production and international trade, together with the entire legal and political framework of the modern state. Any other way of projecting successful globalization and the concomitant enduring peace everywhere in the world is at best only a pipe dream. And that kind of radical reconstitution of the operative principles of the capital system would require the transfer of the effective *power of decision making* to the social individuals on a *substantive* basis in all fields of activity. For capital's preponderant legal and political superstructure, which is incorrigible within its own terms of reference, as the failure of reformism amply demonstrated it in the course of the twentieth century, had been articulated right from the beginning on the basis of the same contradictory and ultimately quite untenable transformation of the *substantive* into the *formal.* Inevitably, that kind of transformation must prevail in every domain of the system's material reproductive dimension, fatefully undermining in the end the historical process. Thus the necessary reconstitution of the historical dialectic is inconceivable without establishing and maintaining human relations on a sustainable ground, within the overall framework of a radically different mode of social metabolic reproduction.

The dramatic expansion of production *for exchange,* under capital's unfolding social order, was feasible only through the satisfaction of two vital conditions:

1. The establishment of a *general framework* of operation for material production which would render possible, as a matter of everyday routine, the *profitable equalization of incommensurabilities* everywhere, in tune with the great expansionary dynamism implicit in the radical shift from *use-value to exchange-value* under the new system. This shift made it possible to bring into the domain of profitable capital-expansion not only the virtually inexhaustible range of *"artificial*

appetites" but even objects and relations formerly unimaginable to be subsumed under the determinations of "prosaic" commercial exploitation, including, among others, the creation and distribution of works of art.

2. The *political ability to secure* the beneficial self-expansionary interchanges of the particular productive microcosms among themselves, within the well-expandable and properly protected boundaries of the idealized market, in sharp contrast to the dangers of arbitrary interference encountered under the conditions of "feudal anarchy." The constitution of the *modern nation-state*, and the final articulation of its inherent logic within the framework of *imperialist rivalry*—ultimately exploding in the form of two devastating world wars—was the necessary consequence of the underlying process.

With regard to the first vital condition, the apparently insoluble problem of *incommensurability* defeated even a giant of philosophy like Aristotle. He perceived with great insight the contradiction inherent in the postulated equalization of incommensurabilities well before a perverse but fetishistically working solution could be provided for it. That kind of solution had been instituted through the practically dominant reductive transformation of the virtually infinite variety of *use-values* into the abstract determinations of uniformly manipulable *value*, under the conditions of *generalized commodity production* many centuries later.

Aristotle's defeat in this respect was unavoidable, despite the fact that he was "the first to analyze so many forms, whether of thought, society, or nature, and amongst them also the form of value."[75] For Aristotle, whose basic category was *substance*, found it impossible to come to terms with the mystifying problem of the formalized equalization of substantively/qualitatively incommensurable objects. The idea of equalization objectively grounded on the labor power of politically equal human beings was well beyond the horizon of thinkers even of his greatness in a productive order based on slavery.[76] Thus Aristotle had to conclude his reflections on the subject of equalizing a house with five beds (the example he used) by saying somewhat naïvely that it is "in reality impossible that such unlike things can be qualitatively *commensurable*, i.e., qualitatively equal.

Such an equalization can only be something foreign to their real nature, consequently only '*a makeshift for practical purposes.*'"[77]

Another fundamental reason why Aristotle could not contemplate the equalization of incommensurabilities was his concept of the human being as a "*zoon politikon*"—a social animal—which implied the necessary integration of humans in their society. This vision could not have been in greater contrast to the image of the *isolated individual* fit for the proper operation of generalized commodity production. Such production was feasible only on the ground of the homogenizing reduction of productive human beings—with their *qualitative/substantive* determinations—to the condition of *quantitatively commensurable abstract labor.* In that way the particular individuals could be conveniently inserted into the—*economically forced* but *formally equitable*—*contractual* framework of capital's social reproductive order. For characteristically in that order the capitalists and the workers, as isolated individuals, were supposed to enjoy a fictional "equality as buyers and sellers," when in actuality they occupied radically different power positions in the process of societal reproduction.

Yet their social positions were rationalized as being formally/contractually equal from the vantage point and in the interest of the unfolding capital relation, in the spirit of the abstract "Rights of Man." Accordingly, in capital's material reproductive microcosms, thanks to the reduction of living human beings to the condition of abstract labor, the practical commensurability of the qualitatively incommensurable use values—by turning them into abstract quantifiable value—became possible not as a dubious "makeshift for practical purposes" but as fully in keeping with the law of value. In this way abstract labor became both the *objective ground* and the *measure* by which the equalization of incommensurabilities could be operated, dynamically subordinating the production of *use-value* to the requirements of *exchange-value* in the fetishistic interest of ongoing capital expansion.

This is how the first vital condition for the dramatic expansion of production for exchange—and therewith the required subsumption and domination of use-value by exchange-value—has been satisfied through the sustainable equalization of incommensurabilities in capital's socioeconomic order.

Fulfilling the second vital condition mentioned above—the *political ability to secure* the beneficial self-expansionary interchanges of the particular productive microcosms among themselves—was equally important for the development of capital's new modality of production as a coherent system.

Understandably, the necessary boundaries within which the internally/materially unconstrainable expansionary dynamics was expected to be maintained on a continuing basis had to be forcefully *secured and protected* from intrusion from *outside*. At the same time, some protection and stabilization had to be provided also *internally,* against the potentially most disruptive consequences of avoidable encroachment by the self-asserting economic microcosms on each other. For in the absence of such all-round beneficial protection some considerable damage would be suffered within the locally and nationally circumscribed boundaries—well-protected boundaries that were, of course, highly relevant for the establishment and for the consolidation of the markets required for expansion in the first place—by the weaker constituents of the capital system's productive microcosms. The emerging and ubiquitously expanding nation-state of the capital system was the obvious legal and political framework and the most appropriate direct as well as indirect promoter of such developments.

To be sure, these dynamic developments of generalized commodity production—which were, thanks to the modern nation-state's all-embracing and constantly growing legislative network, as a matter of paramount importance, not only forcefully protected against intrusion from abroad, but also increasingly regulated in the interest of internal cohesion—historically unfolded through the *dialectical reciprocity* of the material reproductive domain and the legal and political superstructure of the capital system.

Transformations of this magnitude were inconceivable in earlier periods of history. Moreover, socioeconomic developments of this kind would be also in their own more advanced setting totally unintelligible without the *ongoing reciprocal interchange* of the forces involved in shaping the relevant changes of the overall system—as an *organic* framework of all-embracing societal reproduction in which the various parts strongly *sustain* one another—across history. At the same time, in view of the fact that the internally unrestrainable new material reproductive system of generalized commodity production could not be maintained in existence without its dramatic expansion on a continuing basis, it was also inconceivable to confine the corresponding legal and political framework of the modern nation-state to anything less than a comparably dynamic form of unrestrainable power relations.

Thus the state was essential no less for the internal cohesion of the productive units against avoidable excess by their more powerful counterparts (which would be of course detrimental for the expansionary potential of the system as a whole), than for protecting the established order from outside interference, in view of the vital need for *correctively preserving* the dynamic constituent of their—not only expansion-oriented but also expansion-securing—centrifugality. The staggering development and unrestrainable expansion of the modern capitalist state itself, irrespective of how problematical its historical advancement turned out to be in the final analysis, in our own time of potentially catastrophic collisions, finds its explanation in this *objective historical dialectic*—between the *internal necessities* of capital's material basis and the legal and political conditions required under which the *potentialities* of the system could be turned into *reality*—and not in the fanciful brainwork of "occidental jurists" circularly projected by Max Weber.

Naturally, this relationship of dialectical reciprocity between the material basis and the legal and political superstructure was by no means simply a question of the unrestrainably expanding magnitudes involved in their interchanges. It necessarily concerned also their most fundamental *internal determinations,* as the material reproductive domain of the capital system and its legal and political dimension followed their respective course of historical development in close conjunction with each other. Indeed, the reciprocal interchange involved—and at the same time also deeply affected—the most fundamental internal determinations of both the material basis and its legal and political superstructure. Only through such dynamic interchange of dialectical reciprocity could it be made possible for the system as a whole to expand in accordance with its full potentiality, thanks to the way in which the material and the superstructural dimension of capital's organic system could interact and powerfully drive forward one another.

We can see the profound impact of this reciprocity between the material domain and the modern state by focusing attention on the inherent connection between the *universal* exchange relations unfolding under the rule of capital's generalized commodity production and the *formal* determinations that enable (because they *must* enable) the systemically necessary equalization of incommensurabilities. For this relationship, based on the universal predominance of abstract labor in the given social metabolic order, must be sustained at all levels of societal interchanges, formally obfuscating and fetishistically obliterating substantive incommensurability everywhere.

Naturally, this includes the way in which the individuals involved in production and exchange are managed in capital's structurally preordained—and in that sense as a matter of unalterable systemic determination both hierarchical/iniquitous and incurably *antagonistic*—but in another sense *formally equitable* (and ideologically rationalized in the fictitious image of "people's capitalism" as even *harmoniously share-owning)* social reproductive order.

As we know, generalized commodity production and exchange are unthinkable without *universal value-equation* that must be constantly accomplished on the ground of capital's material reproductive practices. The *formal reductive homogenization* of all substantive relations—and thereby the *reconciliation of irrational forms* put into relief by Marx, as we have seen elsewhere[78]—is seminally important in this respect. It is crucial for understanding the profound interconnection between the material reproductive processes and the historically specific constitution of capital's ever more powerful legal and political superstructure required for the sustainable operation of the system as a whole. For, viewed simply from the angle of the particular units, the ever more complex exchange relations of the expanding material reproductive microcosms—arising from the unrestrainable centralization and concentration of self-expansionary capital—generate constantly greater demands for systemic cohesion and support which they themselves, as locally confined productive structures, are totally incapable of satisfying. And the causal implication of that circumstance for the development of the legal and political framework itself would seem to be, quite wrongly, a one-way determination of the overall societal complex by the material basis.

However, precisely because the just mentioned growing demands of the expansion-oriented productive units could not be satisfied at all by

the particular material reproductive microcosms themselves, the historically arising complex exchange relations—which we are all familiar with—
could not be established in the first place without bringing fully into play
capital's legal and political framework as the *necessary condition* of systemic cohesion and development. Without the direct or indirect supportive involvement of the capital system's political dimension even the most
genuine expansionary needs of the reproductive microcosms would have
to remain no more than frustrated abstract requirements, instead of being
turned into effective demands. This again strongly underscores the reciprocal determinations of the historical dialectic in the real articulation of
both the material reproductive basis of capital as a coherent system and
its state formation.

In this sense the unfolding of the state's formal/legal universality and
capital's universal commodification are inseparable. The insuperable *sub-*
stantive structural hierarchy of capital's material basis finds its equivalent
at the level of the legal and political relations, calling for the defense of the
most iniquitous established order at all cost. *Formal* measures and rationalizations, no matter how ingenious, cannot obliterate the *substantive*
inequalities and structural antagonisms.

In fact, the need for apologetic ideological rationalization on that
score becomes ever more pronounced parallel to the move from capital's
ascending phase of development to the descending phase. Accordingly,
Kant still needs no cynicism and hypocrisy when he contrasts the *strictly*
formal equality of the law feasible under the rule of capital with the *sub-*
stantive inequality required for managing the given antagonistic social
order. Thus he writes without any camouflage: "The *general equality* of
men as subjects in a state coexists quite readily with the *greatest inequal-*
ity in degrees of the *possessions* men have, whether the possessions con-
sist of corporeal or spiritual superiority or in material possession besides.
Hence the general equality of men also coexists with *great inequality of*
specific rights of which there may be many. . . . Nevertheless, all subjects
are equal to each other *before the law* which, as a pronouncement of the
general will, can only be one. This law concerns the *form* and not the *mat-*
ter of the object regarding which I may possess a right."[79]

In the same way, Adam Smith is not in the least tempted by the need
to hide: "Till there be *property* there can be no *government,* the very end

of which is to *secure wealth* and to *defend the rich from the poor*."[80] However, by the time we reach "capital's hired prizefighter," Hayek, in the descending phase of the system's development, everything is turned upside down, as we have seen. The exploitative practices imposed on "most of the Western proletariat and most of the millions of the developing world"[81]—defended by the neoliberal state with all means at its disposal against the people who dare to oppose it—are glorified as *"moral practices,"* and we are peremptorily told by Hayek that "If we ask what men most owe to the moral practices of those who are called *capitalists* the answer is: *their very lives*."[82] The particular irony in this respect is that Hayek claims to write in the spirit of Adam Smith while in fact diametrically contradicting him. Contradicting without shame the same intellectual giant, Adam Smith, of the ascending phase of the capital system's development, who did not hesitate to denounce in his time the deplorable fact—imposed today no less than in the past through the pretended "moral practices" of Hayek's idealized capitalists on "most of the millions of the developing world" who clothe the world in appalling working conditions in the transnational sweatshops—by saying that *"the people who clothe the world are in rags themselves."*[83]

Adam Smith perceived very clearly that the unjust property system of his time could only be sustained on an enduring basis if the government of the established order kept on defending the wealth of the rich against the poor. In this way—viewing the world with honesty from capital's vantage point—he realized that the material ground of the system he firmly believed in, and its governing political state, were inseparable from each other. What was impossible for Adam Smith to spell out from capital's vantage point was the radical implication of his own insight. Namely, that in order to overturn the perceived and denounced injustice about those who "clothe the world but are in rags themselves," the material ground and the protective political state of the system, which *stood* together, must also *fall* together.

The increasing preponderance of the legal and political superstructure across modern history is very far from being a development of corrigible contingency. On the contrary, it is due to the state's innermost character and objective constitution. For the modern nation-state is *absolutely unrestrainable* in capital's own terms of reference, as a matter of insuperable structural determination. The complete failure of all attempts aimed at a socially significant reform of the state in the course of the last century and a half speaks unmistakably on this score.

To make matters worse, the structurally entrenched material basis of the capital system is *also unrestrainable,* as well as in a socially significant sense *unreformable.* Again, not as a matter of corrigible historical contingency but as a result of its fundamental structural determination. In fact the material reproductive and the legal/political dimensions of the system have a most paradoxical relationship. For they powerfully contribute throughout their reciprocal historical interchanges to the immense *expansion* of one another, and thereby of themselves as well, but they are totally incapable of exercising a meaningful *restraining* impact on each other, not to mention themselves. The inner logic of this type of development is that, as a result, we are subjected to the ultimately all-round destructive consequences of a dangerous *one-way directionality,* leading toward a potentially suicidal *blind alley.* This is so because a system of societal husbandry which by its innermost constitution and structural determination is incapable of recognizing and acknowledging any *limit,* not even when doing so would be, as today, *absolutely imperative*—in view of the everintensifying *destruction of nature* as well as of the vital energy and strategic raw material resources required for humanity's continued reproduction—can offer no viable solution for the future.

The perverse logic of the capital system is that the material and the legal/political dimension can *complement* each other only in an ultimately unsustainable way. For although the legal/political dimension can *constrain centrifugality* in the interest of *overall systemic expansion,* it is absolutely incapable of introducing *rational restraint* into its own mode of operation. This is so because it is incompatible with the concept of *systemically overarching rationality* required for meaningful restraint.

That is the fundamental reason why the final articulation of the capitalist nation-state's inherent logic had to assume the form of *imperialist rivalry*—exploded in two world wars in the twentieth century—which persists today, despite verbal denials, no less than ever before. Hegel, a century prior to the unfolding of global wars, had no illusions whatsoever regarding the question of constrainability. He stated with striking openness: "The nation-state is mind in its *substantive rationality* and immediate *actuality* and is therefore the *absolute power* on earth."[84] Ideas to the contrary, like the Kantian projection of "perpetual peace" and its proposed instrumentality of a League of Nations, proved to be no more than noble wishful thinking on capital's material ground. As our actual historical experience painfully demonstrated, such a League of Nations could do nothing to prevent the eruption of the Second World War, despite the fact that it was conceived and established in the light of the all too obviously devastating consequences of the First World War.

The untenable logic of capital's material reproductive microcosms is "grow eternally or implode"! The nowadays persistent wishful projection of all-round beneficial "globalization" is the ideological rationalization of that logic. At the same time, the oppressive imposition of the power of global hegemonic imperialism in our time—with its unhesitating engagement in massively destructive wars, including the wars pursued not so long ago in Vietnam and now in the Middle East, and indeed not shirking even from the threat of using nuclear weapons against states without such weapons—is the far from "rational actuality" corresponding to capital's unvarnished logic.

The grave contradiction at the roots of such developments is that in our historical period of materially/productively ever more intertwined global developments we are being offered *globalizing rationalizations* within the horizon of the dominant *aggressive nation-state,* the United States of America and its military-industrial complex, but no viable solutions to capital's antagonisms either in terms of the capital system's material ground or at the level of its *rival state formations.* The painful truth of the matter is that—in view of the necessary historic failure of capital to constitute the *state of the capital system as such,* remaining in its stead inextricably tied to the rival imperialist nation-states' destructive logic even under the most extreme conditions of literally MAD "mutually assured destruction," fully in tune with the structural antagonisms of the system's material ground—no sustainable solution is conceivable within the rationally in no way constrainable framework of capital's social order.

Moreover, the historic failure to create the state of the capital system as such is itself by no means a corrigible contingency. For the globally required legal and political framework of regulatory interaction, even if envisaged as confined to a relatively short period of transition on the road toward a positively working (in the sense of consciously self-regulating) normativity, would need *comprehensive rationality* from the time of its inception in order to become historically sustainable. The capital system, however, is incompatible with anything other than the most restrictive and partial form of rationality. This is why the untenable logic of the capitalist nation-state in our time, asserting itself as before in the form of imperialist rivalry irrespective of how its leading "actors" might change from time to time, remains with us even under the present-day conditions of potentially catastrophic collisions.

Hegel's words are most instructive also in this respect. Not only because he insisted, "The nation-state is mind in its *substantive rationality* and immediate *actuality* and is therefore the *absolute power* on earth." The fact that he expressed this judgment in an idealist form, projecting it speculatively into the timeless "future" of the Absolute's "eternal present," is here of secondary importance. For, by complementing his judgment with the required historical qualifications, it is undoubtedly true that the capitalist nation-state, in its *substantive* self-determination and immediate *actuality* asserts itself—inevitably within the capital system's horizon—together with all of its extreme destructive implications, as "the absolute power on earth." And, to be sure, nothing could be more absolute than the Absolute, not just for Hegel but also in terms of capital's self-definition.

The great problem is not the all too obvious actuality of the capitalist nation-state's absolute—unconstrainable—self-assertion throughout its history but the devastating implications of that uncontrollable self-assertion for our time. In the past the structural unconstrainability in question always took the form of wars of increasing scale and intensity, whenever some limiting constraints were attempted to be imposed by the particular nation-states on one another from the outside. Such wars were even morally justified by Hegel, as we have seen above, without questioning in the least the "Germanic" (including the colonially most successful English) nation-state's absolute unconstrainability as such. Nor was it, in contrast to the present time, totally prohibitive, in strictly military terms, to project in Hegel's time the idealized finality of the nation-state's historic mission for instituting the permanent colonial-imperialist domination of the world by saying that "Europe is absolutely the end of history."

That kind of approach belonged to the *normality* of the colonial-imperialist phase of the capital system's development. Indeed, it happened to be perfectly sustainable under the then prevailing circumstances, prominently theorized even as the *unalterable* correlation between *war and politics* by the outstanding Prussian military strategist, General Karl Marie von Clausewitz, Hegel's famous contemporary.

However, what has become totally untenable in our time is the dominant nation-states' unreformable old modality "to seek and create a *sphere of activity abroad*"[85] through their imperialist wars, on the pretext of the *"inherently indeterminable injuries, however minute,"* which they claimed to have suffered themselves, as Hegel was still willing to spell it out in clear terms, corresponding to the absolutely self-assertive logic of capital's modern state formation. That is what requires a fundamental reexamination and radical structural change today, in contrast to the persistent *material domination* and *political/military undertaking* of countless wars (calculated in the region of two hundred military interventions in the affairs of other states after the Second World War) of the most aggressive nation-state of our time: the United States of America, described as "the only necessary nation" in President Clinton's notorious words. And, of course, such disheartening reality is coupled with the cynical ideology diffused under the pretenses of all-round beneficial globalization.

As we know, the system of modern nation-states, with its most iniquitous structural hierarchy among its members. was historically constituted on capital's *substantive discriminatory material ground*, even if later that system became ideologically rationalized—both internally and in its interstate relations—in the spirit of "purely formal" rationality and the (never instituted) abstract "Rights of Man." Thus the challenge in this regard for the future of humanity is to overcome the *blind unrestrainability* of capital's nation-states by the *rational controllability* of a radically different system of globally viable interchanges in substantive terms. Naturally, meeting that challenge, by instituting a historically sustainable form of *socialist internationalism,* is feasible only through the actual supersession of the grievances suffered by the smaller states in the course of their long historical domination by the so-called "world historical nations."[86] And that is possible only by overcoming at the same time, in enduring substantive terms, the oppressive *structural hierarchy* without which capital's societal reproductive order is inconceivable either in its internal *class relations* or in its aggressive *interstate* practices.

To be sure, the accomplishment of that task is not simply a political matter. The fundamental objective condition of instituting a historically sustainable solution in this domain is the qualitative transformation of the *antagonistic material ground* of capital's socioeconomic order that continues to produce, as a matter of *structural necessity,* the drive to unrestrainable global domination of the weaker constituents of the system by the more powerful not only in exploitative material reproductive terms, under the pretenses of globalization, but also on the political/military stage. It is that profound structural determination, erupting in the form of the destructive antagonisms of our time, that must be consigned to the past on a permanent basis.

Thus the required radical transformation of the legal and political superstructure is inseparable from the *reconstitution of the historical dialectic,* which had been dangerously distorted and ultimately *subverted* in the course of capital's descending phase of development, degrading thereby the once positive self-expansionary drive of the system to the condition of blind uncontrollability.

The key difference in relation to this problem is that the capital system was established in the first place on the ground of structurally safeguarded *susbstantive inequality,* thanks also to the unmitigated large-scale violence of the "primitive accumulation" which was greatly facilitated in its classic form in England by the absolutist state of Henry VIII. In complete contrast to capital's deeply entrenched substantive inequality in all domains, from the direct material to the most mediated cultural relations, the necessary alternative—socialist—mode of social metabolic reproduction cannot be considered historically viable unless it is *qualitatively reconstituted* and firmly maintained in its new social setting on the basis of *substantive equality.*

Stressing this vital contrast between the *substantive* defining characteristics of the historical alternative modes of social metabolic reproduction of our time is all the more important for us because in its ideologically well diffused self-images capital always proclaimed its programmatic adhesion, as far as its legislative terms were concerned, to *contractual equality,* just as in practical material reproductive terms it claimed to regulate the socioeconomic order on the basis of *universal value-equation*. However, as we have seen above in revealing detail, all such practices have been actually pursued on the basis of the reductive transformation of *substantive incommensurabilities* into *formally equalizable* relations only, under the ubiquitous dominance of generalized commodity production and its fetishistically equalizable *abstract labor*.

The profoundly iniquitous and structurally safeguarded *substantive* relations of exploitative domination and subordination could be therefore carried on undisturbed in capital's societal reproductive practices for a very long time, until the onset of some major crises as late as the monopolistic imperialist phase of the system's development. And even then, despite the fact that the erupting crises in question were of considerable magnitude—characteristically attempted to be redressed later by the most powerful imperialist states, although without lasting success, by massive military undertakings, like the two world wars of the twentieth century—pointed only *tendentially* toward the ultimately unavoidable *structural crisis* of the system.

In the meantime, the long persistent normality of universal value-equation, under the dominance of fetishistically generalized commodity production, succeeded in conferring even the halo of "liberty-fraternity-equality" on the ideological conceptualizations of the capital system. The increasingly more preponderant legal and political superstructure of capital, unfolding in the course of history with its inexorably expanding legal jungle that reached its climax in our own time, made a vital contribution to the continued success of this mode of societal reproduction. It fulfilled its problematical stabilizing role in a most authoritarian way in the descending phase of capital's systemic development. Accordingly, it contributed by every possible means at its disposal—including the cynically open legitimation of monopolistic encroachment in the field of economic production, and active involvement in the most blatant imperialist adventurism and violence in the political/military domain, in the name of "democratic equality"—to the ever more dangerous subversion of the historical dialectic.

Prior to the articulation of the modern capital system and its state formation the question of equality did not arise at all in relation to the socioeconomic and political dimension of societal reproduction. As we know, "Greek democracy" could sustain its remarkably advanced political decision-making practices on the ground of *slavery* as its long-enduring material reproductive basis. A form of slavery regulated as a mode of social metabolic reproduction in which human beings could be characterized by a thinker as great as Aristotle as nothing more than "talking tools." Moreover, even at a much later stage of historical development, the feudal state, in its well-known self-legitimatory efforts, did not hesitate to claim *divine lineage* on behalf of its privileged ruling personnel. This way of conceptualizing the world order represented no problem whatsoever, either for ancient slavery or for the feudal system of the Middle Ages. For in both cases any concern with equality, not only substantive equality but even formal, was totally irrelevant to the way in which the conditions of existence of the members of society were actually produced and reproduced on an ongoing basis.

In complete contrast, the capitalist state's concern with equality right from the outset of its historical development was rooted in the *formal equalizations* of its material basis, and as such that kind of concern with equality was both *necessary* and *genuine* in its own terms of reference. The complicating fact was that the *capital relation* itself—based on the alienation of labor and its embodiment in capital—could be *circularly presupposed* in capital's self-serving conceptualizations as the only feasible mode of the "natural" reproductive order, at the level of the system's everyday operative principles. Accordingly, the contractual equality and universal value-equation could be coherently proclaimed to constitute the effective modus operandi of the capital system by its greatest intellectual representatives, including Adam Smith and Hegel. This approach became untenable only when the question of the system's *historical genesis* had to be raised, precisely with a view to reassessing its viability regarding the future, in the light of its structurally entrenched substantive inequality that became contested by a growing class-based social movement in the aftermath of the French Revolution and the Napoleonic Wars.

At that point, when the question of time appeared on the horizon both with regard to the *past* and the *future,* the former circular presupposition of the operative principles themselves—ideologically rationalized and eternalized on the ground that they were in Hegelian "rational actuality" demonstrably working—had to fail to fulfill its customary function. For, in sharp contrast to *formally stipulated equality,* which can be ideologically rationalized under all kinds of totally untenable postulates, as we have seen it done even by a very great philosopher like Kant, *substantive equality,* with its qualitative determinations, cannot be treated *circularly,* so as to vindicate its aprioristic exclusion from commendable social normativity by arbitrarily proclaimed *self-referentiality,* offered as a "conclusive" judgment *by definition.* Inevitably, therefore, once the question of substantive equality as such is raised in relation to the *modern state,* it brings with it the challenge to confront the difficult problem of the necessary *withering away of the state* in its historically constituted actuality. For within the historically determined confines of the modern state—which must be hierarchically ordered both internally and in its inter-state relations, embodying thereby the radical alienation of the power of comprehensive decision making from the social individuals—the very idea of substantive equality is of necessity *structurally negated.*

However, the institution of a substantively equitable social reproductive order represents a fundamental challenge for *our future,* calling for the radical transformation of the hierarchically structured legal and political superstructure itself, together with its practical premises and material presuppositions. As discussed, the great expansion of the capital system was made possible in the first place by the progressive advancement of a system of unchallengeable domination of *use-value* by *exchange-value* through which universal value-equation became the expansion-securing dynamic operative principle of societal reproduction under the rule of generalized commodity production. As a vitally important member of a *dichotomous system,* exchange could exercise a *dominant* role in the material reproduction process, quite irrespective of the negative consequences arising in the longer run from its supremacy over production and over the demands it could impose—"behind the backs of the producing individuals"—even on the available, necessarily finite, natural resources. In the last analysis, a system of this kind had to run out of control once the objective systemic limits of capital's mode of social metabolic reproduction had been activated.

Moreover, what made matters worse was the fact that the alienating domination of human use by the fetishistic requirements of commodity exchange was not sustained simply by the given exchange relation in and by itself. The dominance of exchange over use had its equally problemat-ical *corollaries,* which *together* constituted an ultimately unmanageable system—a system of undialectical dichotomies that asserted themselves with categorical peremptoriness both materially and in the political domain. Indeed, the same kind of undialectical dichotomies, characteris-tic of the capital system as a whole, had to prevail through the domination of *quantity over quality,* of the *abstract over the concrete,* and of the *formal over the substantive,* as what we have seen in the necessarily reifying dom-inance of *exchange-value over use-value* under the established reproduc-tive order's universal value-equation.

To be sure, at the roots of all of these inevitably distorting—even if for the purposes of generalized commodity production absolutely neces-sary—relations of one-sided domination and subordination we find the politically secured and safeguarded *structural subordination of labor to capital,* rationalized through the most absurd but fetishistically for a long historical period well-functioning reproductive practice of formal/reduc-tive homogenization that turns into a commodity and reductively equates living human beings with *abstract labor.* It is by no means surprising, therefore, that the ever more preponderant legal and political superstruc-ture of the system played, and continues to play, an increasingly irrational-istic supportive role in delaying the "moment of truth." That moment nevertheless arrives when it becomes unavoidable to pay for the destruc-tive consequences of the unfolding dangerous developments on a global scale both in the material productive domain and on the political/military plane. As things stand today, given its preponderant power the "democ-ratic state" can fulfill its irrational supportive role by brushing aside with cynically stage-managed authoritarianism—whether "neoliberal" or "neo-conservative"—any concern even about the regularly erupting major military collisions.

In this sense, the radical transformation of the legal and political superstructure, as a literally vital exigency of our time, requires a funda-mental change on a long-term sustainable material basis. That means overcoming the undialectical dichotomous domination of one side of the relations, mentioned a moment ago, over the other, from the ultimately self-defeating domination of exchange over use, as well as the abstract over the concrete, all the way to the historically no longer tenable obliteration of the vital qualitative determinations of any long-term viable mode of societal reproduction by the fetishism of universal quantification and the ensuing equalization of incommensurabilities.

The reconstitution of the historical dialectic on a *structurally secured substantive equitable basis* is therefore not a speculative philosophical postulate but a key objective exigency of our present-day conditions of existence. For the dangerous subversion of the historical dialectic coincided with the increasingly antagonistic descending phase of the capital system's development and the activation of its *structural crisis*, bringing with it the defiance of, and the irrationalistic practical disregard for, even the most elementary conditions of sustainable human life on this planet. Naturally, the legal and political superstructure of even the most authoritarian state, no matter how bloated and protected it might be, not only by its catastrophically wasteful military arsenal but also by its ever denser legal jungle, can in no way permanently counter the pressing character of these objective determinations and exigencies.

Capital's mode of social metabolic control could prevail over a long historical period because it constituted an *organic system* in which the material basis of societal reproduction and its comprehensive legal/political regulatory dimension were inextricably intertwined in a dynamic expansionary way, tending toward an all-embracing global integration. Indeed, for almost three centuries the capital system's expansionary drive could proceed quite unhindered. However, one of the insuperable *structural limits* of this system, burdened with the ultimately self-destructive logic of its *unrestrainable nation-state formation:* the necessity of *monopolistic* developments and the associated *imperialist rivalry* among the dominant states, had to make the system itself historically unviable in an age when the pursuit of global war could only result in humanity's self-destruction. And the other insuperable *structural limit* of the capital system is no less grave. For on the plane of material reproduction its *rationally unrestrainable* self-expansionary drive, heavily promoted by capital's state formation, inevitably reached the point of collision with the objective limits of our planetary resources, calling for the adoption of the qualitatively different societal reproductive practices of the only viable—in a *humanly meaningful way economizing*—economy in our planetary household. Naturally, with regard to the imperative to face up to the challenges arising from these fundamental structural limitations of the capital system the radical transformation of its legal and political superstructure—together with its material basis, in the spirit indicated in this section—is an absolutely vital requirement.

NOTES

1. Karl Marx, *Theories of Surplus-Value,* Foreign Languages Publishing House, Moscow, n.d.,1:275–77. Marx is referring in the last line to Lessing's *Hamburgische Dramaturgie* containing his critique of Voltaire.
2. Ibid., 279.
3. Ibid.
4. Ibid., 278.
5. Karl Marx, *Grundrisse,* Penguin Books, Harmondsworth, 1973, 374.
6. As Kant had put it: "One cannot fashion something absolutely straight from wood which is as crooked as that of which man is made." Immanuel Kant, "Idea for a Universal History with Cosmopolitan Intent," in *Immanuel Kant's Moral and Political Writings,* ed. Carl J. Friedrich, Random House, New York, 1949, 123.
7. Adam Smith, *The Wealth of Nations,* Adam and Charles Black, Edinburgh, 1863, 273.
8. Hegel, *The Philosophy of Right,* Clarendon Press, Oxford, 1942,11.
9. Ibid., 10.
10. Hegel, *The Philosophy of History,* Dover Publications, New York, 1956, 457.
11. Hegel, *The Philosophy of Right,* 222.
12. Marx, *Theories of Surplus-Value,* 279.
13. The Vatican Office of the "Defender of the Faith," for many years headed by the most conservative German cardinal, Joseph Ratzinger, is the contemporary organ in direct succession to "The Holy Inquisition." No wonder that the Latin American representatives of liberation theology, including one of the greatest poets of our time, Ernesto Cardenal, had to be condemned by it, and even threatened with excommunication.
14. Friedrich August von Hayek, *The Fatal Conceit: The Errors of Socialism,* Routledge, London, 1988, 138.
15. "Feel" underlined by Hayek.
16. Hayek, *The Fatal Conceit,* 130–31.
17. Margaret Thatcher's denunciation of the striking British miners in 1984.
18. To name only two of the most important of these theoretical misrepresentations, it is necessary to stress the tendentious conflation of the seminal concepts of *work* (the exercise of the much needed creative potentiality of

human beings even in the most advanced form of a future socialist order) with capitalist *wage labor,* and likewise the vitally necessary production of *use-values* (again an absolutely necessary requirement also in labor's hegemonic alternative order to the established one) and the capitalistically dominant *exchange-values.* Both of these characteristic conflations serve the *eternalization* of capital's historically specific reproductive order, arbitrarily transfiguring it thereby into *"the natural and irreplaceable"* socioeconomic order. The two outstanding figures of bourgeois political economy, Adam Smith and David Ricardo, are most revealing examples of this type of conflation, as discussed at the end of this section.

See also section 8, "The Domination of Counter-Value in Antinomous Value-Relations," of chapter 6 in *The Social Determination of Method,* esp. 154–56, in relation to the Hegelian conflation—in the same spirit—of class-privileged means of *production* with generic means of *subsistence,* as well as *work* as such with *socially/hierarchically divided labor,* justifying them—quite astonishingly for an idealist philosopher—on the ground that "Men are made *unequal by nature"* (in Hegel's *Philosophy of Right,* 130).

19. Marx's emphases.

20. Marx, *Grundrisse,* 278.

21. As we read in *The German Ideology*: "The further the separate spheres, which act on one another, extend in the course of this development and the more the original isolation of the separate nationalities is destroyed by the advanced mode of production ... the more history becomes world history. Thus, for instance, if in England a machine is invented which deprives countless workers of bread in India and China, and overturns the whole form of existence of these empires, this invention becomes a world-historical fact." Karl Marx and Frederick Engels, *Collected Works,* Lawrence and Wishart, London, 1975, 5:50–51 (henceforth MECW).

22. "In the development of productive forces there comes a stage when productive forces and means of intercourse are brought into being which, under the existing relations, only cause mischief, and are *no longer productive but destructive forces"* (ibid., 5:520). "Thus things have now come to such a pass that the individuals must appropriate the existing totality of productive forces, not only to achieve self–activity, but, also, *merely to safeguard their very existence"* (ibid., 5:870).

23. Ibid., 5:42.

24. Ibid., 5:43.

25. "The animal is immediately identical with its life-activity. It does not distinguish itself from it. It is *its life-activity.* Man makes his life-activity itself the object of his will and of his consciousness. He has conscious life-activity. It is not a determination with which he directly merges." Karl Marx, *Economic and Philosophic Manuscripts of 1844,* Lawrence & Wishart, London, 1959,75. Marx's emphases.

26. "History is nothing but the succession of the separate generations, each of which uses the materials, the capital funds, the productive forces handed down to it by all preceding generations, and thus, on the one hand, continues the traditional activity in completely changed circumstances and, on the other, *modifies the old circumstances with a completely changed activity....* This [Marxian] conception of history thus relies on expounding the real process of production . . . It has not, like the idealist view of history, to look for a category in every period, but remains constantly on the real ground of history.... It shows that *circumstances make men just as much as men make circumstances."* MECW,5:50–54.

27. Marx, *Grundrisse,* 329.

28. Ibid., 331.

29. Ibid., 527–28.

30. We should recall in this context Marx's warning that firmly underscored that in accordance with capital's unfolding development "the extension of products and needs falls into *contriving* and ever–*calculating* subservience to inhuman, refined, unnatural and *imaginary* appetites." Marx, *Economic and Philosophic Manuscripts of 1844,* 116. Marx's emphases.

31. Karl Marx, *Capital,* Foreign Languages Publishing House, Moscow,1959, 3:804.

32. As Marx put it: *"Labour as such,* in its simple capacity as *purposive productive activity,* relates to the means of production, not in their social determinate form, but rather in their concrete substance, as material and means of labour." Ibid.

33. Ibid., 800.

34. Patrick Gardiner, *The Nature of Historical Explanation,* Oxford University Press, 1961, 138.

35. Karl Marx, *A Contribution to the Critique of Political Economy,* Lawrence & Wishart, London, 1971, 20.

36. All these quotations, as formulated by Marx, ibid.

37. Marx, *Grundrisse,* 278.

38. The Roman Catholic Church not only has its own special state formation, as well as its most elaborate economic and financial network in the shape of the Vatican in Italy, but it maintains very close interactive links with a multiplicity of states across the world. At the same time, even if somewhat farcically, nonetheless for historical reasons understandably, the head of the Church of England today, in the twenty-first century, is none other than the head of the British royal family.

39. H. H. Gerth and C. Wright Mills, eds., *From Weber: Essays in Sociology,* Routledge & Kegan Paul, London, 1948, 299.

40. See section 3.3 of chapter 3: "Reproduction of the operating conditions of production."

41. The increasingly more problematical requirement of contractuality neces-

sarily implies the provision of an—ultimately unworkable—system of *guarantees* by the rival nation states for securing the projected global capital outlets. Naturally, the state is expected not only to legally stipulate such guarantees, but under the circumstances of sharpening antagonisms also to impose them by military force in an unstable international order, with potentially catastrophic consequences. Against the background of modern imperialism and its violent collisions in the past, including two devastating world wars in the twentieth century, the great historical failure to constitute the global state of the capital system is thus sharply put into relief.

42.   In relation to the important question concerning the required switch from the historically dominant *external* modality of normativity—with its imposition of rules of behavior on the individuals from above—to the qualitatively different *internal* normativity shaped by them in an advanced socialist society, we have to recall section 3.3 of chapter 3: "Customs, tradition, and explicit law: historical boundaries of the legal and political superstructure."

43.   Lenin's frequently quoted writing on *The State and Revolution* could hardly be considered an exception in this respect. A far from completed work, it was written—entirely in Marx's spirit—toward the end of the war, with an optimistic perspective about how the expected "break at the weakest link of the chain of imperialism" would initiate a successful revolution worldwide. The short Postscript added to the first edition, after the revolution (dated November 30, 1917), was still conceived in the same optimistic spirit. However, the imperialist war of intervention and the grave economic and social crisis associated with the attempts aimed at securing the survival of the revolution caused a massive derailment, fundamentally altering the original perspective and pushing the question of the "withering away of the state" completely out of sight in Lenin's final years of life, not to mention its fate under Stalin's leadership of the Party and the state. In the few lines of Lenin's optimistic Postscript he indicated the title of the intended continuation of his work—"The Experience of the Russian Revolutions of 1905 and 1917"—and added: "It is more pleasant and useful to go through the 'experience of the revolution' than to write about it." (Lenin, *Collected Works*, 25:492.) It is a matter of the greatest regret that he could not complete this work. For in the light of our experience of the postrevolutionary state, writing about it in the Marxian spirit, as Lenin always did, would be of paramount importance not only concerning the historical past but also in relation to the challenges that must be faced by the socialist forces in the future. With regard to these developments, see my article "Political Power and Dissent in Postrevolutionary Societies," *New Left Review* 108. (March–April 1978), repr. in *Beyond Capital*, 1995, 898–916.

44.   It is well worth repeating here Marx's words: "The animal is immediately identical with its life-activity. It does not distinguish itself from it. It is *its life-activity*. Man makes his life-activity itself the object of his will and of his

consciousness. He has conscious life-activity. It is not a determination with which he directly merges." Marx, *Economic and Philosophic Manuscripts of 1844*, 75. Marx's emphases.

45. See section 2.1 of chapter 2 on "Social Interaction and Uneven Development."
46. Marx, *A Contribution to the Critique of Political Economy*, 21.
47. Marx, *Capital*, 1:18–19.
48. Ibid., 1:19.
49. Ibid., 1:14–15.
50. Ibid., 1:16.
51. Marx, *A Contribution to the Critique of Political Economy*, 21.
52. MECW, 5:49. Marx's emphases.
53. Ibid., 5:59.
54. See sections 3.2 and 3.3 of chapter 3, and section 4.2 of chapter 4.
55. On this vital issue see chapter 5. of *Beyond Capital*, "The Activation of Capital's Absolute Limits," 142–253.
56. As Marx puts it, in his conception the individuals, including of course the individual capitalists, "are dealt with only in so far as they are the *personifications of economic categories,* embodiments of particular class-relations and class-interests." Marx, *Capital*, 1:10.
57. We will return to this issue toward the end of this chapter.
58. See section 4.2 above.
59. As we have seen, in Marx's words: "Capitalist production is *hostile* to certain branches of *spiritual production*, for example, *art and poetry.*" Marx, *Theories of Surplus-Value,* 1;277.
60. Labor, with regard to its emancipated future perspective of realization, not as a particular sociological entity, but as the *universal condition* of historically viable—because non-adversarial and positively co-operative—societal reproductive practices consciously planned and self-critically controlled by the social individuals themselves. This way of regulating the social metabolism is feasible only on the basis of fully instituting and unreservedly observing the vital operative principle of *substantive equality* in every domain.
61. "Twin Twisters," *The Economist*, July 19–25, 2008, 13.
62. Ibid.
63. The state's ever more dense legislative jungle is the "democratic" legitimator of institutionalized fraudulence in our society. The editors and journalists of *The Economist* are perfectly familiar with the corrupt practices whereby, in the case of the giant American mortgage companies, receiving from their state outrageously preferential treatment that "allowed Fannie and Freddie to operate with *tiny amounts of capital.* The two groups had core capital (as defined by their regulator) of $83.2 billion at the end of 2007; this supported $5.2 trillion of debt and guarantees, *a gearing ratio*

of 65 to one. According to CreditSights, a research group, Fannie and Freddie were counterparties in $2.3 trillion worth of derivative transactions, related to their *hedging activities.* There is no way a private bank would be allowed to have such a highly geared balance sheet, nor would it *qualify for the highest AAA credit rating.* . . . They used their *cheap financing* to buy *higher yielding assets.*" ("Fannie Mae and Freddie Mac: End of Illusions," *The Economist,* July 19–25, 2008, 84.)

Moreover, "With so much at stake, no wonder the companies built a formidable lobbying machine. *Ex-politicians were given jobs.* Critics could expect a rough ride. The companies were not afraid to bite the hands that fed them." ("A Brief Family History: Toxic Fudge," *The Economist,* July 19–25, 2008, 84.) Not being afraid "to bite the hands that fed them" refers, of course, to the American state. But why should they be afraid? For such giant companies constitute a *total symbiosis* with the capitalist state. This is a relationship corruptly asserting itself even in terms of the personnel involved, through the act of hiring politicians.

64. "Fannie Mae and Freddie Mac: End of illusions," 85.

65. "The Present Crisis," quoted from part 4 of *Beyond Capital* (published in London in 1995), 962–63.

66. See in this respect: "Qualitative Growth in Utilization: The Only Viable Economy," in my book, *The Challenge and Burden of Historical Time,* Monthly Review Press, New York, 2008, sec. 9.5, 272–93.

67. Marx, *Capital,* 1:85.

68. See Harry Magdoff's account of the way in which the heads of giant capitalist enterprises unhesitatingly redirected economic activity in their firms in accordance with the political economic requests they received from ministerial sources, in the interest of the centrally planned war effort. Harry Magdoff, interviewed by Huck Gutman, "Creating a Just Society: Lessons from Planning in the U.S.S.R. & the U.S.," *Monthly Review,* October 2002.

69. Hegel, *The Philosophy of Right,* sec. 324.

70. As Marx points out, in the fetishistic equations of the capital system irrationality dominates to the point of absurdity. For

"the relation of a portion of the surplus-value, of money-rent . . . to the land is in itself absurd and irrational; for the magnitudes which are here measured by one another are *incommensurable*—a particular *use-value,* a piece of land of so many and so many square feet, on the one hand, and *value,* especially *surplus-value,* on the other. . . . But prima facie the expression is the same as if one desired to speak of the relation of a *five-pound note to the diameter of the earth.*" Marx, *Capital,* 3:759.

In this sense, nothing could be more absurd than the fetishistic equation of *labor*—the potentially most positive and creative activity of *living human beings*—with *commodity,* as the manipulable "material factor of production" and "cost of production," bought like any other commodity, and dispensed with utmost callousness when capital's self-interest so dictates.

71. See in this respect chapter 2, "General Tendency to Formalism, " in my companion volume to the present one, *The Social Determination of Method,* Monthly Review Press, New York, 2010.

72. Hegel, *The Philosophy of Right,* 212.

73. Ibid., 213.

74. Ibid., 214.

75. Marx, *Capital,* 1:59.

76. "Greek society was founded upon slavery, and had, therefore, for its natural basis, the inequality of men and their labour-powers. The secret of the expression of value, namely, that all kinds of labour are equal and equivalent, because, and so far as they are *human labour in general,* cannot be decyphered, until the notion of *human equality* has already acquired the fixity of a popular prejudice. This, however, is possible only in a society in which the great mass of the produce of labour takes the form of commodities, in which, consequently, the dominant relation between man and man, is that of owners of commodities. The brilliancy of Aristotle's genius is shown by this alone, that he discovered in the expression of the value of commodities, a relation of equality. The peculiar conditions of society in which he lived, prevented him from discovering what, 'in truth,' was at the bottom of this equality." Marx, *Capital,* 1:60.

77. Ibid., 1:59.

78. We should recall in relation to this issue chapters 2 and 4 of *The Social Determination of Method.*

79. Immanuel Kant, "Theory and Practice," in Friedrich, *Immanuel Kant's Moral and Political Writings,* 415–16.

80. Adam Smith, *Lectures on Justice, Police, Revenue, and Arms,* in *Adam Smith's Moral and Political Philosophy,* ed. Herbert W. Schneider, Hafner Publishing, New York, 1948, 291.

81. Hayek, *The Fatal Conceit,* 131.

82. Ibid., 130.

83. Adam Smith, *Lectures on Justice,* 320.

84. Hegel, *The Philosopy of Right,* 212.

85. Ibid., 214.

86. The almost forbidding difficulty with this problem is that equitable relations among states and nations have *never* been instituted in the course of history. Envisaging a socialist solution is feasible only on the ground of a radically different—in its innermost constitution substantively equitable—mode of societal reproduction.

CHAPTER FIVE

Kant, Hegel, Marx: Historical Necessity and the Standpoint of Political Economy

5.1 Preliminaries

In his "Critique of the Hegelian Dialectic and Philosophy as a Whole" Marx suggests that "Hegel's standpoint is that of modern political economy."[1] He shares this position with many others, including—and on the face of it surprisingly—Kant himself, as we shall see later on.

What is important for us in this respect is to understand what kind of historical conceptions are both compatible with and positively helped along by the standpoint of political economy. For it is quite wrong to treat Kant and Hegel, as often done, merely as rationalistic varieties of St. Augustine's openly theological (and not in the least truly historical) philosophy of history. To say that "Hegel's concept of 'the Cunning of Reason' is a substitute for the mysterious and inscrutable ways of God in history"[2] is to miss the point completely. For such a view obliterates without a trace the specificities and genuine historical achievements of the Hegelian position. Concentrating on superficial analogies, it generates the proverbial darkness in which "all cows are black," so as to be able to eliminate the social substance of the Marxian dialectic by maintaining that "the famous law of three stages, which Marx and Comte adopted, too, is a secular revision of the religious dialectic in St. Augustine and Joachim de Flore."[3] Once such darkness descends upon us, it becomes possible to put forward the most astonishing propositions, lumping irreconcilable thinkers together by defining "the intellectual heritage of Marx, Comte, Burckhardt, Pareto, Sorel, and Freud" on the basis of their alleged identity in maintaining that "emotive and irrational factors . . . permeated history and society."[4]

The scholarship behind such theoretical generalizations is extremely shaky. We find in a footnote of the same work: "Herder's major work is the vast study called *Ideas for a Philosophical History of Mankind,* which prompted Kant's review article (1874) entitled 'The Idea of a Universal History from a Cosmopolitan Point of View.'"[5] Naturally, the issue is not the date, which may be an uncorrected printing error and should read 1784. Rather, we are misled on a substantive point, and the reversal of the actual chronology between Kant and his former pupil, Herder,[6] minimizes the importance of history in the Kantian system, making it appear as if it had been a minor afterthought to Herder. Indeed, later on we read: "Descartes specifically excluded history from his *Discourse on Method;* and *this choice prevailed among his philosophical successors, including Kant.*"[7]

Thus we are not concerned here with an accidental slip but with a symptomatic misrepresentation of the real state of affairs that turns the actual relationship upside down between the eighteenth-century's genuine attempt at understanding historical development and the predominance of extreme historical relativism and skepticism from the middle of the nineteenth century onward. Accordingly, a few lines later we are offered the conclusion, which asserts that the investigation of the nature of historical knowledge "did not become a serious concern to either historian or philosopher until the great awakening of history as an empirical and/or scientific discipline in the nineteenth century."[8]

As a matter of fact, Kant's preoccupation with the nature of history was not confined to an occasional review article but constitutes an integral part of his conception as a whole. As with many of his projects, the time that had elapsed between the first germs of his ideas on man and history and the final product was considerable. But even as regards the particular essay on "The Idea for a Universal History with

Cosmopolitan Intent" (*Idee zu einer allgemeinen Geschichte in weltbürg-erlicher Absicht*), its preparation went back to 1783, announced in print at the beginning of 1784; i.e., a fairly long time before Herder's work and Kant's two subsequent review articles on it. To quote an Italian book of exemplary scholarship:

> The issue of 11 February 1784 of the *Gothasche Gelehrte Zeitungen* men-tioned, in an unsigned article, that one of Kant's favourite ideas was that the ultimate end of human history should be the establishment of the best possible political constitution. In this respect, the writer continued, Kant hoped that there would be a historian able to offer a history of humanity from the philosophical standpoint, to show how far or near, in the vari-ous epochs, we had been to this end and how much still remained to be done to reach it. Kant had spoken in these terms in a conversation with a scholar who visited him in Königsberg. Having been drawn into the argument, Kant felt obliged to make clear his ideas on the subject in pub-lic. In the November issue of *Berlinische Monatschrift* of Biester—the Enlightenment periodical of Berlin—appeared his "Idea of Universal History from a Cosmopolitan Point of View," an exposition, in nine the-ses, of a philosophy of history founded on the principle of a progressive and universal coming of the realm of Right.[9]

Kant's review articles on Herder's work—which should not be con-fused with his nine theses on "Universal History from a Cosmopolitan Point of View"—appeared in 1785, in the *Allgemeine Literaturzeitung* of Jena. However, his interest in understanding the history of mankind as a unity sui generis did not stop there. The same preoccupation played a vital role not only in some of his writings that directly address the subject but in his conception of morality in general. Indeed, the two so deeply interpenetrate each other that his view of history is neither understand-able without his conception of morality nor the other way around.

In truth, it is important to draw the necessary lines of demarcation not only between figures like Vico, Kant, Herder, and Hegel, on the one hand, and the pessimistic historical relativism of many thinkers in the nine-teenth and twentieth centuries on the other, but even more so between Marx and the entire intellectual tradition that shares the standpoint of political economy. For the historical conceptions compatible with that standpoint are severely constrained by the inescapable limitations of the standpoint itself—that is, of capital's characteristic standpoint—even in the works of its greatest representatives. What is particularly relevant in this regard is their conception of *necessity* as manifest in the unfolding historical process. To put it briefly, they operate with an idea of "historical necessity"—or "necessity in history"—which, compared to Marx, is *not coherently historical at all.* Not even in the most monumental historical conception of the whole tradition: the Hegelian philosophy of history. Yet, curiously enough, it is Marx who is accused of "historical determinism," of the "idealization of historical necessity," of "economic determinism," and the like.

The main purpose of this chapter is to try to redress the balance in both directions. First, we have to see why the determinations inherent in the standpoint of political economy *in the end* bring a totally ahistorical conceptualization of the *given* structural necessity as *forever* insurmountable necessity, although paradoxically the *subjective intention* of the thinkers concerned is to demonstrate how freedom is progressively realized through the unfolding history of mankind. And second, this chapter will focus attention on the generally ignored aim of Marx's project to challenge not only the shorter- or longer-term impact of capital's historical necessity but of *historical necessity in general.* This is clearly evidenced in the Marxian characterization of historical necessity as *"merely* historical necessity" or *"disappearing* necessity," which, under our present conditions, constitutes an outrage against the positive potentialities of the real social individuals.

5.2 Theology, Teleology, and Philosophy of History

As stressed in chapter 2, looking back from a certain distance at actual historical development—a distance from which the *already consolidated* plateaus stand out as "necessary stages" of the whole itinerary, while the manifold specific struggles and contradictions leading to them (which contain numerous pointers toward possible alternative configurations) fade into the background—one may have the illusion of a "logically necessary" progression, corresponding to some hidden design. Viewed from such perspective, everything firmly established acquires its *positive* sense, and the consolidated stages by definition must appear to be positive/rational—in virtue of their actual consolidation.

The historical images conceived in this way represent a most ambiguous achievement. They are simultaneously historical and ahistorical, and in a specific sense even "theological," in accordance with the contradictory determinations of the social ground from which they arise. For, strangely enough, by treating the historically created presuppositions of the given order as *absolutely* given—and therefore structurally untranscendable—the situation that preceded the realization of the absolutized conditions can be recognized from the latter's vantage point as subject to *necessary historical qualifications,* insofar as the rejected position is considered to be objectively opposed to interests of the more advanced stage, as its anachronistic social adversary. Consequently, a genuine possibility is opened up for depicting the *negated* aspect and dimension of social development as historical in the meaningful sense which envisages their *practical supersession.*

At the same time, since the newly assumed position is uncritically absolutized, from its perspective everything prior to it (or in conflict with it) must appear as strictly subordinated moments of an a priori self-fulfilling teleology. To take an example: both these aspects are in evidence when Kant radically dismisses the restrictive hereditary principle of *feudalism* as contrary to Reason, and simultaneously approves the new irrationality of the *alienation of land by sale,* as well as its fragmentary subdivisions, as conditions that are in perfect harmony with the "supreme reason for constituting a civic constitution."[10]

But even so, one cannot treat the Kantian or Hegelian teleology of historical development simply as the rationalistic translation of St. Augustine's theological conception. For the "theological" aspects of their historical teleology arise from the limitations of a determinate social horizon and not from a consciously assumed theological framework. In other words, the theological elements display the—far from desired—*contradictions* of their approach, and not their inherent positive intent. They come into play at the point where, in accordance with the insurmountable limits of the social horizon in question, history must be *brought to an end,* instead of representing the explanatory framework of the whole theory. Thus they constitute only a greater or smaller *part* of the whole conception—comparatively greater in Kant, that is, than in Hegel—but not the central tenets and unifying principles of the attempted historical explanations, quite unlike the openly and deliberately theological visions of the Divine purpose and intervention in the historical world, from St. Augustine to Bossuet and Friedrich Schlegel, as well as to their twentieth-century descendants.

There is a tendency to treat teleology in general as a form of theology. This is due to a large extent to the long prevailing conjunction of the two in an important current of the European philosophical tradition that formulated its explanations in terms of "final causes" and identified the latter with the manifestations of the Divine purpose in the order of nature. However, the summary equation of teleology and theology is quite unjustifiable since, as will be shown later, the objective teleology of labor is an essential part of any coherent materialistic historical explanation of social development. Such an explanation, dealing with actually unfolding causal factors and not with a priori preconceived schemes, has nothing whatsoever to do with *theological* assumptions, even though determinate *teleological* propositions are inseparable from it.

But even with regard to the philosophies of Kant and Hegel in which some theological elements undoubtedly reassert themselves, it is necessary to put the issue in perspective. To see nothing but theology in their teleological conceptions would be like asserting about Liberation Theology the totally unenlightening truism that it has been influenced by the teaching of Jesus Christ. For whatever the generic truth of such assertions, they fail to grasp the theoretical specificity and sociohistorical determinateness of the respective views. The fact of the matter is, of course, that the liberation theologians have also studied Marx and tried to incorporate some of his ideas into their own conceptual framework. And it is precisely their point of contact with Marx that happens to be the decisive factor under the circumstances. For, obviously, they are not being threatened with excommunication by Pope John Paul II on account of their adherence to the teaching of Jesus Christ.

Similar considerations apply to the assessment of Kant and Hegel. To be sure, no one should deny that their teleological systems are thoroughly incompatible with the Marxian teleology, in view of their *necessary* relapse into a—socially specific—theology. Indeed, this curious relapse into theology fulfills the highly revealing function of freezing history in the Kantian and Hegelian historical conceptions at an ideologically convenient point in time, thereby rationalizing the ahistorical temporality of the present, together with the idealized bourgeois social order. However, the problem that really matters is how to explain the socio-historical determinations behind such relapse, instead of merely asserting the permanence of theological teleology as an a priori assumed condition. For, as we shall see in a moment, in both Kant and Hegel the theology in question is the self-legitimating "theology" of an ahistorically conceived *civil society*, brought into their systems on the ground of ideological determinations, and not for the purpose of asserting the absolute merits of the Christian religious creed.

5.3 The Kantian Conception of Historical Development

Let us have a brief look at Kant's "Idea for a Universal History with Cosmopolitan Intent," which is directly relevant in this respect. One of the most important aspects of Kant's conception of history is that he brings the principle of *work* to the fore, insisting that historical development happens to be so determined that everything "should be achieved by *work* . . . as if nature intended that man should owe all to himself."[11] The paradoxical intelligibility of the relationship between the innumerable particular individuals and the human species, and the strange but coherent development resulting from such relationship is described by Kant in the following terms:

> It is like the erratic weather the occurrence of which cannot be determined in particular instances, although it never fails in maintaining the growth of plants, the flow of streams, and other of nature's arrangements at a uniform, uninterrupted pace. Individual human beings, each pursuing his own ends according to his inclination and often one against another (and even one entire people against another) rarely intentionally promote, as if it were their guide, an end of nature which is unknown to them. They thus work to promote that which they would care little for if they knew about it.[12]

In this way an insurmountable dichotomy is created between the individual and the species.[13] At the same time, the "rationality" of the overall process is secured by Kant in our last quote in a way that anticipates the Hegelian "List der Vernunft" (the cunning of Reason), which is said to prevail over against the conscious intentions of the particular individuals.

As to the Kantian characterization of human beings, it is very similar to that of all the major theoreticians of "civil society," putting the *"antagonism of men in society"* very much into the foreground. To quote Kant again: "I mean by antagonism the *asocial sociability* of men, i.e., the propensity of men to enter into a society, which propensity is, however, linked to a *constant mutual resistance* which threatens to dissolve this society. This propensity apparently is *innate in men*."[14]

Indeed, at the plane of overall historical development Kant gives *highly positive* connotations to the negative traits and characteristics of "human nature." For, according to him:

> Without these essentially unlovely qualities of asociability, from which springs the resistance which everyone must encounter in his egotistic pretensions, all talents would have remained hidden germs. If man lived an Arcadian shepherd's existence of harmony, modesty and mutuality, man, good-natured like the sheep he is herding, would not invest his existence with greater value than that his animals have. Man would not fill the vacuum of creation as regards his end, rational nature. Thanks are due to *nature* for his *quarrelsomeness,* his *enviously competitive vanity,* and for his *insatiable desire to possess* or *to rule,* for without them all the excellent faculties of mankind would forever remain undeveloped.[15]

Similarly, the contradiction between freedom and "egotistic nature" is handled in much the same way as in the writings of his great predecessors who share the standpoint of civil society:

> Man is an animal who, if he lives among others of his kind, needs a master, for man certainly *misuses his freedom in regard to others* of his kind and, even though as a rational being he desires a *law* which would provide *limits for the freedom of all,* his *egotistic animal inclination* misguides him into excluding himself where he can. Man therefore *needs a*

master who can break man's will and compel him to obey a *general will* under which every man could be free.[16]

As we can see, while retaining several elements of Hobbes's approach, Kant goes beyond the latter by incorporating into his own system Rousseau's seminal ideas too. However, the view that historically locates him, with the greatest precision, in the company of the leading political economists of the age, is the role assigned to trade and commerce in the course of historical development toward a more advanced condition of life in "civil society." This is the key passage in Kant's "Idea for a Universal History with Cosmopolitan Intent" on the subject:

> Civic freedom cannot now be interfered with without the state feeling the disadvantage of such interference in all *trades,* primarily foreign *commerce* and as a result [there is] a decline of the power of the state in its foreign relations. Therefore this *freedom is gradually being extended.* If one obstructs the citizen in seeking his welfare in any way he chooses, as long as [his way] can coexist with the freedom of others, one also hampers the vitality of all business and the strength of the whole [state]. For this reason restrictions of personal activities are being increasingly lifted and *general freedom* granted and thus *enlightenment* is gradually developing with occasional nonsense and freakishness.[17]

The "achievement of civil society which administers law [*Recht*] generally" on a world scale represents in Kant's eyes "the highest task nature has set mankind,"[18] and it is brought about by the working of the complex material determinations and contradictory interactive processes he identifies among individuals and "even entire peoples." Naturally, a great deal must be ascribed in this conception to the mysteries of the "hidden plan of nature."[19] However, the mysteries are not derived from some stated or unstated theological requirement. On the contrary, they arise from the *Kantian model of civil society itself,* in which the contradictory individual interactive processes cannot be made intelligible on their own. They cannot be made intelligible at all precisely because of the inherent limitations of the individualistic standpoint which Kant shares with many others. For such a standpoint can only yield the idea of the extreme capriciousness of fluctuating weather conditions, to be set against the actuality of nature's mysteriously benevolent uniformity and productive efficacy, as characterized by Kant himself.

As we shall see, despite its problematical character in other respects, Hegel's approach represents a significant advance over the Kantian philosophy of history. For inasmuch as it depicts an earlier and less consolidated phase in the development of "civil society" than Hegel, the Kantian system remains tied to some abstract moral categories in its attempt to explain the motive forces of mankind's historical development.

It is by no means accidental that Kant insists on the *"primacy of practical reason"* as the all-important structuring principle of his system. For that principle enables him to "resolve" the dilemmas and contradictions of social life through the postulates of the "intelligible world" and the legislative supremacy of *formal universality* over all conceivable constraints of *matter* and *empirical existence.* The same model is applied to the assessment of the world of Right and the relationship between formal equality and substantive inequality:

> Right is the limitation of every man's freedom so that it harmonizes with the freedom of every other man in so far as harmonization is possible according to a general law. Public Law is the totality of external laws which makes such a general consonance possible. . . . The civic constitution is a relationship of free men who, despite their freedom for joining with others, are nevertheless placed under coercive laws. This is so because it is so willed by *pure a priori legislating reason* which has *no regard for empirical purposes* such as are comprised under the general name of happiness. . . . The *general equality* of men as subjects in a state coexists quite readily with the *greatest inequality* in degrees of the *possessions* men have, whether the possessions consist of corporeal or spiritual superiority or in material possession besides. Hence the general equality of men also coexists with *great inequality of specific rights* of which there may be many. Thus it follows that the welfare of one man may depend to a very great extent on the will of another man, just as the *poor are dependent on the rich* and the one who is *dependent must obey* the other as a child obeys his parents or the wife her husband or again, just as one man has command over another, as one man serves and another pays, etc. Nevertheless, all

subjects are equal to each other before the law which, as a pronouncement of the general will, can only be one. This law concerns the *form* and not the *matter* of the object regarding which I may possess a right.[20]

The same orientation guides Kant in his reflections on history. Accordingly, he constructs a much more aprioristic unfolding of the historical process out of his postulates than Hegel, in conformity to the requirements of the categorical imperative.

This becomes clear if we remember that even in the last phase of his philosophical development—when, under the impact of the French Revolution and its equally turbulent aftermath, he tries to face some of the contradictions of the real world in his philosophy—Kant could not get rid of the severe limitations of his aprioristic transcendentalism. He sets up a stark *dichotomy* between the *"moralist politician"* and the *"political moralist,"*[21] opting for the first on account of his conformity to the moral law as opposed to the second who bends moral considerations to suit the statesman's advantage.

Thus the abstract determinations of "duty and ought" *(Pflicht* and *Sollen)* are voluntaristically superimposed on both politics and history. Political actions, just like individual pursuits, are evaluated in accordance with the *formal* principle that directly *universalizes* one's subjective maxim as a general law.[22] The question of right is raised "in relation to an a priori knowable politics."[23] Freedom, equality, etc., are established as "duties,"[24] and "moral evil" is declared to be by its very nature "self-destructive."[25] Similarly, it is stipulated that "human rights must be held sacred" even if it means great sacrifices to the ruling powers.[26]

In harmony with this aprioristic determination of politics—which is also designed to establish "the unity of practical philosophy with itself,"[27] in accordance with the earlier mentioned principle of the *primacy of practical reason* in the Kantian system as a whole—the postulated "moralist politician" is supposed to serve history's own purpose: by pursuing the aim of "eternal peace" not as a "physical good" but as a "moral duty," desired for its own sake and "arising out of the circumstances of acknowledging the duty itself."[28]

Furthermore, the objective finality postulated by Kant becomes necessary in order to underpin the general moral construct, in view of its structural deficiency in attempting to derive the *objectivity* of universally valid law (an abstract formalistic substitute for the interpersonal objectivity of action in the social sphere) from the *subjective maxims* of isolated individuals. On the one hand, it is stated that parallel to the expansion of individual needs we find in history a necessary *decrease* in the possibility of their gratification (an idea very similar to the Malthusian view of socioeconomic development), from which it is deduced that in an *inverse ratio* to the *empirical* satisfaction of the *individuals* grows the *moral* figure of the *whole*, thereby bringing nearer the rule of practical reason, the rule of morality. And on the other hand, nature's original "finality" to make men live everywhere on earth, using *war* as its "despotic instrument" to realize this purpose,[29] is said to be progressively displaced by the teleology of *"reciprocal self-interest"* and the *"commercial spirit"* (*Handelsgeist:* a concept borrowed from Adam Smith) corresponding to it. Accordingly, it is postulated that *"commercial spirit, which is incompatible with war* [*sic!!*], sooner or later will bring all people under its power,"[30] thus pointing in the right direction of history's inexorable march toward moral perfection and eternal peace in the framework of harmoniously coexisting states.

As we can see, Kant's horizon, too, is hopelessly constrained by the "standpoint of political economy," i.e., by the standpoint of powerfully self-asserting capital. So much so that even in the midst of ever-intensifying conflagrations in Europe—and despite the growing evidence with regard to their material determinations—he idealizes "commercial spirit" to the point of completely disregarding that the exact opposite of his wishful expectations (i.e., the total destruction of humankind) might come true on the basis of the extreme negative potentialities implicit in that "spirit."

Thus it is the contradiction between the given historical reality and the idealized "commercial spirit" that produces the Kantian moral construct of politics and history. For such an approach resolves the striking contradictions between the embellished ideal and the cruelly prosaic reality by an abstract discourse on history as a "progressive approximation"[31] to the state of eternal peace and the universal rule of the moral law.

5.4 The Radical Openness of History

Conceptualizing an earlier stage of social development and identifying itself with the Enlightenment attitude to Reason as the ultimate determinant of human action on the universal scale of the species, the Kantian conception pays much less attention to the recognizable characteristics of actual history than Hegel. For the latter incorporates in a strikingly realistic fashion many details of human development into his grandiose speculative scheme.

But even so, no matter how great Hegel's advance over Kant, he fails to conceptualize the *radical openness of history,* since the ideological determinations of his position stipulate the necessity of a reconciliation with the present and thus the arbitrary *closure* of the historical dynamic in the framework of the modern state. (Hence the necessary identification of "rationality" and "actuality" from which the equation of actuality and *positivity* can be derived.) Thus the characteristic "theological" teleology of "civil society," in its circular reciprocity with the bourgeois state, asserts itself as the ultimate reconciliatory frame of reference—and a "point of rest"—of the Hegelian construct.

Just as in the case of Kant, his great predecessor, the final responsibility for the reconciliatory closure of Hegel's conception resides with the ideological determinations, and not simply with the idealism of the Hegelian teleology per se. However, the latter is a most welcome methodological complement and vehicle of the social standpoint of political economy from which the apologetic ideological determinations arise.

To be sure, human history is not intelligible without some kind of teleology, as we have seen in chapter 2. But the only teleology consistent with the materialist conception of history is the objective and open-ended teleology of labor itself. At the fundamental ontological level such teleology is concerned with the way in which the human being—this unique "self-mediating being of nature"—creates and develops itself through its purposeful productive activity.

In this process, labor fulfills the function of active mediation in the progressively changing metabolism between human beings and nature. All potentialities of the socialized human being as well as all characteristics of the social intercourse and social metabolism emerge from the objective teleology of this mediation. And since the labor involved in these processes and transformations is the labor of human beings themselves, the active mediation between the human individuals and nature cannot be considered other than *self-mediation* that, as a framework of explanation, is radically opposed to any theological conception of teleology.

Consequently, it is obvious already at this level that history must be conceived as necessarily open-ended in virtue of the qualitative change that takes place in the natural order of determinations: the establishment of a unique framework of ontological necessity of which *self-mediating human teleology* itself is an integral part.

The *historically created* radical openness of history—human history—is, therefore, inescapable in the sense that there can be no way of theoretically or practically *predetermining* the forms and modalities of human *self*-mediation. For the complex teleological conditions of this self-mediation through productive activity can only be satisfied—since they are constantly being created and recreated—in the course of this self-mediation itself. This is why all attempts at producing neatly self-contained and closed systems of historical explanation result either in some arbitrary reduction of the complexity of human actions to the crude simplicity of mechanical determinations, or in the idealistic superimposition of one kind or another of *a priori transcendentalism* on the *immanence* of human development.

5.5 Critique of the Hegelian Philosophy of History

It is well known that Marx credited idealism—in contrast to traditional materialism—with being the first to conceptualize the "active and subjective side" of historical development. However, in view of the uncritical presuppositions of the philosophers concerned, with regard to the established order, idealism could envisage active intervention in the unfolding history only in an extremely abstract form. That is to say, it had to superimpose its preconceived "categories" on historical events and personalities alike, substituting the "self-development of the idea" for the objective determinations of actual social changes.

All the same, there can be no doubt that focusing attention on the subjective and active side of the multifaceted process of socio-historical interchanges constituted a major achievement on the road to making the overall dynamic of historical development intelligible in terms of *conscious*—even if, as far as the particular individuals were concerned, only paradoxically and contradictorily conscious—human intervention in the complex order of determinations.

It was due to the inner requirements of the "standpoint of political economy" that even the peak of such conception of history—the Hegelian philosophy—had to remain trapped within the contradictions of its necessarily abstract and preconceived teleological categories. For though Hegel boldly asserted that "the History of the World is nothing but the development of the Idea of Freedom,"[32] this grand statement sounded utterly vacuous on account of its merely *contemplative*[33] posture. Furthermore, it also suffered from the self-contradictory character of its apologetic tendency which saw the Idea's ultimate "self-realization" in the modern capitalist state,[34] notwithstanding the internal divisions and antagonisms of the latter. Antagonisms that, to a significant extent, the Hegelian philosophy itself could not help acknowledging.

As a result, Hegel equated the historical development that was supposed to have reached its final completion in the modern state with nothing less than the "justification of God in History." This is how Hegel summed up his vision of historical development:

> The inquiry into the essential *destiny of Reason*—as far as it is considered in reference to the World—is identical with the question, what is the *ultimate design of the World?* And the expression implies that that design is destined to be realized.[35]

However, despite the religious phraseology, Hegel was not expressing here a religious concern as such. On the contrary, he considered it a great historical advance—accomplished by the "Germanic world" on behalf of the whole of mankind, as the climax of the unfolding of "universal history"—that "in the Protestant Church the reconciliation of Religion with Legal Right has taken place. In the Protestant world there is no sacred, no religious conscience in a state of separation from, or perhaps even hostility to, Secular Right."[36]

Thus he put forward a secularized interpretation of history—one culminating in the rational actuality of the Germanic state—as the *true Theodicaea*. These were the final words of his *Philosophy of History:*

> That the History of the World, with all the changing scenes which its annals present, is this process of development and the realization of Spirit—this is the *true Theodicaea*, the justification of God in History. Only this insight can *reconcile* Spirit with the History of the World—viz., that *what has happened, and is happening every day,* is not only not 'without God,' but is essentially His Work.[37]

Others may have had their—strictly theological—view of Theodicaea, but that was of no interest to Hegel. His meaning of the *"true Theodicaea"* was made perfectly clear in his recapitulation of the climax of the historical process which preceded the lines just quoted:

> Feudal obligations are abolished, for freedom of property and of person have been recognized as fundamental principles. Offices of State are open to every citizen, talent and adaptation being of course the necessary conditions. The government rests with the official world, and the personal decision of the monarch constitutes its apex. . . . Yet with firmly established laws, and a settled organization of the State, what is left to the sole arbitrament of the monarch is, in point of substance, no great matter. . . . A share in the government may be obtained by every one who has a competent knowledge, experience, and a morally regulated will. Those who know ought to govern. . . . Objective Freedom—the laws of real Freedom—demand the subjugation of the mere contingent Will— for this is in its nature formal. If the Objective is in itself Rational, human insight and conviction must correspond with the Reason which it embodies, and then we have the other essential element—Subjective Freedom—also realized.[38]

In this sense, what counted in Hegel's eyes as the true Theodicaea was the realization of Objective Freedom in the actuality of the modern state. And the historical process itself was defined as the establishment of the identity of the Objective and the Rational, as well as of Subjective Freedom and the requirements of the Law, reconciling at the same time the particular individuals to the state-oriented "rational actuality" of the present.

To be sure, in this conception the room for real historical determinations—i.e., determinations that would acknowledge the objective weight of the past and the present without blocking off the future—had to be extremely limited. "Activity" itself, in an idealistically respectable sense of the term, had to be made synonymous with *self-contemplation* in order to befit the definitional characterization of "Spirit." For, according to Hegel, "the very essence of Spirit is activity: it realizes its potentiality—makes itself its own deed, its own work—and thus it becomes an object to itself; *contemplates itself* as an objective existence."[39]

Such a definitional determination of the nature of historical development, in accordance with an, a priori assumed, *quasi*-theological finality of "civil society," and its corresponding state, inevitably vitiated Hegel's conception of necessity and temporality alike. "Necessity" was conjured up by a conflation of logic and actuality, superimposing the abstractly preconceived categories of the *"Science of Logic"* on real historical movements and transformations, at times in the most grotesque form.[40] "Temporality," on the other hand, had to be turned in the end from a three-dimensional determination of past, present and future into an essentially *one-dimensional present,* partly for apologetic reasons and partly as a result of the internal conceptual requirements of the Hegelian system dominated by the Logic.[41]

We can see this through the fact that, despite defining History as "the ideal necessity of transition,"[42] Hegel could simultaneously also maintain that "the History of the World travels from East to West, for *Europe is absolutely the end of History,"*[43] in keeping with the glorified modern (Germanic) state in his overall system as the "final aim" of actual historical development. The "necessitated gradations"[44] of this far from open-ended "transition" were all modeled on the Logic[45] that conveniently also lent itself to the apologetic requirements of compressing the dynamic three-dimensionality of actual historical time into a mythically inflated and metaphorically embellished present:

Spirit is essentially the result of its own activity: its activity is the transcending of immediate, simple, unreflected existence—the negation of that existence, and the *returning into itself.* We may compare it with the seed; for with this the plant *begins,* yet it is also the *result* of the plant's entire life. . . . We have already discussed the *final aim* of this progression. The *principles* of the successive phases of Spirit that animate the Nations in a *necessitated gradation,* are themselves only steps in the development of the one universal Spirit, which through them elevates and completes itself to a self-comprehending totality. While we are thus concerned exclusively with the Idea of Spirit, and in the History of the World regard everything as only its manifestation, we have, in traversing the past—however extensive its periods—only to do with what is *present;* for philosophy, as occupying itself with the True, has to do with the *eternally present.* Nothing in the past is lost for it, for the Idea is *ever present;* Spirit is immortal; with it there is *no past, no future, but an essentially now.* This necessarily implies that the present form of Spirit comprehends within it all earlier steps. These have indeed unfolded themselves in succession independently: but what Spirit is it has *always been* essentially; distinctions are only the development of this essential nature. The life of the ever present Spirit is a *circle* of progressive embodiments, which looked at from another point of view *appear* as past. The grades which Spirit *seems* to have left behind it, it still possesses in the *depths of its present.*[46]

However, no amount of metaphorical flourish, not even the one arising from the soil of Hegel's philosophical and linguistic genius, could turn the abstract "self-activity" of Spirit—"returning into itself" through its a priori conformity to the timeless "principles" and categorial requirements of a speculative Logic—into real history. For the seed does not simply fall out of the sky, but comes into being through the actual processes of inorganic and organic matter, before it can reproduce itself as a *new* beginning, and not as an abstract logical coincidence of the *categories* of end and beginning. Real historical determinations have to *account for the genesis and subsequent historical transformations* of social/historical structures, in all three dimensions of actual historical time, instead of conveniently assuming them through the self-referential circularity of "Spirit returning into itself" in accordance with the logically stipulated "essential nature" of its "essential presentness" and "self-comprehending totality."

Comparably to the role of the "primacy of Practical Reason" in Kant's system in general and in his philosophy of history in particular, it was because of the internal hierarchy of the Hegelian system as a whole—with the *Philosophy of Right* and its corresponding state formation at its apex— that the "eternal present" and its manifold circles had to come into dominance in Hegel's conception of historical determination. This is why the *Philosophy of History* had to reach its climax in its apotheosis of the modern state, just as the *Philosophy of Right* had to culminate in an identically circular account of world history as the "self-realization of Reason" in the form of the state. History, according to Hegel, could exist in the past— though even then only *"in the depths of Spirit's present,"* thus anticipating the structures of the *"essentially now"*—but not in the future: and especially not at the level of "civil society" eternally locked into the pseudo-universal politics of the modern state. Thus despite Hegel's boundless admiration for the Greek world—particularly pronounced with regard to art which he could locate in his scheme of things at an earlier stage of Spirit's "self-activity"—he could find nothing positive to say about the political dimension of that civilization. He had to maintain that in politics "the Ancient and the Modern have not their essential principle in common."[47] For if they did, the process of sociopolitical development would have had to be admitted to be inherently contradictory, hence necessarily open-ended, instead of being terminated in its "Germanic form," in a "civilizing" (i.e., imperialistically dominant) Europe defined as "absolutely the end of History."

In this philosophical glorification of the established power relations— which in fact sharply contradicted the Hegelian claims with regard to the historically unstoppable realization of the "principle of freedom"—national and colonial oppression were declared to be perfectly in accord with the inner requirements of "Spirit returning into itself" as "fully developed Spirit." The dominant imperialist states received their philosophical legitimation vis-à-vis the "minor states" they oppressed—and through such legitimation could in principle forever *rightfully* oppress—by saying:

> *Minor states* have their existence and *tranquillity* secured to them more or less by their neighbours: they are therefore, properly speaking, *not independent,* and have not the *fiery trial of war* to endure.[48]

The idea of such "fiery trial of war" as a "life-and-death struggle," said to be necessary because "it is solely by risking life that freedom is obtained"[49]—appeared in Hegel's thought at a much earlier stage. However, in contrast to the *Philosophy of History* as well as to the *Philosophy of Right*, in the Hegelian *Phenomenology of Mind* it constituted only a limited and necessarily transcended *moment* of the objective dialectic of "Master and Bondsman." Indeed, in the *Phenomenology* the Bondsman was able to assert itself against the initially dominant Master in its own way, through the *power of labor,* thereby not merely limiting but totally *reversing* the original relationship:

> For just where the master has effectively achieved lordship, he really finds that something has come about quite different from an independent consciousness. It is not an independent, but rather a *dependent* consciousness that he has achieved.. He is thus not assured of self-existence as his truth; he finds that his truth is rather the unessential consciousness, and the fortuitous unessential action of that consciousness. The truth of the *independent* consciousness is accordingly the consciousness of the *bondsman.* This doubtless appears in the first instance outside itself, and not as the truth of self-consciousness. But just as lordship showed its essential nature to be the *reverse* of what it wants to be, too, bondage will, when completed, pass into the *opposite* of what it immediately is: being a consciousness repressed within itself, it will enter into itself, and change round into *real and true independence.* . . . Through *work and labour* this consciousness of the bondsman comes to itself. . . . The negative relation to the object passes into the *form* of the object, into something that is *permanent.* . . . This negative mediating agency, this activity giving shape and form, is at the same time the individual existence, the pure self-existence of that consciousness, which now in the work it does is *externalized* and passes into the *condition of permanence.* The consciousness that toils and serves accordingly attains by this means the direct apprehension of that *independent being as its self.* . . . In fashioning the thing, self-existence comes to be felt explicitly as *his own proper being,* and he attains the consciousness that he himself exists in its own right and on its own account [*an und für sich*].[50]

Horrified by the explosive implications of the objective dialectic of "Master and Bondsman"—which asserted the adequately self-sustaining existence and "*an und für sich*" character of labor, together with the necessary historical supersession of "lordship": shown to be totally superfluous in terms of Hegel's own account—the author of *The Phenomenology of Mind* desperately tries to take back his conclusion already on the last half page of the chapter on "Lordship and Bondage" with the help of linguistic juggling and conceptual sophistry.

The problem for Hegel is that "by the fact that the form is *objectified* [*hinausgesetzt wird*], it does not become something *other* [*ihm nicht ein Anderes als es*] than the consciousness moulding the thing through work; for just that form is his pure self-existence, which therein becomes truly realized. Thus, precisely in *labour* where there seemed to be merely some *outsider's mind* and ideas involved, the *bondsman* becomes aware, through this *re-discovery of himself by himself*, of having and being a 'mind of his own' [*sich selbst eigner Sinn*]."[51]

Thus we are dangerously close at this point to clearly distinguishing and opposing to one another *objectification* and *alienation*, thereby undermining the conceptual impossibility of labor's self-emancipation through the transcendence of alienation.

Hegel extricates himself from this difficulty by simply *declaring* in the next—and final—paragraph of "Lordship and Bondage" that it is *"necessary" to have "fear and service* in general," as well as "the *discipline of service and obedience*" coupled with "formative activity" in a "universal manner." Thus the *temporal* dimension of the historical dialectic is radically liquidated and its phases become permanent "moments" of the externalized pseudo-universal structure of domination in which labor is "through and through infected" by internalized, rather than external, fear.

To be sure, the Hegelian enthusiasm for "universal formative activity" as an "absolute notion" that ought to extend its mastery "over the entire objective reality"[52] is historical in the sense that it rejects the historically no longer tenable claims of *feudal bondage*—and corresponding idleness—from the standpoint of political economy. However, its criticism of the past is inseparable from the "uncritical positivism" with which the timeless "moments" of structural domination become the defining characteristics of the Hegelian notion of "universal formative activity."

The problem is that while *discipline* is indeed an absolutely necessary requirement of all successful formative activity, it is quite another matter as far as "fear and service" as well as "obedience" are concerned. Nor is there a necessary connection between disciplined formative activity and fear/service/obedience, provided that the activity in question is determined by the "freely associated producers" themselves who also determine the *self-discipline* appropriate to their own aims and to the inherent nature of the activity they embark upon.

Naturally, Hegel, from capital's standpoint of political economy, cannot embrace such perspective. Nor can he find, of course, anything to provide the "universality" of an inherently particularistic and iniquitous system of "formative activity" that retains the domination of one class by another in "civil society." This is why the profound historical dialectic of "Lordship and Bondage" is in the end liquidated partly through the transformation of its actual historical phases into timeless "moments" and logical "categories," and partly through arbitrary declarations (of the non-existent "necessary connections" we have just seen) and equally arbitrary linguistic devices. As an example of the latter it is enough to think of the use to which Hegel puts the expression "mind of its own" [*der eigne Sinn*] in his precarious argument. For he categorically declares that if labor does not conform to the stipulated necessary connection between fear/service/obedience and formative activity, "then it has a merely vain and futile mind of its own [*so ist es nur ein eitler Sinn*]." Indeed, a few lines further on Hegel makes great play about the (strictly German, purely linguistic) connection between "mind of its own" and *"stubbornness"* [*der eigne Sinn ist Eigensinn*], so as to totally discredit any departure from the idea of "universal formative activity"—as wedded to fear, service and obedience—that reasserts labor's permanent dependency.

By the time we reach *The Philosophy of History* (and the *Philosophy of Right*), Hegel's earlier inner doubts, intimated in the *Phenomenology*, completely disappear, and the ideological rationalization of the materially and politically dominant social order's brutal self-assertion through the "fiery trial of war" acquires the anti-dialectical rigidity of an arbitrary metaphysical postulate in the Hegelian conception.

As we have seen, Kant advocated and postulated the universal rule of a "perfect constitution," the successful institution of "eternal peace," and the harmonious coexistence of all states within the framework of a League of Nations equally beneficial to all. He formulated these postulates on the explicitly stated ground that "the commercial spirit is incompatible with war," thus elevating to the level of the so-called "a priori principles of Reason" the wishful thinking and *universalistic illusions* of "enlightened" capital: incurably *particularistic,* in fact, in its objective constitution, to the core.

Hegel, representing—with a far greater sense of realism—a much more consolidated stage in the historical development of capital, had no use for the Kantian illusion of "eternal peace," which was supposed to be established at a certain point of human advancement thanks to the enlightened dictates of the "commercial spirit." He did not hesitate to say quite categorically that "the *nation state* is . . . the *absolute* power on earth," and that the *"universal* proviso of international law therefore does not go beyond an *ought-to-be."*[53] Consequently, according to Hegel, the necessity of settling disputes by war had to assert its absolute primacy on the material ground of "civil society." And he insisted that the realization of the idea of peace—a mere "ought-to-be," even though it was arbitrarily and circularly *assumed* by Kant as the necessary culmination of historical development—*"presupposes* an accord between states; this would rest on moral or religious or other grounds and considerations, but in any case would always depend on a particular sovereign will and for that reason would remain *infected with contingency."*[54]

In this sense, Hegel was anxious to keep the dimension of "ought-to-be" at bay in his account of historical development, and to concentrate, instead, on the dominant tendencies of "actuality," even if in the end he always transubstantiated the latter into specific manifestations of the Idea's self-realizing "rationality." Not surprisingly, therefore, in his discussion of the historically most advanced embodiment of the "commercial spirit" the pride of place had to be assigned to imperialistically expanding England. For, according to Hegel:

> The material existence of England is based on *commerce and industry,* and the English have undertaken the weighty responsibility of being the *missionaries of civilization* to the world; for their *commercial spirit* urges them to traverse every sea and land, to form connections with barbarous

peoples, to *create wants and stimulate industry,* and first and foremost to establish among them the *conditions necessary to commerce,* viz., the relinquishment of a life of lawless violence, *respect for property* and civility to strangers.[55]

And to all those who might have criticized the inherent amorality of his conception, he firmly retorted that their doctrine rested on "superficial ideas about morality, the nature of the state, and the state's relation to the moral point of view."[56]

Since it was Kant himself who formulated the irreconcilable opposition between the "moralist politician" and the morally reprehensible "political moralist," one could hardly fail to see the contradiction between these two outstanding figures of German philosophy in this respect. Indeed, Hegel was thoroughly convinced that his own philosophy represented the radical supersession of the Kantian conception as a whole.

And yet a closer look at the Kantian and Hegelian philosophies of history reveals that the contradiction between the two concerning the ultimate perspectives of development is much more apparent than real. For both conceptions base their conclusions on the material premise of "civil society," assumed by them in a totally uncritical manner as the absolute horizon of all conceivable social life as such.

Hegel, though an acute observer of a later phase of historical development, is not in the least more historical in this respect than Kant, who simply postulates the radical transcendence of the identified contradictions of "human nature" and "civil society" by the beneficial self-assertion of the "commercial spirit" and the ensuing realization of an ideal system of interstate relations. However, while the Kantian "ought" is undoubtedly nothing more than the moralistic counter-image of a reality that he cannot conceivably criticize from the "standpoint of political economy" (which he fully supports, nay idealizes), Hegel has his own way of glorifying the social order of bourgeois "civil society," in conformity to a historically more advanced—and also more obviously antagonistic—stage of development conceptualized by him in a representative fashion.[57]

The generic moral postulates of the Kantian solution are no more telling about his uncritical acceptance of the social horizons of the "commercial spirit" than about the—both on the internal and on the interna-

tional plane—as yet far from fully articulated and consolidated character
of the socioeconomic order which the standpoint of political economy
expresses. By the time Hegel writes his *Philosophy of History* and *The
Philosophy of Right,* well after the conclusion of the Napoleonic Wars and
the consolidation of the new social order, the antagonisms of "civil society" and its state formation are too much in evidence to be able to reassert
Kant's Enlightenment illusions. Thus the contradictorily "indetermi-
nate" determination of the state's behavior through the material interests
of "civil society" must be acknowledged for what it appears to be from the
standpoint of political economy itself. As Hegel puts it:

> A state through its subjects has *widespread connexions and many-sided
> interests,* and these may be readily and considerably injured; but it
> remains *inherently indeterminable* which of these injuries is to be
> regarded as a specific breach of treaty or as an injury to the honour and
> autonomy of the state.[58]

As in Kant's metaphor about the "erratic weather," the *"principle of
indeterminacy"* rules also in Hegel's account of the ongoing developments. And the reason why to both Kant and Hegel the underlying law
must remain the mystery of a quasi-theological teleology is because they
take for granted the absolute permanence of "civil society," in all its con-
tradictoriness, as the necessary premise of all further explanation. The
uneasy coalescence of the multifarious constituents of the historical
process is described by Hegel with graphic imagery:

> It is as particular entities that states enter into relations with one another.
> Hence their relations are on the largest scale a maelstrom of external con-
> tingency and the inner particularity of passions, private interests and self-
> ish ends, abilities and virtues, vices, force, and wrong. All these whirl
> together, and in their vortex the ethical whole itself, the autonomy of the
> state, is exposed to contingency. The principles of the national minds are
> wholly restricted on account of their particularity, for it is in this particu-
> larity that, as existent individuals, they have their objective actuality and
> their self-consciousness.[59]

At the same time, the "world mind" is postulated as the imaginary resolution of the manifold actual contradictions without questioning, however, the social world of "civil society" in the slightest. Particular states, nations, and individuals are said to be "the *unconscious tools* and organs of the world mind at work within them,"[60] and the "individuals as subjects" are characterized as the "*living instruments* of what is in substance the deed of the world mind and they are therefore directly at one with that deed though it is "*concealed* from them and is *not their aim and object.*"[61]

In this way, again, a genuine insight is inextricably linked to an apologetic mystification. On the one hand, it is recognized that there is an inherent lawfulness in the historical process that necessarily transcends the limited and self-oriented aspirations of particular individuals. Accordingly, the objective character of historical determinations is grasped the only way feasible from the standpoint of political economy and "civil society": as the paradoxically conscious/unconscious set of individual interactions effectively overruled by the totalizing "cunning of Reason." On the other hand, though, the stipulated historical law must be ascribed to a force—be it Adam Smith's "invisible hand," Kant's providential plan of "nature," or Hegel's "cunning of Reason"—which asserts itself and imposes its own aims *over against* the intentions, desires, ideas, and conscious designs of human beings, even if it is said to act *mysteriously through them*. For envisaging the possibility of a real *collective subjectivity* as the—materially identifiable and socially efficacious—historical agent is radically incompatible with the eternalized standpoint of "civil society."

This has the welcome consequence from the point of view of the Hegelian conception that history—whose inner dynamism is ascribed to the design of "Reason returning to itself"—can be brought to an end at the ideologically required juncture in actual history, whatever people might think of this solution. For any conscious rejection of the Hegelian idea of the end of history can be readily dismissed with reference to the same "cunning of Reason" as no more than the unconscious individual conceptualization of the hidden ways in which the "world mind"—outwitting, by definition, the particular individual—asserts its own ultimate aim of preserving the absolute finality of its now reached finality. Accordingly, the possibility of any real—i.e., comprehensive—critique of the advocated apologetic scheme is deflected and a priori discredited. And the radically anti-dialectical conclusions that speak of the Europe of Hegel's own time as "absolutely the end of history" can be misrepresented as the final completion of the historical dialectic.

Thus, ironically, despite the significant advances of Hegel in detail over Kant, we end up in his philosophy of history with the fictitious finality of the "Germanic realm," which is said to represent the *absolute turning point*." For it is claimed that in the Germanic realm the world mind "grasps the principle of the unity of the divine nature and the human, the reconciliation of objective truth and freedom as the truth and freedom appearing within self-consciousness and subjectivity, a reconciliation with the fulfilment of which the principle of the north, the principle of the Germanic peoples, has been entrusted."[62]

Hegel hails the developments under the Nordic principle of the Germanic peoples—including the empire-building English, animated, as we have seen above, by the "commercial spirit" as the "reconciliation and resolution of all contradiction," and he sums up his claims as to what is in the process of being accomplished in the following terms:

> The *realm of fact* has discarded its barbarity and unrighteous caprice, while the *realm of truth* has abandoned the world of beyond and its arbitrary force, so that the *true reconciliation* which discloses the *state as the image and actuality of reason* has become objective. In the state, self-consciousness finds in an organic development the actuality of its substantive knowing and willing.[63]

Hegel often protested against the intrusion of "ought-to-be" into philosophy. In truth, though, what could be more blatantly dominated by the "ought" of wishful thinking than his own way of making historical development culminate in the modern state identified with the image and actuality of reason?

One of the most contradictory aspects of the Hegelian conception is its far-sighted grasp of the irresistibly *global* character of the ongoing development and, at the same time, its transubstantiation into an abstract logico/philosophical category—the category of the "world spirit's self-anticipating universality"—through which the objective dynamism of the whole process can be frozen into the static finality of the established present, under the absolute hegemony of the "Germanic peoples." The use of the *Logic* in the service of such end is highly symptomatic. For once the anticipated categorial development is completed—in accordance with the stipulated requirements of the Hegelian "dialectical circle"—and the logico/historical stage of "universality" is reached, there can be no conceivable advance beyond it. From that moment on the "principle of the north, the principle of the Germanic peoples"—declared to be the fully adequate principle of the accomplished stage of universality—acquires its representative significance and historically insurmountable validity. Thus, though the actual unfolding of history is radically incompatible with the idea of its closure, the arbitrary identification of its "Germanic stage" with the category of "universality" successfully accomplishes the apologetic ideological purpose of terminating history in the present. Accordingly, the Hegelian category of "universality" becomes the absolute legitimator of the dominant power relations, as well as the self-righteous judge of everything that fails to conform to its standard favoring itself and nothing else.

We can see the devastating intellectual consequences of the ideological determinations that produce such pseudo-universal rationalization of the most narrowly particularistic social interests in Hegel's discussion of the "African character." He sets out stating:

> The peculiarly African character is difficult to comprehend, for the very reason that in reference to it, we must give up the principle which naturally accompanies all our ideas—the category of Universality. In Negro life the characteristic point is the fact that consciousness has not yet attained the realization of any substantial objective existence. . . . The Negro exhibits the natural man in his completely wild and untamed state. We must lay aside all thought of reverence and morality—all that we call feeling—if we would rightly comprehend him; there is nothing harmonious with humanity to be found in this type of character.[64]

As to the evidence required to substantiate such assertions, Hegel is not ashamed to rely on—what he would elsewhere dismiss with the greatest contempt as "hearsay and popular prejudice," if not much worse—

"the copious and circumstantial accounts of Missionaries."[65] And here is
an example of the "reports" whose intellectual level is not higher than the
worst kind of missionary imbecility which Hegel, nonetheless, incorporates in all seriousness into his "philosophical evaluation" of the "African
character":

> Tradition alleges that in former times a state composed of women made
> itself famous by its conquest: it was a state at whose head was a woman.
> She is said to have pounded her own son in a mortar, to have besmeared
> herself with the blood, and to have had the blood of pounded children
> constantly at hand. She is said to have driven away or put to death all the
> males, and commanded the death of all male children. These furies
> destroyed everything in the neighbourhood, and were driven to constant
> plunderings, because they did not cultivate the land. Captives in war were
> taken as husbands: pregnant women had to betake themselves outside the
> encampment; and if they had born a son, put him out of the way. This infa-
> mous state, the report goes on to say, subsequently disappeared.[66]

All alleged defects and negative traits of the "African character" are
attributed to the fatal absence of any consciousness of universality. Thus
according to Hegel, "The Negroes indulge that perfect contempt for
humanity, which in its bearing on Justice and Morality is the fundamental
characteristic of the race. They have moreover no knowledge of the
immortality of the soul, although spectres are supposed to appear. The
undervaluing of humanity among them reaches an incredible degree of
intensity. Tyranny is regarded as no wrong, and cannibalism is looked
upon as quite customary and proper. Among us instinct deters from it, if
we can speak of instinct at all as appertaining to man. But with the Negro
this is not the case, and the devouring of human flesh is altogether consonant with the general principles of the African race."[67]

If a thinker of Hegel's stature indulges in such absurd racist fantasies,
one cannot simply come to terms with that by circularly asserting that this
is an "error" of some kind on his part. For there is a great deal more to this
ideological eagerness to believe the unbelievable than "naïveté" and
philosophical "error." Indeed, the real motivation behind his assessment
of the "African race" reveals itself in Hegel's discussion of *slavery*. It is full

of elementary logical contradictions for which he would not have hesitated to fail his first-year high school pupils when he taught philosophy at the Nüremberg Gymnasium.

On the one hand he states that "turning our attention in the next place to the *category of political constitution,* we shall see that the *entire nature of this race* is such as to *preclude* the existence of any such arrangement."[68] And again: "Want of self-control distinguishes the character of the Negroes. This condition is *capable of no development* or culture, and as we see them at this day, *such they have always been.*"[69] Yet, though categorically insisting—as a matter of absolute, racial determinations—on the *impossibility* of improvement and advancement with regard to "Africa, the Unhistorical,"[70] at the same time, he can both "oppose" and defend slavery in the name of the—a priori unfulfillable—condition of "gradual maturation," by saying:

> Slavery is in and for itself injustice, for the essence of humanity is Freedom; but for this man must be *matured.* The *gradual* abolition of slavery is therefore wiser and more equitable than its sudden removal.[71]

A "logic" worthy indeed of Ian Smith of Rhodesia at his worst.

At the roots of such blatantly self-contradictory philosophy of history we find not only the arrogant "principle of the north of the Germanic peoples"—dominating the greater part of the world even today—but, again, the glorification of the modern state. For it is in relation to the "inherent rationality" of the latter that Hegel has the nerve to maintain that the "Negroes" are better off in slavery within the framework of the Germanic state than under their inferior "natural condition" among themselves:

> Negroes are enslaved by Europeans and sold to America. Bad as this may be, their lot in their own land is even worse. . . . The only essential connection that has existed and continued between Negroes and the Europeans is that of slavery. In this the Negroes see nothing unbecoming them, and the English who have done most for abolishing the slave-trade and slavery, are treated by the Negroes themselves as enemies. . . . Viewed in the light of *such facts,* we may conclude slavery to have been the occasion of the increase of human feeling among the Negroes. . . . Existing *in*

a State, slavery is itself a phase of *advance* from the merely isolated sen-
sual existence—a phase of *education*—a mode of becoming *participant
in a higher morality* and the culture connected with it.[72]

And that is not all. For within the frame of reference of the allegedly
higher rationality of the Germanic state everything can be turned upside
down, whenever the interest of ideologically justifying the unjustifiable
requires that. Accordingly, we are told by Hegel that if the Europeans
exterminate thousands of Africans, responsibility and blame for such acts
must be attributed to the "want of regard for life" of those who resist their
invaders:

> In the contempt of humanity displayed by the Negroes, it is not so much
> a despising of death as a want of regard for life that forms the character-
> istic feature. To this want of regard for life must be ascribed the great
> courage, supported by enormous bodily strength, exhibited by the
> Negroes, who allow themselves to be shot down by thousands in war
> with Europeans. Life has a value only when it has something valuable as
> its object.[73]

And, of course, the "great courage of the Negroes" is totally worthless
on account of its failure to match up to the aprioristic requirements that
measure the "intrinsic worth" of everything in public life in terms of their
conformity or otherwise to the uncritically assumed interests of the
Germanic state. For "the intrinsic worth of courage as a disposition of
mind is to be found in the genuine, absolute, final end, the sovereignty of
the state."[74] How could one possibly argue against the "image and actuality of Reason" championed in such terms?

The peculiarity of the Kantian and Hegelian philosophies of history
was that they could not content themselves with claiming *necessity* on the
ground of natural determinations. Viewing as they did the object of their
aspirations, the idealized world of the "commercial spirit," from the distance of an economically as well as politically underdeveloped country—
a distance that painfully underscored the fact that their "necessity" was
to a large extent a mere *desideratum* in their own country—they had to
strengthen their claims through references to the "a priori principles of

reason" and to the "absolute determinations" of the "science of logic."
By contrast the classics of English political economy, as we shall see later
on, had no need for the crutches of idealist "logical necessity."
Contemporaries to the unfolding power of capital and of its Industrial
Revolution, they could confidently elevate to the rank of unchallengeable
necessity the alleged characteristics of "human nature" and the prevailing contingencies of the capitalistic mode of production without any further ado. Nor did they need to idealize the modern state. On the contrary, what they were interested in was precisely to secure the greatest
possible margin of action to the self-expanding economic forces themselves. This implied, of course, the most severe curtailment of the state's
power of direct interference in the socioeconomic metabolism, which
was said to be in any case ideally regulated by the benevolent "invisible
hand" itself.

The Hegelian transubstantiation of the particularistic contingency of
"civil society" into "logical necessity" and "universality," and the stipulated identity of such universality with the "principle of the modern
world" was thus also the expression of weakness and a search for ideal
allies under the materially and politically precarious conditions of the
"German misery" (Marx). Paradoxically, however, this precarious position turned out to be a major asset in some ways in the development of
German philosophy. For the enforced distance from the immediate determinations of capital's unfolding dynamism enabled the greatest representatives of German philosophy—above all Hegel himself—to elaborate the
fundamental principles of dialectical thought, even if in a mystified form.
(We shall see in this respect the comparative superiority of Hegel over
Ricardo, with regard to the dialectical relationship between content and
form, in the next section.)

Nevertheless, the idealist rationalization of material contingencies—
and thereby their elevation to the lofty plane of "ideal necessity"—
imposed its negative consequences at all levels of the Hegelian philosophy. Even the most obvious material processes had to be turned upside
down and twisted around so as to be able to "deduce" them from the
Idea's self-determination, in accordance with the ideally stipulated "principle" and "category" of the historical period to which they belonged. As
an example, we may think of the way in which even the technology of

modern warfare was deduced by Hegel from "thought and the universal."
For, according to him:

> This *principle of the modern world*—thought and the universal—has
> given courage a higher form, because its display now seems to be *more
> mechanical*, the act of not this particular person, but of a member of a
> *whole*. Moreover, it seems to be turned not against single persons, but
> against a hostile *group,* and hence *personal* bravery appears *impersonal*.
> It is *for this reason* that thought has *invented the gun*, and the invention
> of this weapon, which has changed the purely personal form of bravery
> into a more *abstract* one, is *no accident*.[75]

In this way, through its direct derivation from "the principle of the
modern world," the material contingency of ever more powerful modern
warfare, rooted in a globally expanding capitalist technology, acquired not
only its "ideal necessity" but was simultaneously set above all conceivable
criticism in virtue of its full adequacy—the "rationality of actuality"—to
that principle. And since courage as "intrinsic worth" was itself inextricably linked to the "absolute, final end, the sovereignty of the state," as we
have seen above, the apologetic circle of history reaching its culmination in
the Germanic "civilizing" state, with its ruthlessly efficacious modern warfare "invented by thought" for the sake of realizing in a suitable "imper-
sonal" form the "image and actuality of reason," was fully closed.

Inevitably, such a conception of history and the state could only produce in the Hegelian system a truncated dialectic, with "Spirit returning
into itself" as its orienting principle and *circularity* as its necessary concomitant with regard to actual historical determinations. The circular conceptualization of the established order, stipulating that "what is rational is
actual and what is actual is rational,"[76] dissolved every contradiction of the
"essentially now" by escaping from the real to the "inward freedom" of
thought activity while leaving the practical world intact, together with all
its contradictions, in its necessary "otherness": as, by definition, the realm
of a permanent—but philosophically irrelevant—alienation.[77] At the same
time, it had to conclude with apologetic resignation that "to recognize reason as the rose in the cross of the present and thereby to *enjoy the present
is the rational insight which reconciles us to the actual*."[78]

If Hegel had to acknowledge that there was "chill in the peace with the world," as he was advocating it, he could always escape from this difficulty by insisting that "there is less chill"[79] in his reconciliation of "Reason" with actuality than otherwise would be. At a certain point, in accordance with his logico/anthropological[80] characterization of the stages of historical development—which suited his apologetic conclusions in other respects, indicating that there could be no conceivable advance beyond the final phase of "Old Age" corresponding to the Germanic state formation—he had to admit that the comparison was inherently problematical. But he succeeded in extricating himself even from that corner through definitional sophistry, by saying that: "The Old Age of Nature is *weakness;* but that of Spirit is *perfect maturity and strength,* in which it returns to unity with itself, but in its fully developed character as Spirit."[81]

However, no such ingenuity could remove *resignation* from the advocated reconciliation with the established world. For the earlier quoted assertion that "the true *reconciliation* which discloses the state as the *actuality of reason*"[82] could not be separated from Hegel's pessimistic "owl of Minerva" metaphor. This conclusion appeared in the same work which reiterated, in the strangest possible opposition to "ought," the acceptance of the chilling imperative of a "peace with the present" by acknowledging that it all happens only by default:

> One word more about giving instruction as to what the world ought to be. Philosophy in any case always comes on the scene too late to give it. As the thought of the world, it appears only when actuality is already there cut and dried after its process of formation has been completed. The teaching of the concept, which is also history's inescapable lesson, is that it is only when *actuality is mature* that the ideal first appears over against the real and that the ideal apprehends this same real world in its substance and builds it up for itself into the shape of an *intellectual realm.* When philosophy paints its grey in grey, then has a shape of life *grown old.* By philosophy's grey in grey it *cannot be rejuvenated* but only understood. The owl of Minerva spreads its wings only with the falling of the dusk.[83]

Thus the recognition of an inherently problematical state of affairs could not be carried any further, since it would have undermined the entire philosophical construct and its social efficacy. As so often in the Hegelian philosophy, the "theoretical interest" of knowledge—a genuine dialectical insight into an objective contradiction—collided with the "practical interest" of maintaining the established order as given, no matter how acute its contradictions.

This is why, ultimately, Hegel's historical conception had to flounder on the rock of his own social horizon—the horizon of "civil society" in tune with the standpoint of political economy—which could offer no solution to the perceived contradictions. For while in *labor*, for instance, he recognized, with a tremendous insight, both the foundation of history and the wretched condition of alienated individuality, he produced a pseudo-solution to this objective contradiction, preserving it in reality while transferring its phantom image to the "intellectual realm" of speculative philosophy, thereby totally emptying it of its actual historical dimension and explanatory power. Since he could see no way out of the contradictory condition in virtue of which "the fully grown man [in Hegel's general logico/anthropological sense of the term] devotes his life to labour for an objective aim; which he pursues consistently, even at the *cost of his individuality*,"[84] he had to end up with the chimera of "Spirit's self-activity" fulfilling its "historical destiny" in the totally ahistorical realm of the "eternally present" as invented by speculative Logic.

5.6 Naturalistic and Dialectical Conceptions of Necessity

The materialist conceptions that originate in the social ground of "civil society"—idealized from the standpoint of capital's political economy— are equally constrained by their characteristic vantage point. It is not surprising, therefore, that Marx is not less critical of the materialist conceptualizations of historical development than of their idealist counterparts. For while Marx's materialist predecessors operate with *naturalistic* models of social life, Marx consciously defines his own position as dialectical, hence irrepressibly historical.

Nowhere is the irreconcilable opposition between dialectical and naturalistic materialism more acute than in their respective conceptions of *necessity*. The dialectical conception puts into relief the *historical* dynamic and *specificity* of the processes concerned. By contrast, the naturalistic approach tends to obliterate the historical specificities and transubstantiate them into claimed *natural* characteristics and determinations.

Marx clearly illustrates this opposition in his critique of political economists, underscoring the apologetic ideological function of their general approach. Thus Malthus, for instance,

> regards overpopulation as being of the same kind in all the different historical phases of economic development; he does not understand their *specific* difference, and hence stupidly reduces these very complicated and varying relations to a single relation, two equations, in which the *natural* reproduction of humanity appears on the one side, and the *natural* reproduction of edible plants (or means of subsistence) on the other, as two *natural series*, the former geometric and the latter arithmetic in progression. In this way he transforms the *historically distinct* relations into an *abstract numerical* relation, which he has fished purely out of thin air, and which rests neither on natural nor on historical laws. There is allegedly a natural difference between the reproduction of mankind and e.g. grain. This baboon thereby implies that the increase of humanity is a *purely natural process*, which requires *external restraints*, checks, to prevent from proceeding in geometrical progression. . . . He transforms the *immanent, historically changing* limits of the human reproduction process into *outer barriers;* and the outer barriers to natural reproduction into immanent limits or *natural laws* of reproduction."[85]

As we can see, the transubstantiation of the historically specific into a timeless "natural" determination, and the concomitant *inversion* of the relationship between immanent limits and outer barriers for the sake of inventing an alleged "natural law," are not simply "mistakes" or "conceptual confusions." On the contrary, they fulfill the obvious ideological function of "eternalizing" the given social/economic order: by transferring its historical, and therefore changeable, characteristics to a fictitiously permanent "natural" plane.

This happens to be the case not only with Malthus, the "clerical baboon," but even with the outstanding figures of bourgeois political economy—including Adam Smith and Ricardo—who are often praised by Marx. Thus Adam Smith treats labor and the division of labor as human *natural* force in general, ahistorically linking the latter to capital and rent, and constructing out of these elements a "vicious circle" of self-sustaining presuppositions from which there can be no escape.

With Adam Smith

"labour is in principle the source of value only in so far as in the division of labour the surplus appears as just as much a *gift of nature*. A natural force of society, as the soil with the Physiocrats. Hence the weight Adam Smith lays on the *division of labour*. Capital, on the other hand, appears to him—because, although he defines labour as productive of value, he conceives it as *use-value*, as productivity for-itself, as *human natural force in general* (this distinguishes him from the Physiocrats), but not as *wage labour*, not in its *specific* character as form in *antithesis to capital*—not as that which contains wage labour as its *internal contradiction* from its *origin*, but rather in the form in which it *emerges from circulation*, as money, and is therefore *created by circulation, by saving*. Thus capital does not originally realize itself—precisely because the *appropriation of alien labour* is not itself included in its concept. Capital appears only *afterwards*, after already having been *presupposed* as capital—a *vicious circle*—as *command over alien labour*. Thus, according to Adam Smith, labour should actually have its own product for wages, wages should be equal to the product, hence labour should not be wage labour and capital not capital. Therefore, in order to introduce *profit* and *rent* as *original* elements of the cost of production, i.e., in order to get a *surplus value* out of the capitalist production process, he *presupposes* them, in the clumsiest fashion. The capitalists *do not want* to give land and soil over to production for nothing. They want something in return. This is the way in which they are *introduced*, with their *demands*, as historical fact, but not *explained*."[86]

Thus the "clumsy" behavior of a great thinker—the blatantly circular presupposition of what must be historically traced and explained—produces the ideologically welcome result of transforming the specific conditions of the capitalistic labor process into the timeless *natural conditions* of the production of wealth in general. At the same time, a determinate *social/historical* necessity—together with the temporality appropriate to it—is turned into a *natural* necessity and an *absolute* condition of social life as such. Furthermore, since the question of capital's *origin* is circularly avoided—i.e., its genesis from the "appropriation of alien labor," in permanent *antithesis* to labor, the inherently *contradictory*, indeed ultimately explosive, character of this mode of producing wealth remains conveniently hidden from sight, and the bourgeois conceptualization of the capitalist labor process, predicating the absolute finality of the given "natural" conditions, cannot be disturbed by the thought of the historical dynamic and its objective contradictions.

In the same way, David Ricardo conceives the relationship of wage labor and capital

> as a *natural*, not as a *historically specific* social form, the creation of wealth as use-value; i.e. [for Ricardo] their form as such, precisely because it is *natural*, is irrelevant, and is not conceived in its *specific* relation to the form of wealth, just as wealth itself, in its *exchange-value* form, appears as a *merely formal mediation* of its *material* composition; thus the specific character of *bourgeois* wealth is not grasped—precisely because it appears there as *the adequate* form of *wealth as such*, and thus, although exchange-value is the point of departure, the specific economic forms of exchange themselves play no role at all in his economics. Instead, he always speaks about distribution of the general product of labour and of the soil among the three classes, as if the form of wealth based on *exchange-value* were concerned only with *use-value,* and as if exchange-value were merely a *ceremonial* form, which vanishes in Ricardo just as money as medium of circulation vanishes in exchange.[87]

Again, the historically specific is turned into the allegedly "natural" and thereby that which is in reality *transient* is given the status of a *natural necessity*. The conflation of "use-value" and "exchange-value"—which we can witness also in Adam Smith—is by no means accidental. For thanks to such conflation, a highly problematical (indeed *contradictory* and ultimately *explosive*) form of wealth—one that necessarily subordinates the production of use-value to the, no matter how wasteful, expansion of exchange-value—can be presented as *"the adequate* form of *wealth as such."* The method used is equally telling. It consists in the undialectical separation and opposition of content and form[88] through which the potentially critical aspect of the given value form (the *duality* of use-value and exchange-value) can be reduced to "merely formal" irrelevance, whereas the apologetic dimension of the selfsame historical value form (exchange-value misrepresented as use-value) is elevated to being a *"material"* and *"natural"* substance, so as to confer upon it the status of an absolute necessity.

The obliteration of the historical dialectic, the elimination of sociohistorical specificities for the sake of producing imaginary natural necessities—in the service of the "eternalization" of the bourgeois relations of production—is one of the principal objects of the Marxian critique. What is implicit in this critique is the concern for the self-emancipation of the associated producers from the fetishistic "power of things" (a constant theme of Marx's writings from his youth to his old age), opposing to capitalistic "reification" the objectively unfolding potentialities of a genuinely autonomous mode of action. Getting to grips with the question of "necessity"—in the sense of both drawing the line of demarcation between natural and social necessity, and determining with precision the historical, hence transitory, character of the latter—is an integral part of this concern.

Referring to Ricardo's definition of circulating and fixed capital in terms of their relative degree of perishability, Marx writes: "According to this [view], a coffee-pot would be fixed capital, but coffee circulating capital. The *crude materialism* of the economists who regard as the *natural* properties of *things* what are *social relations* of production among people, and qualities which things obtain because they are subsumed under these relations, is at the same time just as crude an *idealism,* even *fetishism,* since it *imputes social relations to things* as inherent characteristics, and thus *mystifies* them."[89]

The point is that things do not become capital—whether circulating or fixed—in virtue of their *natural* properties, but on account of being *subsumed* under determinate social relations. If it was really the case, as Adam Smith, Ricardo, and others had claimed, that the historically given mode of production was "the adequate" expression of the *natural* characteristics of things and of the *"natural law"* of social intercourse and production as such, then there could be no way out of the "vicious circle" of a priori presupposing capital so as to live with it forever. The "crude materialism" and fetishistic idealism of the political economists—their capitulation, in one way or another, to the power of things—serves precisely the apologetic ideological end of declaring their vicious circle unbreakable. This is why the task of "demystification" is inseparable from a precise definition of the natural and the social, the "absolute" (i.e., in nature's way enduring) and the specifically historical, grasping the necessities involved within their social/historical parameters, and not as untranscendable absolutes on account of their arbitrarily imputed "natural" ground.

5.7 Need and Necessity in the Historical Dialectic

One of the most important aspects of this complex of problems concerns the relationship between *need* and *necessity,* and indeed the inherently *historical* character of both. Nothing illustrates this more clearly than the changing ratio between natural necessities and social needs in the course of the reduction of necessary labor time and the growing adoption of "luxuries" as social necessities. The necessity involved in such transformations

is itself subject to changes, because needs are produced just as are products and the different kinds of work skills. Increases and decreases do take place within the limits set by these needs and necessary labours. The greater the extent to which *historic needs*—needs created by production itself, *social needs*—needs which are themselves the offspring of social production and intercourse, are posited as *necessary,* the higher the level to which *real wealth* has become developed. Regarded materially, wealth consists only in the *manifold variety of needs*. . . . . This pulling away of the *natural ground* from the foundations of every industry, and this transfer of its conditions of production outside itself, into a general context—hence the transformation of what was previously *superfluous* into what is *necessary,* as a *historically created necessity*—is the tendency of capital. The general foundation of all industries comes to be general exchange itself, the *world market,* and hence the totality of the activities, intercourse, needs, etc., of which it is made up. *Luxury* is the opposite of *nat-*

urally necessary. Necessary needs are those of the individual himself *reduced to a natural subject.* The development of industry *suspends this natural necessity* as well as this former luxury—in bourgeois society, it is true, it does so only in *antithetical form,* in that it itself only posits another specific social standard as necessary, opposite luxury.[90]

It may sound strange to hear that necessity is "subject to changes" until we recall that the natural being to which this condition applies is a unique natural being who introduces a thoroughly new mode of causality into the order of nature through its productive activity. Hence the original natural relationships are not merely modified to a certain degree but can be radically reversed in the course of historical development. This is how that which is for a start naturally necessary becomes *historically superseded* through the production of the *new needs* themselves. Consequently, clinging to the notion of the timeless "natural" is nothing but mystification, which implies the absurd *reduction* of the human individual to an unrecognizably crude, animal-like "natural subject."

The other side of the same coin is that just as the original natural necessity is historically displaced and becomes a *superfluous* and intolerable constraint from the point of view both of the individual and of the social metabolism in general, likewise the formerly superfluous and generally unaffordable "luxury" becomes vitally necessary not simply from the point of view of the separate individuals but, above all, with regard to the continued reproduction of the newly created elementary conditions of social life as such. For through the advance of the productive forces the strictly natural progressively recedes and a new set of determinations enters into its place. Consequently, the removal of the newly acquired and structurally incorporated (diffused, generalized) "luxuries" from the existing framework of production would carry with it the collapse of the entire production system.

This is a far from unproblematical process in that the transformation of the formerly necessary into superfluous, and vice versa, simultaneously removes all kinds of objective constraints and opens up the possibility of not only genuine historical achievements but also that of finding quite arbitrary and manipulative "solutions" to the newly generated problems and contradictions of social/economic life. Hence the necessary distinction between the growth of wealth as the development of the "manifold variety of needs" on the one hand, and the manipulative production and imposition of "artificial appetites" on the other, since the latter arise from the wasteful needs of an alienated production process and not from those of the "rich social individual." For so long as the production process follows its own determinations in multiplying wealth as divorced from conscious human design, the products of such alienated procedure must be superimposed on the individuals as "their appetites," in the interest of the prevailing production system, irrespective of the consequences in the longer run. As a result, the "pulling away of the natural ground from the foundations of every industry" brings with it not a liberation from *necessity* as such but the ruthless imposition and universal diffusion of a new kind of necessity.

5.8 The Conflation of Natural and Historical Necessity

From the point of view of the bourgeois social order this new kind of necessity is just as *absolute* as natural necessity was prior to being displaced by historical development. This is why the political economists cannot conceptualize the true liberating potential of the ongoing social/economic transformations. Instead, they must conflate the prevailing historical necessity with "natural necessity" so as to be able to defend the ultimately *unnecessary necessity* of the capitalist labor process as the *absolute necessity* and untranscendable natural horizon of all social life.

This conflation of the "natural" and the "necessary" is accomplished not for the sake of paying the slightest attention to nature itself but, on the contrary, so as to be able to contradict it in the most blatant fashion: by declaring the self-propelling necessities of the prevailing mode of production to be "natural/absolute," thereby decreeing the unquestionable "naturalness" of even the most artificial appetites that arise from the alienated needs of self-expanding exchange value.

If the arbitrarily stipulated, fixed "human nature"—with its necessary "egotism" (Hobbes, Kant, etc.) and "propensity to exchange and barter" (Adam Smith)—cannot establish the claimed link between "nature/necessity" and the wastefully proliferating artificial appetites, other mythical concepts and arbitrary assumptions come to the rescue. Accordingly, the myth of the "pursuit of *diversity*"—as "implanted by nature into all individuals"—is postulated in order to subsume under the force of yet another apriorism the specific pressures and requirements of even the most parasitic phase of development. Such a priori determination of "diversity," then, conveniently functions as the universal label under which anything and everything can be explained and justified, from the self-serving platitudes and formalism of liberal political theory to putting stripes into toothpaste and shaping like fishtails the wings of motor cars: all in the name of "individual sovereignty" and "consumer sovereignty" of a "free society," in perfect harmony with nature, of course.

The point is, though, that both "natural" and "necessary" must be questioned as a result of historical development. At one end, *natural necessity* progressively leaves its place to historically created necessity, and at the other *historical necessity* itself becomes *potentially unnecessary necessity* through the vast expansion of society's productive capacity and real wealth. Thus historical necessity is indeed "a *merely historical* necessity": a necessarily disappearing or "vanishing necessity" [*eine verschwindende Notwendigkeit*][91] that must be conceptualized as inherently *transient,* in opposition to the *absoluteness* of strictly natural determinations (like *gravity*).

However, natural and historical necessity are inextricably intertwined in the objective dynamic of social development itself, which makes an adequate conceptualization of their relationship extremely difficult. Since the disappearing necessity of historical necessity is visible only from a standpoint able and willing to acknowledge the ultimately *unnecessary* necessity of the given social/economic necessities, there can be no real understanding of the intricate historicization of nature in the human context if the necessarily transient character of all forms of production in terms of which such historicization first becomes possible is denied in order to be able to maintain the *permanent necessity* of the capitalist mode of production.

It is not possible to grasp the meaning of "historical necessity" without simultaneously questioning in the human context "natural necessity" as well. And vice versa: it is not possible to understand the true meaning of "natural necessity"—i.e., the vital distinction between the *absolute* conditions of production, the *elementary* requirements of the social metabolism itself,[92] and the *historically transcendable* natural conditions and determinations of social life—without radically questioning at the same time the historical limits (i.e., the strictly *relative* validity) of all historical necessity. Failing to do so, due to some prevailing social interest, carries with it in all bourgeois historical conceptions—even in the greatest of them, as we have seen in Hegel's case—the contradiction of ending up with a negation of history, despite the original intentions of the theoreticians concerned, substituting thus an idealized "nature," or some other abstract schematism, for real history. In view of these determinations it is by no means accidental that the political economists resort to the conflation of the social and the natural, the historically necessary and the naturally necessary, the sociohistorically transient and the absolute. They cannot have a clear view of *any* of these concepts since it is inconceivable for them to see the rule of capital as an ultimately unnecessary and therefore potentially disappearing necessity.

The conflation of natural and historical necessity and the concomitant obliteration of the inherently *historical* character of all historical necessity in bourgeois conceptions corresponds to the objective processes of capital's social/economic metabolism that ruthlessly subdue everything under their "iron determination," from the articulation of the material infrastructure to the production of art and philosophy as saleable commodities. It is possible to speak in Marxist theory of the quasi-natural law of the capitalist mode of production only because capital itself objectively asserts its inner determinations in this fashion, refusing to accept any limits, and overpowering all obstacles to its own self-expansion.

Ironically, however, liberal ideologists attempt to combine their total capitulation to this "iron necessity" of capital's quasi-natural law—the belief that *"there can be no alternative"* to capital's prevailing processes of productive reproduction—with the mythology of "freedom" as confined either to some lofty imaginary realm, like the Hegelian "self-understanding of Reason" or to the prosaic margins of operating in submission to capital's reified determinations while maintaining the illusion of "consumer sovereignty" and "individual freedom." And since the Marxian theory openly challenges both capital's objective determinism and the corresponding ideological capitulation to its claimed "natural necessity," it is, of course, the Marxian conception of freedom and human self-eman-cipation, and not the targets of its critique, that must appear in this upside-down world of bourgeois ideology as *"historical and economic determinism"* and the negation of freedom.

5.9 The Disappearing Necessity of Historical Necessity

In reality, the Marxian conception of history points in the opposite direc-tion. Far from remaining trapped within the horizon of any determinism, it indicates, in fact, a movement toward the supersession of not just the *capitalistic* economic determinations but of the preponderant role of the *material basis as such.* As Marx puts it (immediately after defining histor-ical necessity as "a *merely* historical, a *vanishing"* necessity), "The result and *inherent purpose* of this process is to *suspend this basis itself.*"[93]

The "purpose" here referred to is not some hidden "destiny," fore-shadowed from time immemorial, but the *objective telos* of the unfolding historical process that itself produces such possibilities of human self-emancipation from the tyranny of the material basis, possibilities that are by no means anticipated from the outset. Nor is it simply a self-propelling material determination that produces the positive result of the suspension of the once completely overbearing material basis itself. On the contrary, at a crucial point in the course of the historical development a *conscious break* must be made in order to alter radically the destructive course of the ongoing process. This condition cannot be emphasized strongly enough.

As we have seen earlier, the historical dynamic of ever-expanding needs and correspondingly growing productive forces pulls away the nat-ural ground from every industry and objectively transfers the conditions of production *outside* them, to the plane of ultimately *global* interchanges. This progressive displacement of natural necessity by "historically cre-ated necessity" opens up the possibility of a universal development of the productive forces, involving the "totality of the activities"[94] within the framework of the growing international division of labor and of the ever-expanding world market. Since, however, the conditions of production are outside the particular industrial enterprises—outside even the most gigantic transnational corporations and state monopolies—capital's "universalizing tendency" turns out to be a very mixed blessing indeed. For though on the one hand it creates the genuine *potentiality* of human emancipation, on the other it represents the greatest possible complications—implying the danger of even totally destructive collisions—in that the conditions of production and control happen to be *outside*, thus, nightmarishly, everywhere and nowhere. As Marx argues:

> The barrier to capital is that this entire development proceeds in an entirely contradictory way, and that the working-out of the productive forces, of general wealth, knowledge, etc., appear in such a way that the working individual alienates himself [*sich entäussert*]; relates to the conditions brought out of him by his labour as those not of his own but of an alien wealth and of his own poverty. But this antithetical form is itself fleeting, and produces the real conditions of its own suspension. The result is the *tendentially and potentially* general development of the forces of production—of wealth as such—as a basis; likewise the universality of intercourse, hence the world market as a basis. The basis as the *possibility* of the universal development of the individual, and the real development of the individuals from this basis as a constant suspension of its barrier, which is *recognized* as a barrier, not taken for a *sacred limit*. Not an *ideal or imagined universality* of the individual, but the universality of his real and ideal relations. Hence also the grasping of his own history as a process, and the *recognition* of nature (equally present as practical power over nature) as his real body. The process of development itself posited and known as the presupposition of the same. For this, however, necessary above all that the *full development* of the forces of production has become the *condition of production;* and not that *specific* conditions of productions are posited as a *limit* to the development of the productive forces.[95]

Thus capital's universalizing tendency can *never* come to real fruition within its own framework, since capital must declare the barriers which it cannot transcend—namely its own structural limitations—to be the "sacred limits" of all production. At the same time, what should indeed be recognized and respected as a vitally important objective determination—nature in all its complexity as "men's own body"—is totally disregarded in the systematic subjugation, degradation and ultimate destruction of nature. For the interests of capital's continued expansion must overrule even the most elementary conditions of human life as directly rooted in nature.[96]

Whether the "possibility of the universal development of the individual" comes to fruition depends, therefore, on the conscious *recognition* of the existing barriers. Accordingly, "the result and the inherent purpose of the whole process" mentioned by Marx cannot be the unproblematical outcome of some material mechanism. Its realization requires both the conscious recognition of the prevailing contradictions/barriers and the ability to institute a new mode of non-alienated social intercourse on the basis of that recognition. In other words, what is at stake is a conscious intervention in the material processes so as to *break* the vicious circle of their self-asserting chaos on a *global scale*, instead of accommodating ourselves to the course of the prevailing material mechanisms in the spirit of a naïve reliance on a new kind of benevolent "invisible hand" or "cunning of Reason," as manifested through the world market and the fully accomplished international division of labor.

Marx's description of the inherent logic of these processes in fact culminates in indicating a mode of social intercourse whose contrast with the dominance of self-asserting material determinations could not be greater. This is how he assesses the ongoing development and its implications:

> There appears here the universalizing tendency of capital, which distinguishes it from all previous stages of production. Although limited by its very nature, it strives towards the universal development of the forces of production, and thus becomes the *presupposition of a new mode of production,* which is founded not on the development of the forces of production for the purpose of reproducing or at most expanding a given condition, but where the *free, unobstructed, progressive and universal* development of the forces of production is itself the presupposition of society and hence of its reproduction; where advance beyond the point of departure is the only presupposition.[97]

Thus just as the pulling away of the natural ground from the foundation of every industry—the ever-receding necessity of natural necessity—

transfers the conditions of production outside them, in the same way the progressively disappearing necessity of historical necessity transfers the positive potentiality of capital's universalizing tendency outside it, to a radically new mode of social production and intercourse. Without a *conscious* break from the *tyranny of the material base* necessitated by this transfer, the "universalizing tendency" we can witness in the ever more chaotic interlocking of the global social intercourse can only assert its *destructive* potentialities, given the impossibility of a viable *overall control* on the basis of capital's own "presuppositions." And no one could seriously describe the project of articulating the conceptions and corresponding institutions needed for a *conscious global control* of the conditions of human self-realization as the spontaneous unfolding of *material inevitability*.

The "free, unobstructed, progressive and universal" development of social life under the conditions of the new mode of production implies the *end of one-sided material determinations* and thereby also a radically new relationship between the former material basis and its superstructure—their effective *"fusion"*—in the new *"realm of freedom."* And this is precisely the fundamental meaning of the Marxian discourse on basis and superstructure. For Marx is not simply concerned with providing a realistic as well as flexible/dialectical explanation of the complex relationship between material structures and ideas, important though such explanation might be in the context of cultural theory. His main concern is to chart the course of human emancipation and the obstacles—material, institutional, ideological—in its way. Naturally, emancipation includes the freeing of ideas, too, from the power of blind material determinations. Indeed it would be a very strange "realm of freedom," one in which everything could be produced freely except ideas.

Just as it is not possible to talk about individual freedom without forcefully opposing the subsumption of individuals under their own class, and not merely their domination by the ruling class, in the same way it is not possible to take the idea of the future "realm of freedom" seriously without envisaging at the same time the emancipation of the various forms of consciousness from the preponderant constraints of the material basis as such. This is why the disappearing necessity of historical necessity is so important in the dialectic of historical development.

NOTES

1. Marx, *Economic and Philosophical Manuscripts of 1844*, Lawrence & Wishart, London, 1959, 152.
2. Hans Meyerhoff, ed., *The Philosophy of History in Our Time*, Doubleday Anchor Books, New York, 1949, 6.
3. Ibid.
4. Ibid., 15.
5. Ibid., 5.
6. In any case, part 2 of Herder's work was published in 1785; therefore Kant could not have reviewed it in 1784.
7. Ibid., 12.
8. Ibid.
9. Augusto Guerra, *Introduzione a Kant*, Editori Laterza, Roma-Bari, 1980, 88.
10. Kant, "Theory and Practice Concerning the Common Saying: This May Be True in Theory But Does Not Apply to Practice" (1793), in *Immanuel Kant's Moral and Political Writings*, ed. Carl J. Friedrich, Random House, New York, 1949, 421.

    Like Rousseau, Kant, too, firmly favors the "middle condition" and opposes the great concentration of wealth. Thus his denunciation of feudal irrationality is linked to a rather romantic critique of that process of concentration, unable to find, however, any practical weapon against it, other than the naïve expectation that "one vote to the owner of any amount of property" might make some difference in this respect. This is how he argues his case:

    > In any case it would be *contrary to the principle of equality* if a *law* established the *privileged status* for those large estate owners as under *feudalism*, without there being any possibility that the estates would be *sold* or *divided* by inheritance and thus made useful for more people. Nor is it proper that only certain arbitrarily selected classes acquire some of these *divided properties*. Thus the big estate owner destroys the many smaller owners and their voice [in the commonwealth] who might be occupying his place. He does not vote in their stead for he has only one vote. ... Not the amount of property, but merely the number of those owning any property, should serve as a basis for the number of voters. [Ibid., 420–21]

11. Kant, "Idea for a Universal History with Cosmopolitan Intent," in Friedrich, *Immanuel Kant's Moral and Political Writings*, 119.
12. Ibid., 116–17.
13. Kant insists on more than one occasion that according to his scheme of things "those natural faculties which aim at the use of reason shall be fully developed in the *species*, not in the *individual*." (Ibid., 118.) This leads him to further dilemmas. For he has to admit that in the rational adminis-

tration of civil society the reconciliation of egotism and justice represents a practically insoluble problem. As he puts it: "The task involved is therefore most difficult; indeed, a complete solution is *impossible.* One cannot fashion something absolutely straight from wood which is as crooked as that of which man is made. Nature has imposed upon us the task of approximating this idea." (Ibid., 123.)

Taking this view, together with Kant's radical exclusion of the consideration of *"happiness"* as a merely *"empirical"* matter from the field of his concerns—characterized in this way in order to be able to concentrate on the vacuous formal principle that stipulates the "general equality of men as subjects" while accepting the permanence of the "greatest inequality in degrees of the possessions men have," on the ground that "material things do not concern the personality" ("Theory and Practice,"417–19)—makes a very disconsolate reading indeed. For such ideas rationalize and legitimate the structural parameters of the established social order as the unquestionable horizon of human life itself.

14. "Idea for a Universal History," 120.
15. Ibid., 120–21.
16. Ibid., 122.
17. Ibid., 128.
18. Ibid., 121. For an analysis of the Kantian concept of "civil society" as an essentially legal/political concept, see Norberto Bobbio, "Sulla nozione di 'società civile,'" *De homine,* no. 24–25, 1968. See also "Kant e le due libertà," in Bobbio, *Da Hobbes a Marx,* Morano editore, Napoli, 1965.
19. Kant, "Idea for a Universal History," 127.
20. Kant, "Theory and Practice," 415–18. As we can see, in the Kantian construct many things are turned upside down. We are told that "the poor are dependent on the rich"—rather than the other way round—so as to confer on the historically established material power relations the permanent solidity of a natural order and the halo of its conformity to the dictates of reason. Accordingly, the ruthlessly enforced relations of dependency are justified on the "rational" ground that "the one who is dependent must obey the other as a child obeys his parents or the wife her husband." Similarly, we are merely told that it is well and proper that "one man serves and another pays," without questioning the dubious historical legitimacy of such a relationship of dehumanizing material dependency, nor indeed of the source of the self–perpetuating wealth a fraction of which is used for paying the "one who serves." Instead, they are circularly assumed as already given, with an unchallengeable finality, on par with the relationship between the child and his parents and the wife and her husband, in the spirit of patriarchy.

Naturally, it would be a wild overstatement to suggest that Hegel can offer a satisfactory solution to such problems. However, at least he perceives them as *problems*—see above all his discussion of the relationship between "Lordship and Bondage" in *The Phenomenology of Mind*—even if the "universal class of civil servants" as the watchdog over the enforcement of the "general interest" in the Hegelian *Philosophy of Right* is devoid of any substance.

21. Immanuel Kant, *Zum ewigen Frieden* (1795), Reclam Verlag, Leipzig, 1954, 80.
22. Ibid., 88.
23. Ibid., 89.
24. Ibid., 90.
25. Ibid., 91.
26. Ibid., 94.
27. Ibid., 87.
28. Ibid., 88.
29. Ibid., 66.
30. Ibid., 73.
31. Ibid., 103.
32. Hegel, *The Philosophy of History*, Dover Publications, New York, 1956, 456.
33. "Philosophy concerns itself only with the glory of the Idea mirroring itself in the History of the World. Philosophy *escapes* from the weary strife of passions that agitate the *surface* of society into the calm region of *contemplation;* that which interests it is the recognition of the process of development which the Idea has passed through in realizing itself—i.e., the *Idea* of Freedom, whose reality is the *consciousness* of Freedom and nothing short of it." Ibid., 457.
34. "In the history of the World, only those peoples can come under our notice which form a state. For it must be understood that this latter is the realization of Freedom, i.e., of the *absolute final aim,* and that it exists *for its own sake.* It must further be understood that all the worth which the human being possesses—all spiritual reality, he possesses only through the State. . . . For Truth is the Unity of the universal and subjective Will; and the Universal is to be found in the State, in its laws, its universal and rational arrangements. *The State is the Divine Idea as it exists on Earth.*" Ibid., 39.

"The State is thus the embodiment of rational freedom, realizing and recognizing itself in an objective form." Ibid., 47.

"Objective or Real Freedom: to this category belong Freedom of Property and Freedom of Person. . . . Real Liberty requires moreover freedom in regard to trades and professions. . . . Government has to provide for the internal weal of the State and all its classes—what is called administration: for it is not enough that the citizen is allowed to pursue a trade or calling, it must also be a source of *gain* to him; . . . Nothing must be considered higher and more *sacred* than *good will towards the State.*" Ibid., 448–49.

35. Ibid., 16.
36. Ibid., 456.
37. Ibid., 457.
38. Ibid., 456.
39. Ibid., 73–74.
40. In this respect a discussion of Hegel's analysis of the "character of the Negroes," together with his advocacy of a strictly "gradual abolition of slavery," follows in this chapter.
41. These two reasons are, of course, deeply interconnected and may be separated only for analytical purposes.
42. Hegel, *The Philosophy of History*, 78.
43. Ibid., 103.
44. Ibid., 78.
45. "Universal history—as already demonstrated—shows the development of the consciousness of Freedom on the part of Spirit, and of the consequent realization of that freedom. This development implies a *gradation*—a series of increasingly adequate expressions or manifestations of Freedom, which result from the Idea. The logical, and—as still more prominent—the dialectical nature of the Idea in general, viz., that it is self-determined—that it assumes successive forms which it successfully transcends; and by this very process of transcending its earlier stages, gains an affirmative, and, in fact, a richer and more concrete shape;—this *necessity* of its nature, and the *necessary series of pure abstract forms* which the Idea successfully assumes—is exhibited in the department of *Logic*." Ibid., 63.
46. Ibid., 78–79.
47. See in this respect Hegel's summarily negative treatment of this problem in *The Philosophy of History*, 47.
48. Ibid., 456.
49. Hegel, *The Phenomenology of Mind*, Harper Torchbooks, New York, 1967, 332–33.
50. Ibid., 236–239. "Form" italicized by Hegel.
51. Ibid., 239.
52. Ibid., 240.
53. *The Philosophy of Right*, 212–213. Hegel is realistic about war almost to the point of cynicism. He writes in *The Philosophy of Right* (210–11):

    War has the higher significance that by its agency, as I have remarked elsewhere [*Über die wissenschaftlichen Behandlungsarten der Naturrechts*], the ethical health of peoples is preserved in their indifference to the stabilization of finite institutions, just as the blowing of the winds preserves the sea from foulness which would be the result of a prolonged calm, so also corruption in nations would be the product of prolonged, let alone 'perpetual' peace. . . . This fact appears in history in various forms, e.g. *successful wars have checked domestic unrest* and consolidated the *power of the state at home*. . . .If the state as such, if its autonomy, is in jeopardy, all its citizens are duty bound to answer the summons to its defence. If in such circumstances the entire state is under arms and is torn from its domestic life at home to fight abroad, the *war of defence turns into a war of conquest.*

54.   Ibid., 214.
55.   Hegel, *The Philosophy of History,* 455.
56.   Hegel, *The Philosophy of Right,* 215.
57.   The dated historical character of the phase conceptualized by Hegel is clearly indicated when he contrasts "civil society" and the state by suggesting that "in civil society individuals are *reciprocally interdependent* in the most numerous respects, while *autonomous states* are principally *wholes whose needs are met within their own borders."* (Ibid., 213.) Today, of course, no one in his or her right mind could assert this.
58.   Ibid., 214.
59.   Ibid., 215.
60.   Ibid., 217.
61.   Ibid., 218.
62.   Ibid., 222.
63.   Ibid., 222–23.
64.   Hegel, *The Philosophy of History,* 93.
65.   Ibid.
66.   Ibid., 97.
67.   Ibid., 95.
68.   Ibid., 96.
69.   Ibid., 98.
70.   Ibid., 99.
71.   Ibid.
72.   Ibid., 96–99.
73.   Ibid., 96.
74.   Hegel, *The Philosophy of Right,* 211.
75.   Ibid., 212.
76.   Ibid., 10.
77.   "A practical interest makes use of, *consumes* [mark it: not *produces*] the objects offered to it: a *theoretical* interest *calmly contemplates* them, assured that in themselves they present no alien element. Consequently, the *ne plus ultra* of Inwardness, of Subjectiveness, is thought. *Man is not free when he is not thinking;* for except when thus engaged, he sustains a relation to the world around him as to *another, and alien form of being."* Hegel, *The Philosophy of History,* 439.
78.   Hegel, *The Philosophy of Right,* 12.
79.   Ibid.
80.   This framework of logico/anthropological deductions is adopted not only

in Hegel's *Philosophy of Right* and *Philosophy of History* but also in his *Philosophy of Mind.*

81. Hegel, *The Philosophy of History*, 108–9.

82. Hegel, *The Philosophy of Right*, 222. The passage continues by claiming that "In the state, self-consciousness finds in an organic development the actuality of its substantive knowing and willing" (222–23).

83. Ibid., 12–13. It is important to notice that the concept of the "maturity of actuality" in this passage—like the "perfect maturity of Spirit" in Hegel's *Philosophy of Mind*—is a thoroughly apologetic concept. Indeed, these two concepts—Spirit's "maturity" and the "maturity of actuality"—are closely linked together and can acquire their full meaning only in relation to one another. Likewise, the organic/anthropological analogy of "The Ages of Man" (again, in *The Philosophy of Mind*) in its linkage to Spirit's unfolding—an analogy that remains a mere externality in that it completely disregards the actual historical determinations and objective presuppositions of *real organisms*—becomes intelligible in terms of the apologetic ideological functions which it has to fulfill in the Hegelian conception.

84. Hegel, *The Philosophy of History*, 223.

85. Karl Marx, *Grundrisse*, Penguin Books, Harmondsworth, 1973,605–7.

86. Ibid., 329–30.

87. Ibid., 331.

88. In this respect we can clearly identify Hegel's superiority in that he produces genuine insights on the dialectical interrelationship between content and form. Significantly, however, such insights are made possible not *despite* but, on the contrary, *because* of the abstract–speculative character of the Hegelian philosophy. For the ideological determinations of the bourgeois "standpoint of political economy" assert themselves at once with great immediacy when one has to descend from the lofty realm of abstraction to a terrain where one must confront the tangible issues of exploitation and domination as manifest in the inner contradictions of the value form. On that terrain, understanding the objective material determinations underneath the changes in form through which, for instance, living labor is transformed into capital/stored-up-labor and dominates itself in a hostile fashion, in the guise of an untranscendable external power, becomes rather dangerous for the beneficiaries of the standpoint of political economy. For the *reversal* of the selfsame transformations—in the sense of living labor assuming control over its own material conditions—might be envisaged under the impact of the persistent and ever-intensifying contradictions. It is relatively easy to see the truth of certain conceptual interconnections when it does not hurt. The whole thing radically changes, however, when revealing the dialectical intricacies and objective interdeterminations of content and form tends to undermine the interests of some apologetic intent. In that case the status quo is much better served if the dynamic of

dialectical transformations can be frozen by opposing the "merely formal" to the claimed permanent "material substance" and by making a mystery out of their stipulated a priori separation.

89. Marx, *Grundrisse*, 687.

90. Ibid., 527–28.

91. Ibid., 831–32.

92. These concepts are centrally important to all serious theory of ecology concerned with identifying the threat inherent in the ongoing economic development with regard to the elementary conditions of the social metabolism itself. The problem is capital's *necessary* inability to make the real distinction between the safely transcendable and the absolute since it must assert—irrespective of the consequences—its own, historically specific requirements as *absolute* ones, following the blind dictates of self-expanding exchange value.

93. Marx, *Grundrisse*, 832.

94. This expression—from page 528 of the *Grundrisse*—refers to one of Marx's seminal insights, articulated in great detail already at the time of *The German Ideology*. In this early work Marx laid great stress on the destructive implications of the contradiction between the forces and the relations of production and concluded: "Modern universal intercourse cannot be controlled by individuals, unless it is controlled by all." Karl Marx and Frederick Engels, *Collected Works,* Lawrence and Wishart, London, 1975, 5:88.

95. Marx, *Grundrisse*, 541–42.

96. In this respect the same considerations apply as mentioned in n. 92.

97. Marx, *Grundrisse*, 540.

CHAPTER SIX

Structure and History: The Dialectical Intelligibility of Historical Development

6.1 Preliminaries

We have seen in the last chapter that in the writings of the great thinkers who viewed the historically given world—and in an *eternalizing way* legitimated its *antagonistic* societal reproductive practices—from the standpoint of capital, including Adam Smith and Hegel, the relationship between *historical necessity* (in principle subject to change) and *natural necessity*[1] was characteristically *conflated*. This strange conflation was accomplished by them because it could yield the kind of value-laden, in strict logical terms fallacious but ideologically most pertinent, rationalizing conclusions in their scheme of things. Such "conclusions" happened to be—as from the adopted standpoint of capital's political economy they *had to be*—well in tune with the objective determinations and self-propelling requirements of capitalist "civil society," idealized by the political economists and philosophers in question. Their ideological rationalizations took the revealing form of transfiguring their indefensible *assumptions* into peremptorily decreed *conclusions*.

This way of theorizing the world by the outstanding thinkers of the bourgeoisie, already in the ascending phase of capital's all-encompassing historical development, was particularly telling in the case of Hegel, as briefly indicated earlier. For, as a great *idealist* philosopher, who defined all of his principal categories in relation to the "Absolute Spirit," Hegel could find nothing even slightly problematical, let alone theoretically inconsistent, about justifying his *ideologically*—and only ideologically— well understandable defence of *historically created and consolidated social inequality* (of *"skill and wealth"* in his words) in the name of *natural* necessity. Thus, in his *Philosophy of Right,* Hegel proclaimed:

> Men are made *unequal by nature,* where inequality is in its element, and in civil society the right of particularity is so far from annulling this *natural inequality* that it produces it *out of mind* and raises it to an *inequality of skill and wealth,* and even to one of *moral and intellectual attainment.* To oppose to this right a demand for equality is a *folly of the Understanding* which takes as real and rational its abstract equality and its "ought-to-be."[2]

Even the assertion according to which "men are made *unequal* by nature" is typically self-serving, fallaciously equating *difference* with "natural inequality." For human beings are undoubtedly made in some ways *different* by nature, but by no means *unequal* in the Hegelian sense of capital-apologetic *social inequality.* That kind of determination is *imposed* upon the class of working individuals by the discriminatory requirements of their established societal reproductive order. But of course Hegel was in no way alone in squeezing morally justifiable claims out of the unjustifiable structural determinations of the most iniquitous capital system.

In all such approaches, championed by the intellectual giants of the bourgeoisie in the ascendant, some key tenets were presented as if they had self-evident truth value, without any attempt at substantiating them, in the interest of declaring the rationally unchallengeable permanence of the established order. At the peak of the intellectual development of the European Enlightenment movement the key ideological tenets assumed in that way by the thinkers concerned ranged from Adam Smith's depiction of the capitalist order as *"the natural system of perfect liberty and justice,"*[3] benevolently managed by the mysterious "invisible hand," through

Kant's proclamation of the incurable *"asocial sociability"* and *"egotism"* of human beings—asserted by him as being due to the unalterable production of humanity from "crooked timber"—all the way not only to Hegel's just quoted pretended "natural" justification of historically imposed and perpetuated *structural class inequality* in "civil society," declared to be in full conformity to the "rational actuality" of the "Absolute Spirit," but also to his mysterious explanatory concept of the "Cunning of Reason" as the fundamental principle of intelligibility of world historical development as a whole.

This way of conceptualizing the world was unavoidable by the thinkers referred to. For what was absolutely incompatible with the standpoint of capital—and it cannot be stressed strongly enough: incompatible not only in the regressive and ever more destructive phase of capital's systemic development but already in its epoch of ascendance—was the vital concept of *structural* change without which a coherent *historical* view of the human world is unthinkable. That is, a historical view *open* toward the *structurally alterable future* as a matter of its innermost determinations. This is what had to be from the start beyond the horizon of capital's representative intellectual figures, and remain so in their conceptions of the world forever, as quite inimical to their system's inalterable logic of hierarchical structural domination and subordination.

Eternalizing the historically created world in this way was by no means a case of feasible corrigibility of a theoretical conception that could be remedied through the process of philosophical enlightenment. Historical intelligibility cannot be derived from the *internal* resources of philosophy alone. Some crucial *objective conditions* must be satisfied as the *sustaining ground* of intelligibility of the actual historical movement.

In order to make it possible to envisage the idea of *structural change* as the required explanatory concept in historical theory, the *real world* itself to which the concept of "irrepressible structural change" refers must be conceived as *objectively dynamic and historically determined* in its own terms of reference. And that necessary condition implies that the adopted historical vision must be *radically open toward the future on the ground of the objective structural determinations of the unfolding development itself.* That is the tangible meaning of the philosophical principle that asserts the *dialectical primacy of social being over consciousness.*

In this sense, the idea of change could not be sustained as truly historical if it were confined to acknowledging transformations only *within* the parameters of the *established structural framework*, no matter how fundamental; for instance, like the qualitative advance represented by the Industrial Revolution in the development of capitalism, in contrast to its historical phases prior to that revolution. In other words, in order to qualify as an *open-ended* historical vision, the necessary key term of reference of *structural change* had to be conceived as *epochal*, embracing in a *dialectical* and therefore *unclosable* way not simply the *given* historical epoch, but *all epochs,* including all those that are bound to arise in the course of the still unfolding human development *in the future.*

Thus the validity of epochal determinations had to be defined in meaningful objective terms. Not as conjuncturally manageable and with the aggravation of the descending phase of a societal reproductive system's development only violently enforceable if it cannot be "subtly" manipulated, but as *epochally sustainable*. Once the *actual sustainability* of the dominant social forces characteristic of a specific historical epoch becomes problematical—as happens to be the case under our own circumstances of capital's ever more destructive reproductive order—the move to a not marginally but fundamentally different set of epochal determinations is objectively activated within humanity's time horizon, irrespective of how consciously, or not, the historical subject responds to the emerging changes. Accordingly, this crucial objective societal requirement of *epochal sustainability* carries with it in theory the necessity of grasping and explaining the problems of human historical development not in terms of some abstract cosmic time horizon but on the ground of the *objective societal/historical dialectic*.

Thus in the Marxian vision the concept of *structurally evidenced historical change*—as the vital qualifier in the constitution of a genuine historical view of humanity's development—had to be defined as *epochal historical change* in the *most comprehensive* sense of the term. That way of approaching the problem was essential for being able to identify not only the *ascending* but also the *descending* phase of development of the given historical epoch, and thereby also the increasingly more problematical aspects of the socioeconomic system within its framework. For the structural deficiencies and ultimately insoluble contradictions of a descending *systemic phase* of reproductive interchange can become properly high-lighted only from the societal vantage point of a more advanced *epochal alternative.*

In this sense, the historical standpoint deserving its name had to combine itself from the "inside" elaborated synthesis of the systemic determinations of the given epochal structural framework with an ability to step "outside" of it, in the interest of an appropriate critical evaluation of the emerging and aggravating epochal limits themselves. And that way of looking at these problems necessarily meant the investigation of the objective dialectic of the *all-embracing*—but at the same time *irrepressibly open-ended*—epochal determinations. That is, it had to mean the adoption of an "all-embracing epochal perspective" in the sense of envisaging the successive development of qualitatively different and potentially more advanced historical epochs of societal reproduction.

"Historical totalization" could not qualify as really historical unless it was oriented toward the *open-ended totality* of feasible human historical development, on the ground of humanity's necessary social metabolic interchange with nature. Such vision of historical totalization was called upon to assess the significance of the *particular* instances and phases of transformation, including the structurally well identifiable move from one historical epoch to the next, in the most comprehensive sense of the objective all-embracing epochal dialectic.

The ability to view the dominant systemic forces both from the "inside" and from the "outside," in the interest of securing a truly open-ended conception of historical development, had to mean not only envisaging change itself but the necessity of *epochal structural change* as arising from the objective *internal dynamics* of the given order. It also meant the necessity of envisioning new epochal transformations at some appropriate time in the future, on the internal ground of the objectively prevailing determinations whose constituents—pointing in the direction of the future—were already at work in the actually existing present, at least in an embryonic form. For, in view of the innermost dialectical determinations of *continuity* and *discontinuity*—that is, *continuity in change* and *change in continuity*—the *historical* dimension of human affairs could not be artificially separated from, let alone apologetically opposed to, the *trans-historical* constituents of change.

The dialectical intelligibility of historical development could not be conceived in any other way. For the *transhistorical* is an integral part of the overall historical transformations. But, of course, the dynamic determinations of the *trans*-historical—whether positive, like humanity's cumulatively emancipatory advancement, or negative, like the exploitative power of *class domination* across a variety of social formations—should not be confused, or speculatively confounded, with the *supra*-historical, in the interest of eternalizing apologetics. ·

Naturally, this kind of always *open-ended epochal progression*—the dialectical unity of the historical and the transhistorical—could not be legitimately defined by some aprioristic principle or preconceived design. Its only feasible objective ground of determination cannot be other than humanity's actually sustainable life span, in its inseparability from the changing—at any particular point in time more or less adequately secured, but as a matter of *absolute* requirement always to be renewed— social metabolic interchange with nature. There can be no historical conception theoretically sustainable as an alternative to that. Not even if the adopted aprioristic principle or preconceived design is metaphysically ennobled as "the World Spirit."

As we have seen, the *closure* of the historical movement could be conceptually envisaged, and made intelligible in its own terms of reference, in the Hegelian system. It could be done even in the form of the idealization of imperialistically dominant Europe as "absolutely the end of history."[4]

We have seen that this conception was spelled out with reference to the "Theodicaea of the World Spirit"[5] and its "Cunning of Reason," which was said to be able to determine—by using the "world historical individuals," like Julius Ceasar and Napoleon, as *its instruments*—the course of world historical development toward the completion of *its own end,* prefigured right from the beginning.

Naturally, that kind of solution—and *any form of closure,* no matter in what way it might be justified—is totally inadmissible when historical analysis is centered on the actual ground of the *objective historical dialectic.* Thus, contrary to accusations leveled against Marx's historical conception,[6] there can be no question of an idealizing closure of history through the arrival of the envisaged *socialist historical epoch.* The socialist world order advocated by Marx as a historical epoch—in Marx's own words described as "the new historic form," in contrast to what he calls its "pre-history"—must be radically open in its comprehensive epochal parameters and corresponding internal determinations, or it could not qualify for being historical at all.

The objective and subjective factors of actual historical development, explained in terms of the *dialectical interrelationship* of the complex material and cultural determinants that constitute the changing overall structural framework of social metabolic reproduction, embracing all epochs of the past and epochally open to the future, all have their own appropriate weight and significance in this respect. That is why the objective historical dialectic cannot be legitimately pushed toward a wishfully projected conclusion even by the most ingenious theoretical scheme. Nor could it be explained by the well-known categories and principles formulated from capital's vantage point, like the "invisible hand" postulated by Adam Smith (and much celebrated even in the twentieth century, with extreme conservative intent), or the Kantian idea of "Nature's Providence" watching over the paradoxically preordained selfish moves of the creature made from "crooked timber." Nor indeed by the most flexible of them in speculatively elucidating world historical events and developments: the Hegelian "Cunning of Reason."

The only way to make dialectically intelligible the course of actual historical development is by adopting as the theoretically necessary point of departure the dynamic transformations of objectively existing need and necessity—and in the first place by *nature categorically imposed*—with reference to the progressive *self-constitution* and potentially emancipatory *self-mediation* of the human agency. That is to say, by accounting in historical theory for structurally meaningful change through the intervention of the *actual human subject of history* not as a fictitiously inflated "sovereign maker" of historical change—to the arbitrary exclusion of the immensely weighty objective conditions, found by the social individuals at their point of arrival, and in a partially modified form left to the next generation both to live with and to modify—but as a vital and genuinely *active part* (and only a part, no matter how important) of the overall process.

In this sense, the challenging problem of dialectical intelligibility in historical theory requires focusing on the actual process of the human being *becoming* the subject of history in a properly defined sense. That kind of meaningful self-constitution of the historical subject takes place in the course of the human being *progressively* developing its ability to significantly overcome—not just in principle but in its increasingly more extended *transformatory practice* over nature and society—the grave limitations of necessity. Not only those of "blind necessity," which happen to be from the outset categorically imposed on humankind by nature, but also the *self-imposed,* and under the productively more advanced conditions of development quite unjustifiable, *historical necessity* arising from antagonistic societal reproductive mediation required by the prevailing but historically superable modality of social metabolic control.

This is what we can identify as humanity's historical process of emancipatory transformation, from the first instances of *genesis* and self-constitution of the active subject of history to its most advanced *full-scale* development. But this process is very far from matching the wishful projection of some linear "progress."

To be sure, the results of this process of the historical dialectic are cumulatively embodied in the overall framework of changing socioeconomic systems, thanks to the complex interdeterminations of the objective and subjective factors at work in epochal structural change. However, the truth is that we are talking about a *historical process* that combines advances and relapses at times in a most bewildering way. For the prevalence of the emancipatory advances of this human historical process is a great positive *potentiality* only. It cannot be turned into *historically endurable actuality* without gaining *conscious control* over the *destructive constituents* of the same development. The destructive constituents, that is, which are as objective parts of the overall *historical dialectic* as the creative human self-emancipatory forces.

Thus, in order to make dialectically intelligible the unfolding course of human historical development, in its openness toward the epochally changing future, all such conflicting forces and determinations—warning in our time about the increasing danger of humanity's potential self-destruction and calling for historically viable reassurances against it—must be taken on board.

6.2 The Dynamics of Need, Necessity, and Epochally
Sustained Structural Change

Cosmic time is *irreversible* in the sense that it follows its own course of unfolding—according to the determinations and transformations emanating from its *objective constituent forces*—on the most comprehensive cosmic scale. That scale is called in cosmology the "universe," but—in contrast to religiously inspired "Big Bang" metaphysics—it should be properly qualified as "the part of the universe now accessible to our actual means of observation."[7] In this objective sense, irreversible cosmic time asserts its inexorable logic in tune with the—by human beings absolutely unrestrainable—interplay of chance and necessity in its incommensurable cosmic setting.

That is very far from being the case with humanity's more or less controllable time horizon. For human historical time unfolds according to its own terms of reference of which *human subjectivity*—from some point onward in humankind's development—is an integral part. Moreover, human historical time can overwhelmingly prevail, for better or worse, only in our *planetary household,* and it can make its impact to some extent in the extremely limited broader interplanetary surrounding around us, compared to the vastness of the universe now accessible to our means of observation.

This fundamental difference makes socially articulated historical time in principle *rationally controllable* by human beings. But, of course, this assertion is also in need of qualification. For on the one hand it is true that human historical time becomes rationally controllable to an increasing degree, in its own setting, across history. However, on the other hand, the unfolding of historical time simultaneously also makes humanity's societal reproductive interchanges—among the members of society and with nature—more or less directly affected by potentially quite devastating *irrationality*. A characteristic irrationality that arises from the class-determined failure of the social individuals to overcome the structural antagonisms of their given form of societal reproductive control. Nevertheless, it must be also stressed here, that the irrationality in question is—again at least in principle—avoidable or superable.

As to the implied fundamental contrast with the irreversibility of cosmic time, human historical time—in which *emancipatory advancement* is a profoundly meaningful and seminally important concept—is not only *reversible,* as evidenced by many advances *and relapses* chronicled in the course of actual historical development, but even *totally destroyable* through the potential *self-destructive activity of the human historical subject.* That is the real meaning of irreversible historical *closure,* and not the speculatively hypostatized "end of history" in the apologetically posited "rational actuality" of capital's "eternal present."

The term "catastrophe" is a prominently *anthropomorphic* concept, applicable in the domain of cosmic time in an *analogical* sense only, borrowed from human society. In the human world, however, the word "catastrophe" has a precise meaning of *overwhelming negative finality.* It stands for the periodically experienced destructive impact of some immense forces—of nature or society—on human life, like a massive earthquake or flood, or in its conceivably most devastating form, for the possibility of the *potential termination of human history itself,* as the *ultimate catastrophe.*

Thus the contrast between human historical time and cosmic time could not be greater also in this menacingly negative, but at the same time epochally most relevant sense. Far from offering the *epochal sustainability* of the now existing conditions, the present stage of development of human historical time imposes on humanity, with unpostponable urgency, a never before seen but *absolutely inescapable* orienting determination. For as a result of a specific type of, historically produced, systemic societal reproductive development, *under the rule of capital,* the *reversibility of human historical time* at the present juncture of history had assumed the form—which happens to be very far from a vague and abstract theoretical possibility—of the *acute practical danger* of the *termination* of humanity's historical time altogether. And to underline the gravity of this *radically new* epochal challenge, all of the required means and potentially all-destructive powers for accomplishing such ultimate catastrophic process are fully at the disposal of capital's actually existing and structurally entrenched irrational vested interests. This is a grave condition identifiable for the first time ever in history.

How did this apparently self-contradictory turn of historical events and developments come about, at the peak of humanity's highest productive advancement? What are the grounds on which the potentially fateful, and on the face of it quite absurd, culmination of history—amounting to the more than feasible total negation and destruction of human history itself—emerged from the course of humanity's productive successes and even undoubted partial emancipatory achievements, like the abolition of ancient slavery and feudal serfdom? Is there any way of rationally accounting for the historical appearance of this ultimate form of irrationality, with a view of effectively countering the immense uncontrollable power of the underlying destructive—and also self-destructive—social forces?

What is quite obvious is that no *natural necessity* could be blamed for the emergence of this acute, historically specific, danger, brought about by the perilous descending phase of the—pretendedly *natural*—capital system, of the destruction of the elementary conditions of human existence itself on this planet. A clearly identifiable danger that in our time represents a slap in the face of Adam Smith's glorification of capital as *"the natural system of perfect liberty and justice."*

This danger, to be sure, is by no means the result of natural necessity. For in terms of actually foreseen natural necessity it would take *billions* of years before planet Earth would be destroyed under the impact of the physical changes inevitably affecting the sun in the far distant future.

Yet, we are talking here not about some rhetorical flourish, devised for the sake of political convenience and corresponding profitable pseudo-green economic exploitation, nor about some mysterious cosmic threat or biblical warning, uttered in the form of "repent . . . or else." What we have to confront in these matters at the present juncture of humanity's historical development, with unpostponable urgency, is indeed harsh *necessity,* even if it happens to be a kind of necessity which is in principle counterable by conscious intervention and—provided that certain fundamental conditions are really satisfied—in due course also historically superable. In fact, contrary to the ideologically motivated distortions and purportedly "objective accounts" of Marxian theory as crude "historical determinism" and "economic determinism," nothing illustrates better the real nature of *historical necessity*—both its objective *power* for inducing significant changes in human affairs and its inherent *limits*—than the Marxian assertion that such necessity must be conceived as a potentially *"verschwindende Notwendigkeit."*[8]

The vital condition that rationally explains the apparently self-contradictory turn leading to the more than feasible destruction of human history itself in our time is not *natural necessity* at all. It is the crucially important fact that through the unfolding of human historical development a *new kind of necessity*—the sui generis *historical necessity* characteristic of significant societal change, with its associated objective *causality* inseparable from the practical realization of more or less controllable *human design,* in contrast to the type of causality manifest in the natural *law of gravity*—made its appearance in the order of nature. By its innermost character this new kind of necessity—grounded on the most complex set of past and present social determinations and dialectical reciprocities, set into motion by the human subject in an irrepressibly objective but changeable, and indeed historically changing, setting—asserts itself in the direction of the open-ended future for as long as humanity is capable of sustaining its conditions of existence as a *uniquely active* part of the planetary order.

Thus, the unfolding of human historical time as *historical necessity* is characterized by the interplay of a great variety of moves and determinations of increasing complexity, from the simplest local to the most comprehensive global, ultimately impacting on the whole of our planet. The manifold manifestations of human historical time range from *anticipations* of societal reproductive objectives to be reached, with the help of *instruments* and modalities of *action* devised for the purpose, to their more or less successful—or even completely failed—realizations, followed by *corrective* adjustments, however primitive at first, feasible under the prevailing conditions of productive development and the corresponding relation of forces.

Inevitably, the active intervention of human beings in attempting to solve even their most limited problems brings consequences with their own logic and objective power of recalcitrance that must be confronted at some time in the future, even if not immediately at the next turn of events. In fact, the absence of an immediate negative impact is often the motivating force for following a determinate course, given the socially/tendentiously determined limitations of insight by the dominant vested interests into the long-term implications and consequences of the adopted action. But, of course, the power of objective determinations cannot be ignored and averted in the long run.

Moreover, the point of departure of the whole process—prior to the progressive unfolding of *historical necessity* set into motion with its own defining characteristics by human beings—is inevitably the order of nature itself, with its *natural necessities* of which our ancestors were a massively dominated part at the most primitive stages of development. Accordingly, it is an elementary condition of historical advancement that the moves involving the first emancipatory steps should carry with them the rudimentary transformation of the given *necessities and contingencies of nature* into a form usable for the satisfaction of an expanding range of human needs.

This means gradually overcoming the originally *absolute constraints* of nature-imposed determinations that at first directly correspond to the requirements of *bare survival.* In other words, in the most obvious sense the unfolding process means *pushing back* the boundaries of the harshest natural necessity. Thus in the course of this development the original *natural necessities*—shared by our primitive ancestors with the animal world—are actively turned into *internalizable human needs.* And the latter can be legitimately called at some point in their course of transformation *humanly internalizable needs,* marking the demarcation line that separates the "unique self-mediating being of nature" from the animal world, qualitatively contrasting it with all animal species whose members are only *"genus-individuals"* (in Marx's words), who fully share their characteristics and limitations regarding their vital reproductive functions with other members of their species.

In this way, on the one hand, the original absolute constraints are overcome with the help of the *activities* and *instruments* devised by the self-mediating being of nature for the satisfaction of the most elementary nature-determined needs. At the same time, on the other hand, this dialectical process of really *active interchange* with nature, with the help of no matter how primitive instruments at the outset, also means the creation and satisfaction of new needs capable of further expansion. This goes well beyond the extreme limitations of bare survival, in accordance with the objective determinations arising from the unfolding historical process itself on the objective ground of both the necessities directly imposed by nature and the *accumulable* strength as well as the increasing *knowledge* represented by the specific functions of the utilized instruments. This is the unfolding dialectical process through which already the most primitive *homo faber* becomes at the same time *homo sapiens,* inseparably, as Gramsci rightly stressed.[9]

Of course, the natural necessities and contingencies always remain the irreplaceable *natural substratum* for the survival of this unique—progressively *self-mediating* and *self-developing*—being of nature, the emergent human being. Equally, the instruments and modes of action used for the satisfaction of the societal reproductive needs of increasing complexity must also fit in with this natural substratum in order to be sustainable at all in the long run. But this combination of the objectively given *natural contingencies* and the societally defined modes of *metabolic interaction* with them, in conjunction with the emerging productive *instruments,* also provide for the self-mediating human being the required scope for advancement, provided that the elementary conditions of the metabolism with nature are not violated. In that way, for a long time in history the objective forces and potentialities of the order of nature itself are positively released and utilized in the interest of productive development, in contrast to the reckless violation of nature around us that we experience in our own time on an ever-growing and frightening scale.

This difference between our present worsening predicament and the more remote past is of course also due to the circumstance that the required material reproductive resources, as a matter of *favorable natural contingency,* were once very far from being threatened with exhaustion by the demand imposed upon them on a planetay scale. But favorable natural contingencies cannot be assumed to be eternal, given the unavoidable impact of human intervention in the order of nature. Consequently, the observance of the rules of properly economizing *rational husbandry* is an *absolute* requirement in a necessarily *limited planetary household.*

This is so because the—by no means forever extendable—limitations of the planetary resources happen to be simultaneously not only our self-evident natural *contingencies* but also the outer horizon of our *inescapable natural necessities.* Besides, the ongoing perilous violation of the natural substratum of human existence itself, which could not be denied today except by the established socioeconomic order's most callous apologists, is not due to some fatality of nature. On the contrary, it can assert itself thanks to the *vicious circle* of capital's boastfully glorified creative or *"pro-*

ductive destruction" becoming *destructive production*, in the service of multiplying *profitable waste* and actively *generating scarcity* on an absurdly expanding scale.

In this respect we witness in the course of historical development a most *paradoxical* transformation of the relationship between humankind and nature through the emergence of the new kind of causality and its assertion in the form of objectively prevailing but by humans instituted historical necessity. For, thanks to the active power of the self-mediating being of nature for modifying its surroundings and putting to its own use, *selectively,* the forces of nature, parts of the originally given system of *natural necessities* are differentiated in the sense that they become only *"contingencies,"* to be utilized by, formerly from the order of nature itself totally absent, *human design.*

The selective utilization of *some* objective forces of nature over against some others makes that kind of advancement possible. Accordingly, on the side of nature itself we find, on the one hand, by human beings absolutely unalterable *natural necessities* and, on the other—precisely thanks to the *selective utilizability* of some forces of nature over against others—in the service of human purposes, a broadening range of pliable *natural contingencies.* At the same time, when we consider the historical transformation being accomplished in the social world, on the side of the *human subject* we find the twofold redefinition of the natural conditions of its self-reproduction as

- directly nature-determined (and in that form persisting) *natural necessities*;

- progressively expandable and qualitatively transformed[10] *natural and human needs.*

However, it is a self-deceiving presumption, perpetuated in the service of capital's antagonistic second-order mediations, that the *natural contingencies* exploitatively used by the ruling order do not remain at the same time *natural necessities,* which should be respected as the *absolutely fundamental substratum of human existence itself,* instead of being abused. Thus at a certain point in historical time, as a result of the transgression of some vital objective limits, the *natural necessities* return with a *vengeance*[11] as potentially all-destructive determinations, reasserting their *primacy*—in the unmistakable form of literally vital *natural necessities*—over the highly irresponsible treatment of natural resources and relations as *"mere contingencies"* that can be trampled upon at will.

Moreover, given the irrepressible objective interrelationship between natural necessities and human needs, the phase in actual historical development when such irresponsibility runs riot—our present time, corresponding in epochal terms to the descending phase of capital's development—is also characterized by the *system-determined subversion of human needs.* As a result, they are subjected to the fetishistic imperatives of capital expansion at all cost, bringing with them the *degradation* of human needs into *profitably manipulated artificial appetites,* imposed upon society in that form for the sake of justifying the production of boundless *waste* and dangerously extended *scarcity.* The authoritarian imposition of the vested interests of the military-industrial complex on our society—with the most active involvement of the "ethical state" idealized by Hegel—is a particularly striking example of both unlimitable waste and artificially produced scarcity under the rule of capital.

The *objective* and ultimately *inviolable logic* of the process of social metabolic reproduction and corresponding interchange with nature— inviolable, that is, in the sense that its gross violation is bound to carry with it potentially catastrophic consequences—is the necessary constitution and assertion of ever more complex and, in its general tendency, advancement-facilitating *historical necessity*, with its own forms of lawfulness, in contrast to the original *natural necessities* into which our distant ancestors are overwhelmingly submerged at the dawn of historical time. To be sure, historical necessity has its own—in some ways also *trans*historically prevailing, but nonetheless in the final analysis *historically transcendable*—constraints, arising from the self-imposed antagonisms of class domination across thousands of years of human history.

Evidently, such long-enduring class domination is the painful negative dimension of the transhistorical continuity of human development. But that is not the end of the story. It would be unconsolably gloomy if it were. The truth of the matter is that at the same time when the structurally enforced power of class domination undoubtedly persists across countless centuries of history, the cumulative character of humanity's transhistorically acquired powers, in the form of knowledge and productive instruments, offers a much more reassuring potential outcome than the permanence of structural domination and subordination. Precisely because—thanks to the fulfillment of some objective conditions made possible by the creation of historically new needs and powers favorable to securing their satisfaction—the determinations of humanity's self-imposed historical necessity (including its negative transhistorical dimension) are in principle transcendable, even if the ensuing more advanced conditions bring new constraints to be confronted in due course. Thus the overall process in question also has the *positive dynamics* of productively unfolding emancipatory transformation.

It goes without saying that the necessity instituted by human beings in the course of history as historical necessity, with its own kind of historically transcendable causality qualitatively different from the absoluteness of the natural law manifest in the form of the law of gravity, for instance, can be both *positive*, advancement-facilitating and -enhancing, and *negative*, even overwhelmingly destructive.

Indeed, the striking negative side of the developments chronicled in thousands of years of human history is the assertion of historical necessity imposed by human beings upon themselves in the form of the *antagonistic* modality of mediating the relationship of the social individuals among themselves and with nature. This form of ultimately untenable antagonistic mediation holds firmly under its rule the class-determined social individuals who are also induced to believe at the same time that their mystifying adversarial way of regulating their socioeconomic interchanges is the result of some *unalterable law of nature*. It appears to them to be a burdensome natural law because those exposed to its power are incapable of controlling it.

However, as the young Engels rightly underscored in a brilliant article,[12] which had a significant and fully acknowledged influence also on Marx, the uncontrollable force in reality is *their own making* and not a nature-imposed law at all. It is the adversarially competitive/antagonistic relationship of the individuals among themselves, corresponding to what Engels in this article called the *"unconscious condition of mankind."*[13]This presumed law manifests its power with undeniable impact on the whole of society, as if it was a genuine natural law, making its damaging impact in the midst of the periodically erupting economic crises all over the capitalist world. And Engels had clearly put it into relief in his characterization of the trade crises of his time, which were treated by the liberal political economists—whose explanatory role boiled down to providing an automatic justification of their system, absolving it of all responsibility—as an insuperable natural law:

> Of course, these trade crises confirm the law, confirm it exhaustively—but in a manner different from that which the economist would have us believe to be the case. What are we to think of a law which can only assert itself through periodic crises? It is just a natural law *based on the unconsciousness of the participants.* . . . Produce with consciousness as human beings—not as *dispersed atoms* without consciousness of your species— and you are beyond all these *artificial and untenable antitheses.* But as long as you continue to produce in the present *unconscious,* thoughtless manner, at the *mercy of chance*—for just so long trade crises will remain; and each successive crisis is bound to become *more universal* and therefore *worse* than the previous one.[14]

Inevitably, it belongs to the inherent logic of these developments that the crises become *more universal* and *worse* as time goes by, increasing the stakes enormously, parallel to the world being brought in its entirety under the rule of "globalizing" capital.

In relatively early stages of historical development, when the impact of human beings on their surroundings is still very limited, given their modest numbers in relation to the totality of nature around them, their adopted reproductive activities can fit in without too much difficulty with the inescapable contingency/necessity of nature. The situation dramatically changes, however, when capital's *destructive production* asserts itself on the whole of the planet, coupled with the system's self-mythology of unqualified *"growth"* as the absolute panacea, although in reality such growth is pursued only for the sake of profitable capital expansion irrespective of the consequences.

That is the point in time when the way of treating the natural substratum of human existence as the "mere contingency of nature" becomes totally untenable, and the continued violation of the rules prescribed by the requirements of sustainable social metabolic reproduction *potentially suicidal*, in contradiction to the pursuit of rational husbandry in the planetary household. That is decidedly the point in time when *"the unconscious condition of mankind"* and the pretended *"natural law based on the unconsciousness of the participants"* must be permanently consigned to the past, together with the ideologically most biased conceptualizations of the dominant socioeconomic practices in the form of "artificial and untenable antitheses," like the phony opposition in political economy between *monopoly* and *competition*.[15]

Under the circumstances of capital's all-embracing domination of societal reproduction on the whole of the planet, the stakes are no longer *partial*. Consequently, the remedies to the identified problems and contradictions cannot be envisaged in the form of *partial corrective adjustments*. Capital's *destructive global encroachment* can only be countered by gaining *comprehensive conscious control* over the blind assertion of historical necessity emanating from the practical imperatives of the capital system's antagonistic second-order mediations in their entirety.

As we saw in chapter 4, Marx in *The German Ideology* characterized the onset of human history by saying, "The satisfaction of the first need, the action of satisfying and the instrument of satisfaction which has been acquired, leads to new needs, and this creation of new needs is the first historical act."[16]

The road from the "first historical act"—accomplished through the creation of new needs—to full human emancipation is, of course, most arduous and full of its own contradictions and antagonisms. The advocated positive outcome is by no means posited as secure in the Marxian conception, in contrast to the aprioristic Hegelian projection of the idealist quasi-theological teleology of World History.

In Hegel the unfolding of world historical development is preordained by Divine Providence. Accordingly, *"Divine Wisdom, i.e., Reason, is one and the same in the great as in the little."*[17] Thus, once this aprioristic presupposition is proclaimed, philosophy must conform to its overall scheme by asserting, "Our intellectual striving aims at realizing the *conviction* that *what was intended by eternal wisdom is actually accomplished* in the domain of existent, active Spirit, as well as in that of mere

Nature. Our mode of treating the subject is, in this aspect, a *Theodicaea—a justification of the ways of God.*"[18]

Here, again, the peremptorily *assumed* "concluding conviction," intended as the "justification of the ways of God," can simultaneously justify and rationalize in an absolute sense capital's untenable modality of *antagonistically mediating* the potentially catastrophic actuality of societal interchanges of the established order. In this way the *existent* can be idealized in the name of Reason, which is equated with "Divine Wisdom" capable of "intending everything in its eternal wisdom" and, by definition, also capable of actually accomplishing everything thus intended. Consequently, we can be legitimately invited "to *enjoy the present*, this is the *rational insight which reconciles us with the actual.*"[19] The ultimately self-destructive antagonistic mediations of the existent represent no difficulty, because in the grand scheme of the Hegelian *Science of Logic* mediation must "bend back its end into its beginning," so as to complete "the circle of circles,"[20] speculatively accomplishing thereby the ideologically required *"transcending mediation"*[21] which leaves the historically untenable antagonistic second-order mediations of the system not only standing but even glorified by its claimed coincidence with "the ways of God." For in the Hegelian philosophical conception the course of history is supposed to correspond to nothing less than *"the essential destiny of Reason"* which is said to be, as Hegel insists, *"destined to be realized"*[22] in the actually existing world,[23] in conjunction with *"Spirit's perfect embodiment—the State"*[24]—a crucial part of his rationalizing conception.

In this Hegelian vision the actually existing "Germanic" (but not narrowly German) capitalist State, representing for him the *"ethical universe,"*[25] could be categorically declared to be *"the Divine Idea as it exists on Earth."*[26] By adopting such a view Hegel wishfully decreed at the same time the ideal solution to the problems and contradictions that might still remain. His solution consisted in stipulating that "Truth is the Unity of the universal and the subjective Will; and the *Universal* is to be found in the *State,* in its laws, its universal and rational arrangements. . . . When the subjective will of man *submits* to laws—the contradiction between *Liberty and Necessity* vanishes."[27]

All this could not be any different in the Hegelian teleology of the self-developing World Spirit because the underlying purpose of world historical development—*destined to be realized* according to him right from the beginning, as we have seen constantly reasserted by Hegel—is the reconciliatory disclosure of *"the State as the image and actuality of Reason."*[28] The legitimacy of the required actual "submission of the subjective will" of the people to the "rational universality" of the purportedly ethical State followed with absolutely unquestionable validity in the Hegelian scheme of things from such an aprioristic ideal design.

In the actually existing world, however, not only the contradiction between *"Liberty and Necessity"* but even the fundamental problems pertaining to the objective differences between *need and necessity* must be addressed and secured on a *materially viable* and *epochally sustainable historical basis.* And that must mean, in terms of a dialectical materialist conception of history—explicitly contrasted by Marx with "naturalistic materialism"[29]—the elaboration of a proper account of the complex interrelationship between the objective and the subjective factors that assert themselves through the *unique,* human-instituted *non-naturalistic causality of historical necessity.*

Accordingly, the objectively sustainable *dialectical intelligibility* of historical development in the Marxian account calls for the understanding of the constitution and transformations of historical necessity by the self-mediating being of nature, the human subject. A form of necessity that is inseparable from human design, no matter how rudimentary at first, in contrast to the grand speculative anticipations and self-reassuringly preordained solutions that can be deduced from the concept of the World Spirit's "eternal present." The latter is, of course, synonymous to world historical totalization by the ideal, speculatively devised Totalizer.[30] In the materialist conception of history, by contrast, the *dialectical intelligibility* of development, unfolding in accordance with the unique causality of historical necessity—amounting up to the present to *totalization without a Totalizer,* to use Sartre's apt expression[31]— can only be sustained by putting into relief not only the *inescapable, materially constraining determinations* of the ongoing open-ended historical process, but at the same time also the genuine *emancipatory potentialities* of the selfsame process. Both the constraining material determinations and the emancipatory potentialities are embodied in the deeply interconnected dimensions—including the most complex cultural/intellectual and spiritual dimensions, as discussed in chapter 4—of the societal reproductive practices pursued by the self-mediating human subject.

Thanks to the emancipatory potentialities of the unfolding development, the historical subject itself—responsible for constituting and transforming societal reproduction through its dynamically extended activity, within the complex dialectical framework of transhistorical continuity and discontinuity—becomes in due course capable of a *conscious overall mastery* of the globally intertwined requirements of social metabolic reproduction. This is what we find anticipated in Marx's discussion of the defining characteristics of "the new historic form," in contrast to the history of antagonistic class societies.

Inevitably, with the global extension of the societal reproduction process, to embrace in its general tendency the whole of the planetary household, the conscious mastery of the social metabolism becomes, and must become, not an abstract possibility but an elementary condition of human survival itself. For without the elaboration and practical operation of an *epochally viable* modality of conscious social metabolic control on a *global scale*—a challenge never faced by humanity before—the *uncontrollability* of capital's antagonistic system of second-order mediations, asserting itself with growing severity already in its much more limited national and interstate setting today, can only result in *chronic structural crises,* perpetuated for as long as staggering from one crisis to the next can be maintained, and *ultimate destruction*. Naturally, the accomplishment of this form of conscious, historically sustainable, overall societal reproductive control is feasible only on the *primary condition* that the historical subject succeeds in securing the *natural substratum* of human existence in the planetary setting with enduring epochal viability. And that requires the practical critical reassessment of historically created *need* and *necessity* within the objective dialectical framework of humanly constituted, and in that way also transcendable—in other words, in a proper sense *historical*—historical necessity.

Both *need* and *necessity* must be conceived in this practice-oriented theoretical framework in an inherently *historical* sense, by putting into relief their dialectical correlations and transformations in the course of human history. At the same time, the relevance of the historical achievements obtained in the course of humankind's development in terms of need and necessity must be defined in precise terms as pertaining to the *individual* as well as to the *collective* subject.

In fact the only way to make *dialectically intelligible* the real character of the historical subject,—with its original constitution on the natural ground[32] from which it must emerge, together with its *changing needs* unfolding from the world of *natural necessity* that dominates at first all living creatures, including our distant ancestors—is the *actual unity* of the particular and the general, the individual and the collective/social. It is not this objectively constituted *dialectical unity* of the individual and the social that needs explanation but the tendentious conceptualizations of that relationship which postulate—and try to justify—the separation, and even the opposition of the two, whatever might be the complicated ideological reasons for devising such images of one-sided subjectivity.

In this respect, the theoretical conceptions elaborated by some major intellectual figures of the bourgeoisie are particularly problematical. For the *eternalizing standpoint of capital*—in affinity with projecting a notion of the *isolated individual* into the most remote corners of the past, in the interest of drawing a direct line of continuity with the commended productive and distributive practices of the capitalist present for all time to come—is incompatible with a consistent historical vision. Thus, in such conceptions, whether we think in this respect of Adam Smith or of his later soulmates, we end up with an ahistorically idealized notion of the "Natural Individual," together with an arbitrarily postulated "human nature," as befits the self-images of a socioeconomic development beginning its ascendancy in the sixteenth century and reaching its maturity in the eighteenth.

> In this society of *free competition*, the individual appears detached from the natural bonds etc., which in earlier historical periods make him the accessory of a definite and limited human conglomerate. . . . this eighteenth century individual . . . appears as an ideal, whose existence they project into the past. Not as a *historical result* but as history's *point of departure*. As the *Natural Individual* appropriate to their notion of *human nature*, not arising historically, but *posited by nature*. . . . The more deeply we go back in history, the more does the individual, and hence also the *producing individual*, appear as dependent, as belonging

to a greater whole. . . . Only in the eighteenth century, in "civil society," do the various forms of social connectedness confront the individual as a *mere means* towards his *private* purposes, as *external necessity.* But the epoch which produces this standpoint, that of the *isolated individual,* is also precisely that of the hitherto most developed *social* (from this standpoint, general) relations. The human being is in the most *literal* sense a *zoon politicon,* not merely a gregarious animal, but an animal which can *individuate itself only in the midst of society.*[33]

Thus the *contradiction* between the actual state of affairs and its theoretical depiction is overwhelming. For the *objective inseparability* of the individuals from their social domain has *never been greater* and more all-embracing for the whole of humanity. At the same time, however, the *illusions* attached to the fictionalized "sovereign" decision-making powers of the *isolated individual* continue to be asserted in political economy with total unreality. As a matter of ever-expanding socioeconomic development the actually prevailing social bonds have never been more intense in all history, in the sense that the earlier *limitations* of the once dominant *local* bonds are progressively *superseded* by the inexorable tendency of the capital system toward *global encroachment* of its reproductive practices. Yet the self-serving image of the one and only viable ("natural") mode of social metabolic reproduction, centered on the postulated "free and equitable" exchange relationship of the isolated individuals, must be perpetuated. This must be done even at the cost of grossly distorting all of the actually existing fundamental determinations that concern the *objective dialectic* manifest in the *necessary unity* of the *individual* and the *social,* as well as in the historically changing relationship of *need* and *necessity,* with regard to the conditions of existence of the social individuals as much as of humanity as a whole. But, of course, this contradiction between the actually existing state of affairs and its conceptualizations from the standpoint of capital's political economy is not without some very important—even if theoretically unjustifiable and practically incorrigible—reasons.

The core of this insuperable contradiction can be made very clear by underlining that, in contrast to the capitalist mystification of wealth emanating from commodity fetishism, *"regarded materially, wealth consists only in the manifold variety of needs."*[34]

In this sense, humanity's productively instituted historical advancement is made possible by pushing back the boundary of strict *natural* necessity and progressively replacing it by potentially emancipatory *historical* necessity and the corresponding creation and transformation of *human need*. Accordingly, "This pulling away of the *natural ground* from the foundations of every industry, and this transfer of its conditions of production outside itself, into a general context—hence the transformation of what was previously *superfluous* into what is necessary, as a *historically created necessity*—is the tendency of capital."[35] But it makes a world of difference in which way the historically changing needs of the individuals, as well as of society as a whole, are treated.

The contrast in this respect between a socialist communal order and the reproductive system subjected to the complete domination of exchange-value could not be greater. In the socialist communal order, described by Marx as "man's *positive self-consciousness*,"[36] "in place of the wealth and the poverty of political economy come the *rich human being* and *rich human need*. The rich human being is simultaneously the human being *in need of a totality of human life-activities*—the man in whom his own realization exists as an *inner necessity*, as *need*."[37] By contrast, under the fetishistic domination of exchange-value over use-value, *need* must retain its *external* character, dominating both the individuals[38] and society as a whole.[39] This is why the historically produced imposition of the *external necessity* of the capital system—a form of necessity whose imposition on the members of society is *absolutely* required for the system's normal functioning—must be theoretically transfigured and practically operated as if it were a *nature-imposed necessity*, emanating from a mysterious natural law. That is the way to fallaciously identify the claimed *absolute* requirement of a *historically specific system* with the unalterable absoluteness of *nature's law*. For by transfiguring the specifically historical in that way the claimed unalterable "natural law" becomes suitable to *idealizing* capital's reproductive order as "the natural system of perfect liberty and justice," in Adam Smith's famous words, decreeing that system to be in full conformity to *"human nature"* as such. At the same time the arbitrarily proclaimed "natural law" can be also used for *absolving* the capital system—on account of its "perfect natural character"—of all blame for the inhumanities identified in it by the same thinkers, who are still willing to acknowledge at the ascending phase of capital's development that "the people who clothe the world are in rags themselves" (Adam Smith again).[40]

The needs of the people who are in rags count for nothing in the idealized "natural system of perfect liberty and justice," despite the fact that they are acknowledged to be the people who clothe the world. The same goes for Hegel's speculatively transubstantiated approach to this problem. Indeed, in Hegel's philosophy the callous exclusion of the working *"needy man"* (recognized by him to be needy) from the benefits conferred upon those who have the structurally secured and safeguarded privileges of *property,* conveniently sanctified and protectively watched over by the Hegelian "Ethical State," is justified on the contorted but most revealing ideological ground that *"property is the embodiment of the free will of others."*[41] The actual historical fact that the capitalist constitution, expropriation, and concentration of property is totally incomprehensible without relating it to the boundless bloody violence of the "primitive accumulation"—with the most brutal role played in it by the emerging modern state, in an astronomical distance from the philosophical legend which decrees property to be the ethically justified and enforced[42] "embodiment of the free will of others"—obviously also counts for nothing in the self-images of the idealized bourgeois order.

The grave corollary of development under the conditions of the productively most powerful system in all history is that the potentially emancipatory advancement must be at the same time *negated* by the *antagonistic modality* of capital's self-expansionary vested interests. For the latter can only prevail in *antithetical* form, by imposing *exchange-value* at all cost on use-value and on the corresponding *human need,* otherwise it would implode as a productive system confined to its nightmarish "stationary state."[43]

Capital, thanks to the structurally safeguarded monopoly of property, in reality embodies not the "free will"—as claimed by the speculative philosophical self-justificatory legend—but the *crucial function of societal reproductive control alienated from the producers.* And precisely because the all-important function of social metabolic control is radically divorced from, and in a hostile alienated form imposed upon, the producers, it must be maintained in that way as an *antithetical* structural relationship, deeply affecting everything, including the production and satisfaction of human needs.

Thus the potentially emancipatory pushing back the boundaries of strict natural necessity and the "transformation of what was previously *superfluous* into a *historically created necessity*" carries with it contradictory results and ultimately self-destructive consequences. The problem is that the objective contradiction between potentially emancipatory advancement for the whole of humanity, and the threatened destruction of humankind through the self-induced degradation of the natural substratum of existence itself in the planetary household, due to the pernicious inner antagonisms of the ongoing development, cannot be solved within the confines of the globally extended capital system. For

> The general foundation of all industries comes to be *general exchange* itself, the *world market*, and hence the *totality of the activities, intercourse, needs*, etc. of which it is made up. Luxury is the opposite of the naturally necessary. *Necessary needs* are those of the individual himself *reduced to a natural subject*. The development of industry suspends this natural necessity as well as this former luxury—in bourgeois society, it is true, it does so only in *antithetical* form, in that it itself only *posits another specific social standard as necessary*, opposite luxury.[44]

Evidently, a society of increasing size and complexity, not to mention a globally integrated society, cannot operate without *exchange* of some kind. But, again, it makes a world of difference what kind of exchange is used for securing the mode of societal reproduction. That can assume the contrasting forms of either

1. the historically sustainable production of *real wealth*, corresponding to the earlier mentioned *"manifold variety of needs"* willingly appropriated by the social individuals, as integral to their self-realization, or

2. the endless reproduction of *external necessity* imposed upon the members of society, in order to perpetuate an *alienated form of exchange relationship* and the corresponding submission of human need to the fetishism of commodity, in the service of capital's increasingly *wasteful, destructive,* and *uncontrollably extended* self-reproduction.

It is a most revealing fallacy, fully in tune with the antithetical determinations of capital's political economy, to *equate reified commodity exchange* with the necessary general requirement of *exchange in general*, so as to be able to predicate through that false equation the absolute legitimacy of exchange-value dominating use-value. As a result, the real *alternative* exchange relationship—the humanly emancipating and liberating *exchange of activities* corresponding to the self-realization of the social individuals, in a freely and comprehensively planned social order—is categorically excluded from the concept of exchange by the false equation in question, which is tendentiously proclaimed as *absolute* from the standpoint of capital's political economy and philosophy. This way of conceptualizing the problem even by the greatest intellectual figures of the bourgeoisie is unavoidable not only because the type of exchange relationship absolutized in it *happens to be* practically dominant in the established societal reproduction process. More important, because from capital's adopted standpoint the de facto historically created but now absolutized exchange relationship *must remain dominant forever* in that form, since it corresponds to the essential defining characteristics and irreplaceable operational requirements of the given mode of controlling the social metabolism itself.

Naturally, this way of equating *exchange as such* with exchange-value is only tenable in antagonistically reproduced *commodity society*, on the imposed *practical premise* separating *ownership* and *control* from productive activity in a historically determinate form. For under the rule of capital, corresponding to a *historically unique* separation of ownership and control from the producers in the societal metabolic process of *generalized commodity production*—which includes the first time ever in history the *universal commodification of living labor*—"Commodities are non-use-values for their *owners* and use-values for their *non-owners*. Consequently *they must all change hands*. . . . Hence commodities must be realized as values before they can be realized as use-values."[45] That is why *reified exchange-value* must absolutely dominate *use*, thereby frustrating the satisfaction of human needs under the supremacy of continued *external necessity* even at the conceivably highest stage of capitalist productive advancement, negating and nullifying at the same time *the emancipatory potentialities* of historical development.

The dangerous *"antithetical form"* in which capital *"posits another specific social standard as necessary"* (i.e. as socially untranscendable) at the highest stage of its historical development, on a *global scale,* is by decreeing—in the name of its pretendedly ultimate *"globalization"*—its own historically attained (but historically *un*sustainable) phase of development as *absolutely unsurpassable.* Yet, what is in the process of historically unfolding under the inexorable tendency of capital's global development carries with it the *explosive entrapment* of the totality of the activities, intercourse, needs, etc. within the framework of the system's antagonistically operated all-embracing second-order mediation: the *world market* prescribing the permanence of undisturbed commodity exchange on a universal scale. And that means the potentially catastrophic reassertion of the *absolute necessity*—the worst kind of *external historical necessity ever created by human beings*—of capital's *uncontrollable permanent self-expansion* directly contradicting the *necessary limitations of the planetary household,* undermining thereby the elementary natural requirements of the societal reproduction process. This is why the great emancipatory potential of productive advancement in all history must be ultimately nullified by the *absolute structural limitations* of the capital system itself at the highest stage if its global development, due to this system's divorce from human need necessarily overruled in it by the fetishistic imperatives of universal commodity exchange.

Capital's immense productive dynamism across history was due to a large extent to its ability to get rid of the constraining shackles hemming in the production process under slavery and serfdom. In this way *formally* emancipated labor appeared on the historical stage—as the "free labor" of *economically compelled* and exploited "wage slavery"—capable of "freely" entering into the capitalistically stipulated and legally sanctioned *contractual relationship* of universal commodity exchange that *had to* incorporate *commodified living labor.*

The necessary *practical premise* of such exchange relationship, positing the subordination of use-value to exchange-value, was the separation of property ownership—and thereby the control of production—from the social class of producers. In this way exchange-value had to acquire absolute dominance. That was necessary because use-values are inseparable from *qualities,* and therefore they are *unquantifiable* for the purposes of generalized commodity production. Only some liberal utilitarian philosophers tried to square the circle of quantifying qualitatively different values for the sake of their own ideological convenience.

However, it was an absolutely necessary condition of generalized commodity production, under the rule of capital, that all commodities should enter the alienated exchange relationship in a *commensurable/quantifiable* way. Commodities had to be *equalizable* in the capitalist exchange relationship, which was impossible through the *qualitatively different*—and therefore incommensurable—use-values corresponding to specific human needs. By contrast, exchange-value, perfectly suitable to disregarding human need, could fulfill the function of *quantification and formal equalization* required by the fetishistic commodity exchange relationship.

Naturally, the separation of exchange-value and use-value applied above all to *commodified living labor* without which the viability of the capital system itself was inconceivable. The ability to *autonomously* use their use-value as producers was *absolutely denied* to the laborers who had been deprived of the means of production necessary for controlling the production process itself. Under the rule of capital everything had to be transacted through the primacy and *supremacy* of the exchange-value of the commodities. They had to be exchanged because of the earlier mentioned fact that "commodities are non-use-values for their owners and use-values for their non-owners." Moreover, they had to be exchanged on a *formally equalized,* even if in some ways bewilderingly fictitious, basis. The absurdly fictitious relationship of "equal exchange" in the bourgeois order is, of course, the pretended "free exchange" between *capital and labor.* For the necessary practical premise of such "free contractual relationship" is the *actual material dispossession* of the class of laborers, and their *hierarchical structural subordination* to the class of personified capital in the societal reproduction process.

Accordingly, the dominance of exchange-value over use-value carried with it

1. the supremacy of the *strictly formal* determination of the exchange relationship in which *incommensurable qualities (use-values),* transmuted into quantifiable exchange-values (in the case of the specific productive skills of the workers transmuted into saleable generic *labor*

power) had to be *formally equated* in the process of ever-expanding generalized commodity production[46] and corresponding capital accountancy; a form of economic accountancy not only *incapable of* but, worse than that, *incompatible with* qualitative human considerations, and

2. in close conjunction with the fetishistic determinations of capital accountancy, *human need* had to be frustrated and subjected to the rule of *external necessity* through the *prerequisite* of a successful commodity transaction. Such transaction had to be imposed on the workers by absolutely inescapable economic compulsion, constrained also by the vicissitudes of the labor market in the form of the insecurity of work opportunities before it could be satisfied even as the producing individuals' elementary need for food and shelter in its alienated, always profit-determined, commodity form.

Nevertheless, the economically compelling determinations of the capital system's *wage slavery* proved to be historically far superior to the politically constraining shackles of slavery and serfdom. For whereas slavery and serfdom *hemmed in* productive development, the economic compulsion imposed on labor acted in the opposite direction, as a vital motivating force for the producing subject's *most active contribution* to the dynamic expansion process itself.

Generalized commodity production, dependent upon the highly self-regulating—and not externally/politically supervised—market framework of exchange, was incompatible with direct political control of productive labor. Economic compulsion, which had to be with painful inevitability internalized—i.e. turned into their own *self-exerting force*—by the producing individuals, was incomparably more effective in that respect. Accordingly, in comparison to slavery and serfdom the economic compulsion and forward drive of commodified labor under the rule of capital proved to be *irresistible,* demolishing all obstacles constraining capital-expansion in the course of the last four centuries of historical development.

The insurmountable contradiction of the system—leading at a determinate point in its unfolding to the activation of its absolute limits—ema-

nated not from some politically imposed external limitation of labor productivity but from capital's innermost systemic character. It was due to
the unremediable objective condition that capital-expansion—in one
form or another, including its most parasitic and chronically wasteful varieties—was, and always remains, not only *irresistible* but also *uncontrollable*. Uncontrollable, that is, to the point of its own potential self-destruction at its antagonistic globalized stage of development.

This is where we can see the necessity of critically reassessing the false
identification of societal exchange relationship in general with commodity exchange, which posits thereby the absolute subordination of use-
value—and corresponding human need—to the fetishistic requirements
of profit-oriented exchange-value and in the end destructively uncontrollable capital-expansion. For in actuality there is a limit to everything,
including *uncontrollability*. That limit is reached when, in the case of capital's self-expansion, the panacea of *unqualified and rationally unconstrainable growth* continues to be idealized and forcibly imposed upon
society by capital in the form of *destructive cancerous growth*.

In this respect the fundamental alternative to the reified system of
exchange-value necessarily prevailing over use-value and need under the
rule of capital is the *exchange of activities*. This is not a question of tech-
nical/technological arrangements. The alienating and *structurally secured
social division of labor* in our society is often misrepresented in that way,
in order to hide the historically untenable character of capital's *hierarchically enforced domination of labor*. By adopting that line, it can be pretended that the capitalist division of labor arises from the absolute necessity of productively advantageous technical/technological separation of
the disparate elements of the labor process. Contrary to such tendentious
conceptualization of these problems, we have to consider here the necessity of a radical *systemic change,* without which any historically viable and
epochally sustainable society of the future—beyond the destructive antagonisms of the present order—is unthinkable.

The radical systemic change from the now dominant fetishistic
exchange relationship to the qualitatively different *communal system*
based on the rationally planned and organized exchange of activities
requires in reality the *liberation* of humanly fulfilling activities in all
domains. That is the real stake, and not some kind of wishfully projected

technological improvement which can be manipulatively imposed, from above, in the ways of the past. In other words, the change in question must embrace and redefine in an emancipatory way the meaning of activities in the material productive field no less than in the intellectual and artistic domain, so as to make possible the realization of the positive potentialities of the self-mediating social individuals.

That kind of change is feasible only on the basis of *substantive equality,* in place of the *substantively most iniquitous* system of mystifying *formal equalizations* belonging to the essential defining characteristics of generalized commodity production and exchange that negate human need everywhere.

The necessary condition of such *qualitative change* is the institution and sustained operation of the communal system of production and consumption by the "freely associated producers." It can only be defined in the form of the fully cooperative exchange of their activities by the social individuals, within the framework of a *substantively equitable and rational organization of labor,* in place of the class of labor being ruled in an authoritarian way, as it always must be, under all conceivable varieties of the capital system, by *the structurally enforced and politically safeguarded hierarchical social division of labor.* This fundamental practical transformation of societal reproduction in its entirety is the only way to achieve the necessary *global integration* of the antagonistically divided forces of society for the first time ever in history.

To quote Marx's characterization of this qualitatively different way of organizing production and consumption:

> The communal character of production would make the product into a communal, general product from the outset. The exchange which originally takes place in production—which *would not be an exchange of exchange-values but of activities*—determined by *communal needs and communal purposes*—would from the outset include the participation of the individuals in the communal world of products.[47]

This all-embracing qualitative change is also meant to overcome the domination of human need by the self-perpetuating *external necessity* inseparable from generalized commodity production and exchange. That system of production and consumption dictates its own rules which must be obeyed by all members of society. As we have seen earlier in a quotation from the *Grundrisse,* under the rule of capital the reified social bonds—assuming the form of the uncontrollable alienated objectification of labor—"confront the individual as a *mere means* towards his private purposes, as *external necessity*." As a result of such complete overturning of the actual relationship between the producers and the control of production, the alienated objectification of labor itself dominates societal reproduction in a most absurd way, ruthlessly imposing on the workers a "fetishistic situation when the *product* [alienated labor: capital] is the *proprietor of the producer*."[48]

The total frustration and alienated domination of human need under the circumstances of commodified living labor can only be removed by historically overcoming the antagonism between production and its alienated control. This is why "in place of the wealth and poverty of political economy come the rich human being and the rich human need. The rich human being is simultaneously the human being *in need of a totality of human life-activities*—the man in whom *his own realization* exists as an *inner necessity,* as *need*."[49] Thus the fundamental meaning of the communal social order of societal reproduction, rationally planned and consciously managed by the social individuals as their cooperative exchange of self-mediating and self-realizing activities, is the epochally sustainable *transcendence* of *external necessity*.

Such *external historical necessity* was in its own time created and imposed upon themselves by the human beings, and not by some unalterable natural law. The latter is self-servingly proclaimed as an economic and political absolute—corresponding to a "natural system of perfect liberty and justice"—from the standpoint of capital's political economy, in the service of *eternalizing* the established social order. In complete contrast, in view of the fact that the necessity in question was created by human beings themselves, that kind of historical necessity can be also historically superseded by them, provided that they radically redefine their present conditions of social metabolic reproduction.

And there is nothing mysterious about that, in total contrast to the allegedly benevolent but utterly mysterious work of the "invisible hand" and its equally mysterious later conceptualizations in bourgeois philosophy, like Hegel's "Cunning of Reason."[50] The reassuring overall solutions of bourgeois philosophy and political economy conceived from the standpoint of capital could not be formulated without a large dose of mystery even at the ascending phase of the system's historical development. The Marxian "Critique of Political Economy"[51]—the recuring subtitle of all of his major works—had to be undertaken in order to remove that *mystery* by exposing its *objective ground of mystification,* ossified in the commodity-exchange relationship. And of course it was necessary to undertake that exposure for the purpose of radically changing the social metabolism pursued under the rule of capital.

In this spirit, the qualitative restructuring and conscious supersession of the established order, with its fetishistic uncontrollability and increasing destructiveness, means securing in a practically viable way—on an ongoing basis, in the form of an open-ended historical order[52]—the material and cultural conditions of societal reproduction. Not in the form of an *abstract collectivity* confronting and dominating the more or less isolated particular individuals[53] but by rendering *conscious* and *humanly fulfilling* the *dialectical unity of the individual and the social.* And that is possible only on the communal basis of realizing the chosen objectives of the real social individuals. For the *"zoon politicon* can *individuate* itself only in the midst of *society,"* as we have seen it stressed by Marx in a quotation above. And of course the most appropriate way of individuating themselves by the social individuals is when they can do that with positive cooperative solidarity among themselves.

This is the tangible meaning of the socialist program aimed at transcending *external necessity* by the *internally embraced necessity* of the real social individuals, corresponding to their *self-realizing human need.* The historically unfolding *necessary unity* of the *individual* and the *social*—for a long time inevitably *imposed* by human beings upon themselves in an unconscious and antagonistic way—is thus a vital constituent of the *overall dialectical intelligibility* of historical development as an open-ended social metabolic process.

Need and necessity are closely intertwined in the actual historical process at all stages of humankind's development, including the highest possible. This is so because the *subject of history* is the *sentient human being,* with nature-determined elemental *needs* imposed on it as *external necessities* for as long as they cannot be progressively overcome by the historic creation of new needs through productive advancement. Any attempt to disrupt or undermine, in the service of some socioeconomic vested interests, the objectively intertwined fundamental relationship between need and necessity can only lead to disaster and to the ultimate catastrophe of humanity's self-destruction.

The deciding issue in this respect is not simply the necessary interconnection between need and necessity, but the relevant implications of the progressive increase in humanity's self-emancipatory power in the course of historical development. For thanks to such historical development the *superfluous, obsolete,* and for the purposes of viable societal reproduction *anachronistic* constituents of once objectively self-imposed historical necessity *can be* successfully consigned to the past—in the earlier mentioned form of *"verschwindende Notwendigkeit,"* that is: "vanishing necessity"—in a humanly sustainable way. The objectively secured and historically sustainable dialectical transformation of *external necessity* into the *internal necessity* of the social individuals' *self-realizing need* is the *positive modality* of achieving that kind of emancipatory change.

On the other hand, due to the social inertia emanating from the deeply entrenched forces of hierarchical structural domination, wedded to the massive material, political and cultural vested interests of capital's personifications, the diametrically opposite course of action may be imposed upon society, blindly defending even the most extreme form of *historical anachronism and destructive obsolescence* instead of consigning them to the past.

The unavoidable consequence of following that negative course of action within the objectively intertwined relationship between need and necessity, at the present stage of historical development, is the perilous *overturning* of the connection between the *absolute* and the *relative* factors: a correlation to which all objective beings—like the human being of nature, with its innermost human as well as natural determinations—remain subject *under all circumstances.* And this perilous overturning of the most fundamental of all relationships takes the form of *irresponsibly relativizing the absolute*—the inescapable natural substratum of human existence itself—for the sake of *absolutizing the relative.* That is, for the sake of absolutizing the capital system's historically attained and *historically anachronistic,* ever more destructive, societal reproductive order.

This carries with it the acute danger of grossly violating the continued *real necessity* of objective determinations and correlations, in conjunction with *real human need*. This is particularly grave at the present phase of historical development. For in relation to real human need it is necessary in our time to adopt some conscious strategies in order to be able to secure their satisfaction in a finite world whose limitations have been put into relief by the prohibitive demand globally—and quite unsustainably—imposed upon them.[54] Yet, instead of the adoption of rational strategies of production and societal reproduction we find the continued subjection of human need to the arbitrarily proclaimed *absolute necessity of capital's catastrophically wasteful yet eternalized rule.*

Significantly, in the Spanish language for instance, the same word—*necesidad*—is used to cover both "need" and "necessity" in their basic senses. Alternative Spanish ways of conveying the meaning of necessity in more specific contexts are offered by the words *imperativo, imprescindibilidad, inevitabilidad,* and also *requerimiento* and *requisito*. A similarly close connection, expressing the relationship between "need" and "necessity," is given in the German language by using the shared root of "*Not*" and "*Notwendigkeit*," while the more specific category indicating the sentient being's given needs is covered by the word "*Bedürfnisse*."

Common language as a rule forcefully embodies and puts into relief the fundamental objective relationships of such categories, often in revealing contrast to philosophical speculation. As Marx wrote with a touch of irony in one of his letters to Engels about Hegel's speculative concern with the philosophical categories: "What would old Hegel say in the next world if he heard that the general *(Allgemeine)* in German and in Norse means nothing but common land *(Gemeinland)*, and the particular, *Sundre, Besondere,* nothing but the separate property divided off from the common land? Here are the *logical categories* coming damn well out of *'our intercourse'* after all."[55]

To be sure, the same kind of relationship prevails between "our intercourse" and its valid conceptualizations in the categories of need and necessity. No theoretical conceptualization can be considered valid unless it faithfully reflects and highlights the objective historical dialectic of the analyzed relations.

However, ideologically motivated distortions are all too frequent. In this respect—hopelessly mystifying the objective relationship between the *natural* and the *historical*—one of the most frequently employed arguments in favor of defending the ruling order, irrespective of how consciously and openly it is formulated with that intent, is to offer a baffling explanation for the contradictions that cannot be denied in capitalist society, by blaming the *"human nature"* of so-called selfishly conflictual individuals for them.

Naturally, that is no explanation at all. It is only a vain attempt to try to run away from the problems themselves, denying at the same time—explicitly or by implication—both their social origin and the feasibility of finding a historically and socially viable remedy to them. For once the vague and generic notion of unalterable *"egotistic human nature"* enters the picture, with the associated presumption of *individualistic conflictuality*, everything can be left in its place in actually existing society. Most conveniently, everything can stay as it is, even if *rhetorical preaching* about the "alas persisting defects" is still admissible for the sake of satisfying the conscience of the "better liberal minds" capable of both spotting the defects and simultaneously exempting themselves from any responsibility for them.

In this way the dialectical unity of the individual and the social is not only obfuscated but completely obliterated in the name of a fictitious "human nature." At the same time, and precisely because a pretended unchangeable *natural determination* is self-servingly posited as the explanatory cause of the conflicts admitted to exist but divorced from their social dimension, the possibility of *historical intervention* for countering and overcoming the undeniable problems some time in the future is a priori ruled out. Thus the obliteration of the necessary social dimension of genuine individuality—put into relief by Marx by saying that "the zoon politicon can individuate itself only in the midst of society"—carries with it the tendentious *negation of history*.

The role of this approach for justifying the unjustifiable in the name of human nature is fairly obvious in relation to the present. However, the abstract philosophical conception representing its ancestry is several centuries old, even if in its origin it did not have the same crudely apologetic social function. Nevertheless, Marx highlighted way back in the spring of

1845, in his critique of Ludwig Feuerbach, the total untenability of postulating a speculative ahistorical and socially vacuous "human essence" as the adopted explanatory framework of the criticized problems. According to Marx:

> Feuerbach resolves the religious essence into the *human essence*. But the human essence is *no abstraction inherent in each single individual*. In its reality it is the *ensemble of the social relations*.
>
> Feuerbach who does not enter upon a criticism of this real essence, is consequently compelled:
>
> 1. To abstract from the *historical process* and to fix the religious sentiment [*Gemüt*] as something *by itself* and to presuppose an *abstract—isolated—human individual*.
> 2. The human essence, therefore, can with him be comprehended only as a *"genus,"* as an internal, *dumb generality* which merely *naturally* unites the many individuals.[56]

Thus the fundamental defect of Feuerbach's conception is his failure to be *critical* of the *"ensemble of the social relations"* that define the real nature of the human being, in the midst of its historically created and changeable social reality. This failure to be critical of the necessary social target of transformation in a period of major crisis all over Europe—a failure due to Feuerbach's adoption of the standpoint shared by bourgeois thinkers—is what induces him to abstract from the actual *historical process*. In the spirit of the adopted standpoint he must postulate, instead, as the explanatory framework of his philosophical critique of religion, "an *abstract—isolated—human individual*," defined in terms of its *"dumb generality,"* speculatively characterizing it as an abstract *genus-individual*, merged generically with some fictitious natural determinations that are supposed to be common to *all genus-individuals*.

Conceptualizing the world in this way, which happens to be broadly diffused in bourgeois philosophy, is of course completely *useless for changing the world*. For the actually existing social world is made to disappear in such conceptions, together with the real social individuals, by the arbitrary postulate of a *fixed conflictual human essence*, in problematical harmony with the existent.

The contrast with the Marxian definition of the dynamically changing nature of the human being as the "ensemble of the social relations" could not be greater. According to that vision, human nature is grounded, to be sure, on the objective foundations given to our most distant ancestors as a *being of nature*. But it is qualitatively changed in the course of history by the *unique self-mediating being of nature*—who is the productively *self-developing human being*—through the ongoing transformation of the *ensemble of the social relations,* in accordance with the dialectical intelligibility of historical development.

The speculative reduction of the individuals into *genus-individuals* eliminates not only the social and historical dimension of the actually existing society, and thereby conveniently its necessarily changeable/changing character, but also the genuine *individuality* of the real social individuals. For it is the productively developing self-mediation of the human individuals among themselves and with nature—in total contrast to the animal world incapable of such productive self-mediation: an insurmountable limitation confining their particular members to the condition of always remaining by nature limited "genus-individuals"— that enables them to *individuate themselves in the midst of society,* and only in the midst of historically changing society.

The revealing absence of historical and social awareness from Feuerbach's philosophy—a defect shared by many other philosophers who adopt the same socioeconomic standpoint of their class—and the necessarily associated failure to be *critical* of the established societal reproductive order, is the principal target of the Marxian critique of the abstractly nature-determined *genus-individual.* It is therefore by no means accidental that Marx's *Theses on Feuerbach* are concluded by forcefully underscoring that "Philosophers have only *interpreted* the world, in various ways; the point, however, is to *change* it."[57]

In regard to the gratuitous postulate of *"egotistic individuality"* as the directly nature-determined explanatory foundation of social development, the only thing it is good for is to obliterate some crucial objective differences, by grotesquely bringing to a convenient *common denominator* the members of the antagonistically opposed *social classes* who in reality have diametrically opposed interests and productive functions. The egotistic behavior befitting the individual members of the capitalist class

is in sharp contrast to anything even remotely feasible for the personifications of labor. This is why Marx argued: "Labour can only appear as wage
labour when its *own* objective conditions meet it as *egotistical powers,* as
alien property, value existing for itself and holding fast to itself, in short as
capital."[58] But, obviously, even the personifications of capital as *"egotistical power"* have nothing to do with *"genus-individuality"* directly determined by nature, nor with *"individual conflictuality,"* which would necessarily apply also to the individual members of the class of labor. If it was
due to nature-determined *genus-individuality and conflictuality,* that
would put the *capital system itself* beyond criticism: the more or less conscious postulate of such conceptualizations. For

> the functions performed by the capitalist are only the *functions of capital*
> itself performed with consciousness and will . . . The capitalist functions
> only as *capital personified,* capital as a person, just as the worker only
> functions as the *personification of labour.* . . . The self-valorization of cap-
> ital—the creation of surplus value—is therefore the determining, domi-
> nating, and overmastering purpose of the capitalist, the absolute driving
> force and content of his action. . . . This is an utterly miserable and
> abstract content, which makes the capitalist appear as just as much under
> the yoke of the *capital-relation* as the worker at the opposite extreme.[59]

Thus, not only on the side of labor is it absurd to postulate the nature-
determined egotism of genus-individuality, in the interest of finding a *fictitious common denominator* between capital and labor, but also on the
side of capital itself. For the selfish (even the most ruthlessly selfish) assertion of the *"egotistic power"* of the individual personifications of capital
for the exploitation of their workers, in the interest of maximizing their
profit, is primarily due to the historically specific *social function* which
they *must* fulfill—"as *alien property, value existing for itself and holding
fast to itself"*—not as a matter of *individual inclination* but on the pain of
being unceremoniously expelled in the event of failing to do so, through
bankruptcy, from their own class which is *objectively* in command of the
societal reproduction process.

The fact that bourgeois philosophy conceptualizes these matters in
terms of genus-*individuality*, attaching to the overall explanatory frame-

work a *vacuous concept of (formal) equality* totally contrary to its substantive sense, speaks amply enough for itself, together with the revealingly *time-bound*—yet in its intent *eternalizing*—character of the adopted approach.

Aristotle had no use whatsoever for designating the working slaves as *human individuals*, not even as "genus-individuals," in that a similar characterization would posit some kind of *equality*. He called them *"talking tools"* without any camouflage of their conditions of existence, because he was clearly focusing attention on their actually given *substantive status* in slave-owning society, in contrast to transubstantiating capitalist *wage slavery* into *real equality* in modern times.

Nor would the feudal lord consider for a moment his *serfs* as his *equals* in any sense of the word. Neither as equals on the ground of "human nature" nor as a result of some institutional arrangement. The magnificent satirical novel by Gogol paints a devastating picture of the social relations in which the serfs could increase the status of the feudal lord simply by their sheer numbers; a circumstance successfully exploited in this novel by a clever and cynical self-promoter who carries on enterprisingly collecting in feudal Russia the *"Dead Souls"* (that is, the recently deceased serfs still nominally surviving in the original titles contained in the coffers of the feudal lords).

No concept resembling *genus-individuality* would be of any use or help either to Aristotle—who unhesitatingly rejected the very idea of *non-substantively equalizable* exchange transactions that would have to equate *qualitatively different* products: he called such transactions "only a makeshift for practical purposes"[60]—or to feudal society.

It is in a sense quite astonishing that the idea of timelessly nature-determined *genus-individuality,* and corresponding *individual conflict-uality,* should be seriously entertained at all as a key explanatory concept, contradicted at the same time by its obvious *historical specificity* relevant only to modern bourgeois society. The reason why it can—and indeed must—be maintained in that way, despite the obvious contradiction in question, is because its constantly repeated postulate conveniently supports the ideological interest of *eternalizing* the capitalist order, proclaimed to be both natural and permanent despite its undeniable historical origin and transcendability. Indeed, that order is proclaimed to be absolutely permanent precisely on the arbitrarily declared ground of its correspondence to nature's requirements. In the service of such overwhelming ideological class interest of the self-legitimating ruling order, there can be, of course, no aversion to relying on *complete mystery* for "explaining" the actual workings of the established order.

In this sense, it must be indeed considered a *total mystery* why the ruling social order does not fall to pieces if it is really *individual conflictuality* that determines its functioning. Why is the outcome *development at all*—not to mention the claimed one and only insuperably advantageous and forever sustainable development—and not *total chaos and disintegration*, due to the nature-determined collision of the egotistic genus-individuals? Those who continue to propound today the idea of *individual conflictuality* as the explanatory cause of naturally advantageous societal reproduction, without further qualifications, are in fact maintaining a totally incoherent notion. This view is very similar to envisaging positive social reform *"little by little,"* without any idea of the *overall framework* in which a multiplicity of fetishistically idealized little changes could make any improvement at all, instead of adding up to complete disaster.

When Hobbes asserted the nature-determined *bellum omnium contra omnes*—the war of each against all—he did not leave matters suspended in that way in thin air. As a great philosopher of his time, representing determinate socioeconomic and political interests, he completed his picture by postulating (and siding with) the absolute unrestrainability of *Leviathan:* the all-powerful State whose role was to bring order into the otherwise self-destructive chaos. Thus the overall conception devised by Hobbes was intellectually coherent, no matter how problematical in terms of its historical sustainability. Naturally, by the time Hegel had put forward his own idea of the "Ethical State" as the necessary corrective to the conflictuality of the individuals in "civil society," at a much more advanced stage of capital's historical development, the state had to be cut down in power to a "constitutional" entity, leaving in the Hegelian vision very little room for the power of arbitration of the ruling Monarch (in his own explicit words almost nothing, as we have seen earlier).

To be sure, the mystery did not disappear from the solutions postulated even in the work of the greatest thinkers of the bourgeoisie who identified themselves with the standpoint of substantively iniquitous capital, at the ascending phase of the system's development. What is relevant, however, is that—unlike the crude apologists of our time—the Adam Smiths and Hegels were not satisfied at all with the proposition that *individual conflictuality* of the *genus-individuals* can be sustained *on its own* as the credible explanatory framework of the successful functioning of the established socioeconomic order. Even if in very different ways, from Hobbes to Hegel, they all offered a *totalizing vision* that would posit the maintenance of the overall system, despite its *necessarily centrifugal* constituent parts. Thus they asserted both the *individualistically conflictual cell structure* of the depicted social order—in its linkages to *genus-individuality,* whether of a straightforward natural kind or of an idealistic speculative variety—and the simultaneous *totalizing cohesion,* posited in terms of some unexplained and unexplainable but necessary general principle or force, like Adam Smith's "invisible hand."

The theoretical function of the projected overall regulator was precisely to assert the permanent sustainability of *the whole*—in Hegel's famous dictum "the truth is the whole"—despite its manifold particularistic (but in their view only individualistic, and not structural) contradictions. The stipulated but unexplainable correctives devised from the standpoint of political economy for making plausible the *totalizing cohesion* of the capital system were necessary for two principal reasons:

1. the *unmentionability* of the really existing *antagonistic class control* of the given socioeconomic reproductive order, based on the structurally secured, brutally iniquitous *material power relations*—embodied in the means of production and control expropriated from the producers—protected in that alienated form by the capitalist state. This happened to be (and of course continues to be) a most iniquitous structurally entrenched *power relationship* of *class* domination and subordination. It *directly* contradicted (and absolutely continues to contradict) the postulated idea of the *equality* of the producers entering—in the spirit of their deliberations that are supposed to arise from their *individual free will*—the required *"equal contractual relationship"* with capital as *free labor,* fully in accordance with the "Rights of Man," and;

2. the necessary *transfiguration* of the structurally safeguarded *hierarchical class domination* and the corresponding irreconcilable *class antagonism* into strictly *individual conflictuality*—the latter as it is supposed to be due to the human individuals being made in general out of "crooked timber" by "Nature's Lawgiver," in Kant's words, or as due to some other aprioristic and forever enduring determination—which would (and conceptually could) both retain the asserted *irreconcilability* in "civil society," on an individualistic basis, and at the same time *justify* the absolute permanence of an *incurably exploitative* overall socioeconomic and political order. To justify it as nothing less than *"the natural system of perfect liberty and justice,"* which was supposed to be insuperably beneficial to all individuals, who in reality were only in a *purely formal sense equal,* and even that with heavily restrictive qualifications.[61]

Since the *real controller* of the social metabolic process could not even be hinted at, let alone openly acknowledged, in its *class exploitative* materially and politically determined *historical specificity,* some kind of unexplainable *speculative overall controller* had to be invented in its place, in order to offer a *reassuring view* of the necessarily timeless ("eternalizable") totalizing cohesion of society. Only that kind of speculative overall controller could reconcile the contradictions inseparable from these conceptions, without any reference to the ultimately *explosive structural antagonisms* of the established societal reproductive order.

We find by far the most elaborate and comprehensive range of speculative correctives to self-referential individual conflictuality in the Hegelian system. Hegel's vision concerning this matter, even if most problematical in its ideologically motivated general orientation, is nevertheless far superior to the later dominant versions of the purely individualistic—yet miraculously all-round beneficial—conflictuality, theorized in the most primitive capital-apologetic fashion, asserting the viability of a societal reproductive interchange which in reality could only result in chaos. In revealing contrast to that kind of apologetics, represented in our own time by the Hayeks of this world, the highly complex Hegelian correctives were conceived from the standpoint of capital's political economy in the system's still ascending historical phase of development, in genuine affinity with the work of Adam Smith who directly influenced the great German philosopher.

Significantly, Hegel elaborated his principal ideas in the aftermath of the French Revolution and the Napoleonic Wars, which also signaled the appearance of the working class on the historical stage as an independent social and political force. For it was in that period that the class of labor started to forcefully put forward its self-assertive claims, beyond the obfuscating constraints of the heterogeneous "Third Estate" of which it used to be a—necessarily disappointed—part. Understandably, therefore, much had to be reassessed in that age of great turmoil to which Hegel was a most acute witness.

The Hegelian correctives to the conceptually incoherent idea of historical/societal development on the ground of "immediate individuality"—explicitly and sharply rejected by Hegel—were fourfold:

1. He had put at the center of his attention, as a way of explaining the course of development, "*the process of the genus with the individual,*"[62] insisting that the "*immediate individuality*" must be made "*conformable to the universal,*"[63] and adding at the same time that "the *genus* is truly realized in *mind*, in *Thought*, in this element which is *homogeneous with the genus.*"[64] By devising the conceptual framework of the ideologically required solutions in this lofty idealist way, yet in full conformity to the ruling order, Hegel could posit in relation to the world of "civil society"—in which individual conflictuality unavoidably and in his view by no means reprehensibly had to prevail—a reconciliatorily unquestioning but most sophisticated philosophical outcome. The latter was accomplished in his system thanks to an imaginary "*dialectical advance*"[65] whereby everything could remain in the existing societal reproductive order exactly as it was before, in harmony with "rational actuality."[66] The claimed "dialectical advance" was, of course, only conceptual, but it was an important step for explicitly distancing the Hegelian approach from the theoretically primitive position of "immediate individuality."

2. The second major corrective introduced by Hegel, in line with Adam Smith's "invisible hand," was the *List der Vernunft* (the "Cunning of

Reason"), representing for him the general principle of overall regulation of world historical development and explaining the events of the past as well as the functioning of the present; a purely assumed principle of all-embracing control that was a priori destined to prevail over the actions of the *particular* individuals. Hegel did not hesitate to call "Absolute Cunning" this postulated principle of overall regulation he equated with *"Divine Providence . . .* working out its own aims," stressing that "Divine Providence may be said to stand to the world and its process in the capacity of Absolute Cunning."[67]

3. And that was far from enough for Hegel, in his attempt to make plausible the functioning of the depicted world historical order, for he added yet another—conceptually most important—corrective to the idea of purely individualistic conflictuality, in his own way of demonstrating the self-realization of the "Absolute Spirit" as the identical Subject-Object of history. This he did by stipulating that the Absolute Cunning of Divine Providence (corresponding to the way in which the "Absolute Spirit" asserted its own power with full adequacy in the human world) was in reality using the outstanding historical figures—the "world historical individuals," like Alexander the Great, Julius Caesar, Luther, and Napoleon—for the realization of *its own ends,* while those individuals were convinced that they were themselves the originators of their own transformatory aims and actions. In this way Hegel could maintain that not only the individuals but also the particular states and nations were "the *unconscious tools* and organs of the *world mind* at work within them,"[68] bringing to what he considered to be an eternally workable common denominator—though doing that, of course, only in a speculative way—the *unconsciousness* of the human beings and their actually existing institutions on the one hand, and the highest conceivable *suprahuman consciousness of the world mind,*[69] on the other, as the ultimate guarantor of the only sustainable order instead of chaos. This is how he proposed to reconcile the otherwise totally untenable, but by Hegel tellingly acknowledged,[70] insuperable *irrationality/unconsciousness* of the eternalized capitalist order of "civil society" and its genus-individuals, together with their particular states and nations, with *consciousness* as such, essential to any viable conception of history.

4. The most important corrective addition introduced by Hegel—for the purpose of justifying the absolute permanence of the material reality of capitalist "civil society," notwithstanding the ineradicable conflict-uality of the "genus-individuals"—was his conception of the *"Ethical State,"* which would subsume the self-seeking reproduction process and the corresponding satisfaction of the needs of the individuals and their society under a higher order fully befitting the World Spirit. Without that, "civil society" would not be sustainable at all. However, thanks to the necessary combination with the higher order of the "Ethical State," the depicted "civil society" itself, in its *given actuality,* corresponding to the requirements of capital's idealized order, became fully harmonizable with the World Spirit's self-realization process. That connection with the "Ethical State"—the latter decreed to be "the Divine Idea as it exists on earth"[71]—removed any shadow of concern about the established order's eternal viability. Indeed more than that, it simultaneously also disqualified the "folly" of the "Understanding"[72] (in the name of the highest dialectical principle of "Reason") about any possible improvement to be introduced into the actually existent through reform aimed at *real equality,* tendentiously dismissed by Hegel as a mere "ought-to-be." For in the Hegelian "Ethical State" a key role was assigned, *by definition* (since it could only be done by definition), to the utterly fictitious *"universal class"* of civil servants, who were idealistically and idealizingly posited as safeguarding the *interest of all,* and thus properly *harmonizing* the world historical order, notwithstanding the insoluble—but through the profound interrelationship with the "Ethical State" ennobled, and thereby legitimately eternalized—contradictions of "civil society."

Paradoxically, in view of the vital explanatory and justificatory role which the "Ethical State" was called upon to fulfill in the Hegelian system as a whole, in an age of world historical turmoil and conflict never experienced before on an even remotely comparable scale, Hegel was challenged to elaborate one of the greatest theories of politics and the state in the course of the entire history of philosophy. For nothing short of that magnitude could be suitable to fulfill the role he consciously assigned, and had to assign, to the state as the overarching pillar of his monumental reconciliatory system. His achievement also in that respect stands in sharp contrast to the pedestrian apologetic concoctions offered by the propounders of "immediate individuality" who were incapable of producing anything even minimally relevant to understanding the nature of the modern state in the descending phase of capital's systemic development.

There was something grandiose about the fourfold corrective overall conception elaborated by Hegel. For he attempted to put self-seeking individuality, and the satisfaction of needs feasible on its basis, in perspective. Indeed, he tried to put them in a world historical perspective, in contrast to being satisfied with the crass apologetics of what he dismissively called "immediate individuality." Hegel criticized such views—a criticism applicable not only to some thinkers before Hegel but even more so to many capital-apologists after him—on the ground that assuming the plausibility of a purely individualistic position was philosophically quite untenable in view of the disregard of that approach for the necessary relationship between the *particular* and the *universal*. And in general philosophical terms Hegel was perfectly right about that, irrespective of how speculative his terms of reference had to be in his idealist philosophical rationalization of the existent.

The insurmountable problem for Hegel had arisen from his conception of *"the universal"* to which everything in the course of historical development and in the actually existing world of societal reproduction had to conform, in order to qualify for the noble status of "rational actuality." For in terms of the *real world* of history and society—in contrast to the speculative domain of his ingenious, and in terms of their idealist coherence most powerful, categorial abstractions, depicting the framework of the World Spirit's self-realization process in accordance with its unalterable *"eternal present"*—the Hegelian *"universal"* tended to coincide with *capital's incorrigible partiality*.

In that world of incorrigible partiality, constituting the necessary societal systemic premise of Hegelian "universality," with regard to the established property relations the great violence that secured their establishment, and indeed the inhuman material and political compulsion required for their continued economic domination and "ethically" state-protected maintenance, had no significance whatsoever. On the contrary, the capitalist property relations, revealingly for Hegel, had to be accepted as *absolutely sacred* in view of the claimed embodiment of the "free will of others" in them, as indicated earlier. That kind of ideological rationalization of historically produced and enforced *incorrigible partiality* as the absolutely unchallengeable principle of *universality* also inevitably amounted   to speculatively subsuming capital's destructive—and ultimately even *self-destructive—external necessity* under the highest and noblest category of *freedom*.[73] Thus the adoption of the standpoint of capital's political economy by Hegel proved to be incompatible with genuine *universality in the actually existing world* even at the ascending phase of capital's historical unfolding.

The long historical development—from the creation of the first new needs of our distant ancestors to the present modality of global societal reproduction—culminated in our time in the antagonistic dominance of capital's incorrigible partiality falsely asserting itself in the name of universality.

The great difficulty for redressing this matter is that any form of concern with the question of universality for thousands of years seemed to belong only to the domain of religious and abstract philosophical discourse. And that circumstance indicated very well the apparently intractable nature of the problem itself. For, on the one hand, the structurally enforced discriminatory/exploitative character of *all class societies* necessarily—and indeed massively—prevented the institution of real universality in the actually existing societal reproductive order. On the other hand, the *direct justification* of incorrigible partiality in genuine theory had to be considered inadmissible. That is, it had to be rejected as the kind of direct justification of incorrigible partiality that would present the violation of universality not simply as the de facto objectively prevailing iniquitous ordering principle of societal reproduction but, unashamedly, doing that as if it was also *de jure*—that is, fully legitimate as well—in the name of the glorified *particular individual.* Naturally, adopting that kind of position would be quite preposterous in philosophical terms. Only an *indirect justification* of the existing state of affairs was acceptable to any serious thinker.[74] And, of course, that form of indirect justification had to include the acknowledgment of the admittedly very difficult but nonetheless unavoidably challenging relationship between the *particular and the universal* at least as a problem, even if only in the form of some speculative philosophical or religious postulates.

To be sure, as far as this fundamental issue of the difficult relationship between particularity and universality is concerned, its solution cannot be envisioned even through the noblest universalistic postulates of philosophy divorced from social transformatory practice. And the social practice required in this regard, to be successful at all, would have to be most radical, advocating an epochally viable transformatory intervention. For in the actually existing world there *cannot be* a *direct relationsip* between the particular and the universal. That relationship, whether we think of the necessary interchange between humankind and nature, or among the particular individuals in society, is always—and *must* always be—*mediated* in some way, in accordance with the historically changing circumstances. Whether we can take seriously the theoretically advocated relationship between the particular and the universal depends entirely on the nature of the prevailing *actual forms of mediation* conceptualized in such theories, and certainly not on the speculative declaratory postulates made of mediation in general.

The grave problem in this respect is that under the rule of capital the necessary *actual* intermediary link of mediation between the particular and the universal is fatefully dominated by the *antagonistic second-order mediations* of the reproductive order in force as a mode of social metabolic control, imposing in that way the system's incorrigible partiality. Accordingly, the unreformably antagonistic character of the capital system's second-order mediations deeply affects both humankind's vital—and potentially suicidal—relationship to nature, and the great variety of interchanges among the individuals in all domains, from the elementary material reproductive activities to the most complicated cultural/intellectual creativity. As a result, all attempts at introducing into human affairs *substantively equitable* organizing principles of *universality* had to be effectively *nullified in societal practice* in the course of modern history. In the last few centuries we have been offered in theory many promises and wishful idealist solutions to the contrary, but they could never be realized in *substantive* terms. Given the actual dominance of capital's antagonistic second-order mediations in the established social metabolic order, it is by no means accidental that the idealized theoretical foundation of the modern state's regulatory practices, claiming universality—as spelled out in terms of the "Rights of Man"—also had to be confined to *strictly formal* measures even in the conceptions of the greatest intellectual figures of the bourgeoisie, at the ascending phase of the system's all-encroaching development, as we have seen it discussed in this study.

On the material ground of the capital system it was impossible to find a viable solution in theory to the challenging problem concerning the relationship between particularity and universality. The best that could be expected from the thinkers who identified themselves with the standpoint of capital was some speculative wishful postulate of purely conceptual "mediation" to which in the real world of the societal reproduction process nothing could correspond. The underlying contradictions and class antagonisms of the system could not even be mentioned in the relevant conceptualizations, let alone defined in concrete social and historical terms as strategic targets for an epochally viable and comprehensive transformatory action. For they constituted the necessary *practical premises* assumed by all such theories.

This is why, in case some of the contradictions were acknowledged at all, in a suitably transfigured form, like individualistic conflictuality and adversariality—as by Kant's characterization of the "asocial sociability" of the human individuals made of "crooked timber"—they were coupled with the pseudo-solution of a priori *rightful* "Nature's Lawgiver" who would mysteriously overcome them, so as to bring even "Perpetual Peace" into the "Commercial Spirit's" ever more destructive world.

The same was true of Adam Smith's version of the "invisible hand." The Master of that benevolent hand was hypostatized as *ex officio* capable and willing to positively resolve the identified problems, and doing that in the same way as whatever other speculative wishful remedies could be projected by other representative figures of the enlightened bourgeoisie as a happy way out of the real contradictions.

Even the most advanced and comprehensive of such philosophies, at the tail end of capital's ascending phase of development, the Hegelian system,[75] could only offer the most abstract imperative of "mediation between the particular and the universal" as a purely conceptual "ought-to-be," in a wishfully stipulated harmonization of the existent with the "rational actuality" of the World Spirit. And when Hegel characterized the unfolding of World History in terms of the advancement of Freedom, he had to define it as "the development of the *idea* of Freedom," disregarding the systematic, structurally secured and enforced gross *violations of freedom* in the world of capital's *far from "rational actuality."* That was, again, an *indirect justification* of the existing order, both acknowledging the unavoidable challenge of freedom as a universally commendable concept and, at the same time, also successfully spiriting it away by confining freedom as such to the *speculative domain of the Idea.*

The reason why the more or less conscious indirect justification of the structurally entrenched and safeguarded antagonistic second-order mediations of this iniquitous system was feasible at all was a historical contingency. Indeed, the unjustifiable theoretical transfiguration of capital's incorrigible partiality into abstract universality was in consonance with the circumstance that, thanks to the scope provided by the global extension of the established mode of production—which happened to be in the more distant past well short of the planetary limits—some of its major contradictions as an increasingly destructive form of social metabolic control could be effectively *displaced* (but of course without being resolved) for a considerable time, and thereby the activation of capital's ultimate *systemic* limits effectively *postponed.*

Inevitably, however, the arrival of the "moment of truth" in the form of *acute crises* on an ever-increasing scale was only a question of time. Accordingly, no one could—or at least no one should—take it for granted forever, as Hegel categorically asserted, that "Europe is absolutely the end of history."[76] For *world historical development* in the actually existing world was asserting itself in a very different way—with its sharpening antagonisms and devastating wars—as compared to its idealized speculative characterizations.

In the actually given world, historical development in due course had put on the order of the day the literally vital necessity to face up to the all-destructive problems of capital's social metabolic control. Thus Marx could rightly argue already in 1845:

> The further the separate spheres, which act on one another, extend in the course of this development and the more the original isolation of the separate nationalities is destroyed by the advanced mode of production, by intercourse and by the natural division of labour between various nations arising as a result, the more *history becomes world history*. Thus, for

instance, if in England a machine is invented which deprives countless workers of bread in India and China, and overturns the whole form of existence of these empires, this invention becomes a *world historical fact*. . . . From this it follows that this transformation of history into world history is by no means a mere abstract act on the part of "self-consciousness," the world spirit, or of any other metaphysical spectre, but a quite *material, empirically verifiable* act, an act the proof of which every individual furnishes as he comes and goes, eats, drinks and clothes himself. In history up to the present it is likewise an empirical fact that separate individuals have, with the broadening of their activity into *world historical activity*, become more and more *enslaved under a power alien to them* (a pressure which they have conceived of as a dirty trick on the part of the so-called world spirit, etc.), a power which has become more and more enormous and, in the last instance, turns out to be the *world market*.[77]

In this way the *real antagonistic powers* at work in the societal reproduction process on a global scale could be unmistakably identified as the universally alienating as well as enslaving phase of *world history*. They could be indicated by Marx as the tangible forces of the *world market*. The same world market that happens to be one of the most iniquitous and all-encroaching *antagonistic second-order mediations of the capital system*. In this way both the practical feasibility and the necessity of transformatory intervention on the appropriate global scale of real world history could be forcefully underlined.

Likewise, the "world historical individuals" had to be, and indeed could be, demystified. Only in that demystified form, as genuine *social individuals*, could the actually existing world historical individuals assume the much needed *responsibility* for their own deliberations and actions, in contrast to being speculatively characterized and strangely glorified at the same time as "the *unconscious tools* and organs of the *world mind* at work within them." For in that lofty idealist form of characterization, as the mysteriously chosen unconscious tools of the world mind confined to the eternalized past and present, they were *good for nothing* as far as humanity's gravely endangered actual future was concerned.

In terms of the really existing phase of world history also the meaning of "world historical individuals" could be made perfectly obvious and tangible. Accordingly, it was put into relief by Marx that the issue could not be tied to a handful of elitistically conceived individuals, who mysteriously appear from time to time thanks to the world mind's "Absolute Cunning." Instead, it had to embrace the *social individuals in general* who, as a result of the unavoidable broadening of their activity everywhere into *world historical activity*, become in actuality *"world historical, empirically universal individuals in place of local ones."*[78] And the ever-intensifying world historical challenge for humanity's survival could only be met by the social individuals, in their capacity as *"freely associated producers,"* provided that they applied themselves to the realization of the tasks which they had to confront with *"communist mass consciousness"* (in Marx's words, formulated already in *The German Ideology*), as required under the circumstances of the capital system's deepening structural crisis.

With the unfolding reality of "empirically verifiable world history," dense with its explosive antagonisms at capital's descending phase of development, the need for *conscious comprehensive transformatory action* has become absolutely imperative. This is so because of the historically unique relationship between capital's mode of social metabolic control and human survival itself. For when the earlier forms of societal reproduction—like slavery and feudalism—reached the extreme limits of their historical viability and had to become untenable, that condition represented no fundamental danger for the possibility of future development and for the destruction of humanity. It is qualitatively different in the case of the capital system. For the activation of capital's absolute limits,[79] under the conditions of the system's global encroachment, directly endangers the very survival of the human species precisely because of the incurably destructive articulation of capital as a global metabolic control of societal reproduction in our time. In other words, the destructiveness inseparable from the activation of capital's absolute limits, if left unchecked, carries with it the total unsustainability of human life on this planet the first time ever in history. That is what needs to be brought under comprehensive conscious control under the present circumstances.

The antagonistic interactive forces of capital constitute an irremediably *centrifugal* overall system, despite all wishful postulates of harmonious globalization. *Conscious comprehensive control* on capital's systemic scale is therefore unthinkable, no matter how great the dangers of destruction and even capital's own systemic self-destruction. Revealingly, in the course of history already at the ascending phase of capital's development, the overall cohesion and control of this centrifugal system could only be speculatively postulated in the form of some kind of *mysterious totalizer,* as done even by the greatest thinkers of the bourgeoisie. Neither *comprehensive* control, nor the *conscious and voluntary* institution of a viable plan concerning societal reproduction could be envisaged in the form of rationally identifiable design and corresponding action.

It was that double hiatus that had to be filled in by the various overarching postulates of a mysterious *supra-human totalizing subject,* from the "invisible hand" to the Hegelian "Absolute Cunning of Divine Providence" working out its own plans through the even more mysteriously projected "unconscious instruments" of the unalterably centrifugal, yet in their very centrifugality idealized, constituent parts. And that kind of wishful "solution" was posited by the outstanding thinkers of the bourgeoisie—who could not imagine any other remedial action to their antagonistic system—well before the threat of humanity's self-destruction, together with the potentially catastrophic military instruments and the actively destructive "productive" practices fully capable of realizing such threat, had been put in their massive materiality at the disposal of capital's personifications. That is, at the disposal of those *in charge*—but by no means *in control*—of the established reproductive order, who have *ex officio,* precisely as devoted personifications of capital's self-expansionary imperative at all cost, the conceivably most irrational vested interest for deploying the powers of destruction.

How could then today anybody invest their faith in such mysterious *supra-human* totalizing agencies and their "unconscious instruments,"[80] or in some projected new varieties of them, asserting that despite everything they would be capable of overcoming the grave dangers tangibly identifiable now? Dangers that are, albeit in a self-serving apologetic way, even officially acknowledged both on the military and on the ecological plane? For the insuperable contradiction between *systemic centrifugality*—which from the standpoint of capital must be always *idealized systemic centrifugality*—and the absolute imperative of a *consciously planned and rationally managed global reproductive order,* would have to be *irre-*

versibly overcome so as to envisage a way out from the now pursued destructive blind alley. To project all-embracing *antagonistic centrifugality* as harmoniously combined with *sustainable globalization* is the most absurd *contradiction in terms.* No one in their right mind could take seriously this contradiction as the viable practical strategy to be pursued in the future.

The sobering fact is, and remains, that in terms of this fundamental structural incompatibility—between the vital requirements of sustainable production in the global planetary household and capital's destructive centrifugality—really there cannot be any alternative to the necessity to establish and adequately secure the social reproductive practice of *epochally sustainable globalization.* Moreover, epochally sustainable globalization worthy of its name can only be envisaged as a societal reproductive order consciously managed by the *freely associated producers* within the social metabolic framework of a *historically open-ended system.* Thus the only feasible way of overcoming the structural incompatibility we must face is this: capital's idealized—ever more destructive—centrifugality needs to be irretrievably consigned to the past if humanity is to survive.

There can be no way of understating the radically different character of the socialist conception which represents the real alternative to the ongoing course of development. For the socialist alternative cannot become viable unless it is strategically envisaged and practically secured as an unreservedly open-ended and consciously managed comprehensive transformatory system.

The human agency in control of the objective *structures* and temporal *processes* of such a system could have nothing to do with some speculative *supra-human* hidden designs and corresponding wishful solutions. We must always bear in mind that our terms of reference concern not the domain of an idealistically hypostatized "ought-to-be" but the tangible— and in our own historical time undeniably endangered—actuality of "empirically verifiable world history."

Accordingly, when we consider the requirements of *epochally sustainable globalization,* what is legitimate and necessary to put into relief is that the unavoidable theoretical corollary of the formerly projected mysterious *"supra-human* totalizer"—in any shape or disguise—is the replacement of the genuine open-ended *historical* conception we absolutely need by a *supra-historical* postulate, said to be benevolently managed by the "World Mind" (or whatever else, including its market-idealizing secular varieties), and the corresponding *closure of history* in the arbitrarily eternalized present.

In the same sense, opting for the frequently projected *"supra-individual"* historical subject, whether in the name of some speculative metaphysical construct or in the form of an alienating abstract collectivity, can only derail the required strategic conception.

To be sure, no coherent historical explanation is conceivable in terms of the "aggregates of particular individuals" who are said to be confronting one another in tendentiously depicted "civil society." But for our future the historically sustainable alternative to that kind of conception—which must be always posited from the standpoint of capital's self-serving political economy—is not the equally dubious *supra-individual* determinacy of so-called "rational actuality" (again fully in tune with capital's mode of social metabolic control), but the *real social individual* who is not only *in charge of* but also *in rational control of* the societal reproduction process. Not the *isolated individual* but the *real human being* whose character is defined by the objectively constituted *dialectical unity* of the individual and the social, as mentioned before. For adopting the idea of the *supra-individual* determinacy of development means at the same time also the acceptance of the postulates of the *supra-historical totalizer* of the allegedly insuperable antagonistic modality of societal interchange and the arbitrary *freezing* of the historical process in the self-contradictory and self-destructive *insuperable adversariality* of the "eternal present."

With regard to the future, openly acknowledging the need for a *rational totalizer*—in contrast to the great variety of failed *mysterious totalizers* propounded in the past—cannot be avoided. As clearly indicated a moment ago, the only viable historical subject capable of being engaged in the necessary rational totalization of the complex global interactive processes under the conditions of capital's deepening structural crisis can only be the *real social individuals*—and it cannot be stressed strongly enough: as defined by the objectively constituted *dialectical unity* of the individual and the social—who are not only *in charge of* but also *in rational control of* the challenges of increasingly more global societal reproduction.

In terms of the categorial "*Daseinsformen*"[81] (Marx) involved in this respect, we find the *real social individuals,* in their actual *historical* as well as *trans*-historical[82]—simultaneously *inter*-individual and *trans*-individual—social reality on one side, and the speculative categorial projections of the "*supra*-individual," the "*supra*-historical" and the "*supra*-human," in the form of various metaphysical constructs, on the other.

Thus, what is appropriate to underline in relation to the present phase of "empirically verifiable world history" is

1. the necessary orientation toward the objective dialectic of *continuity* and *discontinuity*, as the integrative synthesis of all dimensions of historical time, including the *trans-historical* aspects of humanity's social development, in place of the *supra-historical* projections of speculative historical theory, and;

2. the *inter*-individual and the *trans*-individual unity of the particular social individuals, acknowledging the necessary collective dimension of their life when conceptualizing the nature of the historical subject of our time as engaged in the creation of the vital "new historic needs" of

    • the pursuit of properly economizing rational husbandry in our inescapable planetary household and

    • the concomitant radical supersession of capital's destructive adversariality.

Only in that way is it possible to envision historical development in the future in harmony with epochally sustainable structural change.

6.3 Material and Formal Structures of History: Critique of Sartre's Conception of Dialectical Reason and Historical Totalization

It was one of Jean-Paul Sartre's great merits as a thinker and exemplary militant to address the fundamental question of historical totalization in the post–Second World War period. His famous *Critique of Dialectical Reason* was dedicated to the subject, announcing in its already massive first volume the "soon to be followed" completion[83] of this project.

It is important to bear in mind that Sartre's *Critique*—as published by Gallimard in Paris in 1960, with the subtitle of *Theory of Practical Ensembles*—was never intended to offer the complete picture on its own. On the contrary, it explicitly promised the proper elaboration of the categorial framework of *"real history,"* as the necessary complementary and indeed the theoretical climax to Sartre's project. This is how he put it in his Introduction to the published work:

> Volume I of the *Critique of Dialectical Reason* stops as soon as we reach the "locus of history"; it is solely concerned with finding the intelligible foundations for a structural anthropology—to the extent, of course, that these synthetic structures are the condition of a directed, developing totalization. Volume II, which will follow shortly, will retrace the stages of the critical progression; it will attempt to establish that there is *one* human history, with *one* truth and *one* intelligibility . . . by demonstrating that a practical multiplicity, whatever it may be, must unceasingly totalise itself through interiorising its multiplicity at all levels. . . . Then we shall be able to glimpse what these two volumes together will try to prove: that *necessity,* as the apodictic structure of dialectical investigation, resides neither in the free development of interiority nor in the inert dispersal of exteriority; it asserts itself, as an inevitable and irreducible moment, in the interiorisation of the exterior and in the exteriorisation of the interior.[84]

However, there were some very good reasons why this project could never be brought anywhere near its promised completion. The intended analysis of *real history*—in contrast to the philosophical problematic outlined in the first volume of the Sartrean *Critique* only in terms of the *formal* structures of history—refused to materialize in the interminably growing pages of the posthumous second volume; a manuscript amounting to a volume of almost five hundred pages, which in the end was not considered suitable for publication by its author. For whereas Sartre had no difficulties illustrating with most imaginatively used historical material the categories adopted in the published work, accurately defined as the strictly "formal structures of history," the attempted evaluation of particular conflictual situations and major historical developments discussed in the second volume remained firmly anchored, despite his intentions, to the same *formal* categorial framework. Thus in the end not much choice remained to Sartre than to abandon his originally promised comprehensive account of real history as the integral part and *"terminus ad quem"* of his vision of historical totalization.

Yet, it would be quite wrong to see in this outcome the corrigible personal failure of a particular thinker. In the case of one of the outstanding intellectual figures of the twentieth century, as Jean-Paul Sartre undeniably happened to be, the *non-realizability* of an important theoretical enterprise—attempted, to be sure, from a determinate social and historical standpoint—has its deep-seated objective ground and corresponding representative significance. On this particular occasion this is the case all the more because Sartre intended to put forward his conception, in the midst of the turmoil of some far-reaching historical events,[85] as an integral part of a quest pursued with great passion throughout his life in the service of the cause of human emancipation.[86]

In this sense Sartre rejected in the strongest possible terms any idea of a mysterious totalizer, which we have seen advocated even by the greatest thinkers of the bourgeoisie in the ascending phase of the capital system's historical unfolding. He insisted that in any viable historical conception people must be "wholly defined by their society and by the historical movement which carries them along; if we do not wish the dialectic to become a divine law again, a metaphysical fate, it must proceed *from individuals* and not from some kind of supra-individual ensemble. . . . The dialectic is the law of totalisation which creates *several* collectivities, *several* societies, and *one* history—realities which impose themselves on individuals; but at the same time it must be woven out of millions of individual actions."[87]

Another major achievement of the *Critique of Dialectical Reason* is Sartre's elaboration of the categorial framework of what he calls the formal structures of history, as we find them outlined in the work published by Gallimard in 1960, with powerfully depicted historical material, ranging from some key episodes of the French Revolution of 1789 to twenti-

eth-century developments. These formal categories—from the constitution of "seriality" and the "fused group" to disintegrative "institutional-
ization"—as elaborated in the first volume of the Sartrean *Critique*, by no
means could be said to constitute the formal structures of history in general. They are on the whole applicable to a determinate phase of human
history only, in that they encapsulate some characteristic determinations
of social interchange under the bourgeois order. In that way, though, their
potential for illuminating some important aspects of modern historical
transformations is truly remarkable. Indeed, precisely thanks to their formal structuring orientation they are well in tune with some of the fundamental material imperatives of capital's productive order that must subsume under its fetishistically quantifying *formal equalizations* and
abstract homogenizing determinations the most disparate qualities of
societal metabolic interchange in which exchange-value must absolutely
dominate use-value, as we have seen discussed in chapter 4 as well as in
section 6.2 above. Thus the fact that Sartre was unable to complete his
original project of integrating the propounded formal structures of history with his intended account of real history cannot take away anything
from their explanatory value in their own setting.

To understand the insuperable impediments at the roots of Sartre's
project for elucidating the problem of totalization in real history it is
worth quoting a passage from an important interview he gave in 1969 to
New Left Review. As clearly transpires from this interview, even as late as
1969 Sartre was still promising to complete the second volume of the
Critique of Dialectical Reason, although he had already put aside its
nearly five hundred pages way back in 1958. These were his words in the
1969 interview:

> The difference between the first and the second volume is this: the first
> is an abstract work where I show the possibilities of exchange, degrada-
> tion, the practico-inert, series, collectives, recurrence and so on. It is con-
> cerned only with the theoretical possibilities of their combinations. The
> project of the second volume is history itself . . . my aim will be to prove
> that there is a dialectical intelligibility of the singular. For ours is a singu-
> lar history. . . . What I will seek to show is the dialectical intelligibility of
> that which is not universalizable.[88]

However, as the case turned out to be, the drafting of the second volume, which was actually interrupted for Sartre's compelling internal reasons before the end of 1958, was never taken up again. Its abandoned manuscript was posthumously published in French five years after Sartre's death, in 1985, and in English six years later, in 1991.

Nevertheless, the destiny of this major Sartrean project was by no means surprising. My own comment, when Sartre was still alive and fully active, on the just quoted passage and on the anticipated *unfinishability* of his theory of historical totalization—as clearly demonstrated to me by volume one of the *Critique of Dialectical Reason* as well as by the 1969 interview itself—was as follows: "It is extremely difficult to imagine how one can comprehend 'history itself' through these categories, since the problem of history is precisely *how to universalize the singular without suppressing its specificity*. By contrast, however, it is very easy to see the natural transition from history to *biography*, namely from this Sartrean conception of history to the project on Flaubert. For the intelligibility of the *non*-universalizable singular calls for lived experience as the basis of its comprehension. And the reconstruction of the personage through *l'imaginaire* necessarily involved in it,[89] gives us a 'True Legend,' at the highest level of complexity. Some of the fundamental structures of history remain hidden away in the second volume of the *Critique* that *never comes*, for they do not seem to fit into the framework of Sartre's quest."[90]

The insurmountable problem for Sartre was, and always remained, that the way to universalize the singular without suppressing its specificity is feasible only through the *appropriate mediations* that link the—socially defined—multiplicity of particular individuals to their groups and classes at any given time, and to the unfolding societal development across the whole of history. Sartre's answers to the question of *mediation* were always extremely problematical in his conception of historical totalization. And, again, the missing social/historical mediations from his thought were not a *corrigible* absence.

To be sure, Sartre rightly stressed that history is "woven out of millions of individual actions," as we have seen his firm insistence on this issue in an earlier quote. However, despite a claim made explicit in the period of writing and publishing the first volume of the *Critique of Dialectical Reason*—according to which existentialism has been left behind by him in his later development as no more than an "ideol-ogy"[91]—some of the crucial categories developed in his early work, prior to and during the Second World War, and indeed most strikingly in *Being and Nothingness,* remained always dominant in his philosophy. He even took back in 1975 the 1958 assertion about existentialism being merely an "ideological enclave within Marxism,"[92] accepting instead, and in a curious way,[93] the existentialist label again.

The point of seminal importance in this respect was that by his de facto—even if under the given political circumstances not programmati-cally expressed yet persistent—attempt to give an *existential ontological foundation* to his own categorial framework also in the *Critique of Dialectical Reason,*[94] Sartre barred the road to making dialectically intel-ligible the process of historical totalization in real history. Namely, he made it prohibitively difficult to envisage how it could be possible at all for the "millions of individual actions"—in truth always deeply embed-ded in historically most specific and dynamically interrelated social struc-tures—to add up to a network of law-like determinations in the proper sense of *historical* necessity, conceived as progressively changing and in its modality of asserting itself in due course "vanishing necessity." The missing historical mediations played a crucial role in derailing Sartre's intended overall account of real history.

In his problematical attempt to give an ontological foundation to his own "existentialist enclave within Marxism," Sartre had to turn the *emi-nently historical and socially transcendable category of scarcity* into a par-alyzing ahistorical and anti-historical *absolute*, arbitrarily proclaimed to be the insuperable *permanence* and the overall determination and horizon of our real history. He did this by postulating that

> to say that our History is a history of men is equivalent to saying that it is
> born and developed within the *permanent framework* of a field of tension
> produced by *scarcity*.[95]

At the same time, he repeatedly contradicted his earlier categorical assertion according to which *"there is no such thing as man; there are peo-ple."*[96] However, for the sake of the existentialistically absolutized declara-tion of a *perverse reciprocity* between each particular individual and the mythical "Other" who inhabits *every* individual, a direct line of identity was decreed by Sartre to be fatefully prevailing between the ethically both rebellious and at the same time also viciously inhuman individual and the *mythical/demonic man* under the rule of *permanent scarcity*. It is important in this respect to quote in some detail Sartre's words from the first volume of the *Critique of Dialectical Reason*:

> In pure reciprocity, that which is Other than me is also the same. But in reciprocity as modified by scarcity, the same appears to us as anti-human in so far as this same man appears as radically Other—that is to say, as threatening us with death. Or, to put it another way, we have a rough understanding of his ends (for they are the same as ours), and his means (we have the same ones) as well as of the dialectical structures of his acts; but we understand them as if they belonged to another species, our *demonic double*. Nothing—not even wild beasts or microbes—could be more terrifying for man than a species which is intelligent, carnivorous and cruel, and which can understand and outwit human intelligence, and whose aim is precisely the *destruction of man*. This, however, is obviously our own species as perceived in others by *each* of its members in the context of *scarcity*. . . . it makes everyone *objectively* dangerous for the Other and makes the concrete existence of *each individual* endanger that of the Other. Thus *man is objectively constituted as non-human*, and this non-humanity is expressed in *praxis* by the perception of *evil as the structure of the Other*.[97]

This ahistorical Sartrean discourse on "evil as the structure of the Other"—and indeed the "Other" as each and *every particular individual*—in the *Critique* was articulated in such a way that with relative ease it could be incorporated into the existientialist ontological design of his first great synthesizing philosophical work, *Being and Nothingness*. In this way we were told by the "marxisant"[98] Jean-Paul Sartre of the *Critique of Dialectical Reason*:

> I may try to kill, to torture, to enslave, or simply to mystify, but in any case my aim will be to eliminate *alien freedom* as a hostile force, a force which can expel me from the practical field and make me into "a surplus man"

condemned to death. In other words, it is undeniable that what I attack is *man as man*, that is, as the free praxis of an organic being. It is *man, and nothing else*, that I hate in the enemy, that is, *in myself as Other;* and it is myself that I try to destroy in him, so as to prevent him destroying me in my own body.[99]

Naturally, the passionately committed militant intellectual Sartre's *motivation* for constructing this vision of inescapable conflict, characterized as necessarily arising from and ruled by permanent scarcity, inseparable from its existentialist ontological underpinning, was not the submissive defense but the radical negation of the existent societal order. He needed the heightened ontological emphasis for his proclaimed "existentialist enclave" in order to put into dramatic relief the enormity of the struggle that must be pursued against the *"enemy"* Other, paradoxically defined as *"myself"* and *every individual self.* However, by doing so without bringing into the picture the appropriate *social and historical mediations*—indeed by obliterating the vital distinction between historically insuperable *first-order* and capital's to be transcended *antagonistic second-order mediations*[100]—he ended up with *absolutizing the historically relative* against his own critical intentions.

Under the specific conditions of real history asserting themselves in our time, as we are forced to live them *under the structurally determined rule of capital,* the antagonistic second-order mediations must always prevail. They represent a historically in the long run *absolutely untenable imposition and domination* of the established societal reproduction process, with their ultimately destructive and self-destructive implications. The *historical supersession* of such antagonistic second-order mediations, no matter how prohibitive the obstacles to their overcoming might appear under the present conditions, is the key to the solution of the thorny issue—the veritable *vicious circle* in the capital system's *"real history"*—of scarcity inseparably combined with recklessly produced waste on the one hand and the often oversimplified wishful counter-image of "abundance" on the other. The idea of the pseudo-ontological permanence of capital's oppressive second-order mediations, postulated on the premise of historically, already long before capital's appearance, imposed *class domination*, as the necessary structural framework of self-imposing scarcity, is a falsely stipulated distortion. For the *relative* continuity which we can find between the *qualitatively* different antecedents of capital's antagonistic second-order mediations and its own distinctive modality of class-exploitative societal reproductive domination by means of the economically enforced extraction of surplus labor as surplus value, is *trans*-historical—and in that sense *superable*—but emphatically not *supra*-historical.

Once, however, the existentialist ontological underpinning of Sartre's categorial framework asserts itself, offering a vision of some kind of "human condition" inseparable from destructive conflict under the rule of permanent scarcity, the original intellectual motivation of critical negation of this great militant thinker is inevitably pushed into the background. Thus the corollary of *absolutizing the relative*—i.e., absolutizing the historical category of scarcity by turning it into ontologically interiorized permanence—makes its far-reaching negative impact. This corollary of absolutizing the relative in Sartre's existentialist ontological "enclave" paradoxically assumes the form of *relativizing the absolute conditions of human existence* by suppressing its unique character as a *historical absolute*. The actually existing and, this cannot be stressed enough, by no means *ahistorical* absolute constituent of humanity's dialectical determination—namely the forever *inescapable*, and in *that sense*, but not in its particular modality, absolute—*natural substratum* of human existence is the issue here. Its unique determination as a historical absolute remains in force nonetheless. For no matter to what degree this natural substratum might (indeed must) be modified by ongoing human productive development, in the course of the historical creation of *"new needs"* and the corresponding extension of the conditions of their satisfaction, ultimately it always remains firmly circumscribed by nature. And that circumstance also means that inasmuch as it is violated—which continues to happen in our time to an increasingly dangerous degree in humankind's relationship to nature—it must be also unceremoniously, and even punitively, imposed upon society by the objective requirements of human existence itself.

Naturally, this makes absolutely imperative for humanity the positive articulation of a viable and historically sustainable interchange of the social individuals with nature and among themselves, as the changing but necessary social ground of their relationship to nature, if they want to avoid self-destruction. But to do so is possible only by observing the unique and inherently historical character of the relationship in question. Only on that basis is it feasible to redefine in a proper way, especially under the conditions of the intensifying structural crisis of their mode of social metabolic reproduction, the vital relationship of humanity to nature in the necessarily *open-ended* historical framework of development.

Accordingly, it would be self-defeating to identify in any attempted account of "real history" the objective character of the *natural substratum* of human existence—which must be in the course of human development subject to *appropriate* historical transformations,[101] in view of the intervention of, by human beings' instituted and changing *historical necessity* in the order of nature—with the timeless *existentialist ontological materiality of scarcity,* postulated on the arbitrarily assumed ground that *"man is objectively constituted as non-human,* and this non-humanity is expressed in *praxis* by the perception of *evil as the structure of the Other."*[102] To presume and proclaim that "man is objectively constituted as non-human" is an *existentialistically misrepresented prejudgment* of the issue, devised for the purpose of switching immediately, in the same sentence, from the apparently *neutral/objective* meaning of "non-human" to the fateful characterization of the "non-humanity of human praxis" as necessarily carrying with it the "perception of evil as the structure of the Other."

The "objective constitution of man," called in this way by Sartre, with regard to its primary/primitive objectivity, does not and cannot refer at all to "man," nor to an existentialistically projected demonic/mythical "non-human," but only to the *animal* world. In relation to the being that emerges later in history—by constituting itself—as human, it can be legitimately called, from a human perspective, *pre-human,* but decidedly not in a tendentious sense, proclaimed to fit the somber spectrum of existentialist ontology, as "non-human." For prior to the open-ended historical *self-constitution* of the human being—of which "the creation of a new need" is the "first historical act," as we have seen above—there is no such being properly so called as "non-human" in the Sartrean sense. It must be revealingly called by Sartre in that way so that later the being in question should be easily presentable in the spirit of existentialist ontological gloom as "evil," with its structural determination assigned to the "Other" embedded in every individual self, including "myself."

In actuality the natural substratum of human existence itself is not a massive "materiality" but a changing social structural relationship—an always historically specific mediation—of human beings in general with nature *and* among themselves. Thus this inescapable mediation is necessarily constituted and reconstituted through socially specific and historically changing human intervention in the absolutely inescapable order of nature. In other words, it is constituted and reconstituted in the form of the earlier discussed dual causality of nature's own lawfulness on the one hand (which can be dynamically adapted but not violated), and the progressively modified/displaced (and in its *particular* modality in due course "vanishing"/superseded) historical necessity on the other.

In the same sense, the category of *scarcity* is from its inception an inherently historical category, acquiring its meaning from the relationship of its *temporary* (no matter how long) domination over the human beings that under determinate—that is, historically specific and alterable—conditions must suffer its power. This is far from being a self-sustaining power. It must be simultaneously also defined as subject to becoming *historically superseded*, at least in principle. Or not, as the case might be. But *not superseded* only if the projected necessary failure of the human species is absolutized as the all-embracing ultimate catastrophe, amounting to the termination of human history itself. Scarcity makes no sense at all *in itself and for itself as an absolute.* It is always "scarcity in relation to something or someone." Moreover, even in its objective determination as a weighty contingency it makes sense—one way or another—only in relation to human beings who may *suffer or overcome* it, thanks to their own inherently historical determination and self-determination. Unlike humans, animals do not *"live in a world of scarcity."* They just live—and die—as the "species-determinations" of their "genus-individuality" permit and destine them to do.

Scarcity must therefore be understood in its appropriate historical context, as *parasitic* on human history, and not as the postulated *ground* and pessimistically hypostatized *causal foundation* of history. To say with Sartre that history is *"born and developed* within the *permanent framework* of a field of tension *produced by scarcity"*[103] can only absolutize the relative and relativize the absolute. For, in the latter sense, the Sartrean assertion subordinates to the hopeless vicissitudes of demonically magni-

fied and likewise interiorized scarcity[104] the *absolute imperative* of instituting a viable alternative to the established mode of social metabolic
reproduction at the present critical juncture of history. By contrast, in the
framework adopted by Sartre, the gloom of insuperably absolutized anti-
historical scarcity as the ground of historical intelligibility, wedded to the
earlier quoted perverse reciprocity between "myself and the Other in
me," is overwhelming.

The fact that the *imperative* facing human society today for adopting
a radically different mode of historically sustainable social metabolic
reproduction is *absolute*, in direct opposition to capital's destructive pursuit of *unlimitable*—hence by definition always "scarce"— *capital expansion,* does not and cannot obliterate the inherently *historical* character
and corresponding *urgency* of such absolute. For all conceivable
absolutes in the human context are necessarily historical at the same time,
including those concerning the ineliminable natural substratum of human
existence itself. However, by *submerging* the historically determinate
practical imperative for elaborating a viable societal reproductive alternative into the generic pseudo-absolute existentialist ontological projection
of the "permanent framework of scarcity" can only generate desolate pessimism[105] and the noble but impotent "ought to be" as its envisaged
counter-image.[106] There can be no room therefore in the structurally prejudged "existentialist ontological enclave," dominated by permanent
scarcity, for exploring the conditions of feasibility of the required and historically sustainable positive alternative.

The strange result of all this is the diminishing of responsibility for the
capital system itself, notwithstanding its historically overwhelming range
of destructive second-order mediations. Such responsibility is diminished in Sartre's proclaimed "existentialist ideological enclave within
Marxism" on account of the mythically magnified role ascribed by him to
the anti-historically extended generic "interiorized scarcity" made by
"myself as the Other." And that "Other in me" is hypostatized by Sartre
in a form overburdened with the most unreal projection of responsibility
by being characterized in an earlier quoted passage from the *Critique of
Dialectical Reason* as the "demonic double" of not only the human
species in general—called in that quote "a species which is intelligent,
carnivorous and cruel, and which can understand and outwit human

intelligence, and whose aim is precisely the *destruction of man*"[107]—but at the same time of every single individual in their personal capacity. This is a most peculiar way of exempting the capital system of its quite obvious responsibility for being actually bent in our time on the very real "destruction of man" rightly deplored by Sartre himself. Moreover, what makes the kind of existentialist ontological underpinning which we have seen in the categorial framework of the *Critique of Dialectical Reason* rather paradoxical is, of course, the circumstance that Sartre would be the last person to offer such exemption as a matter of conscious deliberation to the inhuman power of capital. No one raises more often in a dramatic way than Sartre himself the question of responsibility in general and the grave responsibility of the intellectuals in particular. His moral indignation and radical negation remain always very intense. But the only historical subject he can appeal to and try to enlist for the fights he is engaged in is the isolated particular individual.

The political dimension of Sartre's approach to history is expressed in a brilliant occasional piece from 1973: "*Elections: A Trap for Fools,*"[108] published in *Les Temps Modernes* in January 1973, and as we learn with precision from the article itself, written on 5 January 1973, shortly before the French general election under Pompidou's presidency.

"Elections: A Trap for Fools" is a very significant article as the political actualization of the Sartrean *formal structures of history,* developed in great detail in the first volume of the *Critique of Dialectical Reason.* For in the Sartrean vision the categories of the *Critique* are perfectly applicable to the electoral situation itself, considered by him a strictly and reprehensibly "formal structure of history."

In this respect it is directly relevant that Sartre's *Critique of Dialectical Reason,* regarding its inspiration, can only be understood in the context of the *dual crisis* of

1. French colonialism in Vietnam and Algeria, and;

2. the deepening crisis of the Soviet type system, including the East German (1953), the Polish (1955–56) and the Hungarian upheavals. Indeed, the Hungarian popular explosion of October 1956 has a greater impact on Sartre's thought than any other contemporary his-

torical event, as evidenced by his major essay: *The Phantom of Stalin* as well as by the *Critique of Dialectical Reason* itself.[109]

The formal categories elaborated by Sartre in the first volume of his *Critique of Dialectical Reason,* arising to a considerable degree from his passionate assessment of this dual crisis, remain to the end the orienting principles of his interpretation of the unfolding political events and of the role to be assigned to the individuals participating in them. This is so irrespective of the fact that he is unable to theorize the problem of totalization in "real history" either in the repeatedly promised but unfinishable second volume of the *Critique* or anywhere else.[110]

The process of fateful "serialization," corresponding to one of his most important formal structures of history, in conjunction with the "practico-inert field," is described by Sartre in "Election: A Trap for Fools" in most vivid terms. Talking about the serialized individual he insists that "a soldier takes the bus, buys the newspaper, votes. All this presumes that he will make use of 'collectives' along with the Others. But the collectives address him as a member of a *series* (the series of newspaper buyers, television watchers, etc.). He becomes in essence identical with all the other members, differing from them only by his serial number. We say that he has been *serialized.* One finds serialization in the *practico-inert* field, where *matter mediates* between men to the extent that men mediate between material objects. . . . *Serial thinking* is born in me, thinking which is not my own thinking but that of the Other, which I am and also that of all the Others. It must be called the *thinking of powerlessness,* because *I produce it* to the degree that I am Other, an *enemy of myself* and of the Others, and to the degree that I carry the Other everywhere with me."[111]

At the same time, the grave consequences of such serialization are graphically put into relief by saying, "Now, these citizens, identical as they are and fabricated by the law, disarmed and separated by distrust of one another, deceived but aware of their impotence, can never, as long as they *remain serialized,* form that *sovereign group* from which, we are told, all power emanates—*the People.*"[112]

Sartre's accusing finger, as we can see, is not pointed at society in general but to every individual. For, according to him, I as the serialized—and indeed actively self-serializing—individual am the guilty one who *pro-

duces the "thinking of powerlessness," and in that way I become "an *enemy of myself* and of the Others." He thereby clearly ascribes responsibility not only to the ruling societal order but directly to each one of us, looking at the same time also for the required remedy in the form of a *direct appeal* to our individual consciousness. Not surprisingly, the article of "Elections: A Trap for Fools" ends with an "ought to be" presented as a *"must,"* by saying, "We must try, *each* according to his own resources, to organize the *vast anti-hierarchic movement* which fights *institutions* everywhere."[113]

The question of *how* the now actually serialized individuals could prevail against the "hierarchic institutions everywhere," as he invites them to do, cannot be addressed by Sartre. Some of his centrally important categories—indicting the power of serialization as such and the necessity of the fused group's institutionally foreshadowed disintegration, as well as the fateful relapse of the particular members of the group into self-imposed seriality—speak eloquently against his own proclaimed imperative. This is the reason why the "ought to be" of the unspecified mode of "organization" of the individuals is strongly contradicted by Sartre's explicit judgment against the feasible success of organization itself. This is expressed with great sincerity in an interview given by Sartre in 1969 to the important Italian political movement, the *Manifesto* group, in these words: "While I recognize the need of an organization, I must confess that I don't see how the problems which confront *any stabilized structure* could be resolved."[114]

The most significant passage in "Elections: A Trap for Fools" which illuminates the political and theoretical roots of Sartre's militant strategic orientation, is his emphatic condemnation of the act of voting itself, in the name of his passionate advocacy of *sovereignty* celebrated also in one of his most important categories, the "sovereign group."

This seminal passage of Sartre's 1973 article on elections reads as follows: "When I vote, I *abdicate* my power—that is, the possibility everyone has of joining others to form a *sovereign group* which would have *no need of representatives.*"[115]

The importance of Sartre's concern with the imperative of sovereignty cannot be stressed strongly enough. The same idea is emphasized—indeed idealized—by him in the immediate aftermath of the defeat of the dramatic May 1968 upheavals in France. In fact Sartre singles out the embryonic appearance of sovereignty as the *great novelty* of the 1968 historical events in general. For he insists in his sharp condemnation of the critics of the student movement, "What I reproach all those with, who insulted the students, is that they failed to see that the students expressed a new demand: the need for *sovereignty*."[116]

Of course, the sovereignty here referred to, wholeheartedly supported by Sartre, is nothing less than the unique social formation that in his view should be—or, in more accurate terms, "ought to be"—spontaneously constituted by all those who reject serialization, in opposition to the "stabilized structures" whose politically favored organizational establishment is turned down by him even in one of his most succinctly articulated political reflections on the subject, presented in the interview conceded to the *Manifesto* group of the Italian radical left. And the mode of constituting such sovereignty, according to Sartre, is either through some revolutionary explosion, like May 1968 in France, or by means of the admittedly problematical organizational form brought into being by the *direct appeal* of the militant intellectuals to the consciousness of the potentially anti-hierarchical individuals in general, who are said to be favorably disposed in that way by their "need for liberty."

The idea that such direct appeal might be able to produce the required outcome is often expressed by Sartre with a confession of self-critical skepticism, even pessimism, as we have seen it earlier.[117] It persists, nevertheless. For the roots of advocating politically commended solutions in the form of such direct appeals to individual consciousness reach back a long way in Sartre's political development. Indeed, as far as the individualistic addressee of political enlightenment is concerned, such views reach back even more so—in fact much more so—not only into the rather remote past of French political and intellectual history but in the philosophical tradition of the European bourgeoisie in general, in terms of its earlier discussed orientation to "aggregates of individuality"[118] in neglect of class reality.

In terms of the political organizational form based on the idea of some direct appeal to individual consciousness shared by Sartre, we have to remember the *Rassemblement Démocratique Révolutionnaire* (RDR)[119] with which Sartre was formally associated in 1948 and 1949. He insisted in an interview given to the Paris edition of the *New York Herald Tribune* that such a movement was addressing itself strictly to the individuals, and not to "constituted groups."[120] Accordingly, the programmatic pieces written by Sartre and his associates about this—far from really influential—movement explicitly stressed the desire to be very different from the established political organizations and parties of the left. It was explicitly stated by Sartre that they are meant to orient their individual supporters, instead, toward the defense of some important longstanding political ideals. In this sense he argued:

> "The question is not to abandon liberty; not even to abandon the abstract liberties of the bourgeoisie, but to fill them with content.... The first objective of the Revolutionary Democratic Assembly is to combine the revolutionary demands with the idea of Liberty."[121]

In this way, under the political circumstances of 1948, the direct appeal to the progressive individuals remained rather vague and generic. But the same form of direct appeal was later put into relief by Sartre in his much more radical interpretation of May 1968, in sharp contrast to the traditional organizational forms and parties. His stress on "sovereignty," in his praise of the students, is most relevant in that respect.

However, the most important defining characteristic of the Sartrean position concerning the required historical alternative is precisely his categorical rejection of the act of voting itself in the passage quoted from the 1973 article. A rejection made on the ground that we have seen a little while ago, namely, "When I vote, I *abdicate* my power—that is, the possibility everyone has of joining others to form a *sovereign group* which would have *no need of representatives.*"

In the form of this direct appeal to individual consciousness of the would-be voters, dismissing the traditional state institutions and the "constituted" political parties, the Sartrean rejection is formulated in the spirit of the best bourgeois tradition of the Enlightenment. We can see its close affinity with Rousseau's radical dismissal of voting and his condemnation of the parliamentary representative political system. This is how Rousseau argues his case:

The deputies of the people, therefore, are not and cannot be its *representatives;* they are merely its stewards, and can carry through no definitive acts. Every law the people has not ratified in person is null and void—is, in fact, not a law. The people of England regards itself as free; but it is grossly mistaken; it is free only during the election of members of parliament. As soon as they are elected, slavery overtakes it, and it is nothing. The use it makes of the short moments of *liberty* it enjoys shows indeed that it *deserves to lose them.*[122]

In the same way as Rousseau's self-deluding Englishmen who foolishly renounce their power in favor of parliamentary representatives and quickly lose their momentary liberty, which they are said to deserve, Sartre's "self-serializing fools," who likewise consent to abdicate their power by voting, instead of "joining others to form a *sovereign group* which would have *no need of representatives*," also fully deserve their fate according to the great French "marxisant existentialist" intellectual.

But even so, Sartre's militant adhesion in the twentieth century to the heroic Enlightenment perspective championed by Rousseau in support of direct democracy in the eighteenth is paradoxical. For Sartre formulates the most radical critique of the bourgeoisie while remaining *within* the bourgeois class horizon. He often even consciously and explicitly states that his sharp critical position is that of an *insider.* Sartre does that so as to be able to denounce as strongly as feasible, from the "critical insider's position," the *mortal danger* posed by the historically given socioeconomic and political reality in which all individuals are, according to him, deeply implicated.

Thus Sartre defines his own position as a *bourgeois with an acute critical conscience* who assumes a position of *open revolt* against the increasing destructiveness of the established order, without the ability to detach himself from the bourgeois integument.[123] The passionate *direct appeal* to individual consciousness is in this Sartrean vision the necessary corollary to his explicit or implicit advocacy of instituting some kind of *direct democracy* whose distant ancestry was supposed to be in tune with the "Rights of Man." His earlier quoted desire to "fill with content the abstract liberties of the bourgeoisie" speaks volumes for itself in that respect. But it also shows the difficulties and limitations of attempting to produce totalization in "real history" within the categorial framework of the "formal structures of history" compatible with a radically intended but in its origin necessarily abstract and formalistic horizon. One conceived in its time within the boundaries of the never realized—and for that matter never realizable—bourgeois "Rights of Man."

Accordingly, it would take the labor of Sisyphus to "fill with content the abstract liberties of the bourgeoisie," and of course to no avail. For the distance from the formal liberties of the bourgeois order to their socialist counterparts which are inconceivable without all-embracing real content—as for instance the question of *substantive equality*—is *literally astronomical*. The actual constitution of a radically different social metabolic order, structurally defined in a *qualitatively* different way from capital's mode of societal reproduction—from its elementary material productive practices to the highest levels of cultural interchanges, together with the corresponding decision-making practices of its substantively equal social individuals emancipated from capital's antagonistic second-order mediations[124]—is required for the realization of such relationships to which the bourgeoisie could not significantly contribute even in the abstract heroic period of its historical past prior to the French Revolution. And that would need infinitely more than to "fill with content the abstract liberties of the bourgeoisie." For the sobering truth of the matter is that those abstract liberties—devised in accordance with the requirements of a *structurally iniquitous* social order, and therefore within their own terms of reference appropriately confined to the *formal/legal sphere*—cannot be filled with socialist content. They are *incompatible* with substantive socialist determinations, notwithstanding the slogan about "filling them with content" adopted from time to time in well-meaning but greatly constrained political discourse.

Paradoxically, Sartre's reformulation of the idea of some kind of unspecified and organizationally undefinable direct democracy is put under heavily accented question marks in relation to any feasible future by his own rather pessimistic account of the constitution and fateful disintegration of the "fused group." Yet, it is retained as an "ought to be." But even as a noble "ought to be"—revealingly enough coupled with his repeated exhortations addressed to individual consciousness to "join a sovereign group which would need no representatives"—the Sartrean idea turns out to be an openly admitted "formal structure" only. A most problematical formal structure that would have to be (but, as it happens, cannot be) "filled with content" in his elusive second volume of the *Critique*, envisaged for making intelligible his apodictic project about the dialectic of "real history."

Sartre criticizes Husserl in the first volume of the *Critique of Dialectical Reason* for his conception of "apodictic certainty." This is how he puts it:

> Husserl could speak of apodictic certainty without much difficulty, but this was because he remained on the level of pure, formal consciousness apprehending itself in its formality; but, for us, it is necessary to find our apodictic experience in the concrete world of history.[125]

To be sure, the way Sartre *intends* to pursue his own project of demonstrating apodicticity in real history cannot be satisfied with the internal resources of "pure, formal consciousness apprehending itself in its formality," within the confines of self-proclaimed Husserlian immanence. However, despite the intended major differences Sartre continues to share important aspects of his own orientation toward apodicticity with the bourgeois ancestry in view of the fact that he never submits the *material foundations* of capital's social order to a sustained critical analysis. He addresses his critical observations to the political and ideological/psychological dimensions only.

Thus it is by no means accidental that Sartre's categorial framework in the *Critique*—including its unfinishable second volume—can only be spelled out in terms of the *formal* structures of history, which undoubtedly happen to be highly relevant to the evaluation of some important aspects of the societal interchanges of capitalist "aggregative individuality," but they are most problematical in relation to overall historical development as "real history." For in the society of generalized commodity production, operated on the basis of formally reductive homogenization and abstract value-equation of all substantive/qualitative incommensurability, capital's perverse formal apodicticity can, to be sure, prevail. But in the open-ended development of real history it can do so only for as long as the antagonistic second-order mediations of the material reproductive system itself can impose the ultimately *self-destructive imperative* of endless capital expansion on the producers through the *substantively* most iniquitous—but formally/legally "equalized" and in that way secured—order of hierarchical structural domination and subordination.

In this sense the perverse but for a long historical stage preponderantly successful *formal apodicticity* of the capital system's *law of value,* with its *rationally unlimitable* self-expansionary imperative as the dynamic material determinant of its *apodictic certainty sui generis,* can *appear* to be insuperable. It can proclaim with categorical absoluteness its own—in reality in historical terms most specific[126] and in substantive terms most limited—insuperability in view of the *total absence* of identifiable *self-limiting* targets of productive pursuit admissible from the standpoint of capital's mode of social metabolic reproduction. This is an incorrigible and dangerously missing, but absolutely necessary, self-limitation. It is due to the fact that—to be a meaningful self-limitation at all—it would have to be defined in *substantive* terms necessarily excluded by capital.

Such *structural impediment* to the vitally important self-limitation is imposed on capital as a historically specific reproductive system in view of its innermost and unalterable material determination that must assert itself in generalized commodity production. For that kind of production cannot operate without *formally reductive universal value-equation.* And that is because such a system must *formally equate* under its most discriminatory exchange relation the qualitatively/substantively incommensurable use-values corresponding to human need. Moreover, this incorrigible determination is further aggravated on account of the utterly *fallacious*—yet as a rule apologetically asserted and perpetuated—*false identification* of commendable productive development, idealized as unquestionably desirable *"growth"* in general, with the *fetishistic absolute* of increasingly more destructive *capital expansion.*

Nevertheless, even if there can be no rationally conceived and instituted limits admitted to capital's self-expansion in its own terms of reference, there are some absolutely vital *systemic limits.* These are twofold. On the one hand, the limits in question arise from the irrepressible antagonistic second-order mediations of the capital system in general, and on the other from the increasing *destructiveness*—foreshadowing at the same time also potential systemic self-destruction—of capital's mode of social metabolic reproduction in relation to *nature*. Indeed, the grave transgression of capital's systemic limits is coupled with devastating military adventurism exercised in the interest of imposing the "globalized" system of *destructive production* (while preaching the self-mythology of "productive destruction") by the imperialistically dominant powers in our ever more precarious planetary household.

Sartre's pessimism is boundless when he calls out in despair: "It is impossible to find a *rational basis* for revolutionary optimism, since what *is* is the present reality."[127] In this way the destructive dominance of the *rationally unlimitable* self-expansionary imperative of the capital system is unhappily interiorized as the apparently undefeatable "rationality of actuality." But capital's *formally equalizing rationality* is in reality *substantive irrationality* that must be imposed with ruthless apodictic necessity in the production sphere as much as in all fields of the political domain—from the most comprehensive state practices involved in safeguarding the internal and international class relations and interests of the established mode of material production to the ideological/political regulation and value-determination of the "nuclear family"—no matter how destructive the consequences in the descending phase of the system's development. No wonder that we are presented with bleak pessimism concerning the future in Sartrean discourse after the bitter disappointment that follows the short-lived enthusiasm of 1968.

This is understandably so because, similarly to Marcuse, also in Sartre's approach too much of the apparent stability of capital's material reproductive order and of its allegedly "integrated" social subject of potential change—rejected by Sartre as unable to overcome the inertia of "constituted groups" and "stabilized structures"—is granted at face value to "organized capitalism." As a result, the wishfully postulated but in actuality extremely fragile social subject of the "ought to be" radical transformation—the allegedly "sovereignty-embodying" French student movement of 1968 for Sartre, and Marcuse's "minoritarian groups of the intelligentsia"[128] (sharply opposed by him to the working class)—offer no more solid ground for envisaging the required changes in the unfolding future than the abstract declaration of *"needs"* which are said by Sartre to be "the needs of every man," irrespective of their social class belonging and corresponding material and ideological determinations.

We can clearly see that Sartre, like Marcuse (who in this respect to a large extent inspires Sartre), adopts the dubious notion of *"organized capitalism,"* contrasting it with "competitive capitalism." Sartre puts into relief the politically challenging novelty of "organized capitalism" in order to call for an "anti-authoritarian" way of approaching the task ahead on the model of the aspirations of French Maoist students, in contrast to the traditional political parties of the left which are in his view anchored to the nineteenth century. These are Sartre's words:

> The classical leftist parties have remained in the nineteenth century, in the time of *competitive capitalism.* But though the Maoist movement is still in its first stages, these militants, with their anti-authoritarian praxis, appear to be the only revolutionary force capable of adapting to new forms of the class struggle in a period of *organized capitalism.*[129]

Marcuse's concern is very similar both in calling for a new social subject of transformation, indicating the militant youth as the embodiment of anti-authoritarian politics, and in claiming that the now established societal reproductive order must be characterized as indefinitely stable *organized capitalism*, in contrast to the past. In both cases the claimed novelty and corresponding power of "organized capitalism" is paradoxically overstated. It is overstated to such an extent that when the somewhat euphoric period of 1968 passes away, together with the idealized expectations attached to its claimed "anti-authoritarian" political praxis, the pessimistic readjustment of the former strategic perspective can only offer in favor of its own support the noble but abstract postulate of the internal *need* of the individuals in the case of both Sartre and Marcuse, coupled with constant references to Kantian imperatives in the writings of the German militant intellectual from the 1960s to his final years.[130]

The Kantian legacy weighs down as heavily on Sartre as on Marcuse. And that is a major part of the problem. For in order to give a *substantive rational foundation* to a positive and historically sustainable alternative to the capital system, it is necessary to extricate ourselves from the established order's formal rationality and corresponding formal apodicticity of gravely iniquitous but pretendedly unobjectionable universal value-equation. Yet in terms of the pretended equitable value-determinations even the absolute human outrage of decreeing capital and labor to be *formally/rationally equal* in the *exchange relation* as individually sovereign "buyers and sellers" can be totally misrepresented, turning into a travesty the real character of the relationship involved. For the pretended equality of *"contractually related individuals,"* who are supposed to regulate voluntarily and freely their interchanges in accordance with the "Rights of Man," is in fact brutally forced upon the *class* of living labor by the *actual power relations* embodied in the originally by great violence instituted,[131] and ever after state-protected, *alienation and expropriation* of the means of production from the producers. Accordingly, with the passing of historical time the idealized and state-legitimated formal rationality—which in actuality (i.e. in the Hegelian "rational actuality" of real history) always amounts to *substantive irrationality*—becomes in capital's descending phase of development ultimately self-destructive in view of the historically untenable but rationally unlimitable imperative of capital expansion.

The formally idealized "Rights of Man"—curiously invoked even by Sartre when he appeals to the idea of the individuals joining "that *sovereign group* from which, we are told, all power emanates, *the People."*[132]—cannot be exempted from the requirement of giving a *substantive rational foundation* to a historically sustainable positive alternative to capital's *formally* legitimated and in the name of its pretended *"formal and instrumental rationality"*[133] peremptorily enforced mode of social metabolic reproduction. Otherwise we must remain trapped by Sartre's—and Marcuse's—utter pessimism.

However, in Sartre's lifework it is impossible to supersede the established order's formal rationality and corresponding formal apodicticity without abandoning the idea that the categorial framework of his "marxisant existentialist" conception, as spelled out in his *Critique of Dialectical Reason,* encapsulates the "formal structures of history" in general, and as such applicable also to a strategic view of the necessary historical alternative to capital's social metabolic order. The unfinishable second volume of the *Critique* does not stand in Sartre's lifework alone. The same fate affected his project announced at the very end of *Being and Nothingness,* concerning the problems of "situated freedom" to be pursued on the *"ethical plane,"*[134] and the work on *"structural anthropology"* whose "early publication" was also repeatedly promised by Sartre in interviews many years before his death, but never materialized.

The reasons for the revealing unfinishability of these major Sartrean projects are very similar. But this is in no way meant to be a negative judgment on Sartre's lifework. Paradoxically, the major projects in question are in fact *complete* in their incompleteness and truly *representative* as integral parts of his great militant intellectual achievement precisely in their unfinishability. For they embody a tireless—even heroic—struggle on his part to radically *negate* the established order *from within* its own class parameters.

Sartre voices the insuperable dilemmas involved by using the same expression about the nature of the enterprise that he tries to pursue as "necessary but at the same time impossible." He says that in different but interrelated contexts. Thus, talking about the most powerful organized political force of the left in France he asserts that "Collaboration with the Communist Party is both necessary and impossible."[135] That sums up very well Sartre's position on the issue, indicating the painful double-sided acknowledgment that, on the one hand, without a major organizational force the advocated objectives cannot be accomplished, yet on the other hand, the force in question is very far from actually promoting the necessary change.[136] The same dilemma is put by Sartre in more generalized terms when he insists, "Ethics is *for us* inevitable and at the same time impossible."[137]

All these paradoxical and self-torturing insights are by no means "publicity-seeking" occasional remarks of which he is accused by his capital-apologetic detractors.[138] They are consistently coupled with the most dedicated theoretical work in composing thousands of pages[139] of his major unfinishable projects, formulated *from within* the horizon of his own class whose conscience Sartre tries to challenge and indeed shake. The unfinishable manuscripts express with great personal authenticity the impossibility to realize the chosen historical task by the reactivation of even the best Enlightenment tradition, together with the once sincerely believed (but never instituted) "Rights of Man" characteristic of its horizon. Sartre's inability to go beyond the *formal apodicticity* of the shared class horizon, confining his own categorial explanatory framework to the *formal structures of history,* despite his explicit promise and conscious efforts aimed at elucidating "real history" both in the political domain and in the world of morality, is inseparable from this connection.

Sartre's writings on ethics, which were not lost, show a repeated attempt to overcome the forbidding practical impediments of the given historical situation in terms of his appeal to the moral imperative, formulated frequently in the Kantian spirit. In a major lecture, written not in his youth but nearly at the age of sixty, he quotes Kant's famous dictum— *"You ought to, therefore you can"*—and insists on the primacy and centrality of *individual praxes* in contrast to collective and institutional structures.[140] However, this attachment to the Kantian legacy and its corollaries is not without serious problems. For the German philosopher, to whom Sartre is deeply indebted throughout his intellectual life, does not hesitate to reconcile the fundamental contradiction between the *formal* requirements of Enlightenment rationality (and corresponding equality) and the most blatant perpetuation of *substantive inequality* even in the domain of the law. He argues in this way:

> The *general equality* of men as *subjects in a state* coexists quite readily with the *greatest inequality* in degrees of the *possessions* men have, whether the possessions consist of corporeal or spiritual superiority or in *material possession* besides. Hence the general equality of men also coexists with *great inequality of specific rights* of which there may be many. . . . Nevertheless, all *subjects* are equal to each other *before the law* which, as a pronouncement of the *general will,* can only be one. This law concerns the *form* and not the *matter* of the object regarding which I may possess a right.[141]

As we can see the greatest moral philosopher of the bourgeoisie in the ascendant, Immanuel Kant, who models the universality and validity of the moral judgment as such on the *"form* of the natural law," can find absolutely nothing wrong with the total denial of substantive equality to the overwhelming majority of the people. Even his reference to the idea of Rousseau's *general will* cannot make any difference in that respect. The insoluble contradiction between the actually existing system of formalized law and the "legitimately" enforced substantive inequality in society and in the state is supposed to be overcome by Kant's peremptory decree according to which the law as such can be concerned only with the *form* and not with the *matter* of the object in question. Consequently it can be most iniquitously discriminatory even in terms of the *"specific rights"* that it may or may not grant to whoever it pleases, and yet qualifying at the same time as fully adequate to the rational requirement of the *"general equality* of men as *subjects in a state,"* justified with reference to its claimed harmony with the *general will*. Although in this way we find in Kant—who was, like Sartre, greatly inspired by Rousseau—a characteristic interpretation of the *general will*, corresponding to the *Sovereignty of the People*, the Kantian advocacy of the materially discriminatory idea of equality, in tune with the established order of private property, is not in conflict with some of Rousseau's most important tenets. For the great French philosopher of the Enlightenment insists with unmistakable firmness that "the *right of property* is the most *sacred* of all the rights of citizenship, and even more important in some respect than *liberty* itself; . . . property is the true foundation of civil society, and the real guarantee of the undertakings of citizens[142] . . . the general administration [embodied in the state] is established only *to secure individual property*, which is antecedent to it."[143]

Naturally, Sartre advocates the *real equality* of all individuals in society, and he can only scorn the "great inequality of specific rights" (in favor of those who can pay for it) imposed by the hypocritical practices of actually existing law. However, he cannot extricate himself from the formal apodicticity of the system oriented toward asserting the primacy and historical viability of the *individual praxes*, in the spirit of the *aggregates of individuality* idealized by the best philosophical tradition of capital's ascending phase of development, including the conceptions of Rousseau, Kant, Adam Smith, and Hegel. Sartre's ever renewed direct appeals to individual consciousness are obvious manifestations of that. This kind of orientation carries with it idealizations of its own kind in relation to the present, as we find it clearly demonstrated in Sartre's greatly overrated characterization of the French Maoist students,[144] who later in fact ceased to have anything to do with an even vaguely progressive, let alone genuine revolutionary, perspective. And, of course, the problems go much deeper than that as far as the question of the necessary historical alternative to the established order is concerned. For the obverse side of the same coin of expecting the required solution from the direct appeal to individual consciousness had to be that far too much was granted by Sartre, exactly the same way as by Marcuse, to the continued historical viability of so-called *"advanced capitalism"* and *"organized capitalism."*

Sartre's historical conception is haunted to the very end by his dismissal of the idea of the "We-subject" in *Being and Nothingness*. As discussed in section 7.3 of *The Social Determination of Method*, according to the Sartrean existentialist ontology

> the oppressed class can, in fact, affirm itself as a *We-subject* only in relation to the oppressing class. . . . But the experience of the "We" remains on the ground of *individual psychology* and remains a simple symbol of the *longed-for unity of transcendences.* . . . The subjectivities remain out of reach and *radically separated.* . . . We should hope in vain for a human "we" in which the intersubjective totality would obtain consciousness of itself as a unified subjectivity. Such an ideal could be only a *dream* produced by a passage to the limit and to the absolute on the basis of *fragmentary, strictly psychological experiences.* . . . It is therefore useless for humanity to seek to get out of this dilemma; one must either transcend the Other or allow oneself to be transcended by him. The essence of the relation between consciousnesses is not the *Mitsein* [being with]; it is *conflict.*[145]

This view of the nature of the "We-subject" as a mere projection of individual psychology is linked by Sartre in the same work to the assertion according to which the conception of humanity is totally illusory, derived from the notion of God as a "radical absence," and thus it is "forever renewed and forever results in failure." Accordingly, "Each time that we use the 'Us' in this sense (to designate suffering humanity, sinful humanity, to determine an *objective historical meaning* by considering man as an *object* which is *developing its potentialities)* we limit ourselves to indicating a certain concrete experience to be undergone in the presence of the absolute Third; that is, of God. Thus the limiting concept of humanity (as the totality of the *Us-object)* and the limiting concept of God imply one another and are correlative."[146]

By the time we reach the *Critique of Dialectical Reason* Sartre is willing to give some tangible meaning to the concept of humanity by saying,

"Our critical investigation must also show *how* the *practical multiplicity* (which may be called 'man' or 'Humanity' according to taste) realizes, in its very dispersal, its interiorization."[147] However, also in this work the existentialist ontological underpinning of the relationship between "myself" and the "Other"—depicted as the interchange in reciprocity between the Other as myself and myself as the Other, in the domain of history "developed within the *permanent framework* of a field of tension produced by *scarcity*"[148]—makes conflictuality insuperable. Also, defining "Humanity" by the term "practical multiplicity"—or, rather, agreeing politely to call Sartre's operative term of "practical multiplicity" by the name of "Humanity according to taste"—leaves the door wide open to an insuperably individualistic account of some vital historical processes. This outcome cannot be helped by Sartre in view of the absence of theorizing in his philosophy the required complex *mediations* (not confined to the circularly deterministic "field of materiality")[149] through which the objective and subjective factors can be brought together, not least by indicating the sustainable constitution of the "we-subject" as the transformatory agent of historical development, in contrast to the fateful necessity of its relapse into self-induced seriality.

We have to consider here a most difficult and somewhat convoluted passage from the *Critique of Dialectical Reason.* Its great complexity is due to Sartre's internal difficulties of trying to find solutions in this important work to the addressed problems within the categorial framework adopted by him. For his categorial framework itself stubbornly resists his attempts at finding the desired solutions. Nevertheless, it is necessary to quote this passage in its integrality because it sums up better than anything else Sartre's general approach to history. This is how it reads:

> In its attempted transcendence of this concrete objectivity (which only succeeds in so far as it is not prevented by the Other), the praxis of struggle awakens, actualises, comprehends and transcends the constitutive praxis of the Other in so far as he is himself a practical subject; and in its action against the Other, on the completion of this very transcendence and through the mediation of the field of materiality, it reveals and produces the Other as an object. From this point of view, the anti-dialectical negation appears as a moment in a more complex dialectic. At first, in

fact, this negation is precisely what is transcended: the praxis is constituted for both as the negation of negation: not only through everyone's transcendence of his object-being, but practically through everyone's attempts to *liquidate* the practical subject in the Other outside and from the outside and to recover his objectivity through this transcendent destruction. Thus the antagonistic negation is grasped by everyone as a scandal which has to be transcended. But at the level of scarcity its origin does not lie in this revelation of scandal: it is a *struggle for life;* thus the scandal is not only grasped in its appearance as scandal, but also profoundly comprehended as the impossibility that the two should co-exist. Consequently the scandal is not, as Hegel supposed, the mere existence of the Other, which would take us back to a statute of unintelligibility. It lies in suffered (or threatened) violence, that is in interiorised scarcity. In this respect, although the original fact is logically and formally contingent (scarcity is only a *materially given)*, its contingency is far from impairing the intelligibility of violence. What is important for the dialectical comprehension of the Other, is the rationality of his praxis. Now this rationality appears in violence itself, in so far as this is not the contingent ferocity of man, but *everyone's* intelligible reinteriorisation of the contingent fact of scarcity: human violence is *meaningful.* And as this violence is a negation of the Other in everyone, negation, in its reciprocity, becomes meaningful in and through everyone, as scarcity turned practical agent, or in other words as human-scarcity. Thus practical negation is constituted as a negation of scandal-negation both in so far as the latter is the Other in everyone and in so far as this Other is interiorised scarcity. From this point of view, what is indissolubly negated by praxis is negation as the condition of man (that is to say, as a conditioning readopted in violence by the conditioned) and as the freedom of an Other. And in fact the scandal of the presence in me (as a mark of my object-being) of the Other's freedom as the freedom-negation of my freedom, is itself a determination in rationality in so far as this negative freedom actualises in practice the impossibility of our co-existing in the field of scarcity.[150]

Thus the dialectical *intelligibility of history* in this Sartrean vision is primarily concerned with the *comprehension* of the "scandalous" dialectical rationality of the Other's praxis, in its threatening "freedom" that must be negated and "transcended" (indeed possibly "liquidated" as practical subject) in the unavoidable "struggle for life." The question of violence is explained as dialectical intelligibility and rationality in terms of the full *reciprocity* at work whereby the objective determinations of conditioning are "readopted in violence by the conditioned." In this way we are always offered by Sartre a definition of the Other as "the Other in everyone": a definition inseparable at the same time from the *comprehension* of violence as *"meaningful human violence."* And precisely because "interiorised scarcity" as meaningful violence involves (and implicates) *everyone,* the antagonistic relationship affecting all human beings must be considered ipso facto dialectically intelligible and comprehensible.

This conception of meaningful historical interchange also carries with it a most problematical definition of the historical agent. In one sense, applying to all individuals, it is the "free"—inasmuch as consciously and actively threatening—"Other in everyone," including of course myself as the Other to the Other. But since this Other in everyone—in its necessary constitution in and through full reciprocity—is "interiorized scarcity," through this "marxisant existentialist" ontological underpinning of the Sartrean vision of *scarcity as such* assumes a quasi-mythical status as the effective agent of history. This strange determination of the historical agent is paradoxically—by directly linking the abstract universal to the abstract individual, in an attempt to demonstrate the "dialectical intelligibility of that which is not universalizable," as mentioned before[151]—due to the "irreducible" (repeatedly commended in that way by Sartre himself) individualistic conception of his philosophy. For due to the fact that the claimed dialectically intelligible violence in history is said to be "a negation of the Other in *everyone,"* negation itself, "in its *reciprocity,* becomes meaningful in and through everyone, as *scarcity turned practical agent."*

In this spirit we are subsequently presented by Sartre with the firmest possible assertion concerning the nature of comprehension, positive and negative reciprocity and intelligibility itself, modeled also at this point in his analysis, in terms of its simultaneously individualistic orientation and abstract universality, on the existentialist life or death struggle of "myself" with the Other. These concluding remarks lead again to the frequently repeated promise about elucidating in the forthcoming second volume of the *Critique*, on the basis of the formal structures discussed in its first, the dialectical intelligibility of historical totalization in real history. The lines in question read like this:

> To comprehend in struggle is to grasp the praxis of the Other in imma-nence, through its own objectivity and in a practical transcendence. I now comprehend the enemy through myself and myself through the enemy.... Comprehension is an immediate fact of reciprocity. But as long as this reciprocity remains positive, comprehension remains abstract and external. Struggle, in the *field of scarcity*, as *negative reciprocity*, engen-ders the Other as Other than man, or as anti-human; but at the same time I comprehend him, in the very springs of my praxis, as a negation of which I am a concrete practical negation, and as *mortal danger*. For each of the adversaries, this struggle is intelligible; or rather, at this level, it is intelligibility itself. Otherwise, reciprocal praxis would in itself have no meaning or goal. But what concerns us is the general problem of intelli-gibility, particularly at the concrete level.... These questions bring us at last to the real problem of History. *If* History is to be the totalisation of all practical multiplicities and of all their struggles, the complex products of the conflicts and collaborations of these very diverse multiplicities *must* themselves be intelligible in their synthetic reality, that is to say, they *must* be comprehensible as the synthetic products of a totalitarian praxis. This means that History is intelligible if the different practices which can be found and located at a given moment of the historical temporalisation finally appear as partially totalising and as connected and merged in their very oppositions and diversities by an intelligible totalisation from which there is no appeal.[152]

However, the insuperable difficulty is that the Sartrean *formal struc-tures of history*—validly applicable in terms of their illuminating political determinations, if coupled with their complementary socioeconomic qualifications, to capital's highly specific and transient stage of develop-ment—cannot yield the dialectical intelligibility of *real history* in general. On the one hand they are made problematical by their existentialist onto-logical underpinning which structurally opposes itself to the "We-sub-ject" even in Sartre's "marxisant" phase of development, and on the other, by the conception of "advanced capitalism" and "organized capitalism," and its militantly with great integrity postulated but socially undefined counterforce. This is what we must consider in the remaining pages of this section.

The first idea that needs reassessment is the concept of *"reciprocity"* postulated by Sartre. He puts forward that idea as part of the existentialist ontological underpinning he intends to give to his own categorial framework. The envisaged Sartrean conceptual framework is meant to account—thanks to his "marxisant existentialist" idea of reciprocity—as fully for the relationship between the particular individuals as for those social formations that should be described in his view as "practical multiplicities," including "humanity according to taste." For Sartre claims that such a categorial framework is the only way to provide the "dialectical foundations of a structural anthropology," formulated first in "synchronic" terms as "the elementary formal structures."[153] This is according to Sartre the necessary conceptual foundation on the basis of which it becomes possible for him to consider "the diachronic depth of practical temporalization"[154] in the promised second volume of the *Critique of Dialectical Reason*, thereby accounting for the "dialectical intelligibility of real history."

Sartre needs the claimed "marxisant existentialist" concept of full reciprocity (and circularity) because in his view the symmetrical relationship between the Other and the individual *subject*—in that the subject must be reduced by the Other, in accordance with the requirement of Sartrean reciprocity, to the status of an *object* and threatened to be destroyed in that way in the course of the insuperable "struggle for life" in the historical domain asserted by Sartre to be "born and developed within the permanent field of tension produced by scarcity"[155]—enables him to postulate at the same time the *negative* but again appropriate and full reciprocity as the necessary condition of dialectical intelligibility. For this way of conceiving the relationship in question makes it possible for him to posit also on the opposite side of the equation the same negative and circular reciprocity through which "the Other in myself" likewise transforms the free praxis of the "Other outside" into the enemy *object*—so as to liquidate it as the rival subject that must be prevented from realizing its own design as "free praxis" and "mortal danger" for me—in the process of my self-assertion as the only acceptable free praxis prevailing against the Other in "interiorized scarcity." This is how I "comprehend the enemy through myself and myself through the enemy" as a result of which dialectical comprehension itself becomes "an immediate fact of reciprocity."[156]

This is perfectly coherent in its own—Sartrean "marxisant existentialist"—terms of reference. The problem is, however, that all individuals in our historically created and in that way maintained societies are constitutive parts of determinate *class* formations. Inevitably, therefore, in the actual *class reality* of real history, as we have to confront it until it is historically superseded by actual societal development—in obvious contrast to the abstractly postulated individualistic account of the permanent enmity between myself and the Other in the Sartrean categorial framework of circularly reciprocal determination and negation—there is definitely not, and there cannot possibly be, any symmetrically conceptualizable relationship of circular reciprocity. On the contrary, we find not only in the present order but also in the class societies constituted across history some system of very far from symmetrical *structural domination* and *subordination* that changes only in its historical *specificity*—from slavery through serfdom to the "wage slavery" of the capitalist order—but not in its fundamental modality of *hierarchical structural domination* without any resemblance to Sartrean reciprocity.

Accordingly, the challenge for the *class of labor* (and of its particular members), in their capacity oriented toward constituting the necessary and only feasible historical alternative to capital's societal reproductive order, concerns the establishment of a *non-hierarchical structural framework* of social metabolic reproduction, to be accomplished on a *substantive equitable* and thereby *historically sustainable* material and political basis. And that involves, to be sure, the task of overcoming within such *qualitatively* different societal reproductive horizon the historically to our own days prevailing, and through its unique vicious circle *wastefully perpetuated,* but at least in principle superable, objective conditions of socially specific *capital-accumulating scarcity.*

Indeed, the now fetishistically enduring vicious circle of scarcity is quite unique precisely in its immense but deliberately promoted wastefulness. Moreover, as such it is supposed to remain operative in its totally untenable cultivated wastefulness and globalizing destructiveness for the unsustainable prosaic cause of *endless capital-accumulation*, in contrast to the somber vision of our "struggle for life" over the existentialistically postulated "mortal danger" embodied in the "Other in everyone," defined as ontologically insuperable *interiorized scarcity*.

After 1968 Sartre confessed that "I have always remained *an anarchist*." When Michel Contat reminded him of that admission, in the interview published under the title of "Self-Portrait at Seventy," this was Sartre's answer:

> That is very true. . . . I have changed in the sense that I was an anarchist without knowing it when I wrote *Nausea*. I did not realize that what I was writing could have an anarchist interpretation; I saw only the relation with the metaphysical idea of "nausea," the metaphysical idea of existence. Then, by way of philosophy, I discovered the anarchist in me. But when I discovered it I did not call it that, because today anarchy no longer has anything to do with the anarchy of 1890.
>
> CONTAT: Actually, you never identified yourself with the so-called anarchist movement.
>
> SARTRE: Never. On the contrary, I was very far away from it. But *I never allowed anyone to hold power over me,* and I have always thought that *anarchy*—which is to say, *a society without powers—must be brought about*.[157]

Revealingly enough, the question of advocating the establishment of a *"society without powers"*—irrespective of the name conferred upon the political creed associated with it, from nineteenth-century anarchism to the present—goes to the heart of the matter. Naturally, it is not enough for a prominent and socially most privileged individual to say: *"I never allowed anyone to hold power over me."*

The really difficult problems are whether, to what extent, and in which sustainable form, the rejection of power exercised over oneself is *generalizable* in its applicability to the present and to the future. For, obviously—and Sartre would have to be the first to admit it—in the case of the overwhelming majority of the people in our actually existing societies today, even simply raising that question, not to mention the major impediments encountered for successfully translating it into their practically sustainable circumstances by the far from privileged individuals, in their capacity as more or less isolated individuals, cannot arise. *Wage slavery* is not very reassuring in that respect, even if the old historical forms of slavery and serfdom have been as a rule successfully consigned to the past, even if by no means everywhere.

Naturally, the fact itself that the issue can be raised at all in our time, and indeed that it could be raised in some form already in the nineteenth century, shows some significant advancement in terms of the *objective dialectic* of historical development, and not only in terms of its comprehensibility and intelligibility. For in the remote past the slaves could be simply categorized as "talking tools" even by a giant of philosophy like Aristotle, as mentioned before. In this sense Sartre's ideal of anarchy that "must be brought about," called by him *"a society without powers,"* can only mean a society in which there is no *separate body* exercising power over the individuals against their aspirations and will. The issue is, then, What are the conditions for the realization of such a society? And that is the point where the question of how to deal with the established social order—described by Sartre and others as "advanced capitalism" and "organized capitalism"—must be confronted. In other words, the fundamental question is: What are the *actually required and feasible leverages* through which capital's social order can be radically transformed in the desired direction?

Nineteenth-century anarchism was dismissed by Marx in no uncertain way. He wrote about Bakunin's book *Statehood and Anarchy*, that its author "has only translated Proudhon's and Stirner's anarchy into the barbaric idiom of the Tartars."[158] And Marx argued, "A radical social revolution is bound up with definite *historical conditions of economic development;* these are its premises. . . . Bakunin understands absolutely nothing of social revolution, only its *political rhetoric;* its economic conditions simply do not exist for him. . . . *Willpower,* not *economic conditions,* is the basis of his social revolution."[159]

But even if we ignore the weighty historical baggage of the nineteenth-century varieties of anarchism, for the sake of an idealized anarchist "society without powers" advocated by Sartre, some fundamental objective determinations and difficulties cannot be disregarded. Especially if at the same time the supposedly inexorable power of "advanced capitalism" and "organized capitalism" is reasserted, so as to be opposed by a direct political appeal to individual consciousness invited "to join a new sovereign group"[160]—illustrated with the example of the French Maoist students—and contrasted with organized parties (and other "stable organized structures") that are said to have "remained in the nineteenth century." Yet capitalism—inseparable from those "historical conditions of economic development" put so powerfully into relief by Marx in all of his seminal works—cannot be overcome at the *political* level only,[161] no matter how genuine might be the "willpower" of the individuals who wish to oppose it in that way.

The key problem in this respect is the *objectively grounded centrifugality* of the capital system itself in its innermost constitution as a mode of social metabolic reproduction. As we have seen it discussed in other parts of this study,[162] the modern state emerged and expanded in relation to that insuperable centrifugality, not least for the purpose of bringing under a feasible degree of control its potentially most disruptive aspects. This epochal historical process was accomplished—on the ground of the underlying material determinations—in the interest of the dynamic expansion of the capital system as a whole, in its inseparability from the increasingly more powerful modern state. That is indeed where we can see a *real reciprocity*. But, of course, this kind of reciprocity is, again, very far from being symmetrical. It is defined by a determinate type of social and historical *interrelationship* in which the *dialectical primacy*[163]—not to be confused with a *mechanical one-sidedness*—belongs to the fundamental material determinations in the sense already discussed above.

Naturally, this type of reciprocally secured development between politics and the economy, on the material reproductive ground of capital's necessary centrifugality, also means that negating the political dimension on its own, in the spirit of even the most idealized conception of anarchism, could only absolutize or exasperate the *systemic centrifugality* of the established mode of social metabolic reproduction, resulting in total uncontrollability. This is why anarchism had to prove to be a non-starter in all of its varieties in the past.

The historically constituted and structurally entrenched reciprocity of capital's fundamental dimensions can only be overcome by radically altering the material reproductive as well as the political dimensions *together,* and doing that on the appropriate *systemic scale*. The *partial material cooperative ventures* known to us—which attempted to change the system through the work of the productive and distributive cooperatives—represented the obverse side of the anarchist political coin. Significantly, despite the good will invested in such cooperatives by their adherents, they could not make a practicable inroad into the structural determinations of capital's social order on other than a minute scale. Not even when the political anarchist and the material cooperative sides of the coin have been brought together, as in Spain, in the anarcho-cooperative enterprises.

Here it is well worth reminding ourselves that Marx never hesitated theoretically stressing the idea, and also passionately advocating it in his pioneering organizational involvement in the international socialist movement of his time, that "the *economic emancipation* of the working class is the great end to which *every political movement* ought to be subordinate as a means."[164]

The same idea, underlining the dialectical primacy of the material basis of capital's social order, was reiterated by one of the greatest intellectual and political figures of the socialist movement, Rosa Luxemburg, when she wrote:

> What distinguishes bourgeois society from other class societies—from ancient society and from the social order of the Middle Ages— . . . is precisely the fact that class domination does not rest on "acquired rights" but on *real economic relations;* the fact that wage labour is *not a juridical relation* but purely an *economic relation.*[165]

In the same sense, it would be a great mistake to imagine that imperialism can be overcome at the political/military level, as many people after the Second World War naïvely started to celebrate the arrival of the age of "post-imperialism." Also in this regard Rosa Luxemburg's words, which highlighted the inescapable and historically evolved economic foundations of imperialist political/military strategies, remain valid to our own days, despite the fact they were written almost a century ago. This is how they read:

> Imperialism is not the creation of any one or of any group of states. It is the product of a particular state of ripeness in the world development of capital, an innately international condition, an indivisible whole, that is

recognizable only in all its relations, and from which no nation can hold aloof at will. Capitalism is incompatible with economic and political divisions. . . . It needs for its development large, united territories . . . and [to] lift the demands and needs of society to a plane corresponding to the prevailing stage of capitalist production and to the mechanism of modern capitalist class rule.[166]

Accordingly, the devastating political-military dangers of imperialism—a system of most iniquitous internal determinations and corresponding interstate relations that can change its historical *specificity* but not its structurally entrenched *substance*—cannot be consigned to the past without radically overcoming the material reproductive dimension of the capital system as an integrated whole.

The *incurable centrifugality* of the capital system can only intensify its contradictions and heighten the dangers necessarily associated with them in an age of globally conflicting vested interests asserted by the dominant monopolistic forces, corresponding to the now prevailing stage of articulation of capital's mode of social metabolic reproduction. Direct political appeals to individual consciousness, even in the most idealized spirit of anarchism, cannot counter the power of the vital material reproductive determinations whose analysis is missing from Sartre's work not only before the *Critique of Dialactical Reason* but also later.

The "formal structures of history" offered by Sartre in the two volumes of the *Critique of Dialectical Reason,* and reiterated in different ways in his subsequent writings, always remained well within the framework of the posited formal determinations, oriented toward an increasingly more elusive *political* advocacy after the great disappointments he suffered following the moments of hope in 1968 and in its immediate aftermath. Sinking into a deeply pessimistic mood in his final years was therefore sadly but perfectly understandable in the case of a combative intellectual, like Sartre, who after the defeat of 1968 could not envision any leverage by which he could "from within" even slightly alter, let alone dislodge from its hinges, as he once hoped, the political consciousness of the class against which he passionately rebelled.

The pessimistic idea that "advanced capitalism" and "organized capitalism" might be able to offer some long-term sustainable remedy to capital's antagonistic second-order mediations could not be of any help in this respect. The necessary point of departure for an alternative approach cannot be other than an attempt to put firmly into relief the *material structures of history*. Not as "given once and for all," in an abstractly posited generality, with unsustainable claims to formally universalizable validity extended to all possible phases of history, but in its *actually unfolding and changing specificity*. And that framework would have to be identified in our time in accordance with the never in the past experienced historical determinations—with their *deeply antagonistic* and therefore in the last analysis unrealizable tendency toward *global integration*—which correspond to the ever more destructive monopolistic material and political/military stage of capital's imperialist articulation as a societal reproductive system, directly threatening even humanity's relationship to nature.

To be sure, this point of departure, in its unavoidable historical specificity and orientation, could offer no a priori apodicticity of any kind for understanding the dialectical intelligibility of historical development "once and for all." Any attempt to do so would be in relation to actually unfolding history a crass contradiction in terms. The idea of postulating a set of eternally valid "material structures of history" in the spirit of some kind of aprioristic apodicticity could only assume the shape of a *straitjacket,* or a *bed of Procrustes,* to which necessarily open-ended real history would have to be arbitrarily tied or imaginarily chained. There can be no general material structures for all conceivable phases of real history, nor indeed any universally extended formal structures. For the real history of human societal existence could not qualify for being history at all by closing its gates to alternative forms of development with the help of some posited permanent structures, be they at a determinate time in history clearly identifiable material structures. Nothing illustrates this proposition better than Marx's explicitly stated insistence that the category of *"historical necessity"* makes no sense at all unless it is understood as historically changing and *"vanishing necessity."*

Moreover, once the objective and subjective conditions for the establishment of a rational *planning process* are consolidated in the course of the historically pursued and sustained socialist transformation, the power of earlier overwhelming *economic determinations* is bound to be greatly diminished. It is put into its place as an integral but *subordinate* part of a conscious *socialist accountancy*. That form of accountancy becomes practicable only in the absence of the predetermined and self-perpetuating *vested interests* of capital's willing personifications who expropriate to themselves the power of *managing* the societal metabolism even if they cannot *control* it, irrationally steering society instead in the direction of *systemic annihilation*. For only the socialist accountancy can confer their proper—and not fetishistically absolutized—weight upon the objectively limiting factors, within the adopted framework of humanly rewarding and *positively interiorized* objectives.

This is so because the real meaning of the words quoted about "the *economic emancipation* of the working class" is the *emancipation of humanity* from the blindly prevailing power of *economic determinism* under which no human being can ever be in genuine control of the social metabolism, not even the most willing personifications of capital. Only through the qualitative transformation of *labor*—from being the alienated and structurally subordinate but necessarily recalcitrant *social class* of the reproduction process into the *universal regulative principle* of humanity's interchange with nature and among its individual members, freely embraced as their meaningful life activity by all members of society—can real human emancipation be accomplished in the course of open-ended historical development. That is the reason why Marx was contrasting to what he called "prehistory" not some kind of Messianic "end of history"—although he is often crudely accused of doing that—but the dynamic process of actually unfolding and consciously controlled "real history." That is, history no longer ruled by *antagonistic economic determinations* but lived in accordance with their chosen aims and objectives by the social individuals as freely associated producers.

In fact the categories called by Sartre "the formal structures of history" are most illuminating for a *limited phase* of capitalistic developments, on account of their affinity with some important material and human characteristics of the formally equalized articulation of generalized commodity production. But they could not be extended to the whole of history, from the most remote past to the indefinite future. That kind of *universal extension*—and corresponding *closure*—is inadmissible not only for the *material structures* of history, which must be grasped always in

their historical specificity, irrespective of how long the underlying determinations can assert themselves in the changing societal domain, but also
for what may be legitimately called *formal structures* in an appropriately
defined social setting. Sartre could be no exception to that. Indeed. Sartre
supplied his own proof for the impossibility of modifying and extending
his own "formal structures" in the postulated way by his inability to complete the original project[167] repeatedly announced for the elaboration of
the conceptual framework of "real history" in the second volume of his
Critique of Dialectical Reason.

The pessimistic idea shared also by Sartre that "advanced capitalism"
and "organized capitalism" represent a significantly different and historically more sustainable phase of the capital system's development than its
nineteenth-century variety, to which the political parties of the left have
allegedly remain anchored, is quite unfounded. The opposite is much
nearer to the by no means pessimistic truth.

The deciding issue concerns the rational restrainability and controllability of any societal reproductive order in relation to the historical actuality and availability of its necessary conditions of reproduction. And the
most uncomfortable truth of the matter in this respect is that a socioeconomic reproductive order, the now established societal order, whose viability depends on *endless capital expansion,* must constantly generate not
only (to a large extent manipulable or even repressible) *subjective* but also
irrepressible objective expectations—both for others and for itself—which
it cannot possibly fulfill.

In this sense, in contrast to capital's existing order, only a *qualitatively* different way of managing the social metabolism, from the elementary material processes to the highest levels of artistic production and
enjoyment, could make a real difference in this respect. And that would
imply a radically different orientation of the social individuals toward
consciously pursued *communal coherence* of their activities, in place of
the now prevailing and potentially disintegrative centrifugality of their
conditions of existence. This is so because for as long as the *antagonistic second-order mediations* of the capital system remain dominant, they
are bound to call for some kind of political super-imposition, instead of
militating against it in the spirit of the anarchistic desideratum of "society without powers."

There can be no such thing as "a society without powers." Especially not in an age of globally unfolding production and societal reproduction. The now established reproductive order is inseparable from its *antagonistic second-order mediations* for the simple reason that they are required for the irrational pursuit of endless capital-expansion irrespective of the consequences. However, this system is bound to produce *recalcitrance* (in the producing individuals), the *superimposition of extraneous control* (in order to defeat recalcitrance, if necessary by violence), and at the same time also *institutionalized irresponsibility* (because of the absence of rationally feasible and acceptable control). It is not too difficult to see how problematical it must be to regulate "advanced capitalist" society on the basis of such practices and corresponding results even on a limited national scale, not to mention the necessity to keep the intensifying contradictions under the lid in their unavoidably unfolding global setting. Understandably, therefore, the only way to sustain a globally coordinated reproductive order on our horizon is by envisaging *cooperatively shared material and political power*, determined and administered on the basis of not simply *formal* but *substantive equality* (an absolute must as the condition of feasibility of a viable future societal order) and the corresponding *rational planning* of their life activities by the *freely associated producers*.

Naturally, this is inconceivable without the appropriate form of *mediation* of the social individuals among themselves and in their combined relationship, as *real humanity* (though not "according to taste"), to nature. However, there is nothing mysterious or prohibitively difficult about advocating a qualitatively different system of societal reproductive mediation. The conditions of its establishment can be spelled out in a tangible way, involving a determined and historically sustained effort to break the *stranglehold of exchange-value* over humanly adopted and gratifying *use-value*, corresponding not to *formally equalizable* and substantively incommensurable as well as callously ignored, but to the individuals as freely associated individuals *directly meaningful human need*.

The basic organizing principle of the kind of societal reproductive activity which is oriented toward such a qualitatively different social metabolic order was described by Marx in very simple terms, with reference to the *communal* interchange of the life activity of the individuals, when he wrote:

The communal character of production would make the product into a communal, general product from the outset. The exchange which originally takes place in production—which *would not be an exchange of exchange-values but of activities,*—determined by *communal needs and communal purposes*—would from the outset include the participation of the individuals in the communal world of products.[168]

Obviously, regulating and freely coordinating their life activities by the individuals implies *ongoing positive adjustments.* The required genuine positive adjustments in a socialist order become feasible thanks to the removal of the structurally entrenched vested interests of the alienating class existence of the past, with its institutionalized irresponsibility under the capital system. Accordingly, the productive and distributive activity of the individuals can be promoted and maintained not by postulating a "society without powers" but by the *fully shared powers* of the members of society, inseparable from the adoption of their *fully shared responsibility.* That is the only viable and historically sustainable alternative to the growing destructiveness of "advanced capitalism" and "organized capitalism."

6.4 Structural Imperatives and Historical Temporality: Critique of Structuralism and Post-Structuralism

Claude Lévi-Strauss—eulogized by one of his devotees as "structuralism personified"[169]—admitted in an interview he gave in 1971 to the prominent French weekly journal *L'Express* that "since 1968 structuralism went out of fashion."[170] What was remarkable in this respect was not the fact that in the 1970s structuralism started to fade away, being pushed out of the limelight by "post-structuralism" and other similarly oriented "post" denominations, like "post-modernity."[171] Rather, the somewhat astonishing circumstance was that after the Second World War the ideology of structuralism had actually acquired an extremely dominant position, and maintained it for well over a decade—from the middle of the 1950s to the end of the 1960s—in European and American intellectual circles.[172]

Of course, this postwar period coincided with the pretenses of *"the end of ideology"*[173] both in America and in Europe. Structuralism, with its claims to represent the ultimate of "scientific rigor" in the field of the "human sciences,"[174] fitted very well into the prevailing intellectual and political climate. Even more strangely for Lévi-Strauss himself, the "non-ideological" aspirations of his celebrated orientation were combined with explicitly claiming to be simultaneously a "marxisant" intellectual, like Jean-Paul Sartre. As late as the 1971 interview published in *L'Express* Lévi-Strauss was still asserting that he was a "marxisant" thinker. In this regard the postwar intellectual prominence of the Communist Party in France, professing its (Stalinistically "updated") devotion to Marx, made that ideological alignment perfectly understandable. At least to the extent of paying lip service to Marx in the case of some important intellectuals like Lévi-Strauss. And even a figure openly hostile to any idea of socialism, Raymond Aron, who championed the American "Atlanticist" perspective and Europe's subservience to U.S. dominated NATO, could not avoid a negative dependency on the French CP's intellectual prominence. All this had changed considerably around the end of the 1960s. The serious decline in the popularity of structuralism, dated by Lévi-Strauss himself to the years immediately following May 1968 in France, and the simultaneous appearance of various post-structuralist ideological approaches, coincided with the new phase in the development of the capital system marked by its deepening *structural crisis*.

However, even Lévi-Strauss's erstwhile claim that he was a follower of Marx, in any sense at all, should be taken with a mountain-size pinch of salt. Not only with regard to his—extremely pessimistic—position recorded in his major interview in 1971,[175] but also in relation to the rest of his work before that date or after. For as regards the theory of the "superstructure" in which he suggested that he had elaborated his own unique version of the Marxian concept—asserting at the same time without any justification that the superstructural domain was left virtually untouched by Marx, who was supposed to have assigned to it only an unfilled "space"—the characteristic approach to the field offered by Lévi-Strauss was incorrigibly *ahistorical*. And nothing could be more alien to Marx's lifework as a whole as well as to any particular aspect of it.[176] In this spirit Lévi-Strauss was not only completely ignoring Marx's fundamental answers to the problems of the superstructure and ideology, conceived by him as *dialectically* linked to, and in that way inseparable from,

the changing material basis of society—as we could see them in considerable detail for ourselves in the course of this study—but offered a *diamet-*
rically contradictory line of approach to the problems elaborated by Marx
always in a profoundly historical sense.

It is also important to underline here that the various "post-structuralist" and "post-modernist" ideological trends could not be considered significantly different in this respect. The extremely skeptical and
problematical attitude to history was by no means confined to Lévi-
Strauss himself. Indeed, the incorrigibly ahistorical approach to their
object of inquiry constituted the common denominator of all kinds of
postwar structuralism and post-structuralism, including the general line
of "structural functionalism" advocated—with Weberian allegiances—by
Talcott Parsons, and heavily promoted for capital-apologetic ideological
purposes in the United States of America.

The major conservative Swiss historian of the nineteenth century,
Leopold von Ranke, coined the famous orienting principle for fellow historians according to which *every age was equidistant from God*. That line of
thought amounted to categorically asserting that whatever might indicate the
signs of historical *development,* in terms of Ranke's views belonged to the
world of illusion and false appearance. The claimed "marxisant" contribution by Lévi-Strauss to elucidating the nature of the superstructure—from
the "elementary structures of kinship"[177] to the "logics of myth"[178] and to
the characterization of the relationship between history and "La pensée
sauvage"[179]—had much the same "equidistancing" orientation in Lévi-
Strauss's "structural anthropology," devoted to the defense of the conceptual
universe of the North and South American Indian peoples vis-à-vis the
thought produced in modern times anywhere. In other words, according to
Lévi-Strauss the idea of historical advancement as such had to be considered
extremely dubious, to put it mildly. Accordingly, it was not in the least surprising that when Lévi-Strauss was asked the question in 1971 by the interviewer of *L'Express*: "So you think that history is devoid of any sense?" his
gloomy answer could only be: "If it has a sense, it is not a good one."[180] In
this way Lévi-Strauss's position was even more retrograde than the historical skepticism of the prominent British conservative Sir Lewis Namier, discussed in chapter 5 of *The Social Determination of Method,* who asserted
that if there is sense in human history "it escapes our perception."[181]

The idea of historical advancement is rejected by Lévi-Strauss in the most romantic fashion by postulating that in the vision of the world produced by the savage mind "the whole of nature could speak to man."[182] His imaginary solution to the gloomily described troubles of our contemporary world was said by him to be the management of *technological* progress in a rather stationary way and strict *population control.* However, Lévi-Strauss pessimistically rejected his own solution as unrealizable immediately after mentioning it, coupled with an endorsing reference to the "utopian" views once advocated by the nineteenth-century reactionary and indeed racist French writer Gobineau,[183] who also turned away from his own projected utopia by ruefully saying that it was unrealizable. But Lévi-Strauss never bothered to spell out the necessary social qualifications concerning even the elementary conditions of feasibility of his proposed solutions which—in terms of their concern with technology and population control—could fit in perfectly well with the wishful commonplaces of ubiquitously promoted capital apologetics.[184] The pessimistic formulation of his comments was voiced on account of the nostalgically deplored "unrealizability" of the should-be "but alas cannot-be" solutions. (Mytho)logically, therefore, Lévi-Strauss could only end his 1971 interview with the earlier mentioned doom-laden tirades against humanity in general,[185] exempting at the same time from all blame the "regimes, parties, groups and classes"[186] whose role is clearly recognizable in our actually unfolding history.

The incorrigibly ahistorical—and in many ways even anti-historical—character of Lévi-Strauss's work is by no means the only sense in which his approach is diametrically contradictory to Marx. An equally serious aspect is his rejection of the Marxian unity of *theory and practice.* In fact Lévi-Strauss presents his opposition to socially committed practice as a commendable virtue when he contrasts his own stance to Sartrean existentialism by saying that structuralism, unlike existentialism favored by the young in and after 1968, is *"devoid of practical implications."*[187]

What is very difficult to understand in this respect is this: Why should one try to elucidate the complex—both substantive and methodological—problems of the superstructure and ideology if not for putting to appropriate *practical use* the knowledge acquired through such investigation? That was indeed the vital concern expressed by Marx with his insistence about the cardinal importance of *practice* in orienting the intellectual enterprise. After all, as we have seen in the Introduction to *The Social Determination of Method,* Descartes forcefully stressed the inherently practical nature and justification of his own engagement with the theoretical challenge of untying the deceptive skeptical knots produced by scholasticism in the field.[188] Short of such practical orientation, what is the point at all of Lévi-Strauss's romantic tirades against humanity, condemning it as "its own worst enemy," if—allegedly—nothing can be done about it, because the "technological and population control utopia" advocated by him (against "population explosion" as the postulated "source of all evil") is said to be "unrealizable"? If really nothing can be done to remedy the identified problems, then also the act of voicing the gloomy romantic laments must be utterly pointless, and in a curious way even self-contradictory.

We can see the self-contradiction in Lévi-Strauss's approach to these issues by recalling a typical passage from *The Savage Mind* on the nature of history. It reads like this:

> History is a *discontinuous set* composed of domains of history, each of which is defined by a characteristic frequency and by a differential coding of *before* and *after.* . . . The *discontinuous* and *classificatory* nature of historical knowledge emerges clearly. . . . In a system of this type, *alleged historical continuity* is secured only by dint of *fraudulent outlines.* . . . We need only recognize that history is a *method* with no distinct *object* corresponding to it to reject the equivalence between the notion of history and the notion of *humanity* which some have tried to foist on us with the unavowed aim of making *historicity* the last refuge of a *transcendental humanism:* as if men could regain the *illusion of liberty* on the plane of the "*we*" merely by giving up the "I"s that are too obviously wanting in consistency. In fact history is tied *neither to man nor to any particular object.* It consists wholly in its *method,* which experience proves to be indispensable for *cataloguing* the elements of *any structure* whatever, human or non-human, in their entirety.[189]

Thus, when it suits the requirements of Lévi-Strauss's positivistic characterization of history, humanity is ruled out of court with the typical exorcising label of *"transcendental humanism."* This curtly dismissive treatment of humanity is even reminiscent of Sartre's earlier seen prewar condemnation of the "We-subject" in *Being and Nothingness*, also re-echoed by some strange "structuralist Marxist" authors. At the same time, in complete contrast to his earlier position, when adopting the tone of the romantic Jeremiads seems to be a more convenient form of discourse, humanity is resuscitated again as the—alas hopelessly deaf or "unwilling to listen"—addressee of Lévi-Strauss's utterly gloomy but in ruling ideological circles curiously welcome and prominently diffused sermon. Not even the faintest memory remains of the once categorically dismissed "refuge of a transcendental humanism" and "historicity" in this updated reference to humanity, well in tune with the newly emerging and appropriately promoted "globalized utopian" and respectably "classless" ideological and political climate.

Lévi-Strauss also claims to be a dialectical thinker. In reality, with the repetitive dualisms and dichotomies of his timeless and rigid structuralist approach he is not only *un*dialectical but also *anti*-dialectical. Opposing continuity and discontinuity in the way in which we have seen it done by him in the last quotation, defining history as a *"discontinuous set,"* is a graphic example of that. Again, nothing could be more alien to the Marxian approach to history in which the dialectical relationship between *continuity and discontinuity* is always stressed as strongly in relation to the material basis as to the superstructure of society.

We can clearly see this also in the following quotation from the *Grundrisse,* where Marx discusses the fundamental issue of the categories, underlining that "Bourgeois society is the most developed and the most complex historic organization of production. The *categories* which express its relations, the comprehension of its *structure,* thereby also allow insights into the *structure and the relations of production* of all the *vanished social formations* out of whose ruins and elements it built itself up, whose partly still unconquered remnants are carried along within it, whose mere nuances have developed explicit significance within it, etc."[190] In this way the meaning of *structure* is illuminated, thanks to the profoundly dialectial conception of continuity and discontinuity in actual historical development from the "vanished social formations" to the most complex organization and relations of production in bourgeois society.

By contrast, Lévi-Straussian structuralism turns the concept of structure into a reified fetish precisely because of its arbitrary dichotomous treatment of history, counterposing even the mystificatorily frozen idea of *"space"* to that of historically unfolding *"time."*

We have seen that Marx had put into relief in the strongest possible terms that "we know only one science, *the science of history*."[191] Lévi-Strauss rejects that approach, to be sure, not by naming Marx (after all, he is supposed to be also a "marxisant" intellectual in the field of the superstructure) but by sharply criticizing sinfully radical Sartre.[192] He writes: "Sartre is certainly not the only contemporary philosopher to have valued history above the other human sciences and formed an *almost mystical conception of it*. The anthropologist respects history, but he does not accord it a special value. He conceives it as a study complementary to his own: one of them unfurls the range of human societies in *time*, the other in *space*."[193] It is a very strange "complementarity" indeed which operates on the premise of the dichotomous separation and opposition of space and time. We have seen in section 6.3 above in considerable detail Sartre's approach to history developed in his *Critique of Dialectical Reason*. It does not resemble in the slightest Lévi-Strauss's strictures against this major attempt at elucidating the dialectical character of historical totalization, irrespective of how far Sartre succeeds in completing to his own satisfaction the chosen very real philosophical task.

To say that Sartre has an "almost mystical conception of history" is nothing more than a gratuitous insult voiced by an anti-historical and anti-dialectical thinker. Sartre, who was in fact most generous in the *Critique of Dialectical Reason* to Lévi-Strauss, was well justified when in his answer to such insult retorted: "Anyone who can write down 'the dialectic of this dichotomy' shows he knows absolutely nothing about dialectic." And we find in the same quotation of *The Savage Mind* the adoption of another anti-dialectical dichotomy—for dichotomies are ubiquitous in Lévi-Strauss's work—also when he crudely counterposes the concept of *method* to that of the *object* (on top of *space* and *time*, as well as *continuity* and *discontinuity*) in his characterization of history, reducing it to the task of *"cataloguing"* the *"elements of any structure,"* and thereby confining to a strictly *subsidiary* position the historian's enterprise; which means in fact demoting it even from its (politely/evasively granted) *"complementary"* role.

Naturally, Lévi-Strauss's real target of censure is not simply Sartre but the left in general, although he is supposed to be, of course, also an intellectual figure of the left. But in actuality the leading French structuralist celebrated by the conservative weekly *L'Express* is no more a man of the left than he is a follower of Marx or a dialectical thinker. He claims that "superstructures are *faulty acts* which have 'made it' socially. Hence it is vain to go to historical consciousness for the truest meaning. . . . In Sartre's system history plays exactly the part of a *myth*. Indeed, the problem raised by the *Critique de la raison dialectique* is reducible to the question: under what conditions is the *myth of the French Revolution* possible?" (his emphases).[194]

Thus, after he conveniently reduces everything in his conception of myth to the proverbial darkness in which all cows are black, Lévi-Strauss—well armed again with his own claim of being *"a man of science"* who stands outside the merely contextual field of history[195]—can proceed to aim his fire at his principal political target by saying that "The *so-called men of the Left* still cling to a period of contemporary history which bestowed the blessing of a congruescence between *practical imperatives* and *schemes of interpretation*. Perhaps this *golden age of historical consciousness* has already passed."[196]

Thus, in view of the prominent figure of French structuralism the only proper thing to do is to abandon any concern with "practical imperatives"—unlike socially committed Sartrean existentialism deplorably favored by the youth in 1968 and after 1968, and disparagingly described by Lévi-Strauss as "an old thing" (*une vieille chose*)—so as to offer in its stead the detached rigor "devoid of practical implications" of the structural anthropologist "man of science." Lévi-Strauss is not disturbed even by directly contradicting himself in the same paragraph by first claiming that he is "engaged in doing scientific work" and immediately adding another one of his bizarre romantic laments by saying, "But I cannot help thinking that science would be more lovable if it did not have to serve to anything."[197] And yet Lévi-Strauss does not hesitate to appoint himself to the lofty status of standing outside the "mere contextuality" of temporally limited contemporary history and above the "faulty acts of the superstructure which have 'made it' socially." But can it be done? And in any case, what does it really mean, if anything?

In truth the textual record shows that—in contrast to the groundless accusation according to which the main tenets of Sartre's *Critique of Dialectical Reason* amount to no more than a myth about the French Revolution still fashionable on the left—nothing could be more mythically inflated than Lévi-Strauss's universal panacea of *"exchange."* It is propounded by him fully in harmony with the well-established conservative treatment of that category—corresponding to a totally ahistorical and wild extension of its meaning—in twentieth-century ideology, including the characteristic role to which it is put in the aggressively anti-socialist crusade by Friedrich von Hayek.[198]

The full structural anthropologist arsenal of kinship is used by Lévi-Strauss for that purpose, even if much of it is considered rather questionable in terms of the evidence peremptorily claimed by him, according to the critical view of those fellow anthropologists who are not wedded to the structuralist ideology of standing "above ideology" in virtue of having "scientifically" deciphered its code through the universalist Mythologics of the Lévi-Straussian superstructure. As the English anthropologist Edmund Leach underscored it, "Many would argue that Lévi-Strauss, like Frazer, is insufficiently critical of his source material. He always seems to be able to find just what he is looking for. Any evidence, however dubious, is acceptable so long as it fits with logically calculable expectations; but wherever the data runs counter to the theory Lévi-Strauss will either by-pass the evidence or marshal the full resources of his powerful invective to have the heresy thrown out of court!"[199]

In this respect, too, we find in the writings of Lévi-Strauss a most disturbing anti-historical conception, motivated by conservative, and indeed reactionary, ideological interests. So much so in fact that at a certain point in the extensive March 1971 interview even the conservative *L'Express* finds the gloomy romanticism too much to take on board and respectfully asks the question: "Isn't what you say very 'reactionary,' in inverted commas?"[200] It is to this question that we are offered by Lévi-Strauss the final answer of his interview, which is utterly reactionary without any inverted commas, condemning humanity altogether as "its own worst enemy and, alas, at the same time also the worst enemy of he rest of the creation."[201] That is the blind alley into which the reader is led by Lévi-Strauss's Mythologics.

The insuperable problem for Lévi-Straussian structuralism is that the concept of *exchange* is inherently historical. Indeed, precisely in view of the comprehensive nature of exchange relations that actually change in the dialectical sense of continuity in discontinuity, and discontinuity in continuity, the most diverse reality corresponding to the term "exchange" is a historical category (a "Daseinsform," i.e. a form of being) *par excellence*. If it is treated in any other way, by obliterating the qualitatively different determinations of its modes of being, this important category becomes fetishistically blurred in a most revealing way. The socially telling fetishization in question takes the form of *conflating* some clearly identifiable aspects of the claimed exchange relations and corresponding values (to be discussed in a moment) into a fallaciously posited one. This is done in more or less conscious conformity—and of course in the descending phase of the capital system's development in much more rather than in less conscious conformity—to the interests of the established socioeconomic and political order.

It is by no means surprising or coincidental, therefore, that in Lévi-Strauss's mythologizing procedure the anti-historical and generic extension of the concept of exchange is associated with crying over the "loss of the sense and secret of *equilibrium*"[202]—the mythical postulate of capital-apologetic modern "scientific" (even "mathematically rigorous") economists and market idolators[203]—and over the "disintegration of *civilization*."[204] For heaven forbid point the finger to the *crisis of capitalism*, let alone to its grave and deepening *structural crisis* of which the explosion of May 1968 was an obvious early manifestation.

In Lévi-Strauss's books, by contrast, the dramatic events of 1968 and their nonconformist aftermaths are interpreted as "an additional sign of the *disintegration of a civilization* which fails to secure the *integration of the new generations* that could be so well accomplished by the societies without writing."[205] He attributes to Marx the absurd idea that "social consciousness *always lies to itself.*"[206] For if it were really true that "social consciousness always lied to itself," in that case the destruction of humanity—in the form of Lévi-Strauss's "cataclysm"—would be an absolute *certainty*, and not a socially produced and socially preventable danger. No "scheme of interpretation," let alone the claimed structuralist deciphering of the code of what is supposed to be hiding behind the "necessary lies of social consciousness," could show a way out of the associated dangers. Objective historical antagonisms and their contradictory incorporation in social consciousness can be consigned to the past only by the radical intervention of the human *historical subject* in the domain of *objective* social metabolic reproduction—and not at the level of mythologics—in response to the prevailing, but by the structuralist man of science dismissed, *practical imperatives*. However, with regard to the human subject and historical agent[207] whose development is envisaged by Marx in the form of actively *overcoming the false consciousness* that must arise from the *objective determinations* of historically specific class antagonism, Lévi-Strauss sets up not just one of his many dichotomies but a hopelessly self-paralyzing *"irreducible antinomy"*[208] between the most comprehensive historical and dialectical categories of *subject* and *object*.

Every criticized phenomenon is presented in Lévi-Strauss's work in an utterly vague and generic form, so as to avoid the embarrassing requirement to name the social specificity of capital's antagonistic reproductive order. In the same way as he was vacuously lamenting over "civilization" in general, he complains that society is becoming "enormous," that it minimizes "difference" and spreads "similarity," and that it fails to escape "abrupt and hard determinism," etc. But he refuses even to mention, let alone to seriously analyze, the tangible character of ruthless *capitalist* determinism at the roots of the deplored phenomena. Instead, he denounces *"progress"* in the most grotesque way, by saying that it brings only 10 percent good while 90 percent of the efforts dedicated to it must be spent on "remedying the inconveniences."[209]

Also, in his wide-ranging 1971 interview given to *L'Express* in the period when in the aftermath of the events of 1968 the organized *reactionary* forces in Paris—actively promoted by the Gaullist regime—openly display their aggressive determination in favor of the most repressive measures, marching on the Champs d'Élysées in the center of the French capital shouting, *"Kill Sartre, civil war-machine,"* and even bomb his nearby apartment,[210] Lévi-Strauss has the nerve to say in the concluding paragraph of his interview, in response to the delicately raised suggestion that his views might sound somewhat reactionary to the readers, that "the terms *'reactionary'* and *'revolutionary'* have no meaning except in relation to the *conflicts* of groups which oppose one another. But today the greater peril for humanity does not come from the activities of a *regime, a party, a group, or a class.*[211] This is what we are asked to believe by the structuralist "man of science." After all, we have been also invited by him to accept, as we have seen above, that—contrary to the foolish beliefs of the "so-called men of the Left," à la Sartre and his socially "non-integrated" followers among the youth—"the golden age which bestowed the blessing of a congruescence between *practical imperatives* and *schemes of interpretation* has already passed."

The contradictory treatment of the thorny issues of the exchange relationship, closely connected with the questions concerning use-value and exchange-value, go back a long way in the various theoretical conceptions formulated from the standpoint of capital. Not surprisingly, therefore, neglecting and even obliterating the historical dimension of the major issues, so as to be able to eternalize capital's societal reproductive order, is a general tendency in this field. Moreover, this tendency is clearly visible not only in twentieth century capital apologetics but also in the writings of the classical political economists.

In this way the capitalist exchange relations are ahistorically universalized (and of course legitimated) through their confusion with a dehistoricized conception of utility. Thus in the case of Ricardo, for instance, we find the baffling conflation of exchange-value with use-value and utility in general. This confounding transformation is accomplished in Ricardo's work by treating the capitalist labor process and the creation of wealth through the—in reality *historically specific*—capitalist exchange relation as *natural* and by assigning, in Marx's word, "merely a ceremonial form" to exchange-value. In other words, for Ricardo:

> Wealth itself, in its *exchange-value* form, appears as a *merely formal mediation* of its *material* composition; thus the specific character of *bourgeois* wealth is not grasped—precisely because it appears there as *the adequate* form of *wealth as such*, and thus, although exchange-value is the point of departure, the *specific economic forms of exchange* themselves play no role at all in his economics. Instead, he always speaks about distribution of the general product of labour and of the soil among the three classes, as if the form of wealth based on *exchange-value* were concerned only with *use-value,* and as if exchange-value were merely a

ceremonial form, which vanishes in Ricardo just as money as medium of circulation vanishes in exchange.[212]

In contrast to such approaches, the importance of grasping the necessary *historical mediations* of both "exchange" and "utility" could not be greater. For the failure to identify the historically specific mediations in theoretical analysis can only yield the profundity of conveniently embellished *tautologies* which, on the basis of their ability to claim (commonplace) "self-evidence" to themselves, frequently constitute only the preliminary step and the "jumping board" to the most arbitrary assertion of ideological vested interests at the next step. "In this sense it is a *tautology* to say that property (appropriation) is a *precondition* of production. But it is altogether ridiculous to leap [in bourgeois political economy] from that to a *specific form* of property, e.g. private property. (Which further and equally presupposes an antithetical form, non-property.)"[213]

It is an obvious tautology to say that exchange is a necessary (and in that sense universal) condition of human society. For how could the multiplicity of human individuals exist and reproduce themselves in their societies without exchanging—*something, sometime and other, somewhere*, and *somehow*[214]—among themselves? For the individuals in question are neither *"genus-individuals,"* nor *isolated* individuals, as depicted in the bourgeois "Robinsonnades" in modern times—living each of them as single individuals on their particular well-stocked desert islands, like Robinson Crusoe, and waiting only for the arrival of Friday to serve them as laboring "hands," in accordance with the ideal determinations of *"nature"*[215]—but inescapably *social individuals* even under the most extreme dehumanizing conditions of *capitalist alienation*. The notion of exchange is reduced to a platitudinous tautology when it is proclaimed as a universal and permanent panacea, devised for the purpose of fallaciously smuggling into the equation as the *necessary premise* of all reasoning in the field the *desired apologetic conclusion,* in the absence of the really vital—inseparably *social* as well as *historical*—dimension of the substantive relationships at issue.

The important category of exchange can acquire its theoretically relevant meaning only when it is inserted into the dynamic historical framework of socially determined *specific mediations*[216] and complex interrelationships through which the *objective changes and transformations* of its modalities—changes ranging from "capillary" alterations to qualitatively/radically different and all-embracing magnitudes—are convincingly displayed. That is to say, changes that unfold in accordance with the dialectic of *continuity in discontinuity and discontinuity in continuity* characteristic of *historical/transhistorical development*. But *development* is what we are concerned with, even if often it is misrepresented as a simplistic "straw-man" *progress*, invented for the purpose of being set to fire with a single matchstick in the service of romantic structuralist laments. Indeed the annals of history show substantive development from the exchange relations of our distant ancestors—who are compelled to live for a long historical period "from hand to mouth"—to the globally interdependent and interactive, as well as potentially *emancipatory*, present and future. The emergence of this emancipatory potential is an integral part of the historical process itself, irrespective of how great might be the—*socially preventable or rectifiable*—dangers that are now inseparable from capital's globalizing modality of social metabolic reproduction and from their *historically specific* and correspondingly destructive second-order mediations. Without the concrete grasp of the social and historical determinations at stake in these matters the platitudinous tautology about "exchange" commended as a universal panacea can only amount to the mystifying apologetics of the established order.

In the same sense, it is quite obvious that in necessarily changing—and not structuralistically frozen and reified—human society there can be no *structure* without *history*, in the same way as there can be no *history* of any magnitude without its corresponding *structures*. Structural imperatives and historical temporality are closely intertwined. For human society is inconceivable without its *dynamic structuring determinations* (often misrepresented as rigid architectural constructs, so as to be able to dismiss the Marxian "base and superstructure metaphor") which secure some kind of *cohesion* even under the conditions of the antagonistic capital system's *structural centrifugality*. The *structural imperatives* may indeed assume the most rigid form under determinate *historical conditions* and assert themselves "behind the backs of the individuals" if need be, as precisely they happen to do that under our own conditions of existence. Accordingly, also the categories of structure and history—as all-embracing and temporally changing structural articulations of the corresponding forms of being (*Daseinsformen*)—are inextricably *conjoined* in actually existing human society.

However, without an inherently dialectical and historical treatment of both of them also the concepts of structure and history are as much in danger of being turned into mere *tautology* as the timeless universal panacea of *exchange*. This means that an adequate conception of their relationship must account not only for the *historical genesis* of any *structure* whatsoever[217] but also for the *process of development* in humanity's history itself, i.e., for its *genesis* and dynamic *transformations*, in accordance with its determination as an *open-ended* framework of societal change; which includes the potential move from antagonistic "prehistory" to "real history" consciously lived and ordained by the non-antagonistically self-mediating social individuals. Otherwise we end up with the earlier seen hopeless dichotomies of *space* and *time*, *continuity* and *discontinuity*, *subject* and *object*, etc., and the reduction of history itself—said to be "devoid of any object" and good for nothing but "cataloguing" the "elements of any structure"—to a desolate collection of data "complemented" by the "anti-progress" mythologics of Lévi-Straussian structural anthropology.

It is necessary in connection with all of these fundamental relations to keep the *objective priorities*—which happen to be both historical and logical primacies—in their proper perspective. In the case of *exchange*, for instance, before one can envisage the exchange of anything, the objects to be exchanged must be somehow *produced*. And so must be the social relations under which their historically specific production becomes feasible. In other words, the question of historical genesis must take *precedence* in these matters, as indeed it happens to be most important also for dialectically settling the question of what may or may not be legitimately considered the *precondition*, in contrast to the *result*, in any determinate relationship. Thus in distribution, analogously to exchange

> the *structure of distribution* is completely determined by the *structure of production*. Distribution is itself a product of production, not only in its object, in that only the *results* of production can be *distributed*, but also in its form, in that the specific kind of participation in production deter-

mines the *specific form* of distribution, i.e. the pattern of participation in distribution. . . . In the shallowest conception, distribution appears as the distribution of products, and hence as further removed from and quasi-independent of production. But before distribution can be the distribution of products, it is (1) the distribution of the instruments of production, and (2) which is a further specification of the same relation, the distribution of the members of the society among the different kinds of production. (Subsumption of the individuals under *specific relations of production*.) The distribution of products is evidently only a *result* of this distribution, which is comprised within the process of production itself and determines the *structure of production*.[218]

As we can see, all of the named factors relevant to the evaluation of the historically always specific productive/distributive relationship are dialectically treated here, fully respecting both the temporal and the structural priorities involved. The same must apply to the assessment of the exchange relationship as much with regard to the most remote historical past as its capitalist modality, as well as to its potential future—absolutely vital—transformation. For it is crucially important for the survival of humanity to institute a radically different—*communal*—exchange relationship in the not too distant future, in place of the fetishistic and destructive domination of use-value (which corresponds to human need) by increasingly more wasteful capitalist exchange-value.

Revealingly, those who mythically inflate the concept of exchange and project its capitalist variety even into the most remote corners of the past, obliterate not only the real *historical* dimension of the exchange relationship itself but also the objective *structural priorities,* so as to block the road ahead, with its *qualitatively different* mode of regulating social metabolic reproduction also in terms of the unavoidable exchange/interchange of humanity with nature and among the particular individuals themselves in society. By defining exchange in terms of the *product* (the *result*) of the process—irrespective of the question of what kind of product is at issue, from material goods to cultural entities—they obliterate all awareness of the specific *productive activities* and the corresponding *relations of production* at their roots, as their necessary precondition, under which the producing individuals are subsumed. They represent the exchange relationship in this way in order to be able to banish from view the feasibility of instituting a historically viable alternative. Thus the *primacy of activity* itself is characteristically wiped out in the interest of eternalizing and *absolutizing* the historically *contingent* capitalist alienation of both the *productive activity and its commodified product.*

In reality there can be no aprioristic apodicticity for projecting the—socially always necessary—exchange relations in the form of *products,* let alone of *commodified products.* The only reason for engaging in such projection—and grossly *violating* thereby both the historical and the conceptual primacies involved—is to harmonize, in the interest of social legitimation, the *commodity form of exchange* with the established, historically contingent *form of property* embodied in the *relations of production,* with its antagonistic second-order mediations. For the given relations of production, ruled by the imperative of perennial capital-accumulation, are incapable of producing and distributing the products in any other way. But the absolutized legitimatory claims of the established form of property and appropriation are historically false. For as Marx had clearly put it into relief in his discussion of property and appropriation, against the eternalizing claims attached to the notion of private property: "History rather shows *common property* (e.g. in India, among the Slavs, the early Celts, etc.) to be the more original form, a form which long continues to play a significant role in the shape of *communal property.*"[219]

Thus, even if the historical primacy of common property is disputed and denied, in the service of the vested interests of capital-accumulation, no one can rationally deny the *primacy of productive activity* itself at the roots of all conceivable forms and varieties of production, from material goods to religious ideas and works of art. This is so even if this primacy can be practically violated, of course, as a matter of *historical contingency,* through capital's mode of class-exploitative *appropriation,* from the time of the "primitive accumulation" to the present. In this sense, advocating the *exchange of activities* as the only viable *historical alternative* and a qualitatively different mode of production and distribution for the future, means *restituting* to productive activity its *ontological primacy,* overturned and usurped by capital's forcibly discriminatory form of expropriating appropriation to which we have been accustomed for a very long time. But it goes without saying that the institution of a qualitatively different exchange relationship, compared to its now dominant form, based in the future on the *self-managed exchange of activities* in a consciously planned and coordinated productive and distributive order, requires the radical transformation of the alienated *property relations* into a *communal type*. That is precisely the reason why in the ideologically dominant theories (and mythologics) of the exchange relations even the mention of the feasibility of production and societal reproduction on the basis of the exchange of activities by the freely associated producers must be avoided like plague.

Nevertheless, the necessity to regulate societal reproduction based on the voluntary *exchange of activities*, in contrast to the authoritarian division of labor inseparable from blindly pursued capital-accumulation, remains the vital *practical imperative* of our historical time, no matter how sharply it contradicts the apologetic structuralist *"schemes of interpretation."* For that is the only feasible way of *reconstituting* the one and only historically sustainable relationship between production and *human need* through restoring *use-value* to its rightful place in the exchange relationship, on the basis of *substantive equality*. That is, a genuine socialist modality of exchange, freed from the wasteful and destructive domination of formally reductive *exchange-value* and, accordingly, viable both in humanity's reproductive *microcosms* and on the *global* scale.

Naturally, *exchange* is very far from being identifiable with historically much more limited *exchange-value*. Nor is *use-value* itself simply identifiable with "utility" as such. For we know very well that use-value is necessarily mediated *and dominated* under the historical conditions of the capitalist production order by exchange-value. Indeed, there are some extremely perverse forms of "utility" under the circumstances of capital's rule over society, graphically exemplified by the "military/industrial complex" and its infernal war machinery whose *"utility"* is only *destruction*, in more senses than one.

However, it is a characteristic feature of the ideological justification of the established order to confound *utility* in general with capital's fetishistic imposition of exchange-value over society. This kind of tendentious confusion can assume particularly conspicuous forms. In this sense, let us take an important example—and in some ways a model of structural functionalism—the most highly revered bourgeois political economist of the twentieth century, John Maynard Keynes. He does not hesitate to idealize in the most contradictory fashion a fictitiously projected future social reproductive order, and to glorify at the same time the prosaic reality of the capitalist mode of production—admitted also by Keynes to be utterly prosaic for the rhetorical purposes of the rather dubious "persuasion" offered by him.

To be sure, Keynes knows very well that the real issue at stake is the imperative of capital accumulation. Nevertheless, on the one hand he insists in his lectures collected in the volume called *Essays in Persuasion*—lectures delivered in the second half of the 1920s—that *capital accumulation* is an absolute necessity for societal advancement, and in this sense he fallaciously confounds the historically specific expansion of capitalist exchange-value with utility in general, projecting in a sonorous way that for a hundred years "we must pretend to ourselves and to everyone else that fair is foul and foul is fair; for *foul is useful and fair is not.*"[220] At the same time, on the other hand, without envisaging the slightest alteration in the dehumanizing reproductive practices of the capital system, he preaches in the same lecture that in the rhetorically projected future society: "We shall honour those who can teach us how to pluck the hour and the day virtuously and well, the delightful people who are capable of taking direct enjoyment in things, the lilies of the field who toil not, neither do they spin."[221] But, of course, he keeps entirely to himself the secret of how we are going to get from the existing "usefully foul" social reproductive order of necessary capital accumulation to the "virtuously hour and day-plucking" society of the future. Disconcertingly though for such Keynesian apologetics, in our days the projected "one hundred years" are nearly up, and we are more distant from the spuriously praised goal of "neither toiling nor spinning society" than when it was disingenuously acclaimed by him from a safe distance of "one hundred years" in his *Essays in Persuasion,* with capital-apologetic devotion.

We find a similarly motivated *conflation* in the work of John Maynard Keynes between what he calls *"useful economic technique"*[222] and its necessary *social structural setting.* Also in this regard, tellingly, the established social structure is always taken for granted, and most of the time it remains also *unmentioned,* so that the semblance of *idealizable neutrality* should be conferred upon the socially articulated economic techniques required for maximizing profitability and capital accumulation. However, the fact is that the idealized *"neutral productive techniques"* are always deeply embedded in a historically specific *social structure* of production and the corresponding control and execution which, under the structurally entrenched hierarchy of the capital system, *necessarily divorce* the control functions of production from labor, in accordance with the established *social relations of production* as their material ground and state-protected legitimacy. "Useful economic technique" taken by itself is, therefore, a self-interested fiction, just like the society in which the "delightful people toil not, neither do they spin."

The revealing conceptual orientation and *vital practical premise* of *structual functionalism* is precisely this kind of mystifying conflation and idealization of determinate socioeconomic techniques and control processes as "purely technical" and "purely economic," and thereby absolutizable. They are the defining characteristics of the claimed "universally valid General Theory" of Talcott Parsons. In addition to that fallacious absolutization, such characteristics are coupled in Parsonian theory with a pronounced *formalist* approach to the discussed problems, so as to make the presented arbitrary postulates—plucked out of thin air—appear "rigorously scientific" in the absence of any supporting evidence. Thus, completely ignoring the actual nature of property rights and corresponding power relations in American capitalist society, we are told by Parsons that "there *must be* a property system which regulates claims to *transferable entities*, material or immaterial, and thereby *secures rights* in means of life in the *facilities* which are necessary for the *performance of functions*."[223]

Nothing could be more vague and more blatantly apologetic of the established order than this kind of analysis of the actually existing class structure and class conflict encountered under the monopolistic concentration of economic and political power in corporate capitalist society. As C. Wright Mills rightly stressed in his sharp critique of Talcott Parsons:

> Grand Theory is drunk on syntax, blind to semantics. . . . The Grand
> theorists are so preoccupied by syntactic meanings and so unimaginative
> about semantic references, they are so rigidly confined to such high lev-
> els of abstraction that the "typologies" they make up—and the work they
> do to make them up—seem more often an arid game of Concepts than an

effort to define systematically—which is to say, in a clear and orderly way—the problems at hand, and to guide our efforts to solve them.[224]

The trouble is that in such theories the ideological vested interests must prevail at any cost. The vacuous "typologies" propounded by structural functionalist theory serve precisely the purpose of eternalizing the vested interests.

Causal explanations of the abstractly posited changes are conspicuous by their absence in this kind of theory. We find instead a systematic conflation and confusion of the subjective and objective factors as well as of the individual and collective spheres of action. And the meaning of it all transpires when the American grand theorist authors tell us—without even mentioning in their earlier analysis the very real fact of the *capitalist exploitation of labor* (that is, exploitation considered in its unvarnished actuality, without the baffling inverted commas)—that the result of the "cycle of structural changes" described by them is that the claimed " 'new economy' has become independent both of the previous 'exploitation of labour' and the previous 'capitalistic control.' "[225] This happy outcome is supposed to sound very good to everybody. For thanks to the curious use of the inverted commas in the quoted lines we must be now doubly reassured that the "exploitation of labour" and the antagonistically contested "capitalistic control" of the economy never really existed and, moreover, that they have now, in virtue of the formalistically postulated "cycle of structural changes," completely disappeared from the (not so new) "new economy."

The "structural functionalist" mystifications, in the service of the fictional "new economy," are designed to divert critical attention from the increasingly problematical and globally exploitative nature of *monopolistic corporate capitalism*. Every social and economic problem—painfully affecting the life of countless millions of people—is metamorphosed into "neutral functional" categories and pseudo-scientific "typologies," so as to be able to offer the semblance of the right and proper "regulation of the claims to transferable entities, material or immaterial, and thereby *secure rights*" that are required for the (generic) "facilities" of systemic interchange and for the (equally generic) "performance of functions." And this is so quite simply because it "functionally must be" so. Consequently we shall live happily ever after in the functionally—and of course also structurally—best of all possible worlds.

In this typologically embellished world the "secured rights" are secured strictly for *"transferable entities"* only, assigned to the domain of utterly fictitious individual "consumer sovereignty," excluding with the firmest possible determination even the most remote feasibility of *real structural change* (i.e. a radical change with regard to the "non-transferable entities" of the means of production to the class of labor) in the hierarchically entrenched and state-protected antagonistic structural order. And we receive this reassuring wisdom on the authority of ideally competent "structural functionalism" that—"in the light of recent sociological theory," as they put it—emphatically denies the relevance of "social class and class conflict." For in such theory, even when it projects its fantasy-typology about the "cycle of structural changes," the real structural determinations of the established social and economic order quite simply do not exist. Accordingly, all "structural changes" must be confined to the well containable "facilities" and "functions" appropriate to the allegedly "non-capitalist control" of the established order.

What is important to bear in mind also in this respect is that the structural functionalist theoretical obfuscation, and ultimate obliteration, of the actually existing structural determinations of capital's social metabolic order is profoundly *anti-historical*. The fundametal ideological purpose of this theory is the eternalization of the capital system often in a fetishistically camouflaged way, travestied in the form of complicated typologies and schematisms depicting invented structures and disembodied functions. But the barefaced social apologetic character of these "grand theories" is revealed from time to time either directly—as we have seen above in the *explicit denial* of class conflict and capitalist exploitation by Talcott Parsons in actually existing monopoly-capitalist society—or indirectly, in his abstract formalist discourse on "transferable entities" and "facilities" required for the permanence of the strictly accommodatory "performance of functions." The established—*historically produced and historically changing*—social and economic order of the capital system completely disappears thereby from view, so that the danger of any *significant change in the future* should also conveniently disappear with it in an aprioristic and irretrievable fashion from the reader's horizon.

The attribution—to eternalized capital—of the "useful economic techniques," as well as of the fetishistically depicted and apologetically transfigured structures and functions of societal development, is a self-serving and utterly false attribution. For it characteristically ignores the *historical dimension* of these problems. A dimension that happens to be seminally important not only for a proper understanding of the nature of past developments—including humanity's tendentiously misrepresented but in reality far from linear "general progress," which is nevertheless very real, notwithstanding all kinds of structuralist and post-structuralist anti-historical tirades against it—but also of the necessary and feasible task for the future. For productive machinery and techniques, in their historically unfolding combination with science and human knowledge in general, including all of their positive and negative potentialities, did not fall out of the sky, as manna from the biblical heaven. They had to be created by—and in the course of structurally secured expropriation also alienated for a transcendable historical period from—the working subject of history. That is, by *homo sapiens* considered as increasingly more skillful and inventive *homo faber,* and not as mystifyingly depicted modern capital-accumulating and profit-maximizing *homo economicus.* Indeed, they had to be created—by the self-mediating human beings in their absolutely inescapable productive interaction with nature and among themselves—as integral parts of the process of *potentially emancipatory* development. A process dialectically intelligible only on the basis of the objective deter-minations of progressively expanding human need and creatively "van-ishing" historical necessity that carries with it humanity's epochally sus-tainable transformatory structural advancement.

To be sure, these transformations are extremely complex and in their innermost character up to our own time also very contradictory. For in the course of historical development the self-mediating human subject of nature and history also imposed upon itself the alienating burden of *antagonistic*—and in many ways destructive—second-order mediations. Nevertheless, the actually accomplished societal productive develop-ments in question, no matter how problematical in some ways, are at the same time also vitally important for the present and for a historically sus-tainable future. They are important in virtue of their objective determina-tions of controllability, provided that we care about seriously confronting and countering the unavoidable dangers implicit in them, instead of pouring out romantic laments about "humanity being its own worst enemy and at the same time the worst enemy of the rest of the creation."

In this context it is necessary to focus attention on some lines from Marx's *Grundrisse*:

> The development of the means of labour into *machinery* is not an *accidental* moment of capital, but is rather the *historical reshaping* of the traditional, inherited *means of labour* into a *form adequate to capital*. The accumulation of *knowledge and of skill*, of the *general productive forces of the social brain*, is thus absorbed into *capital, as opposed to labour*, and hence appears as an *attribute of capital*, and more specifically of *fixed capital*, in so far as it enters into the production process as a means of production proper. . . . Further, in so far as machinery develops with the *accumulation of society's science*, of productive force generally, *general social labour* presents itself not in labour but *in capital*. The productive force of society is measured in fixed capital, exists there in its objective form; and, inversely, the productive force of capital grows with the *general progress*, which *capital appropriates without charge*.[226]

> The entire production process appears as not subsumed under the direct skillfulness of the *worker,* but rather as the *technological application of science*. . . . This *elevation of direct labour* into social labour appears as a *reduction of individual labour* to the level of *helplessness* in the face of the *communality* [Gemeinsamkeit] represented by and *concentrated in capital*.[227]

As we can see in these lines from the *Grundrisse,* the historical process of humanity's advancement and the "accumulation of knowledge and of skill"—which is simultaneously the "accumulation of society's science" and the "general productive forces of the social brain"—is a highly contradictory process, due to the *alienating perversion* of the unfolding objective relationships. It is both positive, in that we see a *general progress* of society and the enrichment of the "social brain" through the "accumulation of society's science," but we must experience at the same time the increasing power of the negative dimension, which is in ever greater need of conscious human control in the dangerously unfolding present and the future. For in the course of this historical development of human knowledge the potentially all-round positive accomplishment of the general productive forces of the social brain is *one-sidedly*—in an alienated form of expropriating appropriation—*"absorbed into capital, as opposed to labour."* It is thereby put to the service of capital's potentially most destructive and ultimately uncontrollable purposes, ruled by the *absolute imperative* of capital-accumulation whatever might be the consequences.

By contrast, on the side of labor, the expanding production process appears not as subsumed under the direct *skillfulness* of the *worker,* but rather as the fetishistic *"technological application of science"*—taken at face value by all capital-apologists—which means simultaneously the *"reduction of individual labour* to the level of *helplessness."* Moreover, one of the most absurd aspects of this alienated form of development and historical advancement is that the ever greater *socialization of the labor process assigns to capital* the *perverted communal dimension* (*Gemeinsamkeit*) of societal reproduction. This is a totally *usurpatory* assignment, sharply contradicted by the innermost nature of capital itself which remains always wedded to the *self-legitimating* control of the *means* of production and asserts its unchallengeable authority to regulate the distribution of the *products* of *social labor.* And in this antagonistic and fundamentally self-contradictory course of development the traditional means of production are historically reshaped by increasingly more *socialized labor* into a form *adequate to capital* in the form of *machinery, science and technology,* carrying with them in actuality an ever greater *domination of labor.*

Obviously, a real understanding of these productive developments is impossible without closely relating them to the antagonistic, and ultimately totally untenable, capital-labor relationship in which they are deeply embedded. And by implication it is, of course, also painfully clear that science and technology must be extricated from this *antagonistic* embeddedness for the sake of making the alternative mode of social metabolic control that we need historically viable. The issue is not social embeddedness *or not,* but what *kind* of—antagonistically articulated or positively enhancing—social embeddedness. It is utterly vacuous to talk about "useful economic techniques" without constantly bearing in mind the necessary implications of the inescapable social roots and articulation of all technology not only in the past but also in relation to any historically sustainable future. For the *necessary corollary* of the development of knowledge and technology, on the ground of the *irreversible socialization* of the labor process, as described in the lines quoted from the *Grundrisse,* is that the *perverse antagonistic appropriation* of the fruits of the social brain by capital must be overcome. And it can be overcome only if the *communality* of production, which is *usurped by capital* in a fetishistic and alienating form, is *restituted* in a rationally viable way to the social labor process itself, assigned to and *consciously controlled by social labor,*[228] in accordance with the positive development and the gratification of *human need*. This is how Marx spells out the *necessary corollary* in question, closely related to the earlier quoted lines, in two important passages of the *Grundrisse:*

> In this transformation, it is neither the direct human labour he himself performs, nor the time during which he works, but rather the appropriation of his own general productive power, his understanding of nature and his mastery over it by virtue of his presence as a social body—it is, in a word, the development of the social individual which appears as the great foundation-stone of production and of wealth. The *theft of alien labour time, on which the present wealth is based,* appears a miserable foundation in face of this new one, created by large-scale industry itself. As soon as labour in the direct form has ceased to be the great well-spring of wealth, labour time ceases and must cease to be its measure, and hence exchange-value must cease to be the measure of use-value.[229]

The growth of the forces of production can no longer be bound up with the appropriation of alien labour, but the mass of workers must themselves appropriate their own surplus labour. Once they have done so— and *disposable time* thereby ceases to have an *antithetical* existence— then, on one side, necessary labour time will be measured by the needs of the social individual, and, on the other, the development of the power of social production will grow so rapidly that, even though production is now calculated for the wealth of all, *disposable time* will grow for all. For real wealth is the developed productive power of all individuals. The measure of wealth is then not any longer, in any way, labour time, but rather disposable time.[230]

In this way Marx forcefully underlines the harmful *historical anachronism* of capital's societal reproductive order that continues to function, in an *irrationalistic* way, on the basis of the *"miserable foundation"* of the *"theft of alien labor time,"* keeping society in the straitjacket of artificially perpetuated but exploitable "necessary labor" measured by, and in subservience to, capital-accumulating exchange-value, instead of being measured by the *needs* of the social individual. For capital, because of its innermost nature, is totally incapable of setting free the immense productive and emancipatory potentialities of *disposable time*. This is because under the rule of capital the social individuals' progressively developing and potentially liberating *"surplus labor"*—which can be transformed into creatively usable *disposable time* if allowed to grow as it could and should—cannot be set free. It must be condemned to an *"antithetical* existence" in its modality of *disposable time* on account of the latter's uselessness for exploitative appropriation and corresponding capital-accumulation on the required and feasible scale. For capital the indefinite growth of *freely disposable time*—in contrast to profitably exploitable but limited "leisure time"—would be even dangerous, amounting to *social dynamite*, since it could not offer for the social individuals any *meaningful allocation* for their freely expanding disposable time within the confines of the established mode of societal reproduction. Accordingly, capital cannot possibly switch from the fetishistic tyranny of *exchange-value* to the consciously regulated production of *use-value* in the service of *human need*. That kind of switch would be feasible only on the basis of the full development of disposable time, which directly contradicts capital's now utterly dangerous historical anachronism as an increasingly wasteful, and at the same time callously inhuman—because need-denying—productive system.

However, this is a necessary *systemic/structural failure* and therefore nothing can be done to remedy it within the framework of the capital system itself. It must remain the painful truth under the conditions of our societal development, despite the already attained positive *potentialities* of science and human knowledge in general. This structurally constraining condition (and contradiction) is insuperable under the circumstances when labor time, rather sooner than later, must cease to be the alienating measure of social wealth, and hence exchange-value must cease to be the crippling and nature-destructive measure of admissible use-value. For the new historical imperative, in place of the ever more destructive and irrational imperative of parasitic capital-accumulation, is that the workers must themselves *appropriate their own surplus labor*, in order to set free for themselves and for society as a whole the creative and emancipatory potentialities of *disposable time*. And that requires a radically different—communal—mode of social metabolic control. For unless the producing social individuals can appropriate their own surplus labor, there can be no chance of releasing from its fetters their own potential *disposable time*, which can conceivably become *disposable* only if their real owners are capable of freely disposing of it. And that inevitably raises the question of *who allocates* the potentialities of d*isposable time*, and *for what purposes* can the planned allocation be brought in a sustainable relationship with the *producers of disposable time* in a positive way. For capital knows only one practicable purpose of "resource allocation,"[231] the profit-maximizing process of capital-accumulation. Only the producers of creatively expandable disposable time are capable of consciously allocating the great potentiality of such time for their own freely chosen *emancipatory purposes*. Otherwise they could have no interest whatsoever in creating it, nor could they be *forced* to produce it, since its production requires the free deliberations of the social individuals themselves, its potential creators. Moreover, without this condition the very idea of producing disposable time would be totally irrational in that there could be no *outlet* for its allocation and "realization" within the systemic confines of capital's social order. In other words, disposable time, in the real—*all-round emancipatory*—sense of its meaning, can only come into existence through its *unhindered full-scale* production by the self-mediating social individuals who *consciously* create it within a qualitatively different structural framework of social metabolic reproduction. That is the only way to overcome its now absurdly straitjacketed *"antithetical* existence," confined to the "miserable" setting of profitably exploited and alienating "labor time" exposed by Marx. In this vital sense, Marx directly counters and devastatingly demolishes the traditional labor theory of value.

This is how Marx actually analyzes in all of his major works the unfolding historical process of societal reproduction, in conjunction with the development of society's knowledge and the corresponding impact of science and technology on the labor process itself. However, we find in the writings of the various capital-apologists a caricaturistic misrepresentation of his complex dialectical and profoundly historical approach. Thus, when Marx clearly stresses, as we have seen, the historical anachronism of capital's continued reliance on the "theft of alien labor time," made necessary for the sake of the profitable exploitation of "necessary labor," and he points out the dangerous implications of this historical anachronism—of which we see in our own time a most graphic example in the potentially all-destructive exploitation of science and technology by the military-industrial complex for its own purposes of fraudulent profit maximization—Habermas glorifies the fashionable and allegedly all-round beneficial so-called "trickle-down effect" of this destructive process, in his opportunistic eagerness to refute Marx. He writes, as if Marx had never even heard of science and technology, that under advanced, organized capitalism "industrial research has been linked up with research under government contract, which primarily promotes scientific and technical progress in the military sector. From there information flows back into the sectors of civilian production. Thus technology and science become a leading productive force, rendering inoperative the conditions for Marx's labor theory of value. It is no longer meaningful to calculate the amount of capital investment in research and development on the basis of the value of unskilled (simple) labor power, when scientific-technical progress has become an independent source of surplus value, in relation to which the only source of surplus value considered by Marx, namely the labor power of the immediate producers, plays an ever smaller role."[232] Not surprisingly therefore Habermas, following his own fantasies, also apologetically asserts on the same arbitrary ground the fictional *"scientization of technology,"*[233] when in reality we are condemned to suffer the harmful consequences of the exact opposite: the wasteful and dangerous *technologization of science* against which the scientists who maintain a strong sense of their social responsibility continue to protest.

Naturally, it is a completely grotesque idea that science and technology—under the conditions of "advanced organized capitalism" revered by Habermas—are an *"independent* leading productive force" and thereby a socially neutral *"independent source of surplus value."* Given their deep-seated embeddedness in the established *structural determinations* of the social order, they are not more independent of their capitalist integument than Habermas himself is of serving the vested interests of capital-apologetics. The *structural framework* determined in any conceivable historical epoch by the *forces and the relations of production,* including any historically sustainable socialist society of the future, can be ignored or bypassed only by the worst kind of social apologetics. It is well understandable, therefore, that Habermas also wants to get rid of these vitally important categories of social being in his self-acclaimed supersession of Marx. Accordingly, he declares that "the category framework developed by Marx in the basic assumptions of historical materialism requires a new formulation. The model of *forces of production and relations of production* would have to be replaced by the *more abstract* one of *work and interaction."*[234] The trouble is, though, that this "new formulation of historical materialism"—which is neither historical nor in the least materialist—consisting in the introduction of the undoubtedly "more abstract," *Parsonian type* and hopelessly vague categorial pair, as advocated by Habermas, renders the whole enterprise of social and economic analysis useful only for the ideological purposes of conceptual obfuscation and mystification.

In truth, the realities behind the much abused notion of "useful economic techniques," as well as the apologetically posited concepts of "science and machinery," are not disembodied entities, manipulable at pleasure in terms of anti-historically projected "functions" and fictitious "structural changes," as treated by Talcott Parsons and his epigones. They are historically produced and historically evolving *Daseinsformen*—i.e. forms of being—which under the conditions of our own societal reproductive existence are not simply *socially embedded* but *unsustainably* embedded in an *antagonistic social metabolic system of second-order mediations.* In other words, under the present circumstances they are intelligible only in relation to a specific type of *social structure* and its corresponding dynamic *historical determinations,* together with their rival *social agencies,* which actually represent objective *hegemonic alternatives* of social metabolic reproduction. It is because of the objective ground of their social and historical determinations that these rival hegemonic alternatives cannot be conveniently reduced to the abstract categorial schemes of *"structural functionalism"* and its aprioristic claims to timeless validity.

If structural functionalism presents its wisdom in the form of the claimed universally valid abstract postulates of Parsonian Grand theory, the programmatic claim to originality by *"post-modernity,"* as spelled out by Jean-François Lyotard—once an adherent of the French left political group promoting the magazine *Socialisme ou Barbarie*—is that it abandons *"grand narratives"* in favor of *"little narratives"* (*"petit récits"*).

On the face of it, this is a big difference. But it stops at the level of a verbal contrast. For the substantive common denominator of the two approaches is their defense of the capital system. They share the theoretical justification of a political stance which is willing to grant the need for "little changes," just like the Popperian advocacy of "little by little," so long as such changes can be safely accommodated within the overall framework of the established *structural order*. For any idea of changing the *socioeconomic structure itself*—and God forbid advocate the idea that such change should be accomplished in an emancipatory way—would have to be peremptorily condemned by "postmodernity" as an inadmissible *"grand narrative."*

According to Lyotard the "modern" is making "an explicit appeal to some *grand narrative,* such as the dialectics of Spirit, the hermeneutics of meaning, the emancipation of the rational or working subject, or the creation of wealth."[235] By contrast to the grand narratives, to be condemned, Lyotard enthusiastically declares that "the little narrative [*petit récit*] remains the quintessential form of imaginative invention."[236] However, if people try to find out what might qualify for the exalted status of the "postmodern" condition, they are bound to be disappointed. For they receive only answers bordering on sophistry, like this: "What, then, is the postmodern? It is undoubtedly a *part of the modern*. . . . A work can become *modern* only if *it is first postmodern*. Postmodernism thus understood is not modernism at its end but in the *nascent* state, and this state is *constant*."[237]

The totally anti-historical skepticism at the roots of this "postmodern" approach—which wants to retain the existing societal order as the overall framework of social metabolic reproduction even when it allows you to take delight in the "quintessential form of imaginative invention" projected in the form of the little changes of its "little narratives"— becomes clearer from another text in which Lyotard tells us:

The thought and action of the *nineteenth and twentieth centuries* are governed by an Idea (I am using Idea in its Kantian sense). That idea is *the idea of emancipation.* What we call philosophies of history, the great narratives by means of which we attempt to order the multitude of events, certainly argue this idea in very different ways: a Christian narrative in which Adam's sin is redeemed through love; the *Aufklärer* narrative of emancipation from ignorance and servitude thanks to knowledge and egalitarianism; the speculative narrative of the realization of the universal idea through the dialectic of the concrete; the Marxist narrative of emancipation from exploitation and alienation through the socialization of labour; the capitalist narrative of emancipation from poverty through technical and industrial development. . . . No matter which genre it makes hegemonic, the very basis of each of the great narratives of emancipation has, so to speak, been *invalidated over the last fifty years.* . . . The great narratives are now barely credible. And it is therefore tempting to lend credence to the great narrative of the decline of great narratives. But, as we know, the great narrative of decadence is there *in the very beginnings* of Western thought, in Hesiod and Plato. It dogs the narrative of emancipation like a shadow. And so *nothing has changed,* except that *greater strength and competence* are required if we are to face up to our current tasks.[238]

Thus, the "postmodern idea," firmly rejecting the "great narratives of emancipation," is supposed to have been *always* there, from the *"very beginning of Western thought."* So that the "postmodern" is not only prior to the "modern" but also co-extensive with the ancient. The only question that remains to be answered, then, is how we are supposed to "face up to our current tasks" with "greater strength and competence."

On this subject the deeply disenchanted former leftist Lyotard's answers are no less baffling and confusing than his diagnosis of the historical situation and of its conceptualizations, past, present, and future. Above all, to be sure, of the present and the future. For in the real world not everybody had abandoned the castigated idea of emancipation "in the last fifty years," nor are they likely to do so in the future. What is, then, the "competent" alternative proposed by postmodernity?

Lyotard offers as his model for action the "language games," combined with locally accessible computerization, and he adds: "The line to follow for computerization . . . is, in principle, quite simple; give the public *free access* to the memory and data banks. *Language games* would then be *games of perfect information* at any given moment."[239] And he also specifies "the principle that any consensus on the rules defining a game and the 'moves' playable within it *must* be *local,* in other words, agreed on by its present players and subject to eventual cancellation. The orientation then favours a multiplicity of finite *meta-arguments,* by which I mean argumentation that concerns *metaprescriptives* and is limited in space and time."[240] And Lyotard's idealized example is this:

> The municipality of Yverdon (Canton of Vaud), having voted to buy a computer (operational in 1981), enacted a certain number of rules: exclusive authority of the municipal council to decide which data are collected, to whom and under what conditions they are communicated; access for all citizens to all data (on payment); the right of every citizen to see the entries on his file (about 50), to correct them and address a complaint about them to the municipal council and if need be the Council of State; the right of all citizens to know (on request) which data concerning them is communicated and to whom.[241]

As an English adage puts it: "Mountains are in labor and a mouse is born." For what is missing here, as everywhere else in the "postmodern narratives," is any awareness of the forbidding difficulties and massive impediments involved in transforming into a *general social practice* the necessary control over the destructive antagonisms of the capital system. That would require a control extended not only over the jealously guarded secrets of the capitalist state itself but also over the state-legitimated "trade secrets" of the all-powerful transnational corporations that are structurally combined with the military-industrial complex.

The postmodern defense of the existent, in its disenchanted tirades against the idea of emancipation in general, and against "the emancipation of the working subject"[242] in particular, excludes even the most remote possibility of raising questions over the *fundamental determinations* of the established order, as "invalidated narratives." It prefers to submit itself to the far from simply "local" structural imperatives and deeply entrenched, *globally exploitative* vested interests of capital's mode of social metabolic control as a *whole*, offering as its own "competent" partial correctives only what can be readily absorbed by the self-legitimatory needs of the *overall* structural framework. The advocacy of "postmodernity" posits the requirement of "strength and competence" for facing up to the "current tasks." However, its *accommodatory localism* constitutes a far cry from the idealized condition of the "games of perfect information." Fittingly, the concluding sentence of Lyotard's *Postmodern Condition* offers to the reader resounding rhetorics only. These are Lyotard's final words: "Let us *wage a war on totality;* let us be witnesses to the *unpresentable;* let us activate the *differences* and save the honour of the name."[243]

6.5 The Law of Uneven Development and the Role of Scarcity in Historical Conceptions

Two major problems of historical development must be considered here, however briefly, before we can move on to the final section of this chapter. First, the *law of uneven development* in the course of historical transformations; and second, the nature of *scarcity* and the prospects of overcoming its destructive dimension in the future.

For understandable political reasons, in the twentieth century the question of uneven development was primarily debated in the context of Kautsky's (and of his direct or indirect adherents') accommodatory—and in theoretical terms shallower than skin-deep—projection of "ultra-imperialism," and Lenin's forceful rejection of it.[244] The recent varieties of the same idea of "ultra-imperialism," under whatever fanciful name, are no less shallow, as well as totally capitulatory to the pseudo-democratic self-legitimatory claims of U. S. imperialism, even when dressed up in left-sounding verbiage. The proposition that a societal reproductive system—whose constitutive parts are antagonistic to the core—should be able to overcome its objective material contradictions through a "globalized" state system, under the permanent domination of the most powerful of them, called "Empire" or whatever else, is too absurd to be taken seriously even for a moment. Only the wishful projection of some apologetic vested interests, cynically promoted by the propaganda organs of the established order, can create the semblance of its possibility; and even that only by disregarding the grave evidence to the contrary, including the pursuit of devastating and historically unsustainable wars.

In any case, it must be also underscored that the law of uneven development across humanity's history asserts itself over a much broader range of problems than the question of changing power relations among the major capitalist states arising from the determinations of their antagonistic social order in the age of imperialism. This must be kept in mind irrespective of how vitally important it is for us to confront—in the interest of humanity's survival—the issue of the potentially all-destructive aspirations of the now most powerful imperialist state for global domination in our time.

In addition to the necessarily changing power relations, the law of uneven development in history embraces the complex interchange between the material basis of society and its superstructure. This relationship includes the dialectical reciprocity between the level of material productive development attained at any given period of history and the various art forms.

The connection between material determinations and the various arts should not be treated in the form of some kind of "one-to-one correspondence" conceptualized through a mechanistic reduction. And that is by no means the end of the story. For another important aspect of this complex interrelationship between the historically given material foundation and the superstructure is the paradoxical unevenness that can be found between some vital legal conceptualizations and corresponding codes of regulatory practice on the one hand, and the general degree of development of a particular society.

Marx made it very clear that in the materialist conception of history all these issues must be taken on board in their full complexity. He insisted that we must account in dialectical terms for "The *uneven development* of material production relative to e.g. *artistic development*. In general, the concept of *progress* not to be conceived in the usual *abstractness*. Modern art etc. This disproportion not as important or so difficult to grasp as within *practical-social* relations themselves. E.g. the relation of education. Relation of the United States to Europe. But the really difficult point to discuss here is how *relations of production* develop *unevenly as legal relations*. Thus e.g. the relation of *Roman private law* (this less the case with criminal and public law) to modern production."[245]

In this important sense, what we are concerned with is nothing less than the dialectical validity—or mechanistic/reductive failure—of a general historical conception that claims to offer a coherent and sustainable overall picture of societal transformations, in contrast to any *abstract* and arbitrary projection of historical development as straightforward *"progress."* And, of course, the aspiration by an all-embracing historical theory to grasp the societal interchanges in their full complexity is very far from being simply a question of *theoretical accuracy*. For a mechanistic/reductive approach carries with it important *practical* implications and consequences for the elaboration of the *socialist transformatory strategies* which may or may not be feasible within its general framework.

Obviously, in this regard the problem is that social transformatory strategies—representing the corollary of the Marxian historical conception and of its orienting principle spelled out by him as the *necessary unity* of theory and practice—cannot succeed by positing *voluntaristic projections* in place of laboriously overcoming, by the adoption of the measures appropriate to the situation, the difficulties and contradictions inevitably associated with the dialectical intricacies of objective structural relationships.

It is much more than a coincidence that Marx is discussing the question of understanding uneven development in the same context in which he puts into relief the importance of making the materialist conception of history truly dialectical. First, he firmly rejects the "accusations about the *materialism* of this conception," stressing the validity of the proper materialist approach by contrasting it with *"naturalistic* materialism." And then, as a matter of clarification he adds the necessary defining characteristic of the type of materialist conception advocated by him: *"Dialectic* of the concepts of productive force (means of production) and relations of production, a *dialectic* whose boundaries are to be determined, and which does not suspend the real difference." The earlier quoted words on *"the uneven development of material production relative to e.g. artistic development"*[246] immediately follow the last sentence, concerned with the vital necessity of always observing the dialectical nature of the problems to be assessed. Accordingly, giving its proper weight to the difficult and at times even contradictory questions of *uneven development* must be in Marx's view an *integral part* of a dialectical conception of history.

The assessment of the various art forms in relation to their material setting across history is all too easily vulgarizable, not only with artistically but also politically most damaging consequences, as amply proved by the Stalinist historical experience.[247] Marx's qualifications in this regard are relevant both for general methodological and for practical reasons. His comments on the issue read as follows:

> In the case of the arts, it is well known that certain periods of their flowering are out of all proportion to the general development of society, hence also to the material foundation, the skeletal structure as it were, of its organization. For example, the Greeks compared to the moderns or also Shakespeare. It is even recognized that certain forms of art, e.g. the epic, can no longer be produced in their world epoch-making, classical stature as soon as the production of art, as such, begins; that is, that certain significant forms within the realm of the arts are possible only at an *undeveloped* stage of artistic development. If this is the case with the relation between different kinds of art within the realm of the arts, it is already less puzzling that it is the case in the relation of the entire realm to the general development of society. The difficulty consists only in the general formulation of these contradictions. As soon as they have been specified, they are already clarified.
>
> Let us take e.g. the relation of Greek art . . . to the present time. It is well known that Greek mythology is not only the arsenal of Greek art but also its foundation. Is the view of nature and of social relations on which the Greek imagination and hence Greek [mythology] is based possible with self-acting mule spindles and railways and locomotives and electrical telegraphs? What chance has Vulcan against Roberts & Co., Jupiter against the lightning-rod and Hermes against the Crédit Mobilier? All mythology overcomes and dominates and shapes the forces of nature in the imagination and by the imagination; it therefore vanishes with the

advent of real mastery over them. What becomes of Fama alongside
Printing House Square? Greek art presupposes Greek mythology, i.e.
nature and the social forms already reworked in an unconsciously artistic way by the popular imagination. This is its material. . . . Egyptian
mythology could never have been the foundation or the womb of Greek
art. But, in any case, a *mythology*. Hence in no way a social development
which excludes all mythological, all mythologizing relations to nature;
which therefore demands of the artist an imagination not dependent on
mythology.

  . . . But the difficulty lies not in understanding that the Greek arts and
epic are bound up with certain forms of social development. The difficulty is that *they still afford us artistic pleasure* and that in a certain
respect they count as a norm and as an unattainable model.[248]

As we can see, the problems discussed here by Marx have a fundamental methodological importance alongside their major practical implications. As in the last paragraph quoted above, it represents a real challenge for the elaboration of a coherent aesthetic conception. A dialectical
conception that must be able to elucidate both the relevance of the specific historical conditions under which the major works of art in question
are created, and at the same time also explain their *enduring ability* to
stimulate the artistic sensitivity of the people who continue to enjoy the
human experiences conveyed in them—by drawing the audience into the
depicted world through their persistent captivating power—even from
the historical distance of thousands of years.

  With regard to the earlier mentioned unevenness of legal conceptualizations and codes of practice in the course of historical development,
Marx's revealing example is the paradoxical *anticipatory* character of
Roman law. For, somewhat astonishingly, Roman law produces the
"juridical person" which can reach its full realization only under the conditions of capitalism. In this respect Marx points out:

  In Roman law, the *servus*[249] is correctly defined as one who may not enter
  into exchange for the purpose of acquiring anything for himself. It is,
  consequently, equally clear that although this legal system corresponds to
  a social state in which exchange was by no means developed, neverthe-

less, in so far as it was developed in a limited sphere, it was able to develop the *attributes of the juridical person, precisely of the individual engaged in exchange,* and thus anticipate (in its basic aspects) the legal relations of industrial society, and in particular the right which rising bourgeois society had necessarily to assert against medieval society. But the development of this right itself coincides completely with the dissolution of the Roman community.[250]

Thus we can see here a double paradox. For the early determination of the juridical person, without an appropriate material ground corresponding to its potential full development, is undoubtedly a most significant anticipation in its own terms of reference, within the realm of the law. At the same time, however, in the sense of the second, superseding paradox, the proper material articulation of the conditions for the general diffusion of the juridical person, carries with it the total dissolution of the type of societal relationships under which the original juridical anticipation was conceivable in the first place.

The discussion of the far-reaching ramifications and implications of the potential unevenness between the material development of society and the various legal conceptualizations and codes of practice does not belong here. Such problems can be properly explored only within the framework of a coherent theory of the state.

What is important to stress here, nevertheless, is that in terms of the Marxian conception an abstract reductive approach—not to mention a self-legitimatory type that voluntaristically postulates the equivalence between the dominant material determinations and the adopted legal regulatory framework—is completely out of the question. Accordingly, one cannot stress too strongly also in this respect the theoretical and practical importance of the law of uneven development which calls—in Marx's explicit words, as we have seen above—for a consistently *dialectical* analysis of these problems.

The first time the question of uneven development was raised by Marx in relation to the prospects of a socialist revolutionary explosion was in the first part of *The German Ideology,* in 1845. It appeared there with reference to the feasibility of dramatic social changes taking place in a capitalistically *underdeveloped* country,[251] as a result of the contradic-

tions of uneven development in a globally ever more closely interconnected system.

Talking about the historical maturation of the contradiction between
the productive forces and the forms of social intercourse Marx underscored that "to lead to collision in a country, this contradiction need not
necessarily have reached its extreme limit in that particular country. The
competition with industrially more advanced countries, brought about by
the expansion of international intercourse, is sufficient to produce a similar contradiction in countries with a less advanced industry (e.g. the
latent proletariat in Germany brought into more prominence by the competition of English industry)."[252] This is so because the less-developed
countries are inevitably "swept by world intercourse into the universal
competitive struggle."[253]

Naturally, we are talking here about a historically most advanced stage
of material productive development that dynamically extends not only
over the various districts and regions of a particular country but over
increasing areas of the world, and ultimately over the whole of the planet.
Even regarding any particular country, this type of—*large-scale industrial*—development cannot possibly be *uniform*. As Marx rightly
stressed: "It is evident that large-scale industry does not reach the same
level of development in all districts of a country."[254]

Consequently, if this happens to be the case with the material productive changes of any particular country exposed to large-scale industrial
transformation, no matter how favored that country might be under a
determinate set of circumstances, how could development in general be
uniform over the whole of the planet? This must be particularly underlined in the case of the antagonistically structured capitalist system in
which the "macrocosm" of the societal reproductive order as a whole is
made up of *centrifugally driven* "microcosms."

It is well known that in every single capitalist country, irrespective of
how privileged and even militarily/imperialistically prominent it might be
or have been at a certain period of its history in the global pecking order
of capital, as for instance Great Britain for centuries, there are zones of the
country in question that are *"underdeveloped"* in comparison to others.
The "North/South divide" is observable in this more limited sense in
every single country, even if, to be sure, in rather different ways in the

privileged ones in comparison to the former colonially dominated parts of the world. For the plight of the latter may be perpetuated for some considerable time under new forms of "neo-colonial" etc. domination and corresponding "developmental aid."

Moreover, the law of uneven development cannot be wished out of existence in the future. It is bound to remain in force—although with *qualitatively* changing potential impact and significance—even under the conditions of a genuine socialist order in a *globally interchanging* world. That is, in a globally integrated and developing socialist order that would be expected to function on the basis of the voluntary determinations of their societal reproductive activity by the freely associated social individuals. To postulate the *uniformity of development* under such conditions of existence would be a most absurd contradiction in terms. For uneven development in an inescapable global order, in conjunction with productive determinations consciously planned and carried out by the social individuals, is well capable of being conducive to positive advancement. Naturally, what decides the issue in this respect is the adopted modality of social metabolic reproduction.

The real concern for socialists—far from the desire of chasing an arbitrarily postulated and self-contradictory uniformity of development—is that the law of uneven development in an inescapably intertwined world should not impose its power in a *blind* and *destructive* way, as it does under the rule of capital's antagonistic second-order mediations, when it must prevail at all cost *behind the back of the individuals*. Thus the real problem for any feasible future socialist order is not a fictitious "abolition" of the law of uneven development—which is inconceivable for a variety of reasons in a globally integrated reproductive order—but the conscious cooperative way of *redressing* its potential negative impact, wherever and to whatever extent such impact might arise. After all, the vital defining characteristic of a non-antagonistic mode of social metabolic control—one operated by the social individuals through a conscious way of mediating their relations among themselves and to nature, in contrast to capital's fetishistic imperatives imposed on them behind their back—is that the members of society are capable of critically planning *and self-critically reassessing* their actions, so as to *rectify* thereby the negative consequences in the spirit of *solidarity*. In the capital system, by contrast, uneven development can run riot because the *causal* determinations must be taken for granted as unalterable. Only some of their manifestations and consequences are accessible to corrective action, provided that they are manipulable on the ground of the *eternalized causal imperatives.*

The destructiveness of the law of uneven development under the capital system—with worsening implications and results parallel to its *global encroachment* on all aspects of life, including nature, belying the absurdity of endlessly propagandized happy "globalization"—is due to a threefold rejection of *control.* This fateful rejection of effective control of the unfolding societal reproductive processes is an objective condition which always remains insuperable within the framework of capital's systemic determinations.

The threefold rejection of rationally planned and critically reassessed control in question, due to the capital system's unalterable practical premises, assumes the form of three fundamental contradictions:

1. between the *productive activity* engaged in by the working class of society and the structurally preexistent *systemic orders* hierarchically superimposed by the personifications of capital on the labor force deprived of the means of production, oriented by the necessary expansionary production targets of the established social metabolic order;

2. between *production and consumption*, in actuality firmly determined by the fetishistic dominance of production over consumption, irrespective of how much consumption may be idealized, as a wishful postulate, even by the greatest figures of classical political economy;

3. between *production and circulation,* due to positing circulation on the ground of the ultimately all-destructive absolutized imperative of unlimitable capital-expansion and accumulation at all cost, and interiorized in this ultimate unsustainability by the willing personifications of capital.

In view of these systemically incorrigible contradictions the possibility of *corrective intervention* even against the potentially most negative impact of uneven development in the natural world—not only in terms of the direct damage inflicted upon the natural environment: the necessary substratum of human existence itself, but also regarding the irresponsible exhaustion of the planet's strategically vital material resources in the longer term—cannot be seriously considered for a moment, let alone effectively instituted. The eternalization of unlimitable capital-expansion, subjectively interiorized—but structurally necessary—by capital's personifications, nullifies all rational assessment of the actually existing limits. The law of uneven development through which a weaker power can set free and maximize its dynamic inner potentialities—through which it can temporarily emerge even as the dominant "superpower" of the world—irrespective of its impact in due course on the overall power relations of the global capital system, is a significant contributory factor in this respect. Dangerously, however, this aspect of the law of uneven development carries with it also great temptations for the pursuit of the most adventurist policies for permanent world domination, as highlighted by two world wars in the twentieth century and the continuing wars of the present.[255]

Another major problem is that the systemic requirements of capital's mode of social metabolic reproduction must be always idealized, no matter how strongly they are contradicted by the unfolding, and by no means uniform, determinations and changing power relations. The *idealization* of consumption, for instance, which is supposed to justify by definition almost anything—fully in tune with the imperatives of endless capital-accumulation—must prevail not only in the period of the capital system's decline but already at the *ascending phase* of capital's historical development. And this must be so even in the case of the greatest intellectual representatives of this societal reproductive order. Thus we are peremptorily told by Adam Smith:

> *Consumption* is the *sole end and purpose of all production;* and the interest of the producer ought to be attended to only so far as it may be necessary for promoting that of the consumer. *The maxim is so perfectly self-evident that it would be absurd to attempt to prove it.*[256]

The sobering but rather uncomfortable truth of the matter, making a real mockery of Adam Smith's *"perfectly self-evident maxim,"* is that even the most wasteful practice of state legitimated production—as we experience it in the form of the *astronomical magnitudes* of material and human resources put at the disposal of the *military-industrial complex* for the purpose of its war-machinery—can ruthlessly dominate idealized consumption in the interest of *perversely destructive* (yet in terms of the universally diffused systemic fiction supposedly "positive consumptive") capital-expansion and accumulation. For in actuality, "the expansion of money, which is the objective basis or mainspring of the circulation, becomes [the capitalist's] subjective aim, and it is only in so far as the appropriation of ever more and more *wealth in the abstract* becomes the sole motive of his operations, that he functions as a capitalist, that is, as *capital personified* and endowed with consciousness and a will. *Use-values* must therefore *never* be looked upon as the real aim of the capitalist; neither must the profit on any single transaction. The *restless never ending process of profit-making* alone is what he aims at."[257]

The insuperable *uncontrollability* of the capital system by human beings is in a curious way even admitted by the great Scottish political economist when he writes that the capitalist is *"led by an invisible hand to promote an end which was no part of his intention."*[258] The mysterious supra-human "invisible hand" is supposed to benevolently accomplish what the individuals themselves are acknowledged to be quite incapable of doing. Moreover, we can find in the same work, *The Wealth of Nations,* even the most astonishing admission that the supra-human invisible hand might not be, after all, always so benevolent or capable as it is supposed to be, indicating thereby the greatest possible trouble for the future, which happens to be our present prophetically envisaged by Adam Smith. In this sense he asserted in *The Wealth of Nations*:

> The progress of the *enormous debt* which at present oppress, and will in the long run *probably ruin, all the great nations of Europe,* has been pretty uniform.[259]

However, such profoundly original visionary insights could not be carried one single step further by Adam Smith. For the required critical reflection on the likely causes and modalities of the calamitous "long run ruin of all the great nations of Europe," manifest not in the form of a biological plague but an economic one, arising from the uncontrollable debt-generating determinations of the necessarily expansionary capital system, would directly contradict another—and an even more fundamental—"perfectly self-evident maxim" professed by this great figure of the Scottish Enlightenment. Namely, that capital's mode of societal reproduction is the "natural system of perfect liberty and justice."

Ironically, the widespread idealization of the established reproductive order as a "natural system" takes care of everything, even of the problem of potentially most destructive *scarcity*, when scarcity is acknowledged as part of the overall scheme of difficult but workable solutions. For once the supreme authority of nature itself is postulated[260] by the ideological representatives of the bourgeoisie as an integral part of the universal explanatory framework and justification of the given relations and processes, even what might appear at first sight as a major contradiction can be readily spirited away.

In this sense, the liberal theory of the state was founded on the self-proclaimed contradiction between the assumed total *harmony of ends*—the ends posited to be necessarily desired by *all* individuals in virtue of their *"human nature"*—and the total *anarchy of means*. And the anarchy of means conceptualized in this way was the allegedly insurmountable *scarcity* of goods and resources that must induce the human individuals to struggle, and ultimately to destroy each other, unless they succeed in establishing over above themselves a superior authority, in the form of the *bourgeois state*, as the *permanent* restraining force of their individualistic belligerence. Thus the state was invented for the alleged purpose of "turning anarchy into harmony." That is, to dedicate itself to the universally commendable task of harmonizing the nature-determined anarchy of means with the wishfully postulated—and equally nature-determined—harmony of ends by reconciling the violent antagonism between these two *natural* factors: unalterable "human nature" and forever dominating material scarcity. And, of course, this reconciliation was asserted in the form of the absolute permanence of the state's externally imposed political power over the individuals.

To be sure, if the factors highlighted in this way were really the unalterable forces of *nature*, and consequently they could not be controlled in any other way than by an external supra-individual political authority superimposed on the individuals constituted by nature itself as antagonistically confronting and destroying one another as warring individuals, in that case the corrective state authority, in its capacity of making harmonizable societal interchanges feasible at all, would have its permanent legitimacy. In that case the Hegelian idealist version of this state ideology—according to which the Absolute Spirit's originally hidden design, establishing the state as the only feasible supersession of the contradictions of conflicting genus-individuals in "civil society," and in this capacity the state being both "Spirit's perfect embodiment"[261] and "the image and actuality of Reason"[262]—would be self-evidently true forever. There could therefore be absolutely no question of envisaging the state's "withering away."

However, the fact that the stipulated "human nature"[263] was itself a self-serving assumption, invented for the purpose of a circular plausibility of its mere assumption by virtue of what it was supposed to "explain" and justify, but that the actually existing *scarcity* was an *inherently historical* category, and consequently subject to feasible *historical change* and potential supersession, had to remain concealed in the liberal theory of the state and "civil society" under the multiple layers of circularity characteristic of such theory. For it was this kind of apologetic circularity, constituted on a merely assumed but totally unsustainable "natural" foundation, that enabled the intellectual representatives of liberalism to move at will backwards and forwards from arbitrary premises to the desired conclusions, establishing on the a priori foundations of their ideological circularity the "eternal legitimacy" of the liberal state. Thanks to such fundamental circularity between "nature-determined" individuals as well as their appropriate "civil society" and the idealized political state—which was supposed to overcome the identified contradictions without changing the existing material reproductive order itself—both capital's state formation and its societal reproductive framework could be assumed as forever given, in virtue of the justifying reciprocity and the thereby projected absolute permanence of their interrelationship.

Scarcity (or "anarchy of means") played a vital role in this scheme of things. It "rationally" justified both the irreconcilability of the warring individuals as "genus individuals"—who, after all, had to assert their self-interest in accordance with their stipulated "human nature"—and at the same time also provided the eternal reason for adopting the necessary corrective measures by the political state for making the *system as a whole insurmountable* by preventing its destructive fragmentation to pieces through individualistically pursued antagonisms. But take away from this picture *"insurmountable scarcity,"* and replace it by something akin to a sustainable availability of productive and humanly gratifying resources, often simplistically referred to as unqualified "abundance," and you witness the immediate collapse of the entire *pseudo-rational self-justificatory construct*. For in the absence of fateful scarcity the allegedly nature-determined genus-individuals have no reason to engage in the postulated "life or death struggle" among themselves in order to survive. By the same token, however, if you accept the proposition concerned with nature-determined—and therefore by definition existentially primary, insurmountable, and all-justifying—scarcity, then you are *entrapped* by a structural framework in which the parts are reciprocally/circularly positing one another, barring thereby any possibility of exit from their *vicious circle*. For in that case you must accept even the fictitious postulate of nature-determined genus individuality, on the evidence that human beings undoubtedly survived with (and despite) their conflicts all the way to the present time in a world of scarcity within the confines of their "civil society" and the state.

In this sense, if the socialist alternative intends to offer a way out of this tendentious entrapment, conceived from the standpoint of capital, it must challenge *all* of its circularly interlocking constituents. That goes not only for a viable conception of historically defined and socially changing human nature—highlighted by Marx as the *"true community of men"*[264] and the *"ensemble of social relations"*[265]—but also for the rest. That is, for the eternalized bourgeois material reproductive order of "civil society" as much as for its state formation, so as to be able to envisage at the same time a radically different mode of social metabolic reproduction. One capable of overcoming the established antagonistic *class relations,* misrepresented in the bourgeois conceptions—even the greatest—as genus determined *individual conflictuality*. For capital's antagonistic second-order mediations necessarily carry with them the perverse irrationality of *eternalized scarcity* even when its original material conditions are productively overcome in the course of historical development.

Paradoxically, despite his passionate detestation of the institutionally secured inhumanities of bourgeois "civil society" and its protective political state, Jean-Paul Sartre cannot break out from the entrapment mentioned above. For it is not enough to negate only two of the fundamental constituents of the perversely interlocking capital system. However, the difficulty is that inasmuch as Sartre wants to give an existentialist ontological underpinning to his conception of humanity's historical development even in the *Critique of Dialectical Reason,* he must present us with a most problematical account of *scarcity* in what he calls his "existentialist enclave within Marxism."

As we have seen in section 6.3 of this chapter, Sartre categorically asserted in the *Critique of Dialectical Reason* that "to say that our History is a history of men is equivalent to saying that it is born and developed within the *permanent framework* of a field of tension produced by *scarcity.*"[266] We have also seen that for Sartre this is not a question of historically surmountable social contingency but a matter of the human being's existential ontological determination according to which "*man is objectively constituted as non-human,* and this non-humanity is expressed in *praxis* by the perception of *evil as the structure of the Other.*"[267] And to make matters worse, this quasi-mythical Other is constituted not simply somewhere outside but also inextricably *in myself as the Other.* Accordingly, we are told by Sartre: "It is man, and nothing else, that I hate in the enemy, that is *in myself as Other*; and it is myself that I try to destroy in him, so as to prevent him destroying me in my own body."[268]

Sadly, given the existentialist ontological presuppositions retained by Sartre to the end, even when he calls himself a "Marxisant" thinker, it is impossible to find a viable solution to the problems of scarcity in his writings. And that goes not only for the first volume but also for the unfinished—and as we have seen above, within Sartre's conceptual framework on principle unfinishable—second volume of the *Critique of Dialectical Reason,* which was supposed to give a dialectical account of "*real history,*" in contrast to sketching the categorial outlines of "the formal structures of history" in the first.

His discussion of scarcity and its human impact in the second volume of the *Critique,* presented with the much admired Sartrean graphic intensity through the example of *boxing,* tends to be in terms of its validity grounded on characteristics of the *past* and, with regard to the present and the future, confined to *individual psychological plausibility* despite the author's claims to general validity. Sartre offers a curiously undialectical "dialectic" of the asserted "interiorization" of the contradictory predicament of the generic "scarce man." For what we receive from him in the second volume of the *Critique of Dialectical Reason* is an unsustainable explanation of the depicted relationship, timelessly projected into the future. It is extended to the thorny—and in the existing societal reproductive order absolutely fundamental—issue of the origin of *profit*, summed up in the Sartrean assertion in this way: "*Profit* springs from the *non-sufficiency of satisfaction* (worker and wage) and from *non-abundance*."[269]

The example of boxing claimed by Sartre to be representative of all struggle is not simply problematical in this respect but quite inappropriate to the characterization of historically determined and capitalistically enforced *structural antagonism*. The vital difference between the Sartrean representation of the "boxers' struggle" and the real antagonism between capital and labor (for which boxing is also supposed to stand) transpires when we read:

> This bout in which the two [boxing] beginners are embroiled, each a victim at once of his own blunders and the other's, has a reality all the more striking in that such *domination of the labourers by their labour*, by producing their future before the eyes of all (they will vegetate at the foot of the ladder or *abandon the profession*), causes it to be seen and touched as a signification and as a destiny. . . . But it is a destiny, in so far as this *domination of the boxers by boxing* is directly grasped as presence of their future misfortune. . . . The social ensemble is incarnated with the multiplicity of its conflicts in such a singular temporalization of *negative reciprocity*.
>
> . . . In a direct sense, the fight is a public incarnation of *every* [Sartre's emphasis] conflict. It relates, *without any intermediary*, to the interhuman tension produced by the *interiorization of scarcity*.[270]

However, in actuality the fundamental difference—that arises from a grave *social antagonism* concerned with two diametrically opposed social metabolic alternatives and not from what could be characterized by the "negative reciprocity of every conflict"—is that labor, as capital's hegemonic alternative, cannot "abandon" the "profession." Its situation is not a *profession* at all but a *structurally determined condition* and a necessarily subordinate *class position* in the societal reproduction process. The *particular worker*—but not labor as such—can *"abandon"* this or that "profession" (in the sense of changing a job), but due to his class situation he is at the same time forced into another one. Labor as a social class cannot do anything like "abandoning the profession."

Equally, the *"domination* of the boxers *by boxing"* is inapplicable to the condition of labor. Labor is dominated *by capital*, and not "by labor," in the Sartrean sense of the boxer being "dominated by boxing." The *domination of labor* is historically most specific, and it is not due to *"scarcity"* and *"technology"* in Sartre's sense, let alone to the "interiorization of scarcity." In fact we are concerned here with a *non-symmetrical* relationship of *structurally enforced domination and subordination,* quite unlike the symmetrical "struggle between two boxers" who agree to cooperate within a voluntarily accepted *set of rules.* In the case of labor the "rules" are *forced* upon the members of the class as a whole (through their structurally enforced domination and subordination), and the—far from voluntarily embraced—"rules" are not forced simply on individual workers but on the class as a whole. But even if the prevailing rules are not *politically* forced upon the members of the class, as they are under the conditions of slavery and feudal serfdom, they are forced upon them nevertheless, as *economically* imposed determinations. Thus the regulatory determinations in question are in the most fundamental sense objectively—materially/reproductively—prevailing rules. Moreover, a significant further qualification is also needed in this respect. For the *ultimate guarantor*—even if only the *ultimate* guarantor—of safeguarding the materially/structurally predetermined and enforced rules of commodity society is in fact the *capitalist state,* with its class-determined legal system and the corresponding law-enforcing apparatus:

> Every form of production creates its own legal relations, form of government, etc. In bringing things which are *organically* related into an *accidental* relation, into a merely reflective connection, they [the political

economists of the descending phase of capital's historical development] display their crudity and lack of conceptual understanding. All the bourgeois economists are aware of is that production can be carried on better under the modern police than e.g. on the principle of *might makes right*. They forget only that this principle is also a legal relation, and that the *right of the stronger prevails in their "constitutional republics"* as well, only in another form.[271]

Sartre needs the ahistorical *absolutization of scarcity*—in the name of *"historical* intelligibility," of all things—in order to make possible for himself the avoidance of elaborating the categories and structures of *real history*. He remains anchored to the *"formal structures of history"* in tune with the existential ontological determination given in his conception even at the time of writing the *Critique* to "evil as the structure of the Other"—and the Other also "in myself"—engaged in permanent interiorized struggle over scarcity.

Sartre's way of linking together *"scarcity," "struggle"* and *"contradiction"* in the modality of insurmountable necessity is also most problematical. For even if in the rather remote *past* we can identify the *necessary* linkage between *scarcity and struggle*, this is not so once *rational control* of the conditions at stake by the social individuals becomes feasible, in conjunction with sustainable productive advancement. Here, again, the example of the boxers is inapplicable. For we are concerned with different orders and types of *rational control:* one *formally consistent* with a voluntarily agreed set of rules devised for the purpose of an—admittedly most lucrative—sport, and the other *substantive,* from the domain of *real history*.

To be sure, in the case of the two boxers their "rationality"—i.e. their voluntary/conscious acceptance of the "rules of their profession"—is inseparable from their claimed struggle. But their "struggle" is not a real struggle at all in the sense of the "life or death struggle" over insurmountable scarcity constantly called by that name by Sartre himself. Nor is it even slightly comparable, in its essential character, to the *antagonistic confrontation*—a very *real historic struggle* over the contested outcome of the *structurally determined antagonism* between capital and labor over their incompatible *hegemonic historical alternatives*. Only a dubious *formal analogy* can be drawn between such fundamentally different forms of struggle, as the structural antagonism between capital and labor in real history and the *consensual ritual* of the two boxers even when they fight over a purse of a hundred million dollars.

Sartre can offer us in the case of the two boxers a *psychologically* plausible picture. Thus he is at his most eloquent when he asserts that "what is certain is that, in every brawl, the deep source is always *scarcity* . . . the translation of human violence as *interiorized scarcity*."[272] And he proceeds with his graphic characterization of the meaning of the boxing match in the same vein by saying:

> The two boxers gather within themselves, and re-exteriorize by the punches they swap, the ensemble of extensions and open or masked struggles that characterize the regime under which we live—and have made us violent even in the least of our desires, even in the gentlest of our caresses. But at the same time, this violence is approved in them.[273]

In this way the depicted particular boxing contest can be generalized by Sartre as representative of all human violence. This is how it appears in the *Critique*:

> *Every* boxing match incarnates the *whole* of boxing as an *incarnation of all fundamental violence*. . . . An *act* of violence is always *all* of violence, because it is a *re-exteriorization* of interiorized scarcity.[274]

Thus a *direct line* is drawn between the psychologically plausible depiction of two *individuals* in a boxing match and the *general conditions* of human violence said to correspond to the *re-exteriorization* of *interiorized scarcity*. Accordingly, in the Sartrean picture the psychological plausibility of the boxing individuals' *motivations,* and its projection ("without any intermediary," as he puts it elsewhere) as the claimed identity between the *particular act* of violence and the *general condition* of necessarily interiorized—as well as violently re-exteriorized—scarcity takes the place of what should be made socially/historically *determinate* and in that sense plausible. But that could only be done in the categorial framework of *real history*, where scarcity occupies its specific, but not absolutizable existential ontological place.

The problem of *abundance* often appears in some form counterposed to scarcity. Sometimes this is done for the purpose of a priori dismissing the possibility of overcoming scarcity any time in the, no matter how distant, future because it is said to be totally unrealistic to envisage the stable institution of abundance in human society in view of the insuperably conflictual determinations of "human nature." No further comments are needed in relation to this position. On other occasions, however, the possibility of overcoming scarcity by abundance is not denied on principle, but nonetheless it is ruled out for the foreseeable time ahead of us on the ground that it would require some productively most advanced *technological* conditions that might perhaps materialize in the distant future. And there is also a third, positively assertive position about the emerging abundance that states "the *conquest of scarcity* is now not only foreseeable but actually foreseen."[275]

Marcuse's position was much the same as the views just quoted from an essay by the prominent Canadian Marxist thinker, C. B. Macpherson. Marcuse insisted that the "utopian possibilities" which he advocated were "inherent in the *technical* and *technological forces* of advanced capitalism" on the basis of which one could "terminate poverty and *scarcity* within a very foreseeable future."[276] He kept on repeating that *"technical progress* has reached a stage in which reality no longer need be defined by the debilitating competition for social survival and advancement. The more these *technical capacities* outgrow the framework of exploitation within which they continue to be confined and abused, the more *they propel* the drives and aspirations of men to a point at which the *necessities of life* cease to demand the aggressive performance of 'earning a living,' and the 'non-necessary' becomes a vital need."[277] And in the same work, written by Marcuse well before sinking into deep pessimism, he postulated a "biological foundation" to revolutionary change, saying that such a foundation

> would have the chance of turning quantitative *technical progress* into qualitatively different ways of life—precisely because it would be a revolution occurring at a high level of material and intellectual development, one which would enable man *to conquer scarcity and poverty*. If this idea of a radical transformation is to be more than idle speculation, it must have an

objective foundation in the production process of *advanced industrial society,* in its *technical capabilities* and their use. For freedom indeed depends largely on *technical progress,* on the advancement of science.[278]

This generously well-meaning unreality was written and published by Marcuse more than forty years ago, and we have seen absolutely nothing pointing in the direction of its realization. On the contrary, we have witnessed recently a devastating crisis of "advanced industrial society," with *food riots* admitted by one of the ideological pillars of the established order—*The Economist*—to have taken place in no less than thirty-five countries, despite all of the significant *technical progress* undoubtedly accomplished in the past four decades. Not even the slightest attempt has been made for the enduring "conquest of scarcity."

The great weakness of the Marcuse-type projections, shared by C. B. Macpherson and many others, is that the positive results regarding the "actually foreseen conquest of scarcity" are expected to arise from the "propelling force" of technical/technological progress and productive advancement. And that could not happen even in a thousand years, not to mention forty or even a hundred. For technology is not an "independent variable." It is deeply embedded in the most fundamental social determinations, despite all mystification to the contrary,[279] as we have seen above on several occasions.

No one can doubt that the sympathy of the people who in this way anticipate the conquest of scarcity is on the side of the "wretched of the earth who fight the affluent monster."[280] But their moral discourse cannot even touch the fundamental objective determinations that so successfully perpetuate the denounced plight of the exploited and oppressed, let alone effectively alter them. To expect from productive advancement, arising from "technical progress" in "advanced industrial society," to move humanity in the direction of eliminating scarcity is to ask for the impossible. The same kind of impossibility as expecting that the capitalist should set a limit to his appetite for profit on the ground that he has enough profit already. For the society Marcuse and others talk about is not "advanced industrial" but only *capitalistically advanced*—and for humanity itself suicidally dangerous—society. It cannot take a single step in the direction of conquering scarcity for as long as it remains under the rule of capital, irrespective of its growing "technical capabilities" and the corresponding degree of improvement in productivity in the future. For two important reasons.

First, because even the greatest technically secured productive advancement can be—and under the conditions now prevailing in our society actually *is* and *must be—dissipated* through profitable *waste* and the channels of *destructive production,* including the state-legitimated fraudulence of the *military/industrial complex,* as we have seen before. And second—what happens to be more fundamental here—because of the objective character of the system of capital-accumulation. We should not forget that *"capital personified* and endowed with consciousness and a will" *cannot be* interested in the conquest of scarcity, and in the corresponding equitable distribution of wealth, for the simple reason that *"use-values* must *never* be looked upon as the real aim of the capitalist. . . . The *restless never-ending process of profit-making* alone is what he aims at."[281] And in that respect, which is inseparable from the absolute imperative of endless capital-expansion and accumulation, the permanent structural impediment is that *capital always is*—and, this cannot be stressed strongly enough, it *always must remain,* as a matter of inner systemic determination—insuperably *scarce,* even when under certain conditions it is contradictorily *overproduced.*[282]

Sartre is, of course, not in the least concerned with the conquest of scarcity and its sustainable replacement by productively generalized abundance. He is firmly negative in that respect, describing the "man of scarcity" as the man who imposes his will and expropriates abundance to himself.[283] The existential ontological orientation and coloring of Sartre's characterization of the insuperable conflictual relationship between myself and my adversaries is retained to the very end of the *Critique of Dialectical Reason* when he writes that "in the field of scarcity an increase in the number or power of my neighbours has the result of increasing the precariousness of my existence. For that power seeks both to produce more (a ceiling though) and to eliminate me. My alteration is suffered, and is what incarnates the transformation in me."[284]

However, Sartre's way of dealing with the problem of scarcity and abundance—by making scarcity the existential foundation *of history,* as its "permanent framework produced by scarcity," as well as of *historical intelligibility,* rather than a (no matter how important) contingent factor *in history,* capable of being overcome under altered conditions at some point in time—does not solve the very real historical challenge facing us. In truth, some elementary qualifications are required for a proper characterization of *abundance* that can be legitimately posited in the context of overcoming the historical *domination of scarcity.* For at a relatively early stage of humanity's historical development the "naturally necessary needs"—which were for our distant ancestors fully in tune with the overwhelming material domination of scarcity—are actually superseded by a much more complex, historically created, set of needs, as we have seen it discussed earlier. To be sure, the productive advancement in question does not represent the end of this burdensome story but, nonetheless, it means a significant move in the direction of conquering the original domination of human life by scarcity. In this sense:

> *Luxury* is the opposite of *naturally necessary.* Necessary needs are those of the individual himself *reduced to a natural subject.* The development of industry *suspends this natural necessity* as well as this former luxury— in bourgeois society, it is true, it does so only in *antithetical form,* in that it itself only posits another specific social standard as necessary, opposite luxury.[285]

Accordingly, consigning scarcity to the past is a long-drawn-out but, despite all obstacles and contradictions, an ongoing historical process. However, precisely because of the *antithetical form* in which this historical development must be carried on in bourgeois society, the real question for the future is not the utopian institution of unqualified "abundance" but the *rational control* of the process of productive advancement by the social individuals, feasible only in a socialist reproductive order. Otherwise the historically no longer justifiable domination of scarcity—in the form of perversely wasteful but profitable *destructive production* in a variety of its capitalistically feasible forms—remains with us indefinitely. In the *absence* of the required *rational self-determination on a societal scale*—whose absence under the present conditions happens to be not a fateful existential ontological determination but a question of historically created and historically superable impediment—even the greatest (abstractly postulated) *"abundance"* would be utterly powerless and futile as an attempt to overcome the domination of scarcity.

Thus we are concerned in this respect with a *historically determinate*—but not permanently *history-determining*—social force and impediment to social emancipation that dominated human life for far too long. It is that structural/systemic impediment that must be radically superseded through labor's hegemonic alternative to capital's established mode of social metabolic control according to the Marxian conception of the "new historic form."

6.6 The Dialectical Nature of Historical Change and Advancement

Historical consciousness, as we have seen it discussed before,[286] is concerned with the perception of change not simply as a lapse of time, but as a movement with a *cumulative* character. This implies some kind of *development*—like, for instance, the emergence of the bourgeois societal reproductive order in contrast to the feudal system—that may be legitimately described in a substantive and for the future important sense as *more advanced* than what preceded it.

Naturally, this means for the relevant philosophical theories also a quest for identifying the *historical agency or subject* of their field of investigation. That subject was defined in the most varied historical conceptions as capable of actively intervening—to be sure, under the objectively *given* circumstances—in societal transformation for the purpose of making a significant impact on the existing state of affairs and through them, in a more comprehensive and lasting way, on the unfolding developments in general.

The historical circumstances to be modified were, and are, of course, always *particular*. But precisely because they are part of an *ongoing process* of transformation (or resistance to it), the genuine historical theories, in contrast to anecdotal accounts and chronicles, must attempt to grasp the complex dialectical relationship between *particularity* and *universality*. For historical events and developments are truly intelligible only if they are elucidated in terms of their broader *"determining*/determined" character. That is to say, if they are depicted in terms that include the significant modifying impact made by the active individual or collective subject on the conditions encountered at the time of entering the historical stage. In this dialectical sense the objectively "determined/determining/determinant" conditions of cumulative change—both as originally found and as significantly modified by the historical subject in a given situation—necessarily transcend in a *transhistorical* direction the limited historical specificity of the events and forces in question.

As we know, the objective universalizing tendency of capital, tending toward an ultimate global integration of its social metabolic order, enabled modern philosophers to interpret the problems of historical change in a very different way from those we could find in ancient Greece and in the Middle Ages. In this sense the eighteenth century, through the work of Vico, Montesquieu, Rousseau, Diderot, Lessing, Kant, Herder, and Goethe, made a giant step in the direction of a genuine historical explanation, reaching its peak in the first third of the nineteenth century in Hegel's monumental philosophical synthesis that conceptualized the world from capital's vantage point.

To the extent to which it was compatible with his social standpoint, Hegel offered an account of historical events and transformations in terms of the underlying *necessities* of an unfolding *world history* and its realization of the idea of freedom, even if he could not conceptualize historical development as *irrepressibly open*. For the ideological determinants of his position stipulated for Hegel the necessity of reconciliation with the "rational actuality" of the present, and thereby he ended up with an arbitrary *closure* of the historical dynamics in the framework of capitalist "civil society" and its idealized state formation. Thus history could be treated as open and objectively unfolding even by Hegel only up to the point in time when it reached the established societal reproductive order, but its shutters had to be pulled down in a totally unhistorical way toward a radically different future.

By the middle of the nineteenth century the dominant mood in bourgeois historical writings was extreme skepticism, which became worse as time went by. Not surprisingly, therefore, dark pessimism tended to prevail in historical conceptions in the twentieth century.[287] This pessimism was primarily due to the more or less explicit recognition and admission by the thinkers concerned that the historical subject with which they identified themselves, capital and its economic personifications, had become most problematical (to put it mildly) as the historically viable controller of the unfolding process, due to the grave antagonisms and the deepening crises of their system.

It is important to underline in this context that one of Giambattista Vico's greatest philosophical insights was spelled out in relation to the question of "making history." At the time of writing his *New Science*[288] Vico expressed his astonishment about the fact that in the past "the philosophers should have bent all their energies to the study of the world of *nature*, which, since God made it, He alone knows; and that they should have neglected the study of the world of nations, or *civil world*, which, since *men had made it*, men could come to *know*."[289] In this way the vital category of "making history" and making the *knowable* "civil world" (or "civil society") acquired its seminal importance in historical conceptions. For Vico realized very clearly that the sense and the *raison d'être* of investigating in philosophy the nature of the historical processes was to be able to *actively participate* in the ongoing transformations, in order to gain a better control over the desired—as well as over the unwanted and to be corrected—aspects of the changes taking place in the "civil world." And of course Vico also realized that the way of *making history* posited by him was unthinkable without *knowing*—that is, without properly understanding—what was at stake in the relevant field of temporal changes and historical transformations.

Naturally, Vico's *"New Science"* of understanding and explaining historical development shared with *epistemology* the interest in combining knowledge with practical involvement. For the *raison d'être* of the philosophical enterprise of epistemology—that is, the theory of knowledge—was to gain an insight into, and a growing control over, the production and advancement of knowledge itself, in order to acquire some mastery over the areas in which the acquisition of better knowledge mattered. Moreover, also moral philosophy was always inseparable from a real concern with explaining and affecting the moral agent's conduct, whether in terms of the Kantian "intelligible world" and its necessary universalization of the personal maxims and choices of the individuals, by analogy with the form of the natural law as explained in the *Critique of Practical*

Reason, or in a more down-to-earth, even directly utilitarian, form. What else could there be then the point of historical investigation if not gaining a better insight into the nature of the historical process for a meaningful participation in the unfolding developments?

It was in this sense by no means accidental that the "New Science" of historical investigation—grounding the idea of *making history* on humanity's firmly asserted *ability to know*[290] the processes involved—was pushed into the forefront of philosophical attention in the ascending phase of capital's epochal development. Nor could it be considered accidental that the descending phase of the capital system carried with it the onset of extreme skepticism and the all-pervasive dominance of historical pessimism in the writings of capital's ideological personifications. True to form, therefore, Vico's great insights had to be totally undone not simply for the purpose of rejecting the views formulated by this great Italian philosopher and pathbreaker of historical interpretation but above all in the interest of "refuting Marx" and *his*—also in a direct practical sense most challenging—concern with making history in the present and in the future. Thus Hannah Arendt tried to demolish Vico's fundamental distinction between making history and making nature—at times doing this in the most absurd way, by claiming that in the thermonuclear processes human beings are "making nature" in Vico's sense of "making history"[291]—while her real ideological target was Marx, dismissed with the grotesque jibe according to which "in the classless society the best mankind can do with history is to forget the whole unhappy affair, whose only purpose was to abolish itself."[292] Accordingly, in this kind of extreme skeptical and pessimistic vision the idea of actively intervening in the historical transformatory process, and humanity's ability to acquire the knowledge needed for that purpose, had to be tied and discarded together, with a view to exclude thereby the feasibility of any radical social change.

Despite all such skepticism, actual trends of development indicate *positive potentialities* for the future, if kept in their proper historical perspective, notwithstanding the dangers for the very survival of humanity evidenced in our time. For, as stressed before, quite unlike cosmic time, which is irreversible, considered from a human perspective, the historical time of humanity is very different on account of the radically new order of necessity—self-imposed but also potentially "vanishing historical necessity"—introduced by human beings into the societal order founded on the primary determinations of nature.

In this sense, human historical time is subject to *reversals* not only in view of the periodic relapses and stagnations or paralyses of development seen in the course of history but even in its ultimate terms of reference, concerning the active human subject's exercise of its power in the course of historical transformations. Thus, there could not be a more ironical confirmation of the *active power* of the historical subject or agency than to note with apprehension its ability, and also its steps now undeniably taken, toward destroying itself through the self-imposed antagonistic modality of social metabolic reproduction—the capital system in its deepening structural crisis in our time. And yet, this mode of societal control is supposed to be the neoliberally postulated predicament and ultimate destiny of humanity to which, as they arrogantly say, "there can be no alternative," disregarding the fateful negativity associated with capital's impact both on nature and in the field of ever more destructive production, as well as on the plane of ceaseless military devastation.

However, precisely because the potentially "vanishing historical necessity" is nothing like a fatality of nature, a consciously pursued active human intervention against the destructive forces of capital's antagonistic second-order mediations is capable of averting the identifiable dangers. For what is historically created and enforced is also amenable to corrective historical change. Indeed, as a matter of countervailing determinations, actual trends of historical development reveal not only the undeniable dangers but also a socially meaningful *advancement* in some important fields and relations.

It goes without saying that the positive trends here referred to do not indicate some homogeneous linear "progress," let alone a journey toward a "Messianic end-station," as it is frequently (and falsely) insinuated by Marx's adversaries. Positive potentialities must be actively converted— and not in the naïve sense of "done once and for all" but constantly reproduced and secured as well—into sustainable realities. This is required even under the most favorable circumstances, no matter how far we may glance ahead in time in the direction of what Marx calls "real history," in contrast to the structural limitations of "prehistory." For the primary consideration that legitimately contrasts the meaningful notion of "real history" with "prehistory" is the posited ability of the human beings to extricate themselves from the structural determinations which compel them under the now prevailing circumstances to order their life activities on the basis of rules and relationships that "work behind the back of the individuals," as discussed before. And the anticipated radically different way of regulating their life by the social individuals in "real history" can only succeed in the form of an *ongoing process*. The necessary change on that score is feasible by overcoming, in a perfectly tangible sense, capital's fetishistic *exchange relationship*, together with the illusions imposed by the individuals themselves, "behind their own back," on *all* of the individuals partaking in the system of commodity exchange.

In this regard we can also see two relevant aspects of historical development that prevails as real *advancement* in comparison to the earlier states of affairs. First, because the capital system's generalized exchange relationship as such, despite its contradictions and structural antagonisms, represents a fundamental *productive accomplishment* in contrast to the major constraints of the previous, far less productive, societal reproductive orders. And second, because the establishment and consolidation of this more advanced mode of economic control simultaneously brings to the fore some historically specific conditions and positive attainments that by their very nature point well beyond the inherent structural limitations of societal reproduction under the rule of capital. Indeed, they point toward a socially more advanced future.

Naturally, the conditions and attainments in question—like the not only juridical but also socioeconomic and political notion of personality, the much more generally shared proprietorship, freedom, and equality, considered in some by no means negligible sense, etc.—make their first appearance in capital's productive and societal reproductive order in a most *abstract* and *formalized* way. This is so because they must remain apologetically divorced from their actually realizable, but by capital denied, *substantive* dimension, so as to be readily *containable* within the commodity system's structurally constraining integument. The abstract formalism of the posited *"Rights of Man"* is a graphic manifestation of this characteristic limitation.

Nevertheless, the fact *is* and *remains* that the conditions we talk about have actually made their historic appearance in capital's reproductive order; and they did so not out of *individual caprice* or *religious inspiration*—as the latter is mystifyingly postulated by Max Weber's "Protestant Spirit of capitalism," in the German thinker's habitual *reversal* of the actual material and cultural orders of determination—but as a result of clearly identifiable *social and historical necessities*. For the great dynamism of capital's historical advancement, embodied in the massive expansionary potential of generalized commodity production, was totally unthinkable without simultaneously setting into motion the conditions and paradoxical attainments which at some point in time—again, under objectively unfolding conditions and antagonisms—had to *turn against* the structurally constraining capitalist integument itself.

Moreover, the necessarily *fetishistic* form that even the greatest "civilizing achievements"[293] of capital's historically far more advanced reproductive order had to assume, due to the ultimately explosive inner antagonisms of the incorrigibly exploitative productive system itself, made it possible to conceptualize and *highlight the irreconcilable contradiction* between the professed *eternalizing claims* and the *alienating and dehumanizing reality* of this historically specific way of ordering societal reproduction and human conduct.

Understandably, this way of ordering human conduct was unavoidable in a system that had to assert itself fetishistically "behind the back of the individuals" in the interest of a *uniquely*—and in the end also *destructively—expansion-oriented* mode of production, driven by the absolute but *blind imperative* of capital-accumulation whose nature and real motivating force had to be concealed, as a necessary mystification, even from capital's pretendedly "sovereign decision making" personifications. At the same time, however, the fact that the most advanced productive system in all history could prevail over against a historically feasible alternative human design only through the fetishistic transfiguration of the potentially creative relationships—which *capital itself had brought to the fore*—carried with it some, by capital insuperable, complications and contradictions. For on the one hand, the capital system was responsible for an *immense social development* and the never undoable[294] effective *socialization of production*, with its relentless tendency toward the *global* scale for its full realization. On the other hand, however, capital was also responsible for activating the simultaneous *direct contradiction* of this great historic accomplishment, due to the structurally prejudged and entrenched[295] *private expropriation and appropriation* of the productive means and the commodified products alienated from living labor. This represented a contradiction of such magnitude and intensity, in its necessary insertion—*as it had to be inserted*, both because of the hierarchically operated and structurally secured *material* purposes of generalized commodity production and on account of their social and political *legitimation* as well as *ideological rationalization*—into the formally "free and equitable" exchange relationship between capital and labor, that not even the thickest layers of commodity fetishism could conceal it indefinitely.

Accordingly, the unfolding socioeconomic development as historical advancement—which is always articulated, on the ground of objective dialectical determinations, in the form of productive or destructive *alternatives*, in contrast to the simplistic positivity of wishful thinking—made it possible to conceptualize and highlight in due course not only the long-term untenability of the ever more prominent destructive contradictions of the capital system but also the *viable historical alternative* implicit in the removal of the fetishistic capital relation itself. Consequently, the *demystification* of capital's incurable fetishism, with its ruthless imposition of the incorrigible systemic imperatives that had to (and for as long as this system survives must continue to) work behind the back of the individuals, could also provide the *strategic program* for an *emancipatory transformation*. That was the obverse side of the work of demonstrating the untenability of capital's fetishism for the future, representing in its necessary strategic orientation an important positive historical advancement.

The critical demystification of capital's all-pervasive fetishism could appear on the historical agenda only at a determinate point in time, at the onset of the capital system's descending phase of development. Under such circumstances the advocated emancipatory transformation could be envisaged not as an abstract moral postulate, however noble in intent, which used to characterize the condemnation of capital's dehumanizing power for a very long time,[296] but as a practically articulated radical socialist conception, with its *objective leverage* deeply rooted—both as the negation of the established mode of control and as its positive societal reproductive alternative—in the fundamental structural determinations of the existing order. And that makes a major difference. For this *objective grounding* of a practically viable alternative societal reproductive order in capital's *necessarily aborted* positive potentialities, constituting thus an *integral part* of the *overall historical advancement*, is an important condition of a successful outcome.

Historical change amounting to significant *advancement*[297] is identifiable in the course of the last few centuries in our world of "accelerating history." It can be denied only by the most retrograde vested interests, whether they are called "neoliberal" or "neoconservative." Moreover, looking more closely at the historical trends in question it also transpires that their significance is enhanced when considered in conjunction with one another, rather than separately. And that is always a methodologically important aspect of the dialectical intelligibility and evaluation of historical development. For "potentially vanishing historical necessity" can assert its objective and subjective determinations only in the form of a variety of necessarily *interacting* forces and conditions, in relation to the always given *structural setting* to which it must adjust itself in an active way, altering thereby at the same time the *overall configuration* of the unfolding historical potentialities and realities.

In this sense, we can see historical development anticipating—or already embodying—real advancement in a variety of important relations. In some cases the full extent of the realization of their positive side is, of course, more dependent on conscious intervention in the future than in some others. However, in all cases referred to here the positive potential, representing major advancement in comparison to the more distant past, is clearly in evidence.

The immense, and without an all-engulfing catastrophe irreversible, *socialization of production* accomplished under the rule of capital, as a far-reaching historic advancement, has been mentioned already. To be sure, a high price had to be paid for it through the universal commodification of all human relations and the fetishistic encroachment of capital's productive development over everything, with the dehumanizing impact of the alienation of societal reproductive control from the people, directly affecting and endangering even the most fundamental relationship of the individuals to nature. However, even this heavy price cannot invalidate the historic accomplishment in question. For whereas the vital socialization of production itself is historically irreversible, its alienating and antagonistic mode of exploitative operation can be overcome and consigned to the past. As a major historic attainment and advancement, the socialization of production can be—and has to be—built upon, and also extended in an appropriate way in a socialist future. Indeed, there can be no other productively viable ground and starting point in that respect, in view of the crucial fact that in any viable future order there can be only a greater socialization of production and not less of it.

The historically developed socialization of production, with all its most diverse linkages in the overall complex of the capital system, cannot be fictitiously wound back under some wishfully postulated and at times quixotically yet tellingly promoted slogan like "small is beautiful." Not even when in the midst of a massive global economic crisis the voice of apologetic wisdom is induced to declare that the dominant financial institutions are now "too big to fail," while in actuality the parasitism and fraudulence in the relevant economic sector as a whole displays its grave failures. The issues at stake call for real alternative solutions, through the supersession of the explosive antagonisms of the irrepressibly globalizing capital system, and not for manipulative conjuring tricks wishfully propounded for putting back the genie into the bottle. The objective tendency toward the realization of the positive potentialities of a fully socialized productive and societal reproductive system on the global scale implies the need for the most comprehensive rational coordination of the complex interchanges, feasible only within a socialist corrective framework. But there is no need for vacuous postulates to be invented for the imaginary ground on which such transformation can proceed. The long historical process of development and productive advancement in the field, notwithstanding its major contradictions, has provided the necessary point of departure. And that point of departure—represented by the given socialization of production—happens to be not only *capable* of corrective extension under the conditions of the unfolding and on the economic plane integrative global interchanges but also *necessary* for it, irrespective of its contradictions.

Closely linked to the domain highlighted by the immense and still growing socialization of production we find another vital historical advancement. This is clearly visible in the development of the productivity of labor itself and in the corresponding potentially great increase of the social individuals' most rewarding *free time,* emerging on a scale simply incommensurable with anything visible in previous modalities of societal reproduction. The full realization of this tangible positive potentiality is, of course, very much a challenge for a historically secured socialist future. Nevertheless, we can identify also in this respect a historically accomplished fundamental difference already. For thanks to the productive advancement in question the basic conditions of societal reproduction have been *qualitatively* modified. They have been shifted away from the *tyranny of necessary labor* trough the appearance of *disposable time* on humanity's practically reachable historical horizon, turning thereby the exploitation of necessary labor time into a long-term totally untenable *historical anachronism.*

Naturally, capital must remain "deaf and blind" to the true significance of these changes, because it must operate on the exploitable basis of necessary labor time.[298] But that circumstance cannot undo the accomplished historical advancement itself. It can only put into relief the growing irrationality of the capital system. For the regulation of societal reproduction on the basis of creatively usable *disposable time*, as opposed to the continued exploitation of historically outdated necessary labor time, is not an abstract desideratum but an irrepressible objective historical trend and a very real possibility under the existing circumstances. Its character is unmistakably defined as representing a *practicable* productive alternative that is fully harmonizable with the need for human gratification. Disposable time exists already in a form necessarily ignored and sidelined by capital. However, as an obvious rational and productively superior alternative to the commodified wage labor system, disposable time can be set free through the conscious design of the social individuals, *in their own interest*, in the planned process of productive development and emancipatory transformation.

The historically emerging and potentially growing disposable time, as the qualitatively different orientation of societal reproduction, is important also in another respect. For it corresponds to the only feasible and justifiable way in which labor—as humanly gratifying activity—can assume its position as the universally valid operative principle embracing and regulating the societal interchanges of every single individual. Significantly, also in that regard, only a historically emerging and practically sustainable advancement could transform what appeared at first as a moral ideal into an effectively adoptable and socially much more progressive productive practice.

In fact the enlightened advocacy of making labor the general ordering principle of society goes back very far in history. Paracelsus, a great intellectual of the sixteenth century, underlined already then the human worth and the fulfilling power of work, insisting at the same time that the wealth of the "idle rich" should be confiscated so that they should be compelled to work.[299] However, there were two prohibitive impediments to making human labor the fully justifiable regulating principle in the life process of all individuals.

First, the soulless *drudgery* of the work practices to which by far the greatest part of humanity had to be subjected in the interest of expansion-oriented societal reproduction and capital accumulation.

And second, the structurally secured and safeguarded exploitative *class system* that enabled the "idle rich" of Paracelsus: the personifications of capital in more precise terms, to exempt themselves from the heavy burden of such drudgery.

Naturally, in the course of its expansionary drive capital instituted massive advancement in commodity production, as well as an incomparably higher labor productivity than what we could find under previous modalities of societal reproduction. Potentially this represented an important step in the direction of alleviating the drudgery of labor practices. Since, however, this productive advancement had to remain strictly containable within the confines of the second impediment, the hierarchical structural domination of labor by capital, the advancement could only be potential, even if measuring labor productivity in terms of capital expansion and accumulation the achievement appears to be absolutely gigantic. Yet the drudgery of labor had to remain virtually undiminished, notwithstanding the great achievements of modern science and technology for improving the instruments of production. This is because the most vital aspect of humanly gratifying productive activity—namely the autonomously exercised *decision-making functions* of the working individuals—is, and must always be, structurally divorced from labor under the rule of capital.

Without radically altering that structural subordination and alienation, there can be no question of realizing the immense potentialities of *disposable time* in the domain of labor productivity and human fulfillment. For disposable time makes no sense whatsoever unless the producing social individuals themselves can *freely dispose* over the allocation and the creative exercise of *their own disposable time*. However, the structural determinations of capital make that impossible in view of the fact that capital is nothing if not the total expropriation of the power of decision making to itself. Thus even the technologically/instrumentally feasible improvement of labor productivity must be confined well within the limiting framework absolutely dictated by the preservation of capital's exclusive decision making powers in conformity to the incorrigible systemic imperatives. Consequently, disposable time must be set free from *both* of the earlier mentioned structural impediments that *together* directly affect the power of decision-making. No amount of technological advancement on its own could do that.

Due to the undeniable historical advancement achieved through the tangible emergence and growth of disposable time as the legitimate and viable general ordering principle of social development—advocated for centuries—the drudgery of labor practices can be permanently consigned to the past. This is now well within our reach, even if it is actively negated by the capital system's structural necessities. Thus, also in this respect, the continued and blindly self-serving—but even in terms of the customarily idealized capitalist objective of ever-improved productivity self-contradictory—negation of the historical advancement in question by capital can only underline the increasing historical anachronism of the established societal reproductive order.

Perhaps the most paradoxical evidence of historical advancement under capital's social order is provided by the role assigned to, and effectively fulfilled by, *equality and freedom*.

What makes this development in some ways unique is that, quite unlike the attitude toward ignoring, sidelining, and even actively negating the great objective potentiality of disposable time, the personifications of capital do not try to deny the role of equality and freedom in their system. On the contrary, they make a virtue of it. Naturally, they do that to a large extent (but far from entirely) for the purposes of legitimating and ideologically rationalizing the allegedly insuperable—and therefore "rightfully" *eternalizable*—character of capital's mode of production and distribution as "the natural system of perfect liberty and justice," in Adam Smith's earlier quoted memorable words. And the thinkers who conceptualized the world from the vantage point of capital could identify themselves without any difficulty and reservation with the role fulfilled by equality and freedom in their social order, in view of the *formal* character of both in the capital system, as we have seen before.

The *substantive* determination of equality and freedom would be, of course, a very different matter. For in that way neither of the two could be *contained* within the structurally entrenched *iniquitous* framework in which the *decision-making functions* of societal reproduction must be, in a categorical and most authoritarian sense, expropriated by capital from the overwhelming majority—the laboring classes—of the people who are condemned by economic compulsion to their hierarchically subordinate position in society.

Nevertheless, the issue itself is of a very great importance. It represents a real historic advancement despite its limitations. For previous modalities of social metabolic reproduction had no interest in, nor any space for, the admission of equality and freedom into their domain. Not even in the *formally limited sense* in which they actually fulfill their meaningful role under the rule of capital. This is excluded because even the formally limited sense in which equality and freedom must function in the capital system is radically incompatible with the fundamental structural determinations of the earlier forms and modalities of social metabolic control. The important defining characteristic in this respect is that even if equality and freedom under the societal reproductive conditions ruled by the overall imperative of capital accumulation are—and must remain—*formally limited*, the actually exercisable powers in question are extended in that limited sense to every member of society. For only the *general extension* of the conditions inseparable from equality and freedom—that is, the all-round recognized proprietorship of, and the free disposability over, the commodities possessed by all individuals, even if such "rightful property ownership" is confined to no more than their saleable labor power—makes feasible the establishment and the dynamic operation of *generalized commodity production and exchange*.

This formally limited but for generalized commodity production necessary extension of equality and freedom to all individuals, representing a genuine historical advancement compared to the past, is also undoable without catastrophic consequences.[300] But decidedly not unchangeable. Indeed, the unavoidable challenge for the future is to make them *substantive* in a positive sense. For without rendering in that way substantive the formally articulated and limited determinations of equality and freedom on which capital's reproductive order depends not simply for its ideological legitimation but altogether for its continued practical operation and expansion, the destructiveness of capital's antagonistic second-order mediations cannot be overcome. But that kind of substantive transformatory intervention in the fundamental structural determinations of the established productive and distributive system would require a *qualitative change* in the modality of social metabolic reproduction in all domains, including humanity's vital relationship to nature.

Considering the major trends of historical change and advancement in capital's epoch it is important to highlight their dialectical interconnections and the *combined* positive potentialities arising from those dialectical interconnections. In this way we can identify a significant expansionary movement toward a relevant transformation also in other respects. Thus we can clearly perceive in modern history an irreversible trend of development from the limited *local and partial* toward the all-embracing *global and universalizable*. The trend of globalization, generally acknowledged and even idealized in our time, would be impossible without it. And the underlying changes are by no means simply formal but major objective transformations involving deeply rooted and far-reaching material determinations, together with the corresponding regulatory requirements also on the plane of internal and interstate relations. This is why the pervasive reality of *imperialism*, and the unavoidable change in its power relations in the twentieth and twenty-first century, is not intelligible at all without the *monopolistic* trends of economic development with which political and military imperialism is combined.

Inevitably, therefore, in conjunction with these constantly redefined interrelationships the tendential move from the *formal* toward the *substantive* enters the historical picture in a most significant way. As a result, the earlier discussed formal determinations of equality and freedom in capital's societal reproductive order become extremely problematical. They are in fact directly challenged from two—diametrically opposed—directions.

The *negative substantive assault* on the formally universalized determinations of equality and freedom, and on their extension to all individuals under the normality of capital's reproductive practices, assumes the
form of the most retrograde and authoritarian attempts to forcibly redefine the *internal* as well as the *international* relation of forces; internally
against labor, of course, and internationally with regard to the relative
position of the most powerful states in the interest of securing and
enhancing the domination of one of the antagonistically competing rival
states, or of a temporarily allied group of them, in the overall system of
monopolistic imperialism. The attempt by Hitler's Nazi Germany and its
allies to achieve global domination at the price of unleashing the Second
World War is a prominent historical example aimed at redefining in a
most retrograde substantive way the formal determinations of capitalist
equality and freedom without altering the fundamental structural determinations of the capital system itself.

In the domain of state and interstate relations the usually idealized formation of the *liberal state* is what corresponds to capital's for a long time sustainable material reproductive order. It is in this respect highly revealing that
today—when the Nazi form of violently redefining the internal and international power relations among the dominant states is no longer practicable for
a variety of reasons, including the catastrophic implications of a new global
war—the most prominent current modality of the relentless negative substantive assault on the role fulfilled by formally limited equality and freedom
in the capital system is undertaken by the aggressive *neoliberal* ventures and
war adventures, indistinguishable from neoconservative designs. These ventures now include the *crass violations* of even some of the most elementary
requirements of regulating the internal and interstate relations of the traditional *liberal state*. And the structural crisis of the capital system in its
entirety, asserting itself now for more than four decades, can only aggravate
these problems. Moreover, the painfully obvious implosion of the *social democratic* movement not only in Europe but worldwide, and the transformation
of its parliamentary parties into center-right and pronounced right-wing
neoliberal entities that openly champion—both in and out of government—
the imperatives of the established order, is part of the same trend of development from the formal to the substantive, actively partaking in the retrograde redefinition of capital's regulatory framework.[301]

Understandably, the much needed *positive* side of the substantive critique of capital's traditional way of confining equality and freedom to the formal determinations of societal reproduction is represented by the socialist historical alternative. The strategic articulation of this alternative in the form of an emancipatory social and political movement coincided with the intensification of capital's contradictions in the descending phase of its systemic development. As we know, the development of this movement was very far from being without its own problems. Inevitably, this development was punctuated by significant successes, including some victorious political revolutions, as well as by some major defeats, from the bloodbath that followed the 1871 Paris Commune to the attempted social reproductive transformation under the Soviet type system. And, of course, the historically suffered failures were due not only to the power of the class adversary but also to the reformist illusions and internal contradictions of the movement itself.

As we have seen above, the non-utopian critique of capital had to start with the demystification of its ubiquitous fetishism, in order to be able to understand what to put in the place of its exploitative productive system. For the utopian wishful counter-images to capitalism tended to remain trapped by the fetishistic confusion and conflation of social relations with things and things with social relations, often confounding thereby also the absolute requirement of the production and appropriation of use-value in all conceivable history with the paralyzing power of exchange-value in commodity society.

In the same way and for the same reasons, the demystification of capital's self-serving formal determination of equality and freedom had to be the starting point also in the constitution of the socialist hegemonic alternative. For in contrast to the reformist illusions contained in the "old litany of democracy" (Marx), understanding the need for the realization of *substantive equality* and the corresponding *free decision-making powers* of the social individuals is vital for the elaboration of a strategically viable historic alternative.

To be sure, the historic advancement that once resulted in the important formal attainments of equality and freedom needs to be defended against the retrograde assaults on them in our time. But it is not enough. For the conditions under which the challenges must be faced have never been more difficult than they are today, under the conditions of our global interchanges dense with contradictions and antagonisms. Nevertheless, the objective historical trend from the *local* and partial toward the all-embracing *global* complements the potentially emancipatory trend from the *formal* toward the *substantive*, strengthening its positive side.

As mentioned earlier, the significance of the dialectically interacting historical trends is enhanced in conjunction with one another, compared to being taken separately. This is particularly pronounced in the case of the undeniable historical trend from the *local* toward the *global* in its relationship to the pronounced trend from the no longer sustainable *formal*—equality and freedom in that way confined—to its necessary *substantive* critique.

The original formal determinations and limitations of equality and freedom are in our time quite untenable because of the impact of globally interacting forces and shifting power relations, with their intensifying conflictuality that generates major counterforces against formal confinement. At the same time, only self-contradictory wishful thinking could suggest that a *global order* can be *harmoniously* sustained on the basis of perpetuating the substantive iniquities and corresponding antagonisms in their structurally entrenched present state. A globally integrated order of societal reproduction could only function in a historically viable and sustainable way on the positive ground of *substantive equality*.

The great intellectual conceptions formulated from capital's vantage point in the period of its ascending phase of development, from Vico and Adam Smith to Kant and Hegel, all tried to come to terms with a forbiddingly difficult problem of historical intelligibility. Despite the differences in the particular terms of reference of their formulations, they all offered in substance very similar solutions to these problems in their varying but always secular form of self-reassuring historical intelligibility, in sharp contrast to trying to find such reassurance in the idea of "Divine Providence" as the theologically conceived and so intended explanatory framework of historical development, in the way in which St. Augustine and others did. Indeed, all of these great intellectual figures of the bourgeoisie in the ascendant conceived their solutions not simply in terms of the flow of time, let alone as the vision of an inscrutably chaotic drift of time offered in the more or less openly apologetic and pessimistic mould of their twentieth-century descendants, but as the embodiment of meaningful historic advancement.

The difficult problem which the historical conceptions of the eighteenth century and the first third of the nineteenth tried to elucidate was: How is it possible to derive a historically coherent order and advancement from the conflictual interactions of individuals in "civil society"? A civil society taken for granted by all of them as insuperably but unproblematically conflictual.[302]

However, considered from a broader perspective it transpires that the historical specificity of capital's material reproductive order, contrary to the way in which it is conceptualized in the form of aggregative individualistic conflictuality in the various bourgeois theories of eternalized "civil society," must be complemented by an appropriate *historical account* of the appearance—i.e., of the complex historical *genesis*—and the always significantly specific (sui generis) transformations of *class antagonism* in the course of history. For the conflictuality of the "individuals in civil society," as depicted in the historical conceptions formulated from advancing capital's standpoint, was in actuality only a *special case* of the antagonisms prevailing through their required variations across class history. As such it exhibited the indelible marks of the *structural determinations* of *both* what it shared with the antagonisms of past class societies and the saliently different but nonetheless class-determined societal reproductive imperatives of its own order. A historically all the way to its time by far the most advanced reproductive order that could—and indeed *had to*—incorporate the historic attainments of formally defined equality and freedom, in contrast to earlier forms of class society, as discussed above.

Naturally, the admission of structurally embedded *class* antagonism was totally incompatible with the conceptions formulated from the idealized vantage point of ascending capital. For that kind of admission would have fundamental implications both regarding the rival aims and visions of *collective social subjects*, as hegemonic historical alternatives to one another,[303] and for their far from finally settled—in other words, still historically open-ended and intensifying—antagonistic class confrontations. "Individual conflictuality in civil society" had no such disturbing implications at all. For whoever could come up on top in any particular conflict among the strictly individual rivals and their enterprises, that could make no difference at all for the nature of the social order itself in which they all operated.

That order was *aprioristically assumed* to be the permanent framework of the "positively conflictual,"[304] in its material productive interchanges insuperable, and only at the level of political state determinations to be corrected, "civil society." And even that kind of requirement for state-legitimated intervention and correction could arise only if the mysterious "invisible hand," postulated by Adam Smith, could not accomplish on its own its even more mysteriously successful corrective deeds already at the level of civil society. Naturally, the Hegelian "ethical" state level was also decreed to operate under the totally benevolent gaze of the mysterious real historical subject. Individual conflictuality could not make any structurally relevant difference in the unfolding changes and transformations of "rational actuality." Especially not if you firmly believed—as the thinkers in question all did and said so, in one way or another—that their actually existing societal reproductive order embodied "the natural system of perfect liberty and justice."

Thus the real *collective historical subject* was a priori excluded from the conceptions of the triumphant bourgeoisie by the absolute *taboo* set against acknowledging the immense role of *class antagonism* in historical development, not only of the past but, much worse, potentially also of the future. The place of the actually existing collective historical subjects had to be assigned to a curious notion of the *individual historical subjects—* called even by the name of "*world historical individuals*"—who were supposed to be both directly *responsible* for the historical impact of their actions, and at the same time *knowing really nothing* about the ground and nature of their own conscious motivations. For they themselves were merely "*tools and instruments*"[305] of a mysterious force behind them, the World Spirit with its "Cunning of Reason" (and even "Absolute Cunning") in the Hegelian historical conception and its various theoretical equivalents in all of the others.

Thus the role assigned to the visible individual historical subject, even when promoted to the exalted status of the "world historical individual"—like Alexander the Great, Julius Caesar, Luther, and Napoleon Bonaparte—could not produce any historical intelligibility on its own.

For this reason the vacuum left by the elimination of the class antagonistic but real collective historical subject had to be filled somehow, although, to be sure, without the slightest hint of *class* antagonism. This is why the hypostatized, totally mysterious supra-human subject—whose tools and pliable instruments the world historical individuals were all supposed to be—had to assume the role of the proper historical actor. Not as a *collective* subject but simply as a *mysteriously inexplanable* yet really active *sovereign subject* of history, and thereby the *ex officio* provider of the proclaimed historical intelligibility of "rational actuality." And this curious solution, whose key constituent was—and could not be other than— a *complete mystery,* had to be propounded in the most progressive historical theories of the bourgeoisie. That is, in historical theories which were not religious/theological projections but in their fundamental philosophical intent thoroughly *rational* conceptions, created by the outstanding intellectual figures of the bourgeoisie in the ascendant.

This outcome was all the more paradoxical, indeed quite astonishing, because the unexplainable mystery was combined in these major historical conceptions with some tremendous insights regarding the nature of real historical intelligibility. Thus Kant, for instance, insisted that the historical development of the human being happens to be so determined that everything

> should be achieved by *work* . . . as if nature intended that man should *owe all to himself.*[306]

In this sense, once you remove the Kantian *"as if nature intended"* clause, with its "as if" proviso, ubiquitous in the work of this great German philosopher, you find an absolutely fundamental principle of historical explanation. One fully consonant with the objective dialectic of historical intelligibility asserting itself in actual development. Hegel, in his own way, embraced the same principle of formative activity in relation to which Marx asserted in one of his "Theses on Feuerbach" that it was the merit of idealist philosophy, in contrast to traditional materialism, to highlight the significance of productive activity for understanding historical development and advancement, notwithstanding the fact that it was done in an abstract idealist fashion.[307]

Hegel's accommodatory "as if" clause, so to speak, was his unjustifiable identification of *all objectification* with *alienation*, violating thereby his own pathbreaking dialectical insight into the nature of historical intelligibility. Through this false equation he was able to take for granted the actually existing world of exploitative *alienation* as necessary/unavoidable *objectification*,[308] properly legitimated by philosophy as such. He could defend the vested interests of capital's established order in this way by categorically dismissing—in the name of the highest dialectical principle of *"Reason"* itself—the idea of *social equality* as a "mere ought-to-be" propounded by the "folly of the understanding."[309] The purely fictitious overcoming of this absolutely inalterable predicament for those who suffered the consequences was postulated by Hegel in the form of projecting the imaginary experience of the pauper in the cathedral, where he was supposed to be "the Prince's equal."[310] And that projection, again, just like the speculative but nonetheless dialectical general design of Hegel's philosophical conception, was not devised for the purpose of offering to the believer a *religious/theological* vision and explanation of the world but in the tangible and rather prosaic service of a "rational"—or, rather, to put it in more precise terms, of an ideologically well-rationalized—*secular social apologetics*.

Not surprisingly, we find an even more pronounced rejection of the very idea of social and legal equality in Kant's philosophy,[311] even if the legitimation and justification offered is very different from Hegel's. Likewise, the other great intellectual figures who played a vital role in articulating a genuine historical conception in the ascending phase of capital's historical development had no real concern with the question of social equality. Not even when they had sympathy for the plight of the poor, as Rousseau and Adam Smith certainly did. For the issue itself was not a "more enlightened" treatment of the deprived but the inherently iniquitous *structural determinations* of the social order not only supported but even idealized by all of them.

The awareness of the irreparably iniquitous structural determinations of capital's reproductive order was completely missing, and *had to be* missing, from the philosophical conceptions formulated from the vantage point of capital even at its most progressive stage of historical development. This is why the solutions to the difficult problem of historical intelligibility: "how is it possible to derive a historically coherent order and advancement from the conflictual interactions of individuals in their society," had to be always aprioristically *assumed* in these philosophical conceptions, built on the shaky ground of the *mysteriously inexplainable*—differently named but in substance identical—and wishfully postulated supra-human historical actor.

Historical intelligibility must remain elusive without fully taking into account the *structural determinations* of the unfolding process, no matter how great might be the contradictions and antagonisms that must be faced by the historical actors in the course of their confrontations. For the "conflictual interactions of individuals in civil society" depicted in the major historical conceptions of the bourgeoisie must be qualified by us in the basic sense that the individuals in question could never fulfill a historic role—let alone the role idealized in philosophy as the rather mysterious intervention in the transformatory process by the "world historical individuals"—as *isolated individuals*. The "conflictually interacting individuals in civil society" are in reality inseparable from the collective social forces and antagonisms which they help to fight out to the historically at any particular time feasible—but always necessarily *open-ended*—conclusion under the objectively prevailing conditions and temporally modified specific circumstances.

In this sense, *historical actors* are *individual and collective* at the same time. Abstracting from the *collective social dimension* of the historical stakes conceptualized by the historical figures can only lead to mystery—like the Hegelian postulate of even the world historical individuals as the "unconscious tools" in the ("invisible") hands of the hypostatized real historical subject—instead of historical intelligibility. Indeed, it is necessary to coherently integrate into the overall picture the fundamental *social interests* and the underlying contradictions the historical subjects try to conceptualize and make use of with greater or less success, even if the objective structural determinations of the far from strictly individual interests carry different degrees and modalities of more or less avoidable "false consciousness."[312] If we fail to do that, substituting in their place some projected *individual motivations*, we are bound to end up with complete mystery. For there is an elementary *categorial* difference between the understanding of an endless number of real or imaginable *individual motiva-*

tions—whose unlimitable variety makes some thinkers[313] run into the hopeless contradiction of trying to treat in a preconceived reductivist fashion the potential *infinitude*—and the *social consciousness* of the necessarily and simultaneously individual and collective historical subjects interacting under structurally determined social conditions.

The great historical confrontation of our time is the *fundamental structural antagonism between capital and labor,* and it remains so until it is fought out by the social individuals to its positive or negative conclusion. That is, a conclusion resulting either in the establishment and irreversible consolidation of labor's historically sustainable alternative metabolic order of societal reproduction, or capital's destruction of humanity itself through the insurmountable contradictions and structural determinations inseparable from the antagonistic second-order mediations of the capital system.

But of course capital cannot act as an *abstract collective entity*, with a mythical consciousness of its own. It shares this characteristic with every collective historical subject, including labor. Nor does capital need the "Absolute Cunning" of the mythical "World Spirit" or "World Mind" in order to be able to impose on society as a whole its objective structural interests corresponding to the absolute imperative of capital-accumulation and the concomitant concentration and centralization of capital tending toward its global systemic integration. "The capitalist as *capital personified* and endowed with *consciousness and will*"[314] does that on capital's behalf. In other words, capital as a historical subject exists and asserts itself through its personifications "endowed with consciousness and will," in accordance with and oriented by the innermost structural determinations and imperatives of its system.

The *objective structural determinations and interests* of the capital system, as the established mode of effective social metabolic control, constitute the *"übergreifendes Moment"*—the "overriding determinant" (Marx)—in this relationship. That is what must be conceptualized by the personifications of capital, fully in tune with the *systemic imperatives* of the established societal reproductive order, whatever might be the personal *motivations* of the individual capitalists. When they fail to do that, capital's *corrective power* overrules them by unceremoniously bankrupting the particular personifications who "step out of line," thereby attempting some fanciful departure from the objective imperatives themselves. Also in this respect, there is no need whatsoever to hypostatize a mysterious "world mind" as the successfully corrective "real historical actor."

The objectively prevailing power of capital as the *successful regulator* of social metabolic reproduction provides its own explanation in terms of the actual sustainability of its regulatory functions, for as long as the structural imperatives behind them remain valid, with a temporal/historical qualification necessarily attached to them in the opposite direction. For once the explosive antagonisms of the system as such produce not simply some periodic conjunctural crises[315] but a *deepening structural crisis* on a historic scale, inseparably from the ever more wasteful constituents of the system's *destructive production* and devastating *encroachment on nature itself*, which happens to cast its shadow on our own predicament, then the fundamental *raison d'être* of capital itself—as the *successful regulator*[316] of all-embracing societal reproduction—becomes not only problematical but *totally untenable*.

Perhaps the greatest achievement of the historical theories conceived from capital's vantage point, above all by Hegel, was the recognition of the transformatory movement toward *world history*, even if this insight was spelled out in a speculative form.

Because the internal antagonisms of the system could not be acknowledged even by the greatest philosophers who viewed the world from capital's standpoint, world history had to be theorized as already accomplished, depicted as the proper climax and closure of historical development under the hegemony of imperialistically dominant Europe. In order to make plausible this conception—which has been mindlessly reconstituted and worldwide propagandized even in our own time in a grotesquely oversimplified and distorted form, with the most reactionary "neoliberal" intent—the objective systemic antagonisms, representing the potentially most disruptive *centrifugality* that remains insuperable within the structural confines of the capital system, had to be *transubstantiated* into *individual conflictuality* well containable by "civil society" and its idealized political state, as we have seen above.

In reality, however, the objectively opposed centrifugal units of the particular "civil societies" and the states—both with regard to their constituent parts as smaller or larger but always conflictual economic "microcosms," and in their more comprehensive but nationally articulated general capitalist material framework politically subsumed under a variety of warring nation states—were themselves riddled with worsening antagonisms. This state of affairs was foreshadowing ever greater confrontations for the future parallel to the objective trend toward imperialistically contested global integration.

The intensification of conflict and antagonism both on the material and the political/military plane was implicit already at the peak of the great bourgeois historical conceptions in the inherently *antagonistic centrifugality* of the dominant material reproductive constitutents and their corresponding rival nation-states. This sobering reality had to be speculatively embellished under the naïve postulate that in Hegel's time[317] established European domination represented "absolutely the end of history," in the German philosopher's words. Thus the transfiguration of real structural antagonisms into individual conflictuality was not simply *speculative* but blatantly *apologetic* and obfuscating. So much so that nothing embarrassing could be perceived of the capital system's actually unfolding trend of development even a few decades from the time of these major intellectual figures through the tendentiously distorting optics of their conceptualizations. Within their postulated terms of reference absolutely nothing could be acknowledged of the already imposed and ever extended ravages of monopolistic imperialism, and even less imagined of the frightful bloodletting of *two world wars* in the twentieth century arising from the irreconcilable antagonisms of the idealized social and political ground of the "world spirit's rational actuality" and its projected "realization of the idea of freedom" in world history. The hypostatized and speculatively idealized notion of the "absolute end of history" under European supremacy was in an astronomical distance from the possibility to understand the acute danger of the *real end of history* emanating from the tangible reality of capital's insuperable contradictions.

The actual *systemic centrifugality* represents now a grave problem for the future. Paradoxically, for a long historical period—indeed throughout the capital system's ascending phase of development—this centrifugality constituted a most dynamic force, positively contributing to fundamental productive advancement thanks to its ability to overcome various kinds of restraints and impediments to capital expansion and accumulation. No other social reproductive formation of the past could be even remotely compared to capital in this respect. For the dynamic power of systemic centrifugality played a crucial role in the actually unfolding world history, and continues to prevail in our time through the contradictory process of *globalization*. But that is precisely where the *systemic contradictions* become clearly visible, demonstrating their *structural untenability*. For a *globally integrated* system—the now emerging *rational imperative* of historically viable and sustainable social metabolic reproduction, in contradistinction to the ultimately self-destructive *blind imperative of endless capital accumulation* to which the expansion of humanly gratifying use-value must be fetishistically subordinated under the rule of capital—cannot conceivably be made to work on the basis of antagonistic centrifugality.

One of the most intractable aspects of this problem is the contradiction between the inherent *material drive* of the capital system, tending toward its global integration not *despite* but precisely *through its centrifugality*, and capital's *state formation*. For the latter is constituted from the outset in the form of conflictually opposed and indeed warring *nation-states,* responsible in the twentieth century and in our own time for massive military explosions and devastations, with the potential destruction of humanity on the horizon as the far from "millennial end-station." Also this aspect of actually unfolding world history has been hopelessly misrepresented and wishfully idealized by the great historical conceptions of the bourgeoisie, as we have seen above.[318]

In reality this is not a corrigible dimension of capital's state formation but a fundamental structural defect whose importance cannot be overstated. For the great *historic failure* of capital in this respect, highlighting one of its absolute limits of viability as a reproductive system, has been its inability to constitute the *state of the capital system as such*, in contrast to the antagonistically opposed *nation-states,* without the slightest ability even today to overcome this fundamental historic failure. Karl Kautsky's absurd theory of "ultra-imperialism" as the postulated solution to this problem amounted to no more than the *apologetic ideological rationalization* of capital's insurmountable historic failure, following the complicitous total capitulation of German social democracy to actually existing and destructive imperialism right from the outbreak of the First World War.

However, the seriousness of this problem regarding the no longer sustainable modality of the old centrifugal relations is not confined to the potentially all-destructive interstate antagonisms of our time through the clash of competing nation-states, as propelled by the underlying material drive of the capital system toward its globally unachievable integration under the domination of even its most powerful imperialist state. In a more general sense the issue concerns the *internal structural relationship* of *all* of the interrelated constituent parts of the emerging global system. This is why the contradictory global trend of integrative development now assumes the form of global instability. The problem is that, on the one hand, the systemic drive toward global integration at the present stage of historical development is *inexorable* as a matter of the underlying material imperatives, manifest also in the form of the explosive and chronically insoluble global economic and financial crisis experienced recently. On the other hand, the vital condition of realization of the required integration—the necessity of its *rational sustainability* not only in the first place but in a genuine epochal historical sense—is sharply contradicted by the objectively for a very long time prevailing conflictual centrifugality itself, characteristic both of the smaller constituent parts of the capital system and of its overall structural framework.

Even the most sanguine advocates of globalization, apart from the lunatic fringe preaching the most aggressive imperialist supremacy,[319] would not seriously assert today that the overall integrative process can be achieved—and, more important, made *permanent*—by the use of force. In other words, they concede that the "globalized" form of interrelationship among the constituent parts must be productively manageable on a long-term basis. And that implies, of course, some kind of *coherence* between the traditionally conflictual, and even antagonistically opposed, *micro-structures* and the *global complexes* under which the constituent parts of the social order must be *restructured* under the conditions of historical development unfolding in our time.

The *concentration and centralization of* capital are inherent characteristics of the most dynamic system of societal reproduction in all history, usually represented—and misrepresented—as unproblematical "growth and development." Yet, the inexorable trend toward globalization is inseparable from the antagonistic concentration and centralization of blindly self-expansionary capital, with the closely related contradictions of monopolistic imperialism. For that reason, this trend is very far from being idealizable. It is quite impossible to envisage a *global macro-structure* capable of coherently integrating into its general framework the conflictually opposed constituent parts driven in their traditional centrifugality by the antagonistic concentration and centralization of capital, based on the uncontrollable imperative of endless capital expansion.

The earlier mentioned elementary requirement of long-term *rational sustainability* as the key defining characteristic of a globally integrated societal reproduction process calls for a *qualitatively* different type of material reproductive and cultural relationship, freed from the preestablished *structural hierarchies* of the *substantively iniquitous* capital system. Accordingly, if the *constitutive cells and the micro-structures* of a globally interacting system are not sustainable in terms of their positive cooperative self-determination, there can be no real expectation of achieving the necessary rational sustainability of the reproductive order as a whole. The two stand or fall together. For it is totally inconceivable to squeeze historically open-ended and dialectically evolving coherence on a global scale out of the determinations of persistent structural antagonisms in its constituent parts.

In this sense, the success of the drive toward global integration is not feasible simply in terms of *change,* no matter how large-scale, let alone of forcibly imposed change, in the mold of monopolistic imperialism. It can succeed only if such change amounts to genuine *historic advancement* in response to the great challenges visible all around us. With the advancing trend of globalization the never in the past seen dialectical complexity of epochally sustainable structural change has appeared on the historical agenda. The objective need for the viable productive integration of its constituent parts carries the positive implication that its accomplishment means fundamental historic advancement.

The hopeful trends pointing in that direction have been discussed in the course of this study, including the necessity to overcome the no longer tenable formal determinations—and the *substantive violations*—of equality and freedom, as well as the creative use of *disposable time*[320] in place of capital's historically anachronistic exploitation of necessary labor time. The growing *hybridization* of the capital system, requiring the complicitous state finance of otherwise structurally unmanageable sectors to the tune of *trillions*—and even *tens of trillions*—of dollars, poured down the drain of capitalist bankruptcy and institutionalized fraudulence with utmost cynicism, point in the same direction. For the underlying objective trend of the capital system's structural crisis can only deepen as time goes by. Moreover, the resources hypocritically handed over to the failing but pretendedly superior "private enterprise system" out of the meager resources taken away from countless millions, for the purpose of "saving the system," can only provide palliatives, despite their astronomical magnitude, but in no way the required structural remedies for the future.

Naturally, historical dialectic in the abstract cannot offer any guarantees for a positive outcome. To expect that would mean renouncing our role in developing social consciousness, which is integral to the historical dialectic. Radicalizing social consciousness in an emancipatory spirit is what we need for the future, and we need it more than ever before.

NOTES

1. It must be recalled here that in the human context also the determinations of *natural necessity* can and must be questioned, as and when some of them are actually modified and potentially even superseded, in the course of historical development. These problems are discussed in sections 5.6, 5.7, 5.8, and 5.9.

2. Hegel, *The Philosophy of Right*, Clarendon Press, Oxford, 1942, 130.

3. Adam Smith, *The Wealth of Nations*, Adam and Charles Black, Edinburgh,1863, 273.

4. Hegel, *The Philosophy of History*, Dover Publications, New York, 1956, 103.

5. Theodicaea, in Hegel's words is "the justification of God in History." Ibid., 457.

6. It is worth recalling the groundless accusations used against Marx by Hannah Arendt and others, discussed at some length in chapter 5 of my book, *The Social Determination of Method.*

7. See chapter 4 on "Cosmogenesis" in an important book by the distinguished Greek theoretical physicist and social thinker Eftichios Bitsakis: *La matière et l'esprit*, Athènes, 2008. As Bitsakis puts it: "Il ne s'agit pas de 'univers.' Toutes ces hypothèses se réfèrent à *la partie de l'univers accessible aux moyens actuelles d'observation*" (135).

8. That is, in Marx's words, "a *merely* historical, a *vanishing* necessity."
    (Marx, *Grundrisse*, 832.) In the same context in which Marx describes his-
    torical necessity as *"merely* historical," he also makes it very clear what
    should be considered *absolute* with regard to the labor process as such. He
    underscores, in a critique of the "standpoint of capital" embraced by the
    political economists and Hegel, that the *objectification* of labor at all times
    in history is an *"absolute necessity of production"* (ibid.), but the *alienation*
    of labor—that is, its *alienated objectification*—is historically specific and
    superable. It is superable even if it is unavoidable under determinate socio-
    historical conditions, when the "monstrous objective power which social
    labour itself erected opposite itself as one of its moments belongs not to the
    worker, but to the *personified conditions* of production, i.e., to capital"
    (831). Typically, what must be considered by the personifications and
    interpreters of capital as unforgivable "economic determinism" is not their
    own totally arbitrary *absolutization* of the historically specific capital sys-
    tem's prevailing alienation of labor, wishfully projected by them as an insu-
    perable determination forever prescribed by nature, but Marx's theoretical
    demolition of its claimed eternal sustainability.

9. See Antonio Gramsci, "The Formation of the Intellectuals," in *The Modern
    Prince and Other Writings*, Lawrence and Wishart, London, 1957, 121.

10. Marx forcefully stressed the dialectical nature of these complex developments
    and qualitative transformations manifest in changing human needs by saying
    that "Hunger is hunger, but the hunger gratified by cooked meat eaten with a
    knife and fork is a different hunger from that which bolts down raw meat with
    the aid of hand, nail and tooth. Production thus produces not only the object
    but also the manner of consumption, not only objectively but also subjectively.
    Production thus creates the consumer." Marx, *Grundrisse*, 92.

11. The *permanent structural presence of basic material determinations* in the
    changing social metabolism, with their deep roots in nature, has been
    strongly stressed in an earlier chapter of this book. For no matter to what
    degree the direct material determinations are displaced in the course of
    human historical development by more advanced productive instruments
    and corresponding reproductive practices, they remain always *latent,* and
    may massively reemerge on the horizon of even the most advanced society,
    including a genuinely socialist one. In this respect it must be kept in mind
    that the jungle may be cleared with great effectiveness, but it is bound to
    reassert its original claim if the necessary conditions for its successful ban-
    ishment are not constantly renewed. See on this issue chap. 2, sec. 2.2:
    "The Problematical Character of Labor's Spontaneous Teleology."

12. "Outlines of a Critique of Political Economy" was written by Engels in 1843.

13. The "Outlines of a Critique of Political Economy" was added as an appen-
    dix to Marx's *Economic and Philosophic Manuscripts of 1844,* Lawrence &
    Wishart, London, 1959,195.

14. Ibid., 195–96.

15. In the same "Outlines of a Critique of Political Economy" Engels also forcefully stressed the interrelationsip between *competition and monopoly*, which is characteristically turned into another one of those "artificial and untenable antitheses" by the liberal political economists. He commented: "Competition is based on self–interest, and self–interest in turn breeds monopoly. In short, competition passes over into monopoly. . . . Moreover, competition already presupposes monopoly—namely the monopoly of property (and here the hypocrisy of the liberals comes once more to light); and so long as the monopoly of property exists, for just so long the possession of monopoly is equally justified . . . Monopoly produces free competition, and the latter, in turn, produces monopoly. Therefore, both must fall, and these difficulties must be resolved through the transcendence of the principle which gives rise to them." (Ibid., 194.)

16. Karl Marx and Frederick Engels, *Collected Works,* Lawrence and Wishart, London, 1975, 5:42 (henceforth MECW).

17. Hegel, *Philosophy of History*, 15.

18. Ibid.

19. Hegel, *Philosophy of Right,* 12.

20. Hegel *Science of Logic,* Allen & Unwin, London, 1929, 2:484.

21. Ibid., 485.

22. Hegel, *Philosophy of History*, 16.

23. Hence the Hegelian reconciliatory equation of "rationality" and "actuality."

24. Hegel, *Philosophy of History*, 17.

25. Hegel, *Philosophy of Right*, 11.

26. Hegel, *Philosophy of History*, 39.

27. Ibid. In another part of his *Philosophy of History* Hegel insisted that there must be a positive disposition of the individuals toward the state, subordinating their opinions "to the substantial interest of the State," because "nothing must be considered higher and more sacred than the good will toward the State" (449).

28. Hegel, *Philosophy of Right*, 222.

29. "Accusations about the materialism of this conception. Relations to *naturalistic materialism. . . . Dialectic* of the concepts of productive force (means of production) and relations of production, a *dialectic* whose boundaries are to be determined, and which does not suspend the real difference." Marx, *Grundrisse,* 109.

30. "Hegel fell into the *illusion* of conceiving the *real as the product of thought* concentrating itself, probing its own depths, and *unfolding itself out of itself, by itself. . . .* The *totality* as it appears in the head, as a *totality of thoughts,* is a product of a thinking head, which appropriates the world in the only way it can, a way different from the artistic, religious, practical and mental appropriation of the world. The *real subject* retains its autonomous

existence outside the head just as before; namely as long as the head's conduct is *merely speculative, merely theoretical.* Hence, in the theoretical method, too, *the subject, society,* must always be kept in mind as the presupposition." (Marx, *Grundrisse,* 101–2.)

31. Developed by Sartre in his *Critique of Dialectical Reason.* More about these problems in sec. 6.3.

32. Marx clearly stated: "The point of departure [must be] obviously from the *natural characteristic;* subjectively and objectively." Marx, *Grundrisse,* 110.

33. Ibid., 83–84.

34. Ibid., 527.

35. Ibid., 528.

36. Marx, *Economic and Philosophical Manuscripts of 1844,* 112.

37. Ibid., 112.

38. That is, dominating the *producing* individuals—who are excluded from the *control* of the conditions of societal reproduction through the structurally entrenched *"monopoly of property,"* as the young Engels rightly stressed it—as much as the fictionalized "sovereign *consumers,"* who must accept and internalize as their own genuine needs the "artificial appetites" imposed upon them by the fetishistic imperatives of the capital system.

39. This domination of social metabolic reproduction by capital's self-perpetuating needs, as *external necessity* to which all members of society must unquestioningly submit, becomes particularly evident at times of major economic crises, when the necessity of securing capital expansion—even in the form of "nationalizing" astronomic magnitudes of capitalist bankruptcy by the state—is imposed on society as a whole. And that requirement of unquestioning submission to the system's dictates must include also the utterly bewildered personifications of capital who at such times of major crisis cry "foul" and shout "socialism" in protest against the adopted emergency measures of "recapitalization" of the necessary organs of continued capitalist reproduction by *their own state*, imposed on society in the interest of the continued predominantly *economic mode of extraction of surplus labor as surplus value* stabilized by state capitalist intervention.

40. Adam Smith, *Lectures on Justice, Police, Revenue and Arms,* in Herbert W. Schneider, *Adam Smith's Moral and Political Philosophy,* Hafner Publishing, New York, 1948, 320.

41. Hegel, *Philosophy of Right,* 128.

42. Even as late as the middle of the nineteenth century, the "needy man" who dared to steal a sheep had to suffer *capital punishment,* by being hanged in England for the "heinous crime." Sir Thomas More wrote with biting irony in his *Utopia* (1516) at the time of the "embodiment of the *free will* in *property"* through the good services of the "primitive accumulation" that "sheep are eating men." Thus the strange appetite of sheep for eating

men—and always the exploited poor—could be kept well satisfied for more than three full centuries of capital's enlightened reign, thanks to *"Spirit's perfect embodiment—the State."*

43. John Stuart Mill admitted that the capitalist system must confront sometime in the future the worrying problem of its "stationary state." But he could only offer a totally illusory remedy by postulating a "more equitable *distribution,*" without altering the *productive* order, which is the necessary ground and primary determinant of all feasible distribution. And, of course, he wanted to keep both production and distribution under the elitistic control of the "better minds" also in his postulated future order. See 751–55 of Mill's *Principles of Political Economy,* Longmans, Green, London, 1923.

44. Marx, *Grundrisse,* 528.

45. Marx, *Capital,* Foreign Languages Publishing House, Moscow,1959, 1:85.

46. A vitally important corollary of this dimension of capital's material reproductive process in the political domain is the corresponding development of the *modern state,* with its *formal equality, liberty,* etc. idealized in the *"Rights of Man."* This strictly formal determination of the "Rights of Man" is in revealing consonance with the radical *negation of substantive equality, liberty, etc.* in the structurally safeguarded, incorrigibly *iniquitous, class relationship* between capital and labor in the established material order's overall societal reproduction process.

47. Marx, *Grundrisse,* 71.

48. MECW, 34:109. Marx's emphases. In the same work Marx also points out that "the *objective conditions of labor* do not appear as subsumed under the worker; rather, he appears as subsumed under them. Capital *employs* Labor. Even this relation in its simplicity is *a personification of things and a reification of persons"* (34:457).

49. Marx, *Economic and Philosophic Manuscripts of 1844,* 111–12.

50. We shall return to some important ramifications of this problem presently.

51. As we know, in his first major work Marx characterized Hegel as a philosopher who shares the standpoint of capital's political economy. See page 152 of his *Economic and Philosophic Manuscripts of 1844.*

52. This is what Marx called "the new historic form."

53. Marx forcefully protested in his *Economic and Philosophic Manuscripts of 1844*—on page 104—against the idea of establishing an abstract opposition between "Society" and the individual. These were Marx's words: "What is to be avoided above all is the reestablishing of 'Society' as an abstraction *vis-à-vis* the individual. The individual *is the social being."* Marx's emphases.

54. This is acknowledged even officially, by capital's personifications in the political field, in the cynical but profitable slogan of "diminishing the carbon footprint."

55. Marx, letter to Engels, 25 March 1868, MECW, Volume 42, p. 557.

56. Marx, "Thesis No. 6 on Feuerbach."

57. Marx, "Thesis No. 11 on Feuerbach." Marx's emphases.

58. MECW, 34:413.

59. Ibid., 388–89.

60. See the discussion of these problems in sec. 4.4.

61. It is worth remembering again Kant's earlier quoted assertion that "the *general equality* of men as subjects in a state coexists quite readily with the *greatest inequality* in degrees of the possessions men have. . . . Hence the general equality of men also coexists with *great inequality of specific rights* of which there may be many. . . . This law concerns the *form* and not the *matter* of the object regarding which I may possess a right." (Kant, "Theory and Practice.")

62. Hegel, *The Philosophy of Mind,* Clarendon Press, Oxford, 1971, 64.

63. Ibid., 55.

64. Ibid., 56.

65. These are Hegel's words on this matter: "*Subjective self-seeking* turns into a contribution to the *satisfaction of the needs of everyone else.* That is to say, by a *dialectical advance*, subjective self–seeking turns into the *mediation* of the particular through the universal, with the result that *each man* in earning, producing, and enjoying on his own account is *eo ipso* producing and earning for the enjoyment of *everyone else.*" (Hegel, *Philosophy of Right,* 130.) It would be very difficult, if not impossible, to devise a socially more apologetic concept of *mediation.* For it is extremely problematical to assert the "*satisfaction of the needs of everyone else,*" accomplished by "subjective self-seeking," when Hegel must concede elsewhere, as he actually did, the existence and the precarious conditions of life of the "*needy man.*" To get out of that contradiction it would be necessary to confront the established order's *antagonistic second-order mediations,* in place of projecting the imaginary mediation between particularity and universality in the abstract, in the name of a purely speculative "*dialectical advance,*" ignoring the historical specificity of *class domination* by the personifications of capital. But, of course, the elaboration of that concept of mediation would be feasible only on the basis of radically redefining humanity's relationship to *wealth,* instead of speculatively glorifying the *class expropriation of wealth* through the high-sounding self-justificatory principle according to which "*property is the embodiment of the free will of others,*" as we have seen in this section.

66. See in relation to these problems a more detailed discussion of Hegel's views in chapter 7 of *The Social Determination of Method,* esp. sec. 7.2: "The Process of the Genus with the Individual."

67. Hegel, *Science of Logic,* 272.

68. Hegel, *Philosophy of Right,* 217.

69. Hegel characterized the "individuals as subjects" not as the real subjects of

history but as the *"living instruments"*—almost like Aristotle had characterized the slaves as *"talking tools"*—of "what is in substance the deed of the *world mind* and they are therefore *directly at one with that deed* though it is *concealed* from them and is *not their aim and object"* (ibid., 218). The big difference with Aristotle was that Hegel described the "living instruments" as *properly human,* putting above them the "World Mind" as the one and only *supra-human* real subject of history who makes the human living instruments act out—in and through history up to the present, in a most paradoxical way—*its own design* of bringing to realization in "rational actuality" its own *eternal present.*

70.   It is important to underlscore here, as one of the major achievements of Hegel as a thinker, that he—more than any other representative figure of the bourgeoisie—acknowledged the insuperable irrationality/unconsciousness of capital's societal reproductive order, even if he combined in a reconciliatory way his account of the *necessary unconsciousness* of the process envisioned by the individuals, including the greatest "world historical individuals" and their "consciously" propounded designs whose real meaning was completely hidden also from them, with his speculative idealization of the "rational actuality" of the World Spirit's "eternal present."

71.   Hegel, *Philosophy of History,* 39.

72.   Hegel, *Philosophy of Right,* 130.

73.   We should recall that in Hegel's view "the History of the World is nothing but the development of the Idea of Freedom." Hegel, *Philosophy of History,* 456.

74.   Only the worst apologists of the established order could openly propagandize the crass notion that "there is no such thing as society; there are only individuals."

75.   We should recall that Hegel died in 1831. Two of his most important works concerned with world history and the state—*The Philosophy of Right* and *The Philosophy of History*—were written between 1821 and 1831.

76.   Hegel, *Philosophy of History,* 103.

77.   MECW, 5:50–51.

78.   Ibid., 5:39.

79.   See chapter 5 of my book *Beyond Capital* in this respect.

80.   We must not forget that the policies pursued by aggressive neoliberal market idolatry, with more or less explicit references to some grotesque version of Adam Smith's "invisible hand" by Hayek and his followers, or the preposterously projected Gorbachevian and other postulates of "market socialism," have been responsible for imposing a great deal of human suffering in the world in the last few decades.

81.   "Forms of being."

82.   The inseparably *structural* and *temporal/processual* relationship of *continuity and discontinuity* can be grasped precisely by focusing attention on

the *trans*-historical dimension of societal development, which should not be confused with the idealist speculative *supra*-historical postulates.

83. In fact, in an interview given to Madeleine Chapsal in 1959 Sartre optimistically asserted, "The first volume will be published within a month, and the second within a year." See "The Purposes of Writing," in Jean-Paul Sartre, *Between Existentialism and Marxism*, NLB, London, 1974, 9.

84. Jean-Paul Sartre, *Critique of Dialectical Reason. Theory of Practical Ensembles*, NLB, London, 1976, 69–71. Sartre's emphases.

85. We must recall that Sartre's *Critique of Dialectical Reason* was conceived and written in the aftermath of some major upheavals in Eastern Europe, particularly in Poland and Hungary.

86. See my detailed analysis of Sartre's overall trajectory as a great intellectual of the twentieth century in my book *The Work of Sartre: Search for Freedom*, Harvester Press, Brighton, 1979.

87. Sartre, *Critique*, 36. Sartre's emphases.

88. Sartre, "Itinerary of a Thought," *New Left Review* (November–December 1969): 58–59.

89. Sartre actually admitted in the 1969 interview that in his most detailed interpretation and reconstruction of Flaubert's life, running into several thousands of pages, he had to *invent*—as if he were writing a novel—the person at the center of his monumental inquiry.

90. Mészáros, *The Work of Sartre: Search for Freedom*, 86–87.

91. As he had put it in the first volume of the *Critique:* "I regard Marxism as the untranscendable philosophy for our time, and I believe that the ideology of existence, along with its 'comprehensive' method, is an enclave within Marxism itself, both produced and rejected by Marxism" (822).

92. See Sartre's interview by Michel Contat, "Self-Portrait at Seventy," first published in *Le Nouvel Observateur*, June and July 1975. In English reproduced in Jean–Paul Sartre, *Sartre in the Seventies: Interviews and Essays*, Andre Deutsch Ltd., London, 1978. See in particular page 60 of this volume.

93. See ibid., 59–61.

94. Although, primarily for political reasons, he tried to qualify in this work the retained elements of the existentialist ontological orientation as an "ideological enclave" only, the truth of the matter is that it was incomparably more decisive than just an enclave.

95. Sartre, *Critique*, 125.

96. Ibid., 36.

97. Ibid., 131–32.

98. Sartre called himself "marxisant."

99. Sartre, *Critique*, 133.

100. On the historical problem of antagonistic second-order mediations, see sec. 8.6 of *The Social Determination of Method*.

101. The perilous implication of certain types of transformations, under the irrational and destructive imperatives of uncontrollable capital accumulation, is not that they modify the relationship of human beings to nature—which is characteristic of the whole of human history—but that they do it in a most *inappropriate,* simultaneously destructive. and *self-destructive* way.

102. Sartre, *Critique,* 132.

103. Ibid., 125.

104. We must return to the intricate problems of scarcity later in this section and more extensively in sec. 6.5 of this chapter.

105. Toward the end of Sartre's most revealing and moving interview, conducted by Michel Contat in 1975, the interviewer puts to him, "In general, your political statements are optimistic, even though in private you are very pessimistic." This is how Sartre responds to Contat's observation: "Yes, I am. . . . If I am *not completely pessimistic* it is primarily because I see in myself certain needs which are not only mine but the needs of every man. To express it another way, it is the experienced certainty of *my own freedom.* . . . But it is true that either man crumbles—and then all one could say is that during the twenty thousand years in which there have been men, a few of them tried to create man and *failed*—or else this revolution succeeds and creates man by bringing about freedom. Nothing is less sure. . . . It is impossible to find a *rational basis* for revolutionary optimism, since what *is* is the present reality. And how can we lay the foundations for the future reality? Nothing allows me to do it." *Sartre in the Seventies,* 83–85.

106. *"Freedom must revolt* against forms of alienation," ibid., 88.

107. Sartre, *Critique,* 131.

108. In English it is published in *Sartre in the Seventies: Interviews and Essays,* 198–210.

109. As Sartre expressed this in his interview conducted by Michel Contat: "This was the period in which I broke with the Communists after Budapest. . . . Writing the *Critique of Dialectical Reason* represented for me a way of settling my account with my own thought beyond the Communist Party's sphere of influence over thought." *Sartre in the Seventies,* 18.

110. The analysis of the nature and contradictions of the Soviet-type post-capitalist experience under Stalin is attempted by Sartre in the second volume of the *Critique* in the same formal categorial framework. This is why Sartre's long descriptions of the chosen particular political events and conflicts tend to go around in circles, repeating at every new turn the same generic assertions about the projected formal structures. This is, above all, what denies Sartre the possibility of bringing to the fore in the necessary categorial terms the underlying material structural determinations that would encapsulate the salient characteristics of the historical totalization that must prevail under the circumstances of the postcapitalist capital sys-

tem, in view of the pursued modality of social metabolic reproduction oriented toward, and likewise constrained by, the *politically enforced extraction of surplus labor*, in sharp contrast to its *primarily economic extraction*
in the form of *surplus value* asserting itself even under the greater part of
the monopolistic phase of capitalism. Until, that is, *hybridization,* with
direct political involvement and massive financial support provided by the
state out of general taxation for the "military/industrial complex" and for
rescuing private capitalist enterprise from ever-escalating bankruptcy,
begins to create some major, and potentially insuperable, complications.

111. *Sartre in the Seventies,* 201–2.
112. Ibid., 203.
113. Ibid., 210.
114. Jean-Paul Sartre, "Masses, Spontaneity, Party," *The Socialist Register,*
     1970, 245. Originally published as "Classe e partito. Il rischio della spon-
     taneità, la logica dell'istituzione," *Il Manifesto,* no. 4, September 1969.
115. *Sartre in the Seventies,* 204.
116. "L'idée neuve de mai 1968," observations reported by Serge Lafaurie, *Le
     Nouvel Observateur,* 26 June–2 July 1968.
117. We should recall in this respect the answer he gave to Michel Contat,
     quoted in n. 105.
118. See on this issue several chapters of the present work, and chaps. 3, 7, and
     8 of *The Social Determination of Method.*
119. That is, the relatively short-lived French "Revolutionary Democratic
     Assembly."
120. See "Revolutionary Democrats," Sartre's interview by Mary Burnet, *New
     York Herald Tribune,* 2 June 1948.
121. Jean-Paul Sartre, "Le R.D.R. et le problème de la liberté," *La Pensée social-
     iste* 19 (Spring 1948): 5.
122. Rousseau, *The Social Contract,* Dent & Sons, London, 1958, 78.
123. Sartre writes in 1972: "Even though I have always protested against the
     bourgeoisie, my works are addressed to it, are written in its language. . . .
     Now, we must say that this work [on Flaubert], assuming that it has some
     value, by its very nature represents the age-old bourgeois swindle of the
     people. The book ties me to bourgeois readers. Through it, I am still bour-
     geois and will remain so as long as I continue to work on it. However,
     another side of myself, which rejects my ideological interests, is fighting
     against my identity as a classic intellectual." *Sartre in the Seventies,* 185.
124. As we have seen, the necessary critique of capital's—historically specific—
     antagonistic second-order mediations is absent from Sartre's lifework. This
     is due to a large extent to his concern to give an existentialist ontological
     underpinning to some of the key categories adopted also in his "marxisant
     existentialist" phase of development.
125. Sartre, *Critique,* 35.

126. In the *"eternalizing"* ideology of the established mode of production the necessary historical limitations of the capital system are denied already at the classical phase of political economy (and philosophy) conceived from capital's standpoint, and of course in the most blatant way in the descending phase of capitalist development. Yet the uncomfortable truth is that in all human history prior to the unfolding of capital's mode of societal reproduction there never existed a mode of production which could not function at all without imposing, at whatever cost, its *imperative of unlimitable expansion*. Naturally, this unique historical condition carries the gravest implications for the future.

127. Sartre, *Sartre in the Seventies*, 85.

128. Herbert Marcuse, "Freedom and the Historical Alternative," in Marcuse, *Studies in Critical Philosophy,* NLB, London, 1972, 223.

129. Sartre, "The Maoists in France," *Sartre in the Seventies*, 171.

130. Already in his optimistic phase Marcuse is trying to model his vision on Kantian ideas in the form of "the work of a *supra-individual* historical Subjectivity in the individual—just as the Kantian categories are the syntheses of a *transcendental Ego* in the empirical Ego." (Marcuse, *Studies in Critical Philosophy*, 217.) And he adds a few lines further on: "Kant's *transcendental construction* of experience may well furnish the *model* for the *historical construction* of experience" (218). However, in Marcuse's final years pessimism becomes overwhelming. We are told by him that "the world is not made for man, and it has not become more human." (Marcuse, *Die Permanenz der Kunst,* Carl Hanser Verlag, München, 1977, 53.) In this sense Marcuse presents the bleakest possible picture by saying that "in reality *evil triumphs,"* leaving to the individual nothing but the "islands of good to which one can *escape* for short periods of time" (ibid.). Accordingly, Kant reappears in this totally pessimistic vision, quoted to sustain Marcuse's explicitly desperate hope attached to art as "a *regulative idea* [Kant] in the *struggle in despair* for the transformation of the world" (ibid., 74).

    In his optimistic years Marcuse insisted that the "utopian possibilities" he advocated and whose success he projected without a sustainable social analysis, were "inherent in the *technical and technological forces* of advanced capitalism" on the basis of which one could "terminate poverty and *scarcity* within a very foreseeable future." (Marcuse, *An Essay on Liberation,* Allen Lane/ Penguin Press, London, 1960, 4.) He also told his readers that "this qualitative change must occur in the *needs*, in the infrastructure of man" (ibid.), alerting people to the point that the stipulated moral "ought" of "the rebellion would then have taken root in the very nature, the 'biology' of the individual" (ibid., 5), establishing in the "organism" itself "the institutional basis for freedom" (ibid., 10) and "the *biological need for freedom"* (ibid., 52). These hopes and expectations, as we can

see, directly linked an overgenerous belief in the technical and technological transformatory power of "advanced capitalism" with the wishful postulate of "the biological need for freedom." Marcuse's disappointment, therefore, had to be quite devastating after the failure of his expectations.

131. One should not forget the immense brutality of *"primitive accumulation"*
under Henry VIII and other "great rulers" in the early stages of capitalist
development, whose unspeakable inhumanity induced Thomas More to
say in his *Utopia* (1516) that "sheep are eating men" in the interest of the
unfolding profitable enterprise of wool production.

132. Sartre, *Sartre in the Seventies*, 203.

133. To use Max Weber's capital-apologetic terms. On this issue see sec. 2.7,
"Formal Rationality and Substantive Irrationality," in *The Social Determination of Method*.

134. See Sartre, *Being and Nothingness*, Methuen & Co., London, 1958, 628.
The fragments of Sartre's ethical work written in 1947 and 1948 were published under the title *Notebooks for an Ethics*, University of Chicago Press,
Chicago and London, 1992; and the French original by Gallimard, Paris,
in 1983.

135. Sartre interview by Simon Blumenthal and Gérard Spitzer in *La Voie com-
muniste*, June–July 1962.

136. The subsequent transformation of the—for a long time dogmatic
Stalinist—French Communist Party first into an unprincipled social-democratic formation, providing active support for President Mitterrand's
capitulatory government, and then into a neoliberal force in full complicity
with the established order, provided a most unhappy confirmation of
Sartre's skeptical judgment. I wrote at the time when "the unprincipled
departure" of some of the major Communist parties—in their more remote
past committed to a Marxist strategic transformation of society—started to
take place: "When a once important historical force, the French
Communist Party, reduces itself to the role of a fig leaf, in order to hide the
nonexistent endowments of François Mitterrand as a socialist, no one
should be surprised that a commensurate shrinkage takes place not only in
its electoral fortunes but, more importantly, in its impact on the unfolding
social developments." István Mészáros, *The Power of Ideology*, Harvester/-
Wheatsheaf, London, and New York University Press, New York, 1989,
53.

137. Jean-Paul Sartre, *Saint Genet: Actor and Martyr*, George Braziller, New
York, 1963 (published in French in 1952), 186.

138. Including François Mauriac and Gabriel Marcel.

139. Sartre's lost writings on the problems of ethics alone, pursued again and
again in different periods of his life, are said to amount to at least 2,000
pages.

140. See Sartre, "Détermination et Liberté," a lecture delivered at the Gramsci

Institute in Rome on 25 May 1964, repr. in *Les Écrits de Sartre: Chronologie, Bibliographie commenté,* ed. Michel Contat and Michel Rybalka, Gallimard, Paris, 1970, 735–45.

141. Kant, "Theory and Practice," in *Immanuel Kant's Moral and Political Writings,* ed. Carl J. Friedrich, Random House, New York, 1949, 415–16.

142. Rousseau, *A Discourse on Political Economy,* Dutton, New York, 1950, 254.

143. Ibid., 234.

144. This is how Sartre generously praised the Maoists, in the spirit of his own, for a long time idealized, conception of what a revolutionary movement of committed individuals should be like: "The militants of *La Cause du Peuple* do not constitute a party. It is a political group [*rassemblement*] which can always be dissolved. ... This procedure allows a way out of the rigidity in which the Communist Party has imprisoned itself. Today the Maoists criticize and break out of the notion of leftism: they want to be the left and to create a broad political organization." Sartre interview by Michel-Antoine Burnier, *Actuel,* No. 28, and *Tout va Bien,* 20 February–20 March 1973.

145. Sartre, *Being and Nothingness,* 422–49.

146. Ibid., 429.

147. Sartre, *Critique,* 64.

148. Ibid., 125.

149. Ibid., 814.

150. Sartre, *Critique,* 814–15. Sartre's emphases.

151. See Sartre, "Itinerary of a Thought," 59.

152. Sartre, *Critique,* 816–17.

153. Ibid., 818.

154. Ibid.

155. Ibid., 125.

156. Ibid., 816.

157. Sartre, *Sartre in the Seventies,* 24–25.

158. Karl Marx, "Notes on Bakunin's Book: *Statehood and Anarchy,*" MECW, 24:521.

159. Ibid., 518.

160. It is revealing that in his critique of the serialized voters Sartre equates, most problematically, their *abstract possibility* with a claimed sovereignty-constituting *power.* He writes: "When I vote, I abdicate my *power*—that is, the *possibility* everyone has of joining others to form a sovereign group" (*Sartre in the Seventies,* 204). Of course, in the circumstances of Pompidou's relatively undisturbed France, way after the defeat of May 1968 which contributed to the consolidation of the Gaullist system, the "possibility of joining others to form a sovereign group" advocated by Sartre is a *purely abstract possibility.* Under the conditions of a massive and

intensifying socioeconomic crisis such abstract possibilities may well become *concrete possibilities,* leading to significant historical change. But it is extremely problematical to call abstract possibilities *real powers* in the absence of such a major socioeconomic crisis.

161. In fact, that is the basis on which the "classical left parties" can be, and should be, legitimately questioned for their *strategic* inadequacy, and not for their alleged "nineteenth-century" political attachment.

162. See in particular sec. 4.4, concerned with "The Radical Transformation of the Legal and Political Superstructure."

163. In accord with the Marxian concept of the *"übergreifendes Moment,"* that is, the factor of overriding importance under a given set of circumstances.

164. Marx's circular addressed to the Federal Council of the Romande Switzerland, *Documents of the First International,* Lawrence & Wishart, London, n.d., 3:361.

165. Rosa Luxemburg, *Reform or Revolution,* Pathfinder Press, New York, 1970, 50.

166. Rosa Luxemburg, *The Junius Pamphlet,* A Young Socialist Publication, Colombo (Sri Lanka), 1967, 62.

167. The main reason offered by Sartre in 1975 for abandoning the *Critique of Dialectical Reason* was that "in the case of the *Critique* there is the additional problem of time, since I would have to go back to studying history." (*Sartre in the Seventies,* 75.) Undoubtedly the historical knowledge mastered by any particular thinker is a contributory factor in this respect. But only *contingently.* The necessities lie elsewhere. The much more serious impediments in Sartre's case, imposing insurmountable difficulties on his projected *Critique,* were not due to the limitations of his historical knowledge but primarily to his "marxisant existentialist" ontological approach to the problems of intelligibility in the dialectically unfolding history of humanity.

168. Marx, *Grundrisse,* 71.

169. "Le structuralisme en personne," Jean-Marie Auzias, *Clefs pour le structuralisme,* Seghers, Paris, 1967, 85.

170. "*L'Express* va plus loin avec Claude Lévi–Strauss," a major interview published by *L'Express,* 15–21 March 1971, 61.

171. Of course, the ultra-eclectic opportunist Jürgen Habermas joins in the fashionable scramble for the invention of catchy "post" labels, talking in a most pretentious and confused way even about *"post-history."* He writes: "Hegel's concept of the ethical totality . . . is no longer an appropriate model for the mediatized class structure of organized, advanced capitalism. The suspended dialectic of the ethical generates the peculiar semblance of *post-histoire. . . .* For the leading productive force—controlled scientific-technical progress itself—has now become the basis of legitimation. Yet this new form of legitimation has cast off the old shape of *ideology.*" J.

Habermas, *Toward a Rational Society*, Heinemann, London, 1971, 110–11. The words "post-histoire" and "ideology" are italicized by Habermas. For a detailed discussion of his work see sec. 1.2 and 3.4 of my book *The Power of Ideology*, Harvester/Wheatsheaf, London, and New York University Press, 1989.

172. Not surprisingly, the wide-ranging promotion of structuralism was associated with empire building and a search for respectable ancestors, from linguistics to ethnography. Even Jacob Grimm was adopted as a distinguished structuralist ancestor. Thus we could read about him in a book on liguistics: "His language lacks precision and he was guilty of gross inconsistencies, but his intent is clear. He was far, far ahead of his time. He was, in fact, one of the first structuralists." John T. Waterman, *Perspectives in Linguistics*, University of Chicago Press, Chicago, 1963, 82.

173. For a documented discussion of these problems see my book *Philosophy, Ideology and Social Science: Essays in Negation and Affirmation*, Wheatsheaf Books, Brighton, 1986; and in particular its Introduction and the chapter on "Ideology and Social Science," ix–xix and 1–56; the latter chapter first published in 1972.

174. Characteristically, Jean-Marie Auzias praised "structuralism personified" by saying: "Structuralism is not an imperialism! It wants to be *scientific: and it is*. . . . Lévi-Strauss's thought is satisfied with applying itself to the *human sciences,* and exclusively to them, eminently and insistently refusing by his own *rigorous practice* any concession to *ideology,* no matter under what kind of philosophy it might hide itself." Auzias, *Clefs pour le structuralisme,* 10–11.

175. See in this respect one of the seminal passages of Lévi-Strauss's wide-ranging interview given to *L'Express* in March 1971, as quoted in sec. 8.6 of *The Social Determination of Method.* In that interview he was asserting: "Today the greater peril for humanity does not come from the activities of a *regime, a party, a group, or a class*. It comes from humanity itself in its entirety; a humanity which reveals itself to be its own worst enemy and, alas, at the same time, also the worst enemy of the rest of the creation."

176. As we know, Marx forcefully underscored in one of his earliest works that "we know only one science, *the science of history*" (MECW,5;28; Marx's emphases), insisting in the same spirit the vital importance of history throughout his life.

177. See Claude Lévi-Strauss, *Les structures élémentaires de la parenté,* Paris, 1949.See also *Mythologiques*: *Le cru et le cuit,* Paris, 1964, vol. 1; *Du miel aux cendres,* Paris, 1966, vol. 2; *L'origine des manières de table,* Paris, 1968, vol. 3.

178. Tellingly, as noted by the English anthropologist Edmund Leach, Lévi-Strauss's monumental discussion of American indian myths does not carry the title of "Mythologies" but that of *Mytho-logiques,* which means the "Logics of Myth." See Edmund Leach's book in the Fontana Modern

Masters series, *Lévi-Strauss*, Fontana/Collins, London, 1970, 10.

179. A book translated into English under the title *The Savage Mind*, George Weidenfeld and Nicolson Ltd., London, 1966.

180. See *"L'Express* va plus loin avec Claude Lévi-Strauss," *L'Express*, 15–21 March 1971, 66.

181. Sir Lewis Namier, *Vanished Supremacies: Essays on European History, 1812–1918*, Penguin Books, Harmondsworth, 1962, 203.

182. *"L'Express* va plus loin avec Claude Lévi-Strauss,",", 66.

183. Joseph Arthur Comte de Gobineau (1816–1882), the racist Orientalist author of *The Inequality of Human Races* and *Les religions et les philosophies dans l'Asie central*, was a friend and for some time the secretary to Alexis de Tocqueville in his foreign ministry, and a member of the French diplomatic service between 1849 and 1877. He was also the inventor of the myth of the "superman."

184. The revealing "utopia" aimed at perpetuating capital's established reproductive order, with at least a modicum of doubt about its realizability, was also propounded in the nineteenth century by the liberal thinker John Stuart Mill, who advocated the institution of the "stationary state of the economy" in his *Principles of Political Economy*.

185. See n. 175.

186. *"L'Express* va plus loin avec Claude Lévi-Strauss," 66.

187. Ibid., 61.

188. This is how Descartes put it in his *Discourse on Method:* "I perceived it to be possible to arrive at *knowledge highly useful in life;* and in room of the speculative philosophy usually taught in the schools, to discover a *practical* [philosophy] by means of which . . . we might also apply them to all the uses to which they are adapted, and thus *render ourselves the lords and possessors of nature*." Dutton, New York, 1951, 49.

189. Lévi-Strauss, *The Savage Mind*, 261–62.

190. Marx, *Grundrisse*, 105.

191. See n. 176.

192. A relevant connection in this respect is that *The Savage Mind* is dedicated to Maurice Merleau-Ponty, who vehemently attacked Sartre for his alleged "ultra-bolshevism" in *Les Aventures de la dialectique*.

193. Lévi-Strauss, *The Savage Mind*, 256.

194. Ibid., 254.

195. Ibid.

196. Ibid.

197. "Je m'efforce moi-même de faire oeuvre scientifique. Mais je ne peux m'empêcher de penser que la science serait plus aimable si elle ne servait à rien." *"L'Express* va plus loin avec Claude Lévi-Strauss," 66.

198. See Hayek's *Road to Serfdom*, discussed in *Beyond Capital*.

199. Leach, *Lévi-Strauss*, 19–20.

200. "N'est–ce pas très 'réactionnaire,' entre guillemets, ce que vous dites là?" 66.

201. Ibid.

202. Ibid., 65.

203. As we are constantly told even today, nothing could be more ideally "equilibrating" in due course—provided that we are able and willing to suffer long enough with patience the unavoidably disruptive and "creatively destructive" crisis periods of the system—than the capitalist exchange relations embodied in the market, even in the historical period of its "globalization." Appropriately, in Lévi-Strauss's view the great passage for North American Indians "from nature to culture" has been accomplished through "the *establishment of commerce.*" (*"L'Express* va plus loin avec Claude Lévi-Strauss," 65.) Also, in the "societies without writing" idealized by him, the embodiment of the exchange relations in the elementary structures of kinship "is the common denominator of politics, the law, and the economy" (63).

204. Ibid., 61.

205. Ibid.

206. Ibid., 63.

207. That is, the historically constituted human subject who could remedy at least in principle the situation by appropriately confronting the problems and contradictions of the real world, including its own, now antagonistically self-mediating but transcendable negative relationship to nature, so as to transform the earlier discussed constraints of historical necessity into a progressively vanishing necessity in accordance with human need.

208. *"L'Express* va plus loin avec Claude Lévi-Strauss," 60.

209. Ibid., 66.

210. Sartre's apartment was bombed not once but twice.

211. Lévi-Strauss, March 1971 interview, 66.

212. Marx, *Grundrisse*, 331.

213. Ibid., 87–88.

214. Of course, what really decides the matter is *what, when, where,* and *how* the human beings exchange in their *specific kind* of exchange relationships in which they engage not only among themselves but also with nature.

215. It is worth recalling that according to one of the greatest political economists of all time, Adam Smith, the bourgeois societal reproductive order is constituted as "the *natural* system of *perfect liberty and justice.*"

216. As such, the second-order mediations are by no means necessarily/aprioristically antagonistic. Indeed, the constitution of the "exchange relationship" between humanity and nature and among the individuals themselves in the form of antagonistic second-order mediations is intelligible only as an *inherently historical category,* which implies their historical transcendability.

217. Sartre rightly criticizes structuralism for "never showing how History pro-

duces the structures." *Situations IX,* Gallimard, Paris, 1972, 86.

218. Marx, *Grundrisse,* 95–96.

219. Ibid., 88.

220. J. M. Keynes, "Economic Possibilities for Our Grandchildren," *Essays in Persuasion,* W. W. Norton, New York, 1963, 372.

221. Ibid., 370.

222. J. M. Keynes, "A Short View of Russia," *Essays in Persuasion,* 301.

223. Talcott Parsons, "Social Class and Class Conflict in the Light of Recent Sociological Theory," in his *Essays in Sociological Theory,* Free Press, New York, 1954, 326.

224. C. Wright Mills, *The Sociological Imagination,* Penguin, London, 1970, 42–43.

225. Talcott Parsons and Neil J. Smelser, *Economy and Society: A Study in the Integration of Economics and Social Theory,* Routledge & Kegan Paul, London, 1956, 272. The interested reader can find a more detailed analysis of these problems on pages 41–48 of my book on *Philosophy, Ideology and Social Science,* dealing with "The Ideology of Parsonian 'General Theory.'"

226. Marx, *Grundrisse,* 694–95.

227. Ibid., 700.

228. That is, not by a workforce now composed of isolated, alienated. and fragmented workers but by the developing *social individuals* who are cooperatively combined into *the social labor force* of a communally organized society.

229. Marx, *Grundrisse,* 705. Marx's emphases.

230. Ibid., 708. Marx's emphases.

231. A concept fetishistically glorified by all kinds of apologetic economic theory, including "structural functionalist" economics.

232. Habermas, *Toward a Rational Society,* 104.

233. Ibid.

234. Ibid., 113.

235. Jean-François Lyotard, *The Postmodern Condition: A Report on Knowledge,* Manchester University Press, Manchester, 1979, xxiii.

236. Ibid., 60.

237. Ibid., 79.

238. Jean-François Lyotard, "Universal History and Cultural Differences," in *The Lyotard Reader,* ed. Andrew Benjamin, Basil Blackwell, Oxford, 1989, 315–18.

239. Lyotard, *The Postmodern Condition,* 67.

240. Ibid., 66.

241. Ibid., 103.

242. Ibid., xxiii.

243. Ibid., 82.

244. See in this respect Lenin's work on *Imperialism: The Highest Stage of Capitalism.* As Lenin stressed: "Half a century ago Germany was a miserable, insignificant country, if her capitalist strength is compared with that of Britain of that time; Japan compared with Russia in the same way. Is it 'conceivable' that in ten or twenty years' time the relative strength of the imperialist powers will have remained *un*changed? It is out of the question. ... Instead of showing the living connection between periods of imperialist peace and periods of imperialist war, Kautsky presents the workers with a lifeless abstraction in order to reconcile them to their lifeless leaders." Lenin, *Collected Works,* Progress Publishers, Moscow, 1964, 22:295–96.

245. Marx, *Grundrisse,* 109.

246. Ibid.

247. The severe negative impact of treating art and literature in a voluntaristic way by Stalin's appointee in the field, Zhdanov, are well known. It is also relevant in this respect that when Lukács—who was persistently critical of mechanical reductivism—dared to suggest, in the spirit of the Marxian idea of uneven development, that "the rabbit on the hill is not a bigger animal than the elephant on the plane," attempting to qualify thereby the relative merits of a higher social formation with the requirement of artistic excellence, he was sharply attacked in the Party press not only in Hungary but also in the central organ of the Soviet Party, *Pravda,* by no less a figure than Fadeyev.

248. Marx, *Grundrisse,* 111–12. The word "mythology" is italicized by Marx.

249. "*A slave* who is in the power of another person, can have nothing of his own." *The Institutes of Justinian,* 2:9, para. 3, trans. J. B. Moyle, Oxford, 1906, 58.

250. Marx, *Grundrisse,* 245–46. Emphases by Marx.

251. Much later, in his correspondence with Vera Zasulich in March 1881, Marx had also put into relief the possibility of a socialist revolution breaking out in such an underdeveloped country, namely Russia, where the anticipated revolution actually erupted in 1917.

252. MECW, 5:74–75.

253. Ibid., 5:74.

254. Ibid.

255. Naturally, the preponderant domination of the world order through uneven development by any particular country can only be temporary. "No doubt the aggressive adventures of global hegemonic imperialism are fully capable of and may indeed actually succeed in destroying human civilization. But they are absolutely incapable of offering a sustainable solution to the grave problems of our time. . . . Only the genuine advocacy of responsibly facing up to the grave problems of capital's deepening structural crisis in the spirit of *substantive equality* (feasible only in a socialist order)—which would make the paradoxically 'small country' of the United States the uncontested *equal* of the big countries of India and China—is an absolute

requirement for the future. For only the generally adopted spirit of substantive equality can offer a historically sustainable solution to the now prevailing and potentially most destructive interstate relation of forces." István Mészáros, *The Challenge and Burden of Historical Time: Socialism in the Twenty-First Century,* Monthly Review Press, 2008, 425–27. First published in Brazil, by Boitempo Editorial, Saõ Paulo, 2007.

256. Adam Smith, *An Inquiry into the Nature and Causes of the Wealth of Nations,* ed. J. R. McCulloch, Adam & Charles Black, Edinburgh, 1863, 298.

257. Marx, *Capital,* 1:152.

258. Smith, *An Inquiry into the Nature and Causes of the Wealth of Nations,* 199.

259. Ibid., 413.

260. This is done even by the *idealist philosopher,* Hegel, as we have seen his revealing, purely ideological way of doing it in sec. 6.1, in defense of the most iniquitous determinations of the established order.

261. Hegel, *Philosophy of Right,* 17.

262. Ibid., 222.

263. As Marx made very clear, in his sharp critique of the approach that postulated the idea of the nature-determined and necessarily warring isolated individuality as the fictitious foundation of "human nature" from which the *political apologetics* of an absolutely permanent bourgeois state order could be readily derived: "*Human nature* is the *true community of men.* The disastrous isolation from this essential nature is incomparably more universal, more intolerable, more dreadful, and more contradictory than isolation from the *political community.*" Marx, "Critical Marginal Notes on the Article by a Prussian," MECW, 3:205.

264. MECW, 3:205.

265. Marx, *Theses on Feuerbach.*

266. Sartre, *Critique of Dialectical Reason,* 125.

267. Ibid., 131–32.

268. Ibid., 133.

269. Jean-Paul Sartre, *Critique of Dialectical Reason,* Verso, London, 1991, 2:424.

270. Ibid., 21–22.

271. Marx, *Grundrisse,* 88.

272. Sartre, *Critique of Dialectical Reason,* 2:23.

273. Ibid., 2:26.

274. Ibid., 2:27–28.

275. C. B. Macpherson, "A Political Theory of Property," in Macpherson, *Democratic Theory: Essays in Retrieval,* Clarendon Press, Oxford, 1973, 138. As we have seen earlier, John Maynard Keynes was rhetorically anticipating—in one of his *Essays in Persuasion*—the realization of the ideal conditions of abundance in the "capitalist Millennium" by the year 2030. But that view, voiced in a lecture in 1930, was not to be taken too seriously.

276. Herbert Marcuse, *An Essay on Liberation*, Allen Lane/Penguin Press, London, 1969, 4.
277. Ibid., 5.
278. Ibid., 19.
279. We may well recall the views of Habermas—one of the most fashionable eclectic opportunist mystifiers in this field—who postulates the "scientization of technology" when in reality so much damage is generated by the fetishistic *technologization of science* in the service of destructive production.
280. Marcuse, *An Essay on Liberation*, 7.
281. Marx, *Capital*, 1:152.
282. It is most relevant here that "if capital increases from 100 to 1,000, then 1,000 is now the point of departure, from which the increase has to begin; the tenfold multiplication, by 1,000%, counts for nothing; profit and interest themselves become capital in turn. *What appeared as surplus-value now appears as simple presupposition etc.,* as included in its *simple composition.*" Marx, *Grundrisse*, 335. Emphases by Marx.
283. "The man of scarcity, seeking his abundance, seeks it as a determination of scarcity. Not abundance for all, but his own, hence the deprivation of all." Sartre, *Critique*, 2:421.
284. Ibid., 2:437.
285. Marx, *Grundrisse*, 528.
286. See sec. 5.1 of *The Social Determination of Method*.
287. See in this respect "Vicissitudes of Historical Consciousness in the Twentieth Century," and " 'If Sense There Be, It Escapes Our Perception': From Ranke and Tocqueville to Sir Lewis Namier and Beyond," sec. 5.5 and 5.7 of *The Social Determination of Method*.
288. First published in 1725 but considerably modified in 1730 and 1744.
289. Giambattista Vico, *The New Science*, Cornell University Press, Ithaca, NY, 1970, 53.
290. A far cry indeed from the pessimistically disqualifying dictum that pontificates "If sense there be, it escapes our perception."
291. Hannah Arendt, *The Concept of History*, 58.
292. Ibid., 60. For a detailed discussion of these problems see chap. 5, and especially sec. 5.6 of *The Social Determination of Method*.
293. In Marx's expression.
294. Never undoable, that is, short of humanity's catastrophic relapse into a most primitive form of barbarism.
295. The structurally entrenched prejudgment in question was instituted through the radical separation of the means of production from labor.
296. The sharp moral denunciation of capitalist alienation appears in the early decades of the sixteenth century in Thomas More's *Utopia* and in the writings of Thomas Münzer.

297. This must be always understood in the earlier qualified sense that acknowledges in all productive advancement the presence of destructive potentialities that must be actively countered in the interest of realizing the positive alternatives.

298. To be sure, capital tries to exploit disposable time, to the extent it is capable of doing so, in the form of "do-it-yourself" leisure activity and its instruments, as well as in the field of "voluntary services" not amenable to the requirements of capitalist profitability. But all that is strictly *marginal* in comparison to the full realization of the potentialities of disposable time.

299. Paracelsus, *Leben und Lebensweisheit in Selbstzeugnissen,* Reclam Verlag, Leipzig, 1956, 134.

300. Up to the present time the countless openly dictatorial ventures undertaken by the dominant states at times of major crises in Latin America, Europe, and elsewhere proved to be relatively "episodic," followed as a rule by the restoration of the normality of capital's commodity exchange relations internally as well as internationally. However, the consequences of abolishing the formal liberties in capital's productive order and in its state regulatory system on a permanent basis would be quite overwhelming. They would amount to a descent into barbarism in a literal sense.

301. The debates directly related to this issue go back a long way in the socialist movement, to the time of the adoption of the Gotha Program in 1875, when Marx and Engels sharply criticized the German social-democratic leaders and their fundamentally misconceived strategic orientation. The illusory reformist programs were always defined in conformity to the regulatory framework of strictly formal equality and freedom. "Nothing beyond the old democratic litany," as Marx put it in his 1875 *Critique.* Understandably, the worldwide social-democratic capitulation to neoliberalism was only a question of time.

302. On the complex solutions to this problem by the major historical conceptions referred to see chap. 5, esp. secs. 5.2 to 5.5.

303. As indeed the bourgeoisie happened to be in its historic confrontation with the feudal order, well forgotten thanks to the historical amnesia following its victory.

304. Postulating the necessarily positive conflictuality of capital's "civil society," from Vico, Adam Smith, and Kant all the way to Hegel, was possible, again, only in the form of another arbitrary assumption. As Kant tried to explain in his conception of the mysterious "hidden plan of nature" (see his "Idea for a Universal History with Cosmopolitan Intent," 127): "Thanks are due to nature for his [the human being's] quarrelsomeness, his enviously competitive vanity, and for his insatiable desire to possess or to rule, for without them all the excellent faculties of mankind would forever remain undeveloped" (121).

305. In Hegel's words "the *unconscious tools* and organs of the world mind at work within them," and therefore the real historical meaning of their

actions, must be *"concealed* from them and is *not their aim and object."* Hegel, *Philosophy of Right*, 217–18.

306. Kant, "Idea for a Universal History with Cosmopolitan Intent," 119.

307. "In contradistinction to materialism, the *active* side was developed abstractly by idealism." "Thesis no. 1 on Feuerbach." The word "active" is underlined by Marx.

308. That is, the Idea's (or the World Mind's) necessary *externalization.*

309. Hegel, *Philosophy of Right*, 130. For Hegel this judgment was doubly damning, not only because it was characterized as a "folly" but also because *understanding* as such represented a necessarily inferior way of knowing, in comparison to the highest principle of dialectical Reason. In the Hegelian conception only Reason could accomplish the necessary dialectical grasp of the Truth.

310. "Er ist dem Fürsten gleich," in the words of the *Jenenser Realphilosophie.*

311. See Kant's reconciliation of social and legal inequality with the "General Will" in his article on "Theory and Practice," discussed in sec. 5.3.

312. On these problems see secs., 4.1, 4.3, and 6.5.

313. Particularly in some psychoanalytic and historiographic approaches.

314. Marx, *Capital,* 1:152.

315. Periodic conjunctural crises belong to the reproductive normality of capital.

316. We must bear in mind here, in order to appreciate the great contrast, that over a long historical period of nearly four centuries capital was not only the *successful regulator* of social metabolic reproduction but the *only viable regulator* of such a vital process.

317. We should remember, Hegel shared his time with the great Prussian military strategist, General Karl Marie von Clausewitz.

318. See the detailed discussion of these problems in sec. 4.4.

319. On some of the latter, see "Symptoms of a Fundamental Crisis," sec. 10.3.1 of my book *The Challenge and Burden of Historical Time,* Monthly Review Press, New York, 2008, 399–407.

320. To be sure, in accordance with capital's fetishistic logic there can be no meaningful use made of disposable time on the required scale. For in terms of that perverse logic it is much easier and more profitable to treat, instead, the working people themselves as readily "disposable people." See Fred Magdoff and Harry Magdoff, "Disposable Workers," *Monthly Review* (April 2005): 18–35.

Index